bio   123915   12.95
                         8.95
                         7.95
                         6.95

MAKING PEOPLE'S MUSIC

MAKING
PEOPLE'S
MUSIC
Moe Asch
AND
FOLKWAYS
RECORDS

PETER D. GOLDSMITH

SMITHSONIAN INSTITUTION PRESS
WASHINGTON AND LONDON

The following companies have generously given permission to use quotations from copyrighted works. From "The Ballad of October 16th," by Millard Lampell and Lee Hays, copyright 1993, from "U.A.W.-C.I.O.," by Butch Hawes, copyright 1942, and from "Put It on the Ground," by Ray Glaser and Bill Wolff, copyright 1947, Stormking Music, Inc. All rights reserved. From "The Dying Miner," words and music by Woody Guthrie, copyright 1947 (Renewed) and 1963 (Renewed), from "Hard Travelin'," words and music by Woody Guthrie, copyright 1959 (Renewed), 1963 (Renewed), and 1972, from "Jesus Christ," words and music by Woody Guthrie, copyright 1961 (Renewed) and 1963 (Renewed), from "This Land Is Your Land," words and music by Woody Guthrie, copyright 1956 (Renewed), 1958 (Renewed), and 1970, Ludlow Music, Inc., New York, New York. Used by permission. From "Rock Island Line," new words and new music arrangement by Huddie Ledbetter, edited with new additional material by Alan Lomax, copyright 1959 (Renewed), Folkways Music Publishers, Inc., New York, New York. Used by permission. From "Passing Through," by Dick Blakeslee, and from "The Same Merry-Go-Round," by Ray Glaser and Bill Wolff, copyright The Sing Out Corporation, Renewed. Used by permission. All rights reserved.

Copy editor: Karin Kaufman
Production editor: Duke Johns
Designer: Linda McKnight

Library of Congress Cataloging-in-Publication Data
Goldsmith, Peter David, 1952–
     Making people's music : Moe Asch and Folkways Records /
Peter D. Goldsmith.
       p.   cm.
     Includes bibliographical references and index.
     ISBN 1-56098-812-6 (cloth : alk. paper)
     1. Asch, Moses.   2. Sound recording executives and
producers—United States—Biography.   3. Folk music—United
States—History and criticism.   4. United States—Civilization—
1918–1945.   5. United States—Civilization—1945–   I. Title.
ML429.A83G65   1998
781.62'13'0092—dc21   97-33293

British Library Cataloguing-in-Publication Data available

Manufactured in the United States of America
05 04 03 02 01 00 99 98   5 4 3 2 1

*T*HIS BOOK IS FOR JOANNA AND BENJAMIN

CONTENTS

ACKNOWLEDGMENTS

This book has required the collaboration of a great many individuals, most conspicuously those artists and producers whose memories of Moe Asch provided me with my most important data. They include Jon Appleton, Guy Carawan, Candie Carawan, Richard Carlin, Sam Charters, John Cohen, Sis Cunningham, Barbara Dane, Jac Holzman, Dave Jasen, Ella Jenkins, Kevin Roth, Ruth Rubin, Tony Schwartz, Peggy Seeger, Pete Seeger, Toshi Seeger, Irwin Silber, and Henrietta Yurchenko. Others who contributed to Folkways in less heralded, but equally important, ways also contributed their time in order to speak with me; they include Ronald Clyne, Robert Fox, Mel Kaiser, Harold Leventhal, and Don Molner. Several individuals answered questions and provided clarification by letter or phone—among them are Asch's sister Ruth Shaffer, novelist and composer Paul Bowles, recording engineer Peter Bartók, and jazz critic Gene Lees. Others with whom I consulted include Ben Siegel, Josh Dunson, Benjamin Filene, Raeburn Flerlage, Bess Hawes, Alan Lomax, Rosalie Sorrels, Studs Terkel, and Dave Van Ronk. Barry Sirota spent an evening with me in Chicago describing the world of Jewish American cantorial "stars" at mid-century. Several writers and producers who interviewed Moe Asch during his lifetime—including David Dunaway, Joe Klein, Guy Logsdon, Elisabeth Perez Luna, and Jon Appleton—provided me with tapes or transcriptions of those conversations. Gary Kenton, who began plying these waters some years before me, was very kind in providing me with taped conversations he had had with Moe Asch, Sam Goody, Fred Ramsey, Irwin Silber, Harry Smith, and Pete Seeger, and in turning over to me other materials he had collected—most notably, the FBI files on Sholem Asch and Moe

Asch that he had procured through the Freedom of Information Act. Professor Eva Mills provided me with materials from the Nathan Asch Collection at Winthrop College, which became the single most important source for the first chapter. Professor Ronald Cohen of Indiana University Northwest took an interest in my project and provided encouragement and support from its inception.

Several individuals with whom I spoke during the preparation of this book—most of them in lengthy interviews but a few in briefer telephone conversations—have since passed away. This list sadly includes Frances Asch, John Asch, Harold Courlander, Sidney Cowell, Kenneth Goldstein, David Stone Martin, Frederic Ramsey, Ralph Rinzler, Earl Robinson, and Adam Spiro. I regret that I do not now have the proper means of thanking them.

Portions of this book were read in manuscript form by Michael Asch, John Cohen, Pete Seeger, Tony Seeger, and Toshi Seeger, and for their written and verbal comments, criticisms, and corrections I am vastly grateful. A great many friends and colleagues have patiently listened and responded to my account of Moe Asch's life; the first of several talks on the subject of Moe Asch was presented at a Master's Dinner at Princeton University's Mathey College in the fall of 1990. I am deeply appreciative of the many ways in which this project was facilitated by the support and friendship of Mathey College's Barrie and Dominique Royce. Other friends at Mathey helped me focus my interpretation of Asch's life and locate his work both historically and politically; conspicuous among them are Harvey Teres, now of Syracuse University, and David Nirenberg and Jane Dailey, now at Rice. Through many conversations, Mary Huber of the Carnegie Foundation for the Advancement of Teaching helped me to sort through problems of interpretation in the writing of biography. Other audiences provided me with important insights and correctives, including Dartmouth College's Jewish Faculty and Staff Association and the Upper Valley Jewish Community. Lee Pelton, Dartmouth's Dean of the College, inexplicably saw wisdom in hiring a Dean of Freshmen whose creative energies would be regularly siphoned away on an apparently eccentric book project and gave me his blessing to dedicate any available time to its completion. Others at Dartmouth listened patiently and offered important theoretical suggestions, especially Deborah Chay in the Department of English and John Watanabe in Anthropology.

The Smithsonian Institution's Office of Folklife Programs now houses the Smithsonian/Folkways Archive, where I was given generous access to all of Moe Asch's papers. I owe a special debt to the past and present staff and administration of the archive, including Tony Seeger, Jeff Place, Lori Taylor, Amy Horowitz, and Mary Monseur. I also spent a highly profitable day in the archive of the Rutgers Institute of Jazz Studies and am grateful to its staff for their assistance.

Early stages of my research were facilitated by a grant from the American Council of Learned Societies. I was able to acquire the rights to several of David Gahr's wonderful photographs through a generous grant from the Goodman Fund of the Department of Anthropology, Dartmouth College.

Moe Asch's son Michael, professor of anthropology at the University of Alberta, has been extraordinarily generous in his support of this project since its inception. Never for a moment did he press me to present his father other than the way in which I came to understand him myself. At times my work forced him to confront painful aspects of his father's life, but if he ever flinched, he never showed it. The cultivation of Michael's friendship has been one of the great pleasures of this project.

In the Smithsonian Press's Mark Hirsch I have had the benefit of an acquisitions editor whose patience is only exceeded by the lavishness of his encouragement. Lizzie Grossman at Sterling Lord Literistic, Inc. has shown far more enthusiasm for this project than I would have expected from an otherwise sensible literary agent. To both of them, I offer bewildered but warm and grateful thanks. Copy editor Karin Kaufman is a writer's dream and made the final stages of manuscript preparation an unadulterated pleasure.

Finally to Fran, who on account of Moe Asch has had to settle for a lot less than my full attention for some years now—a million thanks for your forbearance. I am showing him the door now, dear.

INTRODUCTION

oe Asch was as certain as he was of anything that to comprehend the significance of his work one had to understand the history that had shaped his vision of the world. He considered himself a unique person, formed in the crucible of world-shaking events and by his childhood in a family of immense creativity and worldly intellect. His own account of his life was disclosed to interviewers with remarkable consistency, particularly in the last fifteen years of his life: in June of 1970 he taped two long sessions with Israel Young (proprietor of the Folklore Center, a Greenwich Village institution in the sixties), and the following March he spent an additional three hours answering questions from Tony Schwartz (chronicler of urban street sounds and later a prominent media consultant for national political campaigns), while in the company of his wife Frances. In 1977 an edited transcript of the former was published in *Sing Out!* in two installments as "Moses Asch: Twentieth Century Man," the title aptly capturing the importance of Asch's modernism. Asch was very pleased with the *Sing Out!* articles, despite their many factual errors, and kept copies on hand in his office to distribute to friends and visitors. But essentially the same stories emerged when he was interviewed by David Dunaway in May 1977 for a biography of Pete Seeger, by Woody Guthrie's biographer, Joe Klein, the following December, by Elisabeth Perez Luna for a National Public Radio profile in February 1983, and by four or five others for magazine articles and radio programs.

Moe Asch's father was Sholem Asch, the most widely read Yiddish writer of the twentieth century, and for his second son this was the central fact of his life. Sholem Asch rapidly rose to literary prominence in the early years of the century as a playwright and novelist whose work brought the long-hidden life of eastern European Jewry to international literary and artistic attention. His early plays and novels celebrated in often romantic terms the insular life of the Jewish shtetl while challenging Jewish authority for its self-righteous intolerance of its least fortunate practitioners and its inflexible hold on Jewish thought and behavior in an era in which modern European intellectual currents were liberating individuals from medieval traditions. Later his novels became grand historical panoramas that placed Jewish actors within the momentous events altering Europe's political landscape in the century's first three decades, as well as within the American immigrant experience. Asch hoped from this copious literary activity to earn the Nobel prize, for which he was nominated in 1933. Although few American or European Jews were unacquainted with his work by the nineteen thirties, the novels he began to publish on the eve of the Second World War brought him renown among Christian readers, especially in the States. In 1939 he published *The Nazarene,* the first of a set of novels based upon biblical figures and events that would occupy him for the remainder of his life. These novels were immensely popular among Christians, some becoming Book-of-the-Month Club selections. But although he had intended them to effect a reconciliation between Christians and Jews, they were viciously assaulted by the dominant Yiddish press for their sympathetic portrayal of New Testament figures precisely at the moment when world Jewry was facing its most calamitous challenge. The effect of this assault was that Sholem Asch was eventually driven from the United States and his name obliterated from the rolls of prominent world Jews. Forty years after his death, his name stirs only faint memories among American Jews.

Whereas his father was an artist, Asch's mother came from a family of Polish revolutionaries. His mother's sister Basha was—in his telling—Lenin's specialist in early childhood education and the most important tutor in Asch's own political education. An uncle in Warsaw was executed by the czarist regime for seditious behavior during the Russian revolution of 1905, the year Asch was born. His childhood was spent in exile—in Berlin, outside of Paris, and in New York. The Asch household, wherever it went, became the gathering place of expatriate artists of all kinds. Traveling with Aunt Basha and his brothers from Paris to New York in 1915, Asch observed firsthand the brutal affects of war. On the streets of

Brooklyn, he again observed violence; and as a student in Germany in 1923 he observed the social deterioration that followed from runaway inflation and watched the ominous signs of fascism gathering pace. Through his father, he met Albert Einstein, an encounter that gave him the inspiration to undertake his grand recording project. And as a result of the devastating experience of bankruptcy in the late forties, he developed a business strategy that left him relatively impervious to the vagaries of popular taste and large-market forces.

Through these iconic facts, Moe Asch asked his interlocutors to understand him and his work. There can be no doubt that over time he came to believe in the veracity of the stories he told about himself. Memory, we are told, depends on the sensation of familiarity, and in their repeated telling these stories became very familiar to Asch indeed. Whatever their truth, they are the map by which we understand who Asch thought he was and what he regarded as the significance of his work. He seemed to know that his was a story that would be told, and he worked mightily to ensure that it would be recounted as he would have wished it. The facts of his life as he told them were true in the sense that they enable one to comprehend Asch as he regarded himself; they are a *true* portrait of his own self-understanding. And seeing Asch as he wished to be seen is an important means of interpreting his life and work. But it is not the only—nor necessarily the most revealing—window.

Asch was positioned at a singular crossroad in American history, in the history of the American Left and American Jewry, and in the history of musical and scholarly tastes. He was a man who lived on an assortment of social fault lines that enabled him to see both "inside" and "outside," to understand multiple perspectives and to facilitate a kind of cultural "translation" across ethnic, racial, class, and national boundaries. After the age of ten, he lived most of his life in New York City. In many respects his outlook and orientation was very European, and until his family moved to New York in 1915 the language spoken at home was that of the country in which they lived—first Polish, then German, finally French. But as a consequence he never became fluent in any of these languages, nor in Yiddish. As an adult he spoke and wrote and undoubtedly thought in English, but culturally he remained something of a hybrid, straddling European and American life in ways that were never fixedly one or the other.

The same marginal vantage point pertained to his Jewish identity. Because of his father, he was deeply connected on an emotional level to things Jewish, but for the same reason he was profoundly alienated from American Jewish life. Asch was never observant and never Bar Mitzvahed, worked on Saturdays, and rarely set foot inside a synagogue. Yet although not a part of any Jewish community in the face-to-face sense, he was sufficiently knowledgeable about aspects of Jewish life to be able to appreciate the dilemmas of Jewish existence in the United States and to see Jewish life as it appeared to those who lived it and those who did not.

In politics, too, Asch regarded himself as a man who lived within the world of the American Left—he was a "goddamn anarchist," he told interviewer Joe Klein—yet he was not *of* the Left. If anything, he was a Roosevelt New Dealer, and although he had many friends who were Communist Party members and "fellow travelers" and he supported their right to express their beliefs, he was hostile to the cause of international communism. He contributed money throughout his life to a broad variety of socially progressive causes, from labor unions to civil rights initiatives to the preservation of public art. But he did not participate in political organizations, and here again he understood how the American Left regarded itself as well as how it looked from other perspectives along the political spectrum.

From this set of vantage points at the margins of national, cultural, and political identity, Asch was able to grasp the importance of information that would enable others to understand those unlike themselves. He was in this sense a cultural "broker," who although neither attached to nor invested in a single cultural position, dedicated himself to the process by which others mediated understandings across cultural boundaries. His interests were not identified with those whose music he made available nor with the audience for his records, but with the process of making the sounds of other people comprehensible and significant. Granted it was a kind of brokerage that was limited by the medium of recorded sound; primarily, his was a process by which social elites developed a particular kind of knowledge about those less powerful than themselves through their music. But the communication was not entirely one way. For example, a significant number of rural and inner-city musicians in the United States were able to identify lucrative, national audiences for their music through the release of Folkways recordings. Simultaneously, the recording and marketing process became one important means through which some traditional musicians—and their neighbors, family, and friends—came to regard themselves as the bearers of a unique "culture" that had a value and that could be marketed. It created the terms under which local musicians saw themselves as something other than simply "American" but additionally the exemplars of regional and/or ethnic traditions. As partly intended, it had the effect of enabling those who suddenly understood themselves as "folk" to celebrate the significance of their differences but also—and at least as important—to market that difference to cultural and intellectual elites.[1]

The extent to which Folkways contributed to a group's self-consciousness about its cultural or ethnic distinctiveness must have varied greatly; indeed, rural southern American musicians were most directly affected by the role of Folkways Records in the development of professional careers and in the commodification of their musical abilities. We can only surmise what the effect might have been on indigenous peoples whose tape-recorded ceremonies were released on the Folkways Ethnic series. In some instances, they may have never been made aware of the commercially available recording. In others, however, we can guess that the effect was of a piece with other anthropological "publications" that contributed to the legitimation of "native practice" in the eyes of colonial administrators. In particular, commercial recordings and publications were part of the social process by which a group of people came to see themselves as "folk": ethnically distinct or culturally autonomous. In many instances, a group's consciousness of being "a culture" contributed to their self-defense against colonial administrators and missionaries who sought to undermine traditional practices. Although it is currently popular to characterize anthropology as the handmaiden of imperialism, anthropology has played highly varied roles in different world regions throughout the century. Terry Turner has argued that within the Amazon region the very act of conducting anthropological research has had the effect of undermining colonial administrators and other bearers of dominant ideology by suggesting that the cultural practices of those they were studying had a value that justified their claims to self-determination and social equality. But not all communities succeed in taking control of the processes of cultural objectification, as have the Kayapo of Brazil. The Kayapo operate their own video cameras now; Folkways recordings were invariably made by cultural outsiders who controlled the meanings attached to the sound images, with consequences that could not always be predicted.[2]

A recording, we might argue, carries in our cultural context implications different from that of a monograph or journal article. We are accustomed to thinking of its contents as constituting *somebody's* idea of an aesthetically pleasing performance. Thus unlike a written document, a recording of an ethnographic moment—in addition to bearing information—stamps that performance with an aesthetic value in and of itself for its own sake. Never mind that the idea of aesthetic value may have no currency within that cultural context. And never mind that the Western listener may find the experience of that performance to be an excruciating one. Part of Asch's contribution was to educate the American public about the value of other people's musical traditions and thus to contribute to the growing belief among American intellectual elites in the importance of preserving unique cultural traditions for their own sake. With the rise of environmentalism in the early seventies, indigenous cultures seemed to many to be another kind of exotic and endangered species whose continued existence was desirable on largely the same grounds used to justify the preservation of rare animal species—diversity is good for the planet and for all of those who inhabit it.

As a cultural broker, Asch claimed not to be particularly concerned about the purposes to which his recordings were put once on the market. But neither was he naïve about these purposes. He expected at the very least that his recordings would contribute to international, interracial, or interethnic understanding; and the only time he ever hesitated to release material on political grounds was when he believed that its lack of "truth" would undermine the cause of human understanding. Almost any recorded sound could be regarded as true as long as its creation was not overwhelmingly motivated by a desire to make money or to cause harm to others. He told composer Jon Appleton in 1982 that he would not record "Dixie" or German SS songs or anything else "that can be used against people." Everything else could only have the effect of better informing the public. A good sound recording, he believed, was among the least constrained ways of gaining access to a social world beyond the boundaries of one's own.[3]

I regard this book as anthropological in its basic interpretive apparatus, a reflection of my academic training and the years I spent researching, writing, and teaching about African American religion. The concept of "culture" continues to hold special possibilities for me in the effort to understand forces that shape social life beyond those that are purely personal or utilitarian. But in my view culture has been vitiated by its unselfconscious use in the public realm and by assorted postmodern intellectuals, for whom it has become a shorthand way of referring to taken-for-granted social differences that would better be interrogated rather than presupposed. It is partly the current degeneracy of the term that prompts the attention I periodically pay in this book to the way in which cultural difference has come to be understood in the United States and the role that the collection of folk music on records has played in that process.

The idea of using the life history of an individual as the centerpiece of an anthropological project might well have been regarded as anathema in a field dedicated to the understanding of social life as experienced and understood by collectivities. And yet American anthropology in particular has long used the stories of individuals as a means of conveying the lived experience of another culture. Although this might suggest the importance of identifying an individual who is "typical" within a cultural community, in practice anthropologists have more often focused upon subjects who, as a consequence of being exceptional, throw aspects of their culture into sharper relief. Significant examples include Sidney Mintz's *Worker in the Cane* (1960), Vincent Crapanzano's *Fifth World of Enoch Maloney: Portrait of a Navaho* (1969), and Marjorie Shostak's *Nisa: The Life and Words of a !Kung Woman* (1981). These accounts are intended to assist the reader in understanding a culture "from the inside," to recognize the taken-for-granted assumptions of another cultural reality and by extension to challenge the inevitability of the reader's own cultural presuppositions.

However, Asch's life suggests different possibilities and different problems. If the conventional anthropological biography identifies subjects who by virtue of their power and knowledge reside at the center of cultural practices, Asch's life prompts us to ask about the implications of growing up in the interstices of several cultures and what this vantage point enables an individual to understand about the project of cross-cultural communication and translation. Asch lived through an era in which anthropologists' and folklorists' certainties about the distinctions between *folk* culture and *modern* culture became increasingly doubtful; and much to his credit, he weathered this transition well and learned to bring a healthy skepticism to such oppositions as folk/urban, folk/popular, traditional/modern, vernacular/literary, and authentic/commercial. Having grown up on a set of social boundary lines, he was

inclined to concede to them less import—and to recognize more
fluidity—than many of his more scholarly colleagues.

As I discuss in chapter 3, Asch also began his recording career
during the communist Popular Front era, which bequeathed to
American leftists of varying persuasions a belief that folk music is
inevitably a politically progressive medium. Among the most im-
plausible claims that Asch made to Joe Klein was his contention
that "folk music had nothing to do with politics." In this interview
as in others, Asch attempted to distance himself from political
movements but could only deny an engagement with politics by
defining it very narrowly—the national and international politics of
parties, states, and ideologies. But the politics of social movements—whether concerned with labor, race, gay rights, poverty, or
prisoners' rights—these were causes to which Asch lent the
mechanism of his business with some regularity. When Jon Appleton remarked to Asch that Folkways was associated in the minds
of many with left-wing causes, Asch denied it: "I hope not," he
disingenuously remarked. But whatever Asch's intentions—and we
can concede to his work some ambiguity and to his purposes
some ambivalence—there can be no doubt about the fact Folkways was an artifact of left-wing culture.

In this context, as in many others, the attempt to define *Left*
and *progressive* quickly becomes hopelessly tangled. I have attempted to find more precise terms; Sam Charters has suggested
that I use the term *social moralists* to refer to the loose conglom-
eration of Americans at midcentury who supported racial equality,
ethnic self-determination, and world peace. Although Charters's
term might better describe the interests and concerns of those
who came together over the collection, performance, and dissemination of folk music in the forties and after, it fails to capture
the complex historical traditions that they had inherited (wittingly
or otherwise). Thus throughout this book I resort reluctantly to
the terms *Left*, *leftist*, and *progressive* with the understanding that
the terms are distressingly vague. They include Communists and
virulent anticommunists, New Deal Democrats and New Left lib-
erals, labor union activists, civil rights activists, prowar patriots in
the forties and antiwar patriots in the sixties, internationalists,
Trotskyites, Maoists, Henry Wallace pacifists—they fought with
each other almost as often as they rallied against common enemies. But they all had Folkways recordings in their homes, and
they believed that these records were a reflection of their view
of the world.

This rendering of the life of Moe Asch begins with the literal and figurative journey of his father from the Jewish shtetl of Kutno, Poland, to the worldly life of the Jewish enlightenment (Haskalah) in Warsaw. Although personally driven to escape the highly insular world of his childhood, where life was circumscribed by the dictates of Jewish law as surely as it was by anti-Semitism, Sholem Asch also understood the value of that life as a literary vehicle. He developed an extraordinary capacity to look simultaneously backward and forward; the backward glance was often nostalgic and romantic, but the forward glance was universalistic and idealistic. The understanding and appreciation of tradition would be the means of its own transcendence. But the reconciliation he hoped to effect between Christians and Jews by his so-called christological novels of the forties was not intended to follow from an obliteration of the rich individuality of the religious traditions (although some of his detractors believed that he intended exactly that); rather, it was to result from an understanding of common origins and cultural principles while *simultaneously* marveling at the extraordinarily divergent paths the traditions took.

Moe Asch spent remarkably little time with his father, either as a child or as an adult. His mother seemed to have recognized a need to choose between nurturing her children or nurturing her husband's career, and the latter was the hands-down winner. Sholem and Madya traveled the world together, absorbed in one another and in the society of international literary and artistic luminaries. And yet Sholem Asch was a specter that remained suspended over the life and work of his second son long after the famous father had passed away. Without indulging unreasonably in psychological portraiture, we can see Moe Asch's life as a struggle to come to terms with his parents' neglect and to create a body of work that his father would find worthy.

The insights about the intersection of cultural traditions upon which Asch charted his life work—though he could not perhaps have articulated them in any deliberate way—were pure Sholem. There could never be an incompatibility in his mind between the need to understand the astonishing variety of human cultural behavior and the imperative of recalling the transcendent dignity that unites all legitimate human purpose in the pursuit of self-determination. He had little tolerance of nationalist movements and was not appreciably more patient with Zionism than with American Afrocentrism. The current preoccupation with distinguishing between European and African cultural threads in the understanding of American cultural life would very likely have puzzled him; he had learned to accept the messy confluence of historical influences that had come to make up musical traditions in the United States and would have refuted the notion that culture was something to be owned, loaned, borrowed, or perverted by one group or another. There was nothing less legitimate about Pete Seeger's rendition of the Negro spiritual "Down by the Riverside" than Leadbelly's performance of Gene Autry's "Springtime in the Rockies," and both singers had made these songs their own in the process of incorporating them into their repertoires.

This narrative, like any other, involves a set of choices about what is to be included and what excluded in telling the story of Moe Asch and his work. Some of these "choices" were, in fact, constrained by the availability of written documents and the interest and availability of those with memories of Asch. With a catalogue of almost twenty-two hundred recordings, I was unable to discuss more than a fraction of Asch's total output. The mammoth spoken word portions of the catalogue are almost entirely neglected, and although I endeavored to touch upon all of those musicians and producers whose contributions to the catalogue I regarded as critical to the shaping of the project as a whole, I have undoubtedly neglected some whose omission others would find egregious. Furthermore, I cannot justify all of my choices objectively; some were simply the consequence of my interest and taste.

Alongside the sins of omission are the sins of inclusion. The work of biographers has sustained some particularly heavy shelling lately, most notably from Janet Malcolm, who has accused those who pick over the remains of others' lives of practicing a kind of personal defilement. In *The Journalist and the Murderer,* and still more explicitly in *The Silent Woman: Sylvia Plath and Ted Hughes,* Malcolm has written of biographers as literary predators for whom the dead—now unable to defend themselves—function as carrion for the feeding of their greedy and perverse tastes:

> Biography is the medium through which the remaining secrets of the famous dead are taken from them and dumped out in full view of the world. The biographer at work, indeed, is like the professional burglar, breaking into a house, rifling through certain drawers that he has good reason to think contain the jewelry and the money, and triumphantly bearing his loot away. . . . The transgressive nature of biography is rarely acknowledged, but it is the only expla-

nation for biography's status as a popular genre. The
reader's amazing tolerance . . . makes sense only when seen
as a kind of collusion between him and the biographer in
an excitingly forbidden undertaking: tiptoeing down the cor-
ridor together, to stand in front of the bedroom door and
try to peek through the keyhole.

Specifically, she condemns biographers for trampling over the
rights, feelings, and memories of the deceased's living colleagues
and companions in their haste to construct a likeness that fits their
ideological, literary, or pecuniary needs. Anne Stevenson's biography of Plath, she suggests, was a disappointment to the reading
public and critics alike because she chose to use discretion in her
treatment of Plath's husband and sister-in-law:

To take vulnerability into consideration! To show compunc-
tion! To spare feelings! To not push as far as one can! What is
the woman thinking of? The biographer's business, like the
journalist's, is to satisfy the reader's curiosity, not to place
limits on it. He is supposed to go out and bring back the
goods—the malevolent secrets that have been quietly burning
in archives and libraries and in the minds of contemporaries
who have been biding their time, waiting for the biographer's
knock on their doors.[4]

There may be those who will have wished that I had written of
Asch's accomplishments without having mentioned unflattering
aspects of his business practices and personal relations. I could
not altogether blame them for suspecting that this is one more
effort to bring a great man down a peg. Perhaps we have become
a society that is too jealous of those who gain renown to concede
to them the privacy that the rest of us customarily enjoy. It is as if,
in finding fault in the lives of those we might otherwise celebrate,
we are better able to live with the modesty of our own accomplishments. For my part, I cannot guarantee that my motives are
uncomplicated by personal curiosity or by the desire to tell a good
story. Although there are those who, in tracing the development of
the *idea* of folk music, would concede to Asch far less of a place
than I have, there are also others who—since Asch's death in
1986—have conceded to him rather more of a place and in so
doing have attempted to minimize the significance of his personal
and professional shortcomings. To the latter, his behavior merits a

bemused shake of the head: "That was just Moe! Nothing to be done about it!"

My view, however, is that the achievements of Folkways were partly a consequence of his personality and his troublesome human relations, and another person would have created a different—and arguably more meager—legacy. One finds here questions of *social* process that are worth our attention, concerning the relationship between commerce and culture, about the formation of the idea of "folk," about "authenticity" as a commodity. Asch's personal relations were also his business relations (he socialized rarely, and almost exclusively with individuals involved with Folkways); although he threw up a wall between his private and public life, in the end there was no private life to protect and all of his public transactions were infected by his personal style. Many have commented on the paradox of a man who strenuously supported unions all his life and yet often treated those who worked for him quite shabbily. He regarded himself as a consummate supporter of the arts, and yet artists who worked for him were sometimes paid erratically or not at all. I have no doubt that had he treated others more generously than he did, either financially or personally, he would not have been able to amass his extraordinary archive of recorded sound nor to have kept it available to the public. Whether this extraordinary monument to the creativity and dignity of humankind justified his practices and behavior is for readers to decide for themselves; most of those whose work appeared year after year in the Folkways catalogue assuredly believed that it did. In the end, I must concur with Asch that to understand the accomplishment that is Folkways, one must understand the man who created it. At the same time, if the reader is compelled to come to an assessment of the man, it is important not to forget the far-reaching significance of his work.

1. REVOLUTIONARY BEGINNINGS

*I*n 1899 Sholem Asch left the provincial town of Kutno—left his father, his mother, and his fourteen full and half brothers and sisters—and traveled by boat along the Vistula to Warsaw, then the heart of eastern European Jewish culture. He carried with him a series of sketches he had written about village life, intending to present them to I. L. (Yal) Peretz, the leading Jewish writer and intellectual of his time. These were not his first literary efforts, nor was this his first attempt to find a readership; his first efforts were read and rejected by a publisher when he was just sixteen. Asch had not been put off by the rejection and now, three years later, with new and refined material tucked under his coat, he believed his work was ready for critical scrutiny by the individual most capable of launching Jewish literary careers.

The countryside he surveyed from the boat railing was not altogether scenic; he described it unsentimentally in a story four years later: "The horizon extends endlessly, and there is nothing to stop the eye: long monotonous fields stretch for miles and miles, for the most part covered with scanty grain, and only occasionally cut by the white ribbon of a cart road bordered with infrequent weeping willows."[1] His family was undoubtedly ambivalent about his departure. This was not the career they had chosen for him. His mother, Malka, had come from a pious family. The second wife of Sholem's father, she had intended to prepare him for the rabbinate. His father, Moses, was a prominent innkeeper and cattle dealer and not profoundly learned. But he was deeply religious and would serve as the model for several of his son's literary creations—large, patriarchal figures who commanded tremendous respect for their physical strength, business acumen, generosity,

wisdom, and spirituality.[2] His five older half-brothers were Ha-
sidim, whose piety Sholem would soon parody for its arrogance
and elitism. His full brothers and sisters were more worldly, Jews
who partook "more of the flavor of wheat and of apples than of
the synagogue and the ritual bath."[3] As the family's designated
scholar-to-be, Sholem was superficially closer to his half brothers,
but he was also drawn to the indulgent pleasures of his full
siblings. When he began to seek out like-minded souls in Kutno,
he was drawn to intellectual circles in which German texts were
avidly read and discussed. Encountering a copy of Moses Mendelssohn's German translation of the Psalms in Hebrew characters, Sholem began to teach himself German, ultimately enabling
himself to read German classics.[4] Yet if his parents were pleased at
his progress in the local religious school, they could not help being
aware of Sholem's growing reputation in town as an intellectual
secularist and possible heretic.

Secularism among Jews in a small turn-of-the-century Polish
town was a relative matter. Jews remained a nation within a nation,
physically isolated within the town, and separated from Christians
by language and custom. The community life of the shtetl was
regulated by the authority of the rabbinate and the power of the
wealthier Jewish merchants (though their domination of those
poorer and less learned was not entirely unchallenged).[5] Religion
permeated every cranny of Jewish life, propelling the weekly cycle
of sacred and secular days and the yearly calendar of holy days.
On Friday afternoons the entire Jewish community was mobilized
in preparation for the Sabbath: "The town becomes lively with the
Friday feeling; people run about, hurrying, and anyone can easily
see that this is the eve of the Sabbath, the eve of the great day. Even
the sun seems to move over the town in a special Friday manner."[6]
When the Sabbath arrived at sundown, the flurry of cooking,
baking, scrubbing, bathing, and mending was evident everywhere.
The effort to reach God through prayer, through piety, through
charity and generosity reached its zenith on Saturday, when everything was focused on the setting aside of everyday life: "And the
night grows quieter and darker; Sabbath arrives with silent steps
and spreads restfulness in the summer world."[7]

Learning was exalted above all else in the shtetl, not for its own
sake, nor certainly as a means to material success; rather, it was the
preeminent means through which men (and most decidedly not
women) ascended to states of godliness. Granted, at times Jewish
learning in the shtetl descended to empty pedantry, and there was

at times a concomitant disdain for manual labor, but although wealth brought men honor and prestige, it counted for little without learning—and learning alone was often sufficient to bring men the respect of their peers. Hebrew was the language of the learned. Yiddish, although the universal language of European Jews, was the homely jargon of the street and until the turn of the century hardly thought capable of sustaining a literature. Often Jews were not literate in the languages that dominated the Christian nations in which they lived, although in Russified Poland the learning of Russian was periodically mandated by the state in all schools.

Yet the shtetl was not static; it did not exist outside of history. True, out of a need for self-protection and -preservation aspects of the outside world were kept at arm's length and, until the late nineteenth century, the rabbinate resisted with much success the incursion of secular influences. But no less than any other ostensibly "traditional" society, eastern European Jewry had always been subject to internal and external forces that brought changes to the fabric of social life. And when German-inspired enlightenment ideals began to circulate among eastern European Jews, even the strength of the rabbinate was insufficient to prevent their influence on those less bound by the sacred world view. In Kutno the center for the spread of secular ideals was the home of Abraham Glicksman, whose schoolmate, Sholem Asch, was a regular and enthusiastic guest. There Asch became acquainted with Goethe, Heine, Schiller, and Shakespeare.[8]

Sholem's experience of others—meaning Christians—was limited during his childhood in Kutno. The very sight of church steeples frightened him, and he ventured into Christian areas of Kutno only when necessary.[9] One evening in early June 1886 or 1887, he was passing through the cobblers' lane in the Christian quarter as it was the only route to his favorite swimming place. Out of a fear of dogs rather than of Christians, he dashed from house to house until he was suddenly surrounded by three or four Christian boys his own age. Pulling at his new Passover clothes and threatening him with sticks and the two dogs that accompanied them, they demanded to know whether he had killed Christ. He knew at the time that Jesus was the God of the Christians, but with "Christ" he was unfamiliar. He repeatedly denied any participation in the crime, but as his new coat was increasingly in jeopardy, he finally confessed. The beating that followed confirmed his sense that additional familiarity with Christians would serve him little.[10]

Still, in the 1880s the insularity of the Jewish shtetl had already started to unravel. For a hundred years, Poland had been absorbed within the Russian Empire and its Jews had been subject to an unrelenting pattern of anti-Semitic restrictions. In 1835 Jews of Poland and contiguous areas of Russia were officially confined to an area known as the Pale of Settlement, a region bounded by the Black Sea on the south and reaching the Baltic Sea to the north. By the last two decades of the century, economic opportunities in the resource-poor Pale, where the number of Jewish paupers grew by almost 30 percent between 1894 and 1898, had forced many younger Jews from rural areas to cities such as Warsaw and Lodz.[11] Jewish tailors, weavers, shoemakers, and bakers had been producing goods from small-scale shops for decades and employing significant numbers of their Jewish neighbors, but with increasing competition from urban factory production and growing population pressure within the shtetl, these operations could no longer sustain Jewish life. Jews streamed to the cities, where in the factories many experienced their first sustained contact with Christians.[12] Rural life throughout Europe, and with it traditional ways of being and thinking, was breaking up.

In the year following Sholem's birth, Warsaw was the sight of vicious attacks on Jews that lasted for three days; the army was ultimately called to bring the rioting to an end in less than timely fashion. This was part of a broader pattern of pogroms in the Pale that year and the next. The Russian government, initially attributing the violence to seditious elements in the population who would ultimately channel the resentment of the masses against the Russian upper class, in time blamed Jewish exploitation of the Russian people as the fundamental cause. In the wake of these pogroms, Russia imposed a new set of restrictions on Jews that would remain in place until the Bolshevik revolution. The areas in which Jews were permitted to settle were severely restricted, causing mass dislocations. Jews could neither own nor rent property outside of those towns now officially designated for their settlement. Jewish artisans were harassed by official decree and unofficial violence, and Jewish farmers became an endangered species. The combination of the pogroms and limitations on Jewish civil liberties accelerated the proletarianization of eastern European Jews. In urban factories they were subject to the exploitation of owners, both Jewish and Christian. With the breakup of Jewish life as they had known it, many—their numbers would soon reach hundreds of thousands—turned to migration, primarily to the United States. Others sought alternative solutions, no less radical, which would find articulation in two fundamental (and often warring) streams of Jewish social thought: Zionism and socialism.[13]

As a teenager Sholem could not have been unaware of the wrenching transformations in Jewish life around him, though as the son of a moderately wealthy businessman he may have been touched less than others. Yet although he might have been insulated from the economic implications of the events swirling around him, his reading of German and later Russian and Polish literature placed him among the few in Kutno who were able to glimpse another view of the world and its possibilities. When Sholem's secularism threatened to become a source of embarrassment to his family, they sent him to the home of relatives in a nearby town where he taught Torah to the children and began the careful observations of peasant life that would become the basis of his earliest stories. After a matter of months he moved again, this time to the Vistula River town of Wloclawek, where he supported himself by writing letters for those unable to write for themselves. From there, Warsaw was a river voyage of less than a day.

Sholem believed that he had reached the limit of what he could learn out in the provinces. To spend additional time in Kutno and surrounding towns would mean time lost, and Sholem Asch was ambitious and in a hurry. An autobiographical figure in a novel he wrote in middle age expressed the frustration of the young Asch in being confined to the countryside:

> I cannot learn anything here from anyone. We are so cut off
> from the world here, no books, no teachers. In Warsaw I shall
> be able to learn something, find a teacher, get to know people.
> . . . I cannot accomplish anything while I am an ignorant man.
> I would like to study languages, sciences. I should like to
> know something. . . . And then until I know something—well
> then, I shall know what I must do with my life. Then perhaps
> I shall be able to accomplish something. But here—what am I
> here?[14]

Sholem's immediate goal was a meeting with Peretz and the hoped-for publication of his stories. There could be no question about it: "For Yiddish secular culture, all roads led to the home in Warsaw of I. L. Peretz. He opened his house and his heart to the younger Yiddish writers and intellectuals, . . . in both physical and cultural flight from their youth."[15] Asch fit the bill precisely and, as he had many before, Peretz encouraged him. There was one criticism: Asch had written his stories in Hebrew. The literary language of the rising new Jewish secularists was to be Yiddish. Asch, again undiscouraged, returned to the countryside to rework his stories in Yiddish. When he returned to Warsaw a few months later, he had with him the stories that would indeed start him on the road to international literary fame. Before the end of 1900, Asch had published several stories in Warsaw's leading Jewish newspapers and had gained a reputation as an important new writer.

Asch was quickly accepted among Warsaw's Jewish intelligentsia. Struggling fellow writers were jealous of his meteoric rise, and some would later attempt to discredit his accomplishments.[16] But those with less at stake were pleased to watch his success and to glow in the company of a young man whose enthusiasms and sentimentality would one day be legendary. As part of a broader effort to reconstruct his life as he might have wished it to have been, Asch would later portray the early years in Warsaw as a time of want and degradation, sharing "dark and dank holes" with fellow writers and coming "in contact with human need."[17] But others have insisted that his doting parents would hardly have allowed him to experience discomfort, never mind actual hardship.[18] Peretz undoubtedly helped him out not only by promoting him and his work to those who mattered but also by offering financial assistance and seeing that he was not drafted into the army.[19]

Prominent among those whose company he shared in that first year were the members of the Spiro family. Like Asch, the patriarch of the family, Menachem Mendel, was a product of the shtetl who had been educated for the rabbinate. And like Asch, having glimpsed the broader world of European civilization and literature, Mendel Spira (as he was known) joined the Jewish enlightenment movement called Haskalah. He had moved his young family in the late 1880s to Warsaw, where he initially sought employment as a *melamed*, preparing young Jewish boys for their Bar Mitzvahs. But having cut off the traditional Jewish sidelocks, or *payas*, and sewn them to his hat, he could by removing his hat and pinning up his coat feign the appearance of a modernized European. With this guise he was able for a time to live in two worlds, shifting between the traditional one in which he was a teacher and the modern one in which he attended university and educated himself broadly in

European history, geography, and literature. By the turn of the century, he had been placed in charge of a school established by the city's wealthy Jews to meet the needs of growing numbers of young men escaping from the countryside in search of a more secular education. Spiro's school provided them with a kind of high school equivalence that prepared them for entering the university. In another recasting of his past, Asch would claim that it was to study with this inspiring mentor that he first came to Warsaw. True or not, the meeting with this man and his family was of the first importance in the configuration of his life and career. The Spiros would be the model for the Hurvitz family in Asch's first grand epic novel, *Three Cities,* and their encounter with an aspiring writer, new to Warsaw, is illuminating:

> "Am I addressing Herr Hurvitz?"
> "What do you want?" queried the teacher by way of admitting his identity.
> "I want to study . . . I'm very anxious to study," stammered the stranger timidly.
> "Quite so; very good! But what can I do about it?"
> "They told me in Krasnyshin . . . if anybody wants to study he should go to Herr Hurvitz the teacher in Warsaw, who helps people on. . . . I'm very anxious to study . . . very anxious."

And later:

> The guest . . . was a handsome youngster as well; unlike his predecessors, who had mostly been small and ill-formed, he was of a tall straight figure and had well-cut features of a provincial simplicity, beautiful large dark eyes and a soft down on his cheeks that looked like a continuation of his side curls and gave him a soft youthful charm. But what chiefly recommended him to Frau Hurvitz was the superior cleanliness of his garments, which in that respect were unlike those of all the young men who had previously turned up from the provinces. He wore the traditional caftan, but it was spotlessly clean. His shirt showing beneath his prominent Adam's apple was decently ironed. And the satin ribbon that he wore, in the Chassidic manner, instead of a tie, was smooth and neatly knotted round his neck. It could be seen that this young man came of no poor family, and even in a house so democratic as the teacher's this fact did not fail to make an impression.
> "Why do you want to study"? asked the teacher.

"I want to be an author."

"What do you want to write?" the teacher went on with his cross-examination.

"I've written a drama already and I've brought it with me to read to literary men."[20]

"The visitor," Asch continued, "had to endure the additional ordeal of sitting at the same table with strange girls, blushing to the roots of his hair. The girls, observing his blush, nudged each other under the table and bent low over their plates to hide their smiles from their father." The two daughters of the Hurvitz family are modeled on the daughters of M. M. Spiro. The elder, Helene, is modest, soft-spoken, and, like Matilda Spiro, a teacher in her father's school. The younger, Sosha, is brash, aggressive, and a revolutionary—as was Barbara (Basha) Spiro. In fact, all members of the family old enough to take a position were revolutionaries of one stamp or another. Menachem Mendel and his eldest daughter, Matilda (Madya), did not join any political party and did not engage directly in revolutionary activity, though they remained sympathetic to revolutionary causes. Menachem Mendel's wife, Bruha, also refrained from joining a party but was perhaps the most ardently revolutionary member of the household, eager to wade into the fray when circumstances required it. Isaac, the third child and eldest son, was an anarchist. Basha became prominent among the Social Democrats (Social Democracy of the Kingdom of Poland and Lithuania, or SDKPiL). The SDKPiL was only slightly less radical than the anarchists and militantly revolutionary in its perspective. Its scope was ardently international, and although a significant portion of its membership was Jewish, the party explicitly rejected both the ethnic nationalism of Jewish socialist organizations, such as the Bund, and the Polish nationalism of other socialist parties, such as the Polish Socialist Party (PPS). The latter counted among its members another member of the household, Isaac Weinberg, a teacher in the school and later Basha's husband. The PPS was reformist and patriotic, although its left wing would merge in 1918 with the SDKPiL to form the Polish Communist Party (Communist Workers' Party of Poland, or KPRP).[21] Because they were largely assimilated, none of the Spiros belonged to the Bund, the most prominent Jewish socialist organization, which had spliced together assorted Jewish socialist and labor organizations in 1897 in order to unite Jewish working masses in common cause with the general Russian Socialist Party. Though highly fractious at times, all of these parties cooperated at moments of extreme social turmoil, when it appeared that revolutionary impulses were about to bear fruit.

It was something of a high-wire act to be both a Jew and a revolutionary in Russian Poland at the turn of the century. The status of Jews as a whole could hardly have been more precarious; as the quintessential outsider, they were the subject of profound distrust. Sometimes fired unconsciously by Polish workers and peasants searching for a scapegoat, at others times deliberately manipulated by government authorities to deflect attention from genuine sources of oppression, anti-Semitism had a grip on the culture of Christian Europe. Yet the urbanization of eastern European Jews in the late nineteenth century also suggested to some that economic sources of oppression constituted a second source of the Jewish "problem," which, though related, had to be distinguished from anti-Semitism. Secularized Jewish intellectuals of the cities began to consider the plight of workers—that massive portion of the Jewish and non-Jewish population that, by virtue of having nothing more to sell than its labor, found itself profoundly lacking in the means to determine its own destiny. When wedded to the agenda of Yiddishkeit—the preservation of Jewish language and culture—those who would constitute the Bund looked forward to a transformed "workers' state" in which Jewish "nationalist" autonomy was preserved while Jews simultaneously contributed to the overthrow of capitalism. But for avowed secularists such as the Spiros, who nonetheless insisted that they were Jews in some ethereal sense, the meaning of being Jewish constantly seemed about to evaporate.

Although there would eventually be a socialist Zionism, Jewish Socialists of this era strenuously opposed the utopianism of those who looked to Palestine as the solution to the plight of eastern European Jews. The fight would have to be waged wherever Jews found themselves, and in the company of non-Jewish workers. At times this could place Jewish Socialists in very difficult positions: in the midst of an attempt to incite Polish workers to revolution, they might discover that they had incited them to attack Jews and Jewish property instead. Potential allies were also potential antagonists, and it was not easy to determine what the consequences of agitation might be.

Perhaps in 1900 the family of M. M. Spiro sensed what the consequences of socialist activism would be. To the young man from the provinces, however, the contrast between this family and his own was overwhelming in and of itself without complicating it with thoughts of revolution. The Asches were steeped in centuries-old talmudic lore. They lived close to the land, with little sense of their immediate Christian neighbors, let alone the world beyond the Pale. It was unthinkable that they might share common interests and a common predicament with non-Jews. The changes they were witnessing in their world were entirely undesirable and unwished for. The Asches, with the exception of their renegade son, could not have imagined a family such as the Spiros. A family that read secular literature, that eschewed the observation of Jewish ritual practice, that sought a hastened end to the world of the Jews as they knew it . . . the Spiros embodied Sholem's own transformation from the traditional to the modern.

Sholem might well have been attracted to the impassioned Basha, just as the protagonist of *Three Cities* was moved emotionally and physically by the revolutionary zeal of her fictional counterpart, Sosha. But he ultimately would not be able to share a woman with a political cause, particularly not a cause as consuming as revolutionary socialism. Though sympathetic to the principles of socialism, he did not join any of the socialist parties or participate in the seditious activities of their members. Despite his growing closeness to the Spiro family and his increasingly frequent presence in their house, he was considered one of the "politically uncommitted" writers among the rising Yiddish intelligentsia. And there was another matter. Almost all of Sholem Asch's protagonists would be drawn to maternal figures who could offer unqualified comfort and succor—the Oedipal attraction was often portrayed explicitly. For the career that he envisioned for himself, a supportive woman who could fill all his physical and emotional needs (for which he would otherwise have little time) would be indispensable. The other sister—quiet, demure, devoted to her father's school—would be a far more appropriate spouse for a soon-to-be-famous writer. Matilda Spiro was three years his junior yet, in many ways, more worldly than he. She alone among the Spiros was drawn to the Jewish religion; on Yom Kippur she would be the only member of the family to fast. Though her father was a Hebrew teacher, he did not insist that his children learn either Hebrew or Yiddish. Matilda learned both, but only because it was important to her. Basha never learned a word of Yiddish, being far less inclined than her Bundist comrades to reach fellow Jews through "the jargon." Their brother Isaac, by contrast, came to Matilda one day with an enormous yearly edition of the *Freie Arbiter*

Stimme, the Yiddish anarchist weekly, and asked her to teach him to read it. It had occurred to him that it would be an advantage to be able to "speak as an agitator to Jewish boys."[22] Isaac was the pride and joy of the household—"the best, the most beautiful, the most idealistic."[23]

Matilda was only seventeen when she, with Sholem by the hand, asked her father if she might marry this "gawky, awkward, boy of genius from the provinces." Menachem Mendel had had another suitor in mind—a young Jewish man of wealth[24]—and responded to his daughters request by slapping her so hard that her face remained swollen for weeks. Sholem was forbidden to see Spiro's young daughter.[25] In response, he promptly seduced and impregnated Matilda. As in countless instances throughout his life, he did it not out of cold calculation but out of impetuousness, in the fever of the moment, as a spiteful response to his rejection.[26] The Spiro patriarch thereafter had no choice; in December 1901 Matilda and Sholem were married. Seven months later, in July 1902, their first child, Nathan, was born.

Matilda continued to teach in her father's school, in itself a risky undertaking, as the czarist government had mandated that all schools in the empire instruct children in the Russian language. The teaching of Polish or Yiddish was strictly forbidden. Periodically Spiro's school was visited by Russian officials and his students were examined in Russian; if they were not found to be proficient, Russian teachers were brought in to take over until their Russian language skills were at an acceptable level. In 1902 Sholem returned to Warsaw from Berlin, where he had been consulting a publisher, and was unable to locate his beloved Madya or their infant son. He finally found them in jail, where she was being held for teaching Polish and failing to teach Russian. Although Matilda was not held for long this time, Sholem resolved in the wake of this incident to leave Poland forever. He and Matilda would soon begin a lifelong pattern of extended travel, leaving Nathan and later the other children with members of the Spiro family. It would be ten years before the family left Poland altogether, but Sholem and Matilda were there less and less in the intervening years.

Sholem wrote continuously, despite the disruptive presence of an infant in the house. Nathan was colicky and cried without relief for the first six months of his life. Sholem and Matilda could not hit upon a solution until Sholem one day picked Nathan up by his feet, held him upside down, and spanked him thoroughly. Though obviously without memory of it, Nathan would maintain in adulthood that he had been "so outraged by the indignity that I shut up and after that howled no more."[27]

Sholem published two small collections of stories in Hebrew in 1902, and a book of Yiddish sketches appeared in 1903 to favorable reviews. In 1904 his most important work to date, *The Little Town*, was published serially, and his reputation as an important Yiddish writer was established. That same year a play of his was produced in Cracow. If the Spiros had had any doubts about the prospects of their son-in-law, there could be none now. Their growing respect is reflected in a description of their fictional counterparts in *Three Cities*:

> So the young man was now looked upon as one of the family. Some of the Yiddish periodicals that appeared frequently in Warsaw had published his first literary attempts and these had roused wide attention. A famous Yiddish writer living then in Warsaw and regarded by the young generation almost as their mentor, considered the young man had a brilliant future before him. So the former Talmudist from the provinces saw a great many literary people and soon had won a name as a short-story writer of whom much might be hoped.
>
> When the young writer came to visit Hurvitz in the evening he would often read out his latest story. Hurvitz thought very highly of him and devoted himself with enthusiasm to the general education of the young man, lent him books and frequently instructed him methodically of an evening in various subjects. Under the influence of the visitor the whole attitude to the Yiddish language both of the father and the daughter completely changed.[28]

Revolutionary fervor grew unabated throughout the empire, during the earliest years of the century, fueled by the financial reverberations of the Russo-Japanese War. The empire, and particularly Poland, were drained. By September 1904 Warsaw was in agony. Large numbers of factory workers were laid off—up to 30 percent in some industries—and those who remained faced wage cuts of 33 to 50 percent. As many as fifty thousand in Poland were dependent upon public charities. Food and fuel became so scarce that in the Jewish community, usually able and intent upon providing for its own, the leaders were forced to cut rations to the Jewish poor.[29] In a chapter from *Three Cities* Rachel-Leah, the character based upon Bruha Spiro, leads a tattered crowd of Jewish unemployed to the Jewish community house in order to demand coal and potatoes. At the conclusion of the incident, the official of the community house succeeds in having the crowd turn against Rachel-Leah. She returns home, where she is chided by her revolutionary son: "I told you not to have anything to do with charity. There's only one weapon . . . "

The Spiros continued to defy the Russian authorities by teaching Yiddish and Polish in their school. But this was not the full extent of their defiance. On 13 November 1904 a mass demonstration was organized in Warsaw by the PPS; it was peaceful on neither side. By early 1905 large-scale strikes were envisioned by the assorted socialist parties, and the Spiros contributed to the propaganda machine that sought to excite worker resistance. Pamphlets, a major source of revolutionary propaganda, were printed outside the empire in the thousands and distributed in Russian cities by young runners such as Isaac Spiro, eighteen years old that year, who darted through the twisted streets of the Jewish ghetto and across the broad avenues of the central district. One such pamphlet was printed following 9 January 1905 ("Bloody Sunday"), when masses of workers and their wives descended upon the Winter Palace in St. Petersburg with a petition of grievances, only to be mowed down in the hundreds by the palace guards.[30] The petition read "The great day has come! The revolution has come. . . . Comrades in all towns, take up the battle! . . . Arm yourselves. . . . Let every street become a battlefield! Break into the arsenals! Seize rifles, revolvers." David Hurvitz, the fictional counterpart of Isaac Spiro, is caught by his mother, his pockets bristling with revolutionary pamphlets. Though he insists that he is only passing them along to someone else the following day, she scolds him for endangering himself as well as the remainder of the family, and hides the pamphlets herself in her cooking pots. When necessary, the Spiros hid more than pamphlets; revolutionaries on the lam sought refuge in the Spiro household, where they were concealed until immediate danger passed.

Five days after Bloody Sunday, a general strike was called in Warsaw. A large garrison of Russian troops was stationed in the city, and although demonstrations were initially peaceful, the presence of the troops in the city made violent clashes inevitable. On 16 January alone, sixty thousand cartridges are believed to have been fired on the populace by the Russian troops; sixty-four demonstrators were killed and sixty-nine were wounded (of whom twenty-nine later died). The next day, the government declared that the city was in a state of siege.[31] Things remained outwardly calm in the days that followed, but the lull would not last. Another strike was declared on 27 January and spread rapidly through the city. Factories were closed and violent clashes between workers and troops resulted in still more deaths. The center of the city became a battleground; as many as two thousand were killed, of whom a third were women and children. The Russian troops were described as "wild beasts" who fired upon anyone who ventured out of doors. It would be days before all of the dead were cleared from the street. The street violence was followed by systematic executions of leaders, and a Cracow newspaper reported that ten wagonloads of executed bodies were removed from Warsaw.

The following day, a hundred thousand people were on strike in Warsaw, according to a *New York Times* account—street cars had ceased operation, newspapers ceased publication, and the bakeries were rapidly running out of bread. When the bakeries attempted to resume operation on 7 February, several more workers were killed. That same day, violence was reported in Kutno, and troops were dispatched from Warsaw to restore order in Sholem's hometown.[32] Students in all but two of the city's schools refused to return to class until the government restored instruction in the Polish language. Such nationalist spirit did not altogether bode well: Polish nationalists had begun to attack Germans and Jews, smashing the windows of houses that did not bear crucifixes.

In late February Matilda became pregnant with her second child. It could not have been a more inauspicious time. Warsaw was becoming an increasingly difficult place in which to live. The army garrison in the city had been bolstered. Patrols stopped citizens arbitrarily on the street to examine papers; patrons of certain coffee shops, or passersby in the open street, were capriciously corralled and marched en masse to Town Hall for examination. The streets were hazardous by day and the populace avoided them altogether at night. For those families suspected of seditious activity, even their homes did not provide a haven from the late night knock of the police. The periodic rattle of wagon wheels at night meant that another family had been roused from their home at bayonet point and transported to prison and an unknown fate.

With resistance momentarily quelled by the viciousness of the government's response, the allied revolutionary organizations prepared for another mass initiative on May Day, centered upon a general labor strike. They were not joined in this by Lenin's Bolsheviks, who held that strikes aimed at *economic* advantage subverted the broader goal of mass political insurrection. But the Bund, the Mensheviks, and others persisted with plans for strikes and peaceful demonstrations, and when day broke in Warsaw on 18 April (1 May in the Julian calendar), the glorious spring weather augured well. Almost all businesses in the city were closed, cabs and streetcars were idle, and the streets were filled throughout the day with men, women, and children in festive attire. The police had declared that street demonstrations were prohibited, and the display of red banners was particularly forbidden, but red ribbons and carnations began to appear in buttonholes. "Here and there," Asch wrote in *Three Cities*, "could be seen a smart young lady displaying coquettishly a bunch of red poppies that gleamed provocatively amid the gray, dense, slowly moving throng of working men."[33] Isaac Spiro mischievously dropped bits of red rag from the rooftops to infuriate the police below and darted through the throng, handing out red flags.[34]

Despite massive troop presence, lining the main streets and blocking escape through side streets, there were no confrontations until after midday. Then, between 1:00 and 2:00, a procession of several thousand workmen, red banners boldly unfurled, began to make its way up Zelanas Street singing, "The people's flag is deepest red." When they reached Jerusalem Street they were ordered to halt. They refused, and a detachment of cavalry charged into the procession, driving the workers back with the flat of their swords. The infantry began to fire into the crowd, sending the now-panicky marchers scrambling. Cornered in the blockaded side streets and in courtyards, the demonstrators, including women and children, were attacked with rifle butt, sword, and bayonet. The soldiers cracked heads and limbs, lacerated bodies. When the streets had cleared, thirty-one bodies remained. Nor had the violence ceased for the day. In the late afternoon, a group of workmen fired on a military patrol and the soldiers responded by firing into the passing crowd. Twenty were left, dead or wounded. That night the revolutionaries began to detonate bombs, the first in the midst of a patrol of Cossacks near the train station. Again the soldiers responded by firing randomly at passersby. By the next morning, sixty-two were reported dead; thirty bodies awaited identification at a district police station.[35]

For days confrontations continued between workers and soldiers, but the wanton cruelty of the military response reduced most resistance to small and spontaneous demonstrations or individual acts of heroism. On 20 April (3 May) a police sergeant was killed; the murderer escaped without being identified. The following day a boy of ten jeered at a Cossack, who responded by slashing the boy from shoulder to waist. Workers continued to threaten shopkeepers who attempted to open their businesses, and roving youths stopped the few cabs in operation and ejected the occupants. By 23 April the Polish Socialist Party called for a suspension of strikes—the May Day demonstration had been a noble start, but the time was not yet ripe for revolution.

The Spiros had not been injured in the course of the May Day demonstration, but their position became increasingly precarious. The long-awaited visit of the police came some days after May Day. M. M. Spiro's school was shut down, and both he and his son Isaac were taken away to the Paviak prison. Isaac had been arrested for ostensibly taking part in an attempt on the life of the Russian governor in Warsaw; his father was implicated by association. Menachem Mendel's life was spared, but he was ordered to leave the city; with his wife and three younger children, he moved to Lodz. Isaac, however, was executed.[36] For her part, Basha had become a heroine for having smuggled arms beneath her cloak to various revolutionary checkpoints around the city.[37] Despite the havoc the events had created within her family, she would remain a dedicated revolutionary.

The political situation subsided little in the remaining weeks of spring 1905. Warsaw was said to have been the "most lawless city in the Empire" at the time, the French consul general declaring that the city was "absolutely terrorized by anonymous groups of veritable brigands who distribute proclamations ordering workers on pain of punishment to stop working."[38] The police confined themselves to dispersing crowds at the first sign of their appearance while allowing street violence to go unchecked. Mass violence reached new heights in late May when a young Jewish woman was abducted and forced into employment in a house of prostitution. Initially attacks were conducted by Jews exclusively against brothels but spread to include marauding Polish workers who preyed on the apartments of the well-to-do. Not until the attacks had escalated into full-scale riots, three days later, did the governor general of Warsaw call in troops.[39]

In the summer an uneasy calm descended on the city. The Russian government had made a few concessions to the nationalists on the matter of education, allowing some instruction in Polish. Additionally, a degree of local self-government was instituted as a sop to the democratic impulses of the populace. But the calm could not last long—the masses had been too politicized, and the economic situation continued to push matters to the brink. In September the bribe takers in Warsaw—not ordinarily the most politically conscious of workers—went out on strike. Because of rampant inflation stoked by the Russo-Japanese War, the three rubles civil servants had been receiving for "favors" were no longer adequate. A compromise was reached: the bribe takers made some concessions but received a "raise," and the crisis passed.[40]

Events in October again gave revolutionaries cause for optimism. A railroad strike began in Moscow on the eighth and quickly spread throughout the empire, paralyzing the entire transportation and communication network. In an apparent concession, the czar responded with a manifesto on the seventeenth that purportedly guaranteed a broad range of civil liberties. Political prisoners were promised amnesty; freedom of assembly, speech, and association was to be protected. Most significant, plans for a representative legislative body—the Duma—first outlined by the czar some months earlier, were reiterated with additional provisions for the enfranchisement of previously excluded nationalist groups, including Jews. The Bund remained suspicious of the Duma for many months, boycotting it through the first half of 1906. But there were signs of a weakened government, anxious to create the appearance of democratization.[41]

If there was euphoria in some revolutionary quarters, among revolutionary Jews it was extraordinarily short-lived. On 18 October a series of vicious anti-Jewish pogroms flared in cities throughout the empire, apparently in response to a prearranged signal. Any lingering doubts about police and governmental collusion in previous pogroms were now washing away. Revolutionaries of all stripes were attacked, but as always Jews suffered the worst of it. Violence to life and property continued for a week, with the most disastrous consequences in Odessa, where within a four-day period three hundred people were killed. Here, as elsewhere, striking demonstrators were set upon by armed mobs. Although Jews were prepared to defend themselves against their fellow citizens, they were no match for the troops and police, who openly assisted the counterrevolutionaries.

Still, revolutionary activity continued unabated, reaching its zenith with the bombing of Warsaw's Bristol Hotel in November and an additional series of strikes and demonstrations in the weeks that followed.[42] Although not among the cities most affected by the October violence, Warsaw again made headlines in December when allied revolutionary forces took to the streets for what they hoped would be the final confrontation. The *New York Times* reported that, as of the last day of November, the strike of postal and telegraph workers had effectively cut off communication between Warsaw and the interior. In the days that followed, sulfuric acid was poured in letter boxes and hundreds of bags of foreign mail remained unsorted. Factory workers threatened to strike on Monday, 4 December, in support of the eight-hour work day, and families jammed the Vienna Station in an effort to flee the violence. The governor general proclaimed that all street processions and meetings were forbidden; the carrying of arms or heavy sticks was outlawed, and houses and shops could be closed on demand by the police. Within forty-eight hours the czar was reported to have been preparing to flee Moscow, the scene of what was described as "great incendiary conflagration."[43]

On Saturday, 2 December—in the midst of the turmoil that had plagued that violent year—Matilda Asch gave birth to her second son. The infant was named for his recently deceased paternal grandfather Moses, who, it was said, was killed at the age of ninety by pirates while rafting on the Volga.[44] If Sholem had had his way, his sons would not have been circumcised; he found the custom backward and superstitious. Three years later he drew fire from prominent Jews by siding publicly with the father of a child who had died before he could be circumcised. The rabbinate insisted the corpse be circumcised before being interred in the Jewish cemetery; the father refused. Sholem defended the father's position in an article he wrote for an anti-Semitic daily, but not stopping at the condemnation of the particular instance, denounced the entire rite as "barbaric." The debate engaged most of Polish Jewry. Although Asch was not alone in his position on the specific case, his heresy won the enmity of many prominent Jews who would not soon forget it. Yal Peretz publicly defended his protégé but privately worried that Asch was risking ostracism by his denunciation of sacred rituals.[45]

In the case of his own sons, however, his wife's religious feelings were allowed to triumph. At the bris—the ritual circumcision—a young boy asked about the name that had been given to the infant: "Why Moses, why so outspokenly Yiddish, the unhappy boy . . . ?" Matilda defended her choice of the name. Not only had it been the name of her father-in-law, but "God alone spoke to Moses. He sent through him the Jewish law, and he took out the Jews from slavery, brought them back to their own land. Why, for a symbol like this it is worth to suffer."[46]

As the Asch household prepared to incorporate a new member with as little impact as possible on Sholem and his work, the revolution continued to swirl around them. Warsaw factory workers did in fact strike in large numbers, and within days owners of some smaller factories faced bankruptcy. On Friday, 8 December, an infantry regiment garrisoned in the city mutinied to protest the brutality of its commander, and two days later a hundred of their number led a procession through the city streets, singing revolutionary songs. On reaching Marszalkowska Street, they confronted another infantry regiment whose commander ordered them to fire on the mutineers. The regiment refused, permitting the procession to pass unmolested, and the commanding officer fled. Reports of the mutiny of the entire Warsaw garrison were premature—on Tuesday the twelfth, a patrol of infantry dispersed a procession on Ciepa Street, killing one man and mortally wounding three others. But it appeared that the police and the military would not be able to maintain even the semblance of control in the coming days. "Bands of Socialists" were reported to have invaded the hotels, forcing the servants to strike, and "agitators" filled the streets and declaimed from street corners. The police remained indifferent, and the troops were expected to hoist the red flag any day.[47]

The Spiros, the Asches, and others sympathetic to the revolution found themselves teetering between euphoria and despair. The situation in Warsaw was indeed desperate, and there was no telling whether the consequence would be revolution or repression. Food was still in alarmingly short supply. The streets were altogether unsafe, both by day and by night. Two weeks after the birth of the Asches' second child, Warsaw's chapter of the Bund issued a proclamation "urging preparation for an armed insurrection." At the same time others worried that although "Warsaw has not yet witnessed an anti-Jewish outbreak[,] . . . should such an outbreak occur it would be indescribably terrible."[48] The day following the Bund's proclamation, the leaders of those first to strike—the post and telegraph workers—were arrested. The next day Polish nationalists, calling for the Jews of Poland to be "transformed into Poles," declared an end to the use of Yiddish and the universal adoption of Polish.

On Christmas Eve another proclamation was issued in Warsaw, and a general strike was called for the twenty-seventh. But the work of the Polish nationalists had succeeded in undermining any chance of a broad working-class coalition. Jewish revolutionaries stood largely alone, and even those who remained sympathetic had little stomach for additional resistance. On Christmas the post and telegraph strike finally came to an end, and the city's military governor banned the sale of newspapers, the singing of revolutionary songs, the holding of meetings, and the organizing of processions. The arrest of trade unionists and revolutionaries began the following day, just as word arrived that the Moscow uprising had been crushed. Somehow the empire's military had been set back on its feet and, in an astonishingly short time, it was all over. The moment was not at hand after all; revolutionaries such as Basha Spiro would have to channel their energy in other directions for the next dozen years.

For the next several years, Basha's energy was largely dedicated to her sister's growing family. Sholem had developed a taste for summer retreats in the country, where he could write with fewer interruptions. In the summer of 1906 he moved the family, including Basha, to the Polish countryside near Warsaw, where on Sundays Sholem would hold court for delegations of students who had come from the city to hear him read from works in progress. Matilda directed the preparations for elaborate outdoor picnics. Before leaving for the railroad station, the students would pose for a photograph with the Asch family—Moe (he was never called Moses) a baby in his mother's arms and Nathan apart, looking miffed, already at odds with his family.[49]

Travels further abroad sometimes included children, but as their numbers grew, they were more often left behind, placed in Basha's charge. Sholem developed a particular fondness for Cologne and Zurich, and it was in the latter, that same summer, that he wrote the play *God of Vengeance*, which proved to be the vehicle that brought him to broad attention throughout Europe. In the autumn of 1906 he showed the play to famed stage director Max Reinhardt and to Reinhardt's leading actor, Rudolph Schildkraut, in Berlin; though the author was unknown to them, they took an immediate liking to his play. Reinhardt would translate it into German, and four years later it reached the Berlin stage in a short but highly influential run. Schildkraut subsequently took the play on a European tour, and Asch won his first substantial non-Jewish audience.

Among Jews the play was less warmly received. It concerned a brothel owner and his efforts to prevent his daughter from being tainted by his business. Perhaps drawing on his memory of the violence that followed the instance of forced prostitution the year before, Asch played upon the tension between Jewish custom and the sordid realities of ghetto life. At the play's denouement, the daughter is undone when she is seduced by one of her father's own prostitutes. More shocking still for Jewish audiences was the father's use of a Torah within the walls of the brothel in an effort to invoke divine protection on his daughter's behalf. When Asch showed it to Peretz, his mentor advised him to burn it; Asch ignored him. It was becoming increasingly difficult for the preeminent man of Yiddish letters to defend his protégé.[50]

In January 1907, thirteen months after the birth of their second son, Matilda gave birth to their third, John (Janek). With three small children, Matilda might now have been expected to ease up on the traveling, but she had already made a painful choice between her children and her husband and had opted for the latter. The boys would be looked after by Basha and other members of the Spiro family; they would get by. The care and nurturing of a great talent required a special touch, and this was the task to which Matilda felt appointed in life. The pace of their traveling continued to accelerate, first to St. Petersburg for an eventful production of *God of Vengeance* and, early the following year, to Palestine, where they were feted by prominent Jewish intellectuals. Shortly after returning from Palestine in late August of 1908, Sholem attended the Czernowitz Yiddish Language Conference in what was then Austria-Hungary. The conference was intended to consider the role of Yiddish in Jewish culture and to propose ways of regularizing it and preventing additional "infections" from other languages. The participants did not consist entirely of Yiddish enthusiasts, but Asch was by then among the most prominent of the Yiddishists, arguing for the translation of Hebrew scripture and other classics into Yiddish. The conference closed with a testimonial dinner in honor of Peretz and Asch.

During these long absences, the children were left in the home of Matilda's parents. Though the Spiros may have warmed to the idea of Yiddish under Sholem's influence, they remained cultural assimilationists nonetheless, and in their care the children's first words were Polish rather than Yiddish. The younger boys appear to have received some instruction in the Polish language.[51] But Nathan may have been required by Russian authorities to begin his formal instruction in Russian. As it happened, his children's lack of familiarity with Yiddish bothered Sholem not at all. But other aspects of their lives in this time might have given him pause.

Members of the Spiro family remained active revolutionaries and were persistently under scrutiny by the local police. Moe's earliest memory was of an incident at his maternal grandfather's house. Two czarist soldiers burst in one day and, bayonets fixed, stabbed mattresses and knocked closets apart, searching the Spiro home for escaped revolutionaries. After they had departed, having found nothing, grandfather removed the lids from two apple barrels; each revealed a young man, shaken but unharmed.[52]

As his reputation spread rapidly throughout Europe, Sholem forged another literary connection that would bring him his greatest fame as well as a searing ignominy in his last years. It was no less important a connection for his second son. In 1908 Abraham Cahan, editor of the most prominent Yiddish-language newspaper in New York, the *Jewish Daily Forward*, began publishing Asch's stories, guaranteeing him the broadest possible Yiddish readership. In the following decades, Cahan would employ Asch as a reporter in the United States and Europe and would serialize his novels. Asch's senior by twenty years, he was brilliant as well as imperious and arrogant. For decades he used the *Forward* not only to promote and preserve Yiddish culture but also (and ironically) to assist recent immigrants in their Americanization. He considered himself a superior judge of literature and was himself a writer of note—he is best remembered for his novel *The Rise of David Levinsky*, which he wrote in English. Perhaps most significant, he was a Socialist, and consequently the *Forward* represented the voice of Jewish American labor and its struggle for humane working conditions, better pay, shorter hours, and the end of piecework in the garment trade, which turned homes into agonizing sweatshops for adults and children alike.

The collapse of the 1905 revolution resulted in a further deterioration of conditions for Jews in the Pale. Pogroms continued with the blatant participation of police, the military, and local officials. Jews were expelled from ever larger numbers of towns and cities in the empire; twelve hundred Jews were evicted from Kiev in 1910 alone.[53] By the close of the first decade of the century mass emigration appeared to have no end, though in fact it was in its final years. Many of Sholem's brothers and sisters left Poland in this period in order to establish themselves in the New World. Although Sholem was not yet prepared to make the move—and was undoubtedly spared the necessity of doing so by his literary and financial successes—he capitalized on his *Forward* connection to make a protracted visit to the United States. In late 1909 he left

Europe, this time regretfully without Matilda, who was then pregnant with their fourth child. Cahan placed him on salary and sent him touring around the country. Asch used the experience to produced a series of travel sketches, published in the *Forward,* in which he described the spectacle of Niagara Falls and the Grand Canyon as well as the squalor of New York tenements and sweatshops.[54] He also made his New York theater debut with a play written especially for its Yiddish stage entitled *The Compatriot.*

On 17 February 1910, with her husband thousands of miles away, Matilda gave birth to the last of the Asch children—and, finally, a girl: Ruth. In the summer of that year, Sholem returned to his newly expanded family. There was additional reason to travel the following year, as Reinhardt finally staged *God of Vengeance* in Berlin. In the wake of this triumph, Sholem set off once again, this time alone, and to Switzerland. Madya's mother began to fear what became increasingly evident—that Sholem Asch was developing an independent life, one both international in scope and romantic and sexual in nature. She urged Madya to go after him, which she did, leaving the three boys behind in Lodz. For several months the boys remained in Poland, Moe and Janek living with their grandparents and Nathan some distance away, boarding with friends of the family. That year—1912—their grandmother Spiro died, and Sholem and Madya returned for the funeral. Sholem took Moe, Janek, and their young uncle Adam to stay with Nathan in his boardinghouse for a few days. When the funeral was over, the Asches all finally left Poland together—all save Nathan, who inexplicably remained in Lodz until some time after his birthday that summer, when his father came to retrieve him.[55]

Sholem had not forgiven his homeland for the way it had treated his family during the revolution, and in 1912 he fulfilled a promise he had made to himself years before to leave it. He had not found the United States to be sufficiently appealing during his first visit and chose instead to relocate his household to a large estate in Châtillon-sur-Seine, on the outskirts of Paris. The house at 5 rue Kleber was surrounded by a large garden, and beyond that a high wall, topped by broken glass that caught the sunlight—and kept the curious at bay.[56] Sholem decreed that, from the moment of their departure from Poland, Polish was not to be spoken in the family. Instead, they were to adopt the language of their new home.

Sholem's choice of Paris was not arbitrary. Although he had a larger German readership than French, Paris was rapidly becoming the center of expatriate artistic life, particularly among expatriate Jews from the Pale. The Asch household became a bucolic refuge for young painters attempting to establish themselves in the city. During the week Jules Pascin, Amedeo Modigliani, and Moise Kisling would inhabit the demimonde of Paris art life, spending hours over drink and conversation in cafés of the Latin Quarter such as the Café d'Harcourt on the Boulevard St. Michel. On Sundays they were invited to bask temporarily in the material comfort of an "established" writer—though no more than four or five years their senior, Sholem's success had come so early that he seemed part of a previous generation. Initially they came to see Sholem, but discovering that his moods were unpredictable—if he was immersed in the writing of a novel, he would be more alive to his fictional characters than to his guests—they eventually sought Matilda's company instead. The demure young school-teacher had become gracious and cosmopolitan. An entire genera-tion of expatriate Parisian painters, including Georges Braque and Marc Chagall as well as Pascin, Modigliani, and Kisling, fawned over her and in turn received much-needed nurturance and encour-agement. Elaborate lunches and teas were set out for the artists, who undoubtedly appreciated the nourishment as much as the conversation. A small house in the garden occasionally accommo-dated them overnight. Moe remembered as an adult that Pascin had committed suicide in the garden house, but in point of fact Pascin did not commit suicide until 1930, and then in his own Paris studio, not in Châtillon.[57]

Increasingly the children lived in a world apart from that of their parents. When "father" was not writing he was in the city, meeting poets such as Max Jacob in the cafés. And when home and writing, the peace he required was absolute, the consequences of breaking it calamitous. Moe would recall that he was "very world-minded and children bothered him," but Nathan's recollections were more explicit:

> His concentration and drive were so great that it always seemed it would be an overwhelming catastrophe were he to be interrupted; yet interrupt him we did not only out of care-lessness, mix-up, the ordinary ruckus of our games, but as the French say, *exprès*, on purpose. . . . It may have been out of envy of his importance to us, or the attention he was getting from my mother, as well as something else—a kind of death wish—for my father after all, was something like God, and to

interrupt God in the midst of work which is obviously more important than oneself is to invite annihilation. . . . I was almost fascinated by the moment when he would be pulled from his concentration by our noise, and would at first try to disregard it, to remain somehow in his creative world; but we wouldn't let him. Our whispers became louder and turned strident; somebody pushed somebody else, somebody pushed back, there was a sudden shout, somebody punched, somebody screamed. Then came the break: torn from his work, he pushed himself back from the table; came the moment when existence itself teetered; cowering on the floor we stared up at him, no doubt fascinated by the thunder and lightning about to descend on us.[58]

The house enchanted the boys. At the front gate one rang the bell by pulling on the tongue of a stone lion. Inside a closet they found bullet holes that, they were told, dated from the Franco-Prussian War of 1870.[59] When she could, Matilda would send them outdoors. Moe and John sometimes flew kites together in the garden, but although they were the closest in age, the real alliance was between Moe and his older brother. Nathan was refining his ability to stand up to his father, and Moe doubtlessly admired him for it. John was odd man out, often left in the company of his mother and baby sister. It helped only slightly that Moe and John attended school together, taking the train daily to Paris where, in the company of other Jewish children, they attended a French-speaking Alliance Française. Matilda sent Nathan to a Russian-language school because she had in mind to resettle the family in Vilnius one day, where the children could learn to be proud of their Jewish heritage, and Nathan had the best chance of keeping up with his Russian.[60] But when home again at the end of the day, Moe and Nathan would again pair off.

One incident shattered the peace of their life outside Paris more than any other. Among the abundant rose bushes, the pear, cherry, and fig trees, and the humble rows of brussels sprouts were the bronze-colored, gold-flecked flowers of the reseda plant. Sholem apparently valued these most highly, for one day when the family dog had defecated upon them he exploded at the younger boys, imagining that Moe and John had relieved themselves on the plants. Sholem spanked them long and hard. It was difficult for the children to imagine how he had made such a mistake—had life been so crude in Kutno that children defecated in the garden? They carried the injustice of it with them for a long time.

This episode aside, life for the children would never again be as idyllic as it was during the brief years in Châtillon. In the summers, his taste for spas undiminished, Sholem would take the family on seaside vacations to Normandy. In the summer of 1914, the family enjoyed one last vacation together, and then their life together in France came to a sudden and complete halt. The assassination of Archduke Ferdinand the previous June had toppled the precarious balance of European peace; in early August the news reached Normandy that Germany had declared war on France. There were immediate consequences for the Asch family. Most of Sholem's royalties came from Germany and Russia, and with the outbreak of war his income would be cut off for the foreseeable future.[61] Matilda had been making plans to have the family move to Palestine for an extended visit, and she still contemplated an extended stay in Vilnius, despite her fear of czarist anti-Semitism. But both destinations now appeared to be unfeasible without Sholem's accustomed income.

Sholem seemed to have had a plan in mind for precisely such an eventuality, and it was rapidly set in motion. He wired Basha in Warsaw and instructed her to meet the family in Châtillon. Once there, rapid preparations were made for another trip to the United States. As luck would have it, the Yiddish actor and impresario Maurice Schwartz was preparing a Sholem Asch play for the New York stage, and the playwright's presence would be useful. Additionally, he arranged to be placed on the payroll of the *Jewish Daily Forward*, for which he would write a weekly column, a "sermon" of sorts for the Yiddish-speaking Jews of New York. Having moved Basha and the boys to more modest quarters in Paris, near the Place d'Italie, Sholem sailed for New York from Liverpool, England, on the SS *St. Paul*, arriving there on the seventh of November.[62] Matilda and young Ruth followed a few weeks later.

Through the end of that year and into the next, Basha and the boys waited for the money and instructions from Sholem that would enable them to join the remainder of the family in New York. By the time the funds arrived, the ports in northwestern France had been blockaded by the Germans. Escape was only possible to the southwest, so the four boarded a train in Paris in early July for Bordeaux. The war was already taking a murderous toll on the French army. As their train wound through the countryside, they were periodically left to wait on a siding as troop trains to and from the front rumbled by. Through the open doors of the boxcars, the boys caught sight of limbless men who were being transported from the front in baskets, literally "basket cases." It was a formative moment for two of them. Moe would attribute to this experience his consciousness of "man's inhumanity to man" and date his awakening social conscience to it. John's memory, recalled in old age, bears the mark of dream-sifted impressions. Traversing the rich wine country by day, he saw large baskets of freshly harvested, golden grapes. As the day closed, church bells rang across the countryside. Men and women raced to a town square where, affixed to a church or town hall, there was a poster announcing the start of the war. Waking early the next morning before the others, John peered out the window—someone had neglected to pull the shade—and there, in the predawn light, he saw the same baskets that the day before had been filled with grapes. Only now they were filled with limbless war victims. Of course, the sequence of events does not jibe—if war had been declared only the day before, one could not expect to see casualties already. But a child's imagination could not be expected to generate a more potent image of war's arrival, and of war's ability to transform reality.

Basha, Nathan, Moe, and John sailed out of Bordeaux on the fourth of July aboard the SS *Rochambeau*. On the thirteenth they arrived in New York and were ferried to the immigration center on Ellis Island. They might have been quickly processed and returned to Manhattan were it not for two matters. First, John's eyesight was poor and the medical examiners threatened briefly to detain him. Second, while the *Forward* had sent a clerk to assist Sholem in seeing that his family was quickly processed (Sholem's English was never terribly good), he refused his help. His blustery insistence served none of them well. He misspelled their names and misrepresented their birth dates so that one child was ostensibly born a month or two after another. When the situation threatened to unravel altogether, they summoned Baruch Charney Vladeck, an editor and later the business manager of the *Forward*, to straighten matters out.

If the circumstances were unnerving, their meeting with Vladeck was nonetheless an auspicious one for the boys. And for Basha it must have been a reunion of comrades. Vladeck was born Baruch Nachman Charney in Minsk, 1886, and in his youth had much in common with the Spiros. Arrested in 1904 for his involvement with a socialist Zionist group, he received his political education in prison and subsequently became a Bundist. Early in 1905 he was sent by the Bund to Minsk in order to orchestrate a general strike.

While leading a group of workers across an open plain, he was set upon by Cossacks, who slashed him brutally and left him for dead. After recovering, Vladeck resumed his revolutionary activity, spending another six months in a Vilnius jail and, when released, using his rhetorical talents and extraordinary personal daring to rally workers in several Polish cities. The following year he was a Bund delegate to the convention of the Russian Social Democracy, where the Bolsheviks and Mensheviks had their final falling out. Although most Bundists supported the relatively accommodationist Mensheviks, Vladeck remained a militant and, for his trouble, was taken to lunch by Lenin, who lobbied strenuously for his support. When it appeared that the revolution was not after all at hand, Vladeck left for New York, arriving in late 1908, where the *Forward* greeted him as a hero.[63] The Yiddish paper immediately employed him and sent him on a speaking tour of the United States, and for the next three decades he combined his work for the *Forward* with a vigorous and successful career in New York City politics. In time the Vladecks and Asches became close friends, and Vladeck would come to the rescue of one or more of them on many other occasions.

In the end the Asch boys and their aunt were detained on Ellis Island only a few hours (although the discrepant birth dates would create passport problems for Moe for many years). Already versed in the ways of American bureaucracy, Vladeck was able to assure the immigration and naturalization authorities that no deception had been intended—Sholem had merely wanted to show his sons that he was in charge. By the end of the day they were reunited with their mother and sister at their home in Greenwich Village at 3 Bank Street. Basha remained with them only briefly before she found quarters of her own. Valuing her independence above all, she had acquired training as a nurse in the years prior to her arrival in Paris and now found employment at New York's Mount Sinai Hospital. For their part, the Asches departed almost immediately for a vacation in the New Jersey shore town of Bellmawr. Though Sholem felt financially strapped by the absence of his European royalties and complained about the paltry sum he received from the *Forward* for churning out a weekly column, the Asches' poverty was certainly a relative matter. It did not force them to forego vacations, which were still an established aspect of Sholem's annual routine. He was now writing a play each summer for the Yiddish stage and depended upon the quiet solitude of the beach or countryside in order to concentrate. And whatever their deprivations during this time, there was always a hired cook in the household.

At the close of the summer, Sholem saw that the family was settled again in the city—this time on West Farms Road in the Bronx—and departed on another journey to Palestine.[64] The boys confronted the task of learning another foreign language: father had again declared that the family was only to speak the language of its adopted home. In 1905 the New York Board of Education had established a complex system of special classes to teach immigrant children some English before being thrown in with their more Americanized peers. Moe almost certainly spent the first four or five months of the school year in the "C" class, where with other immigrants of varying ages he was taught the rudiments of English. Once he had a sufficient grasp of the language, he was placed with those approximately his own age in the regular class.[65] (In fact, because of language difficulties, he was a class behind those his age.) On the streets, the Asch boys were immersed in a milieu at once familiar and foreign. Immigrant Jews from the Pale had been crowding into the tenements of the Lower East Side since the 1880s, but by 1915 the Bronx had been an outpost for upwardly mobile Jews for more than ten years. It still had the qualities of a suburb and lacked the stark deprivation of the Lower East Side. Jews here were a bit more comfortable, less inclined to be immersed in either the struggles of Jewish labor or the intellectual and cultural ferment of the tenements.[66] With his comparative wealth, Sholem could not have been expected to subject his family to the squalor of the Lower East Side, although he wrote about it frequently and claimed to understand its essence. Instead, the boys spent their first American year with their economic equals.

The Asch children had been in the company of other eastern European Jews for most of their young lives and, culturally, what they saw and heard in the Bronx must have seemed familiar. In dress, cuisine, gesture—in their common experience of anti-Semitism—they shared much with their neighbors. But there were things that set them apart. The First World War had ended the great tide of eastern European Jewish immigration; the Asches were virtually the last ones through the door. Thus all of their immigrant Jewish neighbors had been here longer. Initially they spoke neither English nor Yiddish; when living in Brooklyn a couple of years later, they did briefly attend some classes in Yiddish, but such education amounted to little. Their tastes were doubtlessly informed by the rarified company they

had kept in Paris. And their acquaintance with Judaism was, ironically, spotty. Although major domestic holidays were celebrated
in the home, the family had never belonged to a congregation
(and never would). And although Nathan had turned thirteen
the summer they crossed the Atlantic, he was not Bar Mitzvahed.
Arguably, circumstances prevented Nathan from being Bar Mitzvahed, but circumstances did not account for the fact that Moe
and John were also deprived of this most fundamental Jewish
rite of passage. It was simply Sholem's desire.

Sholem dictated to his children in other ways as well. A player
piano was purchased for the Bronx house and hoisted in through
a window one day. The boys adored it and spent hours listening
to piano rolls, but Sholem would only tolerate classical music in
the house—popular music of all kinds, because he considered it
decadent, was forbidden. Similarly, the phonograph was in constant use, and father was only too happy to purchase the recordings of Enrico Caruso, but popular records were forbidden. Card
playing was also prohibited—Matilda's first task as the wife of
Sholem Asch was to cure him of gambling and excessive drinking
and, having succeeded, they sought to ensure that the children
would not fall victim to the same vices.[67]

Sholem returned from a tour of several months in Palestine, and
the family moved once again. The city had begun to encroach on
their neighborhood in the Bronx, but rather than moving to still
more remote suburbs the Asches moved back to Bank Street in
Greenwich Village. Here, on the West Side, Sholem was just minutes away from the heart of New York Jewish life, yet also
sufficiently removed to avoid continual encounters with admirers—at least for the time-being. Old routines quickly reasserted
themselves. Each week, as the Thursday deadline for the *Forward*
approached, the tension in the household would expand until it
filled every corner and the slightest sound would spark father's
rage. When the deadline had been met, Sholem would escape to
the cafés, as he had in Paris. Across town at the Café Royale, Jewish
men of all stamps lingered over glasses of tea for hours, lost in
heated political or literary debate. When Sholem Asch entered,
heads turned and his name was whispered. "The great Asch . . . "
With his fame, his erudition, and his imposing figure, Asch inevitably dominated the conversation in the Royale. Others deferred to
him readily out of admiration, if not affection. Occasionally he
would take his oldest there with him. Nathan was proud of the
attention his father attracted in such circles, yet squirmed to hear

his parents speak Yiddish on the streets or to watch them read a Yiddish newspaper on the streetcar.[68]

Just as the Asches lived figuratively (and, during the year on Bank Street, literally) on the margins of Jewish immigrant life, they also lived on the margins of Jewish political life. The *Forward* had been founded in 1897 as a socialist publication and remained for decades the voice of New York Jewish labor. Because a writer's work is largely solitary, Sholem's weekly deliveries of his column to the *Forward* building at 175 East Broadway became one of his primary means of meeting and mixing with others. Politically unaffiliated (although the FBI would do its best in the late forties and early fifties to brand him a Communist because of his associations), he nevertheless was tremendously sympathetic to Jewish socialist precepts, particularly its support of Jewish labor. To a significant extent, for the first three decades of the twentieth century, Jewish "labor" meant garment workers.

There is no single explanation for the overwhelming presence of immigrant Jews in the needle trade during this time. Certainly they had brought some knowledge of it with them from eastern Europe. Additionally, it required large numbers of semiskilled laborers, and its labor requirements had increased exponentially since the growth of mechanization in the industry. Also significant is the fact that many of the employers were themselves Jewish, although often of the previous, German, generation of immigrants. For many recent Jewish immigrants, it was simply less threatening to work for a fellow Jew than for a Gentile.[69] Unfortunately, Jews were no less reluctant than others to exploit Jews. Shops were hellish: crowded, filthy, poorly lighted, poorly ventilated, and poorly heated. The work permanently bent the bodies of young women, at times maiming them. Paying often according to work completed rather than by the hour, contractors were redefining the "task" at the turn of the century so that real wages were actually falling. Through the first decade of the century, the wages of garment workers remained the lowest of any laborers in the city. Although the New York Tenement House Act of 1892 officially outlawed manufacturing in the home, two decades later thousands of tenements were still licensed to manufacture clothing. To make ends meet, entire immigrant families—from toddlers to the elderly—were pressed into the manufacturing of clothes, often from break of day to late at night.[70]

To remedy matters, the International Ladies' Garment Workers' Union (ILGWU) was organized in 1900. Although it included significant numbers of Italian immigrants, it was dominated numerically and politically from its inception by Jews. For almost its first ten years it led a precarious existence, running on a shoestring, flirting with bankruptcy, barely withstanding the raiding of other unions. But a decisive strike in late 1909 and early 1910, propelled by the anger and enthusiasm of its women workers, changed all that. Its settlement in February may have resulted in little of a tangible nature for the membership, but its effect on the strength and spirit of the union was decisive. Jewish class consciousness was galvanized further by the horror of the Triangle Shirt-Waist Factory fire the following year. Still a fresh memory for many when the Asches arrived in New York in 1914 and 1915, the fire claimed the lives of 146 Jewish and Italian girls in a matter of eighteen minutes. With no means of exit (the doors having been locked by management), many jumped from ninth-floor windows to their deaths rather than face incineration. Sholem wrote movingly of the event in *East River,* a novel he published at the close of the Second World War:

> Above her, out of the shattered window, a flaming body fell,
> like a living torch, down to the street below. . . . She threw a
> terrified glance to the street below. . . . She could see safety
> nets held out spread by groups of firemen. She could see bodies falling from the walls of the building with hair and clothing aflame. . . . She could see girls crawling through the
> windows on hands and knees, trying frantically to hold on to
> the bare walls. Others seemed to be hanging in mid-air, their
> falling bodies caught by projecting cornices.[71]

Through the Depression, the ILGWU rested firmly at the core of American Jewish labor, ultimately gaining power not only in the field of labor but also in the political arena.

In 1915 the ILGWU Local 25, the Waist and Dressmakers' Union, established a summer retreat for union members in the Catskill town of Pine Hill. They called it Unity House, and it accommodated fifty in small cabins and dormitories. By the turn of the century, Jews were escaping from the heat of the city to the Catskills in significant numbers. At first the "resorts" consisted of little more than converted farms and farmhouses; later, of course, they became quite elaborate. Laborers rarely had the means of taking "country" vacations, but Unity House was subsidized by the union, which in turn used the opportunity to educate its membership and build union loyalty. The following summer, and probably the next two as well, Unity House solved a perennial problem for Sholem—what to do with the children while he wrote. Exploiting his *Forward* connections, he succeeded in reserving places for his sons and Basha at Unity House while he, Matilda, and young Ruth installed themselves in a nearby resort.

The summers at Unity House showed Moe another side of Jewish life. Here he came in contact with laborers and their children as he never had before. In the evenings they would gather for lectures and discussions—and singing. For the first time Moe heard revolutionary songs, perhaps occasionally in English but more frequently in Yiddish—the proletarian songs of immigrant Yiddish poets such as David Edelstat and Joseph Bovshover.[72]

In 1919 Unity House was moved to a much larger facility in Forest Park, Pennsylvania, but Moe and Nathan returned to the Catskills that summer and the next, just the same. Although with the end of the war Sholem's royalties were again flowing from Europe, he decided that the older boys could now be expected to demonstrate some financial independence. In Kingston, not far from the original site of Unity House, Moe and Nathan spent two summers living and working with migrant fruit pickers. They slept at night in leaky, open-sided clapboard barracks, waking at dawn to pick apples. At night they flopped back into their beds, muscle-sore and numb. Only on weekends did they have the energy to do more than was minimally required to function. On Saturday nights they would join the young migrant workers in a local barn for a dance, where Moe, less interested in the dancing than in the music, would hang out with the musicians. He ingratiated himself by offering to carry the drums. When the dance was over, the musicians would remain, jamming on a saxophone, piano, bass and drum. Moe stayed, too. This was something else new—a first taste of jazz.[73]

During the school year Moe and his brothers would occasionally attend a performance of one of Sholem's plays at the Second Avenue Theater, despite the fact that they did not have a sufficient grasp of Yiddish to follow it closely. The grand sentimentality of an Asch play could be riveting, even if one did not entirely follow the dialogue. Frequently, at the close of a performance, Sholem would address the audience directly, a practice he had started in 1910 when, on his first visit to New York, he had appealed to an audience for the support of a subsidized Yiddish theater.[74] During the war Sholem used these occasions to generate support for Jewish war relief. He could rouse himself into an emotional frenzy in very short order and, subjected to a barrage of shouts, threats, and tears, audiences would throw wallets and jewelry onto the stage. To the poor, unassimilated immigrant Jews of the Lower East Side, Sholem Asch was their "great man," their prophet.[75]

During the 1917–18 school year, Moe broke his leg severely in a fall down a short flight of steps at school. He contracted osteomyelitis, an infection of the bone marrow, and there was some doubt that his leg could be saved. Moe was placed in the care of a surgeon at Flower Hospital, where he remained for the better part of a year. Through the months of operations and convalescence, the pain and tedium were relieved only by the regular presence of Basha at his bedside. Moe had grown closer to Basha than had any of the other children, and in that year in which she helped save his leg, their friendship was cemented. Basha spent much of the time explaining to Moe her philosophy of life, her dedication to socialism, her hopes for a brighter social future. Moe absorbed much of what he heard from Basha, eventually sifting it through his father's skepticism about doctrine and party affiliations. It was also in this year that Lenin's October revolution became the obsessive topic of conversation among New York Jewish radicals. The long-awaited event appeared to be at hand. The Bolsheviks changed forever the landscape of American radicalism, and for at least the next four years, only the bold or foolhardy criticized the new Russian order within Jewish immigrant circles. By 1923 the *Forward* would become an outspoken and energetic critic of Soviet Russia, but much of radical American Jewry embarked on the transformative process that would result in the formation of the American Communist Party. From 1917 to 1920, thousands of Jews returned to Europe from the United States, many among them Socialists who had been biding their time in the States since the failure of the 1905 revolution, waiting for the proper moment to return.[76] Basha may well have been chomping at the bit during the year she nursed Moe, yet she may also have known that this was probably the last time she would ever spend with him.

The leg did heal, although it remained spindly and Moe limped for the remainder of his life. And Basha did leave. Having fulfilled this last obligation to her sister's family, it was time for her to live out her political visions. She had had fewer differences with the Bolsheviks than most other Jewish Socialists; it concerned her little that Lenin was hostile to Jewish nationalist impulses. Now she had no qualms whatsoever about throwing in her lot with socialism's best hope. Sholem and Matilda would see her one last time, in Poland in the mid-1930s. In 1936 Matilda wrote to Nathan, urging him to visit Basha in Moscow, where she was living like an aristocrat. But none of the boys ever saw her again. Stories and rumors of her new life drifted back to the boys through their mother. It was said that she had become a close adviser to Lenin and that she had established the Soviet Union's first day-care system. Given the material comfort of her life in Moscow, this is plausible. She also was said to have had a daughter who became an admiral in the Soviet navy, but of this none of the boys ever knew for sure.

The Asches moved twice more in New York. Their only newly built house was on Avenue J in Flatbush, a bare tract of land near a cemetery at the intersection of Brooklyn and Coney Island. Sholem was attracted by the rose garden that the builder had thought to plant beside the house but did not consider the inevitable expansion of the city around. When construction soon began across the street, breaking Sholem's concentration every hour of the day, the family looked for another home. They settled upon a house at 78 McFarland Avenue, Arrochar, a "queer, marginal," and isolated tract of southern Staten Island inhabited by "Italians, émigré White Russians, and strays from Greenwich Village" (the neighborhood was razed in the 1960s during the construction of the Verrazano Bridge).[77] Here Sholem found the peace he had been seeking since his arrival in New York. The six of them would remain in this home longer than in any other during their short life together as a family.

Moe was entering adolescence and becoming rapidly Americanized. He joined the Boy Scouts; he went to movies with John and Nathan and with their neighbors, the Vertovicci brothers.[78] Sholem continued to travel, often heading west in order to lecture to Jewish communities throughout the States. From these tours he would often return with books for the boys—beautifully illustrated volumes from the West, with stories of life on the range, with the cowboys, among the Indians. Often they recounted events in frontier history, the heroes, the outlaws—Buffalo Bill and Deadeye Dick. Moe took particular interest in these books. Here was his first inkling of an America that was otherwise invisible from the five boroughs of New York.

His curiosity about the broader world was sparked in another way as well. To compensate for the frequent absences of his father and the loneliness that resulted, Moe took up ham radio. Although commercial radio broadcasts did not take hold until the mid-1920s, late in the previous decade there were hundreds of amateurs in the United States who communicated with one another on home-made sets. When the United States entered the First World War, all amateur radio communication was forbidden, but by 1919 Ameri-can amateurs were at it again, piecing together sets according to plans found in various amateur radio magazines and communi-cating around the country by morse code. At the close of the war, army surplus radio parts became available in great quantity, and Moe probably built his own sets from used parts by haunting electronics shops in lower Manhattan. His fellow amateurs in the States were able to relay messages from one coast to the other and from Canada to Mexico by 1920, and the possibilities of interna-tional shortwave communication were discovered at the end of the following year.[79] The new technology opened previously un-imaginable opportunities for communicating across barriers of distance and culture.

Radio electronics became Moe's passion and obsession. By the time he was in high school, it appeared that he would pursue a career in science or engineering. The choice was a fortunate one. In a highly competitive family, he had found a field that was free of other takers—no one else in the family had any facility for technology, least of all his father. Scientific fields were paradigmati-cally "modern," and Sholem had been a proponent of modernity all his life. A scientist was a person of the future; there could be no doubt but that the West was on the verge of technological innova-tions that would alter everyday life in profound ways. Through a field such as electronics, Moe could earn the respect of his father without entering into direct competition with him. By contrast, Nathan's choice of vocation was more fateful. Sholem had forbid-den his children to become writers. Why? Perhaps he wanted them to make their own way, without capitalizing on his name, or perhaps he feared their competition (his writing was riddled with Freudian dilemmas—he was surely conscious of the ways in which sons threatened to "replace" fathers). Whatever the reason, Sho-lem's decree was an irresistible temptation to Nathan, and he became a writer.

Sholem remained concerned about the fate of European Jewry throughout the war and, at its close, the situation appeared des-perate. In much of eastern Europe, social order had broken down almost entirely. Advancing and retreating armies had uprooted hundreds of thousands from their homes, cities had been leveled, and farm production had been brought to a near standstill. There was nothing to prevent the wholesale violation of life and property, nor to check the deadly spread of famine and disease. As in decades past, the peasantry sought an outlet for its anger, fear, and frustration, and Jews were again the ready scapegoat. By war's end as many as a million eastern European Jews were homeless, clogging roads and highways in search of family and friends who might be of help. Their arrival in a town stirred the guilt and bitterness of townsfolk who, even had they been so inclined, could spare little in the way of food or shelter. Anti-Semitism was fueled still further by emergent nationalist movements, and a new wave of pogroms swept across the landscape.[80]

In November 1914 an umbrella organization, the American Jewish Joint Distribution Committee (JDC), had been created to coordinate the philanthropic impulses of American Jewry's many factions—the wealthy and assimilated, the orthodox, the laborites and socialists. Formed under the leadership of Felix W. Warburg and heavily dependent on the generous example of wealthy German Jews such as Jacob Schiff, Julius Rosenwald, Louis Marshall, and the Guggenheim brothers, it held mass rallies in 1915 and 1917 in Carnegie Hall in order to raise badly needed funds. It was under the auspices of the JDC that Sholem addressed the audiences of the Yiddish theaters in his appeals for war relief contributions.

President Woodrow Wilson had declared 27 January 1916 Jewish War Sufferers Relief Day. Herbert Hoover, however, who was to make his mark by supervising famine relief in the years following the war, initially concluded that all European war victims were to be treated alike, and he resisted special arrangements for Jews. But Warburg prevailed upon him, and in exchange for a substantial "contribution" to the general Relief Administration, the JDC was permitted to plan for the rescue of European Jewry. In the end it was a relatively easy matter to raise substantial funds; disbursing them, though, proved difficult. The channels through which relief had been distributed in the war no longer existed, and so it was up to the JDC to develop new ones. Two teams of forty staff members each were assembled and trained in the United States and, on agreement of the government, clothed in the uniform of the American military in order to lend them authority and credibility. Among them were experts in sanitation, child care, and economics, as well as volunteers whose personal qualifications counted for more than professional ones. Lawyers, bankers, clergymen, and scholars came forward to volunteer their services to the relief effort. The presence of American Jews was thought to be particularly important as a source of reassurance to European Jews, whose sense of hope had very nearly run out.

Sholem Asch was among the volunteers in 1920 who stepped forward to distribute relief to his former countrymen. He had been an important figure in the JDC from its earliest years, and his substantial literary reputation among European Jews would prove invaluable in opening doors and establishing trust. There was just one problem: in order to wear the uniform of a U.S. Army colonel, he would have to be an American citizen, and he had not been in the States long enough to qualify for naturalization. Louis D. Brandeis had participated in the first organizational meeting of the JDC in 1914, and two years later was appointed to the Supreme Court. His help was enlisted, and an exception was permitted in the naturalization laws. On 10 August 1920 Sholem, Matilda, and the children gathered in the U.S. district court in New York City, and with Sholem's brother Irving among the witnesses, all six were made citizens of the United States. Then off went Sholem to Europe for a sojourn of several months. The work of the JDC coincided happily with the publication of his collected works in Yiddish by a Warsaw publisher, and consequently the grim work of refugee relief was lightened for Sholem by a warm reunion with Warsaw's intellectual community.

Moe graduated from his junior high school, the Rosebank School, PS 13, on Friday, 24 June 1921. He had risen to the top of his class and was consequently awarded the privilege of delivering the valedictory address. That September he entered Curtis High School. The curriculum assigned to him was standard for the day—English, Latin, math, and civics in his first semester, with science replacing civics in subsequent semesters. Additionally, there were required courses in drawing, music, "physical training," and, in his first year, elocution. He could have studied German or French, and it is curious that he chose not to, given his acquaintance with them. There were also a number of business courses in the curriculum, but it is likely that Sholem would not have approved of such unintellectual pursuits. Moe performed well in music class that first semester, despite his later remembering to have had no interest in or facility for music.[81] And his best grade that semester was in drawing. But in the second semester of his freshman year, his grades began to fall off; he barely passed Latin, and in science—which he must have anticipated eagerly—he did not fare much better.

Sholem returned home to Staten Island after a matter of months, but it was apparent that this most recent trip to Europe had contributed to his growing dissatisfaction with life in the States. He had never found it easy to write here, and his taste for American society was probably not heightened when, in 1923, a performance of his *God of Vengeance* in New York was shut down by the Society for the Suppression of Vice.[82] Sholem began to negotiate a more permanent return to Europe. Nathan was no longer his direct responsibility, as he had recently entered Syracuse University, and it would be an easy matter to bring Ruth with them and place her in a European boarding school. But John and Moe represented something more of a problem. At the end of 1922, Moe still had two and a half years of high school to complete; John had three and a half. A possibility accidentally presented itself to Sholem when he and Matilda were invited to Philadelphia to attend the 1922 premiere of D. W. Griffith's *Orphans of the Storm,* a movie starring Dorothy and Lillian Gish, and Joseph Schildkraut, the son of the famous Yiddish stage actor. They stayed the night with Morris Vladimir Leof, a prominent Jewish Philadelphian and mentor to aspiring Jewish intellectuals, artists, playwrights, and dissidents. In speaking with Dr. Leof about the problems involved in returning to Europe, they were told of a marvelous agricultural school in nearby Doylestown, the National Farm School. It had been founded by Rabbi Joseph Krauskopf at the turn of the century after an encounter with Count Leo Tolstoy, who convinced him to turn Jews into farmers and disperse them across the United States.[83] This was not the vision of a lunatic, but part of a tenacious (and doomed) movement that persisted among a few Jewish immigrants for decades. In the 1920s young American Jews trained there in order to prepare for settlement in Palestine, and Sholem, though not a Zionist, might have been drawn to the image of his sons bringing the sacred soil of Palestine back to flower.[84] And there was another incentive—as the children of a famous Jew, they were given scholarships. The Asch boys could board there for free and finish their high school education. It seemed perfect.

Moe's last semester at Curtis was not a promising one. His grades fell off badly and he failed geometry. Only his science grade was above average. When he was discharged from Curtis, on 7 February 1923, a school administrator reported on his character: in the categories of honesty, courtesy, personal appearance, industry, and responsibility, Moe was rated "excellent," with one added provision: "not very strong physically." He came home to a house full of packing crates. With the exception of personal belongings, the contents of the house were placed in storage. The six of them would never live together again. It was agreed that Charney Vladeck would take some responsibility for the boys and keep an eye on them; through him and the *Forward*, Sholem could send money and messages to his sons. Moe and John were bundled off to the National Farm School, Nathan returned to Syracuse, and Sholem, Matilda, and Ruth sailed for Europe. John could not have been happier with the arrangement—horticulture had been his passion since his memorable encounter with grapes en route to Bordeaux. But Moe was miserable. Despite (or perhaps because of) his summers in the Catskills, he had no great love of the outdoors, and his game leg made the farm work excruciatingly difficult and painful. Within a few months, he left the Farm School and returned to New York in order to present his predicament to Vladeck, leaving young John to finish out his high school years by himself.

Though sympathetic, there was little Vladeck could do but provide him with a steamship ticket. Asch embarked from New York with a passport and a one-year visa (later extended for a second year) that would enable him to visit "all countries" for the purpose of visiting relatives, studying, and traveling. He must have suspected that he would receive a frosty welcome from his parents—they had, after all, gone to considerable trouble to free themselves of the children. Ruth had indeed been placed in a boarding school; they certainly were not going to welcome an errant son back into the household. Sholem once again had a creative solution that would enable both of them to capitalize on Germany's rampant inflation. He would place Moe in a school there and provide him with a monthly sum of money out of his American royalties. If Moe converted a dollar each day into deutsche Marks, he could live comfortably and the money would go very far indeed.

Regardless of his science and math grades at Curtis, it was apparent that Moe had a knack for electronics. Sholem discovered a highly reputable technical school, the Electronische Hochschule in Bingen-en-Rhine, where Moe could learn about the very latest developments in radio technology. The only impediment was the barrier of yet another new language. The alternatives were few and highly unattractive—under no circumstances would he return to the Farm School—so Moe immersed himself in yet another unfamiliar language and culture, and over the next two years learned everything there was to know about the electronics of sound.

2. RADIO DAYS

Asch must have felt that political violence followed him around in Europe, or perhaps that it was simply a constant state of affairs on that side of the Atlantic. In January 1923 some months before his arrival in Bingen, French forces had entered and occupied the Rur basin, barely a hundred miles to the north. French president Poincaré had become frustrated that Germany had not been delivering coal and timber, promised as part of the war reparations, and had consequently seized this rich industrial region.[1] The effect was to exacerbate the inflation that had reached vicious levels in Germany that year. By the end of 1923 the exchange rate was twenty-five billion marks to the dollar. The price of goods would leap dramatically in the course of a single day, so that factory workers were sometimes paid twice a day and given time off to shop before prices jumped yet again. A trip to the bakery required bushels of marks. It was reported that Germans bought two steins of beer at a time, preferring to drink the second one warm rather than risk having the price jump two or three times in the interval.[2] Everyone suffered, though it fell hardest on the sick and elderly whose pensions disappeared in a flash. In the winter of 1923 there were reports of death from starvation and exposure.[3] It was no wonder that Sholem had advised Moe to exchange his dollars on a daily basis.

Stabilization measures, which had a gradual salutary effect, were introduced beginning in 1923. In the short run, however, they fueled frustration and provoked angry responses in some regions of the country. The French invasion of the Rur basin had resulted in widespread unemployment in the Rhineland, and there was

substantial resistance among Rhineland bankers and other businessmen to the introduction of a new currency. A separate Rhenish currency was proposed, and with the backing of the French
and Belgians an armed band took over the town hall in Aachen in
October. An independent Rhenish state was announced, and uprisings followed in a string of cities along the Rhine, including
Wiesbaden and Koblenz on either side of Bingen. Yet whatever the
effects of the new economic measures, most Rhinelanders could
not stomach the thought of succumbing to French domination,
and in November bands of farmers confronted the separatists
near Bonn in a bloody skirmish that left 180 of the separatists dead.
The central players in the independence movement were appre-
hended and brought to trial, and by early 1924 the Rhineland was
again part of the fragile German state.[4]

It was not an auspicious way for young Asch to begin his studies.
He watched a town being shot to pieces in what was likely one of
the October uprisings. On another occasion his passport was
snatched from him, and on still another a girl who had been sitting
beside him on the train was raped by French-employed Senegalese troops.[5] As events swirled around him, he attempted to get
his bearings in an unfamiliar language; his smattering of Yiddish
only got in the way.[6] Still he struggled to understand his instruc-
tors and gradually learned the necessary technical vocabulary to
follow their lectures.

Inflation was not the only problem plaguing Weimar Germany in
1924 and 1925. Only the year before, in November 1923, Hitler had
made his first attempt to seize national power. While the Beer Hall
Putsch had failed and Hitler was now biding his time in prison, the
roots of an ethnocentric nationalism had already taken hold. The
parameters of an idealized Germany had begun to take shape
years before around the "cult of the folk," which celebrated the
human body, its connection to nature, and the purity of the
German race.[7] Now, in the search for the causes of the corrosive
economic hardships, Germans turned to time-tested scapegoats.
Jews were readily identified as the cause of economic and political
chaos, and even before Hitler gained a following, they were being
pushed to the margins of German society. Far from providing a
haven, universities were often at the forefront of anti-Semitic
initiatives. As early as 1919 university fraternities voted to expel all
Jews as well as those who married them, and only a year after
Asch had left Germany the German Students' Organization called
for Jews to be removed from the universities altogether.[8]

Asch's isolation in Bingen was broken during his first year by the proximity of his sister. Ruth's boarding school was only a few miles away in Wiesbaden. She was just a young teenager, whereas he was approaching twenty, but they saw a good deal of each other until, at the end of a year, she rejoined her parents. For their part, Sholem and Matilda were summering in Wiesbaden during the mid-1920s, and consequently Moe was probably with them for some portion of the summer of 1924. Although his parents' wealth would protect them from the growing anti-Semitism for almost another fifteen years, Moe was not so lucky. He looked every bit as Jewish as his father (in fact, looked increasingly like Sholem), and while he might have liked to have been "simply" an American, the option was not his. When on the streets of Bingen or Wiesbaden, he was preyed upon by gangs of nationalist youths who taunted and shoved him.

To compound Asch's problems, the promised dollars did not always arrive promptly from his father. It was not that Sholem was reluctant to send it; more likely he was forgetful or found something on which he would prefer to spend his available cash, such as a work of art. But for Moe it meant stretches of hunger, wondering how long it would be before his father would remember him.[9]

When Moe Asch spoke years later of his growing consciousness of American folk music, he consistently cited three formative moments. The first was his encounter with the folk heroes depicted in the books his father had sent him from the American West. The second were evening gatherings when he and his fellow students shared folk songs of their native countries. The electronics school in Bingen attracted an international student body; German, Dutch, and French students predominated, but others came from as far away as Russia, Brazil, and Argentina. In the charged political climate of the 1920s, the singing of folk songs could not have been an entirely innocent endeavor. For Moe the occasion provoked a defensive reaction. He could only have regarded himself as an American by now, but despite glimpses of a broader Americana afforded by the books his father had sent him, he only knew about a narrow slice of American life. Given the prevalence of anti-Semitism, he would not likely have called attention to his Jewishness by singing the Yiddish songs of his mother, and in any case he would not have regarded them as a symbol of a "national" heritage. The other students insisted that the United States lacked any folk culture—they imagined a primitive wilderness overrun with native savages (or so he thought). Asch sensed that they were wrong but had no way to prove it. The books his father had sent him included "ballads," but they had been presented as literature and Asch had not the faintest idea how one might have sung them.

In 1925 Sholem and Madya settled in a house in the Parisian suburb of Bellevue, and Moe visited them during his school vacations. On one such visit he was ambling along the Seine in Paris when he came upon a book stall on the Quai. Among the books was an original 1910 edition of John Lomax's *Cowboy Songs and Other Frontier Ballads,* which Moe eagerly purchased.[10]

Lomax had been writing down the lyrics of cowboy songs since he was a small boy, growing up in rural Bosque County, Texas, in the 1870s and 1880s.[11] Early efforts to interest fellow Texans in his collection met with rebuff. But while completing a master's degree at Harvard in 1907 he ventured to present some of the lyrics to Professor Barrett Wendell for an assignment in which the students were to discuss literature of their own region. Wendell was enthusiastic and in turn showed them to his colleague, the eminent Shakespearean scholar George Lyman Kittredge. They encouraged Lomax to expand his collecting, first by endorsing a letter he sent to a thousand newspaper editors in the West. Lomax asked the editors to have their readers assist him in making "a complete collection of the native ballads and songs of the West" by sending him lyrics.[12] The results were astonishing, and gratifying. When Lomax had completed his master's degree and returned to his teaching post at Texas A&M, Wendell and Kittredge arranged for him to receive a scholarship that enabled him to go on his first collecting expeditions during his vacations.

For American scholars such as Wendell and Kittredge, the collection of oral ballads—indeed folklore as a whole—was at that time a quaint appendage to the study of "great" literature, occasionally useful for the light it shed on the process of literary creation and dissemination. Folklore was primarily the province of scholars whose interest was almost exclusively in the *words,* and it would remain so for another twenty-five years. The musical settings were of little concern, and the social settings in which they were performed were rarely given a thought. But Lomax had a different project in mind in publishing his cowboy ballads. He ignored basic precepts of folklore scholarship by combining bits and pieces from different variants of a single song according to his personal aesthetic criteria. And he printed musical notation for eighteen of the songs so that they could be heard as they were *sung.* His frank intention was to produce a volume that would stir the interest of westerners in their native culture.

Lomax knew that he would have to overcome the resistance of those who regarded his ballads as cheap, tawdry, and unworthy of serious attention, and to do so he enlisted the help of no less than the former president of the United States. Professor Wendell had previously enlisted Theodore Roosevelt's help in a failed attempt to secure a grant for Lomax from the Carnegie Institute. Meeting in a hotel room in Cheyenne, Wyoming, in the summer of 1910, Lomax and Roosevelt discussed the content of the endorsement that Roosevelt had promised to write of Lomax's collection. For Moe Asch this endorsement, perhaps more than the book itself, became the third (and arguably most crucial) iconic moment in the development of his consciousness of folk music. As he mentally reconstructed and embroidered the endorsement over the years, it became a wholesale validation of folklore and folk song as "the real expression of a people's culture."[13] More than that, Roosevelt ostensively implied that "a people have no culture unless they have folksongs."[14]

But this is not what Roosevelt wrote. Reproduced in Roosevelt's own handwriting on the pages immediately following the dedication (to Roosevelt himself), the endorsement establishes the validity of Lomax's enterprise primarily by noting its continuity with the European ballad tradition: "There is something very curious in the reproduction here on this new continent of essentially the conditions of ballad-growth which obtained in medieval England; including, by the way, sympathy for the outlaw, Jesse James taking the place of Robin Hood." Like Wendell and Kittredge (and perhaps under their influence), Roosevelt saw Lomax's work as a project in oral literature. He added as well that the book *ought* to appeal to people of the West and Southwest because of its historical content, and because it preserved an oral tradition that was being "speedily killed by competition with the music hall songs." There is no suggestion that the songs were part of a living culture, nor that the American people as a whole possessed a valid and sustaining folklore. Nonetheless, *Cowboy Songs* permitted Asch to return to his schoolmates with evidence that the United States was not merely a melting pot but had a "uniqueness" to its culture derived from its many different parts.[15]

In the spring of 1925 Asch had completed two years of study in Bingen. Remarkably, through the distractions and hardships he had managed to learn the fundamentals of radio electronics,

working under a professor who had built the radio communication system in Berlin during the First World War. Having entered the
technical school without a high school degree, he had not progressed far enough to have earned the coveted engineer's
"Diplome," which would have provided him with a good deal of
standing in Europe. But it was not his intention to practice his
trade in Europe, and he had sufficient knowledge to enter *some*
aspect of the electronics field in the United States. In April Field
Marshall Paul von Hindenburg, the aging German hero of the First
World War, was elected president of the Republic. His election
resulted from a coalition of conservative nationalist forces and
symbolized a desired return to Germany's days of glory. Although
Hindenburg's presidency did not threaten the liberal Republic as
thoroughly and immediately as some had expected, it was nonetheless hailed by nationalists who took to the streets in jubilant
and aggressive celebration when Hindenburg's election became a
certainty.[16] Asch was in Berlin, preparing to leave Germany, and
found the mood of the revelrous crowd sinister. He later remembered being knocked down that day by the "hockenkroiz kids";
although the swastika was not much in evidence in northern
Germany in the mid-1920s, he might well have encountered aggressive nationalists in search of conspicuously Jewish targets.[17]

It was an auspicious time to enter the radio field in the United
States, though it did not seem that way to Asch when he returned
from Germany at the end of the summer of 1925. He settled on
Panapple Street in Brooklyn and set about looking for work in
electronics. By then scores of small companies were making radios furiously, hoping to make a bit of hay before being charged
with infringing on General Electric or Westinghouse patents. Asch
would find work with one until a sufficient inventory had been
established—or until lawsuits shut them down—and then he
would be fired and start looking for employment all over again.
For a while he commuted to Jersey City to work for Lee De
Forest, the quirky and litigious inventor whose audion tube made
possible the transmission of voice—rather than just telegraph
signals—through the airwaves.

When Asch became discouraged about ever making a living in
his chosen field, Charney Vladeck once again stepped in to rescue
him by arranging a meeting with David Sarnoff of the Radio
Corporation of America. RCA had been formed in 1919, when the
U.S. government, having seized the American Marconi company
from the British during the First World War for strategic purposes,

succeeded in retaining control of it and the means of developing its own wireless communication industry. They did so by constructing an agreement between the Department of the Navy, the Wall Street banking establishment, and those American corporations with a stake in wireless communication. The involvement of General Electric was particularly important because of the patents it held, and the following year Westinghouse and AT&T came to hold a substantial interest in RCA as well.[18] RCA took over the facilities of American Marconi, as well as its administrative and research staff—including a twenty-seven-year-old commercial manager (and second in command) named David Sarnoff. Sarnoff had gained notoriety seven years earlier by having established radio contact with the sinking *Titanic* and for remaining awake for three days in order to relay messages and coordinate the rescue operation. The story had probably been embellished in the process of establishing Sarnoff within the pantheon of great American entrepreneurs, but it was correct in its essential elements.[19]

RCA was established with the intention of refining and marketing wireless radio telegraphy from ship to shore, from ship to ship, and from continent to continent. In 1920, however, Sarnoff was promoting another idea—the broadcasting of music from a single source to hundreds of thousands of radio receivers in the homes of individual American families. RCA, he proposed, would manufacture the radios. His suggestion was dismissed, but not for long. The following year the Department of Commerce began to issue licenses for commercial broadcasting, and by the end of 1922, 576 radio stations had been licensed in the United States. The demand for home radio sets shot up at a meteoric pace, and although Westinghouse had started the commercial production of home radios in June 1921 no one was really prepared. But Sarnoff had become RCA's general manager in May 1921 and promptly set the company's sails in the direction of radio manufacturing. In June of the following year RCA shipped two hundred thousand radio sets and began to address the backlog of orders.[20]

Asch recalled later that Sarnoff was a friend of his father's, having grown up with him in Kutno, but the fact is that Sarnoff's childhood was spent four hundred miles away in the outskirts of Pinsk, and his slight relationship with Sholem Asch was probably a consequence of mutual involvement with the Joint Distribution Committee. Still, it appears that it was partially on Sholem's behalf that Vladeck set up the meeting. On the appointed day Asch went to Sarnoff's office in the tower of the Woolworth Building (where he had been since the days of American Marconi). Sarnoff was only thirty-five but already generated awe—and occasionally fear—in those around him. Asch, at twenty-one, felt very much the kid.

"Well, what do you know? What's your background?" Sarnoff asked. Asch proceeded to describe a device he had been working on that would permit residents of an apartment building to attach their several radio sets to a single antenna. Sarnoff responded by insisting that engineering was no place for a Jew; he regarded himself as a salesman, and in his view it was only in sales that a Jew could get ahead in the United States. But Asch insisted that his heart was in electronics, so Sarnoff proceeded to arrange a position for him. Ever proud of his telegraphic skill, he eschewed the use of a telephone and instead contacted his chief engineer using his telegraph key: he would be sending a young man over to see him—please find him a position.

Perhaps Asch had succeeded in what he had set out to accomplish—for a time he had steady work and was not dependent on seasonal employment with fly-by-night companies. But other reports of his encounter with Sarnoff were not altogether favorable. Probably through Vladeck, Sholem Asch learned that Sarnoff had found his son to be arrogant and disrespectful. Twenty years later Sholem's brother-in-law, Adam Spiro, an electrical engineer, had come to the United States as a survivor of the Nazi regime. When he approached Sholem for assistance in gaining employment, he was told that Sholem could no longer exploit his connection with Sarnoff—all of his credit with the great entrepreneur had been squandered twenty years earlier, when he had sent his son to see him.

Asch was set to work cataloguing the parts of RCA's first radios, the Radiolas. The competition among various radio manufacturers, and particularly between RCA and Zenith, had become quite keen. RCA had started pouring beeswax into their circuitry so that the radios could not be dissembled and copied without ripping apart all the wiring. For six or seven months Asch catalogued and worked to establish a standardized nomenclature of radio parts. Perhaps absorbing the paranoia that prevailed in the industry at the time, Moe imagined that he was regularly followed home by an RCA agent to see that he did not convey company secrets to a competing manufacturer. Still more improbably, he presumed he was fired because he had learned too much: "We can't afford to have you here." If RCA had been concerned that he might be inclined to sell his knowledge to the competition, they more likely would have retained him and remained in his good graces. But for whatever reason, Asch left RCA.[21]

The remaining years of the decade were not easy ones for Asch. He was employed intermittently building and repairing radios, but he must have had the feeling that he was not achieving what was expected of the son of a famous man. It might have made matters slightly worse that other members of the Asch family seemed to be faring better. Sholem remained prodigiously productive. Though not yet halfway through his literary career, his collected works were published in twelve volumes (in Yiddish) in 1921, and again in 1924 (also in Yiddish) in eighteen volumes. Nathan had not finished at Syracuse but instead returned in 1923 to Europe, where he was greeted by his parents with approximately the same degree of enthusiasm that they showed upon Moe's arrival. They were able to dispense with him thanks to a letter from Madya's brother Olek, the entrepreneur of the family. Olek ran a highly successful shipping firm in Danzig but was in need of a business associate that he could trust absolutely—a nephew appeared to fit the bill. He sent for Nathan, who worked for him for a few weeks, but Nathan chafed under the rigid hierarchy typical of German business firms. At the end of that year, with his aunt and uncle out of town, he fled to Paris, where he quickly fell in with the expatriate literary crowd—Josephine Herbst, John Hermann, Kaye Boyle, Ford Madox Ford, Ernest Hemingway, Malcolm Cowley. Some became Nathan's lifelong friends, correspondents, promoters. By the middle of the following year he was publishing short stories, and two novels followed in short order: *The Office* in 1925 and *Love in Chartres* in 1927, the latter based upon the courtship of his first wife, Lysel Ingwersen.

Moe had never developed his brother's sociability. Despite the adaptability required by the many changes of venue during the first twenty years of his life, he had little social grace; his pleasure came neither from his work nor from the society of others, but from his involvement with amateur radio. He joined the local amateur radio club in Brooklyn, and with the exception of occasional work colleagues, his friends—to the extent that he had any—consisted of fellow "hams." Communicating over the airwaves—likely about radio equipment, antennas, interference, signal strength—Asch was able to remain connected with others at a safe distance. When he did meet fellow hams face to face, as he did at the Amateur Banquet of the Executive Radio Council at the

Hotel Pennsylvania in March 1926, the topic of conversation remained technical matters. They scribbled their call letters on one another's programs with promises of future "conversations" on the air.

The following year, while working at a radio shop, Asch was introduced to Frances Ungar, who had come there with a friend, the wife of Asch's co-worker. Frances was some months older than Moe, and although also the child of Jewish immigrants, she was born in New York City. Her father had been a shop steward in a shirt factory. When Frances was just two, her mother learned that she was the recipient of an inheritance back home in the Austro-Hungarian Empire, and she took her two daughters and son back to eastern Europe to claim it. But when she arrived the inheritance mysteriously evaporated, perhaps confiscated by anti-Semitic government officials. She nonetheless remained in Poland for six years, only rejoining her husband in New York in 1913. Frances, like Moe, was the product of two cultures, an unstable household, and a stormy marriage.

Frances was attractive, though hardly the beauty Asch's mother had been. They began to spend time together, but it was not in Asch's nature to be romantic. He recalled his courtship some years later as a "natural act, like breathing." The owner of the shop where he was working hosted a Halloween party; Moe took Frances, and it was there that he proposed to her. On 18 March 1928 they were married—there did not seem much more to it than that. They moved into an apartment together on President Street in Brooklyn; the first piece of furniture they purchased together was a phonograph.

In late June Moe received a letter at his new place of employment, Walthals Radio Store at 61 Portland Street. On *Forward* stationery Charney Vladeck wrote, "Dear Moe, It is seven weeks now that I have been hunting for you without avail. I have some gifts for you and your wife from mother and I would like to turn them over to you." Vladeck had been traveling in Europe, where Sholem and Madya had apparently received word of Moe's marriage to Frances. They had ladened him with wedding presents for the newlyweds and he was now anxious to deliver them.

Asch worked for less than a year at Walthals. It was again becoming apparent that he found it galling to have to work for others. In February 1929 he received a memorandum from his superior: "Effective immediately we intend to hold you responsible for all cabinet work leaving the place. Any set that arrives in the customer's home in an undusted or bad condition will be checked up and the responsibility will rest entirely with you." This may have been the last straw. Asch quit, despite the lack of any immediate prospects. For some months, he and his wife lived on the salary she made as a clerk at the Bureau of Motor Vehicles, while he did a little radio repair work on his own at home. But grander plans were in the works. With some capital loaned by his father, Asch opened his own radio shop—Radio Laboratories—on Driggs Avenue in Brooklyn in early 1930. Moe and Frances lived in an apartment over the shop. In the early years of the business, Frances did the bookkeeping. Asch had an electronics man by the name of Bluestone to help him out in the store; he was the first of a number of Radio Lab employees, and he did not last long.

By the start of the new decade, Asch had been repairing radios for about four years, and he knew them pretty well. In early July of the previous year, he had received a letter from Sid Rosenkrantz, who had worked with him at Walthals and whom Asch would later employ in his own shop. "I heard about you leaving Walthals," he wrote. "I think you are better off. . . . One thing I can safely say, Moe, is that you taught me servicing." Radio Laboratories was an official servicer of RCA Victor and Stromberg-Carlson radios. The year Radio Laboratories opened, Moe attended Stromberg-Carlson's service engineer's technical school at their factory in Rochester, and they in turn were particularly energetic in sending business to Asch over the years. Radio sales and repair were his bread and butter in the early years, and he was brazen in his eagerness for business, even writing to his former employer at Walthals and offering to perform their repair work for them. Additionally, he sold and installed automobile radios. Public address systems represented another side of the business—an increasingly important one over the next decade.

Asch saw himself as something a good deal more than a radio repairman. He fancied himself an inventor as well, and to that end he continued to tinker with other electronic devices. In the spring of 1929, before the opening of Radio Labs, he wrote a statement testifying that he was the sole inventor of the multiple-antenna device of which he had spoken when with Sarnoff: "I without other help have devised an equipment for aerial installation which is a complete unit in itself and may be used for from two to forty to fifty sets hooked up together." Although there is no evidence that he attempted to patent it, he went to some lengths to protect his rights to it. When he read an advertisement for an outfit that was marketing a similar device, he wrote to them with the hope of collecting royalties. "I believe that you are aware of the fact that I am the inventor of such systems," he wrote, "which have been in use in various localities for three years without a break-down. The royalties on each unit shall be seven cents apiece for the first 3000 units and 5 cents apiece for the next 3000."

Other innovations came to Asch rather more gratuitously. In 1932 he wrote in a draft of a letter to Stromberg-Carlson:

> I have been approached by bootleggers and gangsters to install radio receivers in their automobiles for the reception of these [police] signals. These people know me through the installation of broadcast receivers such as Philco etc. in their automobiles which they use on their trips along the Atlantic Coast. . . . It is but a simple matter to tune them to a higher frequency and I believe some other service stations are going to reconnect by means of. . . . That it is not my principle to do so is not the reason of this letter.

As finicky as he may have been on occasion about the nature of his customers, he recollected some years later that he did a handsome business manufacturing navigational devices for bootleggers. Bootleggers coming in off the coast under cover of dark or in fog were ostensibly able to determine their distance from shore by Asch's device, which measured the relative strength of radio signals from New York's commercial stations. In 1932, he maintained, this provided him with his primary source of income.[22]

New York newspapers in the 1930s ran a regular column for radio enthusiasts; the *New York Sun* had an entire radio section on Sundays, to which Asch contributed a column in December 1930 entitled "How a Service Man finds Troubles by Concentration on Socket Tests." Asch also submitted articles to various radio magazines, with mixed success. An article on antenna installation was rejected by *Radio Retailing* in March 1931, whereas another on receiver installation was accepted by *Radio Engineering* the same month. In fact most of Asch's inventive energy in the early years of Radio Laboratories appears to have been directed at the improvement of radio reception.

For four years Moe toiled away at his radio business, served the needs of the local gangsters, and hoped he might be permitted to weather the Depression. It was not to be. At the end of 1933 he no longer had the means of keeping Radio Labs afloat by himself. "Due to conditions I had to give it up," he wrote in a letter the following February, "and [have] now merged with an allied industry in order to exist."[23] Mearns and Zolnier was a Brooklyn electronics outfit on Third Avenue that specialized in sound systems and microphones. The merged shops retained the name of Asch's company—Radio Laboratories—and moved to new quarters at 8 Fourth Avenue. Harry Mearns and Paul Zolnier were very able electronics men; additionally, Mearns's father was a bookkeeper and permitted Frances Asch to give up her role in the business. Moe and Frances left the apartment above the shop on Driggs Avenue and moved to another on U Street, also in Brooklyn.

The newly configured Radio Laboratories continued to repair radios and to install them in automobiles, but the emphasis of the business was increasingly on the building and installation of public address systems—by 1938 all mention of radio service was omitted from Radio Laboratories letterhead. Mearns and Zolnier undoubtedly expected that Asch would open up new markets for their public address equipment. Asch had a bit of entrepreneurial spirit about him, and in the hope of creating new markets he wrote to various New York department stores in late 1935 urging them to consider the installation of public address systems. He also drafted an article about the barkers at Coney Island and their need for higher quality sound equipment:

> At this stage of microphone amplification technique it is
> very silly to see a barker holding a brown or nickel box at-
> tached to a handle close to his mouth emitting noises that
> are supposed to be words to attract customers to a show
> or exhibit. . . . A lapel microphone that does not hide facial
> expressions and permits the free movement of hands and
> body would be just the thing. . . . People like to be fooled; a
> hidden microphone makes a man stay longer to listen to
> the barker to find out if for no other reason where the
> sound is coming from. Here is where you have a chance to
> sell your story.

It is not clear whether Asch succeeded in getting salesmen to use high-quality systems; these efforts did not in any case open up substantial markets for him. Rather, it was in two other areas that Asch made contributions to Radio Labs' newly configured business—Jewish organizations (especially Yiddish theater) and electioneering. His first major break in the latter came on 31 October

1936, when Radio Labs constructed a sound system for Franklin Roosevelt's triumphant Madison Square Garden speech at the close of his second presidential campaign.[24] Roosevelt was Asch's idol—a politician who represented the best of American democratic ideals. Asch wrote in a letter some months later that "the idea behind the election of Mr. Roosevelt . . . was that the policy of the Democratic party was one which believed in the prosperity and pursuit of happiness of the majority, was by prosperity of the small man, and not the big organizations."[25] Asch and his Radio Labs colleagues bypassed the Garden's house system altogether, rigging their own speakers in the monstrous hall as well as outside in the street for the overflow crowd. It was a big, and important, job.

Electioneering remained a periodic market for Asch's sound equipment through the decade. He discovered a way to rig an amplifier up to a car battery and constructed sound trucks for an assortment of political campaigns—including Roosevelt's—up to the end of the decade. But this was decidedly seasonal work. Steadier work came through an assortment of Jewish and Jewish-dominated organizations, including Yiddish theaters, Jewish summer camps, and Jewish labor unions. Asch was not above capitalizing on his name, and in the 1930s the name of Asch was about as big as it got in the Yiddish theater. But as before, it was the Asch name combined with Charney Vladeck's paternalistic efforts on Asch's behalf that opened doors, rather than any specific involvement on the part of Sholem. On the other hand, he claimed that it was through his father—and by attending his father's plays—that he understood the particular problems and challenges of voice projection in the theater.[26] His first theater work was in burlesque houses, such as Minsky's on Lafayette, where Asch installed sound equipment to overcome the poor acoustics. By the end of the 1930s he was installing and maintaining sound equipment for the most prominent Yiddish theaters, including the Second Avenue Theatre and Maurice Schwartz's Yiddish Art Theatre. The latter was the primary outlet for Sholem Asch's plays, with Schwartz staging at least ten between 1922 and 1938. Schwartz, the most financially (if not artistically) successful of Yiddish theater producers, did everything—acted, directed, managed, produced—all in a flamboyant and entrepreneurial style. Irving Howe described him as "a man of Rabelaisian energies and appetites":

> Idealistic and crafty, imaginative and gross, pure in heart and a bruising "go-getter." . . . To keep his theatre alive over so many

years was itself a triumph of will: he exploited actors, pilfered
ideas from gentile directors, courted financial backers, entan-
gled creditors in promises, used every device of modern publicity to win the Yiddish (and American) public, wrote, adapted,
and butchered plays, and, to make up deficits, went on vaudeville tours in the United States and on Yiddish stock-company
tours in Latin America. . . . Schwartz had no conscious aesthetic program—or he had a dozen, which comes to the
same thing.[27]

Asch was careful to see that he was not among Schwartz's victims.
His contracts with Schwartz (as with others) specified that Radio
Labs was to be paid a weekly sum, through the course of the
theater season. Payday, interestingly enough, was Saturday. That
money was changing hands on the sabbath between Jewish businessmen immersed in the Yiddish milieu suggests the distance
they had traveled from Orthodox practice.

Vladeck's *Forward* connections extended like tentacles in a variety of directions. The ILGWU called on Asch for an assortment
of services. In the spring of 1936 the union hired Radio Labs to
set up a public address system for their May Day rally on the
polo grounds. Late in the summer of the same year Asch was
asked to deliver his "cabinet" to the Manhattan Opera House for
a meeting of the Dress and Waistmakers' Union: "Mr. Hochman
[general manager] is accustomed to speaking on it."[28] In the early
1930s the *Forward* established a radio station for the broadcast of
Yiddish programs. The call letters—WEVD—stood for the initials
of Eugene Victor Debs, the premier American Socialist who had
died ten years earlier. Located first at the Broadway Central Hotel
and then the Hotel Claridge at Broadway and Forty-fourth Street,
WEVD quickly became the primary means of disseminating news
of New York's Yiddish-speaking community and of preserving its
cultural distinctiveness.[29] And of course the political programming
was unabashedly pro-union and socialist. Vladeck saw to it that
Asch had a hand in building the transmitter, and in succeeding
months Asch was responsible for investigating complaints from
listeners of reception problems. "I understand you are to get all
complaints about reception," wrote Anna Goldblatt of WEVD to
Asch in the spring of 1935. "Here's one: Mr. Ackerman, 14 Lawrence
Ave., Brklyn, phoned us to complain that he can't get WEVD on
Saturdays between 6:00 and 7:00 P.M. and on Sundays between
11:00 and 12 noon."[30]

Radio Labs remained busy to the end of the decade installing public address systems throughout the city—from the Downtown Athletic Club in Manhattan to public schools on Long Island. Asch struck off to more northern points when he could, following the summer exodus of increasingly affluent New York Jews to the Catskills. When various New York Jewish organizations developed the means, they established camps for their members in the Catskills. The Workman's Circle was a socialist fraternal organization with a national scope, dedicated to a radical, secular, and integrationist political agenda while remaining, ironically, firmly Yiddishist in orientation. Among its efforts to keep secular Jewish traditions alive was the establishment of the Workman's Circle Camp in Sylvan Lake, New York. In 1938 Asch was contracted to install their public address system. The Kenoza Lodge in Sullivan County contracted for a similar system that same year. The Asches were sufficiently prosperous by then that they purchased their first new car—a DeSoto—and with a schematic diagram and a trunkful of parts Moe drove north to wire the camp office, casino, and dining hall, with speakers in remote locations by the swimming pool and pagoda.

Asch was also becoming active in various professional organizations. Of necessity, he became a member of the International Brotherhood of Electrical Workers, originally as a member of its Radio Technicians local (B-1004) and later in Local 1209. In time Asch became the head of the local's Education Committee and was responsible for putting together educational programs for the local's regular meetings. At best Asch's dealings with unions—his own and others'—were contentious. In the spring of 1936 he wrote Local 1209 to complain of having been subject to extortion by the members of another local who claimed jurisdiction in his area. The local in turn wrote to its membership announcing a mass meeting in order to reveal the "decision of the CIO [Congress of Industrial Organizations] regarding the jurisdictional controversy between Local 830 and ourselves."

A more serious conflict—for Asch personally—resulted from the elections of 1937. The American Labor Party (ALP) had been created the year before by several prominent Jewish labor unionists, including David Dubinsky of the ILGWU, Max Zaritsky, and Sidney Hillman of the Amalgamated Clothing Workers, who represented the "conservative" wing of the Socialist Party. Their intention was to form a party that could contribute to the reelection of Roosevelt in 1937 while offering a slate of third-party candidates for local offices. (It became New York's Liberal Party in 1944.) Charney Vladeck was nominated as the party's candidate for a seat on the city council. In the election that followed (which Vladeck won), Asch provided sound trucks, for both Vladeck's campaign and Roosevelt's New York City effort. On 3 December 1937 Asch fired off an angry letter to his old benefactor, addressed with uncharacteristic formality to "Mr. Vladeck":

> A situation came up to-day which I believe is of vital interest to you. As you know the ALP contracted for Sound Trucks from me and other organizations, during the recent campaign. The standard practice of charges for this type of work is $150 a week. . . . I made a special rate with Mr. Greenberg and Jack Sullivan of $100 a week for the period of four weeks which was the length of the active campaign.
>
> One week after we started operating Jack Sullivan called me and asked if he could break my contract as he could get Sound Trucks cheaper? [sic] than what he was paying me. I was told that Local 306 of the motion operators union had donated trucks at the rate of $15 a day which was the pay of the operators. This made the cost to the ALP of $90 instead of the $100 they were paying me. I called my Union representative and was told that Local 306 has no jurisdiction in the public address field and that the matter should be brought to the attention of Mr. Meany at the State Labor Board. . . .
>
> Mr. Meany told me, this was a week before election that he will look into the matter and when I went up there in person he told me that it wasn't him I spoke to before. He then told me to go to Mr. Armstrong at the ALP. This was the day before the election Mr. Armstrong told me that that is the way things are done and I have to get used to hard knocks like he did when he was a young man.
>
> At the last Union meeting I was called to the floor and publicly denounced for my attitude in not pressing the matter. It seemed that some one in the IBEW wanted to have something "on" George Meany and my case was just what they were looking for. I gathered this from the type of questions that were asked me and the manner of the denouncement. . . .
>
> This brings us up to-day. One of the Sound organizations which was contracted by the Bronx headquarters and who is an AFL member called me and said that he is suing the ALP for non-payment of service delivered. He knew that I was not paid for my work in either the Bronx or Manhattan.

And he wanted me to bring joint action against the ALP. This
puts me in an incomfortable [sic] position as when I will need
his support on questions in union matters not only will he as-
sail me but also question my integrity.
    There is certainly no more need for me to show you the
position the ALP is in the eyes of the IBEW as far as rank and
file are concerned. I also wonder what the other Union organizations the ALP has done business with feel about the unpaid
contracts they hold.[31]

Vladeck responded by forwarding Asch's letter to Jack Sullivan at
the ALP. "Please look into this letter by my friend Moe Asch," he
requested, "and see what can be done about it."[32] There is no trace
of what transpired in the wake of these events, and in any case it
appears to have been the last election for which Asch rented
sound trucks. But ironically, George Meany was assailing the ALP
the following year for proving itself no different from the Democrats and Republicans in withholding support for a shortened
workday.
    Asch consistently claimed to be pro-union, but his business
instincts would frequently put him at odds with union workers
and regulations. At middecade Radio Laboratories happily accepted contracts to wire burlesque theaters because they were
non-union houses and consequently permitted them to spend
long hours experimenting with the varieties and arrangements of
amplifiers, speakers, and microphones without having to charge
union scale.[33] His disregard for union regulations became more
egregious over time as Asch found ways to either bypass them or
flout them altogether.
    In the autumn of 1933 he applied for membership in the Institute
of Radio Servicemen (IRS), and by the following spring he was its
secretary. Throughout the 1930s the radio and electronics industries worked frantically to standardize what was quickly becoming
a patchwork of incompatible parts and designs. The interests of
manufacturers and repairmen were frequently at odds when it
came to standardization and compatibility. For repairmen it was a
boon, enabling them to replace parts easily and fathom new radios
as they came on line, but manufacturers remained protective of
their own technology and far preferred to have their radios repaired using their own parts. Early efforts at standardization in the
radio industry were dominated by the radio manufacturers, with
predictable results. Asch represented the IRS at a meeting of the

Institute of Radio Engineers in Rochester in the autumn of 1934. Among the sessions that particularly interested him was one sponsored by the Radio Manufacturers Association on problems of radio interference and another on "permissible amplifier distortion." With his longstanding interest in antenna installation, Asch undoubtedly had opinions on these subjects. The following spring the Radio Manufacturers' Association, with some dissent, voted to fold its work into that of the American Standards Association by reorganizing as its Sectional Committee on Radio, charged with defining "nomenclature, methods of testing and of rating, specifications for radio apparatus and equipment, and dimensions to secure interchangeability where this may be found to be desirable."[34] For the next three years, Asch participated in decisions concerning radio parts and performance—everything from the length of power cords to the standard color codes to be used on resistors. Ultimately Asch was frustrated by the fact that economic expediency often prevailed over the desire for high-quality sound reproduction.[35]

In at least one instance the work of Asch and his Radio Laboratory colleagues prefigured his interest in recording. Microphones were still in a crude state of development at the start of the 1930s; only five years earlier, in 1925, did the first phonograph records electronically recorded with a microphone appear. Previously, musicians or speakers gathered around a large acoustical horn that channeled the sound directly to the needle cutting the record grooves. Microphone technology in the early thirties was still based on the carbon device that Alexander Graham Bell had invented in developing the telephone the previous century. The carbon microphone consisted primarily of a diaphragm filled with carbon (originally metal) granules that would compress or expand depending on the sound waves to which it was subject. The compression and expansion of the granules would change the resistance within the diaphragm and thus the current that passed through it. It was not a very sensitive instrument; only a relatively narrow band of the sound spectrum was transmitted, with the high end particularly underrepresented, and certain frequencies were emphasized at the expense of others.[36]

Asch claimed to have contributed to a variation on the condenser microphone—the "dynamic condenser"—which worked with a gas-filled diaphragm.[37] It was a vast improvement in terms of sensitivity and was notable for a quality that became the heart of Asch's recording philosophy—flat response. *Flat response* refers to electroacoustical qualities that do not either inadvertently or de-liberately emphasize particular frequencies in the sound spectrum. The condenser microphone was an expensive and fragile device, constantly in need of adjustment. It required a battery-powered source of electricity in order to establish an electrostatic charge within the gas-filled chamber. But its advantages were sufficient to have kept it in use for high-quality recording up to the present, and Asch only abandoned it later in the decade with the appear-ance of RCA's ribbon microphone, which was infinitely more rug-ged and sacrificed little in terms of sensitivity.[38]

In the autumn of 1935 Radio Laboratories placed advertisements in various trade magazines for electric guitars: "Sensational New System for Reproducing the Guitar with Smooth Flowing Power and Quality." Orders came in from some unlikely customers, in-cluding the Tampa Civic Opera Company. Commercially produced electric guitars were in their infancy in the mid-1930s. Several problems had plagued guitarists, especially those in the jazz field. The first had to do with volume: under ordinary circumstances, a guitar simply could not be heard over the din of assorted wind instruments and drums. Consequently, guitars had been relegated to the rhythm section, and soloing was largely out of the question. When electric guitars first appeared, audiences (as well as band leaders) were hostile to a sound so unlike that of the acoustic guitars they were ostensibly trying to emulate. The Gibson Guitar Company had attempted as early as 1924 to market an electric guitar for teachers and musicians, but there was insufficient inter-est and a decade passed before Gibson tried again. This time the public seemed ready. At around the same time Asch used available technology to develop a magnetic pickup, which was secured under the strings near the bridge of the guitar. It does not seem that this was a particularly successful or long-running aspect of the work at Radio Labs. But late in the decade the company became involved with two guitarists who had both the artistic vision and electronic sophistication to envision broader possibili-ties for the instrument. The first was Lester Polfus, a guitarist who had started his musical career playing hillbilly music on Chicago's WLS "Barn Dance" program under the name Rhubarb Red. Polfus came to New York in 1937 to pursue a career in jazz and changed his name to Les Paul. Although Asch claimed to have wired the first Gibson Les Paul guitar, Paul's experiments with solid-body guitars postdated his collaboration with Radio Laboratories.[39] Additionally, Paul had access to Epiphone's guitar factory on Fourteenth Street

on the weekends and consequently lacked neither the facilities
nor the know-how to make his own innovations.[40] What he *did*
need help with were amplifiers. He had joined Fred Waring's
Pennsylvanians, who were playing at prominent hotels all over the
city. Alternating current (AC) had not yet emerged as the industry
standard, and many hotels generated their own electricity using
direct current (DC). Paul needed an amplifier that could accommodate both AC and DC, which was not a simple matter. Radio Labs
succeeded in making an AC/DC guitar amplifier—in November 1939
they filled an order for twenty-five of them from the Gibson Guitar
Company.[41]

Jimmy Smith (not to be confused with the jazz organist of the
same name) was a guitarist who played for various commercial
"society" orchestras, such as the Cliquot Club Serenaders. Around
1938 Radio Labs built a variation on the electric guitar for Smith.
The "electric console" fit inside a case that, when opened, stood on
the floor at about table height. Smith played the electric console
while standing, using a technique similar to that required by a steel
guitar: "[An] adaptation of the Electric Guitar, developed and broadened to include effects of many different instruments. . . . A Special
Instrument, entirely original in design and capable of producing
many pleasing effects . . . a source of entertainment, new, sensational and spell-binding."[42] Smith played for dances and private
engagements, for commercial recordings and radio broadcasts.
Perhaps his most unusual assignment was for the musical
Hellzapoppin', for which Radio Labs also provided the sound system.
A loud, tasteless, clichéd, and vastly entertaining pastiche of vaudeville routines, *Hellzapoppin'* offered Asch and his colleagues a tremendous challenge. The action was not confined to the
stage—actors would wander around the theater, appear in the
audience, hang from the boxes. In each location they needed to be
heard, which required both microphone and speaker. The show
opened on 22 September 1938 at the Forty-sixth Street Theatre.
Radio Labs apparently succeeded in assaulting the audience with
sound. "If your ear-drums are tough enough," began the *Times*
review that Sunday, "lend them to Hellzapoppin for a moment."
The reviewer continued:

> It is a vaudeville freak assembled by Ole Olson and Chic
> Johnson, whose basal metabolism is perfect. Being short on
> wit and humor they are longer on rough-house and skulldug-
> gery than any uproar mountebanks this town has sat down

to for years and "Hellzapoppin'" goes off like an ammunition dump. . . . In lieu of original skill they have immense resources of animal strength and good nature and they have whooped up Hellzapoppin' until it fairly demolished the theatre with its noise.[43]

Hellzapoppin' continued to play well into the 1940s, by which time Asch had left the business of sound equipment.

Through much of the decade Asch heard little from the members of his immediate family. Nathan was in touch infrequently, and when he was it usually was in order to hit Moe up for some cash. After publishing novels to moderate acclaim in 1925 and 1927, Asch's older brother had one more artistic success and then fell on hard times. *Payday* was published in 1930; he dedicated it to his father. The novel recounted a night in the life of a brutal, sociopathic young man mired in a dead-end office job in New York City. Against the protagonist's desperate attempts to wring a night of pleasure from the city, the day's headlines announce the impending execution of Sacco and Vanzetti. Revived recently as an exemplary "proletarian novel,"[44] *Payday* brought Nathan critical acclaim, as well as attention of a less desirable kind. In June 1930 a grand jury indicted the publisher of *Payday* because of the book's "objectionable" content.[45]

About a year later, in October of 1931, Nathan wired Moe from Dallas, where he had run out of money and had been thrown out of his hotel for not having paid the bill. "Can you get hold of some money and wire it to me?" Moe sent him twenty-five dollars. Things might have become desperate for Nathan had his brother John not passed through Dallas on his way to the University of California at Riverside, where he intended to continue his horticultural studies. Nathan elected to travel west with John, and largely on the strength of his father's name he landed a job with Paramount Studios in Hollywood, which he held until 1933. In 1935 he published his last novel—*The Valley*—which met with far less success; by middecade he was again floundering, attempting to cope with a second failed marriage, to figure out what variety of person he was—what kind of Jew, what kind of American.[46]

Asch heard little from his parents, either—Frances could not remember his ever having received a letter from them—and what news he had of them tended to come through Vladeck.[47] His parents visited the States in 1931, 1935, and 1937, primarily under the auspices of the Joint Distribution Committee, for whom Sholem was raising money. Moe was lucky if he succeeded in having a lunch or dinner with them in a restaurant. It was during the 1935 visit that there occurred a rare convergence of family members in New York, with regrettable consequences. Two Asches at a time had a chance of getting on; more was treacherous. Sholem decided that he would bring his children with him on a visit to Abraham Cahan at the *Forward* on the Lower East Side—for what purpose it is unclear. Although they would not have a full-scale falling out for four years, Sholem Asch and Abraham Cahan seemed not to care for each other. The latter was jealous of Asch's literary success and accompanying freedom; for his part, Sholem Asch might have feared Cahan and the power he wielded through the *Forward* (events would prove this well founded). It could not simply have been that Sholem wanted to "show off" his children; perhaps he wanted to demonstrate that he was a man of burdens and responsibilities. In any case, when he bundled Nathan, Moe, and Frances into a taxi cab, the atmosphere was tense. Perhaps intending to ease the tension, Sholem began to brag about his amorous triumphs. One involved a dancer for the Imperial Russian ballet whom Sholem had seduced under the nose of her lover, a grand duke. Sholem's sons were well aware that their father had mistresses in assorted parts of the globe. It was not that he and Madya were unhappily married; perhaps Sholem regarded it as the prerogative of a great artist, whose creative powers required the indulgence of whim and appetite. If it troubled Nathan, he was not in a position to moralize—he had been indulging his own considerable sexual appetite since he was a teenager. Moe was not altogether of the same stamp, and in any case he had his wife with him, who was deeply offended by the conversation. Nathan attempted to stop Sholem by kicking him, to which Sholem responded, "What are you kicking me for?" The visit to the *Forward* was apparently forgettable, but when the Asches reconvened on the sidewalk outside the building, everyone was fit to kill. Unable to hail a taxi, Nathan jumped on the running board of one that was passing by. The driver stopped and made a remark Nathan took to be anti-Semitic, whereupon Nathan grabbed him and tried to pull him out of the taxi and pummel him.

"Don't fight!" yelled Sholem, as he and Moe grabbed hold of Nathan, enabling the driver to swing at Nathan unchecked.

"Don't hold me, hold him!" responded Nathan.

Somehow they arrived back uptown at Sholem and Madya's hotel—all four were in tears.[48]

By 1938 Radio Labs consisted of Mearns and Asch. That year they took on a huge project that would have an immense effect on Asch's career. WEVD was moving to new, spacious quarters at 117 West Forty-sixth Street, and Asch and Radio Labs were hired to build a new radio transmitter. The job was of such a scale that it was apparently easier for them to simply relocate Radio Labs to the WEVD building. Through that year and into the next, Mearns and Asch continued to build and install loud-speaker systems; in fact, it was now easier to reach the Yiddish theaters on the Lower East Side, which continued to be their primary clientele. But once the transmitter was completed, WEVD required Asch's services in a new area—recording. Most music heard on the air in this era consisted of live transmissions. Radio broadcasts had become an important source of income for many musicians, and consequently the Musician's Union fought hard against the transmission of music that had been previously recorded on commercial discs (it would be some years before this matter was settled). But noncommercial recordings made explicitly for radio broadcast were another matter. WEVD had a growing need for recordings of Jewish music—orchestral theater music, Yiddish songs, cantorials—and looked to Asch to fill it. Asch built a recording studio in one portion of Radio Labs and began cutting discs for the use of the radio station.

In 1938 Sholem had an assortment of reasons for returning to the States. He arrived with Madya on 16 May aboard the French liner *Normandie,* and the *Times* reported the next day that he had come to confer with other members of the Joint Distribution Committee about a place to which the imperiled Jews of Central Europe could immigrate. He declared to the *Times* reporter:

> We have to take out 150,000 Jews from Central Europe each
> year for five years. If that can be done the Jewish question
> can be settled. As long as Hitler lasts in power so will the Jew-
> ish question in Central Europe last, unless this emigration be
> accomplished. Palestine could take from 40,000 to 50,000
> Jews each year if the laws were changed and a Jewish State
> established.[49]

He understood better than most the magnitude of the problem facing the Jews of Central Europe and can hardly be faulted retrospectively for having misjudged the numbers. Indeed, his concern for European Jewry was sincere and profound, and it is stupefying that anyone would question his loyalty to world Jewry—as many would in very short order. But Sholem was also worried for his own comfort and safety, and for that of Madya—Hitler's presence was already being felt well beyond the borders of Germany. Early that spring the Asches had encountered German Jewish refugees—albeit of a decidedly well-heeled kind—while vacationing on the French Riviera.[50] His villa in Nice had been left in the hands of John Asch, who over the years had built and tended a beautiful and elaborate garden on the villa grounds. It was not apparent that he would be returning there soon.

There was yet another reason for his coming to America that spring. Sholem was in need of some minor surgery and had planned to take care of it in Vienna. But Hitler's presence there that spring prompted a change of plans. Instead, a week after his arrival in New York, he underwent surgery there. The day before, he spent some hours in his son's studio, drafting letters to friends and family. "Dearest children," he wrote, probably to Ruth and her husband Reginald Shaffer in London, "we have come, we saw and now I am going to the hospital today to make the operation. I am in good hands and God and Doctor Berg will do the rest. Mother behaves bravely and as a matter of fact since we are here after she saw the children and her grand-child she's getting younger. I hope soon that I will behave. Kiss the baby [Miriam]." And to Nathan he wrote: "Dear Nathan, When you will get this letter I will be operated. Doctor Berg is doing the job. . . . Mother saw David [Nathan's son] yesterday and will see again today before I go to the hospital. He is a gentleman, and we are all proud of him. This is your best work so far." The concluding sentence was a barb that Nathan undoubtedly did not miss.

And to John:

> John, I want to write to you but I am upset today. I am going today to the Hospital. We are becoming everyday acquainted with old America. And we believe that here is the place we want to settle. It is difficult to make plans as long as I am not well. . . . I cannot see how I can make up my mind to settle here without you. The boys are dreaming about this that we should sell everything and you should come over. . . . Take care of yourself and inquire about selling the place. It does not look as though we will return there so soon.[51]

Except for relatively brief trips abroad, Sholem and Madya did not leave the States again for fifteen years.

By 1938 Sholem Asch had been a fixture in the Yiddish literary world for more than three decades. His reputation had been established through European and American productions of his plays, through his columns and serialized novels in the Yiddish press, and through books and short stories. On the eve of the Second World War he was the world's best known Jewish writer, a hero to Jewish masses on both sides of the Atlantic. In 1933 he had published *Three Cities,* his sprawling historical novel about the Russian revolutions of 1905 and 1917. The English-language version, incongruously translated from the German translation of the Yiddish, won Asch his first American and English best seller. But there were frustrations; his work had a distinctly middlebrow reputation. With the exception of a few staunch defenders, such as literary critic Samuel Niger (a brother of Charney Vladeck), the respect that he desired from the literary establishment seemed to elude him. Furthermore, Asch believed that he deserved the Nobel Prize and that only a sufficiently broad international readership stood in his way. The previous year he had begun work on a fictionalized account of the life of Christ; by the time he arrived in New York the following spring it was largely complete.

But *The Nazarene* was not simply the consequence of wanting to reach a broader audience. Asch had conceived of its most general outlines during his first trip to Palestine in 1909, when he was struck by the essential Jewishness of early Christianity. It was his belief that he could effect a reconciliation between Christians and Jews by portraying their common origins. Although Asch may have been willfully naïve, he could not have predicted the furor that his book would cause when it was published the following year.

Sholem spent the summer of 1938 recuperating from his surgery and putting the finishing touches on *The Nazarene.* In July Sholem and Madya were staying at the resort and conference center at Camp Tamiment in Pennsylvania, and Frances and Moe arranged to join them there for a weekend. Moe had a long conversation with his father about his business, and about some plans that he had been mulling over to create a market for Radio Labs equipment in England with the help of his brother-in-law, Reginald Shaffer. Ruth's husband Reggie was an English businessman who had recently started selling foreign-made machinery; he thought that he could market some of Moe's amplifying equipment there. Sholem thought the idea had merit and proposed that he put up the capital to start such a venture. Moe immediately wrote to Reggie, suggesting that he determine whether it would be possible to manufacture Moe's designs in England, thereby saving on the cost of shipping and on import duties. He mentioned that "father" was interested in investing in their venture but added that he "would not want his money if there was nothing as far as a money making proposition in it. I don't believe you would either." The following month Reggie responded. It did not look as though it would be easy to sell the amplification equipment in England after all. In the end, nothing came of their collaboration.[52]

Moe and Frances returned to Tamiment in August to spend another few days with Sholem and Madya. At the same time Maurice Schwartz was preparing a stage version of *Three Cities* for his Yiddish Art Theatre that fall, and his intention was to pull out all the stops. With as many as seventy-five people on stage at a time, it promised to be an extravaganza of the first order. It was arranged that Moe would construct the necessary sound sys-tem—almost two thousand dollars worth of equipment was re-quired, not an inconsiderable sum during the late Depression, and it was one of Asch's biggest jobs to date.

Three Cities provided Asch with a rare opportunity to collaborate not only with his father but also with his mother. As rehearsals progressed that autumn and Asch puttered around the Jolson Theater, Schwartz struggled with Madya in order to be allowed to stage the kind of sensation he had in mind. She was a constant and—to Schwartz—meddlesome presence. Madya insisted that he be faithful to the novel's ending; Schwartz wanted to end with the maximum possible effect. Abe Cahan concurred with Madya. Sholem "said he was helpless and would not fight with his wife." It was probably not Madya's anticlimactic ending that caused the critics' disgust. "At 11:10 last night," reported one English-language critic, "Schwartz met his Waterloo at the Jolson Theater." Another reported that "Mr. Schwartz's latest effort, *Three Cities* . . . turns out to be a lowly comic strip conception of the sufferings of the Jews in Eastern Europe. Lacking in dignity, devoid of dramatic unity, burdened with Mr. Schwartz's vulgar direction, it leaves one won-dering what has happened to the Yiddish theatre."[53] The paying public, on the other hand, reacted differently. *Three Cities* was one of Schwartz's outstanding financial successes.

It was the same season that *Hellzapoppin'* had opened, and it is not surprising that a public suffering from the final years of the Depression should be drawn to two such garish productions. A third theatrical production—equally rousing but motivated by considerably different impulses than either *Hellzapoppin'* or *Three Cities*—had opened the previous November and moved that same autumn to more sumptuous uptown quarters. *Pins and Needles* was a musical revue sponsored by the ILGWU's Labor Stage; the cast consisted entirely of garment workers who were granted leave by their employers to participate in the revue. Its amateurishness constituted much of its appeal in the first year, and the *New York Times* reported that it had lost some of it the following year when it moved uptown. But it had gained, the same reviewer reported, in "skill, dash and agile beauty in the acting and staging."[54] Thoroughly working class in both production and theme, *Pins and Needles* sought to stimulate a kind of social awareness in the public, particularly an appreciation of American labor. Musically it was modeled on the Broadway tunes of Irving Berlin, but the song titles betray the serious intention: "Why Sing of Stars Above," "What Good Is Love," "One Big Union for Two," and "Sing Me a Song with Social Significance."[55] The novelty of a revue about labor was perhaps eclipsed by the fact that it was also racially integrated. The *Times* reported that the songs written for "Negro voices" were particularly successful: "After all, joyousness is part of the art of revue-making, and this Negro serenade to the christening of a darky baby is the high point of the light entertainment season so far."[56] Some months later a Louisiana country-blues singer by the name of Huddie Ledbetter joined the revue and in turn was introduced by one of the revue's producers to Moe Asch.

In the entertainment season of 1938 *Pins and Needles* was not unique in using popular cultural forms for political ends. Since the mid-1930s the American Left had been attempting to use art "as a weapon." In a sharp and unanticipated departure from its previous position, the Comintern in 1935 issued a set of directives to the Communist Party of the United States of America (CPUSA) that called for collaboration with Socialists and other former leftist bogeymen, as well as for the Americanization of the party largely through the celebration of homegrown American culture. The movement that followed, the Popular Front, was vigorously pro-democracy and antifascist. Earl Browder, head of the CPUSA, proclaimed that "Communism is Twentieth Century Americanism," and a revised version of the CPUSA constitution in 1938 adopted the tradition of Washington, Paine, Jackson and Lincoln as its own.

Pins and Needles was one manifestation of Popular Front enthusiasm. There were many others, and they took an astonishing variety of forms. Many of those who engaged in socially conscious art were not party members, but their inspiration nonetheless came largely from the party. Arguably, the nerve center of the Popular Front movement was New York, where Jews—many of them now second generation and increasingly secularized—were vastly overrepresented in party ranks and among fellow travelers. It was not that party members and sympathizers represented a majority within New York Jewry, nor that Jews represented a majority within the New York party or among sympathizers. Rather, the number of Jews within New York's radical Left were far greater than their numbers within the general population would have predicted. The reasons for this have been hotly debated by historians, sociologists, and literary and cultural critics. Some have insisted that it is something within Judaism that impels significant numbers of Jews to align themselves with causes of social justice. But, argues sociologist Arthur Liebman, were this so one would have expected the most *observant* Jews to have filled the ranks of the Left. Instead, highly observant Jews tended to be among the most conservative, whereas members of the Jewish Left were highly assimilated (though holding in some important though ill-defined way to a sense of Jewish identity). Liebman argues instead that the significant presence of Jews in the American Left was a consequence of their proletarianization, first in eastern Europe and then in the early years of their American immigration. But although other proletarianized immigrant groups were also a significant presence in the American Left of the thirties—notably Italians—still others, such as the Irish, explored different routes to political empowerment in the new country. It remains a puzzle, though both explanations are illuminating to a degree. Since the beginning of the century, and even earlier, many Jews had come to regard the pursuit of social justice as a duty and calling; while often living precarious existences themselves, many outward-looking Jews transcended Jewish self-interest in recognizing the predicament of other socially marginalized communities. The effort to forge working-class coalitions that transcended boundaries of language, religion, and ethnicity came easily and naturally to the Jewish Left and must certainly have had roots in Jewish social traditions. At the same time, without their own experiences of social, political, and economic oppression in the United States and in Europe, it is unlikely that Jews would have been able to develop traditions of political progressivism to the degree that they did.

Certain aspects of the Popular Front were anticipated in both New York's theater and musical worlds. In 1925 a new Yiddish theatre collective was established, called the *Arbeiter Teater Farband* (Workers' Theater Group), or Artef. Artef was the formation of an assortment of Jewish trade unionists, the Workman's Circle playing a predominant role. The idea of an agitprop theater was already taking root among non-Jewish American playwrights who in the Depression sought to use the popular stage to dramatize the cause of "negro-white unity, popular resistance, and worker solidarity."[57] Additionally, Artef looked to Russia and the party for ideological guidance. But among its special contributions was an appropriation of Jewish folk themes as a vehicle for its message of workers' redemption.

A second precursor of the Popular Front was the Composers' Collective, an outgrowth of the Pierre Degeyter Club (named for the coauthor of the "Internationale"), which in turn was affiliated with the communist-led Workers' Music League.[58] The collective consisted of approximately two dozen classically trained composers who wished to use their talents to promote leftist causes, particularly trade unionism. Among them were several who would be associated with Asch in an assortment of critical capacities in the next two decades: Charles Seeger, Henry Cowell, Elie Siegmeister, Earl Robinson. Their intention was to reach the "masses" through song, but they eschewed two existing traditions of political song that might have been instructive. In the second decade of the century the International Workers of the World (IWW, or Wobblies) established a successful singing movement, largely through the songs of Swedish-born Joe Hill. Hill, framed and executed in 1915 for a murder he did not commit, appropriated popular tunes or hymns and reworked the lyrics for his own purposes. One of his best known songs, "The Preacher and the Slave" ("Pie in the Sky"), was a parody of "The Sweet Bye and Bye."[59] The second tradition was rooted in the music of the white rural South and coalesced around a series of violent communist-inspired strikes that ripped through Appalachia in the early 1930s. Out of the Gastonia strike in North Carolina and those in Harlan County, Kentucky, a singing tradition developed to bolster the spirits of the strikers. A group of creative and defiant songwriters emerged who married southern hymns and mountain ballads to unabashedly radical lyrics—Ella May Wiggins (martyred by vigilantes in 1929), Sarah Ogan Gunning, Jim Garland, and above all, Aunt Molly Jackson.

But the Composers' Collective did not regard either popular tunes or folk songs from the rural South to be particularly useful for an urban proletariat political movement. Charles Seeger wrote in the *Daily Worker* in 1934 that folk songs were too "complacent, melancholy, defeatist, intended to make slaves endure their lot—pretty but not the stuff for a militant proletariat to feed upon."[60] They drew instead upon the European model of workers' choruses and composed songs of stunning musical complexity. Some members of the collective were emerging as important figures in the musical avant-garde, and they could not resist the opportunity they saw to educate the public about new musical forms. The results were songs that were largely unsingable.

The skepticism of the Composers' Collective about the political "usefulness" of folk music was paralleled by an equal skepticism—if not outright hostility—on the part of many leftist critics to the political use of *popular* musical forms. Popular music was indelibly tainted, it was frequently argued, by its association with capital, and consequently could never be the vehicle of a socialist-inspired politic. Both debates implicitly questioned whether folk or popular music constituted "art" and whether they were inherently political in content by virtue of their association with oppressed peoples. Did the music of poor people—particularly rural whites and both rural and urban blacks—necessary have political implications? Did it bear within it an understanding of the predicament of those who were politically and economically disfranchised? Or was it fundamentally escapist or demoralizing? A growing contingent of young, primarily American-born party members had enthusiastically taken up African American music as the supreme embodiment of a democratic, uniquely American music. Their intention was to win an acknowledgment of the contributions of African Americans to American culture as well as to demonstrate the benefits of interracial cooperation.[61]

An event in December 1938 grew out of this optimistic reading of folk and popular music's political possibilities. John Hammond, born to wealth as a member of the Vanderbilt family, had developed a substantial taste for "Negro" jazz (along with Norman Granz he would become one of the two most important promoters of black jazz in the mainstream recording industry). He was never a member of the party and his sympathies for it were short lived, but he remained an uncompromising supporter of civil rights initiatives throughout his life. In the early part of the decade he had introduced jazz programming to WEVD but discontinued his association with the station when the Hotel Claridge insisted that black musicians ride the freight elevator up to the station's penthouse studios and the station (enjoying a rent-free arrangement) refused to contradict the hotel management. In 1938 he conceived of the idea of presenting black jazz in a concert-hall setting, preceded by examples of those black musical antecedents that in his mind demonstrated the origins of jazz in a distinctly African American tradition. It was a revolutionary idea for two reasons. First, by presenting black music in Carnegie Hall, he was insisting upon its stature as art. Second, he intended to show that the black contribution to American music was unique rather than derivative—and this a full three years before Melville Herskovits's heterodox treatise on the African origins of African American culture, *The Myth of the Negro Past*.

Hammond's From Spirituals to Swing concert was preceded the previous month by an event only slightly less remarkable. The Spanish Civil War, widely regarded by the Left as a test of the world's (and particularly America's) will to stand up to fascism, was the cause célèbre of the new, antifascist American Left between 1936 and 1939. Thirty-three hundred Americans were recruited to serve in the Abraham Lincoln Battalion of the International Brigade and were sent to Spain to fight alongside other international battalions and the Loyalists against Franco's fascist insurgent movement. They came from all parts of the United States, although New York Communists predominated, including a large number of Jews and a few blacks from Harlem. Fifteen hundred Americans were killed in the Spanish Civil War, including at least two Harlemites. Although never inspiring Harlem's masses as a whole, the Spanish Civil War became an abiding concern for Harlem's intellectuals. In November Harlem's most prominent musicians donated their services to the Harlem and Musicians' Committees to Aid Spanish Democracy for an all-black concert intended to raise money for the Spanish Children's Milk Fund. Cab Calloway, Maxine Sullivan, Fats Waller, Roy Eldridge, Teddy Wilson, Lionel Hampton, and the Jimmie Lunceford Orchestra played a concert billed as a birthday tribute to W. C. Handy.

The communist press gave the concert a stinging review. "During the entire evening," wrote Martin McCall in the *Daily Worker*, "there was hardly a suggestion of genuine and sincere jazz. Evidently, it was assumed that the audience consisted of jitterbugs, and the hypothetical droolers were given their money's worth of noise and vaudeville." "Jitterbugs," he went on to suggest, were "creatures who are not only hopelessly unmusical, but whose sensibilities lie in their hands and feet."[62]

Perhaps with his own upcoming concert in mind, Hammond fired off an angry letter to the *Daily Worker.* The fact that Eldridge engaged in showy tricks and Waller in his trademark clowning did not mean that the music was any less serious. Here was a lesson in the significance of *performance* in African American musical culture. "I think it highly impolitic," Hammond concluded, "for the *Daily* to be a party to insulting treatment of great Negro artists, who, for the first time, are becoming interested in the cause of democracy in Spain and are contributing their services to help it." The *Daily Worker* quickly backed off, apologizing for McCall's review and fretting that it "could not but feed the white chauvinist contempt with which the upper-class approaches Negro life and art."[63]

To finance his own concert, Hammond had secured the sponsorship of the Marxist *New Masses* with the promise that their ideological perspective would not intrude. He had already gone south by the time of the Handy birthday tribute "to search the backwoods of the South for performers."[64] Intending to recruit Blind Boy Fuller but finding to his astonishment that he was in jail for attempting to shoot his wife, Hammond instead discovered Sanford "Sonny"Terry, a nearly blind young harmonica player who lived next door to Fuller, and he arranged to have him come to New York. Additionally, he found a gospel quartet called Mitchell's Christian Singers. When he discovered that Robert Johnson, whom he had also intended to recruit, had been killed the year before, Hammond booked another blues singer, Big Bill Broonzy, who had also enjoyed some recording success. The program was rounded out with gospel singer Rosetta Tharpe, boogie-woogie pianists Albert Ammons, Meade Lux Lewis, and Pete Johnson, an impromptu New Orleans band consisting of pianist James P. Johnson, trumpet player Tommy Ladnier, soprano saxophonist Sidney Bechet, trombonist Dan Minor, and a rhythm section of Jo Jones and Walter Page, and the Kansas City Six, which included Lester Young and Buck Clayton. The highlight of the evening was the Count Basie Band, featuring vocalists Jimmy Rushing and Helen Humes.

The press reaction to "From Spirituals to Swing" was ecstatic, and this time McCall's review in the *Daily Worker* refrained from criticizing any of the musicians. But McCall did find fault with the producer and the way in which the musicians were introduced. He particularly doubted the wisdom of beginning the program with a recording of African drumming: "What was its particular meaning? Decidedly untenable assumptions were made on the basis of this arbitrarily chosen record. A selection from Bach can similarly be chosen to illustrate a possible source of aspects of popular Negro culture. Ideologically, this was a weak beginning."[65] Mike Gold, a prominent American Communist cultural critic and a *Daily Worker* columnist, had similar doubts about the message implied in the concert. Gold was known to be an aficionado of European classical music, and although he praised the musical content of the concert he took exception to Hammond's claim in the program notes that "hot jazz is uniquely American, the most important cultural exhibit we have given to the world. . . . While the intelligentsia has been busy trying to water our scrawny cultural tree with European art and literary movements, this thing has come to maturity unnoticed."[66] In Gold's view Hammond's remarks took too little cognizance of American literary and theatrical accomplishments, naming particularly Whitman, Emerson, Twain, Hemingway, and Dreiser. And he was no doubt right. But Hammond was being deliberately provocative, and it was shortsighted of Gold not to have recognized the significance of Hammond's position. It was the beginning of a debate about a distinctly American cultural canon and the first suggestion that African Americans might have a place within it. In Hammond's view as well as that of many younger Communist Party members, the very act of putting black folk and popular musicians on the Carnegie Hall stage rendered it political.

There remained a more difficult question, however, implied by this point of view. For *whom* was this music political? There was no particular evidence that most Harlemites suddenly recognized the political implications of their music, nor that they were politicized by it. A slightly different kind of problem attended the efforts of leftist intellectuals to reach *white* urban working classes through music. The white folk music being imported from the rural South and West was unarguably political in content (although questions about its authenticity as a "folk" music would be debated for decades). However, it was *not* the preferred musical fare of northern white workers. By early 1940 a folk music community was taking shape in New York. It included Aunt Molly Jackson, who had been run out of Kentucky and settled on New York's Lower East Side with her extended family. But her music did not attract sufficient attention for her to support a family, and she was left to run a restaurant in order to make ends meet.[67] Oklahoman Woody

Guthrie arrived in New York shortly after New Year's, after having had a successful run in 1937 and 1938 on California's KFVD radio station mixing "country" music (much of it inspired by the Carter Family) with a deliberately "homegrown" populism and a healthy dose of cornball humor. In New York Guthrie and Jackson were embraced by leftist intellectuals, who regarded them as the "real thing," and they were joined by the likes of Burl Ives, Huddie Ledbetter, Josh White, Sonny Terry, and Cisco Houston. But who was listening?

> There is little evidence that a "people's culture" . . . was any-
> thing more than a Party fantasy of what a true image of the
> people ought to be. . . . [But] even if its ruralism was often
> hopelessly at odds with the imagined daily life of urban work-
> ers, the native intonation of the people's culture was accom-
> panied by the genuine enthusiasm of the cadres for the new
> Americanist line.[68]

According to Andrew Ross, it was leftist intellectuals who were listening, and in so doing they constructed an enduring image of what they thought was "truly" American.

Asch probably did not attend the From Spirituals to Swing concert—at any rate Frances Asch did not recall that they were there.[69] It is more likely that he attended the Handy birthday tribute, however, as he had friends who went abroad with the Abraham Lincoln battalion and he consequently identified strongly with the Republican cause in the Spanish Civil War. Even in a lean year he managed a contribution to the Spanish Refugee Appeal of the Joint Anti-Fascist Refugee Committee. He had also encountered Hammond by this time, because they were both involved with a progressive theatrical company at the Public Thea-tre—Asch maintaining the sound equipment, Hammond financing the productions. The various strands of the Popular Front's musical consciousness were coming together at a particularly important moment for Asch. With his father in town, it was increasingly apparent to Asch that he needed to do something of greater importance with his life—something that would make his father proud. By itself the electronics business was not sufficiently crea-tive. He would have to find some other way to make his mark. In March of 1940 he and Harry Mearns dissolved their partnership. It was an amicable split, although in any case he and Mearns had never been much more than business partners—they had had no common social life. The assets of Radio Labs were divided between them, with Asch retaining the recording equipment and the studio. They divided up the outstanding debts, Asch assuming those owed to his wife and father (he arranged to have Mearns pay $50 of the $250 that Frances had loaned to Radio Laboratories over time—she never did see the balance owed to her by her husband). The Gibson Guitar Company stilled owed them $330, which they would use to pay off some of the outstanding debt. Mearns retained the right to the use of the name "Radio Laboratories"; Asch kept the use of the telephone number, and it was Asch who remained in the WEVD building, at 117 West Forty-sixth Street.

Sholem's troubles had begun in earnest the previous summer. *The Nazarene* appeared and was received with thundering enthusiasm by Christian America. It became a Book of the Month selection, eventually selling hundreds of thousands of copies, and Sholem received laudatory letters from Christian theologians. But Jewish America was a different matter. Sholem Asch's effort to celebrate Jesus's Jewishness was not without precedent in Jewish intellectual circles. But Jews had rarely been appreciative of the attempt to claim a place for Jesus among figures of Jewish inspiration.[70] Cahan had warned Sholem not to publish the book and refused to serialize it in the pages of the *Forward*. In part, Sholem Asch was misunderstood. His attempt was not to obliterate Judaism by exploring the common ground between it and Christianity but to effect a reconciliation in the hope of heading off the impending holocaust in Central Europe. Still, Sholem was not entirely naïve—it was also his strong iconoclasm that led him to adopt a heterodox view of the historical Jesus. What he may not have entirely counted on was the significance of his position as the world's most prominent *Jewish* writer. If a minor Jewish writer had attempted the same thing, it might not have caused a ripple. But for American Jewry, Sholem Asch was *theirs*, and the attention he lavished on the figure of Jesus (and later Mary and Saint Paul) was inexcusable.

The hell the furor caused him might have been mitigated had it not been for the campaign waged by Abraham Cahan. It is difficult to construe Cahan's motivations in generous terms: his jealousy had simply boiled over. He was, after all, a "freethinker," a socialist with almost no interest in religion at all. But he became obsessed with *The Nazarene*, immersing himself in Judaica for two years in order to support his claim that Asch had distorted Judaism in order to have it conform with Christian doctrine.[71] Asch's sin, according to Cahan, was in trying to curry favor with Christians. Cahan published column after column on the subject of *The Nazarene*, and eventually a small book in Yiddish. At Cahan's urging, one of his editors published a vicious English-language attack on Asch entitled *The Christianity of Sholem Asch: An Appraisal from the Jewish Viewpoint* in 1953, a measure of the depth and longevity of Cahan's obsession.[72]

The entire Asch family felt the withering effects of Cahan's attack. They shared Sholem's pain in being rejected by the community that to his mind he had dedicated his life to defending. And they experienced his embitterment. Sholem was isolated from a significant portion of the American Jewish intellectual establishment, and all the more so because his primary advocate for the last two decades was no longer there. Charney Vladeck's health had been failing for some time. Two years before his death, he had lost the sight in one eye, and he fretted about losing sight in the other. Despite failing health he assumed his office on the city council in January 1938; that April he underwent surgery, and he was hospitalized again in June for ten days. On Friday, 28 October he had a heart attack in his *Forward* office. Through the weekend Moe and Frances waited in Sholem and Madya's apartment at 765 Riverside Drive for news of Vladeck's condition. On Sunday he died.[73] Vladeck would have understood the nature of Cahan's war on Sholem better than most; he too had been the subject of Cahan's animosity, particularly as his political success kindled Cahan's jealousy. Now Sholem was on his own, and his second son was as well.

The breakup of Radio Laboratories did not mean that Moe Asch immediately suspended his work in the field of sound reinforcement. The political campaigns of 1940 brought him a little work, and he continued to provide sound for a few Yiddish theaters that year. In the spring of 1940 he provided the sound system for the ILGWU's Carnegie Hall convention; in giving him public thanks, the master of ceremonies introduced him as "no one else but Mr. Asch, who is the son of the greatest creative writer of Jewish literature, Mr. Sholem Asch." The applause that followed suggested that Sholem's standing had not yet deteriorated significantly within the Jewish working class.

But Asch's business was now known as Asch Recording Studios, and although much of what he did in the early months was for WEVD, he ran his studio independently of the radio station and paid WEVD a monthly rent. The relationship was symbiotic in several respects. WEVD depended on Asch to record programs that could not be broadcast "live." The station in turn provided Asch with programming that he could record, duplicate, and sell to other stations, to theaters, or to the retail trade. Asch began to keep track of his recording sessions in the back pages of his account ledger. The first recording, dated 13 August 1939, was of the Bagelman Sisters, singers of popular Yiddish songs who would later change their name to the Barry Sisters.

There were very few independent retail record companies at the time; the "big three"—Columbia, Decca, Victor—dominated the retail trade and kept most "indies" from acquiring rack space in the stores. Thus at the start Asch had to content himself with finding other outlets for his recordings. He devised a marketing plan that capitalized on the fact that he was just about alone in the field of Jewish recordings:

> The Asch Recording Studios is today the only organization
> that is active in the Jewish phonograph record field. The de-
> mand for Jewish phonograph records is far greater than the
> production, for the following reasons: 1. Radio stations have
> popularized phonograph records by playing them on their
> programs. 2. Not enough records are produced.

His reasoning might have been pedestrian, but it was also flawless. The station provided him with ideal material "because the best Jewish artists appear on the station's programs causing a greater demand for records by these artists. Since there is no live talent available out of town the demand for Jewish phonograph records has increased ten-fold."[74]

Part of the plan was to simply sell transcribed radio programs from WEVD to other stations. Asch determined that there were about twenty-five radio stations around the country that carried Jewish programs "as a regular policy," and few had at their disposal the requisite "live" talent. Asch proposed to transcribe radio dramas, commentaries, educational programming, variety shows, and "The Jewish Philosopher." Representatives of the *Forward* (WEVD's parent company), he suggested, could act as "factory representatives in contacting radio stations, societies or dealers, or be their own salesmen for these records."

At the start Asch was confined to recording whatever the station's programmers had chosen to air. For a man whose acquaintance with Judaism and Jewish culture was erratic, this did not always prove interesting. Sometimes, however, events caused him to sit up and take notice. Albert Einstein came to the studios a few times to broadcast programs about the rising threat to the Jews of Europe. On one occasion he was unable to come to New York, so Sholem Asch agreed that he would conduct an interview with Einstein in his home in Princeton, New Jersey. Moe packed the necessary remote recording equipment—extraordinarily cumbersome in the days when all recording was directly onto heavy acetate discs—and traveled with his father by train to Princeton. The younger Asch was only there to take care of the technical end of things, but when Einstein had finished with Sholem, he asked Moe about his business.

As Asch later remembered, he told Einstein that he had an idea for recording the authentic sounds of the world's people and making it available to the public. Einstein responded that this was an important and valuable thing to do and urged him to pursue it. It was in some respects a mysterious exchange, and it is difficult to know whether it happened in precisely the way Asch remembered it. Asch, for example, recalled that Einstein was a friend of his father's, but this is an exaggeration. When Sholem sent birthday greetings to Einstein on the occasion of his seventieth birthday in 1949, he referred to "the few occasions I have had the privilege to meet you."[75] And it is difficult to corroborate the claim that he had an idea for a catalogue of world sound as early as 1940. Up until then, and until late in the war, Asch primarily responded to opportunity in his recording ventures. What is certain, however, is that Asch continued to cite this event in the decades thereafter as a turning point in his life. The timing was critical—Sholem had reentered his life but would not remain long. As Nathan had learned over the years, "Father" was frugal in the dispensation of praise. It took the intervention of a third person, with authority and stature, to convince Sholem that his second son was on to something.

Whatever its origins, this was certainly to be a departure from prevailing record business practices. Granted the "majors" would periodically release recordings of no commercial value for tax write-off purposes—RCA Victor released a record of African Music in 1939 and Indian Music of Mexico in 1941, both by ethnomusicologist Laura Bolton. And Asch himself was not inattentive to the presence of a *market* for his recordings. What distinguished Asch's intentions, once he expanded beyond broadcast transcriptions, was that he did not select recording artists with the greatest commercial potential in the broadest possible market; rather, he chose those who were guaranteed to meet the needs of a pre- viously ignored portion of the market, one that was small but well defined. Because for at least two years this was an exclusively *Jewish* market, he had also found a way to address the fact that it was highly dispersed by using the network of *Forward* agents to reach Jews all over the country.

Sometimes he made recordings to meet the demands of a particular customer. Herman Yablakoff's Second Avenue Theatre needed a recording of various sound effects, and Asch obliged him. Another service for Yablakoff resulted in trouble. In October 1940 the J. Roshinsky Orchestra performed several selections on WEVD from *White Flower,* a play running at the Second Avenue Theatre. Apparently unbeknown to the musicians, Asch recorded the performance and provided a copy of it to the theater; it was then played outside the theatre for advertising purposes. Yablakoff received a strongly worded letter from a lawyer employed by the Musician's Union:

> No doubt you will appreciate that it is both improper and dis-
> honest for any one to steal music broadcast by an orchestral
> unit and use it for their own profit, without reimbursement
> to the members of the orchestra and without their knowl-
> edge or consent. It is client's view that you are innocent in
> this matter and have very likely been imposed upon by some
> unscrupulous recording outfit which, in committing such
> practices, is violating union rules and regulations as well as
> the law of the land.[76]

Asch, who in the view of the lawyer was undoubtedly the "unscru- pulous recording outfit," also received a copy of the letter and was asked to submit "all the information and knowledge that you have concerning this matter, at your soonest convenience." Asch was more careful after this to see that such "arrangements" did not violate union regulations and laws—or sent similarly acquired recordings to sufficiently remote parts of the country so that a union representative would be unlikely to stumble upon them. It was the start of a persistent difficulty that Asch had in regarding other peoples' "sounds" as "property." In his view it was all *knowledge,* and according to the Constitution the public had a right to have access to it. He was simply acting as the public's agent in making it available.

Transcribed radio programs gradually gave way to recordings of vocalists and orchestras for the retail market. Asch sometimes recalled that his first retail recording was a reading of his father's Bible stories rendered for children, "In the Beginning." Not surprisingly, he took no shortcuts in arranging for the right to use this material. In March 1941 G. P. Putnam's Son, publisher, wrote to Asch granting him permission to record "In the Beginning" in exchange for crediting them for having published the original book, as well as the payment of royalties. Sholem's English was much too heavily accented, so the stories were read by David Niles. At other times Asch insisted that his first retail recording was by the Bagelman Sisters, and on still other occasions he maintained that "Eli Eli" and "Kol Nidre," two cantorials performed by Cantor Leibele Waldman, constituted his first foray into the retail record trade.[77] Cantorials are Jewish liturgical songs that, following the example of the famous New York Cantor Yossele Rosenblatt in the early part of the century, had been elevated to the level of a soaring vocal art. Enrico Caruso had ostensibly expressed admiration for Cantor Rosenblatt, and there were those who had attempted (unsuccessfully) to entice him to the opera stage. Jews on the Lower East Side clamored to hear the best cantors, some of whom had been attracted to the United States from Europe by exorbitant sums of money.[78] More than half of Asch's first twenty commercial recordings were by cantors, some singing liturgical music, others singing Yiddish folk songs, Palestinian songs, and in one case patriotic songs ("Ich Dank Dir Got Fur America"). Waldman was Asch's most prominent cantor, but there were others—Leib Glantz, Saul Meisels, Maurice Ganchoff.

The arrangement with Waldman may have been typical for Asch's early recordings. Asch calculated that the cost of producing two recordings of Waldman came to $955, of which $105 consisted of royalties for the artist. Waldman himself invested the remaining $850, with the understanding that he would be paid back with interest in four quarterly installments of $261. Asch boldly offered his recording equipment as collateral. Furthermore, he bought a Hammond organ on the installment plan in 1940 so that Waldman could accompany himself. If he were unable to sell enough records to reimburse Waldman for his investment, he would quickly be in hot water. The fact that the whole operation was a bit of a shell game was reflected on Asch's balance sheet for fiscal year 1941: $16.93.

In the spring of 1941 Asch was sufficiently busy with assorted recording projects to hire some staff. His first two employees were

Murray Levene and Marian Distler. Distler was a Jew and a leftist, though considerably more sympathetic to the party than Asch. She was twenty-two years old that year—fourteen years younger than he—and freshly graduated from Hunter College. When Asch's payroll suddenly ballooned to ten that autumn, Distler remained the highest paid employee by far. She had been hired as a secretary, but she soon made herself indispensable to the operation and would remain so for twenty-three years.

On the eve of the Second World War, Asch had a tenuous toehold in an esoteric corner of the recording business. He had released a couple dozen commercial recordings, almost all of them in the Jewish field. The significant exceptions were recordings that he made in May 1941 of Huddie Ledbetter. Leadbelly had been in New York on and off since late 1934, when John Lomax and his eighteen-year-old son Alan, the first to record him, had brought him there. The previous year they had discovered him in a visit to Angola Penitentiary in Louisiana to collect the folk songs of the inmates. It was Leadbelly's second long prison sentence; the first had been for murder, the second for attempted murder. In each instance his sentence was commuted when Leadbelly appealed to the governor in song for his release. The Lomaxes had been instrumental in the second pardon, having presented Governor O. K. Allen with an aluminum disc recording of Leadbelly's musical plea. When he was freed, Leadbelly joined John Lomax in Texas, where he was hired to drive the collector's car and operate the recording equipment on a subsequent field trip.[79]

A second field trip followed immediately on the heels of the first. The Lomaxes' destination was the annual conference of the Modern Language Association (MLA) in Philadelphia. John Lomax had arranged for Leadbelly to perform at the annual "smoker," as well as for the "popular literature" section. Although John Lomax's conception of his collecting had evolved since the days of *Cowboy Ballads*, it remained in the thirties an appendage of literary studies. Lomax would continue to promote Leadbelly to audiences, many of them at universities, which might be expected to appreciate his *literary* qualities. Still, this was hardly business as usual at the MLA. The press took note of his appearances at the conference, so that by the time the Lomaxes and Leadbelly arrived in New York, Leadbelly was greeted as a celebrity. John and Alan Lomax and Leadbelly settled in a home lent to them in Wilton, Connecticut, where they were soon joined by Martha Promise, a woman who had known Leadbelly in Louisiana since she was twelve. Promise and Leadbelly were married a few days later, and the four of them set up housekeeping for the winter while the Lomaxes made various arrangements to display Leadbelly's talent around New York and along the East Coast.

In late January Leadbelly made his first commercial recordings for the American Record Company—six sides of country blues were eventually released on the Perfect and Melotone labels. (While the term *side* is used today, especially in jazz parlance, to mean a single "cut" or "track" on an LP or compact disc, it originated in the 78-rpm era, when a single, uninterrupted performance almost always took up an entire side of a disc.) Through that winter the Lomaxes dressed Leadbelly in prison garb (although not stripes, Lomax later insisted) and brought him before audiences throughout the greater New York area. They augmented the already substantial recordings they had made of him for the Library of Congress with a series of sessions in the Wilton, Connecticut, house. Two segments were staged for the "March of Time" newsreel, one of which had Leadbelly dressed in prison stripes, the other in which he surrenders a concealed knife to John Lomax.[80] Leadbelly finally revolted against Lomax's paternalism following a concert that Lomax had arranged for him in Buffalo. "He looked dangerous," reported Lomax in his account the following year. "The moment had come about which friends and prison wardens had warned me. For we were alone and I carried no arms." As it happened, Leadbelly did him no harm, and the tour proceeded to Harvard, where Lomax's old mentor George Lyman Kittredge offered an apparently unnecessary warning: "He is a demon, Lomax."[81] Leadbelly's collaboration with the Lomaxes effectively concluded at this juncture; he and Martha returned to Louisiana by Greyhound Bus, not to return to New York until 1937.

Perhaps most troubling to later folk singers and folklorists were the arrangements the Lomaxes made to acquire the copyrights to Leadbelly's songs. United States copyright laws allow a songwriter to retain the rights to a composition for twenty-eight years following its composition, at which point the copyright may be renewed for another twenty-eight years.[82] This means that when a copy of the song is sold, in either printed or recorded form, a royalty is owed the songwriter. Performance royalties remained a tangled web for some years. Through the 1930s royalties for songs broadcast "live" on the radio were collected by the American Society of Composers, Authors, and Publishers (ASCAP) and the fees disbursed to publishers, authors, and composers in proportion to the level of their activity within the ASCAP organization (rather than to the particular composer). Only with the formation of a rival organization in 1940, Broadcast Music Incorporated (BMI), did the industry switch to a system of paying royalties to the songwriter in proportion to the number of actual performances. The right to broadcast commercially recorded compositions was hotly disputed by the American Federation of Musicians (AFM), the record companies and the radio station operators through the Second World War.

Folk songs present collectors and performers with a particularly vexing problem. The identity of the original songwriter may well have been lost; immersed as they are in an oral tradition, folk songs inevitably are altered at the hands of each performer. Although it would be another ten years before folk songs were to generate significant royalties for collectors, performers and publishers, some would ultimately be worth tens and even hundreds of thousands of dollars. Should the royalties simply not be collected? Or should they be awarded to the singer who taught it to the collector, to the collector who rescued it from obscurity, or to the performer who added a verse that *might* have been crucial to its eventual popularity? A tangled chain of performing, collecting, arranging, recording, and publishing often resulted in multiple claims to a single song.

The Lomaxes' claim to the copyright to the songs performed by Leadbelly was not entirely lacking in merit. Musicologist George Herzog of Columbia had ostensibly demonstrated that most of Leadbelly's "compositions" had identifiable antecedents. Of the forty-nine songs published in *Negro Folk Songs as Sung by Lead Belly,* "more than half . . . have been published in other collections, in some other version. Others are of white parentage, some are white tunes pure and simple."[83] To his credit, Herzog did not entirely slight the creativity and contributions of Negro "interpreters." At the same time the Lomaxes often sifted and selected through several of Leadbelly's renditions of a single song in order to select a version for publication that would have literary merit. As a consequence of this process, as well as the very act of "collecting" in the field, the Lomaxes claimed the right to copyright the songs of Leadbelly. Only after Leadbelly's death in 1949 was there a successful effort to see that his estate retained some claim on his many songs.

Richard Wright wrote a column about Leadbelly for the *Daily Worker* in August 1937, three years before the publication of his first major novel, *Native Son,* and five years before his famous split with the Communist Party. Wright celebrated Leadbelly's accomplishments as a singer, performer, and composer, maintaining that "the entire folk culture of the American Negro has found its embodiment in him . . . it seems he knows every song his race has ever sung." But Wright goes on to excoriate the role of John Lomax in Leadbelly's recent career: "Here begins one of the most amazing cultural swindles in American history. Lomax . . . beguiled the singer with sugary promises, telling him that if he helped him to gather folk songs from other Negro prisoners in various prisons throughout the South, he would make him rich." Instead, claimed Wright, Lomax exploited Leadbelly unmercifully, compensating him only meagerly for his many performances and not at all for the publication of his songs in *Negro Folk Songs as Sung by Lead Belly.* Leadbelly himself was furious about the way he had been portrayed in the Lomaxes' book.[84] His fee for appearing in "March of Time" was sixteen dollars. Furthermore, he accused Lomax of having sensationalized Leadbelly's image for the purposes of publicity, portraying him as a "half sex-mad, knife-toting, black buck from Texas."

Wright reported that upon returning to New York Leadbelly had joined the Workers' Alliance. "The folks in the Workers' Alliance are the finest I've ever known," Wright quotes Leadbelly as saying. "They are different from those Southern White men." Wright included the lyrics to two new Leadbelly compositions in his column:[85] "Bourgeois Blues," a protest against the segregation he encountered in Washington, D.C., and "The Scottsboro Boys Got Here," concerning a celebrated case of southern injustice that the party had taken up in order to focus attention on its antilynching campaign. Having been largely abandoned by the Lomaxes, Leadbelly found harbor with party members and other leftists, who regarded him as a near perfect exemplar of Popular Front politics.

But efforts to claim Leadbelly as a left-wing icon were only partly successful. Earl Robinson arranged to have Leadbelly sing for a progressive adult summer camp:

> I was so interested and excited by his work that I failed to screen his songs. After an evening of him singing "Ella Speed," "Frankie and Albert," and songs of gun-toting gamblers and bad women, the camp was in an uproar. Arguments raged over whether to censure him or me or both of us. By the next day, things had calmed down and that evening when he

sang his "Bourgeois Blues" and the ballad he had composed
about the Scottsboro boys, the air cleared.[86]

Fred Ramsey, who would become Leadbelly's primary protector
and supporter in his last years, suspected that Leadbelly only
wrote protest songs when coached to do so by various leftists.
Certainly Leadbelly knew his audience, and several events in his
life suggested that he was best off singing what people wanted to
hear. Yet not all of Leadbelly's leftist audiences were as doctrinaire
as Robinson's progressive summer campers. Some realized that
many of Leadbelly's songs could be understood allegorically; without forcing the issue, for example, "Grey Goose" could be interpreted as an oblique paean to the resilience of the African
American spirit in the face of brutalizing southern racism. Others,
such as Richard Wright, understood that the celebration of Leadbelly's traditional repertoire was in itself a political act.

Leadbelly came to Asch through Si Rady and *Pins and Needles*. By
1941 he had twice more recorded for commercial record companies—Musicraft and Victor—but he had largely missed the heyday
of "race records," having spent crucial years in prison while record
companies combed the South for "folk singers," both black and
white. By the mid- and late 1930s, the tastes of black audiences had
moved on to jazz—particularly of the big band variety—and an
emerging, harder-edged, urban blues. Leadbelly was having trouble
making ends meet, and Rady was doing Leadbelly a favor by
finding him another outlet for his music, through Asch.

Just before Leadbelly recorded for Asch, he performed for young
children in the Little Red School House, a private school in Greenwich Village for the children of political progressives. Someone
snapped a photograph of Leadbelly seated with his guitar on his
lap, dressed as always in a suit and tie. At his feet was a crowd of
elementary school children, clapping hands, clearly delighted.

Asch's decision to record Leadbelly was a leap of faith and
imagination, a brilliant and creative move even if Asch could not
have seen its eventual implications. His recognition of the value of
Leadbelly's music, as unfamiliar as he was with the genre it represented, was primarily the consequence of his intuition. It would
mean a foray into a different kind of market, still perhaps
significantly Jewish but one more closely identified with progressive politics than with Jewish religion or culture. For Asch's market
was not to be blacks in Harlem—outside the rural South, black
audiences largely rejected Leadbelly's music as dated and Uncle

Tomish.[87] Rather, Asch would find his market primarily among whites who traveled in left-wing political circles, those who had encountered Leadbelly in *Pins and Needles*, at labor rallies, and at other political events.

Asch recalled that his first meeting with Leadbelly resulted in instantaneous understanding:

> Immediately Leadbelly and I were brothers. I understood him, he understood me, and he utilized me and I was willing to be used because he knew that through me and through my medium he was able to express what he wanted. He was a great intellect. A real, hard-thinking, practical man. . . . He really understood what he was, in terms of America, in terms of music and everything else.[88]

Asch recognized a certain formality in Leadbelly, as well as a nobility and self-respect that was reflected in the care he took with his clothes.[89]

Asch prepared a standard contract that stipulated that Leadbelly was to record at least six selections for him within a period of twelve months. In exchange he would receive a royalty of two cents on each double-faced record that was sold as well as a fee of ten dollars per side for each "master" he recorded. Royalties were to be paid semiannually, and the recording fee within ten days of the session.

Taking his cue from Leadbelly's recent success at the Little Red School House, Asch first recorded Leadbelly singing children's songs. Asch sat behind the glass in his recording booth, operating the recording equipment and cuing Leadbelly with hand signals. The studio itself was only ten by fifteen feet; the door at the back opened into the hallway of the WEVD building. The only constraints on Leadbelly were those of time—these first sides would appear on ten-inch 78s, with a maximum running time of about three and a half minutes. Having recorded before, Leadbelly had little difficulty confining his songs to the time allotted and even managed to introduce some of them with brief spoken remarks. Otherwise he did not receive direction from Asch. In Asch's view Leadbelly knew his art, and it would not be his place to give him direction. In their first session in May, Leadbelly recorded two songs, "Ha Ha This Way" and "Sally Walker." It appears that the recordings were made in one take; given the cost of the acetate discs and the shoestring nature of Asch's operation, he doubtlessly wanted to avoid unnecessary costs. Leadbelly returned to Asch's studio the following month, recording four additional songs, and in July he recorded two more.[90] Of these eight, Asch chose six; using the photograph taken that spring at the Little Red School House as the cover, he packaged the six songs in an album of three ten-inch discs with the title *Play Parties in Song and Dance, as Sung by Lead Belly*. In his notes for the album Asch related that "most folk songs and dances that have been recorded are too difficult and too sophisticated for children. Because of the simplicity and repetition of the words and music in 'Play Parties' the songs and dances are easy to learn and retain their natural charm after many playings."

When the album was issued that autumn it produced an unexpected result. Gossip columnist Walter Winchell took Asch to task for having released an album for the children's market by a known killer. It is difficult to imagine how Winchell thought children might be threatened by Leadbelly's innocent songs, regardless of his unseemly past. But the result was that the album received far more attention than Asch had anticipated, and with the success of some other titles at the height of the Christmas season that year he was forced to hire several people on a part-time and temporary basis to keep up with the demand.

Leadbelly quickly learned that although his recordings for Asch might make him famous (or notorious), they would not make him rich. His royalties for the first six months amounted to $29.52. Asch dispensed small checks to Leadbelly through the following spring, none larger than $10.00 When Leadbelly asked for an accounting, Asch tallied the number of albums sold and demonstrated to Leadbelly that he had actually been overpaid: "THIS LEAVES A TOTAL AMOUNT OF $19.90 WHICH YOU HAVE RECEIVED IN EXCESS OF AMOUNT DUE YOU TO-DATE!"[91]

Asch might have puttered along in this manner for some years were it not for the intervention of the war. But in a matter of months after the bombing of Pearl Harbor, a key ingredient in the manufacture of records—shellac—was declared a critical war material. Record manufacturers were allotted a quantity of shellac calculated at 10 percent of the amount that they had been using in the months preceding the war. Asch had been producing few enough records that his allotment was almost negligible. Without some arrangement for additional shellac, he was out of the record business.

Menachem Mendel Spiro, Asch's maternal grandfather, a victim of the holocaust. (Courtesy of Steve Blum)

Aunt Basha Spiro with her daughter in the Soviet Union, 1930s. (Courtesy of Steve Blum)

Asch family home in Bellevue, outside Paris, around 1925. *Left to right:* Moe, Ruth, Madya, unidentified visitor, and Sholem. (Estate of Frances Asch)

Moe and Frances Asch around the time of their wedding in 1928. (Courtesy of Ruth Shaffer)

Exterior of the Radio Labs shop, Driggs Avenue, Brooklyn. (Estate of Frances Asch)

Asch with collaborators Mearns and Zolnier in the Radio Labs shop, around 1934. (Estate of Frances Asch)

Madya, Moe, and Frances at Camp Tamiment, 1939. (Courtesy of Ruth Shaffer)

Asch and jazz clarinetist Pee Wee Russell, 1946. (Courtesy of the Frank Driggs Collection)

Asch with Leadbelly, around 1946. (Photograph by David Stone Martin, Courtesy of the Martin Estate)

Asch and Fred Ramsey, Leadbelly's loyal champion. (Photograph by David Gahr)

Asch and Harold Courlander, editor of the Ethnic Series. (Photograph by David Gahr)

Sholem and Madya at home in Florida, early 1950s. (Courtesy of Ruth Shaffer)

Moe with Sholem in Israel, a rare visit in his father's last year. (Courtesy of Ruth Shaffer)

Moe with his son Michael around 1957. (Courtesy of Michael Asch)

With Pete and Toshi Seeger in the 1950s. (Photograph by David Gahr)

With Sonny Terry and Brownie McGhee, 1958. (Photograph by David Gahr)

Marian Distler. (Photograph by David Gahr)

Asch at the control booth, 117 West Forty-sixth Street. (Photograph by David Gahr)

With Sam Charters, 1962. (Photograph by Ann Charters)

Ella Jenkins. (Photograph by Bernadelle Richter, Courtesy of Folkways Archives and Collections, Smithsonian Institution)

Woody Guthrie. (Courtesy of Folkways Archives and Collections, Smithsonian Institution)

Woody Guthrie and Burl Ives in New York City's Central Park in 1940. This photo was taken as a publicity shot for Alan Lomax's radio program, *Back Where I Come From.* **(Courtesy of Library of Congress)**

Guy Carawan. (Photograph by Larry Moyers, Courtesy of Folkways Archives
and Collections, Smithsonian Institution)

The New Lost City Ramblers. *Left to right:* Tom Paley, John Cohen, Mike Seeger. (Photograph by Photo Sound Associates, Courtesy of Folkways Archives and Collections, Smithsonian Institution)

With Toshi Seeger and her four-day-old niece Sonya Cohen, Newport, 1965. (Courtesy of John Cohen)

3. ASCH RECORDS

f there was a pattern developing in the recordings Asch made in the year preceding the bombing of Pearl Harbor, it had to do with a kind of principled opportunism. He found markets that were being neglected and met specific demands. On the whole these were markets that either overlapped significantly with his father's audience or with whom he felt some political affinity. Until 1944 most of the recording that took place in Asch Recording Studios was of Jewish music. The "majors" (Victor, Decca, Columbia) had recorded a significant number of cantorials in the twenties, just as they had addressed regional demands for southern country (hillbilly) and southern blues and sacred ("race") music. But with the Depression the majors stopped attending to markets that were defined narrowly by either ethnicity or region. Some of the cantors Asch recorded in the first months of 1942 had been recorded previously by Decca, Victor, and Columbia ten years earlier. Others, such as Leibele Waldman, were too young to have been recorded in that era, and although they were singing with varying degrees of regularity on the radio, Asch provided them with their first opportunity to appear on commercial recordings.

Asch took few chances in choosing "Kol Nidre" and "Eli Eli" to be among his first releases. These were perennial favorites, recorded many times before. "Eli Eli" ("My God, My God") had been written for a Yiddish theater production in 1896; within twenty years it had been so widely performed and accepted that it had entered the standard cantorial repertoire and was mistaken for folk liturgy. In the 1920s it was popularly associated with Cantor Rosenblatt, who recorded it frequently, sometimes with "Kol Nidre" on the reverse side. "Kol Nidre" ("All Vows") had precisely the opposite popular trajectory as "Eli Eli," originating in the liturgical repertoire and entering the realm of secular performance. In choosing to record them together, Leibele Waldman was merely emulating his idol and model, Cantor Yossele Rosenblatt.

Asch recorded many other standards of the Yiddish repertoire, both liturgical and popular. Some were chestnuts from the Yiddish stage; one such song, "Ven di boys velen kimn tsurik" ("When the Boys Will Come Back"), was written for the musical *Oy Sadie* in 1918 and had a renewed poignancy when Waldman recorded it for Asch in the early months of the Second World War (Asch 6026). Chaim Tauber (Towber), a prominent Yiddish theater lyricist, recorded "Mayn shtetele Mohileff" ("My Town of Mohilev"), which he had written in 1936 for the musical *Papirener Kinder* ("Children on Paper: Only in Letters and Pictures"), a familiar story of families separated by immigration (Asch 6018). On the reverse side was "Motl der Operator," a lyric he had put to a folk melody in 1934 that recounted the melodramatic story of a modest sewing machine operator who was killed on the picket line when his shop went on strike.

In a few instances Asch recorded contemporary Yiddish songs that had probably not been recorded before. Some were from recent Yiddish theatrical productions, whereas others were deliberately topical. "Reitiha" (or "Rehteh/ratir" [Asch 6015]) was composed in the year before the United States entered the Second World War and was intended to draw attention to the growing imperilment of eastern European Jewry. Max Kletter, publicized as the "Jewish Gypsy," had been composing Yiddish songs since the early 1930s, and recorded four of his compositions for Asch using a small orchestra (Asch 6006 and 6007).

Leadbelly represented Asch's most significant departure from the Jewish field, although there were a few others. Asch had begun to identify African American cultural production as an area to which he would be particularly dedicated. Early in 1941 he prepared an album entitled *Cavalcade of the American Negro*, which featured a script written and recited by actress Mercedes Gilbert. To publicize the album, he sent promotional flyers to black history teachers: "As teachers of the history of your race you will be proud to play these records for your pupils; that they are of undoubted educational, cultural and of entertainment value not only to the whole negro race, but to every American as well." The record purported to tell the "history of the American Negro from 1610 to the present day" and featured the voice as Miss Gilbert as "the mother of the negro race" and the Jarahal Choral Glee Club as the voices of her children. The album does not appear in later Asch catalogues, which suggests that it was prepared for a special market and dropped when it did not meet with success.

In July Jimmy Smith, who was on Asch's payroll as his "musical contractor" before being drafted into the army, made a recording with an unusual jazz quartet consisting of Smith on his "console" guitar, Mike Widmer on electric tenor guitar, Allen Reuss—a Benny Goodman guitarist—on Spanish guitar, and Leonard Corsale on bass. The release of two sides from that session later that year constituted Asch's first attempt in the jazz field (and a rather strange one at that). Also that year Asch released a beautifully packaged album of records entitled *Tree Top Songs*, which featured a woman named Nell Zurn imitating the sounds of various birds.

Another enterprise in 1941 almost cost Asch his studio. The previous year his uncle Olek had succeeded in escaping from Germany with his wife and daughter Madya, Nathan, Moe, and John met them at the dock in New York. Olek Spiro had left behind his prosperous shipping business and found himself suddenly in a new business environment, immersed in a language he did not understand. He immediately scouted around for a means of taking root and settled upon his nephew's fledgling recording business. Olek understood Asch's intentions in identifying previously untapped markets, and Olek thought he knew of yet another—the Polish expatriate community in the United States. Perhaps Sholem's urging was required, but in any case Asch went into business with Olek.[1] An arrangement was made in August 1941 with an investor who would share the costs of recording and pressing an album of three discs. A singer named Kiepura recorded several sides of Polish melodies in Asch's studio. Asch wrote checks to his uncle all through that summer and into the autumn, amounting to several hundred dollars. Then the deal was suddenly off; Asch was instructed to destroy the masters, the cash that had been dispensed to Olek and his wife apparently spent and a dead loss. Had not it been for a loan from Sholem of close to four hundred dollars, Asch would undoubtedly have ended the year in the red.

It took some months for the effect of the war to be felt in the recording industry. The president of the American Federation of Musicians, James Petrillo, announced at the start of the new year that there would be no strikes until the end of the war (a promise that would appear ludicrous in a very few months). The pace of

Asch's recording continued to accelerate through the winter and spring of 1942; Jewish material, particularly cantorials, continued to dominate his recording log, but he recorded Leadbelly again in January, preparing for a second album that would be called *Work Songs of the U.S.A.* Rumors of an impending shellac shortage did not surface until May.

A hopeful sign for the industry was the publication of *The Jazz Record Book* in March. The author was a man of about Asch's age—Charles Edward Smith—who in 1934 had written one of the first serious pieces of jazz criticism.[2] In this book, as in *Jazzmen* (a book he had coauthored with Frederic Ramsey in 1939), the emphasis was largely on the historical development of contemporary jazz. Smith, and especially Ramsey, had become preoccupied with finding the origins of jazz in the New Orleans marching bands at the turn of the century. By the late thirties they were at the leading edge of what had become a cult of early jazz record hunters. For *Jazzmen* they assembled a group of fellow cultists who undertook to interview "every living jazz musician who could contribute factual material."[3] The Jazzmen Group, as they came to be known, were influential in kicking off a revival of interest in the New Orleans jazz recorded primarily in the 1920s. It in turn sparked the first of several waves of revivalist bands—often white—that sought to recreate the music of the early New Orleans bands. The first and most influential of these was a white West Coast outfit called the Yerba Buena Jazz Band, featuring a trombonist of considerable ability by the name of Turk Murphy. The Yerba Buena Jazz Band imitated the arrangements of King Oliver and Louis Armstrong, and by 1941 they were recording albums that had some commercial success. But for hardcore enthusiasts, only the "true," "original," and "authentic" early recordings—however scratchy—would suffice.

By the time *The Jazz Record Book* appeared in 1942, jazz enthusiasts were firmly divided into three camps. On one end of the spectrum were the revivalists, referred to derogatorily by everyone else as the "moldy figs." At the time of the book's publication a combination of harmonic and rhythmic innovations was launching a radically new movement in jazz known as bebop or, later, simply bop. Its progenitors were alto saxophonist Charlie Parker and trumpet player Dizzy Gillespie, and there were very few white practitioners in its early days. Bebop was played by groups consisting of usually no more than five or six musicians; the small size, in combination with the ability to depart from the melodic and rhythmic center of the music, allowed soloists a previously unimagined degree of improvisatory freedom.[4] The trademark bebop enthusiast was the "hipster," cool and anaesthetized in demeanor, uncompromising in musical tastes, relishing his place at society's margin. Holding the very large center of the spectrum were the devotees of swing, a music dominated by the commercial success of big bands such as Benny Goodman's, Artie Shaw's, and Glenn Miller's and owing an unpayable musical debt to the black bands of Count Basie and Duke Ellington. Some of the swing bands were integrated: Benny Goodman had hired Teddy Wilson in 1936, and Artie Shaw had hired Billie Holiday in 1938. Swing was the preeminent form of American popular music from the mid-thirties through the war—the only era in which popular music was dominated by a form of jazz—in part because it was *dance* music.

In *The Jazz Record Book* Smith did not attempt to list every available jazz record, but he did attempt to cover the full chronological and geographical spectrum within the limits of what he regarded as authentic and substantive. New Orleans would, of course, have to be the touchstone. "At present it is doubtful," he wrote, "if anyone seriously disputes the claim that New Orleans is the birthplace of instrumental jazz." Taking a path down which Hammond had ventured in his introduction to his Spirituals to Swing concert, Smith looked for the origins of the New Orleans style in "the folk music of the American Negro, with its African roots."[5] By this he meant primarily blues and spirituals, both of which he (erroneously) imagined to have been well developed by Emancipation. Both spirituals and blues were widely recorded in the 1920s on various "race record" labels, although the former are entirely neglected in *The Jazz Record Book*.[6] Blues, on the other hand, is given a place of honor with a separate chapter dedicated to "Blues and Boogie Woogie." The blues section per se is dedicated to several female vocalists who recorded with jazz bands—Bessie Smith, Ma Rainey, and Ida Cox. Curiously, Asch did not record any female blues vocalists in the 1940s.[7] Most of the boogie-woogie section is comprised of solo piano recordings, with two future Asch Records artists—James P. Johnson and Meade Lux Lewis— figuring prominently.

Appended to the "Blues and Boogie Woogie" chapter is a section entitled "Long, Long Ways from Home," which opens with a notation about John Lomax's *Smoky Mountain Ballads,* an album of the folk music of Appalachia that RCA Victor had released the previous autumn. Smith makes a plea for the reissue of the "folk blues" material that the majors and a few others had recorded in the 1920s, and presents a sampling of several male blues singers, including several who would later record for Asch. Lonnie Johnson, who had once been a guitarist with Duke Ellington, had been an important blues singer and guitarist since his recordings of the 1920s and was accorded the distinction of having been the first guitarist to solo in a New Orleans band.[8] William (Big Bill) Broonzy had become "the most popular male blues singer" on Columbia's budget Okeh race label. Champion Jack Dupree, a "blues shouter" who played piano, was a new artist in 1942. Others—Joshua White, Joe Williams (Memphis Slim), Sonny Terry—would have their most significant financial success later, with largely white audiences. Three and a half pages are dedicated to the Musicraft, Bluebird, and Victor recordings of Leadbelly, and Smith notes parenthetically that Asch had recently released Leadbelly's play party songs: "These are specially suited to children in groups, but adults will find much of interest in the group games and sukey-jumps."[9] A reviewer of *The Jazz Record Book* noted in the *New Masses* that "the generous inclusion of Leadbelly . . . [,] who as far as I know has never been recognized as a part of jazz, shows the deepening appreciation for the Negro folk qualities of jazz."[10]

Smith had had some success persuading the majors to reissue historically valuable jazz from their vaults, particularly with RCA Victor, which had recently initiated its Hot Jazz series. He was able as a result to include a good many recordings of New Orleans musicians—Louis Armstrong, Jelly Roll Morton, King Oliver—that they had made during the Chicago and New York phases of their recording careers. Big band jazz is also amply represented, organized historically and according to various schools of influence. What is not present in this volume is bebop. Very little of the emerging style had made it to disc, and Smith makes no indication that he recognized its appearance on the horizon.

Except for those few who frequented the right New York nightclubs or who were in receiving range of live radio broadcasts, bebop would remain an unheard revolution until close to the end of the war. In April 1942 two shiploads of shellac from India were sunk and recording industry executives immediately predicted the worst. It was rumored that the War Production Board (WPB) would confiscate 50 percent of the existing supply. Some curtailment of record production was a certainty; *Down Beat* predicted that companies would have to cut some acts from their rosters, and the practice of recording multiple versions of a single song would have to cease. The reclamation of shellac from old records began almost at once; the surfaces that resulted from the reclamation process were rough and noisy, but until a substitute was found for shellac there was little alternative (by August, the Clark Phonograph Company in Newark, New Jersey, was pressing records for a new company—Capitol—using a secret shellac substitute).[11] Nationwide drives were established to collect some portion of the estimated two hundred million records then "cluttering up attics, cellars and closets of the American home."[12] For a short time, the majors cut the shipping of records to a minimum and stopped recording altogether.[13]

By midyear the supply of shellac had been frozen altogether, and then allotments were rationed at 20 percent of the prewar supply.[14] But by this time there was a far more serious problem facing the recording industry. Going back on his previous promise, Petrillo announced in early summer that there would be a ban on recording of all union musicians unless an arrangement could be made to pay royalties for performances played on radio stations and jukeboxes. The fear was not only that musicians were not being adequately rewarded for such performances but also that the use of jukeboxes in bars and nightclubs was depriving musicians of work in what might otherwise have been "live" settings.[15] At first Petrillo had in mind to prevent just those recordings being played on the radio and in jukeboxes, but it quickly became apparent that it was not possible to ensure the sale of records exclusively to private homes—it would have to be all or nothing. The ban would consequently apply to the recording of all union musicians, regardless of the purpose to which the recordings were to be put. In the weeks preceding the announced 1 August deadline, the majors recorded furiously.[16]

The deadline came and the recording stopped. The majors had stockpiled enough new recordings that their releases did not suffer significantly for a few months, but by the end of the year they were reduced to reissuing older performances. And within a year they were desperate enough to issue recordings of their major artists—including Frank Sinatra—backed only by vocal ensembles.[17]

Asch was not immediately affected by the recording ban. Although he occasionally used a union musician to back up one of his cantors, most of the musicians he would be recording in the coming months were not of the kind with which the AFM generally bothered. Between May and July he recorded seven different cantors, which resulted in an equal number of two-sided records in the months that followed. The six sides he recorded of Lead-belly appeared in May as *Work Songs of the U.S.A.* Marian Distler wrote the notes, which were included as a small pamphlet in the album. The notes are not extensive, but she went to some trouble to draw on available sources: Smith's *Jazz Record Book,* Carl Sand-burg's *American Songbag,* and three books of the Lomaxes—*Negro Folk Songs as Sung by Leadbelly, American Ballads and Folksongs,* and *Our Singing Country.* The last, which had just appeared, had been faulted by the *New Masses* for having failed "to make the reader conscious of the very real connection between the songs and the environ-ment that produced them."[18] Distler might not have succeeded in capturing the environment that had produced the songs—at least not as a Marxist periodical might have wished—but she provided sufficient social and historical context to reveal what she (and presumably Asch) regarded as the songs' meaning: "This is the story of America at work. Wherever Lead Belly went, he heard the people singing. He learned their songs and he sings them for us as they are sung in the U.S.A."

The focus of the notes was on the *universal* appeal of the songs, rather than on their particular African American origins. Some of the songs on Leadbelly's second Asch album were in fact work songs in the strict sense; that is, they were used to regulate the rhythm of workers engaged in a collective task. One of these—"Take This Hammer," a tree-chopping song—became one of Leadbelly's best remembered songs. Another equally well remem-bered song—"Rock Island Line"—is not identified as "Negro" despite the presence of stock blues phrases:

> ABC double XYZ,
> Cats in the cubbard [sic] but they can't see me.
> . . . .
> I may be right and I may be wrong,
> But you're going to miss me when I'm gone.©

Two other songs, "Ol' Riley" and "Corn Bread Rough," are identified with slavery. The latter is a marvelous, rollicking dance tune that Leadbelly accompanies on his first instrument, the accordion, rather than his trademark twelve-string guitar. Distler remarks that the nonsense lyrics were used to disguise the song's rebellious implications from the slave owners. In recognizing the "protest" element in traditional African American songs, Distler joined the small but growing ranks of leftist enthusiasts who thought they could detect "political content" in black musical forms that on the face of it seemed largely apolitical.[19]

When *Work Songs of the U.S.A.* was released, Charles Edward Smith reviewed it in Bob Thiele's *Jazz* magazine: "In doing this splendid recording job for the jazz and folk music world, Moses Asch proves himself a true son of his distinguished father, Sholem Asch. . . . The whole album is superbly done. It's a grand job and a 'must' for anyone's record library."[20] Despite Smith's kind words (and what for Asch must have been an extremely gratifying reference to his father), the recording was too esoteric to attract much attention. According to Asch's records, he had sold seventy-three copies of *Work Songs* between May and September; another one hundred were sold by the Fred Gretsch Company, a manufacturer and retailer of records. Combined with the nineteen copies of *Play Parties* that Asch had sold in the same period of time, Leadbelly had earned a grand total of $11.58 in royalties.

It is possible that the meagerness of the sales was partially a function of the shellac shortage. Though Asch may have had sufficient material in his vaults on acetate to keep him going through the recording ban, the shellac shortage was providing him with serious trouble. The solution he arrived at was in finding someone with the opposite problem—plenty of shellac and no material to release. Herbert Harris was a party member who ran a movie house on Forty-sixth Street that played Soviet films. When the Soviet Union pulled its exhibit from the 1939 New York World's Fair, at the time of the Hitler-Stalin pact, Harris was given their stock of Soviet records to sell. A few of the records were renditions of Russian folk songs, including the stunning recordings of traditional Byelorussian songs and dances by the Piatnitsky Chorus, which had appeared at the world's fair that year. But many others were frankly propagandistic, such as "Red Army's Nurses Arrive at the Front" or "March of the Partisans." Harris sold the Soviet recordings out of his Union Square store, Stinson Trading Company. When his initial stock was exhausted, he pressed more. Thus by the time of the shellac shortage Stinson had pressed enough records that he was entitled to a significant allotment. But the market for Soviet recordings—even in the heyday of American communism—was not vast and consequently Harris was looking for additional material to release.

The arrangement made between Harris and Asch appears to have been relatively casual; if documents ever changed hands, they have not survived. Asch's material would be pressed and marketed by Harris under the Asch-Stinson label, and Asch would receive a share of the royalties. The agreement became effective on 27 January 1943. Thereafter, and until the conclusion of the war, all of Asch's material—whether it appeared on the Asch or Asch-Stinson label—was sold through the Stinson Trading Company in Union Square. In these years few people—and the artists least of all—distinguished between Asch and Stinson. It was a single company in the eyes of most, and for a period of three years Herbert Harris became a part of the circle gradually growing up around Asch Records.

Part of this circle resulted from the proximity of a couple of nightclubs to the WEVD building. One was Café Society, which had opened in Sheridan Square in Greenwich Village on the night of Hammond's From Spirituals to Swing concert. Its proprietor, Barney Josephson, had owned a shoe store in Trenton, New Jersey. Josephson had been attending the rehearsals for Hammond's concert, and although he knew very little about music he determined that *this* was the kind of music he wanted to feature at his club.

Josephson's brother, Leon, was a party member, and rumors persisted that the club had been established to raise money for the party.[21] But Barney appeared to have other motivations. His interest was in creating a place where interracial audiences could hear both black and white music. Café Society became the place where the cultural and musical aesthetic born out of the Popular Front came to fruition. Jazz musicians, folk musicians, even comics found in it a haven from racism—and from conformity.[22]

The other nightclub was the Village Vanguard on Seventh Avenue, two cramped basement rooms, their walls covered by the murals of Paul Petroff, which was run by Max Gordon. In late 1941 Leadbelly started what became a six-month run at the Vanguard, sharing the bill with another southern black singer, Josh White. Both had had relatively steady work on two CBS radio programs produced by Alan Lomax, "Back Where I Come From" and "The School of the Air." The former had aired three nights a week and was directed by Nicholas Ray. Most of the other prominent figures in New York's emerging folk music scene—Burl Ives, Woody Guthrie, Pete Seeger—appeared with varying regularity on the show. When it ended, it was proposed to Gordon that he hire Leadbelly on a regular basis. But there was concern that Leadbelly's music and diction were too "rough" for an entire evening of entertainment, and the smoother, more cosmopolitan Josh White was added to the bill.[23]

White was about twenty-five years younger than Leadbelly but had been earning his living as a musician for considerably longer. He had left his home in South Carolina before the age of ten to be the "lead boy" for various blind itinerant musicians. He first appeared on record when only twelve, playing second guitar on a blues number by Joel Taggart for Paramount's race record series. By the early 1930s he was making race recordings under his own name (and under pseudonyms: Pinewood Tom and the Singing Christian) for the American Record Company, which had sought him out as Blind Lemon Jefferson's last lead boy. He had established himself among black audiences when in the mid-1930s he moved to New York and shortly afterward suffered a severe injury to his hand that kept him out of music until late in the decade. When he resumed his musical career it was in a Popular Front–inspired theatrical production entitled *John Henry*, which featured Paul Robeson in the title role and Josh White in the role of his late mentor, Blind Lemon Jefferson. The play closed after a short and disappointing run, but from that time on White's audience was primarily in white leftist circles.[24] His repertoire gradually shifted from traditional blues toward songs of social protest, particularly those having to do with racial injustice.[25]

Josh White and Leadbelly occupied one segment of the growing coterie of New York–based folk musicians. Exactly who and what constituted folk music in the early 1940s, however, might have been a matter of some dispute. The national trade magazines for the entertainment industry—*Variety, Billboard*—considered folk music the province of primarily southern or southern-styled artists such as Eddie Arnold, Red Foley, Gene Autry, and Ernest Tubb, who today would be regarded as "country and western." They were the most commercial incarnation of the regional southern artists whom the majors had recorded for local markets in the 1920s. At times, and undoubtedly at the instigation of their record companies, artists in this category reveled in their ostensive lack of sophistication, playing upon the hokum and hillbilly stereotype of the southern mountaineer. Conspicuously absent from the folk category were black artists. Whether sacred or secular—spirituals or blues—black music was categorized under race records throughout the decade.

Folk meant something else again to the academic folklorists, who were beginning to crawl out from underneath the dominant and dominating umbrella of college literature—particularly English—departments. In 1933 Dr. Erich M. von Hornbostel had arrived from Germany as part of Greenwich Village's University in Exile at the New School for Social Research, an effort to save a critical portion of European intellectual life from the impending calamity of fascism. He had trained a new generation of musicologists at the University of Berlin, who took particular interest in documenting and analyzing indigenous, regional musics that were termed folk. His students included ethnomusicologist George Herzog, who was then at Columbia, and composer Henry Cowell, who had joined the New School in 1930, three years after it had hired its first musicologist, Aaron Copland. In 1931 Cowell recruited his close friend and former teacher Charles Seeger to the New School, so that Greenwich Village quickly became a center for the composition and performance of avant-garde music that drew on American and worldwide folk musical sources, as well as on American jazz and other unconventional sources. Henry Cowell, according to some, was a "born promoter"; among the many events he established in the 1930s to heighten public awareness of musical activity at the New School was an annual folk festival entitled Dances of Many Peoples. The New School composers also constituted the core of the Composers' Collective, which in its idiosyncratic way had set about wedding folk musical forms to a revolutionary political agenda. Copland, Seeger, Elie Siegmeister, and other composers sought to create an egalitarian music by, ironically, casting off cultural particularism in favor of an internationally inspired, universal musical form that would be comprehensible to all.[26] By *folk* they meant musical (and only secondarily lyrical) traditions embedded in the lives of rural peoples—musical forms that, it was presumed, had changed little over decades and remained largely impervious to the innovations of individuals. Through Herzog and Seeger and the generation that they trained in the 1930s and 1940s, the field of ethnomusicology gained a toehold in the academy and added a dimension to the study of folk material that complemented the literary approaches preceding it.

But neither the categories of the music business nor those of the academic world precisely accounted for the folk music that was emerging in New York. For starters, the folk music community in New York crossed racial boundaries, conflating the categories employed by the major record manufacturers and retailers. Additionally, although the material of some performers was sufficiently traditional to satisfy the academicians, other performers, though drawing on traditional musical and lyrical styles, were composing new and often timely political songs. By the late 1930s the Popular Front's message had succeeded in convincing party members and fellow travelers that folk music was the only dependably authentic, democratic expression of the American masses.

As folk music historian Serge Denisoff has described it, the urban "folk stylists" of this generation were sorting themselves into two camps: the Stalinist ideologues and the folk entrepreneurs. The first group eschewed any interest in popular or commercial success, remaining ideologically isolated from the mainstream of American life by adhering to the shifting positions of the party. The latter, though occasionally affiliating with leftist organizations when they seemed the only reliable audience, ultimately were seeking a means of entering the mainstream of the American entertainment industry.[27] In reality it was not that simple. As Denisoff himself recognizes, the political convictions of even the most ambitious of the folk entrepreneurs—Burl Ives being the premier example—were not necessarily matters of convenience. And although those who were the most politically committed—Pete Seeger, Earl Robinson, and Woody Guthrie, for example—were disdainful of the overtly commercial products of Tin Pan Alley, this is not the same as suggesting that they had no interest in some degree of commercial success. All three at various junctures happily collaborated with one or more of the major record labels. Financial considerations may not have been paramount, but it would require a fine degree of psychological discrimination to separate the *political* benefits of reaching a mass audience through RCA Victor, Decca, or Columbia from the *personal* satisfactions that inevitably accompanied them. Woody Guthrie was unquestionably delighted to have his *Dust Bowl Ballads* appear on RCA Victor in the summer of 1940—he kept a scrapbook of the reviews.[28] His political convictions were no less genuine for the personal satisfaction he took from having a product in the mass market.

Denisoff's criticism of political folk singers in the 1940s is closest to the mark when he faults them for ignoring popular musical forms with which the urban proletariat was most familiar, and for promoting southern rural styles that were esoteric and foreign to urban ears. "Folk music," writes Denisoff, "was not the music of the urban working class; they preferred the ditties of Tin Pan Alley."[29] It is true that leftist folk singers of the era found popular song a poor vehicle for political education, but *not* because it was tainted by its affiliation with capital—their own collaborations with the majors had no such corrupting affect. Rather, pop music was obsessed with trivial, escapist, pleasure-seeking themes. Obviously substantive political themes could have been adapted to popular musical forms, and *were* in fact in the case of theater music such as Harold Rome's *Pins and Needles* or the many plays of Marc Blitzstein. Instead, however, folk singers and others of the Left had developed a musical aesthetic that equated simplicity with authenticity. Folk music was people's music precisely because it could be played and sung by anyone and thus held the possibility of a mass singing movement. By this they explicitly did not mean the large workers' choruses that were still being promoted by European-influenced circles as the most appropriate vehicle for proletarian themes. During what Denisoff calls the proletarian renaissance of 1939–42, a "'folk music revival' in miniature" occurred during which the collective singing of folk songs by untrained, unrehearsed voices became normative in leftist gatherings. To put it bluntly, party activists and fellow travelers came to *like* folk musical forms more than popular ones, and they were eager to make converts in urban America.

Was it unreasonable to believe that members of the urban working class might have been drawn to the music of Aunt Molly Jackson, Jim Garland, Sarah Ogan, and Woody Guthrie? Within what Robbie Lieberman has called the "Communist movement culture," the development of a taste for rural southern musical forms was not an insurmountable barrier. Party members often were working class themselves and, like fellow members of the working class, were immigrants and children of immigrants for whom American folk music was initially strange. American popular music was rapidly become a hybrid itself, with diverse influences coming from sources rural and urban, southern and northern, European, American, and African. If party members could be converted to an aesthetic of American folk music, why not other members of the urban proletariate? Though they could not have known it at the time, American Communists were coming to the close of their heyday in the years leading up to the Second World War, and mass conversions through folk music were not to be. Would they have succeeded had they used popular musical forms? It seems unlikely. Besides, when folk musical forms briefly surged to the forefront of America's fickle popular musical taste twenty years later, the most impressive commercial successes were with decidedly apolitical material.

Mike Gold, in the pages of the *Daily Worker*, was particularly energetic in his efforts to find successors to the tradition of the IWW's Joe Hill; as early as 1933 he promoted a search for a musical form rooted in the American vernacular.[30] The fruit of this search took its most explicit form in early 1941 with the creation of an amorphous unit of folk-singers whose constantly shifting membership would come to be known as the Almanac Singers. Its core initially consisted of Lee Hays, Pete Seeger, and Millard Lampell, three singers and social activists who exemplified the broad range of New York's Communist Party culture. By fall they would be joined by this century's most important writer of American folk songs, Woody Guthrie.

Lee Hays was, like Woody Guthrie, the product of southern regional cultures that had transmitted to him a deep appreciation for their indigenous musical traditions. Hays—large and lethargic, articulate, argumentative, and hypochondriacal—had come out of a tradition in Arkansas that melded social activism with the soul-stirring power of old-time preaching. His father, killed in an automobile accident in 1927 when Lee was thirteen, had been a Methodist minister. Hays's mother deteriorated emotionally after the death of her husband, and by the time he was sixteen Lee was largely on his own. In 1934 he met Claude Williams, a radical preacher dedicated to the cause of racial and economic justice for the sharecroppers and mine workers of the Depression South. For the next six years Hays studied Williams's brand of religiously inspired radicalism, first as his ministry student at the College of the Ozarks, then as a frequent visitor to the Highlander School in Monteagle, Tennessee, and finally as an instructor at Arkansas's Commonwealth College. Highlander and Commonwealth were labor colleges with roots deep in socialist and unionist traditions. At Highlander Zilphia Horton, wife of Myles Horton, the school's founder and director, employed folk music in theatrical productions that were intended to teach and inspire workers to empower themselves on the front line of the labor struggle. She taught Hays to value the religious and secular musical traditions of his home state and to employ them in confronting economic exploitation and racial intolerance—to use art as a weapon. In 1937 Williams was named the director of Commonwealth College, and he brought Hays with him as a drama instructor. When the school succumbed to withering anticommunist attacks and closed in late 1940, Hays headed north to lend his hand to the cause of urban union organization.

Guthrie was just two years older than Hays, and his Oklahoma childhood was marked by similar tragedies. Catastrophe would continue to follow both of them to the end of their lives, and if anything Guthrie's stories were the more heartbreaking. The specter of genetic illness and a string of horrible fires haunted the Guthrie family. But unlike Hays, Guthrie at least *had* family and a very big and supportive one at that. His father Charley fancied himself a big man in the small town of Okemah. He was a real estate wheeler dealer and occasionally ran for local office, but he talked too fast and was a bit too fond of practical jokes to allow the Guthries to enter the ranks of Okemah society. In 1904 Charley married Nora Belle Tanner, a lively tomboy who sang the ballads of her mother's native Tennessee in a high, nasal voice. They had two children in quick succession, and Charley's commercial and political future looked assured. Even when their newly completed house burned down in 1909, his star appeared to be rising. A third child, Woodrow Wilson Guthrie, was born in 1912, and a fourth and fifth child came along in 1918 and 1922. Charley's real estate dealings were sufficiently lucrative that in 1918 he was able to buy a substantial house for the family in town and a farm out in the country. But well before the birth of the last child, things had begun to unravel for the family. The oil boom that hit Oklahoma in 1920 left Charley behind, and by 1923 he was broke. At the same time Nora's behavior was becoming increasingly erratic and occasionally alarming. Clara, her eldest, became the target of much of her growing hostility. One day in 1919 Clara doused her clothes with coal oil to frighten her mother, who had forced her to stay home from school. Her clothes caught fire and she died the next day from her burns. Many blamed Nora for her daughter's death, and they blamed her again in 1927 when Charley woke up from a nap to find himself ablaze. A moment before his wife had been standing over him with a kerosene lamp. Charley survived the fire but spent months recuperating in the hospital. Nora was hauled off to the state mental hospital in Norman; most townspeople had long ago concluded that she was mad. She no longer recognized anyone; within two years she was dead. Doctors had diagnosed her as having Huntington's chorea, a rare and little-understood genetic nerve disorder that got its name from the uncontrollable twitching and shuffling that caused the afflicted to appear to be engaged in an odd, solitary dance. Thus Guthrie, like Hays, suffered the humiliation of his mother's mental deterioration and the distressing prospect of being orphaned as a young teenager.

Unlike Hays, religion appears to have played little part either in Guthrie's upbringing or among his adult convictions. He was far more influenced as a teenager and young adult by the show-business pretensions of his many musical aunts, uncles, and cousins, and especially cousin Jack Guthrie, who gained national recognition as a country and western singer before Woody had made much impression at all. Jack and Woody began to appear together on Los Angeles radio station KFVD in July 1937. By September of that year Jack had been replaced by Maxine "Lefty Lou" Crissman, whose husky alto harmonized stunningly with Woody's flat, twangy drawl. Every day for almost two years they sang and recited cornball humor under the paternal guidance of Frank Burke, the station manager. Woody wrote most of the songs they sang, using the musical conventions—and sometimes entire melodies—of the songs he had grown up with. The records of the Carter Family were particularly influential, and Jimmie Rodgers (the "singing brakeman") left his mark as well. But lyrically, Woody was an original. What was more extraordinary was the furious *pace* at which he wrote song lyrics—and later stories, sketches, letters, and novels. Guthrie could write a fistful of songs at a sitting and often improvised new verses in the middle of a performance. If they were not all memorable, enough were to make it a feat of extraordinary proportions. It was as though he had a mania for words, and in his forties that is precisely what it became.

Guthrie, an autodidact, had derived from his father a belief in the power of reading. There were moments in his childhood when he had some guidance in his choice of books, but more often he just read voraciously and indiscriminately, and it was a habit he never lost. Fiction, nonfiction, poetry, history, science, and eventually political theory—it was all thrown into the hopper of his mind and came out as something homegrown, amusing, disarmingly sincere, and insightful. Increasingly observers thought they detected the wordy enthusiasms of Walt Whitman in Guthrie's depictions of American working people. In an 1868 essay entitled "American Vistas," Whitman wrote:

> When I pass to and fro, from different latitudes, different seasons, beholding the crowds of the great cities . . . —when I mix with these interminable swarms of alert, turbulent, good-natured, independent citizens, mechanics, clerks, young persons—at the idea of this mass of men, so fresh and free, so loving and so proud, a singular awe falls upon me.

Woody's political sensibilities were coming into focus in the late 1930s, and in a letter to his sister Mary Jo at this time he wrote:

> The poor folks dont own anything. They are scattered, wan-
> dering, broke hungry, dirty, ragged, hungry-looking and all
> that, but one good thing, they are workers, hard workers . . .
> they're Real People, Real Honest To Goodness People, going all
> over Hells' Half Acre looking for work.[31]

KFVD was much of the source of Guthrie's political conversion. His family could not take much credit for his increasingly radical posture—his father had once written a series of antisocialist, and occasionally racist, diatribes for the local paper. And Woody himself presented some racist material on KFVD until several sharp criti- cisms resulted in an immediate apology and retraction. But Frank Burke was a political liberal and free speech advocate who man- aged the progressive Democratic campaign of Culbert Olsen for governor of California in 1938. Among the commentators on KFVD was Ed Robbin, a correspondent for the *People's World*, the West Coast organ of the Communist Party. Robbin believed that he had discovered in Woody a genuine, unschooled proletarian philoso- pher, and through Robbin, Woody discovered in the party a new and highly appreciative audience. Before long Woody's work for the party began to eclipse his faltering radio show; he sang for frequent fund-raising rallies and meetings and began to publish a column in the *People's World* called "Woody Sez." He was far less naïve and unsophisticated than the image he consistently projected in his performances and writing, but he was still a deeply unconven- tional person who was impatient with much of the decorum that greases everyday social life. And his emerging public image repre- sented the ultimate embodiment of the Popular Front hero. Through Ed Robbin, Guthrie met the actor Will Geer, and through Will Geer, Woody came to New York in 1940.

By all accounts 3 March 1940 was a fateful day for American folk music. Will Geer produced a concert that evening at New York's Forrest Theater—a "Grapes of Wrath" benefit for California's mi- grant farm workers. The program included Aunt Molly Jackson, Leadbelly, Bess and Alan Lomax, Burl Ives, Josh White, Richard Dyer-Bennett, and Geer himself. Guthrie's performance was the showstopper, and Lomax realized instantly that he was in the presence of a folk music treasure. Another performance, reportedly brief and forgettable, was by Pete, the twenty-one-year-old banjo-picking son of musicologist Charles Seeger.[32]

Alan Lomax was by then the folk music archivist of the Library of Congress, and in short order he had whisked Guthrie off to Washington, where in three marathon sessions they recorded hours of songs and stories. Later Lomax persuaded RCA Victor to record Guthrie so that they might have an answer to Columbia's Burl Ives. The resulting album, *Dust Bowl Ballads,* contained some of Guthrie's most memorable songs: "I Ain't Got No Home," "Vigilante Man," "Do Re Mi," and "Tom Joad," a long ballad he had written to the tune of "John Hardy" after having watched the film *Grapes of Wrath* several times in a row. When the album appeared that summer it attracted a moderate amount of attention from the press and very little from the record-buying public. Today it arguably stands as one of the half-dozen most important American folk music albums of that decade—or of any other, for that matter.

While Guthrie was in Washington being feted by the Lomaxes, he came to know young Pete Seeger. In many ways, they were mirror opposites of each other: Seeger tall, shy, disciplined, and ascetic, Guthrie small, irascible, rumpled, and profane—they made an unlikely pair. Though Guthrie was deliberately cultivating his Oklahoman twang and his folksy vocabulary and had little firsthand experience of farm labor, he really *was* a genuine product of the Dust Bowl. He knew poverty first-hand and had been touched by more tragedy at age twenty-eight than most men were in a life time. Pete Seeger was a child of privilege from a once-monied, academic family. His knowledge of folk music came largely secondhand. His mother, Constance, was a classical violinist and had little interest in folk music, and even Charles was a relatively late convert, only recognizing the significance of folk music when it was discovered by the rest of the American Left in the Popular Front era. Pete's parents drifted and then divorced when Pete was eight, and about five years later Charles remarried. His second wife, Ruth Crawford, was a highly accomplished, classically trained composer, a profession entirely dominated by men at the time. Additionally, she had a long and abiding interest in American folk song, and her presence elevated the status of folk music in the household considerably.

Pete Seeger's acquaintance with folk music was the consequence of sustained effort rather than ubiquitous environment, but his attachment to progressive political causes developed far earlier than Guthrie's. His father, a man of principle who bristled at injustice when he saw it, was sympathetic with the Wobblies and was fired from his teaching post at Berkeley as a result of having become a conscientious objector during the First World War.[33] Even after his divorce and the start of a second family, Charles Seeger remained a source of political enlightenment for Pete, taking his older sons on a tour of Lower East Side slums and to a May Day demonstration.[34] Pete discovered the party while a teenager, and he was reading the *New Masses* while still in high school. In his second year at Harvard he joined the Young Communist League, and had he not been both shy and immature perhaps he would have become a premier campus radical. But his sophomore year was his last at Harvard, and by the time he encountered Guthrie two years later, music and radical politics had edged out most other considerations in his life. He remained a man of *ideas* and thus profoundly intellectual, but the vehicle for his ideas and intellect would thereafter be folk music. Pete dressed his ideas in homespun and wished above all to make them broadly accessible. His faithful companion in this endeavor was the five-string banjo, an instrument almost entirely unknown to northern, urban audiences until introduced to it by Pete Seeger.

Guthrie undoubtedly appeared to Pete Seeger to be the "real thing." It is not as evident what Guthrie made of Pete. "That guy Seeger," Guthrie said, "I can't make him out. He doesn't look at girls, he doesn't drink, he doesn't smoke, the fellow's weird."[35] But his passion for authentic folk music was unmistakable, and Guthrie could not have but been impressed by the younger man's musicianship. Though his mother was frustrated in her efforts to make a disciplined violin student out of him, when it came to the music he loved Seeger's dedication was boundless. His musical sensibilities were exquisite, and he had the ability to find the essence of a song—regardless of its culture of origin—and to perform it without subjecting it to his own stylistic interpretations. Guthrie would never be the accomplished instrumentalist Seeger was, although his facility on guitar, mandolin, and even fiddle has sometimes been too readily dismissed.[36]

Pete and Woody's first sustained collaboration resulted from Alan Lomax's discovery of a hundred or more unpublished radical folk songs in his father's collection. Lomax's government job prevented him from becoming associated with the material himself, so he asked Pete and Woody to organize it. In June 1941 they completed a manuscript entitled "Hard Hitting Songs for Hard Hit People," which would finally be published by Moe Asch in the early sixties. Once finished, Woody received one of his frequent attacks of wanderlust and asked Pete to accompany him on a trip south and west. Pete agreed. For Woody this was largely another occasion to check up on his sorely neglected wife and children in Texas, but for Pete and American folk music it was the start of a tradition of pilgrimages whereby folk singers of northern origin went in search of "authentic" America and its music. The South was the inevitable destination—either the white South of Appalachia or the black Deep South of Alabama, Mississippi, and Louisiana. For those who went to touch the holy spots of American folk music, it was a transformative experience.

Though it is possible to overstate the case, the characterization of these travels South as "pilgrimages" is not altogether metaphoric. Seeger's journey south contained many of the features conventionally associated with pilgrimages in the anthropological literature, specifically in the groundbreaking work of Victor Turner.[37] Seeger and Guthrie, the initiate and the initiator, set out in the latter's Plymouth to Virginia and Tennessee. As Turner would lead us to expect from a pilgrimage, many of the normative rules of comportment were suspended, statuses were leveled, and Seeger was liberated from the constraints of his ordinary role in life. The former son of privilege sang in bars and on street corners for his supper (and once for a haircut) and bought paregoric under a false name for a legless hitchhiker.[38] A brief visit to Highlander gave Seeger a taste of the front-line use of music for social change. In Oklahoma City they witnessed the hazards of representing the party in hostile territory. The poverty of the Guthrie home in Pampa, Texas, came to Seeger as something of a shock, and he left Woody there after a few days.[39] It would be too much to claim that Seeger was instantaneously transformed by these few weeks of travel with Guthrie, but it was the beginning of the process by which he learned firsthand of the hardships and struggles of the people about whom he was singing. By partaking (if briefly) of the poverty of the Guthries and others he encountered on the road, he began to establish his legitimacy as a "folk" person who could sing and speak with some authority about the common people of America. His biographer unkindly described Seeger as having a "bad case of proletarian chic" in this era, but Seeger's concerns went far beyond matters of style and posture.[40]

By the time Guthrie met up with Seeger again for any sustained time, Pete had already begun to sing with Lee Hays and Hays's roommate, Millard Lampell. Lampell had come from a working-class, Jewish family in Paterson, New Jersey, and was quickly establishing himself in New York as a clever and witty leftist writer. He harbored no musical pretensions but had developed some taste for southern rural music while earning a degree at the University of West Virginia. When Guthrie dropped in on them in late 1940 (Seeger had more or less moved into the Chelsea flat that Hays and Lampell shared), Lampell became an instant convert to Guthrie-style lyricism. Though Guthrie left New York again for the West Coast, he had irrevocably stamped the young trio with his brand of humor and folksy wisdom.[41]

In early 1941 Communist Party members and fellow travelers were still living with the awkward consequences of the von Ribbentrop–Molotov (or Hitler-Stalin) pact of August 1939. Although the party had long promoted antifascist themes, those who remained loyal after the pact were forced to adopt a pacifist stance that included a denunciation of the European war as a capitalist ruse. It was a confusing moment for the American Left, but Seeger, Hays, and Lampell made the best of it and interspersed their performance of union songs with compositions that denounced Franklin Roosevelt for leading America into war. To Guthrie on the West Coast, they sent the lyrics to some of their pacifist songs. "I read your war songs and liked them a lot," he wrote that spring from Portland. "But you ought to throw in more wheels, triggers, springs, bearings, motors, engines, boilers and factories — because these are the things that arm the workers and these are the source of the final victory of Public Ownership."[42] Guthrie was then in the decidedly unradical employment of the Bonneville Power Administration, writing songs to accompany a promotional film for the hydroelectric project. The month he spent preparing the music is widely regarded as one of the most musically and lyrically productive periods of his life. The songs written for the project included "Roll on Columbia," "The Biggest Thing that Man Has Ever Done," and "Pastures of Plenty."

Meanwhile in New York, the Almanac Singers (as they were by now calling themselves) had become the toast of the Left. The three core members moved to more spacious quarters on Twelfth Street and Fourth Avenue, and this became the site of regular Sunday afternoon rent-raising sing-alongs. They were joined by Josh White, Burl Ives, Sonny Terry, Richard Dyer-Bennett, Aunt Molly Jackson, and others. The Almanacs' loft became the gathering place of New York's folk establishment. In a matter of months, there was talk of making a record. The majors would have nothing to do with music whose appeal was so narrow and lyrics so provocative. In the spring of 1941 Asch's commercial recording operation was barely up and running, and besides he had long been a Roosevelt man and would probably have wanted nothing to do with the pacifism implied in such songs as Lampell's "The Ballad of October 16th." On that date in 1940 the federal government instituted the country's first peacetime military conscription. The meaning of the song's chorus could hardly be mistaken:

> Oh Franklin Roosevelt told the people how he felt,
> We damned near believed what he said.
> He said "I hate war and so does Eleanor but
> We won't be safe till everybody's dead."[43]

It was not until Alan Lomax and his colleagues at NBC approached Eric Bernay, a former editor of the *New Masses*, that an arrangement was made for a commercial recording. Bernay, who had been instrumental in convincing the *New Masses* to sponsor Hammond's From Spirituals to Swing concert in 1938, ran a minuscule recording operation in New York called Keynote Records. Even Bernay was skittish about releasing the Almanacs' provocative songs on his label, so when they appeared that June as *Songs for John Doe* the label read Almanac Records rather than Keynote.[44] Asch might have been more receptive to the Almanacs' second release, *Talking Union and Other Union Songs*, recorded later that spring (Asch would in fact reissue *Talking Union* on LP in the mid-1950s). But the deal had already been made with Bernay (who this time was willing to use his label's name), and besides, Asch's first plunge outside the Jewish market with Leadbelly's *Play Parties* was still some months away.

Guthrie finally returned to New York in June and immediately joined the shifting, amorphous membership of the Almanacs. Their first challenge came on 22 June, when news of the Nazi invasion of Russia meant that their pacifist repertoire was suddenly obsolete. Whereas Seeger had been happier singing pacifist songs, other American Communists were undoubtedly content to be realigned with U.S. antifascist policies. Nazis were again the enemy, and except for the growing volume of cognitive dissonance it must have been something of a relief to many. Russia would soon be a U.S. ally, and it was possible to renew the fragile alliance between Popular Front communism and Roosevelt patriotism. For the duration of the war, New York's left-wing folk establishment supported the U.S. war effort and American fighting men and deferred to the no-strike pledge of the unions.

The Almanacs were forced to shelve the pacifist repertoire, but the union songs were still serviceable. Throughout the summer they increasingly worked antifascist material into their programs. In July Seeger, Hays, Lampell, and Guthrie set out on a cross-country tour in a large Buick and for two months sang in support of a broad variety of labor unions, the CIO prominent among them, in cities from Philadelphia to Los Angeles. Lampell and Hays returned to New York before the others; Guthrie and Seeger remained in the West until well into September.

By October and November there were enough members that the Almanac Singers could perform in two places in the city at the same time. Occasional and not-so-occasional members included Josh White, Alan Lomax's younger sister Bess, Pete Seeger's friend Pete Hawes, and a couple recently arrived from Oklahoma, Agnes Cunningham and Gordon Friesen. Agnes (or "Sis" as she was called) had been active in the Red Dust Players, an agitprop theater company that in the late 1930s had tried to revive the union spirit among tenant farmers and sharecroppers whose Southern Tenant Farmer's Union had long before been driven out of the state. By 1941 anticommunist agitation made it dangerous for Sis and Gordon to remain in Oklahoma; they faced arrest and worse, and so after hiding out for a time "in the eroded badlands, among the scrub oaks and jack rabbits in the gypsum-streaked red hills," they ventured to New York, where there were enough fellow party members to make it something of a haven—at least temporarily.[45] Gordon was primarily a writer and cartoonist, and his chief function in the Almanacs was to carry Sis's accordion and to call Guthrie's bluff when his claims to rural authenticity began to stretch the bounds of credibility.[46]

The shifts in political direction the previous June had less effect on the audience for left-wing folk music than one might have expected. For one, the audience had always been small and would remain small to the end of the decade—even if it seemed bigger in New York than anywhere else. And second, the audience itself was contending with the same shifts of direction that the folk singers were. No doubt the Hitler-Stalin pact was profoundly problematic for certain segments of the party membership, and Jews in particular had difficulty swallowing the party's apparent indifference to the fascist menace in Europe. If Asch had *ever* been sympathetic to the party, it was probably at this juncture that he began to grow cynical about it. Others, however, found ways to rationalize the shifts in political direction. Until the Almanacs unraveled as one or another member was drafted or joined the

Merchant Marines, they continued to find sympathetic audiences at party functions, fund-raisers, and even, on occasion, union halls in New York and points west.

In Harlem as well, party "cultural workers" continued to find audiences, although the circumstances were somewhat different. In part because the strength of the party in Harlem was dependent on its alliance with other progressive black political organizations, the distastefulness of the Hitler-Stalin pact left Harlem Communists in the cold, their numbers dwindling.[47] But the interest of the Left in the artistry of Harlem actors and (especially) musicians was less dependent on its specific political content than was the case with the white folk singers. The party continued to celebrate black artistry as the exemplification of "progressive" traditions in American cultural life. Harlem musicians could continue to appeal to white party members and fellow travelers with only a "muted" leftism, according to historian Mark Naison. Thus Billie Holiday, "by no means a political activist" according to Naison, included a pacifist song in her nightclub repertoire entitled "The Yanks Are Not Coming," for which she attracted the unwelcome attention of the FBI. At the same time Harlem artists were forced to perform a delicate balancing act—what attracted a progressive, well-paying white audience might alienate their home constituency. Harlem audiences wanted to be entertained in their own culturally specific idiom, one that less often resonated with progressive white audiences.[48]

That both kinds of musicians—politically progressive white folk musicians and only mildly politicized black jazz (and folk) musicians—found their way into Asch's studio following the end of the Petrillo recording ban speaks to what they had in common: a progressive, white record-buying audience. As it happened, the ban continued much longer than anyone had initially predicted. Petrillo withstood a tremendous amount of pressure to settle with the record companies, including in the end an order from the War Labor Board that he ignored and a "personal request" from President Roosevelt.[49] For months he held out for a settlement that would compensate union musicians for the loss of employment that resulted from the playing of records on the air and in jukeboxes. Seven months into the ban, Petrillo proposed a solution that required recording companies to pay a royalty for each record made into a union fund for unemployed musicians. It was rejected. In June 1943 Petrillo asked music publishers to cooperate with the ban by withholding copyrights from those engaged in illegal recording—they refused. Later that summer hillbilly musicians on Memphis station WMC defied the ban against radio transcriptions by arguing that the union did not regard fiddle and banjo players as legitimate musicians anyway.[50]

Asch used the same rationale in recording a small number of folk musicians during the ban. One was Wallace House, born on the isle of Guernsey in the English Channel, who had come to Canada and subsequently New York with an international repertoire of ballads. His first aspirations were for the theater, but he made his mark as a performer of ballads and eventually parlayed this into an academic career at Columbia and New York University. In September 1942 he recorded a set of twelve songs for Asch, accompanying himself on guitar. The songs represented six musical cultures, including "Waltzing Matilda" from Australia and "Let's All Drink" from Poland. By the standards of authenticity to which Asch later adhered, this may not have been entirely up to the mark. House could legitimately claim to represent English folk traditions and arguably certain colonial traditions as well, but Mexican, Greek, and Russian folk songs were surely a stretch. On the other hand, when *Folk Songs of the United Nations* was released, Asch's catalogue was otherwise dominated by his Jewish material and the couple of Leadbelly albums, and this represented a first foray into the area of international folk music.

Pete Seeger was one of the few others who recorded for Asch during the Petrillo ban. He appeared in Asch Studios late one night in June 1943. He was on furlough from the army long enough to participate in the *Lonesome Train* recording session at Decca Records, a pacifist folk cantata about the life of Abraham Lincoln, written by Earl Robinson and Millard Lampell. Others involved in the session—Leadbelly, Si Rady—had come to know Asch and his way of working; when at the end of the session Seeger expressed a desire to record some other kind of material, they suggested that he take advantage of the remaining hours of his furlough to go over to Asch Studios and see whether Asch might be interested. Asch was happy to oblige and recorded six songs in six takes, all traditional (mostly southern) tunes: "Cindy," "Devilish Mary," "Hard on the Farm," "Erie Canal," "Old Woman and the Devil," and "Reilly." Asch did not initially claim to understand Seeger as he would Guthrie; he found him to be enigmatic, a mystery that was only revealed slowly, through his music. "We understood nothing of each other right from the start," Asch recalled.[51]

Petrillo did not settle with all of the major record labels at once. The first to come to an agreement with the AFM was Decca, whose president, Jack Kapp, agreed in late September 1943 to a royalty of the kind that Petrillo had been pushing for all along.[52] The other majors would continue to hold out for more than another *year.* But once an acceptable agreement had been reached by one major label, there was suddenly an opportunity for small recording companies to jump into the breach. In an article entitled "Waxing Is Everybody's Biz," *Billboard* reported that dozens of recording outfits had blossomed overnight to take advantage of the crippling effects of the ban on RCA and Columbia. As a trade publication with strong ties to the industry, it is not surprising that *Billboard* questioned the practices of the indies: "Quality, ethics and other such matters simply aren't part of the present set-up of many of the indies. Practice is to record as cheaply as possible, either use bands whose real names can't appear because they're under contract to one of the three majors, or pickup aggregations."[53] None of the indies were reported to have their own pressing facilities, using instead the Clark Phonograph Company in Newark, New Jersey, and the Scranton Record Manufacturer in Pennsylvania. Asch used both, about equally. A list of thirty-three record companies was appended to the article, of which only seven had existed two years earlier. It was predicted that most of the indies would be out of business as soon as the remaining majors were recording again—with the possible exception of newcomer Capitol Records, which was thought to have a fighting chance. Asch Records, though existing in infancy in 1942, was almost certainly counted among the unlikely upstarts. *Down Beat,* with somewhat greater loyalty to the music than to the industry, reported the same phenomena with more sympathy for the independent outfits in an article that same month entitled "Small Wax Firms Record Like Mad."

Asch wasted no time in coming to terms with the AFM, and within a couple of weeks of the first postban contract with Decca, his studio came alive with the sounds of union musicians. Charles Edward Smith was the catalyst through which a string of Harlem musicians began to appear in Asch Studios. The first was James P. Johnson, described alternately as the "father of stride piano," the "grandfather of hot piano," the "daddy of the Harlem piano," and the "dean of Harlem piano."[54] He may well have been all of these things, and his contributions to the development of the "stride" style in the 1920s—with its improvisational advance over its predecessor, ragtime—is unmistakable. But Johnson's consistently overlooked influence as both a pianist and composer went well beyond the Harlem piano styles of the 1920s. His failure to gain the notoriety of his protégé, Fats Waller, was a function of his modesty and lack of showmanship. He is rarely associated with his most famous composition—"The Charleston"—and only recently has there been a renewed interest in his symphonic-scale compositions.[55] In fact, by the late twenties he was scoring music for Broadway shows, including the highly successful "Shuffle Along," accompanying singers such as Ethel Waters and Bessie Smith on recordings, and composing symphonic works for the concert stage—notably "Yamekraw: A Negro Rhapsody," which Fats Waller performed at Carnegie Hall on 27 April 1928. Johnson's significance was initially overlooked by the Jazzmen Group but not by John Hammond, who featured him in the From Spirituals to Swing concert. For the first six months of 1940 he led a band at Josephson's Café Society Downtown (by this time there was also an uptown annex), and he experienced a more significant brush with the Left's cultural workers that same year, when he collaborated with Langston Hughes in an ILGWU-sponsored musical entitled *The Organizer.* Although Johnson was by then attempting to attract attention as a serious composer, the revivalists of the late thirties and forties brought him a new audience that was more interested in his earlier work. In August 1941, however, he suffered a stroke that prevented him from performing through the end of the following year. By the time he arrived in Asch's studio, in mid-October 1943, he had still not entirely recovered his powers of speech, although his playing seemed to be unaffected.[56]

As the session was supervised by Charles Edward Smith, it is not surprising that the focus was on the piano styles that Johnson had pioneered in the 1920s. Four sides appear to have been recorded at this session, one take each of "Boogie Stride" and "Impressions" and two takes of his classic composition "Snowy Morning Blues," which he had first recorded in February 1927. They were, according to Smith, Johnson's first solo piano recordings in more than a decade. He added in his notes to "Boogie Stride" and "Impressions" that these were not merely recreations of his earlier style but were "modern in thought." He made the same claim for the take of "Snowy Morning Blues" that Asch ultimately released:

> Snowy Morning Blues is an entirely new concept rather than an
> attempt to repeat the earlier piano record of it, which was so
> popular with jazz fans. When Jimmy began to play, he seemed
> to be recalling the old recording of it but on second try he

found an entirely new version. "I've got it now," he remarked, and that was the master.

The three sides created an awkward problem as far as commercial release was concerned. Asch solved it by releasing "Boogie Stride" and "Impressions" on alternate sides of one twelve-inch disc (assuring it no jukebox play, because the machines could only accommodate ten-inch discs) and "Snowy Morning Blues" in an odd three-disc album of miscellaneous sides. The album included one side by "Peck's Bad Boys," the unusual guitar quartet he had recorded in 1941 that had included Jimmy Smith and Allan Reuss, the Goodman guitarist. Two of the remaining sides were by Fletcher Henderson's Connie's Inn Orchestra, recorded in October 1931, and the others were of a band fronted by Goodman pianist Jess Stacy, recorded in September 1939.[57] The Henderson and Stacy sides were reissues that Asch had licensed from another recording company. The eclectic nature of the album was implied in its title: *Jazz Variations: A collection of old and new instrumental jazz masterpieces featuring large and small jazz bands and famous soloists, in varied styles.* Smith, in his notes, made little effort to tie the sides together: "Here, then are variations in jazz that take in a lot of territory, both in time and in place. . . . Each side has its place in the jazz story and it is especially gratifying to find old collector's items, such as the Stacy and Fletcher Henderson discs, stacked up alongside such new ones as the new *Snowy Morning Blues*."

Down Beat announced the release of the Asch disc and album in a short article that December entitled "Righteous Jazz Rears Its Head on Discs Again." When reviewed the following February under *Down Beat*'s "Hot Jazz" releases, the Johnson material was praised in extravagant terms: "'Impressions' is easily the most beautiful piano number pressed in recent years. . . . Too much boogie woogie has been recorded in the last few years, but these two cuttings by Johnson are remarkable exceptions." They were slightly less complimentary of the *Jazz Variations* album, describing it as a "strange miscellany of excellent jazz." The Henderson sides they described alternately as "a sterling if somewhat antique arrangement" and "almost sheer corn" and the guitar quartet as the "strangest group ever cut." But Johnson's "Snowy Morning Blues" was singled out for praise, and they deemed it better than Johnson's late 1920s version of the same piece. All in all, they concluded, "this album ought to see the Asch firm off to a good start. Charles Edward Smith deserves a hand for the accompanying booklet."[58]

Nineteen forty-four looked as though it would be the year in which Asch's fortunes changed for good. Although it was not clear how long the recording ban would continue to apply to Columbia and RCA, by the spring Asch had a steady stream of musicians in his studio. Some would become sufficiently loyal to Asch that, for a time, the majors offered little allure. Revenues were up enough by June that he and Frances were able to buy a house in Far Rockaway in Queens. They had by then moved to an apartment on Twelfth Street in Greenwich Village. But the previous April, after fifteen years of marriage, Moe and Frances finally had a child—a baby boy, named Michael. The apartment began to feel small for the three of them, and the Far Rockaway house would permit their son to enjoy the sun and seashore. Their original intention was for this to be their year-around house. But the first winter there proved to be too difficult—the house was not well winterized and the commute to Manhattan was too much for Asch. Thereafter and until they sold the house, they opened it in May and closed it in September.

The arrival of a son in Asch's thirty-eighth year—after many years of childlessness—might have been something of a shock. But Asch had long ago established work habits that were not going to be disrupted by something as apparently inconsequential as a baby. From the start it was clear that Michael was to be his mother's child; Moe seemed to have little time and even less interest. In point of fact, this domestic arrangement seemed to have advantages over the one in which Asch himself grew up. Michael would at least have the benefit of his mother's companionship. Perhaps Asch thought himself more responsible than his father for having brought only *one* child into the world, although it meant that Michael did not have siblings with which to share his loneliness. Like his father, Asch regarded children as ornaments to be displayed only occasionally, when fatherhood might reflect well on him. Sometimes—no more than once a year, perhaps for his birthday—he would bring Mike into his studio and record his voice, or perhaps Mike's early piano playing. The rest of the time, Michael was not welcome in the studio. Among other things, Asch was about to begin a not very well concealed affair with his secretary and eventual collaborator, Marian Distler, which was to last for the next twenty years. Most of the time he could not be bothered with his son.

The first artist of significance to record in Asch's studio in 1944 was Burl Ives. Ives had come to New York from rural southern Illinois, where he had learned mountain ballads from his grandmother by way of his mother. Upon dropping out of college, Ives traveled east and attempted to make a go of it as an actor and singer. In 1937 he recorded an album of songs for Columbia's Okeh label entitled *The Wayfaring Stranger,* which attracted almost no attention at all. After selling a couple hundred copies of the album, Columbia determined that Ives was of no particular use to them, and they destroyed the original masters. But by 1940 Ives was a regular on Lomax's CBS radio programs, "Back Where I Came From" and "American School of the Air," and he had begun to appear in some theatrical productions. A brief stint in the army ended with a physical discharge, and finding himself momentarily broke, he called around to various recording companies to see whether anyone might be interested in recording him. For the modest sum of two hundred dollars, Asch won the opportunity to do so.[59]

In Asch's memory the Ives session was one of the most difficult he ever conducted. Ives, he recalled, could not hold a tune or keep his guitar "straight" and insisted on singing "arty" ballads such as "Brennan on the Moor" rather than letting go and singing the authentic songs of his home state.[60] Within a few months Asch would be making his most important recordings of white folk music, but in February 1944 he was almost new to it. He might have sensed that something was wrong, but he was hardly in a position to know how to fix it. His instincts only took him so far, and his knowledge of music was negligible. Ives must have been equally frustrated; by contrast the entire Columbia session had lasted only an hour and the results had delighted him. Working for Asch, he later conceded, was a mistake.[61] Asch recorded six sides of Ives—none of them acceptable—and then, in exasperation, called Alan Lomax in to supervise the session.

Asch in the meantime resumed a session he had begun earlier in the day with Mr. and Mrs. Siller, who were preparing an album of country dances that would eventually appear complete with a book of dance calls. By the time they had completed three more sides, Ives was ready to go again and Lomax had arrived to get things on track. With the Columbia album unavailable, Lomax was at liberty to have Ives repeat several of the songs from that album. Lomax's first take, a second attempt at "The Wayfaring Stranger," was still not right, and a second take of "The Fox" fared no better. But the third effort, "The Foggy Foggy Dew," was a success, and after that things fell into place. A third try at "The Wayfaring Stranger" went well, and the last four takes were all satisfactory.[62] The album eventually contained "The Blue Tail Fly," which Lomax identified in his notes as "an authentic Negro Minstrel song," and several well-known southern renderings of Elizabethan ballads, including "Black is the Color," "The Foggy Foggy Dew," and "Henry Martin." Asch in the end was well pleased with the album, and in April, as soon as it was pressed, Stinson began to advertise it regularly (and until the end of the year) in the pages of the *New Masses*. Asch and Harris apparently enjoyed enough success with it that Columbia realized they had made an error in taking it off the market. When they discovered that the masters had been destroyed, they mastered it again using existing copies of the record with a predictable loss in sound quality. The repressed Columbia album hit the stores that fall with the title *The Return of the Wayfaring Stranger; Billboard* described it as "an album of dubious worth."[63] The Asch album, entitled simply *Burl Ives* (although it was sometimes slyly advertised as *Burl Ives, the Wayfaring Stranger*), was not reviewed at all in *Billboard*—nor anywhere else to speak of.

In early March, *Down Beat* reported an event in Los Angeles that would prove fateful for Asch.[64] A young and brash jazz promoter, Norman Granz, had started a series of unrehearsed Sunday afternoon jam sessions featuring both black and white musicians. Granz did not dictate musical direction, but he did bring together musicians who did not otherwise play together; his novel "mix and match" approach meant that the musicians were forced to rely primarily on extended improvisation. That summer he presented his jam sessions for the first time in Los Angeles' Philharmonic Auditorium, a venue that until then had been the exclusive preserve of classical musicians. He titled these concerts Jazz at the Philharmonic (JATP).[65]

Of more immediate significance to Asch that month was the appearance in his studio of jazz pianist Mary Lou Williams; Charles Edward Smith was again the likely catalyst. Williams had been a regular at Café Society for approximately a year by then, often sharing the bill with Josh White (at the close of an evening, the two would often ride the subway together back up to Harlem).[66] Other evenings she would leave Café Society for Minton's, where she would sit in with Dizzy Gillespie, Thelonious Monk, Charlie Parker, and others who were hammering out the new bebop style. Williams's own credentials were impeccable. She had spent the 1930s with Andy Kirk's Clouds of Joy band, functioning as both pianist and composer/arranger. Most of the other big band leaders of the era used her arrangements as well, including Louis Armstrong,

Tommy Dorsey, Jimmy Dorsey, Benny Goodman, and Jimmie Lunceford. For six months in 1941 she traveled with the Ellington band as composer and arranger. By 1944 she had total command of the swing style of the 1930s while simultaneously contributing to the harmonic innovations of the 1940s.[67]

Williams first came into Asch Studios on 12 March, bringing with her a sextet that included Frankie Newton on trumpet, Edmund Hall on clarinet, Vic Dickenson on trombone, Al Lucas on bass, and Jack Parker on drums. Asch was deferential to jazz musicians as he was with almost no one else. Because they worked primarily at night, the musicians usually came to Asch's studio around dinner time. A routine soon developed in which, according to Williams's recollections in 1954, Asch would take everyone out for "big steak dinners and drinks. Some deserved this, many did not. In fact, we ruined a couple of sessions from being too high."[68] Whatever the effects of dinner and drinks, the first session resulted in five stunning sides. A little over a month later Williams returned and cut several additional sides of solo piano. Asch released three sides from each of these first two sessions in the late spring on ten-inch single records (Asch 1002, 1003, 1004). Each disc contained one side with the sextet backed by a side of solo piano. *Down Beat* described the piano solos as "the best she has ever waxed" and noted on the sextet sides that Dickenson's trombone "steals the show this time." Later Asch packaged six of the sextet sides in an album entitled *Mary Lou Williams and Her Chosen Five*. Charles Edward Smith wrote in his album notes, "Ensemble piano talent is rare in jazz and Mary Lou Williams has it to an unusual degree. Her acceptance of other musicians is not—here are thirty two bars and I'll be back later—but a really collaborative effort." In an article that July entitled "Mary Lou Socko on Record Date," *Down Beat* reported that the six sides released in the spring "met with terrif [sic] reception" and noted that another Williams album on Asch, with largely the same personnel (except for the notable addition of tenor saxophonist Don Byas) was due shortly. This album actually did not appear until early the following year, as the sessions with Byas only resulted in four useable sides—additional material for the album was recorded that December with a quintet featuring Coleman Hawkins. In between, on 10 August, Williams recorded several sides with a trio of Bill Coleman on trumpet and Al Hall on bass.

In preparing the covers for her Asch albums, Williams introduced Asch to a good friend, a graphic artist named David Stone Martin. Martin worked as a graphic designer with the Office of Strategic

Services, later as the art director of the Office of War Information. Before the war was out he would be going to the Pacific as an artist/war correspondent for *Life*. But in 1944 he started drawing album covers for Asch, and for the next several years his stunning pen and ink drawings were an Asch trademark. Asch recalled that he was the first to put artwork on album covers, but although he may have taken the practice to new heights he did not initiate it. Still, it was enough of a novelty in 1944 for *Newsweek* to comment on it in an article that December. According to the article, some album-cover artwork appeared as early as 1926, and the practice really took root in 1938 with the First Symphony of Brahms on Victor, conducted by Bruno Walter.[69] But Martin was in a class by himself, having invented an entirely new genre of album-cover artwork that succeeded in *visually* capturing the feeling of jazz.

By summer Williams had become Asch's first exclusive artist, an arrangement that delighted them both. Williams developed a fondness for Asch that continued until her death in 1981. To her he was generous and accepting—his studio was available for her to use as she saw fit, and he almost never interfered or gave direction. On only one occasion, when she brought Coleman Hawkins along on a recording date that had been scheduled for piano solo, did Asch demur, and then only briefly. "He never told a performer how to record or what to do. If you only burped, Moe recorded it," she recalled in 1954. Not only did Asch give her the freedom to be creative, but he also brought her more royalties than she was to see from any other recording company.[70] Given Asch's parsimoniousness in other instances, it is difficult to account for his generosity with her. Race alone does not explain it—he was respectful of Leadbelly but paid him no more than was absolutely necessary. Perhaps it was a combination of race and a deference to her gender, a deference evident in his dealings with *some* other women. Asch tended to treat women a bit more graciously than he did men, his relations with them being less competitive. Finally, however, Asch held the very greatest respect for artistry, and Mary Lou Williams had that in abundance.

Although jazz was proving to be a fertile field for Asch in the spring of 1944, projects involving other kinds of music demanded his attention as well. A couple came his way through Alan Lomax, who had been commissioned by the CIO and the United Automobile Workers to prepare some recorded material that might encourage industrial workers in the war effort. It was a rare bit of "union" work in an era otherwise bereft of union activity—the "no strike" pledges of the war left workers all but powerless. In this instance the unions merely wanted to boost the morale on the assembly line by having workers see that their work was as vital to the war effort as that of the soldiers on the front line. Unlike Asch, who eschewed rehearsals because they would ostensibly disrupt the music's spontaneity, Lomax saw some value in working through material before convening the musicians in the recording studio. For the first session he assembled a group of musicians who had been appearing with varying regularity on his radio program—Tom Glazer, Burl Ives, Brownie McGhee, Pete Seeger, Sonny Terry, and Josh White. They worked out some material at someone's home—perhaps Lomax's—and on 11 March reconvened in Asch's studio to record it. Despite the focussed intention of the commission, the session reflected the broader range of Popular Front concerns by including songs such as "Jim Crow" (credited to the Almanacs) and "Soviet Union."[71] The song that appeared to be most applicable to the session's ostensive agenda—"U.A.W.-C.I.O."—also came out of the Almanacs' repertoire in their prowar incarnation:

> It's that U.A.W. C.I.O.—makes the army roll & go,
>   turnin' out the jeeps & tanks, the air-planes ev'ry day;
> It's that U.A.W. C.I.O.—makes the army roll and go,
> Puts wheels on the U.S.A.[72]

A second session that June, sponsored by the National C.I.O. War Relief Committee, consisted only of Josh White and Tom Glazer. It too reflected a broader social agenda. "Here, Citizen CIO," touted the catalogue description, "sings of his hopes for tomorrow."

Arguably the most propitious event of 1944 for the Asch Recording Company was the unannounced appearance of Woody Guthrie in his studio in March. Asch later concocted a half dozen different versions of this first encounter, but they all went something like this:

> "Hi, I'm Woody Guthrie." Sits down on floor.
>   "So what?"

Asch sometimes maintained that he never heard of Guthrie until the moment he walked through his door, but the claim is improbable.[73] Guthrie had written a regular column entitled "Woody Sez" for the *Daily Worker*, a paper to which, according to his account book,

Asch subscribed—as early as 1940. Given the circles he traveled in, Asch could not have failed to have heard about the Almanacs. In February 1943 Dutton published Guthrie's highly fictionalized autobiography, *Bound for Glory*, which sold well and was widely reviewed. Perhaps most significant, Guthrie had been appearing with some regularity over the past couple years on Alan Lomax's CBS radio show, "Back Where I Come From."[74] But Asch's retrospective claim not to have previously heard of Guthrie suggests the extent to which he regarded himself as an intuitive judge of artistic talent. In his most candid moments, he conceded that he had heard of Guthrie from Lomax and Pete Seeger but continued to insist that Guthrie knew more about him than vice versa.[75]

There is no doubt that in his own irascible way, under the right circumstances and with the right people, Guthrie could be very charming. Asch doubtlessly appreciated his irreverence, his skepticism, his Popular Front admiration for laboring Americans. Although Guthrie was capable of playing up his folksiness when the occasion required—turning up the twang for Lomax's Library of Congress recordings, for example—Asch recalled that the "put on" soon evaporated in their first conversation, and except for a slight regional accent Guthrie's speech became quite straightforward, even erudite. They spoke of politics, they spoke of folk music, and above all they spoke of their respective philosophies of life. When they were finished, Guthrie had secured a promise from Asch to record him a few days later.

Guthrie's first session at Asch Studios may have been a trial run. Asch's haphazard "log"—in fact, the back pages of an old ledger in which he scribbled song titles, the artist's name, occasionally the date, rarely the accompanists—shows two titles, "Ain't it Hard" and "Pretty Gals."[76] But three days later Guthrie was back, this time with his Merchant Marine buddy and singing partner Gilbert "Cisco" Houston. Houston was an aspiring actor from California with terrible eyesight and terrific musical sensibilities. He had a rich singing voice in his own right, but recognizing Guthrie's originality, accepted a supporting role when they performed, singing harmony and playing backup guitar most of the time. Asch came to depend on Houston to help Guthrie keep time, get the chord changes right, and remember the verses. By the time Guthrie and Houston appeared in Asch's studio for the first time, they had been performing together aboard ship for some months and had perfected what had previously been a sporadic nightclub act. That winter Guthrie had written from the SS *Sea Porpoise* to Marjorie

Greenblatt Mazia, who would become his second wife and the mother of his fourth child, Cathy Ann: "I really think it would surprise you to hear us play now. We have gotten so much practice you wouldn't recognize us."[77] Houston remembered that their fellow sailors were "starved for this kind of real singing. . . . Even when the ship got hit, the guys were out on the decks singing, 'You Fascists Bound to Lose.'"[78] Guthrie had told Asch in their first meeting that he had a large number of songs he wished to record, and it was primarily the mammoth repertoire that he had developed with Houston that he had in mind. The only condition he made was that Asch permit him to review any material he recorded before it was released commercially.[79]

What followed over the next couple of weeks was a kind of explosion of musical cross-fertilization. Word got around that Asch was holding "open house," and Guthrie and Houston found themselves joined in the studio by Leadbelly, Sonny Terry, Josh White, Bess Hawes, and even Mary Lou Williams and gospel singer Nora Lee King. Guthrie accompanied Leadbelly on several takes and assisted Sonny Terry and Josh White as well. But in late April Guthrie was the dominant figure in the studio, and in most instances the others were accompanying him. The 19 April session included sixty-three takes; although there were a few multiple takes when Guthrie fluffed the lyrics—including four takes of his own "Talking Sailor"—most of the songs were recorded in only one take. In this session, as in the others, Guthrie and Houston reached into their vast reservoir of regional folk songs, blues, recorded country music, original compositions, and even popular tunes (toward the end of the first long session, Guthrie accompanied Leadbelly on an improbable version of "Waltzing Matilda"). Two songs Guthrie had prepared for the Bonneville Power Administration three years earlier—"Grand Coulee Dam" and "The Biggest Thing that Man Has Ever Done"—appeared again in the first long session. Guthrie's "Philadelphia Lawyer" featured a close nasal harmony by Houston reminiscent of the Carter Family's 1920s recordings. "Cindy" featured the singing and banjo playing of Pete Seeger and Houston's high harmony; the song was an old folk chestnut, "a much-traveled young lady," according to John and Alan Lomax, "for the song which celebrates her name has traveled as far as mountain fiddlers and banjo pickers have been able to take it, as far as the highways run, the busses roll, and the fast freight rattles."[80]

The sessions that followed in quick succession—20, 24, and 25 April, and an undated final session at the end of the month or in early May—each had notable circumstances and exceptional moments. The 20 April session featured a handful of sacred songs and an early example of Guthrie's interest in children's music—"Rubber Dolly." Guthrie related the story of Sonny Terry's "Lost John"—a convict on the run—in this session, but it is Terry's harmonica playing and assorted whoops and hollers that convey the story's drama. Leadbelly appears to have walked in on the relatively short session on the twenty-fourth, concluding it with renditions of "On a Monday" and "John Henry." The marathon session on the twenty-fifth was framed by two songs that nicely illustrated Guthrie's song-writing method. The fourth take of the session was "Jesse James," which the Lomaxes described as "the best-known and most singable of all our outlaw ballads."[81] Toward the end of what must have been a very long night, Guthrie sang "Jesus Christ," a song whose melodic and lyric structure was based very closely on "Jesse James." But he had transformed Jesus into a friend of the poor and a subversive:

> Jesus Christ was a man who travelled through the land
> A carpenter true and brave;
> Said to the rich, "give your goods to the poor,"
> So they laid Jesus Christ in his grave.©

Sandwiched in the middle of the session was a song that received no particular attention. It was a recent Guthrie composition that had grown out of his irritation with having to hear Kate Smith's "God Bless America" incessantly on the radio. Guthrie's original refrain was "God blessed America for me," but he later changed it to "This land is made for you and me." Guthrie's populist anthem included a verse that is rarely performed:

> As I went walking, I saw a sign there,
> And on the sign it said "no trespassing."
> But on the other side, it didn't say nothing,
> That side was made for you and me.©[82]

In a biographical essay that appeared in a small book Asch published in 1947, *American Folksong: Woody Guthrie*, Guthrie wrote a description of these early sessions:

> Back in the States after this trip Cisco Houston, Blind Sonny
> Terry and myself went up to the Asch studios. Moe Asch, son

of Sholem Asch, took us in, cranked up his machinery and told us to fire away with everything that we had. We yelled and whooped and beat and pounded till Asch had taken down One Hundred and Twenty Some Odd Master sides (sides that might do to release to the public). We tried hilltop and sunny mountain harmonies and wilder yells and whoops of the dead sea deserts, and all of the swampy southland and buggy mud bottom sounds that we could make. We sung to the mossy trees and to the standing moon, and Moe Asch and Marian Distler worked through their plate glass there in the recording studio.[83]

There is a rather broad hint to Asch in this passage that, three years after the fact, he might consider *releasing* some of these sides to the public. For the unfortunate fact of the matter was that only a handful of these 170 (Guthrie was off by about 50) odd sides had found their way to commercial release by then.

Bound as he was to the army by then, Pete Seeger was not a prominent presence at the Guthrie-dominated sessions that spring. In addition to "Cindy," he appears to have contributed only a supporting role in some of the large group efforts on 19 April, notably the instrumental "900 Miles" and renditions of "Good Morning, Captain" and "Mule Skinner Blues." Yet despite the difficulty he had in fathoming the string-bean young man, Asch trusted Seeger and permitted him to arrange another session, probably in very early March. The Spanish Civil War remained the one recent armed conflict about which leftists felt entirely unam- bivalent, Asch included. Asch recalled later that he had "friends" who were killed while fighting with the Abraham Lincoln Battalion of the International Brigade, although for a person who kept almost everyone at arm's length, "friend" might have meant some- one whose hand he once shook.[84] He was enthusiastic when Seeger mentioned that he knew a handful of Spanish Civil War songs, including a couple in Spanish that he had learned while sitting in on a recording session for a flamenco singer by the name of Vilareno. On twenty-four hours notice he assembled three like-minded folk singers—Tom Glazer, Butch Hawes, and Bess Lomax—rehearsed them on a Saturday, recorded them on Sunday, and was back on his army base by Monday. None had actually been with the Abraham Lincoln Battalion, but both Seeger and Glazer had collected Spanish Civil War songs. Seeger remembered the recording as one of the best he ever made, "full of passion and fire," embodying the spirit of popular democracy and resistance. Each of the three ten-inch discs had a Spanish-language song on the A side and a song in English on the B side. It was a musical monument to one of the international Left's finest, most heroic, and most tragic moments.[85] Back at Camp Sibert in Alabama, Seeger wrote to Asch:

> I can't tell you how happy I was to have been in on those re-cordings—I'd have been glad to do it for nothing. Toshi & I have put the 60 bucks away so maybe after the war it can help finance us when we want to move Almanac work, which is what I still call that kind of singing, tho the Almanacs have been inoperative for some time now.[86]

Six weeks later he again wrote Asch from Alabama: "Of course, Moe, I'm very anxious to know how my voice sounds on those folksongs. They were done sort of hastily in a way—sometimes that's for the best; sometimes not. I usually don't like to hear my voice. Sounds too damn young, effete & tinny. Well, we'll see." Seeger also worried that he might get into some trouble with the army for having his name affiliated with a recording that slandered Franco: "Unless I can receive definite word from someone versed in Army law, I don't think I'd best have my name on those Spanish records."

At the end of April Seeger was again recording in Asch Studios—the contract for 29 April indicated that he would be paid one hundred dollars for three hours of recording, with any additional recording to be compensated at AFM rates. Seeger wrote Asch that summer from the Pacific, "After seeing how poorly Victor plugged Woody's album, and Decca other folkmusic albums, I am thoroughly of the opinion that for a person like myself, it is far better to record for a small company—unless there seems to be a better chance of getting on juke boxes."[87]

After the flurry of folk music in his studio in April, Asch turned his attention once again to jazz, which appeared to be the field in which he was bound to have the most commercial success. In early June Mary Lou Williams returned to Asch Studios for the sessions that featured Don Byas's tenor sax. The four sides that resulted from this session included Hoagy Carmichael's "Stardust," Williams's own "Gjon Mili Jam Session," written for the French *Life* magazine photographer who had been filming jazz musicians during the preceding months, and a Williams-Byas composition entitled "Man O' Mine." It was a stunning session throughout, the piano and sax working together to lush effect.

James P. Johnson also returned to Asch Studios about ten days later—this time with a quintet consisting primarily of a rhythm section (bass, drums, guitar) and the trumpeter Frank Newton. The session was conceived by Charles Edward Smith as a history of New York jazz seen through the playing of "Jimmy" Johnson, and it reflects Smith's partiality to historical styles. When released in late November its six sides represented three historical periods, identified as "The Background," which covers ragtime and other "sportin' house" styles; "Harlem," which includes an extraordinarily rare Johnson vocal on "Hesitation Blues"; and "Harlem on Down," meaning from the late twenties until the "threshold of the modern era." Paul Bowles wrote in the *New York Herald Tribune* the following February that these sides "are unaffected, straight jazz, suave, not entirely devoid of sophistication, (witness "Four O'Clock Groove"), but still without any of the objectionable commercial concessions of the day. They offer good examples of the sort of unselfconscious music so hard to find anywhere around town."[88]

Several other jazz musicians followed Johnson into Asch Studios. Within a couple of days Art Tatum appeared with his trio of Tiny Grimes on guitar and Slam Stewart on bass. They appear only to have recorded four or five takes, and according to Asch's log they broke in the middle for a couple of takes by Cab Calloway![89] Asch never released the Calloway takes commercially, but the Tatum sides appeared as an album of two twelve-inch discs the following January. The larger discs represented something of a tradeoff. Although they allowed the artist significantly more time, they did not fit into the jukeboxes of the day, which consequently limited sales significantly. It was a typical Asch choice in favor of artistic integrity at the expense of commercial viability. Tatum's place in jazz history was made almost entirely on the basis of his solo piano work, regarded as unsurpassed in speed and lightness of touch. Mary Lou Williams is said to have remarked that Tatum was "the greatest jazz musician I have ever heard." The trio with Grimes and Stewart lasted only a couple of years, but this was long enough for the three of them to have come extraordinarily attuned to one another. One jazz historian described them as "musical telepathy experts," and their recording of "Topsy" for Asch in June was a premier example of their musical intuition.[90]

Asch Studios were largely silent in the month of July. Having closed only the previous month on the Far Rockaway property, the

Asches were no doubt anxious to spend some time by the ocean and away from the city's heat. Asch did not always find it an inviting prospect to spend time with family, but he did have his young son at home, and the war afforded a couple of rare moments when an especially large number of Asches were able to convene in a single place. Sholem and Matilda had escaped New York City after only a few months on Riverside Drive and purchased a house in Stamford, Connecticut. The elder Asch may have felt a little less vulnerable there to the barrage of attacks that continued to emanate from the Jewish press. If anything they had intensified in 1943, when he had published the successor to *The Nazarene*, his account of the life of Saint Paul entitled *The Apostle*. Additionally, he had generated further hostility that year by successfully concluding an almost four-year effort to find a Yiddish publisher for *The Nazarene* (Yiddish editions of *The Apostle* and the third volume of the trilogy, *Mary*, have never appeared). Because he was shut out by the *Forward* and other Yiddish-language publications, he was confined to publishing in a party-controlled paper, the *Freiheit*, which would cause him no end of trouble in the McCarthy era. In bucolic Stamford, the elder Asch lived in semi-retirement from public life, tended to his homing pigeons, and took up a new hobby—fishing.[91]

In 1940 Ruth and Reginald Shaffer evacuated their young daughter Miriam from England and sent her to live with her grandparents in Stamford. When things became still more intolerable in England in 1943, Ruth herself joined her parents. Nathan had discovered that the best antidote to his torpor was the army, and John, having finally returned to the States from France, had joined the army as well. One evening sometime before Nathan was shipped to the European Theater, Sholem Asch planned a lavish dinner at a New York hotel for all his children and grandchildren. He was taking solace in an imagined family life that the Asches almost never really knew. His sons' army commissions brought him a great deal more pride than anything either had accomplished in their professional lives—he had put a flag in the window of his Stamford house with service stars on it. He played the patriarch to the hilt, ordering (as Nathan remembered it) bad martinis and carving an enormous turkey. If he was aware of the discomfort of others, he did not show it. But Nathan, far from reconciled with his father, bristled inwardly at his ostentatious display of a role he never really knew. Moe was the only son who was not in uniform and undoubtedly was jealous of the pride his father took in his brothers. And Frances, with her memory of the awful taxi ride just before the war, did her best to conceal her dislike of the Asch men.[92] Ruth returned to England in late 1944 to care for her husband, who had been wounded while serving in the British army; the dinner would stand as the last occasion all the members of the family were gathered together.

Things picked up again in Asch Studios that August. Williams appeared again with a trio of Bill Coleman on trumpet and Al Hall on bass before heading out of town on an ill-fated tour. A week and a half later Langston Hughes arrived in the studio to record a series of poems in what was to be the beginning of a long collaboration between Asch and the Harlem poet. Hughes has been said to have been introduced to Asch by Sterling Brown, a Howard University professor of English, poet, and promotor of African American arts who had been the master of ceremonies at the second Spirituals to Swing concert. But this is unlikely as the two African American poets were not much more than acquaintances who saw each other rarely at this juncture in their relationship.[93] Although it is not certain who brought Asch and Hughes together, their meeting was more or less inevitable. In the summer of 1943 Hughes had spent a few weeks with Nathan Asch at Yaddo, a private and exclusive retreat in upstate New York to which the country's most prominent artists (primarily writers) were invited for intervals of work, conversation, and quiet reflection (other guests that summer were Katherine Anne Porter and Carson McCullers). Asch's attention might very well have been drawn to Hughes by his older brother. It may have been still more likely that Hughes's name came up in conversation with Mary Lou Williams, perhaps at the time of her trio sessions earlier in the month. Hughes had just been asked by the radical Southern Negro Youth Congress to compose an anthem that would be put to music by Williams. He had obliged by submitting a poem entitled "Lenin" that left little doubt about Hughes's admiration for the founder of the Soviet state. Perhaps Williams mentioned this collaboration to Asch and suggested that he record the poet.[94] Elie Siegmeister, the leftist composer, and James P. Johnson, with whom Hughes had collaborated on the ILGWU-sponsored play, *The Organizer,* were also acquaintances Hughes and Asch shared.

Hughes had never recorded for a commercial record company before, and indeed the entire field of commercial "spoken word" recordings was all but unknown then. Asch had first conceived of a "talking book" when he produced *In the Beginning,* his recording of his father's Bible stories for children. But he had not released anything else in this genre at the time of Hughes's recording session. Hughes and Asch were in many respects a perfect match. Asch was no doubt pleased with the opportunity to promote another aspect of African American arts, and particularly a poet who so openly celebrated black folk culture and the black working masses. Hughes, like Asch, was a radical who supported leftist causes without become immersed in them. Both eschewed organized politics, particularly the Communist Party (although Hughes was far more sympathetic to the Soviet Union than Asch).

Another thing bound the two men together. They had both suffered through childhoods in which they were largely abandoned by their parents. What is curious is the extraordinarily distinct ways in which the two had internalized this trauma. Asch had learned to deal with his childhood pain by becoming defensive and crusty; not yet forty, he seemed middle-aged to most who met him and he remained "middle-aged" for decades. No one was allowed to penetrate his emotional armor, and anyone who dared to approach risked falling victim to his volcanic temper. Hughes, by contrast, seemed incapable of anger and avoided confrontation. He was unvaryingly kind, generous, eager to please, and hungry for approval. "In certain ways," his biographer concludes, "Hughes would always be, to an extraordinary though not always clearly identifiable extent, a child."[95] He internalized his anger and frustration so thoroughly that it manifested itself in psychosomatic illnesses of an often severe nature. Though a couple of years older than Asch, he played a perpetually young Peter Pan next to Asch's perpetually middle-aged Scrooge. Both, though, remained intensely private and revealed their inner selves to few.

Asch undoubtedly left the choice of material up to Hughes, who chose some of his better-known poems representing a relatively broad range of subject matter. They were also drawn from the full spectrum of his career, which even then was surprisingly long-lived. He included two of his most beloved poems, "The Negro Speaks of Rivers" ("I've known rivers ancient as the world and older than the flow of human blood") and "Mother to Son" ("Well son, I'll tell you; Life for me ain't been no crystal stair"), which he had written in the summer following his graduation from high school. "The Weary Blues" was the title verse in his first published collection of poems, appearing in 1926, and represented a deliberate effort to capture and preserve the beauty of the blues in formal verse just as Scott Joplin had attempted to notate ragtime in order to enshrine it as "art." A fourth poem, "To Captain Mulzac," he had written early the previous year in honor of the first black skipper in the U.S. Merchant Marine. Only Hughes's radical socialist poems were conspicuously absent, the consequence more likely of Hughes's perspicacity rather than any directive from Asch. In all more than thirty poems were recorded, apparently without the need for additional takes, and all of them appeared early the following summer on four ten-inch discs entitled *Poems by Langston Hughes* (Asch 354).[96]

Hughes's appearance at Asch Studios was followed by that of Meade "Lux" Lewis, a boogie-woogie pianist. Like James P. Johnson, Lewis originally made his mark on recordings in the late twenties, only to fall into obscurity in the intervening years. And like James P., Lewis's career was revived in the early 1940s by the renewed interest in boogie-woogie and other "vintage" jazz styles. Lewis was "rediscovered" by John Hammond in 1935, who had found him working in a Chicago car wash. Hammond featured Lewis among a trio of boogie-woogie pianists in his 1938 and 1939 Spirituals to Swing concerts (along with Pete Johnson and Albert Ammons, Lewis's boyhood friend). After the first concert, Alan Lomax recorded the reminiscences and playing of the three pianists for the Library of Congress. Through Hammond, the trio (along with vocalist Joe Turner) was recruited by Barney Josephson to be among the first performers at the newly opened Café Society, and they continued to perform there—with time out for touring—for more than two years.[97]

Lewis left the trio and Café Society in 1941 and lived and performed on the West Coast for the next several years. When he appeared in Asch Studios in the early autumn of 1944 he was still engaged at a Los Angeles nightclub called Randini's—in fact, one of the six sides he cut for Asch that autumn was titled "Randini's Boogie." Charles Edward Smith was responsible for supervising the session and very likely had made the arrangement for Lewis to come east to record in the first place. Lewis's Asch sides made it apparent that his real strength was as a solo artist. In his years away from the trio he had developed a style that placed less emphasis on the rhythmic left hand and allowed for more freedom and inventiveness in the melodic right hand.[98] Six sides were released from the session that December, just in time for Christmas. When *Down Beat* reviewed them the following March, they were described them as "superlative piano music. . . . The very best Lewis has done in a good decade." The reviewer maintained that Lewis's sides for Asch provided "the answer to those who say Boogie is too monotonous."[99] Lewis was listed in the Asch catalogue as an "exclusive artist," implying a mutually binding contract arrangement that Asch had arranged only once before, with Mary Lou Williams. Certainly it reflected Asch's growing stature in the field as well as the artist's confidence in him; it might also, however, have reflected the softness of the demand for boogie-woogie.

Asch also arranged that summer to distribute some jazz recordings of a young impresario by the name of Bob Thiele, who until then had been selling records out of his home in Forest Hills, Queens. Thiele's recordings would continue to appear under his own Signature label, but Asch (and by extension Stinson) would take care of the marketing and distribution. Early in the autumn Signature released a *Fats Waller Memorial Album*, featuring Waller's compositions performed by, among others, Earl "Fatha" Hines, and with notes by Leonard Feather. By late 1944 Asch-Stinson was also distributing eight individual Signature records, including several sides by a Coleman Hawkins outfit and two by a trio headed by Hawkins drummer Shelly Manne.

In the autumn Asch finally had the means of releasing some of the material from Guthrie's sessions of the previous April.[100] Following the democratic principles that had characterized the Almanacs' recordings, the album that resulted was simply titled *Folksay* and was not credited to any one musician. Increasingly used to refer to the collective expressions of "the masses," *folksay* was a term in the Popular Front tradition. A couple years earlier it had been the name of a dance performance organized by Sophie Maslow, a Martha Graham dancer, which included the lyrics of Carl Sandburg, the folk singing and guitar playing of Earl Robinson and Woody Guthrie, and the dancing of (among others) Marjorie Greenblatt Mazia—it was, in fact, the occasion of Woody and Marjorie's first meeting. After the war the name was resurrected again as the name of a theater company organized by Harold Leventhal, as well as by a folk song and dance company called American Folksay Group of New York, in which Irwin Silber, Fred Hellerman, and other People's Songsters figured prominently. For his *Folksay* album, Asch assembled the eight sides from a variety of sessions that spring, featuring Guthrie, Leadbelly, Josh White, and Sonny Terry.

The four-disc *Folksay* album (Asch 432) featured Guthrie on six of the eight sides, including his own "Biggest Thing," as well as "Dead or Alive" ("Poor Lazarus"), "Who's Gonna Shoe Your Pretty Little Feet" with Houston, "Good Morning Captain" with Houston and Pete Seeger, and "Glory," on which he is joined by Sonny Terry. "Nine-hundred Miles" is an instrumental featuring Guthrie's fiddling playing—scratchy and a bit elementary, but more rhythmically precise and in tune than might have been expected. "Cindy" features Pete Seeger with Cisco Houston. The only other side on which Guthrie is absent is a version of "Don't Lie Buddy" with Leadbelly and Josh White. Guthrie was given the task of writing the album notes (though again, they are not credited to him), and he did so in his typically exuberant style. In them he attempted to establish the significance of folk songs, particularly over "popular" songs, which he regarded as ephemeral:

> Hollywood songs don't last. Broadway songs are sprayed with a hundred thousand dollars to get them going, and they last, we'll say, a few months at most. The Monopoly on Music pays a few pet writers to go screwy trying to write and re-write the same old notes under the same old formulas and the same old patterns. Every band on the radio sounds exactly alike. . . . Several million skulls were cracked while the human race fought its way up. Do the big bands and the orgasm gals sing a word about our real fighting history? Not a croak.

Guthrie is particularly contemptuous of Tin Pan Alley's reluctance to treat the subject of the war, and it is interesting to see the extent to which he conflates the war effort with the struggle of working people: "Hitler declared war on the world and several million good people walked into their graves to keep the world a Union World, but do the gals and the bands play or sing a single note about it?"

Popular music is ultimately implicated in just about everything that is hateful in the world:

> The spirit of work, fight, sacrifice, they cannot sing about simply because their brain is bought and paid for by the Money Men who own and control them, and who hate our Union with all their might. They hate our Folk Songs and our Folk Music. They hate it because it is the Light of Truth and the mind of the racketeer cannot face this Light.

Folk music, of course, becomes the source of the world's salvation, because it is *authentic* and because it celebrates the accomplishments of working people. Guthrie emphasizes the ability of folk music to bridge ethnic and racial boundaries, and he reveals his own resistance to what was a growing orthodoxy within the Left on the subject of musical influences:

> You get a taste here of the blues and ragtime which are heard in all Negro music, yet, here you hear, too, what the White Man has given to American Folk Music. It has been the custom here lately to give the Negro so much credit that you may not think that the White Man added very much. The real truth is that the Negro loves and copies the White Man's music as much as the White Man loves and copies the Negro's.

Interestingly, there was little on *Folksay* that was overtly political. Guthrie's own "The Biggest Thing that Man Has Ever Done," sometimes called "The Great Historical Bum," was as close as the album came to a political song, and although it celebrates a litany of the working man's accomplishments it also has a self-mocking tone. But Guthrie's point is made by the other songs as well. "Not too many 'political points' are preached here," he notes, "because the song and the story itself is the political point." It is the same insight that led John Hammond to put Count Basie's band on a concert hall stage in 1938, yet Guthrie would have had difficulty seeing the connection. Guthrie was enthusiastic about almost every record that Asch ever put out, yet remained conspicuously silent on the subject of jazz. It was, he believed, too dependent on the "Money Men" to ever be above suspicion.

When *Folksay* appeared in late September Guthrie began a ritual that he continued through the release of dozens of Asch and Disc albums—he wrote a very personal "review" of the album and sent it off to Asch. The first went on for three typed pages:

> I listened to this album of records several times on my machine at home. And when I played it through for the first time it scared me. It sounded rough and wild, foggy and windy, like sand and like gravel, it had an oily rattle somewhere in it like a valve knock.
>   I put it back up on my shelf thought I would just forget the whole thing. . . . This was one offspring of mine of which I couldn't say that I was so very proud. . . . A whole day went by before I took it down and played through the records again. And all day I had felt a hot itching to play them because I was scared of them. I listened to the rough places and all of

the rough places were still rough. I sort of wanted to grab
them and melt the wax back through the factory and do
them all over again. . . . I spent the next several hours working out a plan to remove all of them from the market and
pour them back into the mould.

(When) I took the records of the Folksay album and listened to them once more[,] . . they sounded like a fiery young
kid. A hard kid, but a solid one. Wild running, here and gone,
fast traveler, tough. And I like this kid now better than any
smooth one.

Guthrie went on to mention each side in turn, singling out Seeger
and Houston's "Cindy" and Sonny Terry's "Glory" for special mention. When *Down Beat* reviewed the album, the reviewer maintained
that Josh White and Leadbelly's "Don't Lie Buddy" was "worth the
price of the whole album. This is worth fighting for," he added, and
Guthrie seconded the motion: "Well, we knew that before we
made the album. I've not heard the Broadway song yet that was
or is worth fighting for."[101]

In the autumn of 1944, while Asch gleaned the best acetates from
the recording sessions of the previous months for commercial
release—sending the acetates out to be "mastered," preparing album covers and inserts—a group of Asch artists headed out of
New York together on a tour in support of Roosevelt's reelection
bid. The tour was sponsored by the Communist Party, or what was
actually being called the Communist Political Association, as Browder had officially dissolved the CPUSA the previous spring. Communication with the Politburo had become tenuous since the
advent of the war, and Browder had interpreted the wartime
alliance of Churchill, Roosevelt, and Stalin as a signal for a new
cooperation with progressive forces in American politics. The
Communist Political Association was formed in part to lend communist support, welcome or not, to politicians such as Roosevelt.[102] Among its first endeavors was the FDR Bandwagon, which
included the Mary Lou Williams Trio, Woody Guthrie, Cisco Houston, Houston's girlfriend Bina Rosenbaum, an assortment of dancers, and Alan Lomax's secretary Jackie Gibson.

Guthrie and Houston set out first for Chicago, where a rally at
the Chicago Stadium for the Communist Political Association
would constitute a dry run for the full-fledged Bandwagon tour.
On the day of their concert Guthrie roamed around the loop,
looking for stores that might carry his book or Asch records. When

he got too cold, he went to sun himself by Lake Michigan and dashed off a letter to Asch:

> Hello Moe & Harris, Marian, & Everybody—Just a word about Mr. Hammersmark on the fly. He's a good man. . . . He says he has ordered albums from you several times with no reply. You'd ought to at least write him all the dope. He wants all he can get of Josh White Album, Woody Guthrie, Spanish Brigade Album. Maybe you are out and filling orders fast as you can. Maybe you don't feel like you can afford to write letters to everybody about your production bottleneck.[103]

Guthrie also reported playing for a soldiers and sailors' dance the previous night, and that he had had several opportunities to plug Asch albums. Guthrie never seemed to lose patience with Asch, but he wanted to point out that he was doing his part and that Asch's distribution problems were a source of frustration. It could be that Asch lacked sufficient shellac to supply far-flung stores with records on a regular basis. Asch's failure to respond to Hammersmark's inquiries indicated the lack of another commodity: time. Asch occasionally dictated a letter to Distler or simply gave her the gist of a communication and had her compose the letter herself; mostly, however, he found letter writing difficult and far too time-consuming and consequently avoided it altogether.

Guthrie wrote Marjorie that the Chicago Stadium rally was a grand success. The balance of the Bandwagon tour, however, did not go so well. Conservative Republican newspapers sought continually to expose the tour as nothing but a communist front, and they implicated Roosevelt in the process. He addressed another letter to Asch and his colleagues from Indianapolis in mid-October, although the salutation reflected an odd turn that his mind had been taking:

> Moe Asch, Marian, Mr. Harris, Asch Records, Stinson Trading & Finance Corp., Publishers, Printers, Recorders, Retainers, Poets, artists, Scientists, Thinkers, Engineers, Actors, Truckmen, Movers, Swappers, Traders, Composers, Editors, Assiners, Executives, Underwriters, Bondsmen, Insurers, Bailiffs, Attorneys, Shippers, Advisors, Listeners, Comrades and Friends! Howdy!

This time he reported that the show was not going very well. At the first official Bandwagon appearance in Boston, the show had been interrupted by a volley of stink bombs. The show's producer

was becoming discouraged, although Guthrie optimistically ob-
served that he could "make big $$ on that kind of publicity year in
and year out."

In the same letter, Guthrie asked Asch whether he had had a
chance to look through the lists of songs that he had left with him.
Guthrie envisioned the recording sessions of the previous spring as
the beginning of a long collaboration that would result in dozens of
thematic albums. He began to keep lists of songs and tunes,
grouped by category; eventually these lists of future projects would
go on for pages and pages—pioneer songs, cowboy songs, sea
songs, fiddle tunes. He left one list with Marjorie and appended ad-
ditional instructions for Asch: "Suggest to Moe the idea of illustrat-
ing the albums with brush or line drawings, etc., on the outside of
the inside record holders. Show him the samples." To Asch he wrote,
"Tell Marjorie what you think. Tell her what you need next. Whatever
it is, she can do it or get it done. That's why I married her."[104]

Asch continued to gather the best sides from assorted sessions
for album release that autumn. The first of two Josh White albums
appeared (Asch 348), using material from the rich 19 April sessions
("Fare Thee Well Blues" and "When I Lay Down and Die Do Die") and
some additional material that White recorded for Asch that Sep-
tember. The *Down Beat* reviewer was again enthusiastic: "With the
possible exception of Josh's own Southern Exposure album, this
set offers the best jazz vocals of the year!" Asch had arranged to
have Langston Hughes write the album notes.

A second release that autumn, titled simply *Blues,* resulted pri-
marily from the undated session in late spring that had brought
together Woody Guthrie, Sonny Terry, Leadbelly, Josh White, Cham-
pion Jack Dupree, Mary Lou Williams, and Nora Lee King. The
configuration of musicians suggests that Asch had deliberately set
out to make a blues album. He opened this session with nine takes
by Dupree, none of which were usable. *The Jazz Record Book* had
described Dupree as "a new name on the 'Race' lists" and singled
him out for the excitement of his boogie-woogie piano accompa-
niment. In fact, a side that survived, identified as "Stomp Blues"
(later released on LP, Asch AA4), is a magnificently inventive piano
blues. In the absence of drums, someone is beating out a rhythm
on a box or table, and a woman (probably Nora Lee King) punctu-
ates Dupree's playing with shouts and hollers. But the side runs
out midchorus, and perhaps this was one of the sessions that
Mary Lou Williams remembered as having been ruined by Asch's
generosity with drinks over dinner. Dupree never appears to have

recorded in Asch's studio again, but at the end of the evening he was given another chance and a very serviceable rendition of "Too Evil to Cry" resulted for the album. Josh White's two contributions to the album, "TB Blues" and "Careless Love Blues," resulted from just two takes. And Sonny Terry recorded "Lonesome Train" (it appeared in Asch's recording log as "Train Breakdown") in just one take. Mary Lou Williams's presence in the studio that evening may have been a fortuitous accident—she accompanied Nora Lee King on two takes of "Until My Baby Comes Home" (Asch used the first one on the album) and one take of the pop standard "What Is This Thing Called Love." The remaining side—Guthrie and Houston's "Ain't Gonna be Treated This Way"—was culled from the fertile 19 April session. The idea of including Guthrie in a "blues" album was less peculiar in an age in which musical categories were less reified than they are today; in an article about the FDR Bandwagon that October, a *Billboard* writer had referred unflinchingly to "blues singer Woody Guthrie."[105] When the *Blues* album was released some months later, the *Down Beat* reviewer singled out the Josh White and Mary Lou Williams sides as the most successful.[106]

Asch Studios remained moderately busy through the autumn of 1944. In early September Asch made a blatantly commercial recording of hillbilly music with the Cactus Cowboys—what was otherwise passing in the music trade as "folk music," though Asch, of course, had learned better. At approximately the same time, jazz violinist Stuff Smith (Leroy Hezekiah) recorded several sides at Asch Studios for an album of "hot jazz" that received mixed notices in the trade press. *Billboard* described the album as a "long and tedious session of hot fiddle string scrapings." *Down Beat* was a bit more enthusiastic: "That Smith man has ideas to burn, and some of them are pretty thoroughly ignited right on these discs. Stuff sings the last ('Stop, Look'), possibly a mistake. Advanced, this swing!" And Paul Bowles, writing in the *New York Herald Tribune*, declared that the trio had produced "some amusing harmonic adventures which penetrate beyond the old Debussy-Ravel frontier."[107] The notes for the Stuff Smith album were written by Inez Cavanaugh and Timme Rosenkrantz. The latter was a jazz impresario with a rather unusual background. The son of a noted Danish author and nobleman, Rosenkrantz himself carried the title of baron, although his was a rather faded royalty. What little resources he had were spent freely on promoting American jazz on both sides of the Atlantic. He gained a reputation for promoting jazz concerts that were far longer on musical taste than commercial sense. In the coming few years, he and Asch would collaborate on more than one project.

In the middle of November Ruth Rubin arranged for Asch to record several of her Yiddish folk songs, most of which she had learned as a child or later as a collector in the Yiddish-speaking community of Montreal. She and her husband intended to distribute the resulting album privately on their own label (Oriole); they arranged to pay Asch a fee in exchange for which he would record the album and make the necessary arrangements for its pressing and production. Although Mrs. Rubin was primarily an a cappella singer, she was convinced by someone in this instance to record the material with a backup chorus (a decision she later regretted). She and her husband knew little of Asch except that he was the son of the famous Yiddish writer.

As Mrs. Rubin remembers it, the session began inauspiciously. As she began the first song, Asch came charging out of the recording booth demanding to know what it was that she was singing. "They're Yiddish folk songs," she replied, amazed that the son of Sholem Asch would have been so ignorant. "Well I never heard any such thing," he ostensibly replied. It is difficult to know what to make of this exchange; Asch grew up in a Yiddish-speaking environment, and although his own spoken Yiddish was fragmentary he claimed to have heard Yiddish folk songs from his mother. Yiddish folk songs, on the other hand, were distinct from both the liturgical music he had been recording for some years and the Yiddish theater music he had long known. Whatever the source of his surprise, Asch became a great enthusiast of Yiddish folk song.

Six sides resulted from the session, the most famous of which was probably "Zhankoye," a song that came out of Russia in the 1920s during the period of collectivization. Rubin introduced it into leftist folk-song circles through Pete Seeger, and it later became the source of a debate in the pages of *People's Songs Bulletin* on the subject of translation. Mrs. Rubin objected to the way in which Seeger had translated the song and particularly to his addition of a verse that added a political dimension altogether out of keeping with the spirit of the original song. Others predictably defended Seeger's reworking of the song by insisting that folk songs were always malleable and often pressed into service in ways that had not previously been intended or even imagined.

Another conflict that resulted from Ruth Rubin's recording session with Asch had more immediate consequences for both of them. After Asch had pressed and packaged the album, the Rubins came to 117 West Forty-sixth Street from time to time to pick up copies as needed. On one such occasion they noticed that he had packaged a large number of the albums on his own Asch-Stinson label rather than on their private label. The album, in fact, continued to appear in Asch catalogues as *Jewish Folk Songs Sung by Ruth Rubin and Chorus* and was even marketed through Asch's subsequent label, Disc Records, in 1946 after Asch Records had dissolved. Asch had not, of course, paid for the right to use Rubin's material, nor was he paying her royalties. The whole matter resulted in a lawsuit that Asch eventually settled with a sum of several hundred dollars, at a time when he could ill afford it.[108]

The year 1944 ended with a flurry of recording. Asch had branched into classical music and was preparing releases of piano compositions of Bach and Debussy. Mary Lou Williams recorded three more sessions for Asch in December, including two with Coleman Hawkins and one rather enigmatic pair of sides on which she accompanied Josh White. These last—"Froggy Bottom" and "The Minute Man"—may have grown out of their joint appearances at Café Society, but Asch released them with other motives. The proceeds from the sale of the single, two-sided disc were to go to Disabled American War Veterans. Asch's intentions may well have been the very best, but the scathing review in *Billboard* suggested that he would be giving up very little in the way of profits. "For the $1.25 being asked for this disk, it's pure exploitation of the public's patriotic spirit. Josh White . . . romps thru these sides as if he was as anxious to get over the spinning as the listener."[109] On 10 December he recorded an Austrian-born cabaret singer in the tradition of the European chanteuse named Greta Keller, accompanied by the Harry Lubin Orchestra, which had previously made its mark in the Yiddish theater. Given the size of the recording outfit, it could not possibly have fit in Asch's minuscule studio. Perhaps the recording had originated as a WEVD radio broadcast.

The new year started well for Asch, and it appeared as though his recording business was achieving a degree of stability. There were still irritants; he remained in many respects under the thumb of Herbert Harris and Stinson Records, functioning as his own stock boy much of the time.[110] But it was increasingly apparent that some recording sessions of historic importance were taking place in Asch Studios, and the evidence for it was coming in from several different directions. In January *Down Beat*'s "best of" list for 1944 included three Asch recordings—James P. Johnson's "Impressions" and "Boogie Stride" were included under best "hot discs," Mary Lou Williams's

"Lullaby of the Leaves" under best "piano discs," and Josh White's *Blues* album under "best vocal." Additionally, Asch had made the acquaintance of some knowledgeable music critics who reinforced for him the significance of the work he was doing. One was Paul Bowles, known then primarily as a composer (and music critic for the *New York Herald Tribune*), although his musical reputation would soon be eclipsed by his haunting stories and novels of deadly cross-cultural misfirings in the cities and sands of North Africa. Bowles dropped in on Asch at his studio and the two talked about jazz and blues, the things that were happening in Asch's studio, and elsewhere. Another critic was John Lucas, a jazz historian who wrote glowingly of Asch's recordings in the pages of *Down Beat.*

Asch was particularly proud in later years of his recordings from this era featuring Coleman Hawkins. Whatever doubts he had had about the tenor saxophonist when Mary Lou Williams first brought him unannounced to his studio had long been dispelled. Hawkins was an important transitional figure in jazz, with a career stretching back to the late twenties. Because he was among the few swing band saxophonists who played a leading role in the development of the new style, his music is of particular interest to musicologists intent upon tracing the evolution of bebop from its swing antecedents. Although his command of his instrument was rarely equaled and spawned an entire generation of younger players, his lasting significance is based at least as much upon what one musicologist describes as his "awe-inspiring intellectual control over the harmonic aspects of jazz improvisation."[111]

Hawkins arrived late one night in the middle of January; Asch recalled that Hawkins appeared at about four in the morning, when he had finished with his nightclub act. Hawkins was then performing in two clubs, the Three Deuces and the Downbeat, with a quintet consisting of Howard McGhee on trumpet, Sir Charles Thompson on piano, Eddie Robinson on bass, and Denzil Best on drums. The Asch recording date was not impromptu; Hawkins had conceived of it some weeks in advance and was just waiting for the addition of an appropriate trumpet player before carrying through.

As Asch remembered it, Hawkins came to the studio before the other musicians and began warming up on the piano, playing classical pieces until he had achieved a certain state of mind. To Asch this was an instance of the creative artist finding a medium through which he could express himself—a kind of folk music in the sense that *any* genuine expression of the self through music is *folk* music. "[He] got himself involved with what his brain and what his intellect was saying," Asch recalled. "He got rid of those inhibitions and he started then to take his . . . saxophone and started to blow in long patterns until he got the feeling of what he wanted to say and this took him an hour. . . . His life as he expressed it through his musical instrument."[112] Asch's characterization of jazz as a folk music is not as spurious as it may sound; musicologists have long debated whether jazz is best regarded as a kind of indigenous "art" music, a form of popular music, or indeed an evolutionary development of African American musical elements (field hollers, spirituals) that were undeniably folk in origin.[113]

When the others arrived, Hawkins was ready to go. The band worked through six compositions, four by Hawkins (though two were based on the chord progressions of popular songs) and one each by McGhee and Thompson. The performances were not all equally successful. Hawkins's own "Bean Stalking" (the title comes from Hawkins's nickname, "Bean") suffers from an insufficiently supportive rhythm section and a breathtaking tempo that the soloists barely sustain. "Night Ramble," another Hawkins composition, is harmonically innovative and complex to the point of being almost unplayable. Of the remaining Hawkins compositions, "Sportsman's Hop" points most explicitly to the harmonic innovations then being adopted by bebop musicians ("Leave my Heart Alone," by contrast, is the most conventional performance on the album). The McGhee and Thompson compositions both came off well.[114] When they had finished, the sun had come up. The sides that resulted represent a snapshot of an innovative band in the process of giving shape to the new bebop style.

When the Hawkins sides were released that autumn, the response was tepid. *Down Beat,* otherwise dependable in its support of innovative jazz, reported, [The] "results are not sensational, manage to be thoroughly passable, however. . . . The stuff, on a Gillespie-chord kick, sound much better after several spins."[115] Although not mentioned explicitly in the review, part of the problem may have been the sound quality of the recording. Although Asch had recorded jazz ensembles before, he remained hampered by his stubborn insistence on the use of only one microphone. At times, the sound of individual instruments is badly muted, and the rhythm section is occasionally lost altogether. Howard McGhee remembered that Asch "had a funny studio":

> I don't know whether it was on account of the technique of the studio, or whether the ideas weren't coming through, you

never could tell. I knew that sometimes the tracks didn't
sound too clear. It looked like a perfectly normal studio, except that it wasn't too cool, it wasn't too fabulous. Like, when
you walked into Capitol studios, you know that they got
everything to work with. But you wouldn't find that at Asch.[116]

Asch, of course, was still operating on pretty much of a shoestring;
even if he was aware of current technological innovations in the
field of sound, it is not likely that he would have been able to
afford them. Still, what Hawkins and others valued in Asch was the
complete artistic license he afforded them. Without that, these
historic tracks may never have been recorded.

Asch's record releases that month continued to reflect the
eclectic activity in the studio. Tatum's "Topsy" and "Soft Winds"
appeared to wide acclaim. "The hot jazz diskophiles will never
pass this one by," wrote *Billboard*'s reviewer, and "the best example
yet of this crew's work," added *Down Beat*. The first Guthrie album
bearing his name also appeared in January; again culled from the
marathon sessions of the previous spring, it attracted a more
generous reception from the trade press than anyone could have
predicted. "Singing from the heart, rather than the throat, Woody
Guthrie . . . is a folk singer of more than casual interest," wrote
Billboard. "They are all songs of social significance. Songs rich in
democratic content, they appeal to the man in the back street."
The album (Asch 347) contained six songs that ranged broadly
over his repertoire; traditional southwestern ballads were represented, but so were his more topical and provocative songs, including "Coulee Dam" and "Jesus Christ."[117]

Though sales of the new Guthrie were negligible, Asch remained
enthusiastic about Guthrie and his songs, and arranged for him to
return to his studio for several sessions in the spring of 1945.
Guthrie was under some pressure; although he had served three
stints with the Merchant Marines during the war and was twice
torpedoed, he received an induction notice from the army in
March and was going to have to report for a physical. The previous
February he arrived in Asch Studios to begin work on the projected
"fiddle tunes" album. Asch was having some carpentry work done
in order to improve the acoustics of the studio; Guthrie declared
that he "didn't hardly know the joint." Two tunes for the album
were recorded that night, "Rubber Doll" and "Cattle Call," and
Guthrie declared to Moe and Marian in a letter a few days later that
he was working on another couple, including a rendition of "Rye

Whiskey" that he wanted to record without accompaniment in order to "get that old rock canyon ring." The next session, in early March, indeed included "Rye Whiskey" as well as "Woody Blues," which he also wanted to include on the fiddle album: "Down south and out west the folks will think it is at home there, and it might be sort of a nice shock to the big city listeners to hear a blues played on a fiddle in the same way that a breakdown, a jig, a reel, a schottische is knocked off."[118] Other traditional tunes comprised the balance of the early March session, including a couple that he had recorded once or twice before for Asch. Although he may have intended to improve on his previous renditions, more likely he and Asch, with the latter's sketchy logbook, had simply forgotten that they had already been recorded. A subsequent session was a great deal more deliberate. Guthrie was interested in recounting the major events of the day in song, thereby constructing a kind of musical newspaper. Asch jumped at the idea and came up with the title *American Documentary* for what they both imagined would be a long-running series. The fiddle album appeared to be on hold indefinitely.

Guthrie arrived in Asch Studios with four or five songs, all generally about the struggle for the control of labor. One was a well-known western ballad entitled "The Buffalo Skinners," which according to the Lomaxes had migrated from the Maine woods to Michigan to the western plains, where it took on its richest form. Guthrie's rendition adheres fairly closely to the Lomaxes' published version, with the skinners mutinying against their boss when he claims that their advances against pay had outstripped what he owed to them. The "drover" is killed and his bones left to bleach in the desert along with those of their four-legged victims (Guthrie's one likely alteration was in transforming the pesky Indians to "outlaws").[119] There were also two takes of a song entitled "Tubman," about Harriet Tubman, neither of which were ever commercially released in Asch's lifetime. The two real gems of the session were Guthrie compositions relating famous incidents in which miners and their families are killed by company thugs. "Ludlow Massacre" traces events during the Colorado Fuel and Iron strike in Trinidad, Colorado; one early morning in winter 1914 the Colorado National Guard repeatedly raked a makeshift tent village with gunfire, killing several women and children. A slightly less known incident in Calumet, Michigan, occurred during a Christmas party for the copper miners' families in a crowded dance hall; the operators' men incited a stampede by yelling "fire" and locking the doors. Though there was not in fact a fire, several dozen children were crushed in the ensuing melee. Guthrie's "1913 Massacre" stands as one of his most moving ballads. It was not a coincidence that both of these incidents had, at their core, the terror of fire; Guthrie knew it well and would again be haunted by fire before the decade was out.

Asch in the end had only half an album from this session, but he remained determined to release his first *American Documentary*. To round out the collection, he took three songs from the sessions of the previous April—"Pretty Boy Floyd," "Union Burying Ground," and "Lost John," featuring Sonny Terry's harmonica. Altogether the resulting six songs, though varied in many respects, cohered far more than any of the previous Asch collections of Guthrie songs. Half of them treated union themes, and the others touched on the travails of working people. But Asch was intent on determining the meaning of the collection still more explicitly. First he had David Stone Martin prepare a stunning lithograph for the cover illustrating the "burial at Ludlow." Next he asked Ben Shahn to provide him with a few photographs depicting antiunion violence. Finally he began to assemble some historical materials with which to write a set of accompanying notes. Writing did not come easily to Asch; he labored over the research and writing for six months according to later recollection: "I had traveled to Denver, San Francisco and the book shops of New York to get the information as well as the various union archives."[120]

Asch's album notes to *American Documentary: Struggle* (Asch 360) are awkward and uneven, full of elliptical reasoning and overbroad generalizations. And yet they trace a kind of historical analysis that is both radical and undeniably Asch's. He begins with the perversion of the founding father's noble declaration—the Bill of Rights—by a Supreme Court decision that elevated property rights over personal rights. Citing early utopian efforts to transcend the preoccupation with property rights, he maintains that this early American socialism was shortsighted: "Karl Marx was yet to appear on the scene and through his work 'Das Capital,' give the world a practical basis for social understanding." Asch skips quickly ahead to industry's oppression of the working man, to the first efforts to organize labor in the United States, and to the better-known incidents of antilabor violence. This, then, becomes the context of "Ludlow Massacre" and "1913 Massacre."

Several strands of Asch's thought are found here. He would always insist that the principles upon which the United States was founded were sound, just, and noble: "The American Revolution was fought by many as a war . . . to establish a free country with a 'Bill of Rights' where all men created equal might live in the pursuit of happiness." Only when moneyed interests began to pervert these principles was the basis for a just society undermined. Thus the struggle of working people in America has been to restore the country to its original mandate. Another aspect of Asch's notes is curious. To "property rights" he has opposed "personal rights." Although he writes approvingly of labor's collective initiatives, its goal is the liberation of individual will and desire, not the creation of meaningful collective life. He is deliberately dismissive of utopian collectives; they were "fordoomed [sic] to fail, since 'fundamentally this American socialism meant nothing more than a union of homes and labor,'" he writes, quoting approvingly from Robert Allerton Parker's *Yankee Saint*. He was a leftist, he always insisted, an anarchist, and he could invoke Marx as a decisive turning point in man's understanding of his condition. Yet he was a man fundamentally alone, who saw no redemptive power in collective life as a goal in and of itself. His generous "anarchism" warred with an intuitive libertarianism.

On the day that Guthrie was to be inducted in the army—7 May, ironically the day the German surrender was signed—he dulled the pain of leaving Marjorie, their two-year-old daughter Cathie, and his friends at Asch Studios by partaking liberally of the liquor that Asch kept on hand. "I nearly got drunk on your liquor there on my day of enlistment," he wrote to Moe, Marian, and Harris from Sheppard Field, Texas, that June. "I hope your little closet is as full on my day of getting home. The closet will be empty and Guthrie will be full." Guthrie's June letter was a response to a letter from someone at Asch Studios, probably Marian (it has not survived). In it, his loneliness is palpable: "I love all of you and this is serious, I miss your door to stick my head in." Army life was far more disagreeable to him than his life at sea had been. He bemoans the ubiquitous racial segregation and the apparent inability of his fellow soldiers to see the war as an antifascist struggle. Frustrated by his isolation, he inquires about the next Woody Guthrie album ("the Harriet Tubman, etc., bunch") and the use of one of his Asch recordings on a WNYC radio broadcast. He also has heard of some shakeup in the Communist Party and wants to know what they can tell him: "Is there a new line? If so what is? I heard some sort of a rumor that Browder cast a lone vote on some sort of an argument or decision. What was it about? What was the details? Be sure you send me a copy of the Sunday Worker once in a while."[121] Indeed, Browder's dissolution of the party had been harshly denounced in a French communist publication the month before, almost certainly at the behest of Moscow, and in a series of emergency meetings that followed Browder ignored the pleas of his American colleagues to declare the dissolution an error. The following month "Browderism" was officially condemned and the party was reconstituted. In a matter of months Browder was expelled from the party altogether.[122] Guthrie was far more likely to receive news of these events from Distler or Harris, both party members, but Asch's alienation from the politics of the party could not have been so very severe at this time if Guthrie was addressing him as well.

Asch himself was traveling in June, to Chicago and Los Angeles in search of markets for his recordings. The events of this trip, which lasted six weeks, are preserved in a series of letters that he had sent to Distler. Their affair had blossomed the previous autumn; he wrote her then, too, one late night in November (perhaps also while traveling, but more likely from his apartment, with Frances and Michael asleep in adjoining rooms). This letter appears to have been the aftermath of an earlier conversation—or argument—about their political differences and what they meant for Asch Records: "Tonight it has come to me the total difference of perspective and analysis of any subject between us. It seems only on those that you get in your way and I in mine does the thing eventually click. If the result is different then the thing must be bad, and if the result is an unknown then it should be tried." He goes on to characterize her appreciation of Soviet life, with its optimism and its celebration of "big things." She would have him believe that "this is a most wonderful and positive life to live. The [Russian] child is brought up that all the weather, the earth, the sky, man, machine, everything is for his benefit if he uses or gets it to help him. It is only bad when that thing is influenced because of greed . . . and these bad things momentarily blind his eyes and he only sees self gain." Under ordinary circumstances, the large forces of the world are salutary in effect.

In contrast Asch's own view is based on a belief in the possibility of a progressive capitalism, harnessed to the service of humanity. In this view of the world, big things are inevitably the enemy: "Big things are to fight, to kill, to exterminate; the trusts, gangsters, cartels, nations." He visualizes the need for "many small people," rather than "the masses," fighting individually against the "machine." "We call people small and visualize the world to be as composed of 'small people doing big things.'" It is apparent that Asch is not accustomed to expressing himself this way, and the words do not come easily. No doubt Distler, college-educated and immersed in party politics, got the better of him in a battle of words. But Asch has his principles, too. He believes in individualism, in the ability of the "small guy" to make a difference. And, surprisingly, he expresses the need for a God to remind man that there is something still bigger than the "big" and necessarily "bad" forces that threatened to overwhelm him: "We are taught as a child to beware of the 'Boogey man' who will snatch us; to fight the cruel 'bad big Boys' to show that we small can lick the bad big. How different then the boy in Russia who is taught that he is big in the sense that he has the might on his side and that the opponent is small (bad)."

The letters he sent Distler in June and July 1945 show a different side. Asch seems unusually relaxed, remarking on the novelty of air travel and drawing brief sketches of clouds and mountains as they looked to him from the sky. On his first night in Chicago his traveling partner of the next several weeks—George Mendelssohn of Vox Records—took him to the Downbeat, where they heard trumpeter Red Allen and trombonist J. C. Higginbotham. Asch was impressed by the energy and knowledge of Chicago's young jazz enthusiasts and expected that it augured well for his company. The record retailers, however, were another story. With a few exceptions, they were interested in the three major labels and very little else. Asch reported to Distler that Lyon and Healey only displayed Victor recordings prominently; even Decca and Columbia were behind the counter. In a few smaller stores he found copies of his Mary Lou Williams, Art Tatum, and John Kirby releases, and store owners who believed that Asch Records was "here to *stay*. . . . They are crying here for our merchandise." Asch also reported to Distler on some shopping: "I bought a gabardine coat, but slacks are impossible to get; I guess I'll wait until I get to Los Angeles." And in his last letter to her from Chicago, he wrote, "It's time you were lonesome for me. I hope you are. You can imagine how I feel needing to talk to some one."

Asch and Mendelssohn had planned to travel on to Los Angeles by airplane, but with the war winding down, domestic flights were dominated by returning GIs, and they worried about being bumped from a connecting flight in some remote location. So they booked tickets on the Santa Fe Railroad for the remainder of the trip west. It took them three days, and although Asch found the scenery through the state of Kansas deadening, he was enchanted by the Rockies, particularly the Raton Pass on the Colorado–New Mexico border, which he described to Distler in detail: "That night the bar was opened for the first time. I treated the soldiers and had three drinks for Kansas, the Raton Pass and you. Marian I hope you notice you come after the Raton Pass for you are a part of it. A Big part."

Among the first things Asch did in Los Angeles was to attend a burlesque show, the first he had seen in many years. Much of it reminded him of the shows he had amplified years ago in New York, but the four Negro jazz musicians were of a conspicuously high caliber. He stayed to hear them play through three shows and afterward went backstage to talk with the piano player. He was particularly taken by the ability of the musicians to improvise upon the movements of the strip show: "Every movement of the strip, every shake of her breast or thighs or midriff improvised by either a tenor sax, a clarinet, a piano or drums. . . . I have to get this routine down on acetate."

While in Chicago Asch's business interests had been confined primarily to retailing. But in Los Angeles there were questions about manufacturing to consider, as well as several artists he wished to see. He made it a priority to find a West Coast pressing plant that would enable him to save considerably on shipping costs. And many of the musicians he had been recording over the past two years were living in Los Angeles. He met with Earl Robinson, and with trombonist Vic Dickenson, who was sick in bed; and he forwarded regards to Distler from Brownie McGhee and love from Art Tatum. From a young record store owner he learned that Cisco Houston had shipped out to sea again.

It seemed to Asch that Los Angeles and many of its inhabitants had succumbed to a kind of filth and rot of the spirit. To regain his equilibrium he sought out Mexican, Chinese, and African American neighborhoods, which would remind him of the purposes for which he and Distler were toiling. Cowhands, Mexican peasants, Negro musicians—all were at home here, and all had found the means "to defend and fight back white man's 'Progress' and 'Sophistication.' . . . Marian they live what we record." He swung between extremes of disgust with the city's decadence to rapture over the possibilities it suggested for the work that he and Distler had ahead of them. There seemed to him to be an audience here for their "serious honest approach" that they had not even been able to imagine in New York. Tastes in Los Angeles seemed different: "The most popular record here is Mary Lou Williams's 'Gjon Mili's Jam Session' and not 'Star Dust' like New York. Interesting, eh?"

Asch's letters to Distler that summer left little doubt that they were partners and collaborators, in their work as in one another's lives. Whatever passion they had for each other appeared to be inseparable from the passion they had for the work ahead: "It really means that you and I will need to discuss and work and think and do many things we love and that is good. I hope you think so too."

"We have a big obligation," he wrote her in his last letter from Los Angeles, "and a big catalogue to work on and now I'm sure we can be left alone without doubts as to the friends and customers we can build. Boy this sure is enough for a wonderful lifetime ahead."[123]

Guthrie continued to write to Asch through the summer, usually asking for money in exchange for promoting Asch Records to anyone who would listen. In a letter in July he asked Asch to send him fifteen dollars and to put it on his account: "If I have no account get out your bastardly pen and make me one." Two days later he maintained that his promotional pitches were causing him to miss his meals, which he would then have to buy at a cost of eighteen dollars a month: "I will only charge you fifteen dollars a month because Marjorie sends me three dollars a month which just makes the eighteen." In August he inquired again about the *American Documentary* album, appending a list that included "Miner's Christmas" ("1913 Massacre"), "Ludlow Massacre," "Harriet Tubman," and "Lost John," but not "Buffalo Skinners."[124] Another letter told of five ballads he had written based on newspaper clippings about army life and the war, and yet another mentioned additional war ballads, a couple of which he thought might round out the album.

With the announcement of the Japanese surrender in August, Guthrie no doubt hoped that his army ordeal might finally be coming to an end, but the army continued to have plans for him. He had been transferred to a base in Illinois in July in order to attend teletype school, and after a furlough in August that left him sufficient time to go east in order to finally marry Marjorie, he was shipped off to yet another base, in Las Vegas. His letters began to show the confusion and prolixity that had plagued him the year before. He wrote several a day, some as long as forty or fifty pages with hundreds of tiny, neat words on a page. A list of projected albums he wanted to record for Asch topped *seventy* one day and included titles such as "War Heroes of World War Two," "Prostitutes and Gamblers," "Outlaws and Inlaws," "Me," "You," "Cars I Owned," "Reno Jail," "Holidays Around the World," and "Paid in Full." His biographer would describe the month of December as a nightmare in which Guthrie became lost in a maze of tangled thoughts, fruitlessly trying to escape through reams of handwritten words.[125] The stresses of army life and his loneliness undoubtedly contributed to his mental chaos, but at least as significant was the progressive encroachment of the disease he had inherited from his mother.

It is not apparent that Asch had any inkling of the hell Guthrie was enduring. The Asch catalogue was now growing rapidly, and he and Marian had their hands full just seeing to the production of the albums and the filling of orders. Langston Hughes was moderately irritated at the difficulty Asch seemed to have in sending out promotional copies of his album and commented in a letter to his good friend and fellow poet Arna Bontemps in August that "Asch's business is getting too big for his small set-up and limited office force, so I guess they got kind of mixed up."[126] The studio had been active in the spring, leaving Asch with a backlog of acetates that had to be prepared for release. Art Tatum, James P. Johnson, and Mary Lou Williams had all recorded sufficient additional material for new albums of their own. Johnson appeared in February with a trio consisting of Omer Simeon on clarinet and Pops Foster on bass, and again in April and May for solo piano sessions, although only the trio recordings appeared on discs during the 78-rpm era. Tatum, on the other hand, recorded six sides in March that became Asch 356.[127] Williams recorded only once for Asch in 1945, but the resulting sides proved to be among her most memorable. After reading a book about astrology, Williams decided to write twelve short pieces, each dedicated to a different musician born under one of the twelve astrological signs. The *Zodiac Suite* was written intermittently over several months. Portions of it were performed on her weekly WNEW radio program, at Café Society, and later with the New York Symphony at Carnegie Hall. For the Asch sessions she was joined by her rhythm section of Al Lucas and Jack Parker.[128]

Other, more eclectic projects were initiated at Asch Studios that spring and summer, including an album of flamenco guitar by Carlos Montoya and an album of calypso music by the Duke of

Iron. Several traditional ballad singers recorded at Asch in the spring, among them tenor Richard Dyer-Bennett, a singer of European ballads in the "art song" tradition who had recorded previously for Decca. Dyer-Bennet recorded sufficient material for six twelve-inch sides (Asch 461), and along with seventy-year-old George Edwards from the Catskills, Mexican singer Eithne Golden, and Josh White, contributed to a *Ballads* album (Asch 560) that was released that fall as a kind of companion volume to the previous *Blues* collection. A couple of small units led by swing-era musicians recorded albums with Asch. The first was a white unit led by the highly regarded tenor saxophonist Jerry Jerome, best known for his work with Benny Goodman's orchestra, although he also played with Glenn Miller and Red Norvo. The second was a still more interesting band led by bassist John Kirby. Kirby was regarded as among the most accomplished swing-era bass players; he had played with Fletcher Henderson, Chick Webb, and Lucky Millinder. Only a year or two earlier his sextet had been the most popular small jazz group in the city and had demonstrated, according to one jazz historian, that "swing could be polite, musical and commercial all at the same time."[129] "John Kirby has done an album of little pieces for Asch Records," wrote Paul Bowles that June, "all neatly arranged and neatly played."[130]

Hy Zaret was a friend of Asch's who over dinner one evening sang around a dozen songs about army life that he had learned as a GI Asch was delighted and asked him to assemble some army buddies who could recreate the informality of a soldier's singalong in the studio. Over the course of two evenings they recorded thirty parodies based on popular tunes that became an album entitled *Strictly G.I.* (Asch 455). It was surprisingly successful in a commercial sense, although, once again, Asch's "informal" business arrangements led to disgruntlement, as he found himself the subject of a lawsuit by Zaret some months later. Tom Glazer prepared a documentary album about the life of Franklin Roosevelt, and in mid-September modernist poet Alfred Kreymborg, then a contributing editor of the *New Masses*, came to record an album of his own poetry.

By mid-1945 there were other developments in the world of jazz recording that touched Asch's operation directly. *Down Beat* announced in June that Bob Thiele's Signature label, now undoubtedly free of the arrangement with Asch and Stinson, was becoming sufficiently successful to challenge the majors in the hot jazz field; Thiele was thinking of purchasing his own pressing plant.

Another young record company that burned brightly in the commercial jazz market for a few years—ARA (American Recording Artists)—signed Art Tatum to an exclusive contract. Most significant for Asch, Granz's Jazz at the Philharmonic concerts in Los Angeles were attracting a great deal of attention and Granz had started to record them. He formed a record company called Vanguard (unrelated to the classical and folk music label of the same name started by Maynard Solomon after the war) but reported having difficulty in securing pressing facilities. Perhaps he would turn over his masters to one of the majors for pressing and distribution. In September *Down Beat* announced that arrangements were being made to book the first national tour of Granz's "jam session stars."[131]

Either Granz was reluctant to go into business with one of the majors or the experienced record merchants did not see any future in "live" recordings that included the distractions of crowd noise and applause, but whatever the reason, while in New York one day, probably in late October, Granz started looking through the telephone directory for a small-time record company. The first name he encountered was Asch. Having called ahead to make an appointment, Granz arrived at 117 West Forty-sixth Street with a bulky package of 78-rpm discs. He tried first to interest Asch in a singer he had recently recorded named Ella Logan; Asch listened for a few minutes but could not be persuaded. Granz prepared to leave, but Asch asked if he might hear another album that Granz had tucked under his arm. Granz played a recording of "How High the Moon" that he had recorded at a JATP concert the preceding year. It featured, among others, Howard McGhee on trumpet and Illinois Jacquet and Charlie Ventura on tenor saxophones. Asch reportedly "flipped," and it is not difficult to imagine why. It was exciting, energetic, straight-ahead jazz, played by a racially integrated band, no less. But it was also a document of music in its "natural" setting, the spontaneous expression of the musicians without any studio contrivances—exactly Asch's cup of tea. Yes, he wanted to release this record and material like it on the Asch label. He proposed a particular financial arrangement, and Granz returned to his room at the Belmont on Lexington Avenue to consider it.

In 1945 Norman Granz was not yet thirty years old. The son of a Jewish merchant who had lost his department store during the Depression, Granz grew up in ethnically integrated neighborhoods and developed an interest in jazz while collecting records in the years just before the war. When he was discharged from the service in 1943 he began organizing jam sessions in Los Angeles nightclubs, eventually producing the first jazz concert at the Philharmonic in 1944. He resembled Asch and John Hammond in adoring African American music and detesting racial discrimination, but was a far better businessman than either of the older men. His objectives, in their order of priority, were "to make money, to combat racial prejudice, and to present good jazz."[132]

The following day, Granz wrote Asch:

> Dear Moe: Pursuant the deal you offered me yesterday about my Jazz at the Philharmonic records, namely—$2000 to cover costs and 15 cents per record royalty—I accept. However, in view of your cooperation during this deal, I think it only fair that I knock off my commission so that you only pay me $1850 plus the royalty. I'll see that you have the masters, the photograph negatives, and my commentary by the end of next week. If you would draw up the contract and air-mail it, that would be very helpful. Oh yes, Moe, I'd like you to include a clause that if the occasion ever arose that you sold the masters, (though I can't visualize that happening), my royalty rate would be transferred and would be in effect with the other company. Thanks, and good luck. Norman G.

Did he think that Asch would need it? Asch had, in fact, made a very generous offer—so generous that Granz could not accept its original terms in good conscience. Asch had acted impulsively, as he always did, and had gambled the future of his recording company on a very high profile venture.

Asch had another matter to contend with. Although Granz's note did not indicate that he was particularly aware of it, by going into business with Asch he had also entered into a business arrangement with Herbert Harris and Stinson Records. Unquestionably Asch was going to have to get out from under the partnership with Stinson and set up an independent business of his own. At least a couple of things made this difficult. First, aside from the official Soviet recordings, which had almost no commercial appeal, all of Stinson's material was derived from Asch's masters; they would give up their rights to it reluctantly. Second, despite two or three good years in the business, Asch had still not accumulated any capital to speak of and he would badly need it in order to pay Granz as well as to press the quantity of records the public would demand.

To prepare for the impending dissolution of the partnership, Asch began to make an inventory of his masters. On one list he enumerated the masters he had recorded between 9 December 1940 and 3 January 1943, that is, until the time of the partnership. These would be off limits to Harris. A second list consisted of the masters recorded since the partnership and until the present—25 November. Two contracts were ultimately signed by Asch, Harris, Harris's partner Irving Prosky, and their respective lawyers. The essence of the first contract, dated 2 December, was that Asch would sell to Harris and Prosky, for the sum of $6,267, all of the masters on the 25 November list, although, perhaps for sentimental reasons, Asch exempted *In the Beginning,* "Kol Nidre/Eli Eli," and his second Leadbelly album. For a period of fifteen months Harris and Prosky would be permitted to use the name Asch Records while Asch would be forbidden to do so. Prosky and Harris forfeited any rights to Asch Recording Studios, and they agreed to hire Asch, at a weekly salary of $125, in order that he might instruct them in the "method and technique of 'completing records.'" Asch would only be obliged to remain in the employment of Stinson until he had completed the production of three albums: *Adam and Eve*, an album of French poetry licensed from the French Broadcasting Company, Mary Lou Williams's *Signs of the Zodiac,* and a new album of folk songs by Josh White. The agreement also stipulated that Asch would never make or sell any records with the same title and by the same artist as those that he had sold under the Asch-Stinson label. Finally, Harris and Prosky agreed to pay one-third of the settlement on the Ruth Rubin suit, which was still pending.

The second contract, signed on 22 December, stipulated that Asch would sell to Prosky and Harris, for the sum of one dollar, all of the contracts—106 of them—that Asch had signed with the musicians he had recorded during their partnership. Harris and Prosky would assume all of the responsibilities implied in the contracts.

The two contracts dissolving the partnership did not take effect soon enough to save Granz from irritation. The first JATP album, with a single, long performance of "How High the Moon" spread across three twelve-inch sides and a performance of "Lady Be Good" on the other three, would still appear on Asch-Stinson. Granz wired Asch from Los Angeles in the middle of December: "Money due tomorrow for original contract on Jazz Philharmonic album 1100.00 must have it immediately please take care of this matter for me as I can get no satisfaction from Harris at Stinson Trading Company wire money immediately kindest regards Norman Granz." Asch as usual was still not flush. The sum from Harris was being paid in three installments, the second due four days after Granz's cable and the third after the first of the year.

Somehow Asch muddled through the weeks of transition. He would be starting a new company in the new year with almost no catalogue to show for his years of work in the recording industry. He retained the loyalty of a few jazz and folk musicians—almost none of the Asch recording artists made new recordings for Stinson after the partnership was dissolved. And Asch made one more deal that was crucial to his success: the Clark Phonograph Company, which pressed his albums, advanced him ten thousand dollars' worth of credit for the first pressings of his new company. With the credit from Clark and six thousand dollars in cash from Stinson, Asch established a new record company in January 1946 and was again his own man. His contract with Stinson had stipulated that he would no longer be able to capitalize on his name or, by extension, on that of his father. It was just as well. He was no longer operating exclusively in the provincial world of New York Jews where the name Asch carried meaning. Instead he wanted a name that would be instantly recognizable and easily remembered. Although his lawyer advised against it for fear that it could not be copyrighted, Asch chose the name Disc Company of America.

4. THE DISC ERA AND BANKRUPTCY

Two apparently unrelated events in the closing weeks of 1945 set the stage for much of what was to go on at Disc Records during the three years that followed. One was the opening-night appearance of New Orleans trumpeter Bunk Johnson at the Stuyvesant Casino on 28 September. Johnson may or may not have been active in New Orleans music circles at the turn of the century when the bands such as that of Buddy Bolden were creating the music that came to be known as jazz. He fell into obscurity through much of the 1930s and, due in part to bad teeth, played very little music until the following decade. But while preparing the *Jazzmen* volume, Frederic Ramsey and Bill Russell repeatedly encountered his name and succeeded in tracking him down through the mail to his home in New Iberia, Louisiana. Johnson seemed to immediately intuit their purpose and gladly offered himself to them as a living example of the "real thing," the surviving hero of "pure" New Orleans music. Adept at the art of self-promotion, Johnson wrote a series of letters to Ramsey and Russell in which he created a kind of mythology about himself and his place in the Bolden band at the moment the music was taking shape. So eager were they for the "truth" about the origins of jazz that the authors of *Jazzmen* took Johnson largely at his word, and musicologists have since been left to sort fact from fiction in his account of the turn-of-the-century bands.[1] Johnson could be faulted for being a beguiling opportunist, but he was only providing the enthusiasts with what they wanted — "a symbol of something that existed only in their imaginations," according to jazz historian Christopher Hillman.[2]

As luck would have it, Johnson was actually a pretty credible trumpet player, and in a series of recordings in the early 1940s he succeeded in adding measurably to the legend that had first taken shape in the pages of *Jazzmen*. With a new set of teeth paid for with money raised by the Jazzmen Group, Johnson proceeded to play in a series of memorable recording sessions supervised by Russell and others in New Orleans in 1942. Some less successful sessions were recorded in San Francisco in 1944 with the Yerba Buena Jazz Band, but while there he caught the attention of *New York Herald Tribune* music critic Virgil Thomson, whose newspaper column added still further to the Bunk Johnson mystique. To Johnson the recording sessions were a nuisance, but one worth tolerating if it would further his eventual goal—to find work playing in the northern cities. Boston beckoned first, but by late 1945 there were auspicious signs of possible New York engagements.

Bill Russell found a suitable venue for Johnson's music in an unlikely place—the Stuyvesant Casino, located on Second Avenue in the vicinity of the old Yiddish theaters. In New Orleans a band was assembled, including legendary drummer (lately in Chicago) Baby Dodds. The casino's ballroom was rented for a month, and the band was engaged to play every night of the week except Monday. The critics aside (they had little good to say about Johnson's band during the opening performances), the audiences' reception was wildly enthusiastic. Made up largely of intellectuals and middle-class college students—almost exclusively white—they found in the seven black musicians a "purity" of expression that seemed to resonate with the need for something more authentic than was currently available on commercial records and radio. For their part the musicians were puzzled; they had been accustomed to gauging the success of their performance according to the energy of the dancers in the audience, yet despite posters that prominently advertised dancing, the listeners sat unmoved throughout the show. The respectful awe of the white audiences had its condescending aspect. Johnson and band were regarded as period pieces, valued for their ability to reproduce a music decades old and discouraged from any experimentation or innovation that might have contributed to their growth as musicians.

In the audience during the early performances was Frederic Ramsey, a preeminent member of the Jazzmen Group. Ramsey had weathered the war as a conscientious objector and was now making ends meet by writing columns on jazz for an assortment of publications. For him Bunk Johnson's performance was the fulfillment of a dream. Every romantic notion he had ever had about the existence of an "original" jazz form appeared to be embodied in the Johnson band at the Stuyvesant. Was there an element of "wishful thinking" in the reaction of enthusiasts such as Ramsey, as some have suggested?[3] Even had the New Orleans audiences valued "changelessness" as had the northern enthusiasts, it seems unlikely that as creative musicians Johnson and his band would have stood still musically for twenty or thirty years. Furthermore, despite the enthusiasts' celebration of "purity" and "authenticity," the New Orleans musicians had responded in their own way to certain kinds of commercial pressure. They were no less eager than the dominating swing band musicians to please a paying audience. Now a new audience was exerting pressure on them, this time to recreate a music that was passing away.

Still, whatever the motivations for producing the performances, the result was an exuberant and joyful music that was new to the ears of most New Yorkers and decidedly welcome. The crowds at the Stuyvesant thinned in a matter of weeks, and the shows were moved to a smaller room within the same establishment. But then on New Year's Day 1946 Johnson and his band were featured in a concert at Town Hall. To introduce the band Ramsey had written some hopelessly poetic notes, read by Orson Welles to the great amusement of the musicians.

The band's engagement at the Stuyvesant continued until 12 January. Sometime that autumn or early winter Asch came down to hear Bunk Johnson and encountered Ramsey. They had met previously; Charles Edward Smith had brought Ramsey around to Asch Studios as early as 1943 to listen in on some of the early James P. Johnson sessions. Asch told Ramsey about his new venture—Disc Records—and invited Ramsey on board to help arrange sessions and to write album notes. Ramsey agreed. Because Smith was already doing much the same thing for Asch, the extension of an invitation to Ramsey suggests that Asch envisioned a much-expanded operation. In fact, from the two-horse team that was Asch Recording Studios, the tiny space at 117 West Forty-sixth Street would become a noisy bustle of activity in the coming months. David Stone Martin became a regular presence in the office, working over his pen and ink drawings or helping to lay out the 78-rpm album covers. His brother Francis was on the payroll for a while as well, as the director of advertising. Charles Edward Smith and Fred Ramsey rounded out the initial team, and they were joined later by the self-trained ethnologist and ethnomusicologist Harold Courlander and by musicologist and composer Henry Cowell.

The second event that was to have extraordinarily long lasting implications for Asch was a meeting on 30 December in the apartment of Pete and Toshi Seeger in Greenwich Village.[4] Woody Guthrie was there, as was Josh White, Millard Lampell, Lee Hays, Earl Robinson, Bess Hawes, and about twenty other singers and songwriters. Their intention was to form an organization called People's Songs, which would "create, promote and distribute songs of labor and the American people."[5] For the many Communist Party members and fellow travelers who had put their political aspirations on hold in order to support the war effort, all the signs were auspicious. Fascism had been put on the run by the war, and labor, having slumbered through the previous four years, was now prepared to make up for the time lost during the "no strike" period. Or so they thought. The relationship between People's Songs and the party was more ambiguous than, for instance, that of the Almanac Singers; many members of People's Songs were party members, many were not. The organization's mandate was sufficiently vague that there was no need for unanimity on the question of a world workers' revolution. Serge Denisoff has concluded that People's Songs "fit the criterion of a political 'front.' . . . It reflected party policy but appeared to operate outside the Stalinist sphere."[6] However, the conclusions one draws about the ideology of the organization depend on how it is defined. Denisoff's inferences are moderately plausible if one attends primarily to those few who ran the national organization. The broader membership, which by November of that year numbered seventeen hundred, represented an assortment of interests and ideological positions. Although we can safely guess that the membership was united in its opposition to fascism and in its support for world peace and racial justice, there was probably slightly less enthusiasm for labor issues and substantially less for the Soviet state. In the end the common denominator was certainly an affection for a certain kind of music and the Popular Front sentiments that went with it.

People's Songs' antecedents were the Almanac Singers, although the emphasis of People's Songs was less on performances by designated "professionals" and more on the writing, dissemination, and group singing of politically "useful" songs through the formation of People's Songs chapters throughout the United States and Canada. "Hootenannies" became the gathering of choice. And unlike the Almanacs, whose communal aspirations caused them to avoid attributing song-writing credits to particular individuals, People's Songs would be careful to grant song-writing credit where due—this out of both the need to recognize song writing as a kind of labor that deserved to be rewarded and the concern for infringing on existing copyrights.[7] The idiom would naturally be "folk music," defined now as music deliberately lacking in commercial pretensions. Because these were to be largely *new* songs, reprinted in a monthly periodical called *People's Songs Bulletin*, the issue of folk music as the product of an oral tradition was largely elided:

> People all over the world and all over this country have always been making up songs about the things that were on their minds. Work songs, play songs, nonsense songs, religious songs and fighting songs. Put them all together—that's what we call "People's Songs." There's only one thing wrong—or maybe right—with them—they're not commercial.[8]

Pete Seeger would be the national director of the new organization. Lee Hays would be the executive secretary; within a few months, however, he had alienated himself from the People's Songs leadership—much as he had with the Almanacs in 1941—on account of his work habits and general lethargy. Seeger was prevailed upon to request his resignation (a move he later regretted).[9] Hays was replaced by Felix Landau (and later Irwin Silber). The board of directors included a number of musicians with whom Asch had worked, including Pete Seeger, Millard Lampell, Guthrie, Tom Glazer, Bess Hawes, and Alan Lomax, as well as fellow record executive John Hammond and the prominent folklorist Ben Botkin. The board of sponsors read like a who's who of the arts: composers Aaron Copland, Leonard Bernstein, and Marc Blitzstein, actress Judy Holliday and director John Houseman, as well as Lena Horne, Gene Kelly, Elia Kazan, Lincoln Kirstein, Alain Locke, Dorothy Parker, Paul Robeson, Sam Wanamaker . . . and Moe Asch. And almost all of these people had their People's Songs affiliation turned against them by various implements of the McCarthy era.

Asch's later recollections of People's Songs were remarkable for two reasons. First, he claimed that Woody Guthrie had nothing to do with it, "or anything like it." Second, he maintained that his own affiliation with People's Songs resulted from assurances that it would not represent a political position: "The next issue I see is the first issue of the damn thing [laughing] and it really is a revolutionary manifest, and with my name appearing as a sponsor, right? And I objected very strenuously, they had no right to do this to me."[10] Although almost twenty-five years had elapsed since the circumstances he was recalling, Asch's apparent disregard for fact was probably neither a deliberate deception nor the result of a failing memory (he was just sixty-five at the time) but reflected the need—evident throughout his many reminiscences in the 1970s and 1980s—to make the past conform to an image he was creating of himself and his work. The intrusion of politics into folk music, he argued in 1970, was the consequence of pressures brought to bear on various folk singers by their marginalization at the hands of the FBI and others, and the subsequent search for work in those leftist venues—particularly labor unions—where they were still accepted. Actually, while People's Songs offered their services to labor unions for rallies and picket lines, organized labor became increasingly skittish about affiliating with a red-tinged outfit such as People's Songs. Seeger sang for the CIO's national convention in Atlantic City in 1947, but shortly thereafter the organization—once the great hope of the communist Left—took a series of deliberately anticommunist steps, purging leftists from its ranks. Other People's Songsters sang for unions in San Francisco, Los Angeles, Chicago, Denver, and Cleveland, but increasingly these were marginal, communist-led organizations. Robbie Lieberman, overstating the case only to a degree, concludes that "the labor movement never made use or People's Songs in a serious way."[11]

Asch may have felt genuine antipathy toward People's Songs at various moments; perhaps Disc's collaboration with People's Songs was the consequence of Distler's urging, with Asch's agreement earned rather grudgingly. But through most of its three-year existence he promoted his records through its *Bulletin,* and late in 1946 he recorded an album that Lomax produced for the organization. In special promotional deals, the *People's Songs Bulletin* offered certain Disc titles to new subscribers. What was to have been the third anniversary issue in early 1949 (ending up instead the final issue) included greetings from a large number of supporters, Asch included. He complained that his People's Songs affiliation caused him trouble with the House Un-American Activities Committee (HUAC), but Asch was actually spared more than most of those he knew in the McCarthy era. The so-called revolutionary manifest was, in fact, a gentle call in support of common, working people—there was nothing in it that he could have found objectionable. So what was his beef? Moe Asch simply did not wish to be made to stand for something he had not explicitly articulated himself. "For what I stand for, I'll die," he said, "but for what somebody else tells me I stand for, I object."[12] As for Guthrie, Asch probably wanted to remember him as an iconoclast, like himself. Yet although Guthrie avoided organized political movements most of his life, he made a sustained effort on behalf of People's Songs—columns, songs, advice, and his usual promotional zeal—at a time when his health was deteriorating noticeably.

On these two pillars—a politicized folk music and a revived interest in traditional jazz—stood Disc Records. Arguably a third pillar was represented by the Jazz at the Philharmonic recordings that were coming from Norman Granz. There were a number of propitious signs for Disc in early 1946, including a short article in the 25 February issue of *Time* entitled "Offbeat." The *Time* article announced an initial release of ten albums and described Asch as "the No. 1 recorder of out-of-the-way jazz, cowboy music and such exotic items as Paris street noises during the liberation, and little-heard Russian operas." Asch, the article continued,

> has almost a fear of hits and he brushes off commercial jazz
> as if it were an unmentionable disease. Unlike most record
> companies, which have lavished their scarce shellac on
> surefire songs, Asch frequently stops making an album just
> when it is selling well, so he can put out something
> else—which may or may not sell. . . . Asch calls his albums
> "basic music" to distinguish them from popular swing or the
> Gene Autry–Bob Wills kind of folk music.

It was a curious promotional ploy on Asch's part. Certainly there was a small audience that would respond to his call for an "authentic" music of the "folk" as opposed to the music we would today label country and western. But it was disingenuous of him to suggest that he might deliberately avoid hits. Asch might well have refused to release records whose only value was of a commercial kind, and indeed he did release records on the Disc label for highly circumscribed audiences, as he always had. But it was the commercial success of a relatively small number of jazz blockbusters that made possible his excursions into esoteric music and documentary recordings.

The first set of releases was indicative. It included an album of calypso music by Lord Invader, a Trinidadian whose real name was Rupert Grant. Lord Invader had previously recorded for Decca, a fair reflection of the extent to which this otherwise obscure music had become something of a rage among the American record-buying public. Max Gordon had happened upon the music accidently in 1939, and by featuring it periodically at the Village Vanguard he helped create a market for calypso among whites in New York and elsewhere. A second audience consisted largely of Trinidadian immigrants (and some other African Americans) in places such as Harlem.[13] Invader was a legitimate product of Trinidad's "calypso tent" competitions and came to New York after having established his reputation at home. But far from being an innocent from the islands, he had won a substantial settlement during the war over the authorship of the Andrews Sisters hit "Rum and Coca Cola," a song whose popularity was not diminished by the fact that it had been banned by four major radio networks for constituting free advertising and for corrupting the youth by its mention of rum![14] Calypso derived its popularity in part from its novelty, although for aficionados such as Fred Ramsey and Charles Edward Smith it was appealing for other reasons as well. It qualified as a kind of "roots" music, although increasingly the recordings were being made for the tastes of its North American audiences. Its practitioners were famed for their ability to spin satirical lyrics about topical occurrences and other events of immediate interest. One such number, about Lord Invader's trouble navigating New York subways, appeared on his album and generated some free publicity. "Lord Invader . . . had difficulty solving the intricacies of New York's subway system," reported *Down Beat.* "So he turned out a calypso song recounting the trials and tribulations of a stranger in New York's underground maze."[15]

Another calypso artist who recorded for Asch, Sir Lancelot (Lancelot Victor Edward Pinard), was also a member of People's Songs and wrote a letter to Seeger that appeared in the *Bulletin:* "Calypso singers are true people's artists, and Calypsos, like people's songs, come straight from the soul of the people; and too, like People's Songs, they are sprinkled with a fine seasoning of wit and satire."[16] His songs reflected People's Songs themes of democratic patriotism and world peace: "Century of the Common Man," "Defenders of Stalingrad," "Walk in Peace." Unlike Invader, however, Lancelot adopted calypso traditions only once he had moved to New York. Having come from an upper-middle-class family that kept a safe distance from the calypso tents, Lancelot's early musical training was in lieder and arias. As the calypso craze took hold, Lancelot was persuaded to sing calypso at the Vanguard and readily found an audience with the New York left. Back in Trinidad however,

Lancelot was shunned by both his embarrassed family and an unappreciative Trinidadian audience. Before the close of the war, Lancelot had settled in California, where he had a long career in films and commercials.[17]

Also among the first set of Disc releases was a new Leadbelly album (*Negro Folk Songs*), an album of *America's Favorite Songs* with Bess Lomax, Pete Seeger, Butch Hawes, and Tom Glazer, four sides by the New Orleans clarinetist Omer Simeon accompanied by James P. Johnson and George "Pops" Foster on drums, and *L'Honneur des Poètes*, a recording of four French resistance writers—Jean-Paul Sartre, François Mauriac, Paul Éluard, and Louis Aragon—recorded in Paris during the war. The Simeon sides show the influence of the Jazzmen enthusiasts now on the Disc payroll, whereas *America's Favorite Songs* reflect Asch's persistent interest in authentic folk music—"a high degree of authenticity," proclaimed the *Billboard* review.

Not everyone was equally convinced of the authenticity of the music that came from the likes of Pete Seeger. In a *Herald Tribune* review of one of the first People's Songs hootenannies, Seeger was singled out as a "good singer and an excellent banjo player." The review continued: "He has carefully learned what the folk singer does, and gives a good reproduction, especially on the instrument. . . . But he quite apparently is playing at being a mountaineer.[18] It was a criticism to which musicians who took their stand on authenticity were bound to be susceptible. But although Seeger may have been guilty of a certain amount of bumpkin posturing in this era, it is a misunderstanding to suggest that he intended to pass himself off as "the real thing." Seeger, Bess Lomax, and Tom Glazer were admittedly citified *interpreters* who wished to use folk musical forms to promote political ends, not to enshrine a changeless, romanticized folk music. Perhaps their intentions were clouded when they appeared on stage next to performers with rural origins, such as Guthrie, Hays, Sonny Terry, and Brownie McGhee. Yet this reflected the dual nature of their passions—rural folk music and progressive politics—and sometimes the two components did not fit together easily.

Granz was in town in June to supervise the first of what would become semiannual tours of the Jazz at the Philharmonic all-stars, and he met with Asch in order to arrange for additional volumes of the JATP recordings. *Billboard* had announced the release of volume 2, featuring Lester Young in April (the first on Disc), and an album entitled *Boogie at the Philharmonic* with Meade Lux Lewis appeared the following month. Sales were strong, though critics were not universally enthusiastic. Some found the crowd noise to be a gimmicky distraction, and others complained of poor mixing and bad surfaces. What the albums certainly succeeded in doing was to provide Granz with the capital to finance the national tours of his JATP units. Although a mid-June concert at Carnegie Hall featuring Buck Clayton and Lester Young received only a mixed review from *Down Beat,* the effect of the setting on the reputation of bebop jazz was considerable.[19]

Also by April there were clear signs that Stinson was going to make a go of it without Asch, as the company began to release new recordings of its own. But it was also releasing a good deal of material that came out of the collaboration, and it was quickly apparent that the attempts to demarcate clear lines of ownership in the agreements of the previous year had not been successful. Granz was particularly aggrieved that the first JATP album was still available through Stinson; in June *Down Beat* reported that the "ebullient and casually unpressed Mr. Granz" planned to sue Harris and Prosky for an accounting of royalties.[20]

The studio at 117 West Forty-sixth Street was no longer the casual place where musicians could drop in to record a few songs when the spirit (or hunger) moved them—those days were long over. The recording and production schedule quickly filled; Asch continued to do much of the recording himself, but in addition to the material that was coming to him from Granz he was scouting around for other usable masters. The Danish jazz impresario Timme Rosenkrantz had an apartment just east of Asch's studio on Forty-sixth Street to which he often invited jazz musicians and knowledgeable enthusiasts. Sometimes Rosenkrantz used these occasions to record the musicians, and during several evening in 1944 and 1945 he recorded pianist Erroll Garner. A session on 14 October 1945 resulted in four lovely piano solos: "Man O' Mine," "Oh, Lady Be Good," "Don't Blame Me," and "How High the Moon." These he sold to Asch, who in turn released the first three on album, which also included piano solos by Billy Kyle.[21] Another set of masters came to Asch from the somewhat unlikely pairing of Bunk Johnson's band and a gospel singer by the name of Ernestine Washington. The session was originally recorded for a short-lived outfit called Jubilee, whose owners—Herb Abramson and Ahmet Ertegun—would soon found Atlantic Records, the premier rhythm and blues label of the 1950s and 1960s. When the masters became available it was doubtlessly Ramsey who jumped at the opportunity to acquire them for Disc. Though poorly recorded with the singing distorted and the band muffled in the background, the playing is exuberant and of high quality.[22]

Many of those who had participated in the great marathon recording sessions of 1944 continued to record for Asch, but in a much more deliberate fashion and rarely together. In early February Josh White recorded four songs that became an album entitled *Women Blues*. Guthrie's musical interests were largely focussed upon his daughter Cathy Ann, who turned three that same month. Creating music with and for her enabled him to concentrate his creative energy, and that spring he recorded the first of his *Songs to Grow On* children's albums. It was a far more sober affair than the free-wheeling jam sessions with Cisco and the others. Marjorie was an active partner in the studio, making suggestions for words and melodies. The songs included "Wake Up," "Clean-O," and "Put Your Finger in the Air," which are today among Guthrie's better loved. The result was an album of three ten-inch discs entitled *Nursery Days*. Asch had been conscious of the commercial possibilities of "kiddie music" since his first Leadbelly release, and Guthrie's children's recordings reinforced his belief in its profitability and staying power. He was not alone—a *Down Beat* headline that fall proclaimed "Kiddie Albums Flood Market."[23] Predictably, the Left press was ecstatic over Guthrie's first recorded ventures into the field of children's music; the communist *People's World*, which had "discovered" Guthrie in 1938 (and for which Guthrie wrote his "Woody Sez" column), declared, "Disc gets an 'A' for putting Woodie [*sic*] Guthrie to work in the children's field. The result is some of the most delightful children's songs ever recorded."[24] But the mainstream press and music educators were equally enthusiastic. Over the years Guthrie's children's recordings sold consistently better than any of his others. The first *Songs to Grow On* album became part of a series entitled *Young Folksay* for which Asch hired a consultant by the name of Beatrice Landeck, a music educator and folk-song anthologist.

By contrast, Guthrie's political song-writing seemed to have lost its spark. He could still churn out long ballads about working-class struggles, but they tended to be rather literal and self-righteous. A mining explosion in Centralia, Illinois, in March the following year resulted in three ballads that People's Songs published as a twenty-five-cent broadside. Despite his attempt to create a "you were there" feeling, none had the power of "1913 Massacre" and "Ludlow Massacre," recorded during the war. Asch did record Guthrie singing one of the Centralia ballads, "The Dying Miner," although it was not released for almost thirty years. The chorus suggests the extent to which his lyric powers were failing:

> Dear sisters and brothers goodbye,
> Dear mother and father goodbye.
> My fingers are weak and I cannot write,
> Goodbye Centralia goodbye.©

Another attempt at the kind of "musical newspaper" that Guthrie and Asch envisioned resulted from a police attack on a black veteran in the South. The veteran, Isaac Woodward, was guilty of having attempted to use a white bathroom, a crime for which he paid with his eyesight. Guthrie sent the lyrics to "The Blinding of Isaac Woodward" to "Moe, and Marian, and all field hands" on 15 August; at Marjorie's suggestion he had set it to the tune of "The Great Dust Storm" from the Victor *Dust Bowl Ballads* album. He hoped that the new ballad might be part of a second documentary album, and in his cover letter he proposed several other songs that might go with it. The following day he performed it at a rally in New York's Lewisohn Stadium in support of Woodward. Guthrie came on for a crowd of thirty-one thousand following Cab Calloway, Milton Berle, Orson Welles, Billie Holiday, and Woodward himself (as well as many others). Because the ballad was unmanageably long, Guthrie had written it on scraps of paper that kept blowing off the music stand. By the time he had finished, he had lost most of his audience.[25]

If contemporary events were not inspiring Guthrie sufficiently, historical events offered little more. Late in 1945 Asch lent Guthrie several pamphlets about the trial and execution of Sacco and Vanzetti. Having lived through the events as a young adult, Asch, like many leftists, held to them as one of the most unambiguous instances of government persecution of the Left (Asch would later find the circumstances of the Rosenberg trial and execution to be considerably more clouded). Nathan's use of the Sacco and Vanzetti execution in *Payday* was very much on Asch's mind when he suggested to Guthrie that he attempt a ballad about the Italian anarchists. On 2 January Guthrie wrote to Asch: "There is plenty here for a good album. . . . There is a ballad about Sacco, one about Vanzetti, one about the scene of the holdup and killing, one about the arrest and foney [sic] trial, one about all of the screwy witnesses and, one about a general shot of the whole thing, the whole story." For the time being, however, Guthrie thought that *one* Sacco and Vanzetti song would do, and that he would include it in an album of "labor martyrs" with songs about the Haymarket bombing, the Scottsboro Boys, Joe Hill, Mother Bloor (of Trinidad, Colorado), and several others. In the same letter he also proposed a new Dust Bowl album, which would depart from the Victor collection in several respects:

> We can do a better job from every point of view if we do a new one, more progressive, bring in the strike songs, spirituals, of the migrant workers. We can use mouth harp, guitar, singing, maybe a tune or two of old Dust Bowl Ballads, but give it a more organized twist and picture the fights and beatings plainer. We can bring in the big crops, factories, mines, timbers, dams, and building ships and planes, and show how they love you when they need you and hate you when they don't. I have thought a lot about how different I would do those Victor Records if I had them to do over again.[26]

Of the various projects of topical songs it was, in fact, the new Dust Bowl album—*Ballads from the Dust Bowl*—that was first completed. In the end it was the *only* Guthrie album to appear on Disc, with the exception of the children's records. It was *not* more organized than the Victor album, and in fact to fill it out he had included a song—"Talking Columbia Blues"—from the Bonneville Dam project. For most of the material Guthrie dipped into his repertoire of the preceding years and pulled out some gems: "Hard Traveling," "Pastures of Plenty," "Rambling Blues." The performances were clean and energetic. The new version of "Hard Traveling" in particular was faster and more polished than the version he had recorded with Sonny Terry and Cisco Houston in 1944, and he was able to include a seventh verse that was left off the earlier recording:

> I've been walkin' that Lincoln Highway, I thought you knowed,
> I've been hitting that '66' way down the road;
> Heavy load and a worried mind, looking for a woman that's hard to find,
> I've been hitting some hard traveling lord.©

In June he wrote to Asch, Distler, and David Stone Martin inquiring about the new Dust Bowl album: "How are the 'Ballads from the Dust Bowl' going, doing, and being received?" Guthrie was as usual in the midst of several projects simultaneously, including the assemblage of his dozens of song lyrics in poem form for a book that Alan Lomax was compiling. The book of lyrics in turn made him feel that he had a great deal yet to record: "To my way of thinking, we've not yet touched on the bulk of my best things. No, not even with the several jillion masters which we made together with Sonny, Cisco and others." He was performing a good deal as well. And in addition he wrote to Asch and the others about a book that he planned to do with them that would include musical notation for his songs as well as introductions and related stories. This, remarkably, would come to fruition the following year as a thin volume entitled *American Folksong: Woody Guthrie*, published by Disc Records and edited by Asch, and including a relatively unvarnished autobiographical sketch.

To spur Guthrie along on the Sacco and Vanzetti project, Asch gave him a sum of money—he claimed later that it was a couple thousand dollars, but it was undoubtedly substantially less—in order to travel to those sites outside of Boston where the holdup, murder, trial, and executions took place.[27] In March Guthrie began to assemble some notes for the project, trying to imagine what America looked like through the eyes of Italian immigrants in the 1920s. In the autumn he set out to New England with Cisco, who had been sent along by Asch in order to assure the quality of the music. Relying on public transportation, they did their best to visit the relevant locations and absorb the atmosphere. One of them had brought along a snapshot camera, and the photos that resulted—eventually deposited in Asch's office—convey a chilly desolation and aimlessness. Something was not working. Asch had a penchant for universalism that tended to blind him to the fact that musical genres and lyrical contents were not always interchangeable.[28] It led him, for example, to suggest to Guthrie that he write a song in celebration of Chanukah.[29] Guthrie's musical roots in the rural southwest suited him well when writing of midwestern mining disasters and western farm laborers, but the story of two Italian immigrants might well have required a kind of musical setting that Guthrie could not provide.

Upon their return to New York Guthrie did record several Sacco and Vanzetti compositions in Asch Studios, and a three-disc album entitled *The Passion of Sacco and Vanzetti* appeared in the Asch catalogue the following year. But the album was not actually released until Asch issued it on LP in 1960. Guthrie himself knew that the Sacco and Vanzetti material was not working and said as much to Asch in a letter of 4 November:

> I think that the best thing we can do is to postpone the recorded songs based on the frame up of Sacco and Vanzetti. If

it means to delay them from this Christmas Holiday Season unto the next Christmas Holiday Season, I suppose, it must be for the best. To delay the most important dozen songs I have ever worked on is more of a pain to me than it could ever be to you. But, I feel like the trip up to Boston and its outskirts was just a little bit hurried and hasty. I did not get to go to all of the spots and places so plainly mentioned in the pamphlets and books. . . . I just feel rushed, and I don't want this album about Sacco and Vanzetti to feel rushed, to smell rushed, to taste rushed, nor to sound like something rushed. . . . So I say, let's forget about the Sacco and Vanzetti album for the time being. It will be lots better when I get a car and my own way of traveling from one scene to the other one.

Guthrie closed with a scrawling, expanding script that covered the bottom half of the paper: "I'm drunk as hell today, been that way for several days, hope you are the same, Woody Guthrie. I refuse to write these songs while I'm drunk and looks like I'll be drunk for a long time."[30]

Ramsey was meanwhile branching out in an assortment of directions. He was ingratiating himself with Leadbelly in various ways, even taking up residence with Huddie and Martha for a period of time. He wrote the notes for the first Disc Leadbelly release, and would figure among Leadbelly's staunchest support- ers in the few remaining years of his life. In April 1946 a London publisher released a thin volume about Leadbelly that featured two pieces by Ramsey, one a set of reminiscences about the singer's appearances at the Village Vanguard and the other a dis- cography.[31] Another project involved an entire album of drum solos by Baby Dodds in which the legendary drummer attempted to trace the history of jazz drumming. Perhaps it was the Ernestine Washington set that turned Ramsey's interest to still other kinds of southern roots music, particularly gospel. Having become Asch's scout for unusual material, he began to attend large gospel shows uptown in Harlem. From these he arranged to release recordings of two groups of gospel singers—the Two Keys and the Thrasher Wonders—who exemplified the genre as presented in rural southern black churches rather than on the concert stage. The Thrasher Wonders were a young group from rural Wetumpka, Alabama, who had been received in the White House by Eleanor Roosevelt. Two members, Gerhart and Andrew Thrasher, would later sing with the Silvertone Singers and then make the jump to secular music as members of the Drifters ("Under the Board-walk").[32] The Two Keys (alternately called the Gospel Keys or Two Gospel Keys) were elderly women who had sung with the Church of God in Christ—the largest organization of black Pentecostal churches—in Atlanta. "Mother" Jones and Emma Daniel accompanied themselves on tambourine and guitar and had resorted to street singing since coming to New York. When Ramsey and Asch acquired the masters to their recent Jubilee Records session (in the same acquisition as the Ernestine Washington–Bunk Johnson sides), a "manager" materialized who brought Jones and Daniel to another recording outfit where they cut additional sides. However, they had signed an exclusive contract that Asch invoked in order to acquire the other sides as well. Ramsey remembered the resultant legal wrangling as something of a fiasco, but it was becoming "business as usual" for Asch, as it was for most of the recording industry. They had a similar experience with the Baby Dodds drum-solo recording. According to Ramsey another traditional jazz enthusiast, Rudi Blesh, got wind of his plans for a Baby Dodds drum solo recording and before Ramsey could get Dodds to Asch Studios (but after he had made the contractual arrangements) Blesh had Dodds record an album of drum solos in a rival studio. In this instance, however, there seemed to be room for two such recordings, both of which were marketed, though on different labels.[33]

To the extent that the urban record-buying public was accustomed to purchasing gospel recordings—and it was then almost exclusively the provenance of African American listeners—the expectation was that the raw and emotional music of the (originally) Pentecostal churches would be dressed up and smoothed out a bit for the recorded media. Asch and Ramsey probably did not give much thought to who the audience might be for this more "primitive" example of the gospel repertoire, but (if it existed at all) it was almost certainly *not* the record-buying public in Harlem. Record stores in that part of the city were barely on the Disc sales route. Asch did release a ten-inch single record disc of the Thrasher Wonders with the likely intention of garnering some jukebox play, but it was a rare and desultory foray into a market he otherwise ignored. Disc's gospel recordings were—like most of the remainder of the Disc catalogue—intended for white, politically progressive intellectuals. Asch and Ramsey shared an intellectual (and educational) mission to discover the origins of contemporary African American music, and in the unadulterated, non-commercial music of the black church they had found an important thread.

By August 1946, in just over half a year, Disc Records had released an astonishing fifty-four titles. They were easily as varied as the Asch-Stinson list had been, representing the categories of contemporary jazz (there were four Granz titles by this time), traditional jazz, folk music, classical music, and spoken word. Asch had also returned to the field of cantorials, releasing albums by Leibele Waldman again as well as Cantor Jonah Binder. Although Mary Lou Williams would soon cease to be an exclusive artist for Asch, recording sides for Victor late in the year, she was nonetheless represented in the Disc catalogue with a lovely album of piano solos, as well as two unusual jazz recordings of other musicians that she "supervised." *Billboard* described her solo piano improvisations as "sheer melodic beauty," and *Down Beat* reported "an engaging simplicity to Mary Lou's playing which is a welcome relief amidst all the frantic scale players."[34] Two new folk musicians whose interests were more scholarly and artistic than political had joined the Asch roster. Adelaide Van Wey was a classically trained alto who had developed an interest in the creole (mixed French, Spanish, and African) songs of Louisiana. Although she did not qualify as a traditional singer, for her contributions to the preservation of Louisiana culture she would later receive an award from the city of New Orleans. Frank Warner was becoming the preeminent collector of songs from the Hudson River Valley and would over time become one of the most important performers and disseminators of traditional songs of the northeastern United States.

Disc recordings were attracting attention from a number of quarters. Asch received a fan letter from a Chicago disc jockey who had been involved with that city's People's Songs chapter. In July Studs Terkel wrote:

> You might tab this letter . . . "A Platter Jockey's Discovery." I'm passing this info to you for what it's worth . . . because the recordings of your company are most directly involved. . . . I can judge only from my personal experience . . . but here's my point, gentlemen. Folk music, the real stuff, done by real artists, such as those whose stuff you've been waxing, is definitely on the upbeat with the public. If adequately plugged and promoted, it can be as COMMERCIALLY socko as any Hit Parader. What was once my hunch is now my firm conviction.

> Folk music pays off. A midwestern radio audience of campus
> kids, boilermakers, and stenos is proof.[35]

Terkel mentioned the letters he had received in response to records by Leadbelly, Burl Ives, Woody Guthrie, Josh White, and
Richard Dyer-Bennett. "Aunt Nancy" (later popularized as "Go Tell
Aunt Rhody") with Seeger on the *America's Favorite Songs* album had
been a particular hit. In addition to periodic mention in the national press, Disc recordings were being reviewed in newspapers
in San Francisco, Pittsburgh, and San Antonio.

Asch began to lavish considerable attention on the Disc catalogue itself, printing it as a substantial booklet that included descriptions of the records, excerpts from reviews, and dozens of
lovely, playful drawings by David Stone Martin and Ben Shahn. His
brother Nathan wrote to him from San Francisco that September
in order to thank him for having sent a check, and to praise the
catalogue:

> Thanks for the check, and for your catalogue, which is beauti-
> ful, dignified and serious. It is possible, as you have done, to
> make even so commercial a thing as a catalogue, something
> in itself and not quite commercial. There is a new book of po-
> ems by Cummings, which has a line in it, "A salesman is an it
> that stinks," and by corollary, how much more stinking is the
> usual inanimate salesman, the catalog. More power to you.
> You are doing something which is good and which I respect.[36]

Nathan went on to describe the satisfaction he took from the
book he was working on (a book that was never published) and
concluded by saying that he thought he was "living a rather happy
life now." His tentativeness bespeaks the difficulty that both of the
older Asch children had in finding pleasure in life. Nathan found
periodic contentment in his friendships with both men and
women but remained a relatively tormented person much of his
life. Moe, by contrast, was frequently uncomfortable in the presence of others, and remained an emotionally stunted, socially
isolated person. And like Nathan, he continued to be tormented
about the worthiness of his work. Nathan's soothing words about
the dignity and seriousness of his catalogue have embedded
within them the hovering presence of "father," to whom the work
of his sons was constantly offered up in hope of receiving a
casually tossed bone of approval.

Things were going so well for Disc that summer that there was talk of incorporating it. Each artist who recorded *exclusively* with Disc would be entitled to a "participating certificate" for each Disc album recorded, entitling its holder to a portion of the profits though not a share of the company's "stock." There were in fact some exclusive Disc artists. Legendary bluesman Lonnie Johnson had signed with Disc the previous month, and although there was certainly less formality in the arrangements with Guthrie, Seeger, Leadbelly, and other folk artists, they were exclusive Disc artists in the sense that few other labels would have had much interest in recording them. The plan was careful to involve the musicians in the artistic decisions of the company while retaining for Asch maximum "freedom of action as to management and finances."[37] Nothing came of the plan, although its socialist overtones are an interesting reflection of Asch's political convictions. Although the plan did not specify that royalties were to be eliminated, the implication was that payments were to be made partly on the basis of the number of albums an artist had recorded rather than the number of albums *sold*. It is not hard to see why some of the more ambitious Disc artists may have found the plan less than enticing. And because it did not have the effect of raising capital for Asch (which he would soon need) and deprived him of some of his autonomy, it could not have remained attractive to him for long either.

Stinson remained a substantial irritant to Asch. Among the Stinson releases the previous spring that no doubt galled Asch was a portion of Mary Lou Williams's *Zodiac Suite*. Also, Harris was not consistently fulfilling the terms of the artists' contracts that he had taken over from Asch, and Asch was taking some of the heat for it. In June, for example, *Down Beat* reported that the "'ebullient and casually unpressed Mr Granz,' as one of the New York dailies called him[,] . . . was planning to sue Stinson Trading for an accounting of royalties on his first Jazz at the Philharmonic album." Late in the year Asch received a letter from a lawyer representing Burl Ives regarding nonpayment of royalties. And there were others.[38] In August Joseph Corn was preparing a suit against Harris and Prosky on behalf of Asch. Their primary offense was in having pressed and sold a dozen of Asch's Jewish titles that predated the original Asch-Stinson agreement and thus should have been off limits to Stinson. Asch apparently received the information from the pressing plant, because Corn knew the precise number of each title as well as the dates on which they had been pressed—on five dates that February a total of more than forty-three hundred discs were pressed contrary to the agreements of the previous December. It took the remainder of the year for the suit to be settled, but for Asch it was well worth it, for it became the means by which he began to reclaim many of the titles he had relinquished to Harris and Prosky the year before. The new agreement, signed in January of the following year, called for Harris and Prosky to deliver quantities of albums as punitive damages—several dozen, for instance, of the Burl Ives and the first JATP albums, which were to be delivered to Asch at no cost, and another six hundred of various jazz titles to be sold to Asch at wholesale prices. More significant, Prosky and Harris agreed to deliver to Asch the masters to five albums: Guthrie's *American Documentary*, Kreymbourg's recordings of poetry, *Strictly G.I.*, the Langston Hughes album, and the Greta Keller album. Thereafter these albums would be Asch's property, and Stinson would be forbidden to press or sell them.[39]

The relationship with Granz remained for the time-being a mutually beneficial one, although the music was still not consistently winning the admiration of critics. Volume 3 of JATP, recorded the previous January, appeared in time for Christmas that year. The *Down Beat* reviewer complained of the sound quality as well as the playing of almost everyone—Charlie Ventura, Dizzy Gillespie, Mel Powell, even Lester Young, none of whom he found up to their usual quality. Only Charlie Parker escaped criticism. "Granz is a colorful character who, despite the many enemies his sometimes bumptiousness makes, has accomplished something in jazz presentations," the reviewer noted. "But if he is going to charge $3.40 for two records . . . they must be better recorded and better jazz than this."

The reviewer also chides Granz for having used pseudonyms for two of the performers: Dizzy Gillespie is identified on the album as "John Birks, 'dizzy' trumpet," and Mel Powell as "Joe Jackson, 'mellow piano.'" Granz had ostensibly complained once about other manufacturers who engaged in precisely such attempts to get around musicians' contractual obligations to other firms. "How now, Norman?" inquired the reviewer. In reply Granz claimed that Powell and Gillespie had been under contract to him and that they had *preferred* to use the pseudonyms. Granz's defense became particularly disingenuous with the appearance of JATP volumes 4 and 5, featuring "Shorty Nadine" on the piano. Released around New Year's and June 1947, respectively, these would be the last volumes of the JATP series to appear on Disc. Both were taken from masters recorded at the 2 July 1944 JATP concert in Los Angeles. "Shorty Nadine" was the nickname of Nat "King" Cole's first wife; Cole was already under contract to the fledgling Capitol label at the time of the 1944 JATP concert and consequently chose his wife's nickname for the Disc release in order to avoid jeopardizing what would become a lifelong collaboration with Capitol. For their part, executives at Capitol probably cared little about Cole's appearance on Disc because it did not infringe on his rocketing career as a vocalist on Capitol. The *Billboard* reviewer of the albums perpetuated the deception, but in *Down Beat* Cole was openly identified as the pianist on the session: "Throughout this entire album Nat shows himself not only a superb soloist but a rhythm man capable of driving yet holding down even such madmen as [Illinois] Jacquet who squeals rather inanely on the last side." The other standout soloist on volumes 4 and 5 was Asch's old Radio Laboratories customer, Les Paul. *Down Beat* still complained about Granz's recording but held out some hope for the future of "live" recording: "Despite its very bad editing, execrable balance, abortional taste, and poor surfaces, there are spots in this album which justify the concert theory of recording, at least in part."[40] The twelve sides of these two volumes not only launched Paul's career as a guitarist and established Cole's credibility as a pianist (despite his lasting reputation as a singer) but also became enduring jazz classics of the war era. They are technically masterful, full of energy and inventiveness, and they created a huge audience for Granz's music.[41]

Granz presented Asch with one other set of Nat Cole sides for which pseudonyms were *not* used—perhaps because, having been recorded in 1942 they predated the arrangement with Capitol (as well as the JATP recordings). They featured Cole at the piano, Illinois Jacquet (saxophone), Shad Collins (trumpet), J. C. Heard on drums, and Gene Englund on bass. The four twelve-inch sides were ostensibly recorded "primarily for the personal kicks of the musicians" themselves and never really intended for commercial release. *Down Beat*, as usual, did not like them: "This is not a particularly good album and while part of the fault lies with one of those sessions that just didn't jell, supervisor Norman Granz should be stood in the corner pondering on the fate of little boys in too big a hurry to balance a group properly."[42] Whatever their merit, Asch apparently wanted the Cole sides badly and paid Granz handsomely for them.[43] His plan was to have them shipped to stores in time for the Christmas shopping season, and he consequently had a very large number of them pressed. Although much of the Disc audience was still in New York City, Asch had a network of distributors that would eventually reach west to Denver and Seattle, north to Pierre, South Dakota, and south to Richmond, St. Louis, and El Paso. Perhaps due to delays in pressing production, the timing of the shipments became critical. The first snowfall of the year arrived on Friday, 20 December, and though there were not massive accumulations, traffic was snarled for hours throughout the city and 113 flights were canceled at La Guardia. Then the weekend intervened, and by the time Asch was able to have the records loaded onto outgoing flights, it was too late. The unneeded inventory languished in his warehouse for months.[44]

Thus Granz's albums were tying up vast amounts of Asch's capital and threatened to swamp what was still a very modest operation. Yet they continued to represent only a fraction of the projects coming out of 117 West Forty-sixth Street in the autumn and winter of 1946–47. Asch's release of ten-inch discs by legendary blues singer and guitarist Lonnie Johnson in August and September constituted a rare foray into the world of commercial jukebox sales. Lonnie Johnson was a sophisticated guitarist who could hold his own with a jazz band when necessary. He had been a commercial success in the race records market of the 1920s and had recorded most recently for Bluebird, Victor's race label, but was between contracts when Asch encountered him.[45] Asch uncharacteristically supported the first Johnson release, "I'm in Love with Love" and "Tell Me Why," with two advertisements in *Billboard*. The first began "Big Blues News for Smart Juke Boxes." The second read "August 31 we announced 'Big Blues News'—Now we Say Big Blues Scoop! for Wise Juke Boxes. . . . Lonnie Johnson recording exclusively for Disc is sweeping the juke box front with two blues and guitar originals." There was some wishful thinking implied in the latter. But what is more interesting is the fact that Asch was making *any* attempt to reach a jukebox audience. This was different from his Gospel Keys albums or his Bunk Johnson/Ernestine Washington albums, which in their raw "authenticity" were really aimed at educated, politically progressive white audiences. With the Lonnie Johnson release (and two additional singles that followed) Asch was attempting to reach audiences such as those in Harlem that had been listening to Lonnie Johnson for decades. The fact that he did not often reach out to this audience suggests that it did not meet with much success, and this in turn need not have come to him as a surprise. Asch did not have any sales experience with the black record-buying public. Still more significant was that Johnson, like Leadbelly some years earlier, was in *this* instance playing a kind of blues no longer considered contemporary among African American audiences, who were currently hot on "jump" and "jive" music.[46] Interestingly, only a little over a year later, in 1948, Johnson scored the biggest hit of his life with "Tomorrow Night" on King Records, which stylistically represented an early rhythm and blues recording.[47] By then Asch and Johnson had fallen out rather badly—over royalties, as usual. Johnson wrote to Asch on AFM stationery in May of 1948:

> This is to let you know that I have nothing else to say to you in regards of my royalty. It's in the hand of my attorney and Local 802 of New York. Now I will see if you give them the run around like you been giving me since 1946. . . . You promised me that I would get my royalty and a full statement and you know when you answered my letter you didn't intend to pay me so you pay my attorney; good luck cause you will need it.

In a reply a week later Asch defended his payment practices and insisted that with the exception of an accounting of royalties which was due shortly, he had paid Johnson fairly. Although Asch could be as angry and defensive in a letter as he often was in his speech, in this instance he was conciliatory and measured. In fact, their relationship was not spoiled, and Asch recorded a demo of Johnson in the 1960s while on a trip to Chicago.

Ramsey and Charles Edward Smith continued to keep Asch Studios busy with various recording projects. The Disc catalogue divided most jazz artists between "innovators in jazz" and "perpetuators in jazz," and Ramsey and Smith's projects invariably fell among the latter. They included several white "traditionalists," including pianist Joe Sullivan, clarinetist Pee Wee Russell, and cornetist Muggsy Spanier. All three had come out of Chicago and its very accomplished (mostly white) traditional jazz bands. Sullivan had led a racially mixed band in the only possible venue (Café Society) during 1939 and 1940, and it was also a racially mixed quartet that he brought to Asch Studios—Sidney Bechet, "Pops" Foster, and George Wettling. One critic, while unkindly describing Sullivan as a "thoughtful but not very adventurous pianist," nonetheless described the Disc sides as among his best.[48] Spanier and Russell graced each other's albums and, under Charles Edward Smith's direction, attempted to recreate their work of the 1930s. The Russell album was generally well received by the *Down Beat* reviewer, who described it as "strictly a Village gathering." Vic Dickenson's trombone playing was singled out for particular praise, and both Spanier and Russell were described as in "better than usual form." The reviewer added that in his notes Charles Edward Smith had remarked that "Pee Wee sings just like he plays. If I were Pee Wee, I would smite him dead for that crack."[49] Spanier's recording unit was ungenerously described as "the old faithfuls again" in *Down Beat*, whereas *Billboard* reported hopefully that "jazz diskophiles will find this set much to their liking."[50]

People's Songs was attracting some national attention by the winter of 1946–47. *Time* had reported a People's Songs hootenanny that had drawn an audience of a thousand the previous April, and the *New York Herald Tribune* reported on another the following month. In December of that year *Down Beat* displayed a photograph of several prominent People's Songsters, including Woody Guthrie and Leadbelly, who were in Chicago at a preconcert party for Josh White.[51] Despite any lingering ambivalence Asch may have had about the organization, he knew that its membership coincided almost exactly with his audience. A half-page advertisement on the back page of the November 1946 issue of *People's Songs* bore the banner:

OUR "SINGING TOMORROWS" ARE HERALDED BY PEOPLE'S SONGS TODAY *DISC* HELPS TO OPEN UP NEW SOURCES OF MUSICAL MATE-RIAL IN MANY RECORDINGS OF *People's Songs* ARTISTS

In the same issue the first People's Songs record album was announced—Asch would be releasing *Roll the Union On* the following 10 December; any People's Songster who signed up six new members would receive a free copy of the six-sided album. It had been recorded at Asch Studios and featured Pete Seeger, Lee Hays, Dock Reese, Hally Wood, Butch Hawes, Lou Kleinman, and Bess Lomax Hawes. A full-page advertisement for the record appeared in *People's Songs* in February–March 1947. And although it bore Asch's address, it was released on the Union Records label—and appeared in the Disc catalogue on Asch Records! (By then the one-year restraint on the commercial use of his own name had lapsed.) Asch apparently created the Union Records label in order to release material of an explicitly political nature, although it was certainly not all radical in nature—among the Union Records releases was the 1933 inaugural address of Asch's political hero, Franklin Roosevelt. But by his use of at least two alternate labels for the People's Songs album, Asch seems to have been trying to protect Disc from political repercussions. The songs on *Roll the Union On* were not, finally, so very radical; none were either pro-Soviet or procommunist, although two of them—"Listen Mr. Bilbo" by New Yorkers Bob and Adrienne Claiborne and "The Rankin Tree" by Lee Hays and Walter Lowenfels—skewered two of the more venomously racist and anti-Semitic congressmen currently in office. Most of the songs celebrated working people and unions. "Put It on the Ground" was a tongue-in-cheek jibe at American patriotic propaganda:

> Oh, if you wanta raise in pay, All you gotto do is
> Go and ask your boss for it, And he will give it to you.
> Chorus: Put it on the ground, Spread it all around,
> Dig it with a hoe, It will make your flowers grow.
> For men who own the industries, I'm sheddin' bitter tears;
> they haven't made a single dime, In over thirty years.
> "The cost of livin' aint so high," I told my wife Miranda,
> "This talk of cost of livin' bein' up, Why it is Rooshian propaganda."
> It's fun to work on holidays, Or when the day is done;
> Why would they pay us overtime, For having so much fun.

As harmlessly sophomoric as they seemed, lyrics such as these would soon be getting several People's Songsters in trouble with the former FBI men and self-appointed vigilantes who founded Counterattack in May 1947—and later with HUAC. Counterattack published a weekly newsletter that compiled the names of those who were thought to be affiliated with "the most important aspects of Communist activity in America."[52]

As if he did not have enough to keep him busy, Asch became involved in the production of a concert in the fall of 1946. In fact, an entire concert production outfit was established—Folkways Concerts—although there is no evidence that there were any concerts after the first, on 26 September at Town Hall, featuring Leadbelly. Bina Houston, Cisco's wife, had a hand in the arrangements, as did Fred Ramsey. Originally the concert was also to have included Cisco Houston, Brownie McGhee, and Sonny Terry, but either out of economy or principle the producers eschewed the smorgasbord approach of the "hootnanies" [sic] and settled upon a concert with just Leadbelly and Terry. "Folk music," the producers maintained in their program,

> should NOT be a heterogenous potpourri, but rather an integral representation of one artist or group. Therefore it is FOLK-WAYS intention to present concerts featuring homogeneous ensembles or individual artists whom we feel have enough of value to convey to maintain audience interest. . . . FOLKWAYS CONCERTS intends to pass on the attendant economy in talent expenditures to our patrons.

Asch paid Leadbelly in cash following the concert and in order to avoid future misunderstanding had Leadbelly write across an envelope "received in full all moneys in connection with Town Hall concert" and sign his name. In point of fact, Leadbelly was continuing to feel agitated over his financial dealings with Asch. The following month he wrote to Asch, "I don't think you are treating right about the records I made for you" and demanded that Asch send him a check for $150. Three days later Leadbelly was writing to Asch again, offering to sell his rights to all of the recordings he had made for Asch (with the exception of those in the possession of Stinson) for the sum of $700.[53] Matters continued to deteriorate between them until, threatened by lawsuit, Asch agreed to settle with Leadbelly for an unspecified sum of money the following June.[54]

Leadbelly was facing considerable financial pressure that fall and winter, after his calamitous attempt at a Hollywood career the previous year. Neither his records sales nor his occasional concert appearances provided him and Martha with steady income. Woody Guthrie, by contrast, was facing a calamity of a very different sort, though one that was almost as familiar to him as insolvency was to Leadbelly. On Sunday, 9 February, Marjorie left little Cathy Ann—who had just passed her fourth birthday—alone in the apartment on Mermaid Avenue while she ran across the street for a moment for some oranges. She was then pregnant with her second child (it would be a boy, named Arlo) and was concerned about getting enough vitamin C. Woody was away performing for a union audience in Elizabeth, New Jersey. In the five minutes that she was away, some faulty wiring in an old radio caught fire, and although the ensuing blaze was quickly extinguished Cathy Ann was burned over most of her body. Her parents kept a vigil at Coney Island Hospital through the night, but by morning she was dead.

The effect on Woody and Marjorie was immeasurable. They attempted to put up a brave front and even appeared at a scheduled children's concert several days later. But the combination of this event and the progressive encroachment of Huntington's disease, though still undiagnosed and usually mistaken for drunkenness by those around him, left Guthrie broken. He remained energetic—the disease in fact generated a kind of manic and slightly scrambled mental activity—and in the ensuing months worked furiously on a book entitled *Seeds of Man,* which derived from a section that had been cut from *Bound for Glory.*[55] He also performed periodically for People's Songs, though he was increasingly selective about the occasions, and somewhat to the relief of Marjorie he began to travel again. In April 1947 he wrote to Asch, Marian Distler, and "the Martins" from Spokane, Washington. A radio station was playing his Bonneville Dam recordings, and he was certain they would promote an album of Pacific Northwest songs if Asch were to release one:

> There is an endless spring of good material in every part of
> our country, jobs been done, disasters, battles and so on and
> such an album as King Columbia folksongs and ballads
> would cause half of these people to grab up their pencils and
> commence scratching around to make up some song that's
> been running them crazy for twenty years. . . . I wish our next
> album could be on this very track. It would even hold lots of
> appeal in other parts of the world, maybe it could turn out to
> be a Grownup Songs to Work On. Think it over.

There would not be another Woody Guthrie album. But this did not prevent Guthrie from churning out additional ideas. In June, home again in Coney Island, he wrote to "Dear Discs" about his discovery of some ballads he had written while in the army, based on his collection of newspaper clippings. "I'd put lots of my faith," he wrote, "if not all of it, in them to make a good album to match some of the kids songs." He proposed that this album of GI songs, and the Pacific Northwest album, be his next two projects. In the same letter he also noted that he and Marjorie were working on an illustrated book of his *Songs to Grow On* (it would not appear in print until 1992) and closed with a scribbled note about a couple of Sacco and Vanzetti songs he had found to round out that as yet unreleased album. The letter was signed Woody, Marjorie, and Cathy (Little Woody or Little Marjorie) Guthrie, though Cathy had been dead for more than four months. Two days later he wrote again, proposing an album of songs about Abe Lincoln: "Hey Disc—I made you my promise some good long time back that I was going to look through my shelf of good books and fish out this Modern Library one which is full of the life and writings of Abe Lincoln, amongst which, I run acrost and copied out these three poetic ballads made up by him." He proposed putting the lyrics to music and adding three songs of his own "about things that happened to Abe, and during his time here. . . . My three, and Abe's three, will make up a whangdangdoozier of an album dedicated to maybe the fullest grown man we ever did have for President."

Guthrie wrote again on 5 July, as he and assorted dancing and folk-singing well-wishers waited for Marjorie to give birth. Guthrie had been playing a new Disc release entitled *Folk Music of the Central East* for everyone who came in the door, and he was wildly enthusiastic about it: "I can't understand one single word of this Central Eastern lingo, but by hearing these songs I know more about our humanly race than I could learn by reading a thousand Congressional Reports." The album was the first release to result from Asch's recent collaboration with Harold Courlander. Richard Dyer-Bennett had introduced Asch to Courlander, a neighbor who traveled in similar leftist, folk music circles. Courlander had a number of recordings of authentic folk music that he had recorded on site in Haiti, Cuba, and Eritrea (then part of Ethiopia) and was mildly interested in finding a way to have them released commercially to the public. He had been working through ethnomusicologist George Herzog, then at Columbia University, who had arranged to have one set of the recordings pressed for commercial sale. But Herzog had not the faintest idea of how to distribute them, and relations between Courlander and Herzog were strained. Some negotiations with Columbia Records had also bogged down—they were put off by the magnitude of the project that Herzog had had in mind—so Courlander was receptive when Dyer-Bennett suggested that he approach Asch.

Courlander represented a dying breed of self-trained ethnographers whose enthusiasm for and sensitivity to world ethnic music resulted in some of the most important collecting of the midcentury. He considered himself a *writer* first and went to Haiti straight out of the University of Michigan, in 1932, in order to provide the setting for an extended piece of fiction he envisaged. Little had been published in English on Haiti at the time, with the exception of W. B. Seabrook's *Magic Island* three years earlier, which provided a sentimental and occasionally condescending view of island culture.[56] Courlander was soon intrigued by the music and ritual of Haitian vodun, and it became the abiding passion of his life. His first stay lasted for six or seven months, and although it was another two years before he returned, thereafter he managed a yearly visit until the end of the decade. He initially transcribed song lyrics and melodies by hand, but by 1939 the inadequacies of this method convinced him to bring along a cumbersome disc recorder—"portable" if you had a donkey, he later recounted. Until his work was interrupted by the war, he recorded a steady stream of singers and musicians in an isolated room at the back of the hotel where he stayed, accumulating over four hundred sides of Haitian music alone. Additional trips to other Caribbean islands—particularly Cuba in 1941, where he was also able to record—allowed him to place Haitian religion in the broader context of the Afro-Caribbean world. By the time he published *Haiti Singing* in 1939 he had firmly subscribed to the notion—only just gaining meager currency through the work of linguist Lorenzo Dow Turner, the anthropologist Melville Herskovitz, and a very few others—that much of Negro culture in the New World was African in origin. And when it came to parts of the Caribbean, such as Haiti and Cuba, it was possible to think of them as extensions of a broadly conceived African cultural area.

In 1942 Courlander had an opportunity to perform war-sensitive work for an aircraft company in Ethiopia, and he seized it as a chance to learn more about the African origins of Afro-Caribbean culture. He sent his disc recorder on ahead with a convoy of ships that was torpedoed off the coast of Madagascar, and he was in Ethiopia several months before he was able to locate another recorder. In the meantime, he had been making the acquaintance of a broad range of Eritrean, Ethiopian, and Sudanese singers, orators, and instrumentalists, many of whom came to Courlander's makeshift recording studio in a bunker on the edge of the airfield. When Courlander left Eritrea in 1943 war regulations prevented him from bringing the forty-five acetates he had recorded back with him. So he left them with a local importer-exporter in two wooden crates, with instructions to have them shipped to the States at the close of the war. In 1945, through the efforts of the Office of War Information (for whom he was now working) and his colleague Henry Cowell (then OWI's music consultant), Courlander was able to trace and recover one of the boxes of acetates; the other never appeared.[57]

Asch not only agreed to release Courlander's recordings from Haiti, Cuba, and Ethiopia but also initiated an entire Ethnic series, of which Courlander was to be editor. *Down Beat* announced the inauguration of the series in March, describing the initial series as "authentic folk music from Haiti, Cuba, Russia, Ethiopia and other musically 'neglected' points," recorded "on location."[58] "Besides their own intrinsic power and value," read the Disc catalogue entry, "these recordings provide a means of increasing the pleasure which listeners may derive from other, more recent music which man has made; latterday folk music and the classics themselves take on new meaning, depth and beauty when heard in association with the age-old music of the Ethnic Series." This was to be a project of preservation and education—much of the music would require hardy ears, and few Western listeners would likely listen to the material for the pure aesthetic pleasure of it—*Billboard* descried them as "an educational rather than a musical set . . . of interest to anthropologists, folk-lorists and perhaps dance students."[59] It was the songs' social *meaning* that was of importance, and this was revealed through the notes. Courlander undoubtedly knew better than to regard the music he had recorded as changeless or "age-old" (probably someone else—perhaps Francis Martin—had written the catalogue entry); in fact, the Ethiopian material included songs and poems about the war.

The Ethnic series was described in all of the Disc literature as "the Folkways of the World on Records." Under the Disc label the series consisted of just five albums, of which three were Courlander's. Courlander wrote the notes for his own recordings, and they were thorough and scholarly. His notes to the *Cuban Cult Music* album (Disc 131), for example, reveal his recognition of the music's African sources. Cuban popular music, he contended, was not substantially African in origin. The conga, the rhumba, and the son were no more Afro-Cuban than boogie-woogie was Afro-American: such music was the creation of the descendants of Africans *in America,* and to regard them as such discredited neither the creators nor the music. But there certainly was music to be found on Cuba that was African in origin:

> For years there has been a raging controversy in Cuban musical circles as to the origins of the national musical idiom.

From a social point of view the final issue of that controversy is not important. But it is a matter of great interest that there *is* such a thing as Afro-Cuban music, and this album presents some of the evidence. . . . African traditions have survived strongly, in some respects, to this day. Music and dancing of the African variety have persisted in the *cabildos* or societies organized by the Afro-Cubans. A great many of these societies have a religious basis, while others are survivals of secret or social organizations which existed previously in Africa.

A fourth album, *American Indian Songs and Dances,* had been recorded in Wisconsin by Charles Hofmann, who also wrote his own notes. It was probably Asch, rather than Courlander, who acquired the fifth recording, perhaps through the Soviet connections he had made when collaborating with Herbert Harris. *Folk Music of the Central East—USSR* consisted of vocal and instrumental music covering a wide geographic area, including Armenia, Azerbaijan, Bukhar, Georgia, and Uzbekistan. Because the music came to Asch without notes, Courlander employed his OWI colleague Henry Cowell to write them.

In January 1947 Asch was being pressed to pay taxes on Leadbelly's Town Hall concert. Although this could not have been a particularly large sum, in a very short time Asch was facing mounting bills from a number of directions. There were also inauspicious signs in the industry as a whole, particularly for indies such as Asch. "Indies Losing Out in Wax Race," read a *Down Beat* headline in May. "Big 4 Control Industry, 300 Indies May Soon Be Holding Collective Bag." The article maintained that only a handful of independent record companies had their heads above water, and Disc was not mentioned among those few whose prospects looked good.[60]

Asch received another blow that was devastating. Although Granz had reported the previous June that he intended to release at least twenty albums through Disc, a year later he announced his first JATP release on Clef, his own label. The original agreement with Asch had expired on 31 March, and although a press release from Disc implied that it was Asch's decision not to renew the contract, it is not clear who was ultimately responsible. Perhaps Asch felt that he was paying too much for the JATP recordings and that he could acquire them himself with less capital outlay. Granz could have as easily determined that he would be better off not having to share the profits from the recordings. Asch would continue to market JATP volumes 2 to 5, the Nat Cole album, and an album by the "hip" class clowns of jazz, Slim Gaillard and Slam Stewart entitled *Opera in Vout*.[61] The following month, in April, Granz was attempting to retrieve the JATP masters. Asch, apparently anticipating Granz's maneuver, sealed the masters in a package and deposited them in Corn's safe. When Granz phoned Corn from his New York hotel for the masters, Corn replied (by letter) that he could not comply since Granz had not provided him with master numbers:

> I do not know what is in the package; if I opened it, I probably could not recognize the masters claimed by you. However, if you will send me a list of the master-numbers, I shall insist that Mr. Asch permit me to open the package and examine its contents, or take it back unopened; I will then inform you of the disposition—and, should I be permitted to open the package, you will be informed which, if any, of the masters listed are in it.[62]

At the end of 1949 Granz was still trying to recover the original JATP masters from Corn.[63]

The loss of his source for Disc's best-selling albums would have been bad enough by itself, but another setback hit Asch personally as well as commercially. In the preceding years David Stone Martin had defined the field of album-cover art with his work for Asch and Disc Records. There was growing recognition that cover art helped to sell records, and Martin's work had helped to distinguish Disc albums as classy, intelligent productions.[64] But that spring Granz succeeded in luring Martin away from Asch. Martin joined Granz in California and drew covers for Granz's various labels—Clef, Norgran, Verve—for the next several years. *Down Beat* described Granz's maneuver as "a choice bit of larceny." Granz responded in a letter the following month:

> I understand our humorless friend Asch flipped when he saw the item about David Stone Martin doing my album covers. I cannot understand that because we agreed he would let Martin do my covers if I made an album of Sholem Asch's *East River* (in thirty volumes yet). . . . Check with Asch and ask him if since JATP left his theme song is Goodman's old recording of "Slipped Disc." On the other hand, better not, you'll never get another Baby Dodds album to review.

Down Beat reported that Asch and Martin had been "screaming bloody murder" because due to a typo Martin had been referred to in the previous story as a Disc "executive" rather than a Disc "exclusive." "Both Martin and Asch were heard growling faintly in the distance."[65] But this could not have been the primary issue. Granz's cutting jokes suggest that he and Asch had had a falling out. True, Asch was not known for his sense of humor, but Granz's allusions to Asch's esoteric releases and to Sholem suggest that he knew how to hit Asch where it hurt.

From the point of view of the record-buying public, Asch's separation from Granz did not appear to have any immediate effect on Disc Records. In fact, in the remaining months of 1947 and into early 1948 the pace of new releases from Disc continued to accelerate. One more JATP recording appeared at the end of 1947, a single record featuring Charlie Parker, Lester Young, and Howard McGhee ironically titled *After You've Gone* (finally, and largely too late for Asch, the JATP recordings were receiving positive reviews). Granz's place in the Disc catalogue appeared as though it might be taken by Timme Rosenkrantz, who provided Asch with some masters from an outstanding concert he had produced at Town Hall in June 1945. In early 1948 Asch released two albums from the concert, one a trio featuring saxophonist Charlie Ventura, and the other a quintet featuring xylophonist Red Norvo and saxophonist Don Byas. Rosenkrantz had easily as much taste as Granz, but a lot less business sense. The concert itself had been a financial failure, and it is likely that he had hoped to recoup some of his losses by selling the masters to Asch. *Down Beat* far preferred the Byas-Norvo sides to the Ventura.[66]

As before, much of the jazz Asch continued to record in his own studio was traditional. One set of sessions was supervised by jazz historian John Lucas, who had written favorably about Asch releases in a *Down Beat* column on the roots of contemporary jazz. Expanding upon the precedent established by Charles Edward Smith in *The Jazz Record Book*, Lucas cited both blues and folk song—secular and sacred—in the development of contemporary jazz. His list of recordings that documented these early influences included Asch recordings by Leadbelly, Josh White, Jack Dupree, and, somewhat surprisingly, the *Folksay* album.[67] Lucas ventured into record production with two albums of Dixieland music by trumpeter Doc Evans. These were deliberately intended to be historical recreations, and Lucas used some of the best white revivalists currently in New York, including pianist Joe Sullivan and drummer George Wettling, both of whom were familiar with Asch Studios. It was a sign that things were slipping in Asch's operation—and a sign of things to come—that the two Doc Evans albums were released without the advance publicity that would have been required to place the recordings in some context: "Why Moe Asch released two albums at once upon an unsuspecting public with no publicity or effort to explain anything about Evans is a little confusing. But then again, that's Moe Asch."[68] Asch *was* exploiting other means of promoting his albums. His staff wrote radio scripts for at least two series, one entitled "Milestones of Jazz" and the other "Folkways of the World." Each show presented several Disc sides—sometimes from a single artist, such as Doc Evans, or sometimes from several—sandwiched between a bit of historical commentary. Most of these shows appeared on WEVD, but at least one found its way as far west as WKNX in Saginaw, Michigan.

There was no longer a parade of beboppers into Asch Studios, as there had been during the war. Only Mary Lou Williams remained faithful, if not exclusive. Her last projects for Asch in this era consisted of a session she supervised for Milton Orent, a bassist friend who had been a staff arranger for the NBC studio orchestra, and two sides of her own with a quartet featuring trumpeter Kenny Dorham ("Kool" and "Mary Lou"). The Orent session included a medium-sized orchestra whose members had been with Woody Herman's Herd.

Asch initiated a collaboration with the Santa Monica Symphony Orchestra, newly formed by Hollywood studio musicians who needed an outlet for their serious musical aspirations. A studio violinist named Louis Kaufman, for instance, who had performed on the soundtracks of Hitchcock's *Suspicion* and Gregory Ratoff's *Intermezzo*, was featured on a Disc release of Saint-Saëns' third violin concerto.[69] Under the direction of Jacques Rachmilovich, the Santa Monica Symphony Orchestra recorded several symphonies by late-nineteenth- and twentieth-century Russian composers—Khachaturian, Tchaikovsky, Prokofiev, Rachmaninov—which Asch released inexplicably on the Asch rather than Disc label. Other classical releases resulted from Asch's continuing relationship with the USSR's Bolshoi State Orchestra and Moscow State Philharmonic. A complete production of Tchaikovsky's *Eugene Onegin* appeared in two volumes consisting of seventeen twelve-inch discs!

Asch's growing involvement with the New York musical avant-garde was probably the result of Henry Cowell's influence. Cowell was very likely responsible for Disc recordings of John Cage's revolutionary "prepared piano" pieces, yet Asch himself was the catalyst for recording a set of lyrics by Charles-Henri Ford put to music by Paul Bowles. The resulting *Night Without Sleep* grew out of Asch's friendship with Bowles. Predictably, a mainstream trade publication such as *Billboard* could not fathom it: "The songs and their singing is just as esoteric and emotional as the titles indicate, all taking their cue from the dream world. The psychiatrist will have to figure out this set, for even the accompanying booklet with the song lyrics doesn't help much in the confusion." Two of the six sides consisted of excerpts from an opera that Bowles and Ford had written based on the life of Denmark Vesey, who had led a slave insurrection in South Carolina in 1822.[70]

Night Without Sleep, its accompanying booklet filled with photographs and drawings, suggests the extent to which artists of the avant-garde encouraged the convergence of musical, literary, and visual artistic endeavors. Bowles's career is indicative, his growing reputation as a composer soon to be eclipsed by his writing. Since 1943 he had been publishing work with Charles-Henri Ford's prominent avant-garde magazine *View,* whose contributors included surrealists André Breton, Marcel Duchamp, Max Ernst, René Magritte, André Masson, Pablo Picasso, and Salvador Dali.[71] As a dedicated modernist, Asch could not have helped but to have been attracted to this happy intersection of art, literature, and music. It drew him into the orbit of his father's work, making explicit the connection between the labor of father and son. Although Sholem's stylistically conventional writing hardly seems avant-garde in retrospect, given his origins (and those of his original readership) in the shtetl, he most certainly was pushing at the boundaries of the known and knowable. Bowles, fascinated by the musical cultures of North Africa and South America, was pushing boundaries both through musical and literary technique and by offering Western readers a glimpse of cultural settings in which the taken-for-granted "sense" of the world seemed to be missing. His approach to other cultures was precisely the opposite of Courlander's—and, indeed, that of most ethnographers—where the effort was to render the "other" comprehensible. Bowles, in his writing for *View* and later in his novels such as *The Sheltering Sky,* sought to show the Westerner knocked off center by his encounter with cultures that he could not fathom. In a special issue of *View* on "tropical America" that Bowles edited, he deliberately rendered Latin American culture as strange and incomprehensible. A half century later Bowles's attention to the violent and grotesque in other cultures may seem ungenerous, although he prefigured the contemporary recognition of the difficulty in "translating" one culture for another. But neither, in the end, represented Bowles's real intentions. The encounter with the culturally unfamiliar was for Bowles, other avant-gardists, and soon the emerging Beats (Allen Ginsberg, William Burroughs, Gregory Corso) a way of casting off familiar cultural moorings in order to better explore their own unfettered mental activity.

It was all grist for Asch. He would not have cared whether the apprehension of other cultures was used to build bridges between people or explore the dark edges of an individual's inner world. They were not in any case mutually exclusive activities. Whatever people made of it, there was only danger in withholding information about the unfamiliar from the public—not in making it available. The unlikely meeting of New York's avant-garde and the ostensively "timeless" music of the world's traditional populations made perfectly good sense to Asch. The former made use of the latter, and Asch made use of it all.

With the demise of the JATP deal Asch began to realize—a bit too late—that the only hope he had for competing against the industry giants was to recognize small, easily targeted markets with which the majors could not be bothered and to meet the specific and dependable needs of those markets. Folk music constituted one such market. Another market was among various dance enthusiasts; Asch released eight volumes of his Ballroom Disc Dance series, which presented music for the fox-trot, waltz, rumba, samba, and tango played by "smart Society bands." Two volumes of square dance music were released, one without calls by Paul Hunt and his Rock Candy Mountaineers and one with calls by New Englander Ralph Page. Later, in the Folkways era, there were recordings for modern dance and ballet. These were low risk ventures; Asch was essentially guaranteed of an audience for them before they were released. A few other recording executives were following a similar strategy. "In the extremely specialized esoteric, or purist hot jazz field, small waxeries like Disc, Dial, Circle, and Bluenote continued to chalk-up satisfactory sales in their limited market," reported *Billboard* in June 1948, when ironically, Disc was in dire financial straights. "Disc is an 'art' label, specializing in highbrow stuff," and while classical music was still dominated by the majors, Disc, Vox, and Concert Hall were making "significant inroads."[72]

In February 1948 there were some superficially hopeful indications of Disc's fiscal health. *Billboard*'s list of "Advance Record Releases" listed an astonishing total of twenty-one new Disc releases. But it was mostly elusive. The list, for example, included ten single discs of calypso music, but eight of them had been among the three previously released Disc albums of calypso music. Asch had five single-disc releases on the "Hot Jazz" list, but three had again been taken out of a previously released album (*Muggsy Spanier and His Orchestra*). Only Mary Lou Williams's quartet sides with Kenny Dorham and two sides by pianist Lennie Tristano and his quartet were actually new. Three releases of Jewish material appear to have been genuinely new, as well as a Charles Ives Quartet and an addition to the Ethnic series entitled *Dances of India*. A Prokofiev symphony had been previously released. The fact that Asch was taking several of his albums apart and selling the discs separately—without the cover art, without the notes—suggests that he was under some pressure to raise capital.

There would be a few more Disc releases in June and July: a couple of sides of Brownie McGhee, a few calypso recordings, and another Soviet classical recording. Two more sides of Red Norvo, from Timme Rosenkrantz's 1945 Town Hall concert, appeared to little acclaim. "Surprised Moe Asch let this one come out," wrote the *Billboard* reviewer about the Norvo-Byas sides. "Entire first side is muddled by poor recording."[73] All of the recordings released in 1948 were either made before the start of the year or involved non-union musicians because the American Federation of Musicians was again on strike. Petrillo had called a recording ban at the start of the year, once again over royalties from the playing of records on the air and in jukeboxes. The original agreement that had ended the war-era strike had run out, and the drafting of a new one was being severely hampered by the recent Taft-Hartley Act, which in the name of preventing "acts in restraint of trade" was having a hobbling effect on unions in many industries. This time the ban continued until almost the end of the year, when Petrillo and the majors found a way around Taft-Hartley regulations that forbade the payment of royalties directly into a union welfare fund by recording companies.

Asch could have continue to record folk musicians. The AFM had only just recognized the harmonica as an "official" instrument and most other folk instruments were still not on the map. But no additional Disc releases were announced after July, and in fact Asch had come up against serious financial and legal difficulties many months earlier, the first signs of which seemed trivial on the surface. In preparation for the release of Elie Siegmeister's album *American Legends,* in February 1947 Asch ordered a thousand copies of the album notes from the Edward B. Marks Music Corporation—or so he thought. Marks thought Asch had ordered two thousand copies, and although they delivered only a thousand, they had printed two thousand and expected payment for the full number of $550, with interest, by March. Asch only acknowledged owing them $275. The matter dragged on for some months. In December the lawyer for Marks attempted to reach a compromise, but when that failed Marks sued Asch. On 16 January 1948 Asch was served with a summons and was ordered to appear in court within five days.

There were other signs that things were unraveling that winter. Asch received a letter in December from his lawyer, to whom he had been indebted for at least a year. An agreement by which Asch was to send his lawyer a hundred dollars a month until his debt had been paid off had broken down, and now the lawyer was discontinuing his services: "I have tried in the last few weeks to talk to you on the telephone, but as always, you do not reply, nor do you extend the courtesy of a return call. . . . Because of all this difficulty, I believe it best that I do not represent you further in any matters that you may have."[74] In late February Asch pawned a guitar. Though he was unlikely to have owned one, perhaps it had been left in his studio some months before by a forgetful musician. In any event Asch never reclaimed it—the pawn ticket was among his papers when he died. In March BMI requested that Asch return a contract for the licensing of the *String Quartet in C Minor* by Sholem Secunda, a preeminent Yiddish composer. Asch had either been unable to make the recording or, more likely, had neglected to pay for the license.

By the first of March Asch's list of "payables" comprised more than five pages. There were dozens of small sums, under $50, owed to suppliers, freight companies, advertisers, and utility companies, and several dozen more for sums between $50 and $200. Asch owed money to most Disc recording artists and record producers; Guthrie, Leadbelly, and Mary Lou Williams were owed slightly more than $200 each. Others, to whom Asch was paying union scale, held notes for a good deal more: $742.50 to Slam Stewart, $371.25 to Lennie Tristano, more than $1,000 to Illinois Jacquet. David Stone Martin, Harold Courlander, Norman Granz, John Lucas—Asch was indebted to all of them. Having lost the lawsuit filed against him by Edward B. Marks, Asch also listed the full amount that they claimed from him—$550—among his payables. Additionally, he was unable to make payments on the large outstanding loans, including $38,000 to the Clark Phonograph Company and $32,000 to his father. Asch had attempted to set up a repayment schedule for the large sum his father had loaned him at the time he was first establishing Disc. The previous May he had sent seven checks to his father's publisher totaling $3,000; these would be cashed monthly to the end of the year.[75]

The following month, Asch wrote to the Allied Record Manufacturing Company in California, a record pressing plant to which he owed about $12,000:

> In reply to your letter of April 14th, please be advised that we are going through a reorganization. My liabilities are in the neighborhood of $225,000. . . . I have been receiving financial assistance from one of my large creditors an eastern pressing concern to whom I owe $70,000, and I am doing everything possible to keep anyone from losing anything. However, it is going to require a great deal of patience. I have some 128 creditors and 98% of them are willing to cooperate 100%.[76]

Asch's "large creditor" was George Erlinger, who was in the process of assuming ownership of Asch's masters and existing stock. Asch wrote a letter the following day to attorneys in Chicago to inform them that the Disc Company of America had ceased to distribute records and that this function had been taken over by a new entity called "Disc Distributing Co., Inc." under the direction of Erlinger.

In June Asch flew to Chicago for a record manufacturer's convention. He had probably attended the convention at Erlinger's behest to see whether they could move some Disc Records in the midwest and recoup a portion of their losses. Asch met with various salesmen he hoped might promote "their line." He also had a meeting with an attorney for Lonnie Johnson who was attempting to get out of his exclusive arrangement with Disc so that he could record for King Records, an independent rhythm and blues label out of Cleveland that would soon be a major player in this new field. Asch had another meeting over lunch with Martha Gleicher, a woman who had been on his payroll during the collaboration with Granz. She had since gone to work for Granz but was willing to return to Asch, presumably in order to help Erlinger reestablish Disc in the jazz field. Asch must have known that Disc was unsalvageable by this point, however, and nothing would come of his attempts in Chicago to resuscitate it. Having run out of funds, Asch rode a bus back to New York, a long and uncomfortable trip for a man who had rarely had to forego creature comforts.

Later that month it was announced that Asch's assets would be put up for auction. There was not much to squabble about by then. The marshall's office prepared the following inventory: electric fan, electric clock, piano, RCA microphone, floor lamp, twelve pictures, shelvings, Woodstock typewriter, two steel filing cabinets, clothes cabinet, two desks, five chairs, desk lamp, fluorescent lights, six recording instruments, record albums. The first auction was scheduled for 21 June in Asch Studios, but by paying a fee of one dollar Asch was able to have it postponed by a week, and throughout the summer Asch paid the weekly fee and evaded the auctioneer.

It was a terrible time for Asch. The worry, stress, and long hours took a horrible toll. He could not face the prospect of failing; it would have confirmed his most worthless feelings about himself, particularly the feelings of disapproval he ascribed—perhaps without foundation—to his father. Although it was not an Asch family trait to complain or show weakness, Asch's health deteriorated. His wife tried to keep him home in bed, but Asch insisted on going to the office; a physician who lived upstairs gave him an injection each morning for an unnamed illness so that he would have the strength to face the task of sorting out his business affairs and fending off his creditors.

As Asch was facing the worst ordeal of his adult life, the American Left appeared to be in the midst of its most hopeful campaign since Eugene V. Debs's last run for the presidency in 1920. Henry Wallace had been Franklin Roosevelt's vice president during the latter's third term (1941–45) but had been dumped from the Democratic ticket in 1944 for holding views that were too progressive even for the New Deal administration. Banished a second time (from the office of secretary of commerce in Truman's cabinet) for a 1946 Madison Square Garden speech in which he argued for a conciliatory approach toward the Soviet Union, Wallace determined that the ragged legacy of the New Deal could only have a future in a third-party candidacy. The Progressive Party was launched that spring. Wallace focused much of his attention on civil rights and the support of labor, but it was his position on the Soviet Union that drew the most attention from the national press. While attempting to forge a broad coalition of political

progressives, intellectuals, working men and women, and marginalized racial minorities, he was painted as a tool of the Communist Party.

There were many things that distinguished Wallace's third-party
run for the presidency that year, but among the most conspicuous
was the use of music in the campaign. In June his *New Republic*
column was dedicated to a discussion of folk song:

> In my early years, I had never thought much about music as a
> political force. . . . Now, I am becoming convinced that when
> the people are deeply moved by the impulse to take construc-
> tive action, they sing. . . . Traveling around the country in this
> political year, I am more and more impressed with the sing-
> ing, and the singers, for the New Party.

He held up the singing of Paul Robeson for particular praise, and
mentioned several exemplary songs, including Guthrie's "Roll on,
Columbia" and a recent ballad by Dick Blakeslee entitled "Passing
Through":

> Was at Franklin Roosevelt's side,
> Just awhile before he died.
> He said, "One world must come out of World War II."
> Yankee, Russian white or tan,
> Lord a man is just a man.
> We're all brothers and we're only passing through.[77]

Through that spring and summer and into September, Wallace's
campaign would be conspicuous for the absence of the traditional
brass band and for the ubiquitous presence of folk singers, especially People's Songsters and, preeminently, Pete Seeger and Paul
Robeson. At Alan Lomax's urging People's Songs gave up almost all
of its other activity for six months and threw its support and
energy into the Wallace campaign; dozens of songs of widely
varying quality resulted. The first, and one of Wallace's favorites,
was "The Same Merry-Go-Round" by Ray Glaser and Bill Wolff,
which appeared in the April issue of *People's Songs Bulletin*:

> If you want to end up safe and sound,
> Get offa the Merry-go-round;
> To be a real smarty, Just join the Third Party
> And get your two feet on the ground!

Many more appeared in a special People's Songs publication entitled *Songs for Wallace,* which appeared in June with a second edition in August. Paul Robeson contributed a parody of "Get on Board" entitled "We'll All Join Gideon's Army." Other parodies included "Skip to the Polls," a reworking of "Skip to my Lou" and an updated version of a Negro spiritual, "Great Day!" by the students at Highlander. E. Y. (Yip) Harburg, best known as the lyricist of "Over the Rainbow," contributed three songs, one of which—"I've Got a Ballot," to the tune of "I've Got Sixpence"—drew Guthrie's contempt:

> How a man . . . could expect such a shallow jingly and insincere number as "I've Got a Ballot" to touch the heartstrings and conscience of the hard-hit masses, is a problem beyond me. I never did hear a living human being call his vote a "magic little ballot." People I have seen call their vote a number of things, none of which are nearly as cutiepie, as highly polite, as flippant, as sissy nor effeminate as this song.[78]

Guthrie's own contribution, "The Wallace-Taylor Train" set to the tune of "The Wabash Cannonball," was lyrically stronger than much of what he had been writing and suggested that his creative powers had not entirely deserted him.

Asch was undoubtedly sympathetic to the Wallace campaign, and despite his tangled business affairs he may have contributed a little of his time to the Progressive Party effort.[79] Wallace was, after all, the living embodiment of Franklin Roosevelt's New Deal politics, the only political movement about which Asch seemed to be entirely unambivalent. But through that summer, as his bankruptcy became increasingly inevitable, there was little to distract Asch from the desperateness of his situation.

As devastating as the prospect of bankruptcy was for Asch, there was one sense in which its timing was fortuitous. That July Columbia Records released its first catalogue of long-playing (LP), 33 1/3-rpm records. In a very short time it was apparent that the technology in the recording industry was about to change in a significant way and it would be up to the bold and well capitalized to declare the direction it would take. Columbia staked its claim on ten- and twelve-inch albums that accommodated on a single disc the same amount of material as four-, five-, and six-disc sets of 78s. The first benefits of the new system would be in saved storage space, but it was hoped that the fidelity of the new LP would also surpass that of the 78.[80]

Victor did not respond until the following March, when they announced that they would stick with the one-song-per-side format of the 78, but on a seven-inch, 45-rpm disc with a large hole in the middle. Decca's president, Jack Kapp, could not make up his mind whether to throw in his lot with the LP or the 45 and some weeks after Victor's announcement opted for a shortsighted compromise—they would remain with the 78-rpm format but with compressed grooves that would accommodate up to five minutes of material.[81] Asch later recalled that Kapp committed suicide over his indecision on this matter, and in point of fact Kapp died at the time of these deliberations (25 March 1949) at the age of forty-seven. But he was reported to have died of a cerebral hemorrhage, and Asch's characterization of his death as a suicide reflects Asch's own impatience with human frailty and his tenacious belief in the ability of individuals to determine their own fate.[82] In any case Asch himself was forced by circumstances to sit out the rpm battles, and by the time he was in a position to enter the controversy himself it had largely been resolved in favor of the LP (the 45-rpm "single" would, of course, become the staple of the pop market).

One way or another, Asch was intent on remaining in the record business. To do so he worked several fronts simultaneously. The primary one involved the creation of an elaborate fiction that had as the central player his secretary and lover, Marian Distler. The outlines of the fiction were worked out in several typewritten drafts, the purpose of which was to establish that Distler had left Disc Records, first to work for Erlinger and shortly thereafter to go into business for herself. The new business was to be called Folkways Records and Service. According to the story they had agreed upon, Asch was to advise her "on the creating of a new record company" for which she would pay him in cash; also, he would be allowed the use of space in "her" premises—his old studio at 117 West Forty-sixth Street—for a desk and his books in order to keep running the Disc Company of America. Distler would "take messages for him in connection with any matters which pertain to his own operations, concerning either the defunct Disc Company or any other business which he is able to conduct."[83]

According to the application Distler filed with the city of New York on 16 September for the collection of sales tax, Folkways had been established the previous 1 May. She had also been trying since the previous January to sign a contract with the AFM that would permit her to record studio musicians, and on 15 April she succeed in securing a contract signed by Petrillo. A corporation was established whose board included George Mendelssohn, president of Vox Records, and it was Mendelssohn who put up the cash that enabled Distler to purchase the Disc assets when they finally were auctioned in August. Jack Kapp also pitched in to get Asch up off the bottom by placing him on a salary of seventy-five dollars a week. In a curious way, Asch had won the admiration of his fellow recording business executives, and they apparently felt an obligation to see that he remained in business. Perhaps they felt, as John Hammond was to express it some years later, that Asch was the "conscience" of the recording business: he released what was important and deserved to be heard, regardless of its commercial merit. If others could not always stick to such high principles, they were at least pleased that there was someone else around who could.

Asch meanwhile had been declared bankrupt on 15 January 1949 on a petition filed against him the previous October by various printing concerns. On Thursday, 27 January, Asch was called to a meeting in the U.S. District Court House in order to appoint a trustee, to elect a committee of creditors, and to examine the various claims against his assets.[84] *People's Songs Bulletin* recounted the demise of Disc in a column in the same month entitled "It's a Hell of a Note." Asch had told the columnist that his mistake had been in "putting too much time and money on popular jazz and classical records." Although his intention had been to use the fast-selling items as a means of introducing the public to the rest of his catalogue, he realized now that "'good' records should be sold to a small circle of persons who will buy them, and gradually widen that circle as the quality of the records becomes known." The column also mentioned complaints of bad record surfaces and that some artists considered the album covers too "artistic" to appeal to the "casual customer." Finally, however, the culprit was the big record companies, who sold records as they would soap, without any regard for artistic merit: "Moe Asch wanted, and still wants to put out the Authentic, as contrasted to the Commercial in people's music. He is to be congratulated for his defeat at the hands of the major companies as well as for his significant contribution to American people's culture." Turning down an offer to work for a major label, Asch would continue to associate with another "small firm."[85]

That Distler's status in Folkways was a fiction—and that Folkways was to be Asch's business in every significant sense—was reflected in a letter that Guthrie sent to *both* of them on 16 August: "I think your idea for going ahead on under your new name Folkways is the best piece of news I've had or heard, apart and aside from our general lectures and spouting offs and mares, studs, jacks, the lack of penises in the movies, and so on."[86] Additionally, a *Billboard* item at the end of 1949 entitled 'Folkways, New Label, Headed by Moe Asch' failed to mention his partner altogether.[87] Distler contributed her name, her good sense, fabulous energy, and every waking minute to the success of the new enterprise. She was unswervingly loyal to Asch and defended him with the persistence of a terrier, but creative decisions remained largely his.

Still, it would be some months before Asch would be able to give Folkways his undivided attention. Bankruptcy proceedings had still not gone forward, and Asch was desperately trying to raise cash by every available means. The first Folkways project was not a Folkways record but the rerelease of several of the Guthrie and Adelaide Van Wey *Songs to Grow On* on 78s on a short-lived Asch label called Cub. *Billboard* announced the debut of the new "kidisk label" in late November, noting that the new disc, on unbreakable plastic, would be marketed through the mail and in the "specialized store trade."[88] It appeared at first as though George Mendelssohn was going to be the means by which Cub would be marketed. His Vox Records operation initially handled the masters and arranged for the pressings. And there were other signs of Mendelssohn's assistance. In May 1948 Leonard Feather had agreed to make available to Asch several Charlie Ventura masters he had recorded at a Carnegie Hall concert in April.[89] A three-way contract was drawn up in late August between Feather, Mendelssohn, and Distler (Asch, with his bankruptcy still unsettled, was conspicuously absent); terms were set for the marketing of the Ventura masters on a new label called Solo, officially owned by Mendelssohn but administered by Distler and, of course, Asch.

A small number of Solo titles were, in fact, manufactured and marketed by Asch and Distler in the months that followed, including some square dance records (probably by Piute Pete, "the greatest hog caller east of the Rockies"), blues, gospel, and Latin jazz.[90] However, Mendelssohn's role in Asch's finances was soon eclipsed by another recording business entrepreneur based in Hollywood named Paul Reiner. Reiner was president of Black & White Records, a small, independent label that had a very big novelty hit in 1947 called "Open the Door, Richard." The song, recorded by former Lionel Hampton saxophonist Jack McVea, derived from a highly suggestive black comedy routine, and although it came out of the rhythm and blues tradition it was phenomenally successful among the white record-buying public as well.

Reiner was one of a growing number of Jewish entrepreneurs who had become involved in the promotion of rhythm and blues music through the establishment of several independent record labels: Savoy, Aladdin, Chess, Regent, Herald, Atlantic—and Black & White. They had become immersed in black music to the extent that, according to some, "they went black . . . talked black, affected black mannerisms, and some of them married black women." They were like Asch in several respects—dedicated to the music in part because they identified with the rich culture of a socially marginalized people. And they recognized a market that was largely being ignored by the majors at a time when many fields of communications—book publication, journalism, broadcasting—were still largely the provenance of white men from monied and well-positioned families.[91]

Reiner had been running Black & White since the close of the war, his wife Lillian functioning as vice president. He and Asch were corresponding during the spring of 1948 in an effort to come up with a mutually beneficially business arrangement.[92] Their negotiations broke off before the summer, but they were on again in the autumn. Reiner had been involved in distributing Disc records in California as well as in seeing to the manufacture of certain Disc items such as the Santa Monica Symphony recordings. In December they had hit upon an arrangement. Reiner was to manufacture recordings on the Cub label from masters provided by Asch; Reiner would then be the West Coast agent for Cub and would pay a royalty to Asch and Distler on records sold. Asch in turn would establish a sales route within a five-hundred-mile radius of New York for the purposes of distributing Black & White recordings. For his trouble Asch would be paid a weekly salary for the first four months of 1949 and a percentage of the money collected from the sale of Black & White recordings. Asch's situation in New York was complicated by the fact that Reiner already had a sales agent in New York City by the name of Larry Newton. But Newton had little time to spare to Black & White because he was in the process of setting up his own R&B label, Derby Records, not far from Asch in the West Forties.

It could not have been easy for Asch to become a salesman again, peddling records as he had electronic equipment almost twenty years earlier. He approached the big chain stores—Kresge, Woolworth, Macy—in an effort to have them carry the Cub line, which by late winter numbered eleven titles and included (in addition to Guthrie and Adelaide Van Wey) recordings by Fred Hellerman and Cisco Houston. Black & White children's records were promised, too, but were slow to appear. In February Asch reported to Reiner that his "New York sales situation for the metropolitan area is snafu." Newton had become too busy with his own enterprises to devote time to Black & White sales, and Asch had discovered that confidence in Black & White among salesmen and store owners was low. There were also by then six Solo records, including blues by Sonny Terry and gospel by the Silvertones, successors to the Thrasher Wonders (Folkways at the time consisted only of Courlander's Ethnic series).[93] Reiner agreed in March to have Asch take over the New York office of B&W Distributors, but by April they were again coming apart. Bills were due and a large quantity of records suddenly were missing, and there were disagreements over who was responsible.

In June Reiner terminated his business relationship with Asch. There was an exchange of angry letters, with Distler as usual taking Asch's part against Reiner: "Regarding Moe Asch, I take personal exception to the fact that you say your relationship with him cost you $5000.00 because I know that to the contrary he has devoted his time (if not in your office, outside) to making as good as possible, relations between your organization and the distributors and dealers." Reiner attempted to be conciliatory, especially to Asch: "I received a letter from Marian . . . and I can't help feeling that a foundation is being laid for dissatisfaction—for a hurt feeling." But Asch, in a letter that crossed Reiner's in the mail, wrote, "The climax came today when Miss M. asked me about a letter she got from you mentioning some $3000 which you had no accounting for. Together with the heat here plus the fact that I feel I have been kicked around enough by you and miss M. have just reached the boiling point where I'm going to do a little complaining." And Distler appended a note on the bottom: "I am *really* tired of seeing Moe Asch kicked around and I am particularly amazed that you also have taken this means of showing your appreciation for what he has done."[94]

Reiner was in the midst of serious financial difficulty and by summer would be out of the record business altogether. One contemporary described Reiner as a novice in the record business who expected all of his releases to succeed as well as "Open the Door, Richard" had: "Reiner began rushing out record after record, and he literally released himself out of the business. He put out so many new records that he quickly ate up every cent he made."[95] Reiner liked and respected Asch a great deal and was unhappy about the falling out. "Moe, I would like very much to maintain your friendship," he wrote at the end of June. "It means more to me than just so many words and financial matters, believe me, do not enter it at all."[96]

After a long silence that caused Reiner to fear the worst, Asch finally wrote him in early August. His first bit of news concerned his bankruptcy: "I have been cleared at last from bankruptcy and discharged which leaves me free to start fresh. You can imagine what the last weeks have been like without any regular income." Asch had learned of Reiner's departure from the record business and wished him well in his new venture (he had started a builders' hardware wholesale company). "With me," he added, "the problem is that I have invested all my time, effort and money in this damn record industry without any cash assets to show for all the years I have put in."

"After all this," Reiner responded, "I wish you would take my advice and forget about records. . . . I don't make money [in the new business] but I don't lose blood every day to the vampires which make up the majority of the record population."[97]

Henry Wallace's presidential bid came to an unhappy ending, with Wallace garnering far less than the 5 percent of the popular vote that his supporters had predicted. The final tally brought him less than a million votes—half of which were from New York alone—and a fourth-place finish behind segregationist Dixiecrat candidate Strom Thurmond. Wallace's pathetic showing could be blamed on any number of factors. There is no question but that the songs generated by People's Songs, based primarily in the folk genre, succeeded in inspiring the small number of already-committed political progressives. But, despite People's Songs' insistence that the general populace was eager for songs from a more authentic traditions, the party's avoidance of popular musical forms did not help them. It was an irony that has not escaped historians—precisely at the moment when it was *most* important to reach the broadest possible audience, a group of cultural workers who prided themselves on populist sensibilities opted for a musical form that was esoteric and that they took to be intrinsically superior to popular music.[98]

Although musical style probably made little difference in the final tally, the vilification of the Progressive Party in the popular press and the related persecution of the party by the House Un-American Activities Committee certainly did. HUAC had been gearing up for an assault on the "communist menace" since the close of the war. That July—after the Democratic and before the Progressive Party conventions—the national secretary and board of the CPUSA were indicted by a New York grand jury for violating the Smith Act, an obscure rider on the 1940 Alien Registration Act that made it a crime to knowingly advocate the overthrow of the U.S. government by violence or force.[99] By the mid-1950s, a significant number of the prominent folk singers would be called up before HUAC: Burl Ives, Josh White, Pete Seeger, Oscar Brand. Some of them were highly cooperative witnesses who eagerly denounced their former comrades—Josh White reported publicly that he had been "duped" into working for organizations whose communist affiliations were unknown to him (while privately he maintained that he had been blackmailed into making his denouncement). Ives was similarly cooperative. Brand had distanced himself from the party in 1946 and had withdrawn from People's Songs and consequently was spared from having to "name names." But he was branded by left-wing folk circles as a "stoolie" nonetheless.[100] Others, like Seeger, took highly principled positions the cost of which varied considerably. "Throughout the late Fifties, Seeger's legal troubles shadowed his career," says his biographer. Seeger himself demurs: "I had a great time going from college to college getting ever bigger audiences, and the picketlines of the John Birchers only helped sell more tickets. We got along fine."[101]

People's Songs only outlasted the Wallace campaign by a couple months. The February 1949 *People's Songs Bulletin* was to have been a "gala Third Anniversary issue," and a large number of supporters had intended to take out advertisements and greetings—Asch was among them, as well as Harvey Matusow, who was later revealed to be an FBI informer in People's Songs and folk-song circles generally. But People's Songs had run out of money and could not continue. Although the abysmal failure of the Wallace campaign was not the immediate cause of People's Songs' demise, it had made it all too clear to the American Left exactly how marginal it had become at that historical moment. Many had little stomach for new campaigns, additional battles. The New York leadership reconstituted the organization as People's Artists and shifted the focus from a broad-based membership to the work of a much smaller group of performers and songwriters. Additionally, accord-

ing to Robbie Lieberman, People's Artists was "more overtly ideological and dogmatic than People's Songs had been" and more
explicitly a vehicle of the "Communist movement."[102] The following year, 1950, People's Artists started publishing a successor to
People's Songs Bulletin entitled *Sing Out!*—the title having been taken
from "The Hammer Song" by Lee Hays and Pete Seeger.

But in 1949 the first People's Artists event was planned as a large
outdoor concert featuring Paul Robeson at the Lakeland picnic
grounds in Peekskill, New York. It was scheduled for Sunday, 27
August and was billed as a benefit for the Civil Rights Congress.
Robeson would be joined by Seeger, Guthrie, and Lee Hays. But the
local chapter of the American Legion got wind of the event and
mobilized a mob of right-wing protesters who repeatedly attacked
the concert organizers with rocks, clubs, knives, and brass knuckles
while screaming anticommunist slogans. The concert never even
began. For some hours Howard Fast, chairman of the concert, and
about forty additional men and boys fought off the mob while the
police looked on. Finally the presence of the press compelled the
police to allow the concertgoers to retreat without additional
injury.[103]

Robeson had been unable to come within miles of the picnic
grounds on the first night. Pete Seeger, who drove to the concert
with his mother, was also caught in a long, unmoving line of traffic.
When he attempted to enlist the help of a police officer in getting
to the picnic grounds in time for his performance, he was told that
there was not going to be any concert. But Robeson, appearing
before a gathering in a Lenox Avenue ballroom in New York a few
days later, vowed that he would hold the concert the following
Saturday. With assurances of protection from some labor unions,
he succeeded in staging a concert for a defiant group of supporters—thirty thousand of them according to organizers, about half
that according to the *New York Times*. The crowd consisted of "a good
percentage of Negroes," noted the *Times*, and "chances were that far
more than half of those there were Communists," though the
"paper of record" declined to suggest how it was that they distinguished Communists from others.[104] The leadership of the International Fur and Leather Workers Union organized a ring of
protectors in military fashion around the crowd in order to keep
the protesters at bay; they were joined by nine hundred law
enforcement officers from as far away as the Canadian border. The
police claimed to have confiscated three hundred baseball bats
from the concertgoers, and managed to keep peace among several

hundred anti-Robeson demonstrators. The concert took place without incident; Seeger opened with "T for Texas" and "If I Had a Hammer" before Robeson appeared for a performance that lasted about an hour and ten minutes.

But the roads leading out of Peekskill were lined with Legionnaires and other nativists lying in wait. Pete Seeger was driving his Jeep station wagon with a couple of friends, his father-in-law, and his two small children. They waited an hour to get out of the gate, and when he arrived at Division Street Seeger was told that he had no choice but to turn right. Within fifty or a hundred feet he noticed glass on the road and warned everyone to be prepared to duck. Baseball-sized rocks had been placed at intervals of a couple hundred yards, and the cars and buses, unable to move more than about twenty miles per hour, were pelted mercilessly from the picnic grounds to the interstate. Two rocks came through the windows of Seeger's Jeep; his son Danny, crouched under the back seat of the car, was showered with broken glass. Seeger stopped by a policeman who was standing within sixty feet of one of the rock throwers and rolled his window down an inch (it was too shattered to open further). "Aren't you going to do something about this?" he asked. "Move on, move on," was the policeman's reply. The buses returned to Harlem and other New York City locations with broken windows and bloodied and badly shaken riders. Several dozen were injured. A thousand concertgoers were stranded for much of the evening when fifteen bus drivers refused to drive through the gauntlet of rock throwers, and in the end several buses returned to New York with volunteer drivers. The instigators of the violence were never identified, although Seeger felt certain that the Klan had been involved and that it could not have occurred without the cooperation of the local police—some of them perhaps Klansmen themselves. The event came to be known as the Peekskill Riot and arguably stands as the nadir of the folk-singing Left.[105]

Asch did not attend the concert at Peekskill. It would not have been like him to go so far out of his way for such an obviously partisan political cause. And in any event, his fragile game leg would have made it risky to get in the middle of a large and volatile crowd. However, if he was worried about attracting the unwelcome attention of the FBI for his many leftist connections, he need not have. Despite his Union Boys and Lincoln Brigade recordings during the war and his People's Songs affiliation afterward, the FBI did not take any notice of Asch until the mid-1950s, and even then it was slight. Astonishingly, it was not Moe Asch but his *father* who attracted the attention of the FBI—and as early as 1946. His greatest crime was probably in having published his stories in the communist *Freiheit* after he had been denied access to the *Forward* and every other Yiddish-language periodical in the United States. FBI agents acquired a copy of his *East River* in 1946 in order to inspect it for possible subversive content, following the appearance of a newspaper review that emphasized his portrayal of exploited factory hands and Jewish radicals. Although an FBI memo in July 1949 concluded that Sholem Asch was not a security threat, his case was reopened in 1950 as a result of a newspaper article that reported his *resignation* from the Jewish Cultural Alliance (Yikuf), an organization thought to have Communist sympathies, if not affiliations. He was called before HUAC several times in 1952.

In the years following Peekskill Pete Seeger drifted from People's Artists. For one he had left the party, in part out of a growing uneasiness about membership in a secret organization but more for the fact that he could as easily—or more easily—reach people without the assistance of the party. The liability of even mild party involvement was becoming all too apparent to everyone in the Left; the People's Artists office was frequently under FBI surveillance, and several leftist folk singers were approached to become undercover agents.[106] Seeger's growing priority was to "get America singing" by any possible means—though folk songs, of course. In late 1949 Seeger's vehicle would become a group called the Weavers, in which he was joined by Ronnie Gilbert, Fred Hellerman, and his Almanacs compatriot Lee Hays.[107] The following year the Weavers were responsible for the country's number one selling record, "Goodnight Irene." It appeared on the Decca label and was produced by Decca's house arranger, Gordon Jenkins, who succeeded in smoothing off the song's rough edges. Asch could not have helped but feel ambivalent about the Weavers' success—here, finally, was the source of success and stability that had eluded him through nine years in the recording business. Would Asch have found them sufficiently "authentic"? Some thought they were not: Irwin Silber wrote acerbic columns about the Weavers in early issues of *Sing Out!* But Asch would not be among the most doctrinaire on the subject of folk authenticity over the years. Had his timing simply been wrong? Harold Leventhal, the Weavers' manager, could hardly have been expected to bring the Weavers to Folkways. Asch's label barely existed at the time, and Asch had neither the capital nor the distributing mechanism to handle hits of any kind. And would Asch have wanted them? He had learned one very painful lesson from Disc that he would never forget: genuine commercial successes in the recording business brought with them tremendous risk. He did not have the money to finance the hits, nor to absorb the cost of the bombs. And most of all he worried about the effect of hits on the remainder of his catalogue. *Time* magazine's characterization of Asch had been off the mark in 1946, but it was true now—Asch had a fear of hits.

The man from whom Seeger had learned "Irene"—Huddie Led-better—had died the previous December. Although he did not precisely die a pauper, as some have maintained, it would be years before any of his descendants benefited from the success that others musicians gleaned from his music. That same month Woody Guthrie was doing time on an obscenity conviction (sexual obsession had become one symptom of his disease, and for some months he had been writing outlandish letters to various female acquaintances). With his mind increasingly chaotic and his behavior ever more erratic, Guthrie was no longer a creative presence in New York's folk music world. Alan Lomax would shortly be undertaking a decade-long self-imposed exile in Europe that would allow him to ride out the McCarthy era in relative peace. The Weavers were the exception that proved the rule: "real" folk music in America was on the skids. And Asch, in typical fashion, seized the moment to put all of his energy behind a folk music record label.

5. FOLKWAYS IN THE FIFTIES

F olkways might have been a three-way partnership. Asch invited Courlander to come in with him and Distler on the enterprise, but Courlander declined out of concern for getting immersed in projects that did not interest him. He agreed instead to remain involved by continuing to edit the Ethnic series. Asch asked him whether he had any ideas for what they might call the new company. Courlander proposed *Folkways*, a term already at hand, as the brochure for the old Disc Ethnic series carried the slogan "the folkways of the world on records" and they had used it for the brief-lived concert series. Ethnic Folkways became the title of Courlander's own series. He had free rein with it, and over time he began to think of the series as a kind of recorded encyclopedia of world music.

Through the 1950s and until he left for Washington, D.C., in 1960 Courlander worked alongside Asch. Between them there was great respect—even a degree of measured affection. Though sometimes the target of Asch's intemperate outbursts (Courlander recalled having made Asch furious by an offhand remark about some statements of Pete Seeger's that he considered silly), Courlander could hold his ground and even return it in kind when necessary. At brief intervals Courlander worked at Folkways pasting brochures and the like in order to make ends meet, but Asch never made him feel like an employee. Occasionally Asch would slip a title into the Ethnic series that Courlander would not have accepted; in Courlander's view Asch "did not know his way around the music" and had little sense of what constituted good documentation. Still, Courlander edited 95 percent of the titles that appeared on the Ethnic list in those ten years and remained proud of the work the two of them did.[1]

Although Folkways gained its broadest audience in the early to mid-1960s when the folk music revival peaked, every significant category of musical, documentary, and sound recording that Asch issued in the 1960s had been initiated in the Folkways catalogue in the 1950s. It was in the 1950s that Asch established his production, sales, distribution, and marketing strategies that—with only rare interruptions in the later 1960s—became the lifeblood of Folkways Records. Keeping in mind all of the formative experiences leading up to the demise of Disc Records, the fifties must still be regarded as the era that gave birth to Folkways.

At first glance, Folkways seems an unlikely child of the fifties; Asch's iconoclasm would appear at odds with the era's notorious conformity. Although David Halberstam's book *The Fifties* may stand as the definitive summation of the era in the public imagination for the foreseeable future, he startled no one when he suggested that Americans in the 1950s "were optimistic about the future. Young men who had spent three or four years fighting overseas were eager to get on with their lives; so, too, were the young women who had waited for them at home."[2] The prosperity that many enjoyed in the postwar years appeared to give little cause for protest.

As always, though, the view from New York looked a bit different. As the great exodus to the suburbs redefined the meaning of the good life for millions of Americans, many remained behind—either by choice or by necessity. Asch himself was a steadfast New Yorker, a vantage point from which things did not appear rosy. Indeed, the fifties were terrible years for many leftists. As it turned out, the Peekskill Riot was only the opening act of American anticommunist hysteria. Senator Joseph McCarthy spread his venomous and irresponsible accusations, and any of Asch's associates who had a public life found their career opportunities narrowing and the vehicles for political expression dwindling. Within the Folkways circle, Pete Seeger's 1955 HUAC appearance, his contempt of congress trial six years later, and the dismissal of the case finally in May 1962 were followed most carefully. But Henry Cowell, Earl Robinson, Sis Cunningham and Gordon Friesen, Millard Lampell, and a great many others were haunted by the effects of their decades-old political idealism and youthful political affiliations.

Asch's parents moved from Stamford to Miami Beach in 1951 and remained there until 1953, when they began to split their time between Nice, London, and Israel. In the relative isolation of their Miami Beach compound, where Sholem spent hours fishing from the end of his dock, the continued carping of the *Forward* group grew fainter. Still he was the victim of a "physical offense" on the beach itself one day in the fall of 1953 by an "extremist, Yiddish-speaking group" (though a leading member of Miami's Jewish community was quick to point out that the group did not represent the sentiments of the community at large).[3] And as the attacks in the Jewish press slowly diminished, the House Un-American Activities Committee began to demand an explanation for Sholem's arrangement with the *Freiheit*. The FBI had been tracking Sholem and interviewing his neighbors prior to their move south, and as a result he would be summoned several times to testify despite his many anti-Stalinist proclamations over the years.[4]

There was very little romance left in the communism of the Old Left in the 1950s. Khrushchev's revelations about Stalin at the 1956 Twentieth Party Congress thinned the already meager ranks of the CPUSA; most were surprised and horrified to discover that the cause that had consumed their youth was corrupt, rotten, and fraudulent, and the shock that followed left many bitter or numb, cynical and politically disengaged for years.

Other, younger New Yorkers took a stand against the conformity of the era, yet felt far less beleaguered than their older comrades. College students in 1950s New York often encountered an intellectual, interpersonal, and sexual atmosphere that was profoundly liberating. Their rebellion was far more Freudian than Marxian, more likely to be marked by entering psychoanalysis than by joining the Communist Party. But arguably it was the start of a social revolution for which the generation of the following decade happily—if undeservedly—took full credit. Interpersonal relationships were analyzed in minute detail, sexual relationships took shape outside of marriage, women could imagine themselves with careers first rather than making themselves over into the perfect 1950s housewife. Interpersonal discovery was accompanied by a mingling of artistic influences; writers and painters looked to jazz innovators Thelonious Monk, Charles Mingus, and John Coltrane for inspiration.[5] The musician David Amram recalled that "there was a cross-pollination of music, painting, writing—an incredible world of painters, sculptors, musicians, writers, and actors, enough so we could be each other's fans. When I had concerts, painters would come, and I'd go play jazz at their art gallery openings, and I played piano while beats read their poetry."[6] From the perspective of New York's young literati of the 1950s, the label "Silent Generation" seemed hardly to fit at all. "Our fifties were far more exciting than the typical American experience," wrote Dan Wakefield in 1992, "because we were in New York, where people came to flee the average and find a group of like-minded souls."[7]

In his midforties by the opening of the decade, Moe Asch had settled firmly into his middle years. His sensibilities derived far more from the Popular Front and the New Deal than from the postwar rebellions of the Beats and their allies. His view of life, politics, and people had solidified long before, and he would make only minimal concession from here on to changes in popular taste. Yet Folkways Records also made a peculiar sense in the New York of the 1950s. It was a nonconformist endeavor and ran against the grain of the self-satisfied fifties in many of the same ways as New York's young artists. Asch was unlikely to have been surprised or disenchanted by Khrushchev's 1956 revelations; he had already recognized a false hope in the idealism of the party and had turned to artistic expression as the arena of his rebellion. There would be little of an overtly political nature in the Folkways catalogue through most of the decade. To some Asch was playing it safe during the hazardous McCarthy years, but Asch would have argued that in presenting the artistic expression of common people throughout the world with dignity he was promoting a political agenda with its own significance. Moe Asch's 1950s was neither a decade of political trauma nor of stultifying conformity, but a decade of exploration and artistic innovation.

In 1950 Asch and Distler were still occasionally shipping Disc records, probably in violation of bankruptcy arrangements. But the new outfit was up and running by early 1949, just as it was becoming apparent that the new long-playing format was going to prevail and ultimately eclipse the old 78s. For a couple of years, Folkways recordings were issued in both formats, and the releases in Courlander's Ethnic series were primarily on 78s. An early Leadbelly reissue appeared on a ten-inch LP as well as in a set of three seven-inch 45s, and *Songs to Grow On, Vol. 2: School Days* was originally reissued by Folkways in all three speeds. Nonetheless the change to LPs was a certainty and for the next several years provided opportunities for Asch to reissue in the new format records of his own (and others). In many cases the 78s had become unavailable. But like collectors of the 1980s and 1990s who temporarily bolstered the languishing recording industry by replacing worn LPs with CDs, the record-buying public in the early fifties was eager to replace cumbersome 78s with LPs that usually cost less than the equivalent set of 78s.

Among the first albums to appear on long-playing records were Pete Seeger's *Darling Corey*, Woody Guthrie's *Songs to Grow On*, and *Take This Hammer*, the first volume in what was intended to be a Leadbelly memorial series. There were immediately questions of ownership. In April 1949 Distler responded to an inquiry that Guthrie had received from the AFM regarding recordings on the Cub label. Distler assured the AFM that Folkways was the producer of Cub records and that the recordings in question had been made in the Asch Studios some years earlier and subsequently sold to her by Guthrie.[8]

Despite signs as early as 1938 that the major record labels were going to make their studio and field recordings of the 1920s and 1930s available once again, most of the historic jazz, race, and hillbilly recordings of this era remained out of print in the early 1950s. Asch and Fred Ramsey hit upon the idea of issuing an anthology of jazz on LP that would trace its history from the rural South to the big bands of the urban North in the mid-1930s. In his 1954 catalogue of LP jazz, Ramsey contended that he and Asch had undertaken the Folkways History of Jazz series "purely as an experiment" and that it represented a "stop-gap" measure in the fight for jazz reissues.[9] Ramsey added that

> its editorial policy . . . has been never to glamorize, never to depart from or distort a strictly chronological sequence in order to make jazz as it was recorded either better or different from what it really was; in a word, to report. Our goal was to gather these loose strands of old recordings together so as to present a literal anthology of jazz on record, comparable to literary anthologies in the strictest sense of the word.[10]

The allusion to literature reflected Asch's sense of himself as a "publisher" as well as Ramsey's own first professional identity as a student of literature. Issued over a period of four years (1950–53), approximately in chronological order, the History of Jazz series earned Asch the reputation in the recording industry as a pirate of others' material. Yet he and Ramsey made efforts to determine the ownership of the original recordings and to arrange for royalty payments when they were successful. Sometimes they heard from the owners of the masters only after the recordings had been reissued, but then readily agreed to pay royalties.

Asch justified the reissue of others' material with a clause in the U.S. Constitution regarding the public's right to information. He and Ramsey reasoned that if the original owners of this historical material would not make it available to the public, then it was their duty to do so. It was particularly exasperating to them that the major labels not only were unwilling to make historically significant material available, having concluded that it no longer made good business sense to address small, regional markets, but also in a great many cases actually destroyed the original masters. Asch and Ramsey made new masters from existing 78s, most of which came from Ramsey's own collection.

The first three volumes of the jazz series—*The South, The Blues,* and *New Orleans*—were issued in 1950. They reflected Ramsey's belief that the origins of jazz were to be found in the rural folk music of the urban South, a contention that would lead to a quest for the wellspring of jazz in rural Alabama a few years later. Woody Guthrie was presented with a copy of the *South* volume, along with some of Folkways' other early releases, and in late December he fired off one of his personal, always glowing reviews: "Your Jazz album vol #1 South is as good as if I'd put all my favorites all together by my own hand," he wrote modestly on 2 December. "Every groove is too good to waste." In the same letter to Folkways he described Seeger's *Darling Corey* as "the very best of Pete Seeger this far in this world" and *Songs of Mexico* as "the best 30 minutes I've spent anywhere all around Mexico." He concludes by paying homage to his own *Dust Bowl Ballads.* Asch had rereleased Guthrie's old Victor recording on Folkways with the title *Talking Dust Bowl,* including in the album notes an essay by his brother John Asch on the subject of soil erosion. "My Grapes of Wrath songs sound like Tom Joad would love to hear it," wrote Guthrie.[11] His own notes for the LP were prepared the previous May: "I just beat my way from NYC to L.A. and then back home again here in Coney"—a trip biographer Joe Klein described as a "particularly disastrous crossing."[12] But Guthrie reported in his exuberant and increasingly redundant style that he had found the Dust Bowl much as he had left it and called on the record buyer to "listen to these songs and to ask your own heart what kind of work you can do to help all of the refugees which you hear of in this Album."

Asch credits RCA Victor for the original recordings but credits himself with production and editing. Discussions about the re-issue of *Dust Bowl Ballads* had apparently been in progress since 1948, when LPs were just taking hold. That July RCA's A&R man wrote in response to Guthrie's letter of June of that year to inform him that the company had no immediate plans to reissue the album but that it was "entirely conceivable" that they might do so when "the market is in better shape." He added that Guthrie was free to record with other companies, but this was undoubtedly not the permission that Guthrie was seeking.[13] That permission never came, so Asch forged ahead with the reissue and endured the legal threats that ensued in the following years. RCA eventually conceded that the Folkways reissue of their recording posed little financial threat and allowed two versions of the album to be marketed simultaneously.

In the fall of 1950 Guthrie placed a series of urgent telephone calls to Asch and Distler, apparently to see whether they could arrange to copyright the song "So Long It's Been Good to Know Yuh," one of the original Dust Bowl ballads, in his name. The Weavers were about to record it for Decca to the accompaniment of Gordon Jenkins's lush choral and string arrangements. Guthrie wanted to secure the royalties to it before they were "swiped" by the Weavers, Decca, or Pete Kameron, who as an associate of Harold Leventhal was now simultaneously Guthrie's business manager and an employee of the Richmond Organization, a song publisher who had recently recognized the profits to be made by copyrighting somewhat altered versions of traditional songs.[14] Asch placed his business on hold for a day, much to Distler's disgust, while Distler herself painstakingly picked out the notes to the tune on a piano and marked them down on a piece of music paper.

Guthrie seems then to have remembered that he might have actually filed a copyright for "So Long" back in 1940. Asch blew up at Guthrie in the Folkways offices for having wasted his time and sent Guthrie and his wife scurrying to retrieve the original copyright certificate. "My respects [sic] for everybody in your office the other day didn't change towards nor against anybody present before nor after our confab ended," wrote Guthrie in his version of an apology. The Guthries ransacked their apartment in search of the certificate, which Guthrie now believed he might have filed prior to the Victor recording sessions that May. When it materialized Guthrie delivered it triumphantly to his publisher, Pete Kameron, who was in the midst of helping with the Weavers' Decca session. Kameron assured him, he reported to Asch, that the copyright certificate would supersede any claims Victor might have to copyright ownership.[15]

The entire charade over the copyright certificate infuriated Asch, who was increasingly impatient with Guthrie. Courlander later recalled that Asch was developing some "very negative feelings" about Guthrie, and although Asch felt very sorry for him and the things that had happened in his family, he could not abide his arrogance.[16] Asch spent an entire weekend preparing draft after draft of a response to Guthrie. When he finally sent it, he accused Guthrie of double-crossing, because he knew all along that the song had already been copyrighted:

> Now you fornicating bastard you write about the ashes (no pun) of your fire brought forth a phoenix in the form '40 copyright to this song—well you darn well know that a copyright is never lost as long as it is registered in the Library of Congress even if you lost your copy, and Marjorie has more than enough business sense to know this.[17]

But Asch concludes his letter by reminding Guthrie of the series of albums they had once discussed that would have Guthrie relating important events of the previous year as a kind of musical newspaper. "I am interested in experimenting with that now as the long playing medium will fit this type of material," he wrote. "And as I am sure no other company can do it and in my estimation the Woody Guthrie of before this last trip to California (the ramifications of which are many) is the only person to transcribe in a true light these happenings. In spite of Congress, the McCarthy Bill, or the War in Korea." Guthrie sent an uncharacteristically brief response: "You ought to hire out as a foreign ambassador and a humorist both. . . . No heavy hard feelings, Woodrow."[18]

In December, the day after he sent his capsule reviews to Asch, Guthrie responded to Asch's request to revive the talking newspaper project in a long letter: "I'm outlining and working out the twelve talking news blueses as per our last few elbow rubs." But his letter dwells primarily on the possibility of resurrecting some of his unrecorded GI ballads from the previous war, and the memory of those experiences sends him off on a loopy recollection of his dreadful experiences: "Ten or twelve numbers about being inducted, bootcamp, shipped over, foxholed, dugout, dusted off, shipped here & shipped yonder, shipped back home (Missions done with), then shunted, shuttled, scuttled, fuddled, and herded and huddled off to dwell on edges of psychotic quonset huts." Asch surely knew that Guthrie's talking newspapers were never to be.[19]

The significance of the "Service" in the company's title (Folkways Records and Service)—another Courlander suggestion—soon appeared to mean that Asch would produce records and other teaching aids on demand for the needs of individual clients. In the early years Folkways distributed educational filmstrips that often accompanied records of Native American or Mesoamerican music. Instructional dance records became one of the first means of meeting specialized "niche" markets, and his first customer was Guthrie's wife Marjorie. She had opened her Marjorie Mazia (her stage name from Martha Graham days) School of Dance a few blocks away from their apartment with some of the royalties Guthrie was earning from "So Long." Earl Robinson would teach guitar there for a while after being blacklisted in Hollywood. *Dance-a-Long* (7651) consisted of simple piano pieces of varying rhythms and an accompanying booklet of texts and line drawings showing the various movements that parents might encourage their children to emulate as they danced to the music. Marjorie could sell copies at her school so that the children could continue to practice their dancing at home.

Other commissioned recordings took Asch in more unexpected directions. The Museum of Natural History needed a recording of a tropical rain forest that they could play to accompany a new exhibit. Asch and Ramsey met with a curator at the New York Zoological Society in order to acquire "clues as to sounds one might expect to hear in a tropical rain forest." They then spent some hours together in the Central Park Zoo recording animal sounds and eventually repaired to Ramsey's apartment, where they reproduced the sound of rainfall in Ramsey's shower by lining the bathtub with newspaper. The recording that resulted entered the Folkways catalogue as *Sounds of a Tropical Rainforest in America* (6120). Few doubted the album's authenticity, although a possibly apocryphal story circulated about a museum curator who on hearing the recording remarked, "Ah, I think I detect a Yankee cricket."[20]

Asch became a one-man sales force. He cultivated his relationship with Sam Goody, who readily took at least one of every release that Asch issued. But Asch quickly learned that there was more to be gained by concentrating on settings where scholars, librarians, and music educators congregated than on record retailers, who showed only the mildest interest in his esoteric offerings. In mid-July 1950 Asch traveled to Cleveland to exhibit his recordings at the American Library Association meetings, setting up a Folkways booth at a cost of ninety-five dollars. For the next four and a half decades—almost until his death—the long hours he spent in the Folkways offices were punctuated several times a year by trips to various exhibition sights. He became a fixture among the exhibitors at the conventions of the Music Library Association, the Society for Ethnomusicology, the American Anthropological Association, the American Library Association, and the Modern Language Association. Although he would take orders throughout a convention, aficionados learned that he would sell off the records he had shipped ahead for the exhibit at reduced prices at the close of the convention, and in that way avoid the cost of shipping the records back to New York.

On an Eastern Airlines flight in April 1952 Moe asked a stewardess for a piece of stationery and wrote out a marketing strategy for the young label. Librarians were to be among his chief clients, as they could be counted on for decades to purchase spoken word, language instruction, children's, and any number of musical recordings. Among teachers his records would be useful not just for music educators but also for social studies teachers. He envisioned Folkways recordings in use in curriculum development, in teacher training, in workshops, conventions, exhibits, and demonstrations. The third leg of his marketing strategy would be museums: aquariums, science and natural science museums, art museums. Asch could expect educators in all three settings to recognize his intentions and support his work, however obscure or esoteric it might appear to mass audiences.[21]

At times it seemed that the more obscure a recording, the happier Asch was about releasing it—at least he could not be accused of pandering to mass-market tastes. Courlander was recovering musical recordings from every imaginable part of the globe. When he acquired them from the individual who had recorded them, it was usually an easy matter to ask the anthropologist or ethnomusicologist to write the accompanying notes. Those who were sensitive to the social context in which the music had been recorded often wrote careful descriptions of rituals, ceremonies, work settings, and social relations. When the recordings arrived without notes, he often called upon Henry Cowell to write them. Cowell's notes were more musicological than anthropological, but he could be counted on for accuracy and thoroughness. An early record set for which Cowell wrote notes consisted of Ukrainian songs and dances—the 78s came directly from the Soviet Union, and Courlander and Asch simply pasted blue Folkways labels over the original red ones. Another was Béla Bartók's original recordings of Hungarian folk music, which Asch had acquired from Bartók's son Peter.

Cowell had started work as early as June 1949 on a compendium of world music with the working title "Music of One World," reflecting the internationalism of the Left in the early postwar years. His project was almost entirely independent of Courlander's supervision and reflected Cowell's eclectic and idiosyncratic musical taste. "The music of some peoples of the world will sound extremely strange on first hearing," he wrote in the notes to the resulting five-volume *Music of the World's People.* "Yet all of this music contains richly rewarding values. That which may seem raucous at first may come to sound beautiful on further hearing; and at the very least, it will be found to be full of meaning and feeling. There is no better way to know a people than to enter with them into their musical life." Cowell declined to organize the recordings by race, style, history, or geography. This was simply a "sampling of widely contrasted musics from many levels of culture and many parts of the world. It is a series which may be started but never ended."[22] The first side of the series begins with a girl's chorus from Madagascar, followed in turn by musical examples from Ireland, Georgia, Greece, Japan, Nigeria, India, France, Russia, Bali, Arabia, Tahiti, Tibet, the United States, Iceland, and Spain. In 1952 Percy Grainger wrote Cowell to tell him that the "album of exotic records put out by you is simply glorious—I . . . just want you to know how much I admire the selection."[23]

Courlander delighted in Cowell's eccentricity. On one occasion Courlander and his wife went to Henry and Sidney Cowell's Village apartment to hear Henry play some of his prepared piano pieces. At one juncture Cowell offered them beers, neglecting to mention that he did not actually have any in the apartment. He then disappeared, leaving the Courlanders in the company of Cowell's blustery wife, Sidney, who was busy mending a suit of Henry's long underwear. Cowell himself returned an hour later in a much subdued state but with beers in hand.[24] The Cowells and Courlanders thereafter saw a good deal of each other.

Meanwhile Courlander was not content to remain solely the editor of other people's work, and he planned a new recording project of his own. Confining himself to a limited area within the United States, he was determined to see whether it might be possible to describe all the types of "Negro" music to be found in a single community or set of related communities. He hoped additionally to be able to "compare musical concepts and practices with those found elsewhere in Afro-America, including the Caribbean."[25] With some funding secured from the Wenner-Gren Foundation for Anthropological Research he drove south from New York to Alabama in the early months of 1950 in the company of his wife. They had a few leads provided him by Alan Lomax, the most useful of which was the suggestion that they look up a white, part-time librarian in Livingston, Alabama, then in her seventies, by the name of Ruby Pickens Tartt. Tartt helped Lomax and his father record African American material during a field expedition in 1940, and Courlander recalled that Lomax probably provided him with Tartt's name because he had led Lomax to believe that he was primarily gathering material for a novel. Tartt was introduced to traditional black church music as a child by her father and had earned a reputation in the region for being a bit peculiar on account of the passion with which she pursued her interest in Negro music. Immediately intuiting Courlander's purpose, Tartt introduced him to her favorite singers and helped him overcome some of the suspicion he generated among local blacks, who initially took him for an FBI agent. Although she herself did not care for blues music, she helped him discover a number of additional singers. The most prominent find was blues singer Rich Amerson, to whom Courlander would devote two volumes of the resulting Folkways series, *Negro Folk Music of Alabama*. Among their other discoveries was Dock Reed, who would become an important singer in the civil rights era. Courlander repaid Tartt by arranging for Wenner-Gren to provide her with her own tape recorder, and by permitting her to write the album notes for what would be the sixth volume in the resulting series, *Ring Games Songs and Others* (4474). Courlander recalled that Amerson's "Black Woman" was among the most frequently cited recordings in the set, but the most enduring contribution probably came from the school children whose "Green Green Rocky Road" became, in various forms, a folk standard.

The results of this field trip fueled Courlander's recording and publishing career for the next several years. Much of the material eventually appeared in his classic *Negro Folk Music U.S.A.*, published in 1963. Unlike Ramsey, Courlander did not regard jazz as African-derived, a conclusion that in his mind did the form no discredit. But much of the music he encountered in Alabama in January and February 1950 did appear to him to suggest African origins. In his notes to the first two albums (*Secular* [4417] and *Religious* [4418]), released later that same year, he remarks that "the controversy of African vs. European elements in the Negro music of the United States still goes on. It is hoped that these recordings will help to shed further light on the study of origins." The hand clapping he noted in both church services and children's games seemed to him to have obviously West African precedents, as well as the responsive singing he found in religious, work, and children's settings. Additionally, the use of vocal punctuations by preachers and work gangs, falsetto vocal styles, and the "ring shout" all appeared to Courlander to reflect African survivals. A particular find during his travels was a hollow-log drum of conspicuously African origins, although it had since been converted into a storage bin.[26] At the same time he cautioned the listener that his intention is not to "create the impression that the music is 'African'":

> The notation of African atavisms is intended only to point out the complicated and composite nature of American Negro music. In the end it has to be recognized that regardless of the sources of inheritance, the American Negro has produced over the years a music that is clearly his own. It is familiar to all of us, yet easily distinguishable from other musical trends in America. It has maintained its own identity and integrity in the midst of the nervous disorders with which our musical life has been afflicted.[27]

Courlander was not, in fact, a devotee of popular American music and lamented the "deformation that [Negro folk music] has undergone in the process of popularization at the hands of its admirers." Though less reverential of authenticity than Fred Ramsey, he was nonetheless among the pursuers of the "genuine article." And *Negro Folk Music of Alabama* was certainly that—it would stand as some of his very best fieldwork, and among the works of which he would be most proud.

Sometime in 1950 Harry Smith was making his way across country from California to New York with several hundred vintage 78 records in tow. Arriving penniless at Penn Station, his first thought was to sell some of his records in order to secure food and shelter. It was suggested to him that he approach Moe Asch, who might have some interest in buying some of them. A meeting was arranged.

Smith was a small, hunched man with a high, pinched voice whose extraordinary intelligence and creativity could be both highly disciplined and hopelessly broad-ranging. Due to his stature he was employed through much of the Second World War at a Boeing plant near Seattle, installing radar parts in the narrow tail

sections of bombers. He spent a considerable portion of his earn-
ings buying up 78s during the shellac shortage.[28] His taste was
fundamentally that of a collector, that is, he sought out a record
because he had seen or heard a reference to it, because it was rare
or exotic or interesting, or because it had a particular relationship
to a recording that he already had. His first records were blues to
which he had seen references in books such as Odum and
Johnson's *Negro Workaday Songs*, which included lists of recordings.[29] He found his way to hillbilly records through an interest in
Irish music, and the internment of Japanese Americans during the
Second World War produced a windfall of rare recordings of Japanese music.[30]

At the end of the war he was, as he later recalled, "making a
desperate attempt to study anthropology" at the University of
Washington.[31] His impulses kept bringing him back to the collection of artifacts, whether material or aural, that when viewed
collectively might reveal something about the culture of the people that produced them. In the mid-1950s this led him to a fascination with content analysis that, much like Alan Lomax's
cantometrics, attempted to draw conclusions about a culture and
its people from the number of times particular words (or categories of words) occur in their song repertoire. Thus, unsurprisingly,
he found the word *food* appearing with increasingly frequency in
rural southern recordings of the Depression.[32] But at heart he was
a structuralist inclined to a much more subtle methodology. In the
early 1980s he half-facetiously described Claude Lévi-Strauss as
"probably the world's greatest living novelist," recognizing that his
appeal was largely in the inventiveness of his interpretations of
myth. Like Lévi-Strauss, Smith's interest was in the patterns that
emerged from a series of related artifacts, and to that end his
collecting ultimately encompassed Kwakiutl and Salish house
posts, painted eggs, string figures, patchwork quilts, and records.

Smith's formal study of anthropology eventually floundered,
perhaps because he found other ways of communicating—
through objects and film—far more interesting and effective than
the written word. He moved to Berkeley and then San Francisco,
occasionally lecturing on jazz and making avant-garde films that
would be the source of his notoriety outside the folk music
world. In Berkeley he lived downstairs from Professor Bertrand
Bronson, whose work on Chaucer in the mid-1930s had evolved
into the study of Samuel Johnson in the forties and eventually
to a fascination with Child ballads (so named for the eminent

nineteenth-century ballad collector Francis J. Child) and other ballad forms. Smith and Bronson swapped records, sometimes with
the collaboration of Bronson's wife at opportune moments when
Bronson was out of town. Thus to Smith's interest in the cultural
context of folk song was added an appreciation for its formal
properties. But Smith's imagination led him eventually to approach song neither narrowly as literature nor entirely as a window to the understanding of other cultures. Smith could
conclude that his "projects are only attempts to build up a series
of objects that allow some sort of generalizations to be made—regarding popularity of visual or auditory themes."[33] Yet he did not
undertake the fieldwork or the writing that would have allowed
him to make generalizations of this order about his collections.
Rather, like the Beats with whom he would eventually join forces,
the exploration of alien cultural forms in the end was a self-ref-
erential project. Smith was finally more interested in what patterns of cultural artifacts told him about himself than what they
suggested about the people who produced them. Folk music and
folk art was "good to think" in the Lévi-Straussian sense that it was
grist for his own artistic imagination. Collecting was itself an artistic endeavor for Smith, because the arrangement of the collected
objects followed the dictates of his own idiosyncratic imagination.
Although Asch may have glimpsed the modernist possibilities of
folk music back in the Disc era, Smith was surely among the first
(perhaps with Paul Bowles) to directly implicate folk music in an
avant-garde artistic vision.

Smith's appearance and manner reminded Asch of the Woody
Guthrie of a decade earlier (Smith was taken to hear Guthrie at a
longshoreman's hall, probably when Guthrie was in Seattle with
Pete Seeger in September 1941).[34] He lacked Guthrie's abrasive
self-confidence but could be equally arrogant and eccentric. Asch
would eventually allow Smith to take advantage of him more than
Guthrie was ever permitted, and his affection for Smith was more
enduring. On the other hand, Guthrie was too self-possessed to
be bothered by Asch's intemperate outbursts, whereas Smith was
sufficiently put off by Asch's shouting that he steered clear of him,
sometimes for years at a time. "He can scare me to death," recalled
Smith in 1983. "I don't like being yelled at."[35]

Smith and Asch had different recollections of the transaction
that resulted from their meeting; Smith's is probably the more
plausible. Asch would recall that Smith came to him with the
express purpose of issuing an anthology of his old 78s on LP: "He

came to me and said: 'Look, this is what I want to do. I want to lay out the book of notes. I want to do the whole thing. All I want to be sure of is that they are issued.' Of course I was tremendously interested."[36] Smith, though, was certain that his initial intent was to sell records, and that it was Asch's idea to issue an anthology.[37]

In May 1952 Smith signed a formal contract with Folkways for the production of a three-volume anthology that would parallel and complement Ramsey's jazz series. He was originally to be paid two hundred dollars as an advance against royalties, with the first one thousand albums to be sold royalty free. But eventually Distler agreed that he would receive his twenty-cent royalty on each album, beginning with the sale of the first one. A small work space was cleared for Smith in the tiny two-room office at 117 West Forty-sixth Street, and he began the work that would consume him for the next several months. Smith recalled that Asch supervised his work daily: "I'm just naturally worthless, and he's not too good, either," Smith remarked some years later.[38] Asch would later claim that his supervision consisted of providing Smith with a peyote button every few hours, from which Smith would draw some degree of his inspiration. Apocryphal or not, devotees of Smith's *Anthology of American Folk Music* have detected a visionary, dreamlike quality in the booklet of almost thirty pages that Smith produced to accompany the records.[39] In his protracted unwrapping of *Anthology,* folklorist Robert Cantwell describes it as "a kind of curriculum in mystical ethnography" and a "memory theater" that

> achieves its ends aurally—working as a kind of solvent on the fixed distinctions of continuous rational space, with its visual-tactile gradient, and transforming it into an altogether dynamic, discontinuous, and irrational space: a multifarious, simultaneous universe, all of its differentiations uncertain, its boundaries permeable and its forms protean, the ephemeral world whose perceptual surface we must continually penetrate to construct a palpable reality, one that always partakes of our own experience.[40]

It is unlikely that Smith imagined that he was quite as disinterested in the social context of the songs as Cantwell's long postmodernist digression seems to suggest. And certainly if Smith did regard it as a "project of detextualizing folk music," those musicians who used *Anthology* in subsequent years to develop their revivalist repertoires most assuredly did not. But Cantwell is surely right that in the arrangement of the music and notes within *Anthology* we see the operation of a lively avant-garde imagination for which folk music has become, above all, a mental plaything.[41]

For each of the eighty-four musical selections in *Anthology of American Folk Music* there was an entry, which included the title and the artists and any other information found on the original label, the recording date, the instrumentation, the original issue number and the master number where available, either a synopsis of the song if a ballad or key words or phrases for other songs, other information about the song, its subject, the artist or the circumstances of its recording, a discography of other recordings of the song, and a bibliography citing references to the song in one or more of the forty-nine volumes Smith consulted for the project. The alphabetical index included titles, artists, first lines, subjects, alternate titles, and quotations other than first lines.

The innovations in the notes are many. Smith appropriated dozens of small etchings from the late-nineteenth- and early-twentieth-century music catalogues from which he worked—pictures of musical instruments, musicians, pointing hands, anonymous bearded men along with reproductions of the original record labels, record envelopes, and sheet music—and scattered these throughout the notes. It was a style of illustration that was quickly picked up by *Sing Out!* and others and became identified with a particular kind of whimsical, folksy publication.

Perhaps most innovative of all were the categories Smith used for the music. He abandoned entirely the racial and regional categories that had dominated the recording industry for decades—none of the records or volumes were identified as blues, race, hillbilly, or other such markers of race and region. Rather, the volumes were divided into ballads, social music, and songs. It was a startling departure, reflecting Smith's lingering anthropological curiosity about the social context of the music as well as of the racial cross-fertilization of musical styles in the rural South.

All of *Anthology*'s selections came from Smith's collection and were mastered for LP by Peter Bartók, universally recognized by those who worked with Folkways in the early years as a top-notch sound and recording engineer. It is not known whether Asch conceded engineering responsibilities to Bartók because there were other growing demands on his time or because he recognized the fact that he himself was not able to keep up with the rapidly changing technology. Whatever the reason, Asch was increasingly remote from the actual recording until, by the start of the following decade, most of the recording and mastering responsibilities had been handed over either to Bartók or Mel Kaiser of Cue Studios, which had moved in across the hall from Folkways in the WEVD building.

The impact that *Anthology* was to have on American folk music was still some years off. In one of the last letters he would send to Asch, Woody Guthrie, as usual, was among the first to express his delight with it. Guthrie had spent the better part of 1952 in various psychiatric wards, as it became increasingly apparent that he was suffering from something more than just alcoholism. By autumn his doctors had finally and firmly identified his disorder as Huntington's chorea. When he was permitted to leave Brooklyn State Hospital in September he bolted for the West Coast and Will and Herda Geer's compound in Topanga Canyon, where he met a young (and recently married) woman half his age named Anneke Marshall. With the symptoms of Guthrie's illness momentarily subsiding, Anneke fell in love with Guthrie and they ran off together—first to New York, and then with Jack Elliot to the home of Stetson Kennedy in Beluthahatchee Swamp, Florida. Guthrie wrote to Asch and Distler from Beluthahatchee in May 1953, noting with pleasure the mention of his Folkways recordings in an issue he had seen of *My Baby* and describing Kennedy's anti-Klan crusade. He signed it "NO HARD FEELINS SPITEN ALL SADBAD RUMORS. YRS TRLY . . . I ME WOODY."[42] Perhaps Guthrie was thinking of the rumors of his illness, inherited from his mother, which he still vainly refused to recognize as a death knell. Two weeks later, he was the victim of another Guthrie family fire, which he caused by pouring gasoline on their barbecue pit. His right arm and hand were badly burned and then poorly treated and would never be serviceable again.[43]

Guthrie and Anneke lurched back across the country, making a brief stop in Mexico, where he procured a quick divorce from a still-reluctant Marjorie. Back in Topanga Canyon, with Anneke pregnant but increasingly alarmed about Guthrie's condition, he tried to resume writing his book *Seeds of Man*. Without the use of his right arm, he typed in capital letters, sending a last, tragic letter to Asch and Distler. It is concerned entirely with his accidental discovery of *Anthology:* "I trapsed around ten dozen trips & times all up and all down the geographical confines . . . trying my best to locate some little suitable present or a giving gift of some keen klassical kind to buy to give over to little Anneke." He happened upon the third volume of *Anthology* but played it for some weeks without noticing that it had come from Folkways: "I played these albums over & over several hundreds of times by this later date without so much as ever taking so much ass one good look at the damn labels to find out who & which recordy company put them out." The records were a magnificent hit with their neighbors in Topanga:

> Every house & every famm damily up here loves only just one earthly article more than they love their homes or their houses or their batch of kids or their cars or their farms & their trucks & their tractors & their properties both public and private which article as I just said is my three elpeed al-bums of Blind Lemon and the Carter Family. And I & her did spell out one little word on one of our best albums here just a while before daybroke this mornin. It went. Let me see. It went ahhhh. It ahhhhh. Went Ahhhh. Went something like. Went some thing like ahhhhhhh. Ohhhhh. Like Ohhhhhhe. Folkways. Record & Service Corp. Didnt say which damn kind of service. Just said Folkwayses. Folke Wayes. Er some sucha domn thing. Folk something. Folky something. Folkwayed. Er Folkslayed. Noope. Folkways. Yep. Folkways. That was it. F o l k w a y s.[44]

Some recordings largely fell into Asch's lap; others he tenaciously kept after. One of the latter was an idea in the early fifties for a recorded anthology of Negro poetry. Eight years had elapsed since Asch had issued an album of Langston Hughes's poetry on Asch Records; in 1952 he reissued the album on LP for the first time, with Sterling Brown (whom Asch had also recorded in the forties) reading several of his own poems on the other side. Arna Bon-temps was employed to write the notes — "and was paid!" he wrote to his friend Hughes.[45] The same year Asch commissioned Bon-temps to edit the *Anthology of Negro Poets,* for which he would be paid fifty dollars. Asch intended to include the most prominent African American poets of the twentieth century, all reading from their own work. He had acquired four sides of Claude McKay reading his poetry from some time in the early forties and hoped to get the rights to a commercial recording of James Weldon Johnson's "God's Trombone" that had been made for the now-defunct Ma-jestic label. He wrote to Johnson's widow in April and described the plan for the anthology as well as the nature of his operation. She seemed initially responsive but came to see Asch the following

October to report that the recordings were now owned by MGM and she could not sell him the rights.[46]

In September 1952 Hughes wrote Bontemps:

> Look here, Moe Asch, Folkways Records, wants me to record two poems for his anthology of Negro Poetry in records, which he says you are the editor of, or the poem-selector. He wants to record next week, so let me know which two poems of mine you think best, by return mail. I'd suggest the best known: "Negro Speaks of Rivers" and "I, Too, Sing America"—or else, if we want one rhymed lyric one, in place of the latter, "Refugee in America."[47]

And in December he wrote a similar letter to Margaret Walker.[48]

The following July Bontemps, still trying to line up his poets, wrote Hughes: "Moe Asch, whom I saw on the Coast, still hopes to bring out that anthology of Negro poets on records. Isn't there anything you can say to Margaret [Walker] and Gwendolyn [Brooks] to bring them across?" Hughes responded: "My suggestion is to PHONE Margaret and Gwen re recordings. Otherwise you'll never get a yea nor nea. They don't answer me, either. I wrote them once as you requested. Have I heard a word? no."[49] This apparently worked; when the album finally came out the following year the poetry of Walker and Brooks constituted the second side.

Hughes had meanwhile begun work on a series of projects of his own for Asch. They signed an agreement in July 1952 for a recorded selection of Hughes's *Chicago Defender* column featuring the fictional Jesse Semple, or "Simple," his naïve but inadvertently wise commentator on contemporary race relations. Entitled *Simple Speaks his Mind,* the album was released in early 1953. Hughes wrote Asch:

> Please forgive me for being so long in thanking you for the recordings of "Simple" and Sterling Brown which you sent me. I'm delighted with them, and it was very good of you to send me several. They are very clear, and friends seem to like. Let's hope they sell somewhatly. I'll be by to see you soon regarding the other things we wanted to do. Spring deadlines have kept (and are keeping) my nose to the grindstone. I'm nothing but a literary sharecropper. I wish you would record me some gospel songs.

The *Simple* recording, however, was pulled from the market and never appeared in a Folkways catalogue, perhaps because of copyright difficulties. Instead, Asch released a recording in the early sixties entitled *The Best of Simple* (9789), a selection of Hughes's columns read by Melvin Steward to coincide with a published anthology of the same name.

The "other things we wanted to do" included four recordings for children that would be released over the next couple of years. Some were tied in with book projects that Hughes was working on. Despite almost thirty years of prominence as black America's leading poet, Hughes was having difficulty making ends meet and had indeed become a "literary sharecropper." Several children's books in 1954 made modest contributions to his income. *The Story of Jazz* (7312), which first appeared in a 1954 catalogue as *The First Album of Jazz*, was derived from *The First Book of Jazz*, published contemporaneously. Hughes admitted to Bontemps that "what I really know about jazz would fill a thimble," so he called upon David Stone Martin, Marshall Stearns, and John Hammond (among others) to review his text.[50] With the help of Mel Kaiser, Hughes took portions of twenty-seven musical selections and connected them with a narrative that traced the development of jazz from African drumming through slave shouts and hollers to New Orleans, big band, and bop. Most of the musical selections came from Ramsey's jazz series.

A second children's book project was turned into a Folkways recording in 1955. Hughes's *First Book of Rhythms* became *The Rhythms of the World* (7340) the following year. Here too, with the help of Kaiser, Hughes drew on existing Folkways recordings, mostly in the Science series, to illustrate the ways in which musical rhythm is derived from sounds in nature. Hughes's *Dream Keeper and Other Poems*, a volume for older children published in 1934, became a Folkways recording of the same name that year (7774).

Yet another record for children, *The Glory of Negro History* (7752), which appeared in its first few years in the Folkways catalogue as *American Negro History*, enabled him to draw upon the research he had conducted for *Famous American Negroes* and *The First Book of Negroes*. These books—one for juveniles and the other for younger children—had been severely edited by Hughes's publishers, who had required him to delete any mention of racial prejudice in the entries of prominent black Americans such as Ralph Bunche and A. Philip Randolph and to delete altogether the entry of W. E. B. Du Bois (Josephine Baker was deleted from *The First Book of Negroes* after the first edition, when it was suggested that she might have been a Communist). Although it is unlikely that Asch would have placed similar strictures on Hughes, *The Glory of Negro History* is also conspicuously lacking in any mention of Du Bois. This is all the more remarkable as there is a lengthy passage about Du Bois's longtime adversary, Booker T. Washington, as well as a section on the Niagara movement (which led to the founding of the NAACP) of which Du Bois was the most prominent member! Perhaps the omissions on the recording simply followed from those in the written text, which were in themselves compromises Hughes made without a battle in order to secure his livelihood. In any case the recording does not shrink from mentioning violence, prejudice, and discrimination. Also, in the year of *Brown v. Board of Education* there is ample intimation that things are getting better. The closing passage, by Mary McLeod Bethune, is unstinting in its reality, as well as in its message of hope:

> We have known what it is to suffer; we are prepared to understand suffering. We have known what it is to be underprivileged; we are prepared by history to redeem others from want. . . . I have always believed that some day we would find greater peace and harmony among the many elements which make up the American people. There is now before us an unparalleled opportunity. This is our day! Doors will open everywhere, the floodtide of a new life is coming in.

Hughes wrote Asch in September 1954 to report that he had secured actors Hilda Hayes, then appearing on Broadway in *King of Hearts,* and Clayton Smeltz to sing on the recording and to read the narration; the final recording would feature the voices of Ralphe Bunche and Mary McLeod Bethune. "You must send a 'History' record to Mrs. Roosevelt," Hughes wrote Distler when the record had been released. "She's a great friend of Mrs. Bethune and so will probably adore our ending (Also she once gave a third of her column to my poems)." Historian John Hope Franklin, then at Howard, was also to receive a copy of the recording, as well as Bethune and Bunche.[51]

Thus with Langston Hughes Asch became the progenitor of "books on tape," though, granted, in highly abbreviated forms. Again, this time in 1958, the release of Hughes's novel *Tambourines to Glory* coincided with a Folkways LP release of the same name (3538). The books undoubtedly helped the sales of the albums; it is unlikely that the albums did much for the sale of the books. Asch's contribution to Hughes's livelihood was undoubtedly modest, although happily "off the books." Although there is some evidence of a periodic accounting of royalties, Asch appears to have paid Hughes in the same paternalistic fashion he had Woody Guthrie, often in cash. "Langston received his money by calling up whenever he needed it usually to pay out to someone in need," wrote Asch sometime after the death of Marian Distler in 1964, apparently in an effort to regularize the royalty arrangements.

Asch also sought out Tony Schwartz, a sound engineer and collector of folk music and an enigmatic variety of urban folklore. Schwartz was a self-proclaimed "gadgeteer" who was developing a reputation in New York for amassing a huge tape library of folksong performances that he had started to tape off the radio from Oscar Brand's WNYC shows in the late 1940s. Folk singers began to drop by his apartment in the early fifties to hear selections from his collection and to add performances of their own, with the clear understanding that they would not be used for commercial purposes. Schwartz also hit on the idea at this time of collecting spontaneous performances of New Yorkers at work and play on the streets. He installed an airplane battery in the back of his Renault, attached an early Magnacorder to it, and from the Magnacorder ran seventy-five-foot cords for his microphone and headset. Parking his car at the curb and slinging a box containing a VU meter and volume control around his neck, he ventured onto playgrounds and into work sites.

Schwartz's work was deliberately noncommercial, which must have appealed to Asch instantly. Asch immediately understood the purpose of Schwartz's work, and its spontaneity fit perfectly into Asch's idea of the authentic. At the same time, the idea that in 1952 one might find authentic folklore on the streets of New York was relatively novel. Schwartz provided Asch with the first concrete evidence that folklore was not an exclusively rural phenomenon, nor was it necessarily tainted or corrupted when transplanted to urban settings. Schwartz's first Folkways release, *1, 2, 3 and a Zing Zing Zing* (7003), captured children's rhymes, chants, songs, hymns, and games on playgrounds and on street corners, in public schools, in play centers, and in homes. The children on it represented a variety of races and nationalities. "In the 'folk process,'" wrote Schwartz in the album notes, "songs are generally passed along from adult to child. In street games and songs the process differs: they are passed from child to child."

If unconventional, Schwartz's work was not unappreciated by established folklorists. In the fall of 1953 Schwartz was at work on his second Folkways project, *New York 19*. Ben Botkin and William Tyrrell, writing in *New York Folklore Quarterly*, proposed that Schwartz's work exemplified "downstate" folklore, which although differing from "upstate" folklore was no less worthy of study. Upstate folklore, they argued, consists of that more conventional folk expression heard from "'those who live simple, unnoticed lives.'"[52] Downstate folklore, they emphasized, was not to be confused with the "city-billy singers" and other symptoms of the corrupting influence of New York's "publishing and entertainment mill." Rather, it was the "sounds of our times," derived from "complicated and confused ways of life." Whether rural life was, in fact, any less "complicated" than urban life might have been a matter of debate, but the inclusion of urban cultural expressions went a long way toward broadening the definition of "folklore" beyond an assemblage of relics from an idealized and vanishing rural past.[53]

For *New York 19* Schwartz confined his collecting to the area defined by his postal zone, a portion of West Midtown that included Hell's Kitchen. Schwartz was developing an ear for significant moments in the lives of those who worked and played on the streets of New York and he had learned how to win the trust of those he encountered. Ben Shahn was among those who warmly admired Schwartz's work. He wrote to Asch in July 1954 in order to express his appreciation and to ask him to send copies of *New York 19* to several friends: "Please tell Tony Schwartz he's my kind of artist—hard-boiled and beautiful."

Shahn also reminded Asch that they had not seen each other "for a Hell of a long time. Why don't you come out soon (to Roosevelt, NJ), and while you are here you can look over some drawings and what-not and see whether there's anything you need."[54] Asch used a Shahn drawing that year for the cover of an album of *Jewish Freilach Songs* (6809) by Prince Nazaroff, an appropriate and predictable match of graphic and audio material. Less predictable was the use to which Asch had put a Shahn drawing the previous year of trumpeting angels—it graced the cover of a recording that Marshall Stearns had made in the Bahamas of *Gospel Songs* by the Missionary Quintet (6824). The eclectic combination of Shahn's identifiably Jewish drawings and Afro-Caribbean singing reflected Asch's iconoclastic disregard for nationalist boundaries. Of more interest to Asch were the thematic continuities uniting people across ethnic lines, yet another reflection of the internationalist impulses of the American Left in the 1950s.

Asch's affiliation with Stearns dated to the late forties, when

Stearns was attempting to get his Institute of Jazz Studies off the ground. Stearns had written Asch to elicit his participation in the project at a time when Asch was in no condition (financially or organizationally) to look much beyond his own immediate concerns. The position of executive secretary was available "for anyone who can raise the money. How about you?" queried Stearns.[55] Asch did not bite. Stearns had been a professor of Renaissance poetry at Cornell but had allowed his passion for jazz to overwhelm his original professional identity. The institute was finally established in New York City in 1953, by which time Stearns was teaching at Hunter College. Stearns enabled jazz studies to get its first toehold in the academy, ultimately establishing the institute as an autonomous entity within Rutgers University at Newark. Although Asch would never again be able to release the kind of commercial jazz that he had in the Disc days, there developed a symbiotic relationship between Folkways and Marshall Stearns that enabled Asch to remain affiliated with the world of academic jazz studies. Folkways became an outlet for the Afro-Caribbean material Stearns would periodically collect on field expeditions. When his book, *The Story of Jazz*, appeared in 1956 it included an outline for fifteen lectures on the history of jazz, which included lists of illustrative recordings from commercially available LPs, a great many of them on Folkways. Despite competing recorded jazz histories by then on Riverside, Decca, and Capitol, Stearns touted Ramsey's jazz series as "the best-edited and widest-ranging series on jazz to date."[56] Almost all of the examples of African and Caribbean music listed for the "jazz prehistory" lecture were taken from Folkways recordings.

Asch did get involved in professional organizations when it served his business purposes. He was present at the American Anthropological Association meetings in the fall of 1953 when a group of anthropologists (including Helen Codere and Melville Herskovits) and musicologists (including David McAllister, Bruno Nettl, and Willard Rhodes) first met to discuss the formation of the Society for Ethno-musicology. The society's journal, *Ethnomusicology*, listed new Folkways releases from its inception, and Asch sensibly retained his membership in the society through the decade. He also allowed his involvement in the Music Library Association to extend beyond immediate marketing opportunities. At the summer meeting in Miami Beach in June 1955 he presented a lecture demonstration entitled "Folk Music," in which, with Marian Distler's ample editorial assistance, he used samples from seventeen different Folkways albums in order to illustrate both the diversity

of world music, as well as songs and instrumentation that transcended cultural boundaries. "Just as there are differences in national cultures, so are there similarities." He traced a handful of
songs (including "Wimoweh") through several musical traditions to
suggest ways in which cultures remade songs to fit existing cultural conventions—and ways in which songs retained the character of their culture of origin despite having been made over. It was
neither the similarities that overwhelmed the differences nor vice
versa, but the peculiar sensation of hearing songs that were at
once familiar and unfamiliar. Asch cleverly flattered the music
librarians by permitting them to hear what the performers of the
songs often did not hear themselves—the irony of their unwitting
and often naïve appropriation of unfamiliar traditions:

> Librarians are the best evaluators of folk music. In the classic
> literature of a civilization, people accept as its truest repre-
> sentation and expression those values which have been tried
> and tested by time. So is it also with folk music. The popular
> hit parade, as well as the ten best sellers, may reflect the
> moods of many people and document the present. But the
> preservation of the true and lasting culture that makes a peo-
> ple great and gives them a heritage worth saving is the duty,
> as well as the pleasure, of those who know how to work with
> ultimate values. It is they, therefore, who must be responsible
> for the maintenance and accumulation of recordings of the
> best and most typical music of the world's many peoples.[57]

It is unlikely that the librarians had ever been subject to a sales
pitch that appealed so directly to their most noble self-image.

Throughout the 1950s Asch had less and less time to become
directly involved with individual projects and increasingly left the
actual recording to others. Those projects in which he did immerse
himself tended to call upon historical and literary, rather than
musical, perceptions. Starting with *Ballads of the Revolution* sung by
Wallace House (5001) and released in 1953, Asch produced a series
of recordings, each on two ten-inch discs, that illustrated specific
eras in American history through songs of the period. The second,
Ballads—War of 1812 (5002) also featured House's voice, while Her-
mes Nye performed *Ballads of the Civil War* (5004) and Pete Seeger
recorded the set *Frontier Ballads* (5003). Asch wrote the notes for all
of these, painstakingly constructing the historical context of each
song using encyclopedias and a few standard secondary texts. The

songs were not, by and large, ballads; nor were many of them folk songs but popular songs of their day. Asch intended these specifically for classroom use rather than for folklorists, so there was no attempt to identify the songs' sources and whether they represented a specific variant or a combination of several. There is less evidence of Distler's editorial polishing in these notes, and they suggest the extent to which Asch remained uncomfortable with written English, resorting often to tired figures of speech. Yet these albums imply what is made more explicit in an album that Asch devised with Charles Edward Smith in 1958. *The Patriot Plan* (5710) consists of recitations of fifteen primary documents from the colonial era (read by Wallace House) intended to trace the origin of democratic principles in the United States. As Asch had suggested several times before over the course of almost twenty years in recording, traditions of tolerance and individual freedom are deeply rooted in American history. Again intended for classroom use, *The Patriot Plan* was not a radical project, but its appearance in the earliest years of the contemporary civil rights movement gave it additional significance.

Fred Ramsey continued to plan large-scale projects in which Folkways was implicated one way or another. Asch arranged for the publication of Ramsey's *Guide to Longplay Jazz Records*, reserving the bulk of the publisher's advance for himself as well.[58] Ramsey also had hours of Leadbelly on tape, from a series of very informal sessions he had held in his apartment in the year before the bluesman's death. By the autumn of 1948 the commercial recording companies had long lost interest in recording Leadbelly. Ramsey had remained one of his staunchest supporters, and he recognized an opportunity when he got his hands on one of the early tape recorders. Tape had solved the problem of tangling that had plagued the older wire recorders and shared with wire the ability to record continuously for an hour or more without interruption. With the advent of LPs Ramsey hoped that Leadbelly could be encouraged to sing and reminisce at length.

Leadbelly, as it happened, needed little prompting, recognizing immediately the possibilities of the new technology. In late September he came to Ramsey's place for dinner with his wife Martha. Because this was only intended as a preliminary meeting, he had left his guitar at home. But as the operation of the tape recorder was explained to him, he began to sing a cappella. Ramsey had hung his New York apartment with drapes in an effort to approximate the sound-dampening environment of a recording studio, although in the first session he had only a crude voice microphone at his disposal. By the end of the first evening, Leadbelly had recorded thirty-four songs, accompanied by Martha's singing on a few, which stretched back to the field hollers and shouts of his youth. In subsequent sessions the following month, they were joined by Charles Edward Smith, whose voice could be heard on a few choruses, and Asch had lent Ramsey one of his fine old RCA microphones. Leadbelly allowed himself to free associate, one song reminding him of another until he had compiled a catalogue of early twentieth-century African American folk and popular song as filtered through his memory and unique musical sensibilities. In all more than ninety songs were recorded, often with one leading directly into another or separated by a brief spoken commentary from Leadbelly.

It was not until 1953 that Asch had the means of issuing Ramsey's Leadbelly recordings. When he and Ramsey looked in the boxes of tapes, they found that some of the tape had adhered to the next winding and much of it had to be repaired. Peter Bartók undertook the task of redubbing the original recordings onto new tape and managed to rescue almost all of it. Ramsey then edited the tapes for three two-record sets (twelve sides) but later discovered that by eliminating separations between the bands the material could be compressed onto eight sides. Although some fidelity was lost in the process, given the crudeness of the original recordings, there was probably not too much fidelity to lose. They became—as Leadbelly could not have known but Ramsey undoubtedly suspected—*Leadbelly's Last Sessions*. Ramsey prepared the notes for the recordings as an article that he sold to *High Fidelity* magazine and then reprinted them in the albums notes with the magazine's permission—a clever practice that served him well in several subsequent projects.

With the editing of the eleven-volume jazz reissue series completed in the spring of 1953, Ramsey turned to a still more ambitious project. With Asch's support, he had just secured a Guggenheim Fellowship in order to investigate "Afro-American music between 1860 and 1900."[59] His plan was to take recording and photographic equipment south to Alabama, Louisiana, and Mississippi and search for music in locations sufficiently remote that he might be confident of its having been shielded from modern, popular influences. It would be important, of course, that Ramsey distinguish his project from Courlander's, but he felt that his approach was altogether different. Courlander, he mistakenly believed, was a trained anthropologist whose interests were primarily in documenting music as part of an entire way of life. Ramsey's focus would be almost completely on the music and its historical development. Specifically, Ramsey was intent on testing his hypothesis that the origins of jazz were to be found in the rural folk music of the South, and his mission was to trace these origins to their wellspring. "My purpose was to explore and document the Afro-American musical environment in as many areas within these states as possible on a relatively limited budget," he wrote three years later for *Ethnomusicology*:

> In so doing, I hoped to tap sources that would provide needed information for assessing musical activity in the pe- riod 1860–1900. This span of years was selected because I felt that it had witnessed the development in and around New Orleans, Louisiana of a dance music which later evolved into the form, or forms of a form, which is now called jazz.[60]

Ramsey drove south in April with his wife and young child and was soon sending tapes and long letters about his experiences back to Asch. In his first week of recording he was intrigued by the way in which one elderly informant distinguished between the gospel music of her youth and contemporary gospel music in 1954: "They sing 'em with the jazz."[61] He could not have been more delighted that she had volunteered the term "jazz" without his prompting, and that it suggested to her a kind of innovative reworking of traditional musical forms.

In the weeks that followed, Ramsey recorded hours of sacred and secular music. He believed that he had found the equivalent of Courlander's Rich Amerson in the person of Horace Sprott, a sixty-eight-year-old farmer and blues singer who to Ramsey might prove to be as important to the history of American music as Leadbelly. He tried to interest Asch in the idea of bankrolling a concert of Sprott and some of the other singers he had encoun- tered for New York audiences, although the idea ultimately came to nothing. A gospel singer he encountered, Dorothy Melton, seemed to Ramsey to have a voice of professional quality—"it is quite possible that there is a singing career in store for her"—and he wondered in a letter to Asch whether she might go in the Marian Anderson or the Ella Fitzgerald direction: "The thing to do would be to find someone in New York who would understand exactly what to do with her voice. A talented musician like Chick Webb could have done it."[62] Ramsey was also very pleased with some recordings he made of the Starlight Gospel Singers, although he wondered whether their use of some contemporary gospel innovations would make them suitable for Folkways. Later he overcame his misgivings:

> Although they are modern, and very much in the current gos-
> pel tradition, you can tell they have 'country' ways about
> them, and that some of the style goes back a lot farther than
> just modern gospel songs. The old people frown on this style,
> but the young ones are taking it up eagerly. . . . Just as with
> contemporary Calypso, I feel that they should be presented
> for exactly what they are—the thing that is going on, now,
> among poor Negroes in remote country districts. Ten years
> from now, this kind of presentation will assume its proper
> perspective.[63]

On those rare occasions when Asch responded, he did so with enthusiasm: "The tapes you sent are still the best reminder that rural America still lives come hell high water or McCarthy."[64] Nor did Asch have qualms about issuing material that might have been influenced by commercially produced records; the Starlight Gospel Singers would appear as the eighth out of the ten-volume set that resulted from Ramsey's trip south, distinguished from the singing of more traditional gospel music with the designation "youngsters."

Ramsey attempted to avoid retracing Courlander's steps, but he discovered not only that Courlander had actually covered the ground pretty thoroughly but that there were other researchers out there who were starting to make the field a bit crowded. In one instance he discovered that a couple of women, grant and tape recorder in hand, had preceded him by a matter of days. He wrote to Asch to suggest that, should they get in touch with him about producing material for Folkways (and he was almost sure that they would), Asch ought to request that they make an agreement with Ramsey to avoid treading on one another's territory.

In his final days in Alabama Ramsey encountered a phenome-non he surely regarded as the "missing link." To his utter delight, he discovered that there was a tradition of brass band music in rural Alabama stretching perhaps as far back as the plantation era and used for the purpose of secular dancing:

> Here is either a parallel development to the early days of jazz
> in New Orleans, or one that might conceivably even precede

it. Negroes might have had brass instruments in their hands
on the plantations before allowed to in New Orleans. At any
rate, it's a tradition that no one seems to have stumbled on
before—perhaps because of its deep country origin. . . . Look
at the Buddy Bolden Band picture in *Jazzmen* and you'll see
this band. Hear our tapes, and you'll hear it.[65]

When Ramsey finally moved on to New Orleans the competition
from other field recorders became still more alarming. He found a
virtual cottage industry of musicians-turned-interviewees, "spouting names, dates, personnel like librarians on an outing. It is all very
pat and not at all reliable. I have avoided these boys like the
plague."[66] He found the city full of intrigue, rife with rumors about
fraudulent recording sessions and unpaid musicians. Though
earning a reputation as something of an eccentric, Ramsey plied
other waters, recording gospel, blues, and folk music while constantly on the lookout for the rural connection in all of the New
Orleans music. "This town is far too sophisticated for my project
and I'm going out to the country to do most of my work," he wrote
Asch.[67] Not that he wished to *"take away* from New Orleans," but
his evidence suggested that the majority of New Orleans musicians came from the country or from families that had moved to
New Orleans from the country.[68] One set of leads resulted in a
lifelong obsession: the search for the "true" story of the Bolden
band. Sadly, he was scooped in 1978 with the publication of Donald
Marquis's *In Search of Buddy Bolden: First Man of Jazz,* although he
continued to work on the Bolden material into the 1990s.[69]

Ramsey troubled himself a bit over the title of the series. At times
he wanted it to reflect the highly regionalized nature of the music,
perhaps by citing the county in which they had been recorded. At
other times he wished the series might reflect his broader purposes, and in one letter to Asch he suggested that it might be titled
"The Roots of Jazz" to complement the History of Jazz series.
Ultimately the series appeared as *Music from the South,* which
satisfied neither of Ramsey's criteria but reflected Asch's discomfort with racial labels.

One of the field recorders Ramsey met in New Orleans was Sam
Charters, who understood better than most what Ramsey was up
to and was sympathetic to Ramsey's search for the authentic and
offbeat. Although Ramsey would later express reservations about
the way in which Charters appeared to him to muscle in on others'
discoveries, in their initial encounter Ramsey was encouraging and

provided him with some suggestions for regions he might work in and "some methods of research."[70] Charters was interested in finding a skiffle band to record, and Ramsey too was enthusiastic about skiffle and wanted to see it represented on Folkways. That autumn Charters wrote Ramsey, offering him the opportunity to hear a recording of a skiffle band he had made in Selma, Alabama. Ramsey forwarded the information to Asch with a strong endorsement. He recalled that Charters's equipment had been crude and consequently the sound quality might be disappointing, yet he regarded the material as potentially important and urged Asch to audition it. Ramsey thought that Asch had previously received some related material from someone else and suggested that it be combined with Charters's material on a ten- or twelve-inch LP. "I leave up to you what you can offer Sam, but I'm writing immediately to say we want to hear it. . . . Will it be out of line to say there's around $50 in it for him?"[71]

Back home in New Jersey, Ramsey was beginning to feel frustrated about working with Asch and Distler. He would frequently send album notes or ad copy to the Folkways offices from his new home in Stockton only to find some weeks later that the material had been mislaid and several days' work consequently lost.[72] And then there was the matter of money. Without the release of the albums there would be no royalties, and Folkways seemed to be hopelessly slow in getting things released. With his cash reserves dwindling, Ramsey approached Bill Grauer of Riverside Records late in the autumn to see whether he might be interested in releasing some of the *Music from the South* material—perhaps more expeditiously than Folkways. Asch quickly got wind of a possible transaction between Ramsey and Grauer and had his lawyer fire off letters to both of them, calling on them to desist.[73] For Ramsey it was a hard, fast slap in the face that taught him never to attempt anything behind Asch's back. But the following March Ramsey was again writing to Asch in painstaking detail about the royalties owed to him that had not been paid.[74]

In the mid- and late 1950s Ramsey and Courlander were becoming the old guard of rural southern music enthusiasts. A younger group of devotees were being introduced to folk music in college folk music clubs and elsewhere. They were more attentive to white, rural southern than to African American music, and perhaps as a consequence their motivations were less ideological. The most important among them—John Cohen, Ralph Rinzler, Mike Seeger—were becoming credible musicians themselves, and their close scrutiny of vintage recordings was partly a means of establishing their own musical repertoire. Each came to folk music from a slightly different angle. Cohen's parents were old Jewish leftists, living in the radical Sunnyside community in Queens, and had been introduced to American folk dancing at a settlement camp on the Lower East Side. Rinzler came under the influence of an uncle—his mother's brother—who had been a student of Kittredge's at Harvard and who introduced him as a child to American folk song as a living literature. Seeger, the half-brother of Pete and son of composer Ruth Crawford Seeger, was interested in the music and its history first and never regarded folk music as the overt political vehicle that his half brother recognized. Still, these three followed parallel and often intertwined paths for decades and made some of the most important contributions to Folkways' traditional American list.

Mike Seeger, through his mother and father, had learned that southern mountain music was still very much alive in the hills just beyond their Washington, D.C., home. By the early 1950s Mike was already amassing a library of tapes he had made of traditional singers and instrumentalists. While his sister Peggy was starting to get caught up in the early manifestations of the folk-song revival, "Mike was involved in the survival of stuff that was still around," remembered Ralph Rinzler, "and that interested me infinitely more."[75] Rinzler and Cohen, on the other hand, were collectors of old 78s; at the politically progressive Turkey Point camp in the summer of 1948, Cohen was introduced to three records by Irwin Silber's sister Elaine—Alan Lomax's *Mountain Frolic* and *Listen to Our Story*, and Woody Guthrie's *Dust Bowl Ballads*. Two years later, as record stores were divesting themselves of 78s for a pittance, he discovered recordings of Charlie Poole and others in an out-of-the way place in San Francisco.

Cohen started college that fall of 1950, spending one miserable year at Williams, redeemed only by the discovery of Library of Congress folk music recordings in the college library and a five-dollar banjo in a local shop. He transferred to the studio art program at Yale the following autumn and within a year met up with Tom Paley, who was already becoming legendary within the Washington Square folk music scene. Paley and Cohen started sings at Yale in the mid-fifties, checking first with Pete Seeger to determine whether they could publicize them as "hootenannies" (Seeger assured them that the word was in the public domain). In the summers Cohen retreated to the hills outside Woodstock, New

York, to work at Camp Woodland. Woodland was run by Norman Studer, who taught during the year at the Little Red School House in the Village. It was a haven for the children of those who had been blacklisted (they got free tuition) and for others, who were introduced there to traditional musicians and storytellers from the surrounding Catskill region.

Rinzler was meanwhile a student at Swarthmore, where he quickly found a place for himself in its energetic folk music club. In 1953 Mike Seeger and his sister Peggy came to Swarthmore to perform at the college's folk festival. Later Peggy sent Rinzler a copy of Pete's banjo manual—then still distributed in its mimeographed form—and Roger Abrahams, a year ahead of Ralph at Swarthmore, found a banjo for him. By the time Peggy invited Rinzler up to Pete and Toshi's place in Beacon, New York, that July for a housewarming, Ralph had already achieved some proficiency with the instrument. Rinzler, like many before and after him, came to exult in the music while contributing his labor to the building of the Seegers' homestead. Rinzler remembered Will Geer and Charles Seeger Sr. being there, as well as Pete's mother Constance. Invitations to Beacon were freely given, and it felt to some as though they had been asked into the inner sanctum of folk music.[76]

Mike Seeger made a connection for Rinzler between the living folk music he was hearing and playing and the academic, archival material Rinzler had started to explore through his uncle. Once Rinzler understood that the oral "literature" of the southern Appalachians was a living and evolving tradition, he became intensely curious about its parameters. Throughout his life he asked himself, How big is this body of music? What is its historical and geographical range? Who and where is its audience? Where and when does it shade off into some other musical genre?

With Mike Seeger's growing collection of tapes, Rinzler soon understood how much bigger this music was than he had first imagined. Mike had a tape of the Stoneman Family and planned to combine it with some recordings he had made of J. C. Suthpin and Louise Foreacre for a Folkways release. Much of the information he needed for the notes was in his head, but he lacked the means of conducting the necessary additional research. Rinzler agreed to undertake the research and write the notes. Using the Lomaxes' exhaustive scholarship as a model, he traced the literary and historical origins of the songs and their variants, as well as previous citations, in the written and recorded literature.

The *Stoneman Family* album appeared on Folkways in 1957 (2315) and was the means by which Rinzler first met Asch. "I had never encountered in my life anybody who was so intimidating," Rinzler remarked of his first encounters with Asch. If he was not shouting, he was curt. Rarely was Asch ingratiating, although he could be charming when he wanted something from someone. Mostly, Rinzler recalled, one was careful not to overstay one's welcome with him. As often as not, Distler was the subject of his wrath; Asch would roar at her, causing her to contort her face in a painful, exaggerated display of deference. Sometimes, out of frustration, she would in turn yell at Rinzler and the other members of Folkways' younger cohort. The untethered display of anger horrified Rinzler.

Cohen, Rinzler, and Seeger were all captivated by Harry Smith's *Anthology* when it appeared. Cohen was perhaps best prepared for it, as he had been collecting vintage records for some years. For the others it was nothing short of astonishing. By 1956 Rinzler and Mike Seeger had partially exhausted what *Anthology* had to offer them and were eager to see the rest of the collection from which it had been extracted. They learned that Asch had purchased the collection and sold it in turn to a friend of Charles Seeger's, Carl Sprague Smith, a leading beneficiary of the New York Public Library. Smith had in turn given the collection to the library, so Rinzler and Seeger approached the music librarian, William Miller, to see whether they might listen to it. Miller informed them that that would only be possible once the collection was catalogued, a process that could take several years. The only solution seemed to be for Rinzler and Seeger to take on the cataloguing project themselves as volunteers. Rinzler taught himself what he needed to know about cataloguing and began the painstaking process of recording the necessary information on hundreds of three by five cards. In exchange they were permitted to take the recordings home—a few at a time—in order to tape them overnight. Suddenly the parameters of the music were several times larger.

Both Rinzler and Cohen recalled Asch's efforts in the mid-fifties to retrieve the ownership of copyrights to songs that had been appropriated by popular English skiffle bands. Using acoustic guitars and homemade rhythm instruments, skiffle bands of the mid-fifties played hopped-up versions of American folk songs, particularly those of Woody Guthrie and Leadbelly. It was the first of many instances in which British musicians found success by refashioning distinctly American musical forms and selling them back to American audiences. Initially skiffle bands were associated with the British Left but soon appeared on the British pop charts as decidedly nonideological novelty acts. Rinzler recalled a taped session with Libba Cotten intended to establish her authorship of "Freight Train" over the royalty claims of Nancy Whiskey, Charles McDevitt's Skiffle Band, and Topic Records. Cohen repeated a story, long in circulation, about the unannounced appearance of Lonnie Donegan's manager in Asch's office one day. Donegan had become skiffle's best-selling recording artist, having transformed Leadbelly's "Rock Island Line" into a hit in January 1956 and scoring later in the year with "John Henry."[77] The manager inquired about royalties due his client for songs recorded by a certain "Leadbelly," including "Rock Island Line." Asch found the suggestion preposterous: "I'll tell you what," he suggested to the unsuspecting hustler, "you come back here this afternoon, and I'll have all the records here. And I'll break them over your head one at a time!"

John Cohen first recorded for Folkways when he was asked to accompany Guy Carawan on Guy's first album in early 1958. By then Asch had ceased recording altogether in his own studio. In 1953 Mel Kaiser had opened Cue Recording Studios in the WEVD building. It was fortuitous for Asch, because he was finding it increasingly difficult to keep up with the purchase of rapidly evolving recording equipment. Moreover, Asch's offices were so badly overrun with boxes of records and papers that there was virtually no room left in which to record anyway. Asch made an arrangement with Kaiser to loan him his cutting lathe indefinitely, and in exchange Asch would be allowed to use Kaiser's studio evenings and weekends. The cutting lathe was a fine old piece of machinery that Asch had used to cut masters for the old 78s. Kaiser had it retrofitted to cut LPs as well. The cutting lathe cut grooves in an acetate disk, and from this "lacquer" a "master" was electroplated. The master—the negative of a record as it had peaks rather than valleys—could technically have been used to stamp records. But in order to protect it, record manufacturers typically introduced two additional steps, making a "mother" disk from the master and then any number of "stampers" from the mother. A successful recording could require forty or fifty stampers. Kaiser was pleased to have the lathe—it would have been too expensive a piece of equipment for him to have purchased, and he would otherwise have had to send out the work of cutting "lacquers" from tapes to other outfits. Asch, on the other hand, was free to record again when he wanted and pleased to be able to have Kaiser record those artists in which Asch desired no direct hand.[78]

Cohen did not speak with Asch until he came to Folkways one day to retrieve his free copy of Carawan's album. Asch, stepping into an elevator as Cohen stepped out of it, saw Cohen with the new album and asked him what he thought about it. Cohen replied that it had some good things, but about other things he had some questions. "Me too," responded Asch. End of conversation. Some weeks later they talked again, this time about Cohen's delight with the early sessions of Woody Guthrie, Cisco Houston, Sonny Terry, and others. Cohen lamented that records no longer captured that kind of lively spontaneity. Asch explained to him how Guthrie and Houston had been playing for crowds in the bars up and down Eighth Avenue just before coming in to record for him and consequently were warmed up and energetic. Around early summer Cohen came to Asch once again to tell him of a wonderful musical encounter he had had with two other musicians. To his way of thinking, the three of them had recreated the energy, spontaneity, and authenticity of the wartime sessions they had been talking about.

"Who are the other characters?" asked Asch.

"Mike Seeger and Tom Paley," Cohen replied.

"OK, I'll record you."

Asch was willing to record the group that became the New Lost City Ramblers on the basis of their individual reputations. Although Paley had not previously recorded projects for Asch, his Washington Square reputation undoubtedly preceded him—Asch could not have failed to have heard of him. In the fall of 1958 the three went into the studio with Asch in the control booth. It would be the only time Asch himself recorded the Ramblers. Mike Seeger did not care for the experience—Asch's characteristically "flat" sound did not appeal to him, and there were a few multiple takes, despite the high value that Asch placed on spontaneity. John Cohen, on the other hand, took great pleasure in working with the legendary Asch. As they prepared to perform "Crossed Old Jordan Stream" Cohen, apparently concerned for Asch's religious sensibilities, warned him apologetically that it was a gospel hymn. Asch had released an album of the Fisk Jubilee Singers in 1955 (with an exquisite lithograph by Aaron Douglas that the group's musical director, John W. Work, acquired especially for the cover), so he was not unfamiliar with the genre and took some pride in his knowledge of Christian musical forms. "Yeah, I know," he responded. "That Jubilee stuff." Cohen broke down in laughter at Asch's unintended joke. It had sounded like "Jew-billy" to Cohen, a mischievous encapsulation of the incongruity of Asch and Cohen toiling together over the music of poor white Appalachians. The others, Asch included, could not imagine what had set him off.[79] In the years that followed the albums the Ramblers made were recorded either by Peter Bartók—a recording engineer they found to be outstanding in every respect—or by Mel Kaiser at Cue, who according to Cohen made them nervous.

Cohen, Rinzler, and Mike Seeger continued to mix performing and field collecting in various measures over the next several years. Although Rinzler joined the Greenbriar Boys in 1959 by taking the place of departing mandolinist Paul Prestopino, he was less interested than the other two in his own musical career and more dedicated to promoting the musical careers of others. When pressed by Bob Shelton to record with the Greenbriar Boys on Vanguard, Rinzler agreed to do so on the condition that the album include substantial notes that would lead the listener to the original sources of their material. In that way he might be able to justify putting himself forward as a vehicle through which "real" bluegrass might get a hearing.

In April of the following year Rinzler performed at the Union Grove fiddle convention with the Greenbriar Boys, and he had an epiphany. He heard a band there playing music that was different—something akin to bluegrass but distinctive. After the performance he stuck around to ask the band some questions: "Why is your music so different from everyone else's here? What are you playing, and where did you learn it?"

Rinzler's attention was directed to the banjo player by one of the other musicians: "This guy here is a neighbor of ours, and he kind of coaches us on his songs."

"Who's he?" asked Rinzler.

"He's Tom Ashley," responded the musician.

"I've heard of a Clarence Ashley who sang a song called 'The Coo Coo Bird,'" Rinzler said, thinking of the legendary Columbia recording that had been reproduced in the Harry Smith collection.

"Why that's me," replied the banjo player. Ashley had recorded for Victor under his nickname (he had been known as Tommy Tiddywaddy as a child for his mischievousness) and had reverted to his Christian name when he recorded "The Coo Coo Bird" for Columbia.

Rinzler went racing off to find Mike Seeger, who was also in attendance at the fiddle convention. "Mike, Clarence Ashley's here—he's in that room." Seeger responded as though he had been hit by a lightening bolt. The vintage music that they had worshipped from a distance of thirty years proved to be a *living* music. It was almost too much to imagine.

Ashley performed a Bill Monroe song for their tape recorder later that weekend, before the conclusion of the fiddle convention. And Rinzler acquired Ashley's address and telephone number and a promise to be allowed to record him later that year. Rinzler traveled south again early in September, arriving at Ashley's home in eastern Tennessee for Labor Day. He came bearing a full set of the Harry Smith collection, intending to present it to Ashley as a mark of his knowledge of and interest in the old music. But to Rinzler's dismay, Ashley introduced him to a blind electric guitarist by the name of Doc Watson, who had earned a considerable reputation on the local rockabilly circuit. Ashley had imagined that Rinzler would record his singing to the accompaniment of Watson's electric guitar playing, but Rinzler would not hear of recording an electric guitar. He asked Watson whether he would be willing to use an acoustic guitar instead. Watson responded in a way that indicated that he, too, had standards. He did not own an acoustic guitar and would not, in any case, record with an unfamiliar instrument lacking the light touch of an electric that he depended upon for various effects. "Just the idea of having to deal with an electric guitar so depressed me," recalled Rinzler some years later. Ashley meanwhile had neglected to practice even a single banjo tune, despite his promises to Rinzler the previous spring. So Rinzler drove off to retrieve Jack Johnson, a banjo player he had heard with Ashley at Union Grove, who lived three hours away in North Carolina.

The following day Watson was still among the collected musicians. Rinzler and Watson drove over to Ashley's daughter's home together, where the recording would take place. Rinzler played some old-time banjo tunes on the ride over. Watson asked to have a turn at the banjo and "proceeded to play the hell out of it," as Rinzler recalled. The result was "an extraordinary cognitive dissonance. How could a guy who played imitation Nashville on an electric guitar also play 'Tom Dooley' in the way that the late G. B. Grayson recorded it, totally different from the way that the Kingston Trio had made it a hit two years earlier?" As it turned out, Watson had grown up with many of the musicians represented on Harry Smith's *Anthology* as friends, neighbors, and relations. He had not previously regarded himself as a "folk" musician, but as he was soon to discover that is precisely how a public—of which he had no knowledge—would soon regard him.[80]

Watson, of course, was permitted to join the others for the session that day, and for those that followed. Rinzler and his engineer Gene Earle probed for the old tunes and weeded out the performances of Eddie Arnold, Roy Acuff, and even Bill Monroe material. Nineteenth-century parlor ballads and sentimental songs were within the permissible range, but Rinzler continued to press them for songs with pedigree that were free of commercial taint.

Rinzler brought the tapes of the first Ashley sessions to Maynard Solomon at Vanguard; he had hoped that they might bring the musicians a little income, which is why he did not take them to Folkways from the start. But Solomon was patronizing when he heard them and saw no commercial potential, so Rinzler took them to Asch, who offered to release them immediately. "Of course I'll put it out," agreed Asch. "I'll give you a hundred dollars." The first volume of *Old Time Music at Clarence Ashley's* was released in 1961; a second volume, the result of subsequent recording sessions, was released two years later (2355 and 2359). When Watson emerged over the next couple of years of touring as a premier solo artist and a unique talent, Solomon was only too happy to sign him to Vanguard.

John Cohen's search for authentic rural southern music had a slightly different cast than Rinzler's. "Tradition" was not an end in itself for Cohen, somewhat to Rinzler's puzzlement, but was one element in an artistic collage that might easily include Beat poets and abstract expressionist painters. Cohen had been introduced to the Beats by his neighbor on Third Avenue, the photographer Robert Frank. Frank had traveled with Kerouac on one of the latter's famous cross-country car trips and in January 1959 started shooting a film based loosely on the third act of Kerouac's play *The Beat Generation*. The shooting lasted six weeks and resulted in a twenty-minute classic of the Beat era—and a forerunner of the underground cinema of Warhol—entitled *Pull My Daisy*.[81] Frank's photographs would later grace the covers of several New Lost City Ramblers albums, but on this occasion he asked Cohen to take the still shots during the filming. At its conclusion he arranged for Cohen to take photographs at the wrap party—many of the major players in the Beat scene would be there, including Alan Ginsberg, Gregory Corso, Larry Rivers, and David Amram. With Frank's encouragement Cohen offered *Life* magazine the right of first refusal to the party photographs. *Life* had been looking for ways of presenting the Beats to the general public and consequently gave Cohen six hundred dollars for the photographs (although they never used them). Cohen used the money to finance a trip to Kentucky, where he hoped to initiate a recording and photography project on mountain music and musicians. He was afraid that the woods of Kentucky would be crawling with collectors that summer, but to his delight the only other collector he encountered was Alan Lomax, who was tracing steps he had traveled before. Cohen's great discovery on this trip—and arguably his most important discovery of a single traditional musician—was Roscoe Holcomb. Holcomb appeared on about a third of the cuts on the resultant album, *Mountain Music of Kentucky* (2317). Cohen had copied the tapes at Mike Seeger's home, on the way back to New York, and tried to interest the Library of Congress in acquiring a copy. He spent another six months editing the tapes and writing the notes, using the model of Rinzler's fine notes for the *Stoneman Family* album as his standard. The *Journal of American Folklore* reviewed the album approvingly late in 1960, noting that the recording was excellent and the material "well balanced. . . . Cohen's notes, concentrating on style, performer, and background, are generally well done, and Cohen shows understanding and sympathy in dealing with the folk of the depressed areas around Hazard (Kentucky)."[82]

There was, as usual, little in it for the musicians. But with the formation of the Friends of Old Time Music (FOTM) in December 1960, Cohen had the means of creating a live audience for Holcomb. FOTM was the creation of Cohen, Rinzler, and Israel (Izzy) Young, joined in short order by Jean Ritchie and Margot Mayo. In February 1961 FOTM presented its first concert, at Public School 41 in Greenwich Village, to a capacity crowd of four hundred. The bill included the New Lost City Ramblers, the Greenbriar Boys, and Jean Ritchie, all of whom waived their customary performance fees in order to pay the travel expenses of the guest performer, Roscoe Holcomb, from Daisy, Kentucky. Holcomb's visits to New York became a periodic event over the next couple of years, and they inevitably included a visit to see Asch. It would be difficult to imagine two men from more disparate backgrounds, yet they developed a respect and fondness for one another. Asch would ask Holcomb how he was doing and, in his usual paternalistic style, slip him a ten or twenty dollar bill. Holcomb would later remark to Cohen what a wonderful guy Asch was. "Hello Moses, how is the boy? fine I hope," Holcomb wrote Asch in 1965 after the release of Holcomb's album, *The High Lonesome Sound* (2368):

> This leaves me not feeling too good; have a very bad cold.
> Moses I would like to have about 20 records 'the hi an lone-

some sound' if you'd care to send them to me I hope this
isn't asking you too much, Moses. I haven't got the money
now but will settle with you when I come up for the concert.
Tell Every Body hello. So Moses be a good little boy from your
friend Roscoe Holcomb.[83]

Mike Seeger had meanwhile acquired an impeccable ear for music
that had historical pedigree, technical virtuosity, and unassailable
aesthetic value. Of the three he was also the one who was most
persistent in perfecting his own musicianship. Thus he owed few
apologies for including a little of his own playing on compilations
of otherwise traditional musicians, such as Snuffy Jenkins and
Smiley Hobbs on *American Banjo Scruggs Style* (2314) and Don Stover,
Earl Taylor, Tex Logan, and Chubby Anthony on *Mountain Music
Bluegrass Style* (2318, released in 1959). The former resulted from a
letter to Seeger from Asch around 1957 in which he suggested that
Seeger consider putting together an album illustrating the Scruggs-
style music. Mike worked out the technical distinctions between
Scruggs's playing and that of Jenkins and others and illustrated
them with examples from his collection.[84] Rinzler again wrote the
notes, placing Scruggs's innovative three-finger style in the broader
context of Monroe's transformation of hillbilly music into bluegrass. *Mountain Music Bluegrass Style* was released in 1959, around the
same time as Alan Lomax's *Folk Songs from the Bluegrass* on United
Artists and might have suffered in comparison to the release by
the veteran collector. But despite Lomax's extensive notes on the
songs on his release, reviewer D. K. Wilgus in the *JAF* preferred the
Folkways release for being "more informative and useful in presenting a number of artists—generally recorded without studio
gimmicks—and a full discussion of the style by Mike Seeger."[85]
Folklore scholarship was in the process of being enriched by
musically accomplished aficionados whose interests complemented the literary orientation of the older school.

Perhaps Seeger's most surprising recording project in this period
was the first Elizabeth Cotten album. "Libba" had been employed
as a "domestic" by Ruth Crawford Seeger since the late forties,
when the composer discovered her working at a department store
counter in Washington, D.C. It was not until 1952, when Libba was
almost sixty, that the Seegers discovered she was an accomplished
banjoist, guitarist, and songwriter. Playing a conventionally strung
guitar upside down and left-handed, she had developed an intri-
cate two- and three-finger picking style that greatly influenced the

playing of Mike, his sister Peggy, and subsequently a good part of the revivalist generation. The first album, *Negro Folk Songs and Tunes,* included the classic "Freight Train" and led to folk festival performances at the University of Chicago in 1961, in Philadelphia in 1963, and in Newport in 1964.[86]

Most of the musicians whose careers were revived by their exposure on Folkways recordings were pleased by the way in which their performances were captured on LP. One rare exception was Buell Kazee, a singer and banjoist from eastern Kentucky three of whose recordings for Brunswick in 1928 and 1929 were reissued in Harry Smith's *Anthology.* Folklorist Gene Bluestein "rediscovered" Kazee in 1956 and recorded an interview that was interspersed with bits of song and banjo playing. Kazee claimed to have been surprised and disturbed when he learned that Bluestein had edited the tape and sold it to Folkways, which had released it as *Buell Kazee Sings and Plays* (3810) in 1958. Kazee had said things in the interview that he had not intended for public release, and he was embarrassed by their inclusion on the record. More than that, many of the songs he performed were only fragments or incomplete renditions and he did not feel that they were sufficiently representative of his repertoire. And, as usual, there was no contractual arrangement and Kazee had to resort to threats before he could shake a royalty payment loose from Asch. "He wasn't going to give me anything. . . . I finally had to sell it to him. I beat him around until I got one royalty check—a hundred-and-some dollars. It was about two years before I got that. Then I got one a year or two later, after browbeating him, and finally I told him to make me an offer and I'd sell it to him."[87]

Sam Charters had been plying other waters—sometimes literally. In the summer of 1958 he set out on a collecting trip in the Bahamas with Ann Danberg, later his wife and Jack Kerouac's sensitive biographer. Charters had by then released five albums on Folkways—his Music of New Orleans series—but it was apparent to him as well as to Asch that there would be many more. He wrote to Asch from the Caribbean that summer about his excitement at having found a fife player who performed quadrilles and his discovery of "improvised two or three part polyphonic singing."[88] But his real find that summer was the dazzling and eccentric guitar playing of Joseph Spence.

Although the resulting three volumes of *Music of the Bahamas* may have been Charters's most important contribution to the Folkways catalogue (3844, 3845, 3846), there would be a great many others. In

January the following year he found Sam "Lightnin'" Hopkins in Houston, and with the promise of three hundred dollars received Hopkins's verbal agreement to record for Folkways. Hopkins had had some commercial success in the immediate postwar years but had apparently ceased to record in the second half of the fifties. His guitar was frequently in and out of the pawn shop, and Charters had to rent one for the session.

Charters set up a portable Ampex recorder in Hopkins's apartment and began the session. At the conclusion of the second number, Hopkins declared that he had finished; it had been so long since he had recorded, he claimed, that he was unfamiliar with the LP format. It took some time for Charters to explain that the record he had in mind would require several additional songs. Once Hopkins had determined the length of the recording Charters wanted, he placed his wrist watch beside him and proceeded to play until the necessary amount of time had elapsed. At the conclusion of the session, Charters paid Hopkins and promised to mail him a copy of the release.

Asch released *Lightnin' Hopkins* the following summer (3822). John S. Wilson praised it lavishly in his *New York Times* review, comparing it to Alan Lomax's discovery of Jelly Roll Morton.[89] Asch dutifully sent a copy of the album to Hopkins, but it was never claimed at the Houston post office. The lack of a contract with Hopkins became a problem for Charters in very short order, particularly once a Houston promoter recognized an opportunity to right an apparent wrong and make some money in the bargain. "I am much disturbed that M. is bothering you about Hopkins," Charters wrote Asch. "As I've told you M. is simply a leech on Hopkins hide." Charters had also learned that Hopkins had actually recorded for Decca and Mercury in the preceding four or five years and thus probably knew more about contemporary recording and royalty practices than he had initially let on.[90] Hopkins himself wrote to Folkways the following November:

> I was thinking I was going to get a share of the money that was made, and that would be right. I think any that sell your records they are suppose to give you part of the money made. If you don't agree, I ask you to stop the records. This company doesn't have a contrack [sic] like they should and they don't have my permission to be selling my songs and my singing on records. They didn't send me a copy of my records; I did think they would send me one. I have another

record coming out that is paying me royalties so I see no reason for not getting a share from you all.[91]

Asch responded to Hopkins, explaining that his was a small company and that he believed that the three-hundred-dollar advance
might reasonably cover the lifetime of the record. After all, there
had been some considerable investment on the part of Folkways in
production costs, including the graphics "which I think you must
agree," he wrote Hopkins, "is a beautiful job in jacket, cover and
pamphlet." Asch, however, was prepared to offer him twenty-five
cents per record royalties after the sale of three thousand records.
The songs would remain the property of Hopkins, but Asch reminded him that he was not to sing the same songs for another
label.[92] Additional letters were exchanged with the promoter and
lawsuits threatened. The following October Hopkins signed a contract entitling him to twenty-five cents royalty on all albums sold.
Charters later claimed, with much justification, that whatever the
royalty arrangements, it was Hopkins's Folkways album that "introduced him to the modern intellectual audience for the blues," an
audience his race recordings would never have reached.[93]

Although Charters eventually contributed to many different
parts of the catalogue, country blues became his special niche. In
1959 he released the first recording for Folkways' subsidiary label,
RBF (Records, Books and Film) entitled *The Country Blues*, intended
as a demonstration record for his recently published book of the
same title. Like Harry Smith's *Anthology* and Fred Ramsey's History
of Jazz series, it consisted of reissued recordings from the twenties
and thirties, usually appropriated without any arrangements with
the original labels. In his introduction to the new series, Charters
made the dubious claim that "the American copyright laws permit
the reissue of any of these older performances, the only restriction
being that the name of the company not be used in any notes or
advertising."[94] The first of the RBF series included Blind Lemon
Jefferson and Washboard Sam, country-blues musicians who were
relatively well known to aficionados in the late fifties, as well as
artists then relatively obscure, such as Bukka White and Robert
Johnson. D. K. Wilgus lamented in his otherwise favorable review
of *The Country Blues* that the recording was released with very little
discographic information, speculating that perhaps this was a
function of copyright problems.[95]

The growing interest in previously obscure country-blues artists
prompted Don DeMichael, then *Down Beat*'s Louisville correspon-

dent, to invent a local musician by the name of Blind Orange Adams. He had intended it as a private joke between himself and the magazine's editor, Gene Lees, but Lees had published the first notice of Blind Orange without a thought, and after that the fictional character took on a life of his own. DeMichael continued to mention Adams's activities in his column; he rented a post office box and created a fan club, and interested collectors began to write letters of inquiry. One of them was Asch, who expressed an interest in recording the "legendary" blues singer for Folkways. Had he consulted Charters he would likely have avoided falling victim to the hoax. But DeMichael and Lees were having too much fun with it and encouraged Asch to pursue the matter. Lees had in mind to have saxophonist Eddie Harris record an album of blues vocals—Harris could produce a parody of a blues vocal that Lees found immensely amusing. But over the course of the correspondence Asch became suspicious and insisted on meeting Adams. The jig was up, and as Lees recalled it, DeMichael killed off his fictional creation in a car accident.[96]

Family life intruded very little into Asch's work world. He frequently did not return home until well into the evening, often having eaten dinner at La Strada on Forty-sixth Street, his most frequent lunch spot, where he had his own table and where he was known to the waiters as "Mr. Asch." In the summers Frances and Michael went on vacation, often to the beach, once to a dude ranch—in 1952 they went to Cuba for two months, and the following year to Provincetown, Massachusetts. Asch would join them for an occasional long weekend. In the late fifties Michael went off for the summer to Lincoln Farm, a work camp in New York state, while Frances stayed in the city.

In 1956 Michael prepared to be Bar Mitzvahed. The Asches had never belonged to a synagogue, so Frances chose the closest temple, which happened to be Orthodox and which was where Michael's friends were having their Bar Mitzvahs. Michael had started to prepare for the ceremony in the preceding year but had not up until then attended Sunday school or Hebrew school. The Bar Mitzvah itself was Frances's idea, and she was surprised when Sholem Asch accepted their invitation to it, because throughout his life he had not been much of one for Bar Mitzvahs. Of course the event took on a new importance with the announcement that the famous man would be attending. Sholem and Madya had ceased residing in the United States in 1953 and for the next two years divided their time between Nice and London, near Miriam and Reginald. In 1955 they were invited to settle in the town of Bat Yam, a suburb of Tel Aviv. There were still protests from some Israelis who continued to regard Asch as an apostate; nonetheless, the Asches settled in Israel in February 1956, and within a couple of months Sholem was traveling half way around the world for his grandson's Bar Mitzvah.

The Bar Mitzvah was scheduled for the spring, around the time of Passover. The week before the ceremony Asch was in Washington, D.C., at a convention. Frances had gone out on a brief errand, leaving Michael alone in their apartment at 29 Fifth Avenue in the Village, and as she returned she was assaulted by a man in the lobby of their building and beaten badly, particularly around the head. She spent the remainder of the week in the hospital, but plans for the Bar Mitzvah proceeded apace. She would appear at the Bar Mitzvah with a bandage on her head, which obscured her vision in one eye. Sholem arrived with the usual fuss, but without Madya, who had been ill.

The members of the Orthodox congregation were neither pleased nor honored to have Sholem Asch in their midst. They first attempted to bar him from the synagogue altogether, maintaining that he was not a Jew. After some discussion they relented, but they would not permit him to have an aliyah, an honorary portion of the weekly Torah reading. Finally he insisted on being allowed to come forward in order to say a prayer for his wife, and although congregants threatened to block his way onto the bema, ultimately he was permitted to do so. Although he had very little investment in the ritual itself, he was going to be sure to receive his due. Thus Sholem succeeded in making himself the center of attention, overshadowing his young grandson. "I want you to know, Michael," he pronounced in obvious earshot of the assembled friends and relatives, "that I was a dying man and I came to your bar mitzvah."[97]

The following January in Bat Yam, Sholem suffered a stroke. His English-language biographer (relying on the Yiddish reminiscences of Sholem Asch's last secretary) reported that all four Asch children learned of their father's illness from the international press and immediately wired to determine whether their presence would be helpful (Ruth would in fact go). But this is unlikely. When he passed away, just seven months later while in London on a visit with Ruth and Reggie, only John came from the United States for the funeral. There was later a memorial service in New York—in death the attitudes of even his most hardened enemies softened considerably and the eulogies were generous—and Moe was present. But at the time of Sholem's death, Asch seemed to take astonishingly little notice. He did not call Michael at summer camp to inform him of his grandfather's death; Mike instead learned of Sholem's death from his counselor, who showed him the obituary from the *New York Times.*

A year later Asch spent a couple of weeks in San Francisco and visited Nathan and his wife Carol. He reported in a letter to his mother that his brother and sister-in-law had thrown a cocktail party "where many celebrities were present"—although he was not sufficiently impressed to name any of them specifically. During his conversations with Nathan it came out that "the family," probably meaning Nathan and John, had long been under the impression that Moe had borrowed a substantial sum from their father some years before and that the outstanding balance remained available to other members of the family whenever they might be in need. His brothers had been laboring under an unfortunate misconception for more than ten years, and when Asch returned to New York in August 1958 he sent the family a letter to clarify the nature of his financial arrangements with their late father. Ten thousand dollars had been put up in guarantee of a loan when Disc was founded in 1946; when the company went bankrupt in 1948, Asch had arranged to pay back the sum he owed his father at the rate of one thousand dollars a year in two annual (spring and winter) installments. At the time of his death, Sholem had been paid nine thousand of the ten thousand dollars he was owed. Asch was prepared to present them with the canceled checks. Thus the "widely spread" rumors of favoritism shown and monies yet owed were untrue. In the copy of the letter that he sent to his mother he included a cover note in which he mentioned "the formal style of Bar-Mitsve [sic] that we had Michael go through." Apparently Nathan had heard of Sholem's surprise over the Orthodox ceremony. "This will be a subject of another letter," he assured Madya, although it is not clear that he ever wrote it.

Asch had a surprising amount of company in the recorded folk music field during the mid-1950s. Bill Grauer's Riverside label, previously dedicated almost exclusively to jazz and blues, began to release other kinds of folk music recordings, from both the field and modern interpreters. In 1955 ethnomusicologist Alan Merriam produced an album for Riverside entitled *Voice of the Congo.* JAF reviewer Bruno Nettl found the recording every bit as scholarly as

William Bascom's parallel release on Folkways, *Drums of the Yoruba of Nigeria,* with rather more entertainment value for the layman.[98] Jac Holzman started Elektra Records as an extension of a modest retail record business and was soon recording many of the same artists as Folkways—Ewan MacColl, Jean Ritchie, Ed McCurdy, Jack Elliot, Oscar Brand. In 1955 he released his first recording of Theodore Bikel, then a well-known film and television actor who would become one of Holzman's steadiest recording artists. Simultaneously he was releasing field recordings from Cape Breton and studio recordings of traditional Haitian musicians. But Holzman's interest was soon focused upon more commercial recordings, and when a series of records entitled *When Dalliance Was in Flower and Maidens Lost Their Heads* by Ed McCurdy began selling in the tens of thousands, it was apparent that his strategy would be different from Asch's.[99]

Yet another competitor in the mid-fifties was Stinson Records, which was energetically releasing albums under the direction of Herbert Harris's son Bob. Ken Goldstein wandered into Harris's Union Square store one day, and Harris asked him whether he would assist in preparing some old masters from the Asch-Stinson days for LP release. Goldstein looked at the masters and declared most of them unusable because they had corroded badly. Harris replied that some of them could be cleaned up and for others they could use clean copies of the records themselves. Harris paid Goldstein five dollars per LP for selecting the material and writing the notes. Among the early Stinson reissues that Goldstein supervised were several volumes entitled *Folksay* that drew upon the 1944 sessions in Asch Studios. On one of the Folksay volumes Harris included several contemporary cuts—including a calypso-inflected version of the traditional southern song "Tom Dooley"—by a small band consisting of Roger Sprung, Bob Carey, and Erik Darling.[100] The release of the old Asch-Stinson material on Stinson LPs infuriated Asch and he attempted periodically to take legal measures to halt it. But there was sufficient ambiguity in the buy-out arrangement in 1946 that he was never able to establish his exclusive rights to the material that he and Harris had released during the war.

Goldstein was in the process of turning a passion for folk music into an academic career, first as a graduate student in anthropology at Columbia and then as one of the first students of American folk music in the University of Pennsylvania's doctoral program in folklore. Through the mid-fifties Goldstein recorded, produced, and wrote notes for perhaps 350 records on Riverside, Stinson, Elektra, Folkways, and, toward the end of the decade, Prestige. Much of the early recording took place in the kitchen of his apartment in the Bronx. Among his first recordings for Folkways was an album by the singer Paul Clayton entitled *Folksongs and Ballads of Virginia* (2110). Goldstein believed that Clayton was an ideal singer of folk songs because his voice was altogether lacking in color. The very blandness of his singing allowed the songs to speak for themselves without the distraction of the singer's interpretation.[101] It was a scholar's perspective that was at odds with the views of Jean Ritchie and others who believed that a singer's interpretation was an important aspect of the folk process. It was also a view that would become increasingly incompatible with the commercial impulses of the recording industry.

Through 1957 and 1958 and into early 1959 Goldstein produced and edited dozens of albums for Asch. It did not appear that Asch would turn down any project he pitched to him, even when Goldstein himself thought they might be of dubious value. As a favor to his friend Lori Holland, Goldstein proposed that Asch release a recording of her renditions of Scottish folk songs for women. He was certain Asch would turn it down, but he did not. Most of these recordings represented regional American folk songs, including a tape he edited of a young singer from Idaho named Rosalie Sorrels. Goldstein recorded Dave Van Ronk's first album in his home studio (*Dave Van Ronk Sings Ballads, Blues and a Spiritual*, 3818). "It would never have been made if I hadn't made a complete nuisance of myself to poor Kenny Goldstein," recalled Van Ronk. "He probably recorded it just to teach me a lesson."[102]

In the spring of 1958 Goldstein was at work on a project for Folkways that would trace nineteen versions of a single traditional song—"The Unfortunate Rake"—as a means of demonstrating the cycle of a song through its many ethnic and regional variants. Asch proposed to Goldstein that they arrange to have a singer such as Sam Hinton perform the variants, but Goldstein wanted a combination of traditional and revivalist singers who might better demonstrate different performance styles. Asch was able to think of five variants already available in his archives (of which Goldstein used four) and gave Goldstein access to the remainder of the archive to retrieve what he could.

In the fall of 1959 Goldstein set sail for Scotland with his wife and three children. He had won a Fulbright to study Scottish folk songs and to complete his dissertation research, and he expected to record an entire series of Scottish albums for Folkways. Asch had by then placed Goldstein on a weekly salary of twenty-five dollars, which was reduced to fifteen for the summer with Goldstein's understanding that it would be boosted back up to twenty-five in the fall. But Distler had reported to Goldstein that the summer had been a bad one for Folkways and consequently they would not be able to increase his salary until the first of December. For the first few weeks in Scotland the checks arrived more or less as scheduled. Among Goldstein's first discoveries was a Scottish variant of "The Unfortunate Rake" that he wanted to add to the otherwise completed project, and he wrote to Asch and Distler to have them send him a copy of his original notes so that he could appropriately incorporate the new notes with the old. Asch had decided as well that he would rather include Brownie McGhee's version of "Gambler's Blues" than Dave Van Ronk's, which would also require some reworking of the notes. Through the late fall, as the weather turned colder and damper, Goldstein wrote long and increasingly plaintive letters to Asch and Distler about the high cost of food and fuel. He pitched ideas to Asch for an album of songs and recitations in the Buchan Scots dialect, as well as recordings of London and Scottish children's songs and games, but in response to these and to his reminders for the "Unfortunate Rake" notes he heard nothing.

Distler finally responded in January, reporting that Asch had found it impossible to read through all of Goldstein's lengthy letters. She had no recollection of having promised to increase Goldstein's stipend, which in any case was part of a growing advance against future projects. "I do not deserve to be conned by you or anyone else," she wrote. Asch would not be able to commit himself to any recording projects until he had an opportunity to hear them, and it was not possible to commit still more funds to projects unless they could bring an "immediate cash return."[103] Yet another letter from Goldstein crossed Distler's in the mail. He had had to cancel a lecture series in Aberdeen because some records he had requested of Folkways for demonstration purposes had never arrived. Plans for recording sessions also had been scrapped due to a lack of commitment from Asch, and Goldstein was starting to have difficulty feeding his family and keeping them warm.

Asch and Distler meanwhile got wind of a possible partnership in a new record company between Goldstein and singer—folklorist Harry Oster, which resulted in a threatening letter in which they reminded Goldstein of Folkways' right of first refusal to the Scottish material. Additionally, they accused Goldstein of having accepted money for several projects that had never been completed—"The Unfortunate Rake" album, Rosalie Sorrels's album, an album of "American Broadsides" by Paul Clayton, and album of Child ballads by Jean Ritchie. Clayton and Sorrels were asking to have their tapes returned. "To date," Distler wrote, "all we have had from you are letters complaining that you need more money for your home and wife and children which you erroneously imagine we owe you or can afford to give you without anything in return."[104] The checks stopped altogether and Goldstein fired off a frantic letter. He had never agreed to enter into a partnership with Oster and had only discussed undertaking some free-lance editing work of the kind that he had been doing for other labels for years. Goldstein insisted that the weekly checks were payment for work that he had already completed for Folkways and not in anticipation of new material. To produce tapes that Asch might audition he would need a commitment from Folkways as well as funds to pay the performers. "The Unfortunate Rake" *could* be completed if they would only send him the notes, and his work on the Sorrels and Clayton *had* been completed—it was only up to Folkways to release them. The Jean Ritchie album had never been completed because she had never gotten around to recording with Asch at Cue Studios, as they had arranged:

> Moe has been good to me in the past, and I have always re-
> turned his kindnesses by being one of his best and most ar-
> dent supporters and suppliers of materials for Folkways. I
> hope you will see fit to answer this letter as soon as possible,
> letting me know which of the two projects . . . you are inter-
> ested in and if I should go ahead and record them, as well as
> seeing a continuation of my weekly checks.[105]

"To put it succinctly," Distler responded, "we simply do not have time to carry on lengthy correspondence whether it concerns monies, production and/or etc. You have had sufficient occasion to know how Moe Asch works. Namely, that he auditions a sample of the material and if it meets with his approval he either assigns completion of the work to someone or carries it through himself."[106] The checks resumed (although only fifteen dollars per week), but a long and important working relationship had been permanently soured. Asch released an album entitled *Traditional*

Singer from Aberdeenshire, Scotland (3519) by a singer named Lucy Stewart, which Goldstein had recorded during his Fulbright year, but although it appeared in the catalogue as volume 1 of a series, it was the only album from Goldstein's Scottish fieldwork that Folkways ever released.

As important as children's recordings were for Asch during the difficult years of the late 1940s, by the mid-1950s Asch found this portion of the catalogue growing at only a modest rate. Guthrie, of course, had ceased to make new recordings of any kind. Charity Bailey, who had taught songs to Michael Asch at the Little Red School House and who had made charming contributions to the second volume of *Songs to Grow On,* appeared for a while as though she might fill the void created by Guthrie's departure from recording. In February 1952 she signed a contract with Folkways for a ten-inch album entitled *Music Time* (7307) that she would record the following May, with the help of writer Eunice Holsaert. The contract stipulated that Folkways would retain the right of first refusal for any additional recordings of "similar type teaching material" that she might make. Bailey was classically trained and accompanied herself on both guitar and piano. And although African American, her repertoire was eclectic and did not peg her to any single ethnic tradition. On this album, as on *Follow the Sunset* (7406) released the following year, Bailey depended on the writing of others, and she did not make her third (and last) album for Folkways for more than fifteen years.

Pete Seeger had recorded *American Folk Songs for Children* (701, 7001, 7601) in 1953, which derived from his stepmother's book of the same name; Asch initially released it on three 45-rpm records.[107] Pete followed this with another half dozen children's records before the decade was out, including his enduring *Abiyoyo,* originally released in 1958 as *Sleep-Time Songs and Stories* (7525). Still, although Seeger preferred to sing for children because they tended to like songs he liked—rather than in nightclubs, where audiences were likely to demand to hear a kind of pop music that never interested him—he was never primarily a children's artist for Folkways.

A third children's recording artist was originally recruited to the label for other purposes. Asch heard some acetate recordings in late 1951 or early 1952 that a French Canadian singer named Alan Mills (real name Albert Miller) had dubbed from his own folk-song performances on international shortwave radio bands. "I have listened to your recordings and I find them most satisfactory. The ones I would be interested in . . . are the French-Canadian folk songs and I could use these as is."[108] *French Canadian Folk Songs* (6929) appeared that year, as did a second Mills album, *Songs of Newfoundland* (8778). Mills thereafter became a prolific Folkways artist, appearing on sixteen albums over the next ten years. Almost half of these albums were for children, starting with *French Folk Songs for Children* (7208) in 1953 followed in short order by *French Folk Songs for Children in English* (7018).

Still, the full flowering of Asch's children's list would have to wait for the fortuitous meeting of Ken Goldstein and a thirty-two-year-old African American woman named Ella Jenkins at Chicago's Gate of Horn in 1956. Jenkins had grown up in a family of Christian Scientists with eclectic musical tastes; the records of her youth included Cab Calloway, Little Brother Montgomery, Big Bill Broonzy, and Danny Kaye. She moved to California in her early twenties in order to complete her college education at San Francisco State and there absorbed an assortment of musical influences, particularly Latin American and Afro-Cuban rhythms. When she returned to Chicago in 1951 she incorporated her growing interest in exotic musical styles with her job as program director for teenagers at the YWCA. In the mid-1950s, for a period of two and a half or three years, she hosted a live television show on WTTW that enabled her to introduce her audience to a range of Chicago-based folk musicians—Josh White, Big Bill Broonzy, Velucia, Odetta. By 1956, when she stopped working for the YWCA, she had committed herself to working full time with her music.

Jenkins wanted to know from Goldstein how she might reach audiences. She had experience as a performer for young people, as an organizer of events; she had a passion for rhythm and rhythm instruments of all kinds, and had begun to accompany herself while in California on an odd instrument called the baritone ukelele. Goldstein suggested that she consider putting out a record—she could prepare a demo of three or four songs in a Chicago studio and see whether Moe Asch might have some interest in it. The record could then, in turn, be the means by which she introduced herself to school audiences and others.

In 1957, with her demo in hand, Jenkins traveled to New York for her first meeting with Asch. On her way up to the studio she ran into Odetta. "Make sure you get some royalties," Odetta cautioned Jenkins on learning that she was about to meet with Asch. The old office at 117 West Forty-sixth Street was small and cluttered. Asch took Jenkins's demo into the control booth and listened to her four songs. When he emerged, Jenkins's anxious anticipation was rewarded.

"Well you know," she remembered him saying, "I think you have something rather interesting going on here. I would like to see you expand things; I would like to see you add some instrumentation. What I heard, I really liked. In the meantime . . . let's sign a contract." Asch had Distler draw up a standard contract with a duration of three years. "I want to hear from you soon, and let me know what you're doing," Asch called after her as she left the office.[109]

Elated, Ella Jenkins returned to Chicago to record the remaining songs that would complete her first album, a ten-inch disc for Folkways entitled *Call-and-Response: Rhythmic Group Singing* (7638), which appeared in the catalogue before the year was out. The cover featured a black-and-white photograph of Jenkins performing for a group of children. The songs included chants she had written using nonsense syllables that, nonetheless, sounded as though they might have been African in origin. One song was, in fact, deliberately identified as African. It was an innovation that few would appreciate until many years later. Here was an African American artist presenting African material to young children as a teaching tool and source of inspiration. With revisionist history in its infancy, African culture was rarely regarded in the later fifties as having been a source of contemporary American Negro life, and it would be another ten years before significant numbers of African Americans derived any positive sense of cultural identification from it. African history was still popularly regarded as savage and lacking in cultural accomplishment. For Ella Jenkins, however, African culture was vital and highly usable.

When *Call-and-Response* was released, Jenkins promoted it energetically around Chicago. She would typically volunteer to play for its students if a school agreed to purchase a copy of her album. "If you come to Chicago this summer," she wrote Asch in April, "I would like to show you what I have done to publicize the album as well as the name of Folkways." Asch typically did not respond to her letters, even as she began to plead more insistently that he keep to the terms of their royalty agreement. Asch did go to Chicago for the American Library Association meeting that summer of 1958, where Jenkins had a chance to discuss her promotional efforts with him and to ask that she not be charged for promotional copies of the album sent to her. Asch promised that she would not be, although it would require additional letters before the sum of $15.60, deducted from her royalty check, would be restored to her. "It was nice seeing you again," she wrote to Asch after his Chicago trip, "and I hope one day, perhaps in New York, I'll get to know you as a person—so many people speak well of you and tell me how wonderful you are to know. We shall see." Jenkins had started to think about a second album and hoped that Folkways might be interested in releasing it, but experiences of the preceding months did not make her confident that they would be.[110]

In August Jenkins began touring summer camps, performing for children and selling copies of her album where she could. A royalty statement for the first half of the year had still not materialized, so she paid Folkways a visit to see what could be done. Distler promised her a statement within two weeks, but in late September Jenkins once again had to resort to a letter: "I realize that the 'Call-and-Response' album is only a small item in your big company, however . . . I should at least have the same consideration contract-wise, as any other artist. This is probably a very busy time, with fall releases; however, I'd appreciate your handling my tiny bit amidst it all."[111]

Jenkins was coming up against the fact that Folkways was not set up to enable touring artists, who depended on album sales for any significant portion of their income, to profit from the arrangement. She was finding that she never received a royalty statement without having to write Asch and Distler several reminders, and even then she could not feel confident that the royalties reflected the number of albums actually sold. Asch and Jenkins had as warm and collaborative a relationship as he was able to have with any artist, but financial matters never stopped intruding on it, occasionally threatening to sour it altogether.

There were other issues for Asch to confront in 1958. By the end of the year the number of albums in the Folkways catalogue was approaching five hundred. The original album numbering system, which had used numbers of one, two, and three digits, was getting to be a problem and was converted to a four-digit system that allowed Asch to bring greater clarity to his categories. The 4000 series would be Courlander's Ethnic Folkways Library, restricted to field recordings, and the International series (6800, 6900, and 8400 through 8886) would consist of recordings made by professional musicians or others who were not necessarily immersed in the musical cultural traditions they performed. The American folk music he had been releasing since the Asch label days was now found in the 2000 series, with no allowances made for ethnic or racial distinction, the 7000 series consisted primarily of children's recordings, and spoken word—an increasingly important part of the label—became the 9000 series. Nine years later he would be forced to adapt several five-digit series.

In the last couple years of the decade Asch was also branching into areas that fit awkwardly into his existing categories. In 1958 he released an album entitled *Sounds of New Music* (6160) that included compositions by Henry Cowell and John Cage, among others. Asch inserted it into the "science series" as he did a subsequent album of electronic music, *Highlights of Vortex* (6301). One of the composers represented on the first album, Roger Maren, was speaking to Asch in the spring of 1959 about new projects, and Asch suggested that he see whether Cage might be interested in making an album dedicated entirely to his own work. Maren in turn wrote to Cage, who, as it happens, had just been speaking with pianist David Tudor about preparing an album that would consist of the ninety stories Cage was then reading for public lectures, accompanied by Tudor's performance of some of Cage's piano work (along with several radios for "noise elements"). Cage telephoned Asch, and they set up a recording date at Cue Studios.

On the day of the recording session, Asch was out of town. Tudor had by then decided to dispense with the radios but added some sounds on magnetic tape as well as whistles and an amplified slinky. Mel Kaiser spent about an hour and a half adjusting the sound levels. Just as the recording finally began, Kaiser abruptly interrupted it.

"What's the trouble?" asked Cage.

"You shouldn't pause the way you do between words; you should just speak naturally."

"But this is what I have to do. I tell one story a minute and, when it's a short one, I have to spread it out. Later on, when I come to a long one, I have to speak as rapidly as I can."

"O.K., I'll just keep my mouth shut."

At the conclusion of the first side Kaiser declared that he was beginning to understand what the performance was about, and that they had better do the first side again. He had been trying to adjust the sound levels during the performance so that Cage's speaking voice would not be drowned out by the music. But Cage explained that just as one's view of a person across the street might be periodically interrupted by a passing vehicle, so the stories might be periodically obliterated by the music—it was intentional. They went on to make four LP sides. When Asch returned to New York and heard the tapes, he expressed his delight to Cage. Cage, too, was pleased with the results.[112] Asch released the two-record set, entitled *Indeterminacy: New Aspects of Form in Instrumental and Electronic Music* (3704). It appeared in the catalogue sandwiched between two other two-record sets, a historical survey of world music by ethnomusicologist Curt Sachs entitled *2,000 Years of Music* (3700) and a Sam Charters compilation of traditional blues singers entitled *The Rural Blues* (RF-202). It was twenty years before Asch was persuaded to make a new category in his catalogue for "electronic music" in order to consolidate recordings that were scattered among several unrelated categories.

It was becoming apparent in 1958 that although some aspects of the business were going very well, others, particularly marketing, were getting away from Asch. His customers were spread out around the United States and abroad, and he could not reach them effectively through traditional retail outlets. The conventions allowed him to reach educators, but not the nonprofessionals who still represented a significant portion of his market. At the same time he was not entirely unaware of who they were. For years albums had been shipped lacking the all-important album note inserts—they had run out of the particular insert and needed to reprint it or they had been temporarily mislaid—and a postcard inserted instead instructing the buyer to write Folkways and the notes would be mailed when they became available. Using this ploy Asch was able to compile a file of names and addresses of potential customers—perhaps ten thousand of them. Asch did not have the organizational creativity to capitalize on them, but Irwin Silber did.

Silber was thirty-three years old in 1958 and had been an effective (if doctrinaire) political organizer for more than ten years. In July 1947 he had been appointed executive director of People's Songs in order to replace Felix Landau (Landau in turn had replaced Lee Hays the previous November when Hays's inertia threatened the coherence of an organization that was growing faster than its organizational structure could bear). As People's Songs metamorphosed into People's Artists (largely a booking agency for left-wing folk musicians and other blacklisted performers) and the *People's Songs Bulletin* was replaced by *Sing Out!* in May 1950, Silber remained in charge. It was in part through the People's Artists' hootenannies of the earlier 1950s that the fragile Old Left kept its cultural identity alive and (barely) visible during its most embattled years. The number of subscribers to *Sing Out!* had fallen to just a thousand in 1954, and in 1957 People's Artists disbanded.[113] Neither the organization nor its publication had constituted a living for Silber, Pete Seeger, and the few stalwarts who donated their time to keep the movement alive. Silber wrote for the *Daily Worker* for a while, until it ceased to be a daily, and then as a copywriter for a publisher until his appearance before the HUAC in June 1958 made it improbable that he would work much longer in the "legitimate" press.

When Silber approached Asch for a job in 1958, things worked out better than he might have predicted. Silber and Asch had crossed paths in the late forties, during Silber's association with People's Songs, but their association really only began when Pete Seeger suggested to Asch that he have Silber write the notes for Seeger's *American Industrial Ballads* (5251), which was released in 1956. This would be Silber's "foot in the door" at Folkways; he recalled that Asch was very pleased with the notes, as was Seeger.[114] In the tradition of the Lomaxes and Harry Smith, Silber took care to identify the origin of the twenty-four songs on the album, and to flesh out the historical circumstances under which they were written. But he distinguished his ends from those of scholarly folklorists:

> For many years these folk songs were looked at askance by traditional scholars and folklorists. We will never know how many of these songs were irretrievably lost because they did not meet the strict and arbitrary definitions imposed by folk song collectors. In recent years, however, as folksong and folk-lore have moved out of the domain of an interesting hobby and into the area of historical and sociological research, this body of protest material has achieved a new respectability.[115]

Silber next asked Asch whether he might be interested in a project of his own—a collection of *Songs of the Suffragettes*, performed by Elizabeth Knight, a People's Artists activist (and heir to the Kresge department store chain) who had a deep, full-throated voice. Silber collected the songs and had Knight record them with Mel Kaiser at Cue. The album was released in 1958.

When Silber took the next step and suggested to Asch that he hire him full time to take care of the marketing end of things, his timing could not have been more fortuitous. The first signs of the folk music revival could be seen in the growing Sunday afternoon crowds of singers, pickers, and listeners in Washington Square. Izzy Young had opened his Folklore Center in April 1957 on McDougal Street in order to sell music books, periodicals, records, and musical accessories. In very short order it became the central gathering place for folk music enthusiasts in the city—what Young termed "folkniks." Within a matter of weeks, he was producing what would become a legendary string of small but memorable concerts. Pete Seeger was not yet quite forty and had left the Weavers in 1957; he and the other Weavers were already the *éminence grise* of the folk music world. The brief stir they made on the hit parade in early fifties with "Goodnight Irene," "So Long It's Been Good to Know Yuh," "Wimoweh," "Kisses Sweeter than Wine," and "Tzena Tzena" came to an end as they fell victim to the blacklist in 1952; they disbanded that year, reunited in 1955 for the legendary Carnegie Hall concert, and toured extensively from 1956 to 1958. But when the group outvoted Seeger's objections to recording a Lucky Strike commercial, Seeger suggested that Erik Darling be hired in his place. When folk songs again appeared on the hit parade, it was primarily as hopped-up renditions by country singers, dismissed by the folk purists as hopelessly ersatz. "Kisses Sweeter than Wine," this time performed by Jimmie Rodgers, spent twenty-one weeks on *Billboard*'s hit parade in 1957 and early 1958. The Kingston Trio's "Tom Dooley," which Dave Guard had learned from the Stinson recording by Roger Sprung, entered the top thirty in October 1958 and spent five weeks in the number one spot during November and December.[116] The following July a rendition of "The Battle of New Orleans" by Johnny Horton also became a number one hit for six weeks and spent a total of twenty-one weeks on the top forty (Horton had married Hank Williams's widow and would himself die in a car crash in 1960). An effort by Asch to market a competing version by Pete Seeger and Frank Hamilton was not successful. That same month the Kingston Trio's "M.T.A.," to which Jacqueline Steiner and Bess Hawes held the copyright, made it to number fifteen on the Top Thirty. The relevance of this to Asch's Folkways may not have been immediately apparent to those on the outside, but something big was just over the horizon. Asch might have been excused in 1958 for feeling that the world—or at least New York—was beginning to come around to his view of things.

Asch had already rented a space around the corner from 117 West Forty-sixth Street; he envisioned an auxiliary marketing operation there that he would place under the RBF umbrella, expecting that it would eventually encompass more than simply records. Books would, in fact, represent a significant element in the Folkways "cartel," as Silber would later put it; films never developed much beyond a few filmstrips for classroom use and the film that Pete Seeger made of steel-drum artist Kim Loy Wong. But initially RBF was set up to enable Sam Charters to issue blues recordings that had been previously issued on other labels, without jeopardizing Folkways with the kinds of royalty problems that followed from Ramsey's History of Jazz series and Harry Smith's *Anthology.*

Asch established Silber in the new space in September and assigned him to the immediate task of preparing a mailing for the Christmas season. Silber had experience working with mailing lists, and he immediately sent Asch's card file of names and addresses to a company that put them on stencils that could readily be made into address labels. The catalogue at that juncture included a description of every record; it was huge and expensive to mail. Silber culled through it and made a selection of titles that he would feature in a special Christmas-edition catalogue, with rewritten or shortened descriptions. He worked out special packages of combined albums and instituted a sales price for orders of multiple albums. Christmas 1958 was Folkways' best season to date.

Silber joined Asch with one condition—that he bring *Sing Out!* with him. Asch's response to this surprised Silber; he not only provided Silber with the space from which to operate *Sing Out!* but also asked to become a partner in the operation. He and Silber would each own a 45 percent share in the magazine; so that neither would have controlling interest by himself, Pete Seeger would hold the remaining 10 percent. Asch's share of *Sing Out!* cost him twenty-five hundred dollars. He also agreed that he would not meddle in editorial policy, and although he certainly expressed himself at times, he never forced the issue. Even in 1958 *Sing Out!* was attempting to be many things to many people, and the tensions that resulted would become gradually more apparent—and more problematic—over the next few years. Surely it was a vehicle for the marketing of folk music, and Folkways benefited as much as its emerging competitors (chiefly Elektra, Vanguard, Prestige, and Riverside). It was also the means of expanding the interest in traditional musical forms, an enterprise some found grossly at odds with the growing commercial viability of the genre. Finally—and most particularly for Silber—*Sing Out!* held the possibility of increasing the means by which folk music was pressed into the service of politically progressive causes.

For a short while Asch brought Silber along to a few conventions—the American Booksellers' Association, the American Library Association, perhaps the Modern Language Association—in order to initiate him into Folkways' particular brand of salesmanship. When traveling together, Asch seemed to Silber a different person. He spent money freely on the best hotels and the best restaurants and showed a public face that was both gracious and erudite. Silber was amazed by Asch's ability to hold his own in wide-ranging conversations with customers about literature, linguistics, and music. Asch liked to be able to sell at least one set of the entire catalogue while at a convention, and occasionally he succeeded in selling three or four. It was Silber who instituted the practice of selling off the display records at the close of the convention, which saved the cost of shipping them back to New York and brought in ready cash, which Asch loved. Over dinner with Silber, Asch occasionally revealed a private side that included rarely seen uncertainties and anxieties. In Silber's view, Asch was a very lonely man who was painfully aware of his own lack of social skills. In those social settings that he could dominate—whether in his office, in one of his regular restaurants, or when playing the salesman—he was capable of being relaxed and affable. Asch avoided social settings in which the control of the situation was relinquished to others, most especially music clubs, which (to the puzzlement of many of his artists) he assiduously avoided all his life.

Silber would recall having been very close to Asch, without denying that they could become furiously angry with one another. Distler was another story. She regarded Silber as a threat to her relationship with Asch and to her control of the company, and they plainly did not get along.

Silber made no secret of the fact that, for him, folk music was subordinate to political ends. It was a view that would get him in increasing trouble with others in the Folkways and *Sing Out!* circle in the 1960s. But in the late fifties, Silber did not depart significantly from Asch on those progressive political ideals that seemed just barely permissible in a politically repressive era—internationalism, pacifism, and interracial understanding. In his first full year as a full-time employee of Folkways, Silber arranged to release a 1954 recording of a hootenanny that encapsulated these themes. *Hootenanny Tonight!* (2511) was hardly a radical manifesto, but it documented the kind of event that kept the New York folk music community alive during some of its leanest years by exploring the possibilities of understanding and appreciating unfamiliar musical cultural forms, and by finding common ground on which individuals of disparate cultural backgrounds could stand. In its eclecticism it was not the kind of effort that folklorists could be expected to appreciate. In discussing this album in conjunction with Pete Seeger's *Gazette* (2501), D. K. Wilgus remarked,

> Moses Asch is correct in defending his right to issue such material; and the material is in a province that legitimately and necessarily belongs to the folklorist. But no one should assume that the liberal tone of most of these pieces is an accident, or that this is the only tradition of contemporary topical song. When Dave Arkin's 'State of Arkansas' is considered, so must be songs expressing other opinions on the integration problem—and they do exist. The folklorist's personal opinion of the Ku Klux Klan should not exclude its songs from notice. No one expects Pete Seeger to sing such songs. But the student of folksong has a different problem and cannot let the noise of one group deafen him to the singing of another. The study is no place for barricades.[117]

There certainly was a selection process at work in determining what might appropriately be a Folkways product. Asch would deny that there were ideological grounds for the inclusion or exclusion of a particular title, and that his intention was other than to simply make material available to the public that the public could then interpret as it pleased. But those who came to him with recording projects—and those who constituted the better part of his market—were interested in documents that were at least neutral toward, if not sympathetic to, the liberal causes of the era. And this if nothing else contributed to the shape of a catalogue, which by the late fifties constituted the aesthetic touchstone of the American Left.

There were other developments in the fall of 1958 that suggested folk music was about to become a commodity over which some might find it sufficiently lucrative to fight. Alan Lomax had returned from his self-imposed exile in England and quickly set about restoring his primacy in the realm of published folk music. Among those in his sight lines was Pete Seeger, who had, in Lomax's absence, recorded several dozen songs for Asch that Lomax claimed as his own, as the collector. Although Lomax's motivations were undoubtedly varied, his purpose was in part to establish his authority in the creation of an American folk-song canon. He had described his 1947 *Folk Song U.S.A.* as "the first attempt to set up a canon for American folk song," and as in any canon formation there needed to be either explicit or implicit claims over the right to determine what "belonged."[118]

The idea of copyrighting folk songs was galling to those who thought the songs should simply remain in the public domain. And then there was the question of whether the collector was entitled to profit from material that he had, in fact, learned from someone else. But at the same time there were legitimate arguments on the other side. If a folk song became the source of a hit record, *someone* would be entitled to the publishing royalties—perhaps the collector might as justifiably be the recipient as anyone else. Certainly Lomax was more entitled to royalties than the performer, who had simply helped himself to the song from Lomax's published collection. The Lomaxes often published a version of a song that was a distillation of several versions they had collected, and this in itself could be regarded as a creative process. And without the collectors, who would ever have heard the songs in the first place?

Lomax was disturbed that Seeger had recorded so many of "his" songs without his having received any copyright credit on the records. He pressed Seeger to write a letter to Asch with a long list of songs, requesting that Lomax's copyright be duly acknowledged in subsequent recordings. "Alan and I have been talking over the past years of recording work I have been doing for you," Seeger wrote,

> and I wish to acknowledge in this letter to you the songs from Lomax books and Lomax sources which I have recorded for your company. . . . It was not my intention, of course, to violate the copyright on the Lomax arrangements of these songs in doing these recordings, nor did either of us suspect that these recordings of mine would put these copyrights into question to any extent. Now that we all see third parties using these recordings of mine as a primary folk source we wish these acknowledgements had been made clear on the records, so that the work of the Lomaxes will be recognized and pirated no further.[119]

Seeger was among those disinclined to regard genuine folk songs as property and reportedly wrote Asch very reluctantly.[120] Asch acknowledged Seeger's letter with a one sentence reply, indicating only that he had read it.[121] But matters did not rest there. Lomax

had retained the Richmond Organization to represent his published interests, and Howard Richmond wrote to Asch at the end
of October: "Would appreciate it if you or Marian would call me in
connection with clearing up the matter of proper licensing. Rest
assured that there is no financial problem involved here, but rather
a serious copyright matter which can be rectified very easily."[122]

But Asch would not concede so readily. Seeger had taken some
of the songs, it seemed to him, from Ruth Crawford's *American
Folksongs for Children,* the contents of which had been properly
copyrighted by Doubleday. Other songs appeared to have been
learned from Woody Guthrie recordings that were made for Asch's
own labels. And then there was the sticky ethical question of
whether Lomax owned the copyright to songs that he collected
while employed by the Library of Congress. Asch wrote Richmond:

> Let me make very clear to you the following: We will be
> happy to acknowledge Alan's claim of collection or arrange-
> ment or synthesis of folk material recorded on the Folkways
> label in every case where the recording artist tells us directly
> that he has learned the song and the version he or she per-
> forms from one of the Lomax collections and where no
> other claims conflict with the Lomax claim. I certainly feel
> that Alan and all other collectors of folklore (myself included)
> are entitled to both recognition and, where possible, financial
> remuneration for their efforts. But I cannot make blanket con-
> cessions nor agree to sweeping claims without a more careful
> analysis of the specific material.[123]

The matter never was—nor could it be—satisfactorily resolved. In
many instances it would be impossible to determine the extent to
which Seeger had learned a song from one source versus another.
It was similar to any other question of intellectual property; but in
the case of folk music the evidentiary trail was often very long, and
sometimes very cold.

6. I COULD'VE HAD JOAN
The Folk Revival

*T*he folk revival of the first half of the 1960s was built upon a set of paradoxes that preoccupied those who had been dedicated to the popularization of folk music in the preceding decades, Asch included. There was first the uncertainty about what it was that constituted folk music, which turned into a series of endless debates, played over and over with numbing frequency in the pages of *Sing Out!* During the many years in which the marketing of folk music remained a marginal and esoteric enterprise, the competing interests, motivations, and definitions were largely suppressed—Asch, Lomax, Seeger, Charters, Silber, and others were all interested in assuring "the music" an audience, and there was too little at stake to worry over what belonged and what did not. The audience for traditional Appalachian singers, revivalist, bluegrass, blues, gospel, and international performers appeared to be homogeneous; as eclectic as the many musical forms surely were, they seemed to fit together by virtue of their authenticity. It would have been anathema to the interracial and internationalist Zeitgeist of the late fifties and early sixties Left to have contemplated a fracturing of the audience or performers along ethnic or nationalist lines. But as performers, managers, impresarios, record-business entrepreneurs, and others began to glimpse the possibility of establishing careers based upon the marketing of "folk music," the question of what belonged loomed larger. When Pete Seeger sought to unplug Bob Dylan (backed by parts of the Butterfield Blues Band, Al Kooper, and Barry Goldberg) at the 1965 Newport Folk Festival and all but prompted a fistfight with Dylan's manager Albert Grossman (Seeger later maintained that the sound system was terrible and had been muffling Dylan's words), the debate may have received its most lucid representation. Yet although the debate became an increasingly irrelevant one to the recording industry, for which authenticity was just one more marketing device, editorial policy at *Sing Out!* as well as programming decisions for Newport and at the proliferating coffee houses and college folk festivals remained preoccupied with questions about the parameters of the genre.

Half brothers Pete and Mike Seeger exemplified contrasting positions. Pete, having developed his ideas about folk song in the era of "my song is my weapon," was ostensibly content to judge a song according to whether or not it "worked," that is, according to whether it moved individuals and (more important) collectivities to a deeper understanding of themselves and the human condition. (Never mind his periodic hostility to popular musical forms that might have "worked" and reached far broader audiences.) Mike, though not perhaps his polar opposite, is a half-generation younger and reflects both older and younger positions in the debate. For him a song's utility was less important than its authenticity, judged according to criteria of historical and cultural pedigree. Whereas Pete made little effort to imitate the vocal style of those whose songs he was singing, Mike, in Robert Cantwell's description, both "imitates and reinvents the traditionally strained, nasal, wood-grained mountain vocality, marking it with authenticity while at the same time claiming it as something both original and exotic." In casting himself in performance as a rural period piece, Mike Seeger, in Cantwell's view, conveys not only an unabashed romanticism but also a set of unspoken questions about the relationship between his own privileges of birth and the social and economic predicaments of the songs' originators.[1]

Asch, always the *bricoleur,* was content to use whatever criteria were at hand. He insisted that the recordings he released had to be "legitimate"—they had to express the truth. But by his own admission his definition of authentic was expanding the longer he was in the business. His earlier inclination was to regard folk music as an exclusively rural phenomenon; later, particularly under the influence of Tony Schwartz, he conceded that legitimate folk expression existed in the city as well. He also came to regard jazz and blues musicians as "folk": "Folk may mean any human being that expresses himself, let's say in a vocal or musical sense. Creating through music a picture of life that reflects that person's experiences and life patterns." A studio, and the promise of royalties, was not sufficient to cause Asch to consider whether the context might be constraining the performance. However, a live performance for a paying audience was. Asch hated coffee houses, and his artists were sometimes hurt by his refusal to attend their performances. His stated objection was that the context was antithetical to genuine folk expression: "You never see me in these damn places because the guy down there is singing to the audience for the purpose that they paid money like a prostitute."[2] It was equally likely that he felt uncomfortable in these settings, as in any social setting he could not control through his personal authority. Asch released very few nightclub recordings; notable exceptions included George Pickow's magnificent Folk City performance by his wife, Jean Ritchie, in the company of Doc Watson and several recordings of Pete Seeger, including those in which he was accompanied by Memphis Slim and Willie Dixon at the Village Gate and by Sonny Terry at Carnegie Hall. Still, Asch might have considered that any musical performance is constrained by a host of social factors, and individual or collective self-interest is as likely to be a part of a performer's motivation in *any* setting as other apparently "generous" motivations. As Raymond Williams maintains in *Marxism and Literature*, artistic production is a kind of material social production that does not depart from any *other* kind of production in the requirement of labor and the manipulation of materials: "'Thinking' and 'imagining' are from the beginning social processes. . . . They become accessible only in unarguably physical and material ways: in voices, in sounds made by instruments, in penned or printed writing, in arranging pigments on canvas or plaster, in worked marble or stone."[3] Playing or singing music must be regarded as a kind of work, and although its place in a given system of exchange might seem tangential, it is not necessarily any more "genuine" for being "freely given," nor less so for coming with a price.

Finally, though, when pressed Asch was content to verify the legitimacy of a recording simply on the grounds that he "said so." At times he privileged social expression, at other moments individual expression. When asked in a revealing interview for *Popular Mechanics* in April 1961 entitled "PM Interviews 'Mr. Offbeat'" about the meaning of "folkways," Asch first speaks about the individual expression of a writer, such as James Joyce. The interviewer then asks him about his criteria for editing a tape, and Asch concedes that because a tape inevitably includes more than can be contained on an LP, choices are made according to what *he* is trying to say about the complete life of a people. The magazine's electronics editor tries to engage Asch in a discussion of recording technique, but Asch's interest is in the ways in which tape recording conveys individual and collective meanings. "We all had 'causes' when we were young," he tells his interviewer. "Now there are fewer causes. People are lost and look for communication and association." In his fifty-sixth year, in an effort to have his interviewer understand the relative importance of individual and social expression, he (perhaps unintentionally) conveys surprising insight into his own struggle to define his place: "The only way to be a family is to know what a family is. This business of running from the family to a society is a terrible thing. We are a social people and should try to be a part of others, but individual understanding is also necessary. We should not try to hide from ourselves."[4]

At the start of the decade, Asch, Maynard Solomon of Vanguard, and Jac Holzman of Elektra could only have been impressed by their own prescience in having prepared the ground for the explosion of interest in folk music. But why just then, after having toiled in obscurity for so long? One market reality was undebatable: the burgeoning market for folk music was a youth phenomenon and, more particularly, an artifact of the tastes of college students. Cantwell has eloquently demonstrated that many distinct (if occasionally related) cultural, scholarly, and political threads had contributed to the shape of American folk music on the brink of the sixties revival—romantic traditions of American pastoralism found in vaudeville and minstrel traditions, the literary interest in an authentic American vernacular, the Left's construction of an American masses (the "workers" becoming the "people" in the Popular Front era). And this meant that folk music, as it was understood in the early sixties, carried with it a set of largely unspoken and often unrecognized presuppositions. These included its valorization as the authentic expression of a people's struggle for self-definition in the face of dehumanizing, modernist incursions—honest, pedigreed, uncomplicated, unambivalently righteous. But for the college students of the early 1960s this history was largely irrelevant and uninteresting; folk music was for them, as Cantwell argues, merely a usable past conveniently malleable for contemporary purposes. Thus Joan Baez, appearing on the cover of *Time* magazine on 23 November 1962, declares to an openly cynical reporter, "I don't care very much about where a song came from or why—or even what it says. All I care about is how it sounds and the feeling in it."[5]

And what were those contemporary purposes? A second paradox of the sixties revival was that the meaning of folk music for those who had kept it alive through the fifties appeared to become much more elusive in the hands of baby boomers. Cantwell has offered perhaps the most plausible explanation for the sudden commercial success of folk music in the early sixties. Folk music, he argues in *When We Were Good*, was becoming the vehicle through which the children of the fifties expressed their discontent with the bland, comfortable, safe, suburban lives that their parents had created for them. In moving out of the city, their parents had deprived the privileged children of the baby boom of the means of bumping up against those whose class, racial, ethnic, or national differences might have provided both a sense of danger and fascination. More than that, the suburban enclave, constructed on the model of corporate rationalism and individual advancement, had undermined the "'communities of obligation,' ethnic and agrarian, in which traditional knowledge and value had been seated."[6] Cantwell looks back fondly to a prewar era in which community life had not been eroded by the commercial excesses of communications technology. Yet in having been isolated from ethnic and class differences, baby boomers could not help but look on those unlike themselves with some uneasiness. Far more comfortable images of differences were provided through television images of cowboys and Indians, through summer camp depictions of noble savages and intrepid pioneers, and through public school textbook portrayals of folk heroes. Upon entering college, when one's discontent with the self-righteous superiority of the parental generation comes to a head, folk music—with a host of preconstrained meanings—became the means of constructing a different kind of "self." It was a readily available vehicle for the articulation of their sense that "the world had been gravely mismanaged by the parent generation . . . [and] the nagging fear that the future might at any moment be withdrawn."[7] Folk music enabled college students to ground themselves in a value-rich past while resisting the transitory, expendable mass culture they had inherited from their parents.

Cantwell follows Simon Frith in recognizing the extent to which the meanings attached to commercial songs in the later twentieth century are ineffably tied to understandings about the people singing them.[8] Although Dylan overtly rejected the mantle of generational spokesman, he and Joan Baez could not have been naïve about the relationship between the images of themselves that they created for public consumption and the acceptance of their music by American college students. But whereas Cantwell is savvy about the ways in which the idea of a romanticized "folk" constitutes a cultural construction that has been made and remade throughout the American twentieth century for an assortment of political and cultural purposes, he is less self-conscious about the presumed existence of an Edenic era in American life when neighbors knew one another and individual striving took a back seat to communal obligations. He can argue that "the old free America was of course an artifact too, of the poetic imagination," but if it was *only* an artifact of the cultural imagination, what was the nature of the cultural transformation in the late fifties that required the folk music response? If the rootlessness of the modernist mentality does not contrast in some substantive way with an earlier cultural reality, what was the need that the revivalist vision was addressing? And finally, if in his postmodernist detachment Cantwell sees only an elusive, culturally constructed past rather than a materially constituted reality, then the apparent vacuousness of the fifties can be no less a construction of our present cultural imagination.[9] The "response" constituted by the sixties folk revival, we might surmise, is an artifact of youthful alienation that was no more salient in the Eisenhower years than in any other decade of the twentieth century; it only took another form, and we are still left to ponder why it took the form of folk music in the early sixties.

In the end, for Cantwell, American society has come unglued in the late twentieth century, and rock and roll—just as *his* parents' generation predicted—was the sure sign of its demise. Simon Frith, on the other hand, posits a relationship between the meaning of early sixties folk music and late sixties rock and roll that has them fulfilling similar functions—if in radically different ways—in the articulation of the space between youth and leisure. He is less sanguine than Cantwell about the fixity of musical meanings; and Frith is particularly dubious about the ability of the makers of popular music—both performers and music business executives—to retain control of the meanings of the "product" once it falls into the hands of consumers. In a third paradox of the sixties revival, some folk ideologues undoubtedly fussed about how commercialization would pervert the meaning of folk music; the legacy of the Frankfurt school caused the Old Left in the sixties to presume that the mass market would fabricate "needs" in the public that it would then meet with products that existed primarily in order to sustain capitalism. But the meaning of folk music was undergoing changes in the sixties that were being driven by cultural and political forces rather than by the marketplace. Consumers rather than producers of folk music would determine its meaning, in both conscious and (more often) unconscious ways. When *Sing Out!* asked twenty-eight folk musicians, record producers, and folklorists in 1966 to discuss the significance of folk songs on Top Forty radio, the reaction was mixed. Folklorist Tristram Coffin eluded the problem by maintaining that once popularized a folk song can no longer be considered folk music. Sam Charters took the opposite perspective by denying the distinction altogether: "Dammit—How long will it be before the intellectual world—and I have to include folklorists in this group—realizes that the Top Forty is our folk music?" Many thought that the commercial success was good for folk music in rescuing it from its insularity and giving it a broad audience. Most of the others agreed that Top Forty radio had become a great deal easier to take since the addition of Dylan and Baez, and the performers among them would have been delighted to have heard their own songs on the car radio. Lee Hays curtly announced that "a song can be good and commercial and I wish more of mine were both."[10] Perhaps those who embraced the marriage of folk music and Top Forty and began to hope that they were becoming indistinguishable slightly overstated their case; there remained differences between a music that had evolved in the preceding decades with very little relation to the mass market and a music that was defined primarily in relation to the means through which it was marketed. Folk music, as it was understood in the early sixties, had gained a fragile but loyal audience through its exposure in summer camps, college outing clubs, and (somewhat later) college coffee houses. It was not created with a mass market in mind and would survive once its brief flirtation with the mass market was spent. Pop music—and rock as its most recent incarnation—was, in the words of Simon Frith, "inseparable from the mass market in its conception": "Pop music is created with the record industry's pursuit of a large audience in mind; other music is not. . . . That classical or folk music can be listened to on records is accidental for its form and content; it is only pop music whose essence is that it is communicated by a mass medium."[11] Cantwell, too, making the case for early rock and roll as a kind of folk music, fails to note that in its dissemination through the media of radio and the 45-rpm record rock is a different kind of phenomenon than the folk music revival of *any* era.[12]

Commercialization was a matter of concern to Asch, but not for any of the reasons cited by others. The scale of his operation was sufficient to handle a mildly successful record, including sales of up to a few thousand copies. But more than that and a single record would swamp his meager staff and facilities; he lacked the capital to supply the volume a hit record would have demanded or—the lesson from his Disc fiasco—to absorb the returns in the event of a potential hit that flopped. In later years he claimed that he was offered the opportunity to sign Joan Baez. This is unlikely, because her manager, Manny Greenhill, undoubtedly knew that Asch did not have the means of handling a genuinely popular artist. Perhaps he had received a copy of Baez's demo tape, which had been sent to the other prominent folk music labels. Still, Asch might be taken at his word when he maintained that he would not have signed a popular artist because it would have prevented him from attending to all of the many esoteric projects that together formed the identity of Folkways Records: "I was offered Joan Baez, all the hit people, but I couldn't use them, because then my label would be known as the pop label of Joan Baez and nobody would buy the country musician from my label, because you couldn't differentiate what I issued."[13]

It would become ironic—but not surprising—that just as the antiwar movement in the second half of the decade was becoming the most popular left-wing movement in American history, folk music was losing its hold on the American Left and falling off the popular music charts. Folk music had sustained the Old Left, but at its greatest popularity it was unable to sustain the New Left for long. Yet the battle was not lost as thoroughly as some might have thought. Through the sixties and early seventies, rock and roll was suffused with folk music values of authenticity and originality; its meanings remained attached to the images projected by those who performed it and to a sense of identity between the performers and their audiences. Frith has challenged the argument of Charters (and others) that pop music is the folk music of today by suggesting that the youth audience for rock is a community only in an ideological (rather than material) sense: "It describes a shared state of mind but not a cooperative way of life."[14] The connections rock musicians made with their audiences were fleeting, occasionally apparent when encountering them through live performance but invariably slipping out of reach when the medium of communication became primarily the LP. Yet the same conundrum existed for the folk performers of the first half of the sixties. Were recordings primarily a means of sustaining or recovering the memories of live performances, or were live performances primarily a means of reinforcing the meanings that listeners had derived individually and privately from listening to LPs? With the success of folk music recordings in the early sixties, the process by which listeners derived meaning from folk music could not help but have changed. The meanings listeners attach to any music (and particularly song) is invariably related to the circumstances in which it is first heard. If songs are initially encountered while an individual is part of a live audience or a group sing—whether in a concert hall, coffee house, summer camp or camping trip—then the meanings are apt to be connected to the experience of that collectivity. But records heard in private settings by individual listeners or small groups will become the vehicle for other kinds of memory associations. Just as pop songs—particularly before MTV began to package listeners' musical associations for them—trigger memories of the circumstances or relationships that provided the context of initial listenings (consider the ubiquity of teenage couples with their designated "our song"), folk music recordings also could become a medium for the encapsulation of private and personal meanings. Frith is certainly correct that "rock . . . is rarely a folk music" in the ways that folk music had conveyed meaning before the revival; but in that sense the folk music of the folk revival was rarely a folk music either. Frith, too, is attached to a definition of folk culture—"created directly and spontaneously out of communal experience"—that is a contemporary cultural and scholarly fabrication, having increasingly little to do with the revival audience of the early sixties.[15]

On Friday, 25 May 1962, Asch received a phone call from his brother John, who had just received a telegram from Ruth informing him that their mother had passed away. Asch told his brother to come meet him at the Folkways offices so that they could phone Ruth. When he arrived Asch shooed everyone else out of the office. John did most of the talking when they succeeded in getting Ruth on the line. He learned that the burial would be on Sunday afternoon. Next they called Nathan in California, who seemed not to know how to react. He asked Asch whether he should send a telegram to Ruth and, if so, what should he say, then he promptly hung up. On a plane to London the following day, Asch wrote an account of the preceding day: "Everything was done mechanical. I knew there would be a reaction but I had to finalize the routine before I could bear to think of the consequences of the death."[16] Asch returned to New York early the following week; there was no visible ripple in his routine, but with the death of Madya the remaining connection to the ancestral generation was severed. The reality of his parents' neglect—his childhood spent largely in the care of others, the long silences when he was an adult, the absence of phone calls or letters—receded into history. Asch was now at liberty to create his own mythology about his parents and their role in his life, without any living intrusions.

At the start of the decade Asch received a boost from the popular press that augured well. It came in the form of an article in *High Fidelity* in June 1960 by Robert Shelton, the music critic of the *New York Times* whose glorious review of a nightclub appearance by Bob Dylan two years later would be credited with launching Dylan's career. Entitled "Folkways in Sound . . . or the remarkable enterprises of Mr. Moe Asch," Shelton's article described Asch as a "doggedly creative, self-made intellectual who combines an almost mystical idealism with the cynicism of a visionary living in a brass-tacks society." Shelton wrote of Asch's father, his immigration to the United States, his German training in radio technology, his entry into and variable experiences in the record business of the forties. He understood Asch's dedication to spontaneity, to documentation, and to content over form, while acknowledging the complaints about technical quality and surface noise that had dogged Folkways recordings for years. At times, he conceded, performance quality is sacrificed for the sake of acquiring otherwise unavailable material: "Asch will often buy tapes from downright incompetent singers who know material no one else has come forward to record . . . musically it may be an excruciating experience." A few years later, another *High Fidelity* writer would define torture as being locked in a room for twenty-four hours while being forced to listen nonstop to Folkways recordings. But the general tone of Shelton's article was far kinder. He mentioned Asch's notorious temper, but also his tremendous generosity. A competitor described Asch as "courageous" and wished he could take Asch's aesthetic chances. Quoting a woman who works in record sales, Shelton concluded by suggesting that Asch's collection will have far more enduring value than that of any of his more commercial competitors; it will stand in fifty years, he declared, as a document of our contemporary life.[17]

Echoing Shelton's florid descriptions, Sam Charters playfully addressed a letter the following month from Scotland to "Dear pert, redheaded Marian Distler. . . . I haven't heard from you—or from heavy-set stoop-shouldered amiable Moses Asch, either. . . . I assume you're busy autographing copies of *High Fidelity*."[18]

At the start of the folk revival, for many of those who would become its stars, the "real thing" was to be found on Folkways. Bob Dylan's deliberate recasting of himself as the young Woody Guthrie was the consequence of his immersion in Guthrie's Folkways recordings during his short-lived college career at the University of Minnesota. Having been befriended by Paul Nelson and John Pankake of the *Little Sandy Review* in the spring of 1960, Dylan took advantage of Pankake's absence from Minneapolis one weekend to make off with a major portion of his record collection. When Nelson, Pankake, and Tony Glover came to his apartment the following week to confront him about it, they found several dozen albums, including some of Guthrie's Folkways releases as well as one of Libba Cotten's Folkways albums and Mike Seeger's compilation, *Mountain Music Bluegrass Style*, released just the previous year.[19] The following year, now in New York, Dylan spent countless hours listening to the available recordings of folk music. For some weeks he slept on the couch of Carla Rotolo (his girlfriend Suze's older sister), who at the time worked for Alan Lomax and consequently had a mammoth record collection, including most of the Folkways catalogue. During the day, while Carla was at work, Dylan immersed himself in her record collection in search of material for the album he would shortly record for John Hammond at Columbia. She remembered his listening to Smith's *Anthology*, as well as to recordings by Woody Guthrie, A. L. Lloyd, and Ewan MacColl. When Dylan's first album appeared it included Blind Lemon Jefferson's "See That My Grave Is Kept Clean" from *Anthology* as well as "Baby Let Me Follow You Down," which although credited to Eric Von Schmidt, appeared to owe something to Ramsey's recordings of Horace Sprott.[20]

Folkways recordings were gaining a hearing among a group of young folk music enthusiasts who would soon smooth and polish the songs, the instrumental and vocal styles, and present them to an audience of previously unimaginable proportions. Of the many factors—social, economic, political—that made this possible, the easing of the climate for left-wing sentiments cannot be discounted. Asch had taken great care in the fifties to ensure that he would not be susceptible to governmental and quasi-governmental forces of right-wing censure. He and (more particularly) Marian Distler had encounters with FBI agents in middecade that convinced them of the wisdom of not attracting unneeded attention.

The FBI had opened a file on Folkways in 1955 because in monitoring the mail from the People's Republic of China to U.S. citizens they had discovered that Asch had received a "pro-Chinese Communist publication" entitled *China Reconstructs*. That autumn agents procured a Folkways "Polish language" recording (*Polish Folk Songs and Dances* [6848], released the previous year) that they concluded had "definite pro-Communist propaganda value":

> The majority of the songs contained in the aforementioned were new songs. [Deleted] one song depicted miners in the coal regions of Poland, singing the praises of existing conditions in Poland today as compared to before. [Deleted] was of the opinion that these records were undoubtedly made in the United States from tapes procured from Communist occupied Poland. [Deleted] upon determining the contents of these records, [Deleted] destroyed or returned the records to the Independent Records Distributing Corporation.

An agent later snooped around the hallways of 117 West Forty-sixth Street, provided a description of the Folkways offices from the outside, but was frustrated in his efforts to read the titles of the many records, books, and pamphlets that he observed in the outer office. Emboldened the following year, an agent spoke with Marian Distler and learned that Folkways was "one of three major producers of folk music in the United States, the other two organizations being Stenson [sic] Records Company and Electra [sic] Records Company." In an effort to make available folk music recordings from throughout the world, Folkways had procured recordings from several communist countries; but the agent was assured that the Soviet records were manufactured from old recordings, the source of which was in the United States. Because the agent did not speak the languages heard on the recordings from the Soviet Union, Poland, Czechoslovakia and Rumania, he could not "completely follow the contents of the records." He nevertheless concluded that he had "uncovered no information which would cause [him] to believe that the records are made to propagandize the Communist form of government. [Deleted] in some instances, the songs depict the hardships of certain peoples in various countries and could probably be construed as being of certain propaganda value. [Deleted] did not believe this could be true inasmuch as most of these songs are a great deal older than the Communist form of government practiced in Russia and the satellite countries."

Ultimately the agent concluded that he "did not have any reason to question either the integrity or loyalty of Miss Distler and that [deleted] she was engaged in a solely legitimate enterprise and [deleted] does not believe that she has any intention of propagandizing the Communist form of government from the music manufactured by her corporation."[21]

The FBI's file on Folkways was marked "closed" in February 1956, and the bureau did not bother with Folkways again until 1962. There were plenty of Folkways releases that year that the FBI might have considered worthy of attention, including Asch's 1959 interview with W. E. B. Du Bois (5511), a second volume of Spanish Civil War songs (5437), and a documentary recording of the House Un-American Activities Committee hearings (5530). They might also have found it curious that having received an order for records from Barry Goldwater Asch used the opportunity to see whether the conservative senator and future presidential candidate might be interested in recording a documentary about his life (he was, but it did not come to anything).[22] What revived the bureau's interest in Folkways, however, was its having learned that the Fair Play for Cuba Committee had contacted the company to determine whether it might be interested in producing records of Cuban revolutionary songs. This in turn seemed to take on some significance when in early 1964 the FBI learned that Folkways was preparing to release a recording that had been made of Lee Harvey Oswald's mother, Marguerite, reading from letters written to her by her late son (Asch was still being protective of Folkways in 1964 in releasing the album on the affiliated Broadside label [BR 401, later 5532]). But the bureau apparently made no additional inquiries about Asch or Folkways until a final episode in November 1965, which backfired quite badly on the FBI. On 5 November two agents confiscated three folk music books and a "combined record album-guitar instruction book" from a music store in Washington, D.C. The books were all Oak Publications, and included *Lift Every Voice*, with an introduction by Paul Robeson, *The Bells of Rhymney and Other Songs from the Singing of Pete Seeger*, and *Broadside*. An alert clerk in the store telephoned a *Washington Post* reporter, Leroy Aarons, who immediately went to speak with the store manager and then phoned the local office of the FBI. The store manager had probably called the bureau himself, following a complaint some months earlier by a customer, and told Aarons that the publications were not "in keeping with the [store's] image." The bureau office refused to confirm or deny the visit of the agents. The article that appeared in the *Post* the next day was entitled "FBI Checks FolkSongs—Then Mum's Word." A subsequent editorial in the *Post* entitled "On Censoring Folk Songs" excoriated both the music store and "criminal law enforcement officials" for attempting to regulate American cultural taste. "The White House," wrote Edward de Grazia,

> might, for example, try to conceive of ways to stimulate, not
> still, peaceful discussion, controversy and dissent where it
> may appear and whatever its political and artistic form. It
> could even begin by asking itself and its law enforcement
> agencies how, under the Constitution, it can be any legitimate
> part of the business of Government to investigate folk and
> civil rights songs.[23]

In the margin of the FBI file page containing the editorial clipping, someone (very possibly Hoover himself) had written, "We should never have gotten into this."

Subsequently Asch and Silber received a request from the U.S. Commission on Civil Rights, Technical Information Center for a copy of *We Shall Overcome*, one of the books (according to the *Post* article) that had led to the complaint to the music store's manager. The commission thought "it would be a valuable addition" to their library and proposed that they be sent a complimentary copy. Asch and Silber could not resist the opportunity to tweak the nose of the bureau and forwarded the request on to the FBI along with a copy of the original newspaper article. They suggested that as the FBI was investigating the book, perhaps the bureau was in the best position to honor the request. A lengthy internal FBI memo followed, concluding that because "several of the protest singers featured in the books . . . are strictly no good, it is felt the letter from Silber and Asch should not be acknowledged and that no further action be taken concerning this matter."[24]

Even before the close of the fifties Asch began to venture gingerly into the area of topical songs with Pete Seeger's first *Gazette* album (2501) in 1958 (a second volume appeared in 1961). Asch had never given up on the idea of creating a musical newspaper of the kind that he had discussed with Woody Guthrie; he introduced the notes to both volumes with a statement of purpose that enabled him to present controversial songs while distancing himself from their political perspectives:

I have always believed that it is the duty and privilege of publishers of materials that reach a wide audience to make available to the general public as great a variety of points of view
and opinions as possible—without the heavy hand of censor-
ship or the imposition of the publishers' editorial view. It is
with this point of view that Folkways Records and Peter
Seeger have collaborated on this new album of contemporary
topical and political songs—believing that the complete documentation of American life makes the issuance of such material our public responsibility. To those who believe in the free
and uncensored expression of not only their own beliefs, but
the opinions and ideas of others, I dedicate this album.[25]

Neither album was confined precisely to "contemporary" political
songs; the first volume included Guthrie's "Pretty Boy Floyd," "Roll
on Columbia," and "Reuben James," as well as the People's Songs
classic "Banks of Marble," and the second included Guthrie's "The
Dying Miner" and Leadbelly's "Bourgeois Blues." But they also included contemporary songs of the "ban the bomb" movement
(Tom Lehrer's "The Wild West Is Where I Want to Be" and Vern
Partlow's "Talking Atom") and the civil rights struggle (Malvina
Reynolds's "Battle of Maxton Field," Dave Arkin's "State of Arkansas"), suggesting that American topical songwriters were about to
come in out of the chilly decade of the fifties. Each printed song in
the notes was accompanied by a reproduction of relevant contemporary newspaper headlines.

For the second Gazette album Seeger presented two contemporary ban-the-bomb songs from England, where leftists were
spared the indignity of reactionary persecution and where, as a
consequence, topical songwriting had begun to flourish somewhat
earlier. Ewan MacColl had been writing songs in support of labor
since the early thirties, and although his interests had turned
largely to experimental theater as a vehicle of political protest in
the intervening years the appearance of Alan Lomax in England in
the early fifties revived MacColl's interest in folk song. Lomax
introduced him to folk and blues recordings from the United
States, and they had long conversations about the uses of folk
song in social and political movements. Together they briefly
formed a skiffle group; when Peggy Seeger visited England in
March 1956 to visit Lomax (on a trip that included the 1957 Moscow
Youth Festival), she was introduced to MacColl (her future husband) and joined the group as well. MacColl was intent on insti-
gating an English folk revival and to that end joined forces with

A. L. (Bert) Lloyd, who had been introduced to him by Lomax. Their movement would depart from the stuffy academicism of Britain's turn-of-the-century revival (in turn inspired by collectors and composers such as Cecil Sharp, Ralph Vaughan Williams, and Percy Grainger) which looked to the preservation of highly romanticized, rural English folk forms. MacColl and Lloyd both had radical origins and were explicitly uninterested at the start in the preservation of a "pure" English folk music. Thus in its earliest phases the folk revival in Great Britain deliberately drew upon American musical forms and was carried along by the whimsical, trad-jazz sounds of washboards, homemade basses, tenor banjos, and acoustic guitars. Only when skiffle began to forsake its left-wing origins and to become the source of highly popular novelty songs such as "Does Your Chewing Gum Lose Its Flavour on the Bedpost Overnight" did MacColl realize that he had created something of a monster—a British folk-song revival that had embraced American folk music to the almost complete exclusion of traditional British forms. He and Peggy Seeger subsequently introduced a policy in their folk clubs requiring singers to sing only songs from musical traditions to which the singers themselves belonged. English singers were forbidden to sing African American blues; nor could an American singer perform a British ballad. To writer Robin Denselow, MacColl's naïvely nationalist posture created a rift between British folk music and more popular musical forms that was not healed until the eighties; perhaps, had MacColl been less dogmatic about hybrid borrowings between traditional English folk song and other music styles, it would not have taken British and Irish rock and roll so long to shake its infatuation with American blues and to embrace the musical styles—as in the work of Billy Bragg, U2, and the Pogues—that were at their fingertips.[26]

Peggy Seeger and Ewan MacColl might have posed a peculiar problem of ethnic musical origins when they began to perform as a musical team. But in producing their own "Gazette" albums—*New Briton Gazette* volume 1 in 1960 and volume 2 in 1962—they were able to elide the problem by performing songs of their own composition (although they did sometimes use traditional English and Irish and even a "Negro" melody). Pete Seeger, touring England in the fall of 1961, was impressed with the topical folk music that he heard from his half-sister, from MacColl, and from others, particularly the songs written for the annual Aldermaston March in protest of the atomic bomb. Upon returning to the States, inspired to rekindle topical song writing as he had known it in the forties, he found two others in a similar frame of mind—his old compatriots Sis Cunningham and Gordon Friesen from the Almanac days.

Cunningham and Friesen had had a very difficult time of it in the fifties. Friesen was blacklisted and consequently altogether unable to get work as a news writer. They had scraped by with an assortment of demeaning office jobs and lived (until the early sixties) in New York City's Frederick Douglass projects. There was virtually no audience for Sis's singing or her songs. But with the gradual political thaw at the start of the decade, there were encouraging signs for topical folk songs. Now and then *Sing Out!* published songs on the subject of nuclear disarmament, racial integration, or youthful alienation, and in the first year or two of the decade Pete Seeger, Malvina Reynolds, and an occasional letter writer would muse about the possibility of a publication dedicated exclusively to topical song writing.

Cunningham remembered some years later that the idea came from Malvina Reynolds, although her husband had previously credited Pete Seeger.[27] In any case Cunningham acquired a mailing list of about three hundred possible subscribers from Seeger and wrote them in order to assess the strength of interest in a magazine of topical songs. The response was good, and in February 1962 the first issue of *Broadside* magazine was produced on a mimeograph machine in Cunningham and Friesen's apartment. It included the lyrics to Bob Dylan's "Talking John Birch Paranoid Blues." Dylan, and the other folk singers who appeared in Cunningham and Friesen's apartment for the regular *Broadside* meetings in its early years—Tom Paxton, Len Chandler, Peter LaFarge, Phil Ochs, Mark Spoelstra, Bonnie Dobson—usually found their way there through Gil Turner, the emcee at Gerde's Folk City. Turner wrote in the first issue: "Topical songs have been an important part of the America's music since Colonial days. . . . *Broadside* may never publish a song that could be called a 'folksong.' But many of our best folksongs were topical songs at their inception." And Friesen added:

> How do we know that young people all over America may not be writing topical songs right now? It's just that we're not hearing about it. The big commercial music publishers and recording companies aren't interested in this sort of material. We may just be assuming that songs like this aren't being written and sung. God knows, there isn't much of an outlet for them.[28]

Dylan remained a regular participant in the *Broadside* group for about a year and a half, and a great many of his songs at this time—including "Blowin' in the Wind," "Masters of War," "With God on Our Side," and "Don't Think Twice"—appeared in the magazine even before they were heard on stage. Shortly after the first issue, Cunningham and Friesen moved to an apartment in the West nineties, which became the regular site of the meetings, a place for folk singers to hang out, critique each others songs, hone their musical and song-writing skills. For some it became a place to sleep and eat, occasionally for as long as six months. Cunningham, Friesen, and Seeger became surrogate parents—or perhaps proud doting aunts and uncles—to the rapidly successful new generation of songwriters and singers. Dylan's songs became a regular part of Seeger's performing repertoire within a few months of the first *Broadside,* and Seeger cast himself as Dylan's champion—as he had been Guthrie's for the preceding twenty years.

Asch followed the progress of *Broadside* carefully, and was important in sustaining it through regular advertising in its pages (rather than fill up a precious page with advertising, Asch would instruct them to place a notice at the bottom of one page: "This Page Paid For by Folkways Records"). Within the first year he had approached Cunningham about recording an album of songs by the singers and songwriters appearing in the pages of the magazine. Asch invited Cunningham up to his office for a meeting—the first time these longtime compatriots met—and proposed a series of albums. They would appear on a separate label, Broadside Records, so that they might be distinguished from Asch's own Folkways productions, an arrangement intended largely to protect Asch and Folkways from the possible consequences of releasing inflammatory material. As a business fiction it was not particularly well veiled; the record labels bore the inscription "Produced with the cooperation of Folkways Records" as well as the usual "copyright by Folkways Records" (the latter, Asch insisted, represented the copyright of the label only, although it did sometimes prove useful, or entangling, when there were questions about the ownership of songs). Aside from the cover of the first album, which consisted of a collage that Asch himself designed of the *Broadside* covers from the first year of publication, the production of the genuine Broadside albums would be altogether in the hands of Cunningham and Friesen. But this did not prevent Asch from periodically adding miscellaneous titles of his own choosing to the Broadside series whenever controversial material made it preferable to protect Folkways.

The singers associated with *Broadside* agreed to forego royalties so that they could be used to sustain the magazine. Friesen recalled that Asch advanced *Broadside* the grand sum of one hundred dollars for each of the first four albums.[29] If this did not suggest that Asch had any particular confidence in the sales potential of the albums, it was probably also consistent with the royalty arrangement. Asch agreed to pay Broadside a flat royalty for each record sold—five cents for the early records—rather than a percentage, with the effect that proceeds dwindled dramatically for the magazine despite Asch's raising the price of his records year after year. Cunningham was irked by this for some years and in the 1970s finally approached Asch to see whether he might agree to convert the flat-fee royalties into percentages.

On the day of the recording session some of the singers gathered at the Kettle of Fish before heading up to Mel Kaiser's Cue Recording studio. The Kettle of Fish—or simply, the Kettle—was upstairs from the Gaslight and in the previous months had become the place where Ochs, Dylan, and others would gather to play cards, drink, and argue politics.[30] Asch had arranged for the studio time, and at Cue the group had grown to include Ochs, Dylan, Gil Turner, Matt McGinn, Pete Seeger, Peter LaFarge, Mark Spoelstra, and Happy Traum. Dylan, by then under contract to Columbia, playfully chose the pseudonym "Blind Boy Grunt" for his Broadside recording credits. The album opened with Turner's New World Singers performing Dylan's "Blowing in the Wind," and four of the remaining fourteen songs were also Dylan compositions. Blind Boy Grunt is heard singing "John Brown," "Only a Hobo," and a fragment of work in progress entitled "Talkin' Devil" that was attached to "Hobo." Although Dylan's dominance is the most conspicuous feature of the album, it was also Phil Ochs's recording debut.

The loosely defined Broadside group continued to attract some of the Village's most promising folk singers (as well as many whose stars would not rise). Though Dylan fell away quickly after the first year, others came to take his place. Eric Andersen took up residence in the Friesen household for about six months. Cunningham and Friesen recorded hours and hours of songs on a four-track recorder in their home and some of these became the basis of subsequent albums. Pete Seeger recorded a couple of albums' worth of material at Cue, some of which became *Broadside*

Ballads Vol. 2. When it was released, Toshi Seeger wrote Asch from Tokyo about it:

> I'd say that it isn't an "entertaining" album but a "thinking" one—Those who want amusement and distraction won't like it and will be critical, and those who want a "Pete Seeger" album will be critical. I would say that here Peter is a means to convey the new songs and material—but that eventually there will be some better singers or performances. Seems to me that Peter could have done a better job—or that some just weren't for him to perform. But nevertheless as a Broadside #2, representing Broadsides, it's good and many thanks that there is a Folkways who is willing to issue it.[31]

For perhaps a couple of years *Broadside* was an important source of material for recording artists, not all of whom necessarily cast themselves as folk singers (Nina Simone's "Mississippi Goddamn" appeared in the pages of *Broadside* around the time of its commercial success).

Some who were already emerging as major players in the New York folk music scene were not altogether enamored of the *Broadside* group, and this was so not necessarily because the quality of songs was uneven or because they were politically provocative (although they were both), but because of the group's political pedigree. Dave Van Ronk, for one, would have nothing to do with *Broadside.* An unrepentant Trotskyite, he felt a certain amount of contempt for an organization that was the modern-day descendant of the Popular Front, People's Artists, and other groups he regarded as fronts of the Communist Party.[32] Cunningham and Friesen had actually left the party at the end of the previous decade, although they might still participate in a tenant's organization that had party origins. But the taint of party affiliation was to have little effect on those whose careers would blossom during or shortly after their early *Broadside* work. In the next couple of years Maynard Solomon would sign *Broadside* veterans Eric Andersen and Buffy Sainte-Marie to his Vanguard label; Jac Holzman would sign Phil Ochs and Tom Paxton to Elektra. Asch only succeeded in keeping Native American singer Peter LaFarge—who had first recorded for John Hammond on Columbia in 1962—within the Folkways sphere. Peter was the adopted son of Oliver LaFarge, author of *Laughing Boy,* the classic tale of Native American life. He was a fragile and troubled young man who succumbed to alcohol and depression in 1966, perhaps the first casualty of folk revival fame.

The irrelevance of party affiliation for the commercial recording industry was apparent as early as 1960, when Columbia Records signed Pete Seeger. Seeger was shortly to go on trial for contempt of Congress, a charge stemming from his appearance before HUAC in August 1955 and his refusal to answer questions on First Amendment grounds. On 4 April 1961 he was found guilty and sentenced to ten years in jail (he never served time, and the verdict was overturned the following year). For the next year Seeger was greeted at concerts by American Legion picketers and in Nyack, New York, was prevented from performing at the local high school because of his refusal to sign a loyalty oath. If the recording industry was going to be skittish about associating with any "Reds," Seeger would be the one. But John Hammond had recently rejoined Columbia Records and was charged with signing new talent, and he wanted Seeger to be among the first (Aretha Franklin was another). Hammond had long ago proven his bona fides as a liberal, especially on racial matters, and he was undoubtedly sympathetic to Seeger's commitment to internationalism, peace, and racial equality. But he signed Seeger to Columbia in 1960 primarily because he believed that he would sell records: "I was sure the growing interest in folk music in the United States would make him popular with young people." Goddard Lieberson, president of Columbia Records, was sufficiently uneasy about signing Seeger that he checked with a corporate vice president at CBS, the parent company. Seeger, he was told, would have no place on CBS television (and would not three years later on ABC either, with the advent of "Hootenanny"), but Columbia Records was free to do what it wished.[33] Seeger was reluctant to leave Asch, who had been exceedingly loyal to him in the preceding fifteen years, but he was attracted by the opportunity to reach far larger audiences. Asch could see that, too, and must have watched the departure of his most important artist with a mixture of regret and pride. The agreement with Columbia stipulated that should Seeger have material that Columbia "could not use," he was "free to take it to a smaller label." Thus Folkways would continue to release Seeger material through the years of his Columbia contract, including a great deal of material that had been accumulating unreleased on Asch's shelves.

Dylan was also among Hammond's early acquisitions for Columbia. Later Dylan maintained that he had approached the three major folk music labels—Folkways, Vanguard, and Elektra—when he first came to New York in 1961 but that none showed the least interest in signing him. He felt particularly rebuffed by Folkways, the label of his hero and model:

> I went up to Folkways. I says: "Howdy. I've written some songs." They wouldn't even look at them. I had always heard that Folkways was a good place. Irwin Silber didn't even talk to me and I never got to see Moe Asch. They just about said "Go." And I had heard that *Sing Out!* was supposed to be helpful and friendly, bighearted and charitable. I thought it was the place. It must have been the wrong place, even though *Sing Out!* was written on the door.[34]

Dylan spared Asch his worst contempt, claiming later that within the *Sing Out!* crowd he was the only one he respected: "Moe Asch, who is old and hip. He's the only one who knows that he's not a clown, that the whole world is not a circus. He knows."[35] But Dylan was, in fact, at the "wrong place" if he had attempted to approach Folkways at all. The offices of *Sing Out!* were by now in a separate building, around the corner from Folkways. Silber did not have any role in signing new artists to the label and can only surmise today that he must have told Dylan to go to 117 West Forty-sixth Street. But Dylan appears not to have encountered Asch until the Broadside recording session some months later. Perhaps it was useful for Dylan to portray himself later as a victim of the folk music establishment, but subsequent events suggest that Dylan was fabulously ambitious even in his earliest days in New York and likely had his eye on a deal with a major label from the start.

Dylan's first album on Columbia—recorded in late 1961 and released in early 1962—consisted almost entirely of unremarkable renditions of traditional folk songs that he had learned from records and from other singers. There were very few contemporary songs; the lone exceptions were his own compositions, "Talking New York" and the moving "Song to Woody," written in waltz time. Nothing on the first album could be called "topical." But the second album, appearing a year later, was a different story. *The Freewheelin' Bob Dylan* included "Blowin' in the Wind," "Masters of War," "A Hard Rain's A-Gonna Fall,""Talkin' World War III Blues," and "Oxford Town," an account of James Meredith's efforts to be admitted to Ole Miss. The influence of *Broadside* is all over the album; with *Freewheelin'*, Dylan became the successor to Woody Guthrie and the preeminent writer of "protest songs" in the early sixties.

At the time the idea of protest songs and folk songs were inextricably linked. Although conceptually distinguishable even then, in the minds of the record-buying (especially college-student) public they were one and the same thing. It was not actually that all or even most of the best-selling folk artists of the early decade were singing political material; Judy Collins's early albums rarely included overtly political material, and Joan Baez's only departures from traditional ballads on her earliest albums were the songs of Bob Dylan. But the idea of folk music bespoke authenticity and commitment, and commitment in that era was fundamentally associated with Old Left themes of racial equality and internationalism. Still, the examples of Baez and Collins or, in still sharper relief, the deliberately commercial and apolitical albums of the Kingston Trio and early Peter, Paul, and Mary, suggest that there might have been a folk-song revival that had no particular connection with political themes. Why then did the folk revival become a political song movement in its most protean stages, and what did that mean?

It is tempting to suggest that protest songs were simply a convenient and available medium by means of which college students of the early sixties could articulate their sense of alienation from the mass culture of their parents' generation. For Robert Cantwell, the protest tradition was simply "good to think" in the Lévi-Straussian sense: "Unlike the bohemian 1920s, the mode of the 1960s seemed more like a collective adolescent quest than a political or even a cultural revolution. . . . The folk revival had no political agenda, beyond being vaguely against racism and war."[36] The idea of folk was particularly useful because there was a venerable tradition in the United States (and in Europe, an influence Cantwell neglects) of appropriating it as a means of challenging modernism. But the example of ballad singers such as Joan Baez and blues singers such as Dave Van Ronk suggests that there were other available folk-inflected vehicles with which to think about one's youthful difference besides protest song. Even if, as Cantwell maintains, the folk revival was fundamentally "about" youthful alienation (a dubious and untestable proposition at best), that is not a sufficient explanation for why protest music became its most readily identifiable form in the early sixties. As the civil rights movement "morphed" into the antiwar movement in the latter half of the decade, and campus unrest came to a crescendo with the revelation in the spring of 1970 of the U.S. invasion of Cambodia, one might still argue that political protest was the vehicle through which college-aged youth expressed, in Cantwell's terms, "a culture of personal rebellion." But that kind of postmodern cynicism does not rest well. A satisfactory account of sixties youth rebellion will have to consider both the personal motivations of those enacting the universal struggle of separation from the parent generation and the socially embedded process of confronting the social injustices of the postwar era. Young folk singers and their audiences in the early sixties acted out of a range of motivations—personal and collective, selfish and noble. Like all human beings, their behavior stemmed from an assortment of occasionally contradictory impulses, and the effort to establish the "real" one is surely chimerical. It is worth considering the possibility that protest songs expressed the genuine social concerns of some significant number of college students (and others) in the early sixties, and that these concerns were more than an incidental vehicle for enacting a generation's personal rebellion.

Broadside magazine became the means by which the private act of song writing was transformed into a growing repertoire of immediately recognizable protest songs. The recordings on the Broadside label accelerated that process very slightly, if at all. They provided a modest income to help the magazine remain solvent, but it was via the far more commercially successful recordings of the individual singer-songwriters—Dylan, Buffy Sainte-Marie, Phil Ochs, Tom Paxton, Eric Andersen—that the songs entered the American song vernacular.

The success of the commercial folk music recordings spurred the demand for public settings in which to hear live renditions of the songs, and the live performances symbiotically encouraged the sales of the records. The Friends of Old Time Music represented one end of a growing spectrum of live folk music presentations. In time it would introduce New York's folk music audience to Doc Watson, Bill Monroe, Joseph Spence (the astonishing, eccentric guitarist discovered in the Bahamas by Sam Charters), and Memphis bluesmen Gus Cannon, Willie Borum, and Furry Lewis, who had last recorded in the 1930s before Charters brought them out of obscurity in the final years of their lives.

Izzy Young's store, the Folklore Center on MacDougal Street, had opened some years earlier in 1957 and remained the gathering point for folk musicians and aficionados through the folk revival. Young originally sold books about folk music, and then records and musical accessories; the Folklore Center held small concerts and became the nerve center of the early revival. Here singers met one another, exchanged songs, debated endlessly about folk music, and spread word of their coffeehouse engagements.

As folk music boomed in the Village, bar and coffeehouse proprietors quickly recognized it as a way of attracting customers. Max Gordon's venerable Village Vanguard, associated primarily with jazz, booked some folk acts when there was money to be made from it, including Peter, Paul, and Mary (until Gordon felt he could no longer afford them). Mike Porco had purchased an Italian restaurant in the Village in 1957 called Gerde's and a couple years later was approached by Izzy Young and Tom Prendergast with the idea of their booking folk music for him. Gerde's became The Fifth Peg until Porco fell out with Young and Prendergast, and thereafter it was Gerde's Folk City. Bob Shelton introduced Porco to Paul Rothschild—who would become Jac Holzman's premier producer at Elektra—and Rothschild suggested that Porco establish a weekly Monday evening hootenanny. It was the rapid success of the hootenannies that caused folk music to take hold at Folk City, and within the first couple years of the new decade hootenannies were running other nights of the week at Fred Weintraub's Bitter End and Clarence Hood's Gaslight.[37]

There were parallel developments in other cities. Cambridge's Club 47, opening in early 1958, also started by presenting jazz. The proprietors could not be convinced to try folk music until, in 1959, a friend of Boston University freshman Joan Baez agreed to rent the club for a night to show them what Baez could do.[38] In Chicago Albert Grossman had opened the Gate of Horn and booked singers such as Odetta and Bob Gibson, whom he also managed. The Old Town School of Folk Music was teaching guitar chords to housewives and future rock stars and presenting concerts by Big Bill Broonzy and Win Stracke. New York remained the place where emerging folk talent went to be recorded, but there were open mikes and hootenannies in most of the major cities of the Northeast and Midwest where performers sharpened their singing and playing. Folk festivals on college campuses that had started in the fifties—at the University of Chicago, Swarthmore, Oberlin, and elsewhere—remained vibrant in the sixties and introduced many college students to folk music. But starting in 1959 and into the second half of the next decade, the premier national event was the Newport Folk Festival.

Newport had hosted a jazz festival since 1954. Its impresario, George Wein, conceived of adding folk music to the schedule five years later, on the weekend following the jazz festival. Folk music had previously drawn audiences at other outdoor concert settings, including the elite summer home of the Boston Symphony Orchestra at Tanglewood and the Chicago Symphony's summer stage at Ravinia in suburban Highland Park. The bill for Newport's first summer ran from the thoroughly commercial (Kingston Trio) to the esoteric (gospel choirs and a Nigerian drum and dance team). It also included one of Holzman's most successful recording stars, Theodore Bikel, as well as Ellen and Irene Kossoy and the New Lost City Ramblers, and Bob Gibson introduced Joan Baez to her first large audience. Asch competed with Maynard Solomon and Jac Holzman for the rights to release the recordings from the first two folk festivals; predictably, Vanguard and Elektra released the more commercial material, or what Silber in his album notes referred to as the "Crowd-Pleasers of Newport." Asch himself combed through the remaining tapes and released two albums of Newport's "authentic" performers, defiantly entitling them *The Folk Music of the Newport Folk Festival*, despite the fact that they included revivalists such as Pete and Mike Seeger, the New Lost City Ramblers, Guy Carawan, and Alan Mills in addition to Brownie McGhee and Sonny Terry and a few other arguably traditional singers. Silber wrote that "there is a thread running through these two discs which Moses Asch has pursued with the doggedness of a blood-hound. The thread is folk music, and while there was not too much of it at the Newport Folk Festivals, it appears in abundance on these two recordings."[39]

The earliest Newport Folk Festivals were sufficiently momentous that Asch went to see for himself, and he participated in a workshop discussion about folk music that John Cohen remembered later for Asch's typically mangled syntax and tortured reasoning, as well as the marvelous good sense he made out of the moral issues surrounding the recording of folk music.[40] Asch wrote a "personal statement" for *Sing Out!* a short time later, in which he described his project of reclaiming the "genuine" in American culture. The enemy was the mass media—manufacturers, advertisers, song pluggers—under whose influence Americans "dressed, acted, wanted and behaved" in homogeneous ways. The old means through which one generation communicated its warnings and guidelines to the next were becoming obscured: "The lessons of the past, the heritage of the past, the people of the past, their experiences, their lives, their songs became un-modern and so obsolete." As a consequence it became his responsibility to "dig deeper and have an understanding and weigh the 'accepted' with the genuine."[41]

The doyennes of Newport society had been looking for an excuse to dislodge the scruffy summer music festivals from their midst for years and found it in the form of a minor riot during the 1960 festival. But the folk festival returned to Newport with a vengeance in 1963 and remained through five turbulent and memorable summers. Pete and Toshi Seeger and Manny Greenhill helped Wein to establish the eclectic synthesis that characterized the festival through 1967, and Ralph Rinzler became the primary schedule organizer. It was Rinzler's particular delight to bring the "rediscoveries" up from the South—those recording artists from the 1920s and 1930s, long presumed dead, who appeared on Harry Smith's *Anthology* and, by now, in other reissue series. The 1963 festival included Clarence Ashley, Dock Boggs, and Mississippi John Hurt.

Asch's son Michael turned twenty in 1963, and was an undergraduate anthropology major at the University of Chicago. Independently of any connection with his father, he had struck up a friendship with Phil Ochs. At Chicago he played some tapes he had of Ochs in an unsuccessful effort to get Ochs on the bill of the University of Chicago Folk Festival. Back home in New York during the summer before his senior year, he traveled up to Newport with Ochs, Ochs's brother and manager Michael Ochs, and Arlo Guthrie. Ochs had not yet signed with Elektra, and his only recording credit to date was his one song on the first Broadside album. Gordon Friesen and Sis Cunningham (who edited the program notes) had arranged to get Ochs onto an afternoon workshop, and despite an emergency room visit earlier in the day for a crushing headache, he managed to perform four songs, including "Talking Birmingham Jam," for which he received a standing ovation. Ochs later cited this response as the starting point of his career.[42] He and Mike Asch also sought out Joan Baez on the festival grounds, hoping she might consider recording one of his songs, but it did not happen.

It was telling in and of itself that Michael Asch's connections with the burgeoning Village folk scene were the product of his own interest and initiative rather than his father's. In addition to Phil Ochs, he had struck up a friendship with John Hammond Jr., who had been a classmate at Elizabeth Irwin High School, and he spent time with Izzy Young at the Folklore Center. But the "regulars" at Folkways—Irwin Silber, Sam Charters, Pete Seeger, Fred Ramsey—were not well known to him. Least well known might ironically have been Marian Distler, whom Michael remembered having met only once. Asch, as in so many other ways, was careful to keep the various parts of his life separate. Yet during his son's early years he did bring him up to the office from time to time. In 1946, when Mike was just three, his early speech was captured on acetate in Asch Studios in a conversation with Distler and his father. Later, when he was eight and nine, his father recorded his early efforts at the piano in the studio. But as he got older and was more likely to understand what was going on between his father and Distler, Mike was not welcomed into the offices. Not until after he had finished college would he spend any sustained time at Folkways. Throughout his childhood and through high school, Mike and his mother continued to eat dinner by themselves. Asch would leave their apartment at Washington Square Village early in the morning and would not return until well into the evening. Weekends, too.

Asch and Distler were locked in a personal and professional partnership that did not mellow over time but became increasingly volatile. The introduction of Irwin Silber into the partnership did not sit well with Distler; although their political sympathies might have been closer than either one to Asch's, they did not like each other and made little effort to pretend otherwise. Most visitors to the office could not help but notice the stream of vicious abuse that Asch piled upon Distler all day long. "Marian, you're stupid! You're stupid!" Sam Charters recalls hearing Asch scream.

There was another side to their relationship. Early in the fall of 1963 there was a party in Distler's Manhattan apartment. Most of the key players in Folkways were there, including Pete and Toshi Seeger, Harold Courlander, Henry Cowell, Jean Ritchie, Langston Hughes, and Sam and Ann Charters. Asch was there, too, but not Frances. Seeger remembered it later as a house-warming party for Distler, who, he thought, had just moved into a new apartment that was likely financed by Asch. The mood was congenial and festive, and Seeger recalls it as having been a rare opportunity to encounter Distler as a person. Charters, too, recalls a sociable evening, with Asch playing a solicitous cohost (this appeared to be the place in which Asch was genuinely at home), but he remembers as well the disturbing reason for the gathering. Charters's wife Ann was reading palms that evening, but when she asked to read Distler's, Distler smiled and held up her hands in two little fists: there would be no reading of her future. Her wrists were plainly bandaged. The evening was a celebration of Distler's return home from the hospital after a suicide attempt and a long confinement for depression earlier in the fall. In September Courlander had written to Asch: "I'm very sorry to hear about Marian. Is it something serious?

Would appreciate your letting us know a little more, and also what is the hospital."[43]

It was not her first attempt. During this or perhaps the previous attempt, she had called Sidney Cowell, who had tried her best to talk her out of it. Distler did not hold Asch directly accountable for her desperation, but Cowell had the impression that he was at the heart of it. Distler told her that she hoped Asch might move in with her one day and share the apartment he had arranged for her following her hospitalization.[44] But Asch seemed to need the pretense of marriage and family and continued to return home at night to Frances and Michael. Distler's third suicide attempt, on 25 January 1964, was fatal. She was forty-five years old and had worked only one job—and had entered into only one romantic relationship—throughout her adult life. As was then customary, the *New York Times* reported the cause of death as pneumonia. The obituary ran half of a page-length column and recounted her part in the establishment of Folkways. Silber recalled having written most of it himself: "Miss Distler had few interests outside the company and folk music in general. Lately she had been trying to learn to play the dulcimer." Asch attended the funeral with Sidney Cowell, and he unexpectedly held her hand through the brief ceremony. When it was time to view the body, Asch refused. "That's not Marian up there," he muttered to Cowell.

Those who wrote Asch in the following weeks expressed their profound shock and sadness over Distler's death. Most never knew the circumstances of her death and were surprised she had been ill. "I was terribly sorry to learn of Marian's death when I arrived home on Monday," wrote Guy Carawan a month later. "I had no idea this had happened."[45] It is not possible to even guess what affect it had on Asch. There is no evidence that he personally assumed any responsibility for her death; he denied to Charters that her death was a suicide. Nor is it imaginable that he discussed it in detail with anyone—there was no one in whom he confided, at least once she was gone. Charters surmises that he treated Distler as he did because he felt entitled to as the son of a famous man who had mistreated many who were close to him as well. His son Michael did not believe that his father had much of an interior life—most of what there was could be found in plain view. But for weeks following her death Asch would not touch Distler's desk—her sweater remained draped over her chair, her glasses on her desk.[46]

The affect on Folkways of Distler's death was not immediate. In 1964 Folkways was entering its most commercially successful year.

Sing Out! appeared to be doing fine, buoyed as it was by the extraordinary success of Oak Books. Oak had started as a reprint series of songs from *Sing Out!* and had grown in very short order with a list that included several musical instruction books, collections of ethnic and regional musical culture, the Carawans' magnificent collections of civil rights songs and other documents of the folk revival.

Langston Hughes was among those who had come to know Marian Distler and to appreciate her vulnerable humanity. He had not made records for Folkways since the flurry of recordings that were intended to accompany his children's books in the mid-fifties, but he stayed in touch with Asch and Distler by periodically dropping in on the Folkways offices to collect royalties. It was the customary arrangement that, according to Asch, consisted of his contacting Distler when he was in need of money, "usually to pay out to someone in need. The last such payment was made (in cash) just before the death of Miss Marian Distler in 1964."[47] He was sufficiently a presence in the Folkways offices that some of the other Folkways regulars, such as Sam Charters, would count him a friend and recall his gentle charm and generosity years later. Hughes would also frequently send a card to Distler and Asch when he traveled. One from June 1962, mailed from Uganda, where Hughes was attending a writers' conference, read "Dear Moe—This is the big game country—but I am NOT on safari. Hello to Marian, Langston."[48]

Two weeks before Distler's death, Hughes's gospel music rendering of the civil rights struggle, *Jericho–Jim Crow,* opened in the sanctuary of the Greenwich Presbyterian Church. The play was directed by Alvin Ailey and William Hairston and included among its cast twenty-two-year-old Gilbert Price, who quickly became a close friend, protégé and traveling companion of Hughes in his last years. Although the play's run was comparatively short, the critical reception from the New York press was extraordinarily positive. In April Hughes sent a card to Asch: "Dear Moe: If you would like to see my Jerico–Jim Crow (maybe again) before it goes into limbo . . . come as my guest this Saturday night . . . and simply mention my name at the box office. There will be two seats for you. It would be nice to have my friends around when the swinging singing finale knocks itself out!"[49] Asch apparently did go, and he responded with a proposal to record the musical numbers for a Folkways release. *Jerico–Jim Crow* (9671) appeared as a two-record set late in the year, with notes that neglected to mention the contributions of the show's composer, Jobe Huntley (whose name was also inadvertently omitted from the sign outside the theater).[50] When Gilbert Price received highly favorable notices early the following year for his performance in *The Roar of the Greasepaint,* Hughes sent Asch a copy of selected quotations from the reviews with an appended note: "Dear Moe—these might make a publicity item for our 'Jerico' record—which, by the way, I like very much, and am delighted to have on Folkways."[51]

Harry Smith entered Asch's life once again in the spring of 1964. That winter he had gone to Oklahoma to make a movie, "but got separated," as he later reported to John Cohen. At the suggestion of a woman from the Oklahoma Historical Society, Smith had gone to Anadarko, reportedly a "real Western town." His first evening in the town he struck up a conversation "with some talkative but, according to the police, rather unsavory characters in one of the local bars" and spent the next week in jail under suspicion of having stolen guns from a local restaurant.[52] His cellmates were primarily Kiowa Indians from whom he learned of a rich tradition of songs used to accompany the peyote rituals of the Native American Church. Smith had a genuine anthropological interest in the Kiowa; he modestly told John Cohen that he was "trying to found new sciences, to entirely overhaul anthropology and turn it into something else."[53] But the presence of peyote was an important additional incentive. Smith chose to record the singers in his hotel room in Anadarko or in the singers' homes, rather than in the context of "meetings," primarily in order to be able to record their commentary on the songs (which became the basis of his notes) but also in order not to jeopardize his informants because the ritual use of peyote remained illegal.

So the recording of peyote ritual songs became the new focus of his investigation, and for this he would need a tape recorder. In March Asch wired Smith a hundred dollars, to be used in part for the rental of a Wollensack tape recorder from an outfit in Oklahoma City, and he wired an additional thirty dollars to Smith in Anadarko the following month as an advance against royalties. When Smith had concluded his recording he mailed the tapes back to Asch in New York and, on returning to New York himself in May, wrote a letter on Folkways stationery promising to edit the tapes for release on ten long-playing records. He also dutifully noted that he remained in possession of the Wollensack and promised Asch two American Indian paintings that he had in his possession at the Hotel Earle as collateral. Late that month Asch started to receive bills from the equipment company in Oklahoma City for the cost of the tape recorder. By August, unable to locate Smith, Asch resigned himself to having to pay for the tape recorder. It would be almost ten years before the edited tapes and notes would be complete, but *Kiowa Peyote Meeting* did appear in the Folkways catalogue as a three-record boxed set. (Smith alluded in his notes to the possibility of additional volumes, but like the apocryphal fourth and fifth volumes of the *Anthology of American Folk Music*, they never materialized).[54] Smith's notes did not resemble those he had written for *Anthology*, as he now regarded his pains-taking references to published antecedents "outdated." Rather, he focused upon the unique features of a given performance, on the singer's knowledge of a song's history, and the songs' place within the peyote ritual. David Evans, in his review for the *Journal of American Folklore*, found Smith's notes enthusiastic yet scholarly and objective. He only regretted that having recommended that the listener imbibe peyote before listening to the songs, Smith failed to include any in the box set.[55]

Shortly after the peyote songs were finally released, Allen Ginsberg was in Harry Smith's room at the Hotel Chelsea, where Smith recorded Ginsberg singing "First Blues" and other songs for eventual Folkways release. Ginsberg remembered that Smith used an old Wollensack tape recorder.[56]

In 1964 the folk revival was still a sufficiently finite phenomenon that it seemed possible to compile a representative sampler. Asch and Jac Holzman of Elektra collaborated that year in the produc-tion of a four-record set entitled *The Folk Box*, released on Elektra but drawing on the discography of both Elektra and Folkways. Robert Shelton compiled and annotated the collection and wrote an introduction in which he described the enterprise as "a basic anthology of American folk expression." His intention was to pro-vide an illustrative sampling of the past ten years of the folk revival, "a curious, exciting often ironic and inconsistently-laden movement. If we look to causes and effects of this revival it is possible to see it as one of the most wholesome trends to have ever effected American mass culture."[57] Asch's role was largely confined to illustrating the accompanying booklet with the kind of antique drawings that he and Silber had been using to ornament Folkways album jackets and notes for some years, with a photo-graph by Fred Ramsey and a drawing of Ben Shahn's thrown in for good measure. The completed project was announced in a full-page advertisement in the *New York Times*, and perhaps *The Folk Box* provided a little useful exposure for some number of Folkways artists, including the New Lost City Ramblers, Mark Spoelstra, and Pete Seeger, for which they were undoubtedly pleased. On the other hand, Harold Courlander gently inquired of the propriety of their having used his field recordings without his permission. Asch responded by pointing out that the contract Courlander had signed with him for the original recordings did not limit their use for other purposes as long as they were only leased rather than sold. In fact, he added, Courlander himself had used material from a great many other Folkways recordings for the anthologies he assembled.[58]

Newport 1964 was the most successful folk festival to date, as far as attendance was concerned. The biggest audience that Newport had ever seen appeared for the Friday night concert, during which Joan Baez brought Dylan on stage for an encore duet of "It Ain't Me Babe." Dylan's solo concert, regarded by critics as a decidedly lackluster affair, was on Sunday evening. Several of the songs were from his forthcoming *Another Side of Bob Dylan*, which would mark his decisive turn away from topical song writing. Paul Wolfe declared in *Broadside* that Dylan was no longer the premier troubadour of protest song and that that honor now belonged to Phil Ochs, for whom Newport 1964 was a triumph. Paul Nelson dedicated a column in his *Little Sandy Review* to the Newport festival, lamenting that among the festival's two hundred performers the traditional singers received pitifully little notice.[59]

But it should have surprised few who followed popular musical trends that it would be the revivalists rather than the traditional musicians who attracted mass attention and fueled the growing folk music industry. Vanguard had signed many of the artists who dominated Newport 1964—Joan Baez, Eric Andersen, Buffy Sainte-Marie—so it followed that Maynard Solomon would again release an album of the festival's most popular acts. Asch, on the other hand, was starting to feel rather neglected, both by artists and by the growing folk music establishment. On Christmas Eve he started a letter to Toshi Seeger, finishing it the following day. The previous day, 23 December, his brother Nathan had died in California of lung cancer. All of the anger, hurt, and sadness he felt over his brother's death was poured into his letter to Toshi.

The letter ostensibly concerned a battle he was waging with Pete's manager, Harold Leventhal, over copyright ownership and Toshi's efforts to find a more secure and profitable home for the copyrights to Pete's songs. The letter revealed Asch's contradictory impulses—his principled desire to protect "the people's" right to the cultural material that sustained them and his self-protective instinct to defend his business interests:

> You should know . . . that we here at OAK or FOLKWAYS are now at the point of being aggressive regarding the rights due us, the respect due us and a general understanding of our po-sition regarding copyright, publishing, issuing, merchandising, advertising, selling, producing and any other facet of commu-nicating through records, tapes, videos, television, radio, books, notes, pamphlets etc., etc., the world as known to OAK as Folk-music and to me as a People's culture and expression. For I take great pride that I am a documenter and a deposit rather than an owner with property rights.

Asch condemned those who turned the people's culture into a commodity for their own gain and warned Toshi of playing with the devil: "Hell and God and Devil and heaven become confused and interchanged. When Howard Richman [sic] took my name and commercialized Folkmusic and Pete was associated with them (him?) this was alright. But now . . . I want to tell Howard Richman [sic] and all that jive to go to hell."[60]

But although copyright ownership was the occasion for the letter, Nathan's death was its subtext. "I guess I can philosoph(ize) since Nathan died and I can reflect," he wrote. The year was ending just as it had begun, with a gruesome, wrenching death. Asch's stormy relationship with his older brother had mellowed consid-erably in the last years. They had seen each other rarely, talked on the phone only occasionally, and never wrote, but Nathan's death left another large hole in Asch's sparse emotional life. He admired Nathan tremendously, and regarded him as far more of an intel-lectual than himself.

The following month he sent a similarly intemperate letter to Pete Seeger, complaining that Rinzler had attempted to extort money from him in support of the festival by ostensibly suggest-ing that Folkways artists such as the New Lost City Ramblers would not otherwise appear on the program. He claimed to have been "knifed" by Vanguard over the rights to the festival recordings, and he was angry that Jean Ritchie, having defected to Elektra, had the nerve to ask for rights to some Folkways material for use in a music book she was publishing, despite his having previously advanced her money for the production of a children's record that she had not yet completed. After all that he had done for folk music to support it through its leanest years, where was his due? He closed his letter to Pete that winter this way: "I am happy I am not Newport. I am happy I am not ELEKTRA. I am happy I am not Vanguard. I am happy I am not Columbia. I am happy I am FOLK WAYS. For how long, God how long?"[61]

Just as Asch appeared to be achieving a stability in his business that he had never previously enjoyed, he was also displaying new depths of bitterness. It puzzled many that he could be so gracious and amiable one moment and so vicious and combative the next. A few understood that he felt unappreciated—for whom had he worked all of these years if not for those who produced and purchased his records? Hadn't he given his artists and producers free rein to do whatever they wanted? And hadn't he kept his promise to assure the perpetual availability of every single recording, regardless of sales figures and fluctuations in popular taste? It was the latter, of course, that ultimately prevented him from making a third promise to his artist and producers, that is, to be able to make even a modest living from their Folkways recordings. Perhaps no one saw the sadness and loneliness. He had not acquired the social skills to sustain friendship, or he had forgotten them, or he would not risk becoming vulnerable in the ways that friendship required.

Folkways did more than a million dollars of business in 1964, shipping tens of thousands of records. But shipped albums are not sold albums, as it is always the retailer's prerogative to return unsold albums to the manufacturer. In 1965 between forty and fifty thousand albums were *returned* to Folkways, and Asch was again in the bind of having too much product and too little cash.[62] His operation did not have the means of weathering the market fluctuations, and if he was going to meet the high demand that he occasionally received for a small number of titles, he was going to have to find another means of doing so. His first attempt was to briefly revive his old Disc label as a separate means of marketing his most commercially successful albums. In the spring of 1964 his lawyers conducted a copyright search to make certain that the Disc name could still be used. They advised against it—there were too many similar names (Duodisc, Melodisc, Dictation Disc, Dynadisc, Ameridisc). But Asch ignored them and prepared a press release the following January: "Disc is back! Disc Records, the leading and influential giant of folk-blues-jazz, which rode the crest of popularity during the mid-forties, thanks to the keen devotion of GIs returning from WWII, is back on the record scene again!" For the first time since the inception of Folkways he departed from his somber black record jackets with the pasted-on labels and created some slightly slicker jackets for albums by Woody Guthrie, Cisco Houston, Leadbelly, Pete Seeger, and Memphis Slim. With higher volume, he was able to keep the per unit cost of the new Disc LPs down and to deliver significant quantities of these titles at short notice. He also priced them competitively (unlike Folkways records, which were promoted as a "premium" line, retailing for about a dollar more than the going price). But this did not solve the problem of the returns.

A solution appeared fortuitously when Arnold Maxim, president of MGM Records, decided that his label needed a way of breaking into the growing folk music market. Folkways would collaborate with Verve, an MGM subsidiary label that Norman Granz had sold to MGM in 1962. Perhaps the label's past affiliation with his old collaborator made the prospect of associating with a commercial powerhouse less difficult for Asch to swallow. Maxim first approached Asch in 1963 about a licensing agreement between MGM and Folkways that would allow the former to release various Folkways titles. Asch was uninterested at the time but ran into Maxim accidently at Chicago's O'Hare Airport on Christmas Day 1964, in all probability changing planes on his way to Nathan's funeral. His ability to deal with adversity and setbacks was waning, as he approached sixty, and the prospect of being liberated from financial anxiety was now a highly tempting one.

The negotiations went on for three months, but the resulting arrangement seemed uncomplicated: Under the supervision of Jerry Schoenbaum, MGM/Verve would have the right to license those records from the Folkways catalogue that it deemed commercially viable. They would be repackaged under the name of a new record label, Verve/Folkways, and they would be marketed and distributed by MGM. Those records Verve chose to release would then be deleted from the Folkways catalogue, and Folkways would receive royalties on copies sold. Additionally Asch would prepare unreleased material from his archive for Verve/Folkways release, and new artists and recordings could be added to the Verve/Folkways list with Asch's approval. The initial release would consist of five previously issued Folkways albums and five albums dedicated to recordings of Pete Seeger, Woody Guthrie, Cisco Houston, Leadbelly, and the New Lost City Ramblers culled from unreleased material in the archive.

The arrangement did not sit easily with all Folkways artists and producers, and rumors started to circulate that Folkways had simply been sold. Asch distributed a mimeographed letter describing the new collaboration and his continuing involvement with all releases in the hope that it would allay concerns. Despite Asch's reassurances, some Folkways artists and producers worried that they would lose the control over their work that they had so highly valued when working with Asch. Why else would they have put up with the haphazard royalty payments? Certainly Verve would not be giving them free rein over cover art, and notes for the Verve/Folkways releases would be confined to the back cover. Sam Charters, for one, was not sure that he would be comfortable submitting material to Asch under these terms.

Newport 1965 is quite reasonably remembered as the occasion of Dylan's "going electric." There certainly was no more earthshaking a moment in the folk revival. Whether Dylan's appearance with electric accompaniment was merely too loud and too poorly mixed for Pete Seeger's ears or whether Seeger regarded it as the shattering of his best hopes for folk music may not ever be definitively determined. Probably it was a bit of both. His biographer reports that Seeger later described Dylan's music on the night of 25 July as "some of the most destructive music this side of hell."[63] The audience was hostile; so were a great many writers. Articles in *Sing Out!* and *Broadside* both condemned Dylan's "defection." But although Newport would endure for two additional summers and Joan Baez would have hit records into the next decade, dusk had started to descend on folk music's day in the sun of American popular culture. At the time Dylan's digression into rock appeared inextricably linked to his abandonment of topical song writing; both appeared to be the consequence of his being lured into more lucrative musical directions, and the latter followed inevitably from the former. The next couple of years would not bear this out, however, as rock became more stridently political than its folk music predecessor had ever been. Particularly with the escalation of the war in Vietnam, it was rock that became the critical means of expressing discontent with American foreign policy. As Robin Denselow has argued, it was not rock music that ended the war in Vietnam, "but music played an important role in helping to reflect and reinforce the antiwar mood in the USA."[64]

Broadside still had some notable moments ahead. Janis Ian was a sixteen-year-old Broadside regular who, having been passed over by several labels, signed with Verve/Folkways and had a huge hit in the summer of 1967 with "Society's Child"—her song of interracial dating remained on the pop charts for almost three months. She had also sung some songs for Cunningham and Friesen's tape recorder prior to her recording contract with Verve/Folkways, and she appeared on a Broadside release entitled *The Time Will Come* (5306) that same year under the name "Blind Girl Grunt," singing "Shady Acres."

Cunningham and Friesen had also taken in Jimmy Collier and Rev. Frederick Douglass Kirkpatrick, two singers and civil rights workers who had come to New York in March 1968 to help organize Martin Luther King's Poor People's Campaign in Washington, D.C. Kirkpatrick ended up living with them for almost three years. He was from Louisiana and had been working with King's Southern Christian Leadership Conference (SCLC) for the past couple of years. Collier was an activist from Chicago who had worked with the NAACP and the Congress of Racial Equality (CORE) before joining King for the Selma-to-Montgomery March in 1965. Collier had written a song in 1966 entitled "Burn, Baby, Burn," which on careful listening did not really endorse the destruction of inner-city property. But many understood it that way, and King once suggested to Collier that he stop performing it. King was far more enthusiastic about Kirkpatrick's "Everybody's Got a Right to Live," which he had written explicitly for the Poor People's Campaign. When King was assassinated in Memphis on 4 April Kirkpatrick and Collier redoubled their efforts on behalf of the Poor People's Campaign, scheduled now for mid-May.

Asch had been hearing about Collier and Kirkpatrick—Shelton had mentioned them favorably in a concert review that spring—and phoned Cunningham to see whether he might arrange to come uptown to hear them. Toshi Seeger assured Cunningham that Asch would never actually venture up to the apartment on Ninety-eighth Street to hear the singers, but he did. Cunningham recalled that Asch was polite, almost formal, and terribly enthusiastic about the songs, especially the "strong" ones.[65] It was shortly after King's assassination, and the album that was subsequently recorded at Cue become a way for Asch to memorialize the slain civil rights leader. Gordon Friesen wrote the notes, referring to the singers as "in the tradition of using music as a weapon for ideas, practiced earlier in this country by such groups as the Hutchinson family of abolitionist days, and in more recent times by the Almanac Singers and the singers in the Henry Wallace campaign."[66] The album cover bore the inscription "Our KING Will Never Die."

Broadside's most notorious recording project grew out of the hare-brained "Dylanology" and "garbology" of Alan J. Weberman. Weberman had become a minor Village celebrity by sorting through Dylan's garbage and drawing various conclusions about Dylan's life and politics based upon its contents. Between 1968 and 1971 Weberman made a thorough nuisance of himself by leading delegations to Dylan's home at 94 MacDougal Street, staging a loud rally on his doorstep, and distributing misinformation about Dylan to anyone who would listen (and, for a time, a great many did, including members of the national press). Initially he wanted to show that although Dylan's lyrics were no longer overtly political, there remained hidden political messages in many of Dylan's songs for those able to crack the code. Later, when he was unable to provoke the reaction from Dylan that he wanted, he became vicious, spreading tales about Dylan's ostensive drug dependency, ultra-Zionist sympathies, and other fabrications.

Friesen, for some reason, found Weberman's analysis of Dylan's lyrics intriguing, and started to print some of his interpretations in *Broadside* in 1968. Perhaps he was attracted to the idea that Dylan had not abandoned his political convictions after all. Friesen was particularly fascinated by Weberman's convoluted explication of "John Wesley Harding," and published a long interview with Weberman in which the Dylanologist claimed to uncover all of the hidden autobiographical meanings.[67] But the published exegesis was apparently not enough for Friesen. Part of Weberman's campaign to liberate Dylan from his own less-noble impulses consisted of a series of late-night telephone calls to him, which he taped. Dylan not surprisingly was abusive, and Friesen decided that this was sufficiently interesting to release it as a commercial recording. Asch concurred. *Bob Dylan vs. A. J. Weberman* became Broadside album 12. "The commotion that [Weberman] created did have one crucial result," wrote Friesen for the album notes. "It forced Bob Dylan to emerge from behind his curtain of mystique to confront Weberman. In this appearance he revealed himself as just another mortal like the rest of us instead of a mystical God enshrouded in the clouds. In that emergence lies the importance of this album."[68]

Cunningham later recalled that Asch and her husband found the album funny. Dylan did not. Asch heard from someone at Columbia that Dylan was unhappy that the record had been released.

Lawyers became involved and lawsuits were threatened. *Bob Dylan vs. A. J. Weberman* became the first record deliberately deleted from the Folkways catalogue, although not before it had circulated sufficiently to result in a number of bootleg pressings.

Asch continued to use the Broadside series for his own projects, when he feared that the content might be sufficiently controversial to cause trouble for Folkways. He liked a group of irreverent and often outrageous musicians who called themselves the Village Fugs. Formed by two "hippie poets," Ed Sanders and Tuli Kupferberg, in late 1964, the Fugs were performing occasionally around New York in art galleries and theaters, and in April 1965 Asch signed a contract with Ed Sanders for the production of *The Village Fugs*, volume 1, an album recorded by Harry Smith. The Fugs' music consisted of a potent blend of rock, Beat poetry, psychedelic drugs, antiwar sentiments, and theater. They appeared in several hundred off-Broadway theater productions in the second half of the decade and were the frequent companions of Allen Ginsberg, who wrote elegiac notes for the first album: "The Bible says that when Christ comes back, 'every eye shall see.' Now every ear can hear, and when the Fugs break thru the monopoly blockade, and their image is broadcast on National Television . . . every eye shall see." The album included overtly political material such as Kupferberg's "Kill for Peace," as well as songs such as "Boobs a Lot" that were intended to be as offensive as possible. Sanders later claimed that their lyrics required them to keep the American Civil Liberties Union on "permanent retainer."[69]

It was a rare foray for Asch into rock music. Not that the idea had not come up before. Charles Edward Smith had been trying to convince Asch to record an album of "neighborhood rock and roll groups" since 1957. In a memo that year Smith proposed that Asch consider a recording that "would follow the development of one or more groups in a documentary fashion," with the intention of presenting the music within the broader social context of Harlem youth:

> As I see it, there are two major angles to Rock and Roll—one
> is that even when by professionals, bands and so on, it is in
> response to the needs of youth who want to dance to music.
> . . . The second angle is that neighborhood groups made up
> their own "bands of voices," imitating the riff style as it was re-
> emphasized in jazz (out of blues originally) by, for example,
> Count Basie.[70]

Four years later Smith was at work on a two-record album of reissued rock and roll recordings of the fifties, representing the early work of Little Richard, Johnny Otis, Laverne Baker, and Frankie Lymon, among others. Neither of these projects saw light of day, despite the intelligent case that Smith made for their inclusion in the Folkways catalogue as a kind of contemporary folk music of urban youth. Asch's lack of enthusiasm for the reissue project might have been the consequence of jitters over royalties. Later developments suggest that he was not opposed to rock and roll on either principle or aesthetic grounds. Charters believed that Asch would have loved to have been a player in the burgeoning business of rock, if only he had had the financial means.

The release of *The Village Fugs* was announced in *Sing Out!* in early 1966. "Out at Last! The Recording Debut of the Village Fugs," read the advertising copy. When Asch expressed his distress at the appearance of "dirty words" in *Sing Out!* the following year, Izzy Young called him on it. "But yet you were the first one to record the Fugs," he told Asch. "That's different," Asch replied. "I was recording the Fugs but I wasn't selling the Fugs to twelve-year-old girls!"[71] There was, in fact, a disclaimer in the advertisement: "Not for the young and immature." But of course Asch could not have been sure who precisely was purchasing the records he released.

Mike Asch was among those who had little doubt about the importance of rock both commercially and aesthetically. In the spring of 1965 he graduated from the University of Chicago and began work for anthropologist Sol Tax in one of his "action anthropology" projects (an anthropology based upon putting the discipline's insights to work in the improvement of indigenous people's lives) in Oklahoma. But the threat of the Vietnam draft caused him to return to New York in the hope that by taking a few courses at Columbia and Julliard he might stay out of the war. Now that Distler was out of the picture Asch could take his son into the business, and thus Michael began an internship at Folkways that fall that lasted eight or nine months. Michael remembered it as a congenial collaboration with his father, who endeavored to acquaint his son with the many parts of the business. They would go to lunch together and talk about Folkways. It was the most sustained period of time they had spent together since Michael had graduated high school in 1961, and as it turned out, the most time he would ever again spend with his father. Michael was intrigued by it all, although uneasy about mastering the business end of things. Asch had him work his way through the archives, partly to audition unreleased tapes that had been sent to Folkways over the past several years. One of the first results was an album that was intended to demonstrate the folk origins of rock. Asch incongruously placed the album, *Roots: The Rock and Roll Sound of Louisiana and Mississippi* (2865) in the History of Jazz series. Michael did not, in retrospect, find it substantive, but it was one of the earlier attempts to locate the origins of rock and roll in traditional southern vocal styles.

Michael also handled some of the daily correspondence and functioned as an A&R (artist and repertoire) man at some of the recording sessions at Kaiser's Cue Studios. One such session came about as a consequence of an encounter between Asch and Lionel Hampton's manager, whose offices were down the hall. With Charles Edward Smith handling the production, Hampton recorded an album of vibraphone pieces in ensemble settings for Folkways entitled *Jazz Man for All Seasons* in which he demonstrated a variety of historical jazz styles (2871). Michael saw the album through the production process, as he did many others in the course of the months he spent there.

If there was a moment when Michael might have entered the business, this was it. But the Vietnam War again intervened and he discovered that his part-time student status would not be sufficient to keep him out of the draft. He applied and was accepted to the graduate program in anthropology at Columbia. It was not that he had ever particularly intended to become an academic, but there did not seem to be many choices. Five years later he was headed to the University of Alberta to take a teaching post, his wife Margaret remarking on the irony of being paid to go to Canada just as hundred of others were stealing across the border to avoid the draft. Michael would be involved in a few more Folkways projects. In 1973 he assembled a double album of forty-nine selections of North American and Eskimo music culled from sixteen previously released Folkways albums. An approving reviewer in the *Journal of American Folklore* remarked that the album was intended to demonstrate the "utilitarian and functional nature of the music [and] . . . in his purpose he succeeds admirably."[72] But there were few of these projects, and most of them, like this one, had some bearing on his academic scholarship. There would never be another viable opportunity for him to enter business with his father.

Meanwhile Asch was dutifully preparing new albums for release on the new Verve/Folkways label. Among the first was a collection of live Pete Seeger recordings entitled *Pete Seeger on Campus*. MGM expressed concern that this would get them in trouble with Columbia, to whom Seeger was still signed as an exclusive artist. Asch responded by pointing out that he was entitled to release any recordings of Pete that predated the arrangement with Columbia, and in fact he had released three previous "live" recordings of Pete since the start of the Columbia deal:

> As you must know I would do nothing to jeopardize Pete's contractual obligations or income. As a matter of fact when Columbia rejected his version of Little Boxes and I used the record, when the song became a hit I permitted Columbia (John Hammond) to use the record as a single, this sold many copies both to Malvina Reynolds, the author, Pete Seeger, the singer and Columbia Records, the producer, who all made a lot of money.[73]

Another recording that Asch prepared for Verve/Folkways was an album of Woody Guthrie sides culled primarily from the massive April 1944 sessions with Cisco Houston, Sonny Terry, Pete Seeger, and others. Entitled *Bed on the Floor* and released in late 1965, Stu Cohen, *Broadside*'s record reviewer, described it as the "'worst of Woody.' The songs are for the most part good, some like 'Slip Knot,' are great. However the record technically is so bad it is difficult to listen to the songs, let alone appreciate them. This record should be listened to only by people who know how good Woody can be when recorded well." Asch fired off a furious response:

> I usually ignore criticism good or bad about the records I produce. But I thought that *Broadside* would have enough sense to understand its moral obligation to help BIG COMPANIES whenever they go out on a limb and issue an unreleased album such as the Woody Guthrie. . . . It is impossible to have a worst of Woody or a worst of Asch or a worst of any folk. You have no right to judge being no God, of what is good folk or bad folk. Folk is people and all folk or people are good. . . . Technicals be damned. Broadside be damned. Be slick. Be correct.[74]

Asch still regarded himself as a recording engineer of some accomplishment, and this criticism hurt his pride.

In addition to printing Asch's letter, Friesen responded to him in a private letter and tried to explain that it was Cohen's view that modern recording technique might have enabled Verve to clean up the recordings considerably. Friesen added that because Verve might be marketing Guthrie to a larger audience than had heard him previously, it was especially important that the record reflect well on him in both musical and technical respects. Asch responded to Friesen by taking full responsibility for the recording—"I approved the Verve Folkways release of Woody. Verve does not do anything without my OK"—and by stating his belief in the importance of "true sound" that is not falsified electronically in order to sound "good." "The only obligation I have to anybody," he declared, "including Woody or Broadside[,] is to be true to them and not in the image of those who wishing to be liked by all become the mirror of 'all.'"[75]

By late in 1965 it was already apparent that the Verve deal was not functioning as Asch had hoped it would. In particular, Verve was releasing a great many things on Verve/Folkways without Asch's OK. Jerry Schoenbaum announced in December that he would be expanding the Verve/Folkways line beyond the "folk staples" from Asch's catalogue in order to increase its "market appeal," a sure sign the revival was faltering. He had recently sponsored a "blues bag" festival at the Café Au Go Go and had signed some of its most successful acts to the label, including the Blues Project. He had also come to believe that some of the most promising "folk music" was being produced in the off-Broadway theaters;[76] the following year, much to Asch's surprise, he released on Verve/Folkways the original cast album of *A Hand is on the Gate*, an off-Broadway production directed by Roscoe Lee Browne and featuring folk singer Leon Bibb as well as James Earl Jones and Cicely Tyson. By the middle of 1967 Schoenbaum had signed Tim Hardin, Laura Nyro, Richie Havens, Gordon Bok, and Janis Ian to Verve/Folkways. Asch received some royalties on these recordings, but quite belatedly and at a much lower rate than he received on those that came out of the Folkways catalogue. A hundred five thousand copies of the Blues Project's *Projections* album brought Asch a little over $2,000, and the more than 112,000 copies that Verve/Folkways sold of Janis Ian's single "Society's Child" was worth $374.01 to Asch. Over the course of a year, *A Hand Is on the Gate* sold 1,317 copies, which brought Asch just over $25.00.

Not long after Asch had signed the agreement with Verve, he made another arrangement, this one with Scholastic, for the marketing and distribution of the noncommercial material in his catalogue that was of no interest to MGM. Scholastic was a highly successful publisher of educational materials for elementary and secondary schools. Much of the growing spoken word material in the Folkways catalogue seemed well suited for school use, and of course Asch had remained active in the children's record market without interruption since the mid-forties. Indeed, the educational market showed signs of becoming very promising for Folkways at middecade, and Scholastic thought that they recognized a good fit.

Scholastic's agreement with Asch, which was much like Verve's in that it was a lease agreement that entitled them to press and market recordings from the Folkways catalogue on the Scholastic/Folkways label, took effect in the spring of 1966. It was unlike the Verve agreement in that they took over nearly the entire Folkways inventory and catalogue. Asch's own office became a place for the production of new albums, whereas sales and distribution shifted almost entirely to Scholastic for the duration of the agreement. Asch was provided with an office in the Scholastic building at 50 West Forty-fourth Street, to which he repaired for at least part of most work days. An article in *Scholastic Teacher* in November 1966 entitled "Scholastic's Remarkable Man of Sound" began, "There is a new name on a door at Scholastic's headquarters in New York." The article repeated most of the apocryphal stories about Asch's life—his father's early theatrical triumphs, the household in Paris that swarmed with artists on the eve of World War I, electronics training in Germany, the encounter with Sarnoff, the advice of Einstein. These stories were becoming the means by which Asch presented himself to others; they were to be understood as the blueprint of his work, his person, and his importance.

Asch's supervisor at Scholastic was Morris Goldberger, a vice president and publisher of the General Book Division. Asch was charged with coming up with new ideas for educational recordings, such as the American Adventure series, which consisted of song excerpts from various Folkways recordings strung together by a historical narrative. Goldberger did not find Asch an easy man to work with; his reactions to things both negative and positive seemed so theatrical that Goldberger sometimes doubted Asch's sincerity. Goldberger became part of the group of colleagues and collaborators whom Asch took to lunch at La Strada, but he found that socializing with Asch was an unpredictable affair: conversation could be warm and engaging, or it could be tense. A planned meeting for drinks with their wives following a Carnegie Hall concert did not really click and did not lead to further socializing.[77]

The other problem for Scholastic in working with Asch was that he had an assortment of "special" arrangements with his steadiest retailers that Scholastic had difficulty honoring. Asch had developed his business practices in a previous age, when far more was based upon cultivating personal relationships and favors were exchanged on the basis of a handshake and without resort to formal record keeping. Folkways was an infinitesimal part of the Scholastic operation (though their first real venture into the audio market), and they were not going to depart from their own highly bureaucratized business practices simply to enable Asch to save face with his preferred customers. Friction was inevitable.

In other respects, however, Scholastic was supportive of Asch's goals and mission. In May, shortly after the inauguration of the collaboration, John Studebaker, Scholastic's vice president for Curriculum, received a letter from a high school principal in Georgia inquiring about Scholastic's involvement with Folkways. The principal had learned from an article by the Christian Crusade that Folkways had the "largest [inventory of] Communist Folk Music in the country on phonograph records." The article had particularly cited the songs of Hans Eisler, the East German composer and Communist who had died in 1962 and whose songs were available on a 1964 Folkways release by Columbia professor of English Eric Bentley (5433). Asch was told of the principal's letter during a Scholastic budget meeting, and he replied to Studebaker by letter a couple days later:

> I wonder why the Christian Crusade did not state that in the booklet accompanying the record we have documented Eisler and labeled him a Communist. Therefore anyone using the album would be able to put the facts before the student with a background and the purpose of the songs. How else can one learn about the enemy but by his own words and actions. . . . Perhaps if we were to understand and apply this knowledge and expose it to our students we could appreciate the dangers of any enemy of democracy so that we would be more prepared to keeping [sic] the concepts and freedom of our constitutional government.

Asch's anticommunist indignation might have been partly manufactured for the occasion (he had befriended plenty of party members over the years without describing them as "the enemy"), but his defense of his right to release material of *any* ideological stripe without being personally associated with it was not. The purpose of the album notes was to provide sufficient social or political context for the recorded material so that a listener could arrive at his or her own conclusions about the songs' significance. Of course, it would require a diligent teacher to draw students' attention to the notes.

Studebaker's response was brief and dry: "I am sorry you were put to the trouble to write me about the letter from the principal in Georgia. I understand the basic theory upon which you have worked so commendably for many years. I do not expect a release by the Christian Crusade would bother us very much."[78]

Asch's output of new recordings started to fall precipitously, from 103 in 1964 to 66 in 1965, 47 in 1966, and 38 each in 1967 and 1968. These would have represented a significant amount of productivity for a modest-sized commercial label, but for Asch they were indications that his creative work was drying up. There were a few important exceptions and a small number of his most loyal musicians and record producers who continued to sustain him. The New Lost City Ramblers had gone through personnel difficulties earlier in the decade. Tom Paley had left for Europe in 1962 to take up his on-again, off-again career in mathematics; Mike Seeger and John Cohen decided that they could not wait indefinitely for Paley to choose between his academic and musical careers. They approached Doc Watson about joining them in Paley's place, but he declined. Ultimately it was fiddler Tracy Schwarz who stepped in. This prompted a letter from a lawyer for Paley, who informed them that they did not have the right to continue to use the name New Lost City Ramblers. Asch paid Paley a sum of money to extricate Cohen and Mike Seeger from any obligation to him and to enable them to continue under the old name.[79] Still, when the Ramblers next released an album, in 1963, they titled it *The "New" New Lost City Ramblers with Tracy Schwarz*, so that there would be no confusion.

After 1964 the New Lost City Ramblers recorded only sporadically, but they continued to tour a great deal and their record sales continued to represent an important (if not altogether critical) portion of their income. Although a Ramblers album was released on Verve/Folkways, they found their album sales falling precipitously in this time, and Cohen wondered in a letter to Asch whether perhaps these partnerships were diverting his energy:

> I think I realize how your energies have been going towards
> Verve and the other arrangements you have with Scholastic,

but I do not like to think that our sales on Folkways should stop on account of this. I know that this is not intentional on your part, neither do you desire it; yet faced with the prospects of no returns from our records I don't know what to think. I know that we are plenty busy with concerts, and judging from the continued growth of Sing Out, the folk music audience has not disappeared . . . [and] neither has the interest in traditional music.[80]

The Ramblers were in England in February 1967 and tried taking matters into their own hands. Cohen had spoken with Jerry Schoenbaum before leaving New York and had gotten the impression that the Verve arrangement was about to fall apart. The various leasing arrangements seemed to Cohen not to provide the record companies with any incentive to promote their albums. Nathan Joseph's Transatlantic label had the British rights to Folkways recordings but released the Ramblers' albums on Extra, Transatlantic's poorly distributed budget label. Cohen found copies of the Ramblers' albums abundantly available on the Ember label, but these were bootlegs and did not pay royalties. The solution seemed to be with England's Fontana label, which appeared to have the means of marketing them adequately. When Fontana offered to sign the Ramblers, Cohen wrote excitedly to Asch for a response.[81]

Asch's response was swift and unequivocal. Because the Ramblers had an exclusive contract with Folkways, any contract with Fontana would have to be cleared in writing by him—otherwise Fontana would face a lawsuit. Asch would demand a quarter of any royalties they made from the British label, and he warned the group not to allow recordings for Fontana to be licensed to any other label or to be sold outside of the United Kingdom. "Do not do anything rash[.] Follow these instructions," he wrote in conclusion. "I fight for you as long as you play fair with me."[82]

Suitably chastened, the Ramblers did not sign with Fontana. Instead they made an additional couple of albums for Folkways, *Modern Times* (31027) and *New Lost City Ramblers with Cousin Emmy* (31015), both released the following year. They would be their last recordings until well into the following decade. Individually the Ramblers would continue to work on Folkways projects, including Mike Seeger's album of songs of the industrialization of the South, *Tipple, Loom and Rail* (5273), with thorough and scholarly notes by Archie Green. The contrast it made with his half brother's famous *American Industrial Ballads,* recorded almost ten years earlier, was suggestive. Both were intended to be "true" to the originals in their own way, but the older recording did not recreate either the singing style or the instrumentalization of the originals. Mike Seeger, however, went to considerable lengths to recreate the originals musically, and although he inevitably placed his own stamp on them, it was with the understanding that the significance of the songs was to be found—in part at least—in the style in which they were performed. Although the older half brother presented the songs for what they could illuminate about contemporary social predicaments, the younger half brother recreated them as a means of transporting his audience to a previous era, when there was little in the way of romance but a great deal of hard-headed dignity. The result was one of Folkways's stunning, and now largely forgotten, gems.

Most of the Folkways releases in 1967 and 1968 came to Asch as largely completed projects; his role was confined to the final production process. Ann Charters brought him the notes and edited tapes of a benefit reading for the New York Workshop in Nonviolence in the spring of 1966. Asch released it as *Poems for Peace* (9765), although the poems (by Allen Ginsberg, Peter Orlovsky, Ed Sanders, and others) were a reasonable illustration of what Todd Gitlin has described as the era's tension "between the radical idea of political strategy—with discipline, organization, commitment to results *out there* at a distance—and the countercultural idea of living life to the fullest, *right here,* for oneself."[83] John Cohen prepared an album of songs by George Davis (*When Kentucky Had No Union Men,* 2343), who had made a questionable claim to the authorship of "Sixteen Tons," a song usually attributed to Merle Travis. Projects that involved Asch more directly were the exception and consisted primarily of archive material from his rapidly receding past. A volume of Cisco Houston songs was assembled from the archive, and in 1967 Asch asked Pete Seeger to prepare a reading of Sholem Asch's *Story of the Nativity.* In his album notes for the latter, Asch maintained that in 1942 he had asked his father to write an English language rendering of the story of the birth of Christ, explicitly to be recorded as a follow-up to *In the Beginning,* the children's record of Old Testament stories. "I waited twenty years for the right voice to tell this story," he wrote. "The voice of a professional actor or announcer would not do. Sholem Asch's *Nativity* must be told, I felt, by someone with an affinity for art and the folk idiom, and with a deep sense of social understanding as well." Asch described

the finished recording as a collaboration between three generations—his father, himself, and Pete Seeger.[84] Asch could not have
failed to notice how rapidly his father's work had faded from the
public eye in the ten years since his death. *The Story of the Nativity*
was the first of a handful of projects Asch undertook on behalf of
his father's memory, and the album notes reverently recount his
father's theatrical and literary triumphs. Though arguably Asch's
most overt expression of the pride he took in being the son of a
great writer, *Nativity* might also have contributed to the rumors
about his father's conversion to Christianity and disavowal of
Judaism. But it is unlikely that Asch worried about it for a moment:
it was precisely the kind of iconoclastic gesture that both he and
his father would have appreciated.

Some time in late 1966 a sidewalk grate collapsed under Asch
near his Forty-sixth Street offices. His leg, long weakened by
osteomyelitis, was fractured very badly and Asch spent several
weeks in the hospital. It was not until late spring of the following
year that he was free of a cast. During Asch's hospitalization, Silber
took over the running of Folkways. He had not been particularly
involved with the record end of things in the past couple of years
since *Sing Out!* and, more particularly, Oak Books had demanded
more and more of his time. With Distler's death, the way might
have been cleared for a closer partnership between Silber and
Asch, but it did not happen that way. Silber had traveled to Cuba
and had returned to write about Castro's communist regime with
considerable enthusiasm. His interests were turning away from
folk music and history to the international revolutionary struggle,
particularly in Vietnam. Although sympathetic with Silber's politics,
Michael Asch thought that he was inappropriately turning *Sing Out!*
into a propaganda vehicle, and Asch, although he probably did not
disagree with Silber either on the political questions, also fretted
over the direction "the folk song magazine" had taken. Michael
Asch had no doubt that his father opposed the war in Vietnam,
and although it was never a topic of conversation between them,
he supported his point with the recollection of a particularly
disastrous Passover seder. It took place at their home in April 1967,
during the weeks leading up to the Six-Day War in the Middle East,
with a handful of relatives and friends. One guest had a son in
Vietnam; others were ardent Zionists. Asch was no more sympathetic to Zionism than he was to black nationalist movements that
sought to establish their identity with allusions to Africa.[85] He
attempted to turn the Exodus into a metaphor for the black

struggle in the United States, and by the time they reached "next year in Jerusalem" the whole thing had deteriorated into an angry shouting match.[86]

But although Asch did not disagree with Silber on most political issues, he was unhappy that *Sing Out!* was being increasingly diverted from the exploration and celebration of folk music by its growing focus on the war. Then in his "Fan the Flames" column in the November 1965 *Sing Out!* Silber reprinted selections from Woody Guthrie's *Born to Win* (which Robert Shelton edited for publication that year) on the subject of folk songs, high prices, censors, sex, and song writing, in that order. The passage on sex derived from Guthrie's sex-obsessed period in the early fifties, which some have surmised was a symptom of his illness: "If there is a prettier sight on earth than those patched hairs between your legs, I've never seen nor heard about it. If there is a prettier sight than this long and viney root that stands up here between my legs, I've certainly never seen that."[87] Silber later regarded his inclusion of this material as a reflection of the growing sexual revolution in the country, as well as perhaps some things he was going through in his own life.[88] It infuriated Asch, who removed himself as the magazine's consultant for the "international section," as well as Toshi Seeger, both of whom felt the material had no place in a magazine that reached a broad audience, including adolescents. Silber thought they were just being puritanical. The incident became prominent among an accumulation of things that suggested to Asch and Silber that it was time to dissolve their partnership.

Prior to his accident, Asch had already started the negotiations that would extricate him from both *Sing Out!* and Oak Books. In January 1967 Silber drew up a report of "books in the works" and prepared a schedule for the completion by spring of those already in production. They included books by Sam Charters, Peggy Seeger and Ewan MacColl, Malvina Reynolds, a book on drumming in the Americas, and the old 1941 Guthrie/Lomax/Seeger project of political songs entitled "Hard Hitting Songs for Hard-Hit People." Other books were not yet in production but soon would be, and still others would never see light of day (including John Cohen's book of photographs from his fieldwork in Peru, much to his intense disappointment). Oak Books was by now a very lucrative business. Asch and Silber sent a letter to all of their Oak collaborators to explain that Oak was being sold to Music Sales, Inc., "an energetic music book publishing company," justifying it primarily on the grounds that although business was good, rising costs were making it increasingly difficult to sustain a small publishing business. Music Sales would take over all royalty obligations starting in October, although Silber would be retained as a production supervisor for five years and his approval would be required on all new Oak titles in that time. By year's end, however, Silber had largely departed the world of New York folk music to become an editor at the *Guardian,* a radical newsweekly.

Asch and Silber made out very well from the sale of Oak, but *Sing Out!* was left high and dry. In Oak's seven-year existence, it had been the primary means of sustaining the magazine financially. Members of *Sing Out!*'s advisory board bought the magazine from Asch and Silber and set themselves up at a new address. It faltered badly in the following months, and Pete Seeger felt that Silber was largely to blame. "I feel if you are trying to kill *Sing Out!* . . . you are doing a good job," he wrote angrily to the former editor.[89] A subsequent editor accused Silber of having kicked the props out from under the magazine. But Silber later insisted that he had warned them that the magazine could not be self-sustaining, particularly if the new owners made themselves its salaried employees.

Asch thumped around on his leg cast for several months; finally in May, with much relief, it was removed.[90] Free of this distraction, free of *Sing Out!* and Oak Books, and free of Irwin Silber, Asch was able to take stock. After two and a half years the Verve arrangement was proving to be unsatisfactory in almost every respect. Asch's lawyers began to document the violations of the agreement, the most egregious being MGM's failure to provide royalty statements. Late in the year, the contract between Folkways and MGM was allowed to expire, but it would be an additional half year before Asch could satisfactorily extricate himself from the collaboration. The sell-off provision of the expired contract allowed MGM to sell the remaining Verve/Folkways inventory at the conclusion of the agreement. The label had been doing sufficiently well for MGM that they were not prepared to let it die altogether. The result was the Verve/Forecast label, which would continue to market those recordings and artists that Schoenbaum had signed himself. But according to Asch's lawyers, MGM was still marketing recordings that derived from masters owned by Asch, in some instances having merely pasted a Verve/Forecast label over the Verve/Folkways logo on the album jacket. Jack Weinstein at MGM maintained in response to Asch's lawyers that the company had "'shown good faith' in changing the label credit," but Asch doubted that there was much advantage to Folkways in having its records marketed under another company's logo. A lawsuit was threatened, but in the end there was too little at stake to justify it.[91]

To the dismal list of deaths that touched Asch in the sixties—Cisco Houston in 1961, Madya in 1962, Nathan Asch and Marian Distler in 1964, Henry Cowell in 1965, Peter LaFarge in 1966, Langston Hughes in May 1967—was added one more in the fall of 1967. On 3 October Woody Guthrie finally succumbed to Huntington's chorea. Asch had never once visited Guthrie in the thirteen years he was hospitalized. The twitching shell that remained of the great songwriter was of no interest to him; as far as Asch was concerned, "he was not Woody Guthrie at that time." Asch had shown up at the ceremony in 1966 that marked the presentation of the Conservation Service Award by Secretary of the Interior Stewart Udall to Woody Guthrie, and he permitted himself to be photographed with Harold Leventhal, Marjorie Guthrie, and Udall. But Guthrie himself was too ill to attend. Later Asch claimed not to have known of the nature of Guthrie's illness until after his death, when Marjorie Guthrie began a campaign to increase the medical community's knowledge (and the public's awareness) of Huntington's disease.[92] His interest was in the living, vibrant Guthrie who remained accessible through his recordings. Marjorie seemed to be among those whose patience for Asch was almost infinite, and over the years, as Leventhal fumed about the difficulties he had in procuring royalties for the Guthrie Children's Trust Fund from Folkways, Marjorie would urge him to leave off Moe. Perhaps she knew that there was not that much money to be gotten out of Folkways; perhaps she knew that there was little hope that Asch would ever develop even marginally rational accounting practices. Asch continued to argue with Leventhal that he had given Guthrie a great deal of money during his lifetime as an advance against royalties, and thus he felt little financial obligation to Guthrie's estate.[93] But Asch paid a price for his recalcitrance, as he was rarely given much consideration in the many homages to Guthrie that followed his death.

Asch's collaboration with Scholastic stumbled along for another couple of years, but both parties had long since recognized that Asch was not the sort to work comfortably within the confines of a conventional business bureaucracy. Asch began to look for other outlets, which resulted in his traveling with Harold and Natalie Leventhal in spring of 1968 to Paris, where they had arranged to meet up with Pete and Toshi Seeger, who were just concluding a lengthy world tour. Their stated purpose was to discuss Seeger's projects for the coming year, although Asch was also looking for ways to revive his European distribution and had scheduled a meeting with the French Chant du Monde label. One very late night Toshi took them all to an open-air market, where she scandalized the others slightly by eating an enormous platter of escargots and other less easily identified French delicacies. Another evening she left a message for Asch at his hotel room: "Peter's taking a walk, Harold has conferences with Essex Music, etc., Natalie [Leventhal] and I are going to buy perfume and French panties for Mika and Penny—tomorrow a.m. *Who* do you wish to join?"[94] As the note intimated, Asch was the odd man out, in more ways than one. Later in the trip he blew up at Natalie when she dared to express an opinion about some difficulty he was having with his son.

At the turn of the decade the Folkways-Scholastic collaboration came apart, perhaps more amicably than the Folkways-MGM agreement, but with two additional complications. First, Scholastic owned the Folkways inventory, and Asch did not have three hundred thousand dollars to purchase it from them. An agreement was reached by which Asch would pay ten thousand dollars each quarter for the next ten years; in 1985, the year before his death, he made the last payment. Second, just as the dissolution of the Stinson partnership in 1946 had deprived Asch of his commercial name, so was he unable to operate under the Folkways name until he was clear of Scholastic. Some years earlier Asch had created a commercial entity called Pioneer that helped to preserve the independence of certain aspects of his operation. In 1970 he became Pioneer Record Sales, with three subsidiary labels: RF (what had been Records, Books and Film, only there were no longer any books, and films had always been a fond hope) for Sam Charters's reissues of vintage material from other labels, Broadside for those records still occasionally produced by the topical song magazine and any other politically sensitive material Asch wished to assign to it, and Asch Records (and the Asch Mankind series, equivalent to the Ethnic series) for new recordings of all kinds. The repeating patterns appealed to him; at sixty-five, when most men retired, he was alone in business once again, under the name of his first record label, left to his own devices. His father's son, waging a lone war on behalf of truth and knowledge, stubborn and unbowed. Like his father, he had the will and the determination to prevail; unlike his father, he would stay to fight the forces of philistinism at their source . . . whatever, or whomever, they were.

7. RECORDING THE CIVIL RIGHTS MOVEMENT

hen the civil rights movement came to flower with the Montgomery bus boycott in late 1955 and 1956 Asch had finally found a political cause about which he could be entirely unambivalent. His dedication to African Americans and African American culture had been evident as early as 1941, when quite without precedent he recorded Leadbelly. And in the intervening fifteen years, without interruption, he released records of black jazz musicians, bluesmen, and poets. Through the southern field projects of Courlander and Ramsey, through Ramsey's jazz reissues project, and through scores of other recordings—contemporary and historical—Asch had assembled an unparalleled document of the development of black music.

The source of Asch's dedication to the cause of African American civil rights is not easily traced. His father—the great reconciler of "races"—might well have provided the philosophical underpinnings of Asch's racial egalitarianism, but he was not otherwise a role model. While lunching at the Tavern on the Green around 1951, Sholem made a racist remark that caused his son to seethe. On the cab ride home with young Michael, Asch let his anger fly. How to understand this man? He could write with sympathy and understanding about Moses's black mistress (Sholem's *Moses* was published that year), but with blacks he encountered in his own life he could be thoroughly bigoted. More likely Asch's racial attitudes are attributable in part to the Zeitgeist of the Popular Front era, but some of them can only be ascribed to Asch's profound humanity—whatever the many contradictions.

Asch was not troubled by the question of whether black music was de facto protest music or whether it was politically retrograde.

He undoubtedly believed that everything he released was an en-
nobling reflection of the human spirit, particularly his recordings
of African American cultural production. Yet it remained the question that preoccupied many of those who wrote about black
music at midcentury and after.

The meaning of slave songs—that inevitable touchstone of any
discussion of African American music—has been a matter of debate since collectors such as Thomas Wentworth Higginson and
Lucy McKim Garrison began to bring the spirituals of the Sea
Islands to national attention during the Civil War. The prevailing
position until the turn of the century was that slave songs were an
uncomplicated reflection of the slaves' Christian ethos of deference, subservience, and deliverance from worldly suffering upon
death. There was no hint in the predominant scholarship that
slaves resisted the self-image that had been pressed upon them
by slave owners and southern apologists—happy, childlike, incapable of fending for themselves in a civilized world or of fashion-
ing an independent ideology. Only with the publication of W. E. B.
Du Bois's *Souls of Black Folk* in 1903 was the debate enriched by the
suggestion that there were meanings in the "sorrow songs" that
departed from the hegemonic view of slave life:

> They are the music of an unhappy people, of the children of
> disappointment; they tell of death and suffering and unvoiced
> longing toward a truer world, of misty wanderings and hid-
> den ways. . . . Through all the Sorrow Songs there breathes a
> hope—a faith in the ultimate justice of things . . . that some-
> time, somewhere, men will judge men by their souls and not
> by their skins.[1]

If Du Bois did not immediately change the terms of the debate, he
at least set the stage for the political rehabilitation of slave spirituals. In the late 1930s two black scholars, Sterling Brown and John
Lovell Jr., advanced the idea that the spirituals not only reflected
slaves' recognition of their exploitation but also served as coded
messages of resistance.[2] The most famous example may be the
interpretation of "Follow the Drinking Gourd" as an instruction to
runaways to use the Big Dipper as a signpost to freedom.[3] Undoubtedly the spirituals were sufficiently malleable that they
meant different things in different places and in different circumstances and could be used to carry explicit information at times.
But for critics of this school of interpretation, attaching specific and

invariant meanings to particular spirituals emptied them of their subtlety and their ability to carry multiple meanings. The crude functionalism, particular of Lovell's writing, resulted from an insistence upon finding a deliberate "use" value in the spirituals that elided the more important ways that spirituals served the slave community through the adaptability of their many meanings.

To some scholars, such as John Greenway in his *American Folksongs of Protest,* the "deliverance" the spirituals invoked was fundamentally an otherworldly one, and if there were latent references to earthly freedom they did not become evident to the slaves until the Civil War.[4] A more persuasive interpretation has been made of the spirituals' salvation theme by Albert Raboteau and Lawrence Levine, who have argued that the separation of "this-worldly" and "other-worldly" into distinct domains is a peculiarly Western cosmological construct that does not sufficiently reflect the highly African-influenced cosmology of slaves that saw heaven and earth, the sacred and secular, as highly permeable realms. Levine holds that "these songs state as clearly as anything can the manner in which the sacred world of the slaves was able to fuse the precedents of the past, the conditions of the present, and the promise of the future into one connected reality."[5] And Raboteau concludes that "categorizing sacred and secular elements is of limited usefulness in discussing the spirituals because the slaves, following African and biblical tradition, believed that the supernatural continually impinged on the natural, that divine action constantly took place within the lives of men, in the past, present and future."[6] But surprisingly, even given the apparent synonymity of their positions, Levine and Raboteau arrive at different notions of the role of protest in slave songs. Thus Levine concludes that "there was always a latent and symbolic element of protest in the slave's religious songs which frequently became overt and explicit," whereas Raboteau cautions that they should *not* be regarded as "coded protest songs."[7]

There is more agreement over the fact that at times songs gave slaves a kind of license to comment upon their condition that would not have been available in everyday speech. Anthropologists and ethnomusicologists have noted the ways in which song permits the articulation of satire, insult, and criticism in cultures as diverse as that of the Eskimos and some Africans.[8] Slave songs often enabled the expression of hate, frustration and anger—the ridicule of masters, mistresses, patrollers, overseers. They were an expression of the slaves' moral superiority, of their ability to "put one over" on their temporal superiors, and they are often thought to have contributed to the slaves' psychic survival.[9]

In many respects the explication of slave songs remained the interpretive standard even as attention shifted to the possibility of "protest content" in African American secular music of the twentieth century. If a people as thoroughly at bay as African American slaves were unable to muster a tradition of protest music, then it is unlikely that their descendants would have done so. If, on the other hand, slave song was protest music par excellence, then its influence must surely have been felt upon all African American protest music that followed. John Lomax saw neither a connection between slave culture and the subsequent development of African American song, nor the presence of a substantial protest tradition in *any* era of African American musical history. "Slavery," he wrote in the *Nation* in 1917, "has been a thing of the past these many years, and, after all, as a part of the race history, formed but a brief interlude—an episode—between many generations of barbaric freedom and the present status of liberty in a civilized land. The bulk of the negro's songs are not dead tradition of slavery days." Lomax argued that the fundamental theme of Negro song was "self-pity," the primary source of which was a feelings of racial inferiority:

> And it seems further credible that he has come to lump the troubles for which he himself is largely to blame along with the inevitable hardships of his situation until he has grown to regard himself as the victim of hard luck, generally abused by everybody; and, at least in many instances, he seems not averse to nursing his gloom a little.[10]

Lomax's comments were not particularly shocking in 1917, especially coming from a southerner who would prove himself a champion of Negro folk culture as "art." And that his position was credible even among whites who regarded themselves as politically progressive, is suggested by the appearance of this piece in a prominent liberal weekly.

But developments in African American song over the next two decades demonstrated that Lomax had been wrong on both scores—the protest tradition, though arguably latent during the preceding decades, remained available to African Americans as circumstances demanded. And its connection to musical traditions dating to the slave era were unmistakable. Songs with deliberate protest messages were not particularly evident in African American political organizations of the late nineteenth and early twentieth centuries, largely because the movements of this era—the women's club movement, the NAACP, even Garvey's United Negro Improvement Association—were dominated by middle-class pretensions.[11] But as soon as there were political movements that reached the black masses in significant numbers and recruited leaders from their ranks, the role of protest songs grew accordingly. In the sharecropping South of the 1930s working people's movements took two primary forms—the Southern Tenant Farmers Union (STFU) and the Communist Party. Founded in 1934, the STFU shared with the party a dedication to socialist principles, to the eradication of the most vicious kinds of labor extortion in the South, and to the elimination of racial bigotry. But although there were efforts to create an alliance between the organizations in the years immediately following the organization of the STFU, party affiliation (and its accompanying indictment of the American government for its ostensive collusion in the exploitation of southern workers) left many STFU leaders feeling skittish, and it never happened.[12]

Both organizations ultimately fostered a politicized musical culture by drawing on traditional African American musical forms, most of them sacred in origin. The violence that southern Communists encountered throughout the South required a considerable degree of secrecy, and consequently there was little group singing among the party's organized *urban* workers. However, the more isolated meetings of the CPUSA's Share Croppers' Union (SCU) adopted patterns of group singing from their worship services, which opened and closed with song. Borrowing from sacred musical forms, spirituals such as "We Shall Not Be Moved" were reworked with appropriate messages of worker resistance. "Give Me That Old Time Religion" became "Give Me That Old Communist Spirit" ("It was good enough for Lenin, and it's good enough for me"). Party leaders may have been uneasy about the appropriation of sacred musical forms, even in reworked versions, preferring instead that SCU meetings open and close with songs from the standard party repertoire ("The Internationale" and the Wobblies' "Solidarity Forever" by Ralph Chaplin). The party's musical preferences were also illustrated by the kind of songs published in their *Southern Worker,* which like "Autumn Blues" and "The Bedspread Blues" in 1936 were usually based on secular musical forms. But the use of spirituals and hymns persisted, and with the establishment of the Popular Front the party's unprecedented (and un-Marxian) recognition of the black church's revolutionary history resulted in the embrace of spirituals as vital protest music.[13] The STFU was simultaneously developing a still more vibrant musical tradition, largely due to the song writing of talented individuals such as John Handcox, whose "Roll the Union On" became a staple in leftist circles for decades.[14]

The repressive postwar years reduced socialist- and communist-led mass black organization in the South to a whisper. In 1951 the Alabama legislature enacted the Communist Control Law, and the last remnant of Alabama's Communist Party disbanded. But less than five years later Alabama's black working class was again mobilizing, and this time there was no mistaking the role of the black church and sacred musical forms. Martin Luther King's leadership of the Montgomery Improvement Association assured the presence of religious themes and imagery throughout the bus boycott. In almost every respect the civil rights movement became the "singing movement" that leftists had been seeking in vain since the era of the Popular Front.

It is not an easy matter to identify the start of the contemporary civil rights movement. Organizations such as the NAACP and the National Urban League had been toiling away behind the scenes for decades in an effort to curb racial violence, break the barriers of racial segregation, and set the foundation for some degree of economic justice. According to Aldon Morris, however, the civil rights movement of the 1950s and 1960s departed from previous efforts in that it was (1) mass-based, (2) church-centered, and (3) focused upon collective, direct action. Although the Montgomery bus boycott is a convenient bench mark for the start of the movement—particularly because it witnessed the emergence of Martin Luther King Jr.—it had a predecessor in the somewhat less successful bus boycott in Baton Rouge in 1953.[15]

From the start the Montgomery bus boycott and its successors drew on traditional African American sacred music with the firm conviction that it had always been a music of resistance. The utility of this music was enhanced by the fact that its improvisatory structure made it highly adaptable; many were of the call-and-response type, inviting song leaders to substitute their own lyric inventions at critical junctures. Thus when Martin Luther King substituted "We are moving on to victory" for "Give me that old time religion," he was following the customary use of the music in every respect.[16] The form came to be known as a "zipper song," suggesting the easy substitution of an improvised phrase for a customary one.

In addition to black sacred music that derived from the slave era (spirituals) and from traditional hymnody that had both black and white origins, there was from the start a role in the movement for gospel music. Gospel derived from the joyous, Holy Ghost–inspired Holiness and Pentecostal movements of the early twentieth century. In an era in which black church music was becoming increasingly staid—as many traditional black Baptist and Methodist churches attempted to emulate the decorum of middle-class white churches—Holiness and Pentecostal churches were throwing off middle-class restraint in favor of a dancing, hand-clapping, singing, shouting, and stomping worship style. These were the signs of an exuberant and personal encounter with God that had been the hallmark of slave religion. The music that came with it employed musical instruments that middle-class black churches had banished from their services, as well as inventive musical styles such as jazz and blues. Gospel remained a music that allowed room for the incorporation of contemporary African American musical styles.

Shortly before the start of the Montgomery bus boycott, in 1954, three elementary school girls began to sing church music together. Mary Ethel Dozier, Minnie Hendricks, and Gladys Burnette Carter came to be known as the Montgomery Gospel Trio. They were called on to sing at the church meetings that over the twelve months of the boycott became the primary source of both information and spiritual regeneration for the weary members of the black community. Their material came directly from the established spiritual and gospel traditions, but in the application of these songs to the situation in Montgomery they took on a new poignancy. One of their popular songs was the spiritual "Keep Your Hand on the Plow (Hold On)." Within a year the lyrics would be altered to "Keep Your Eyes on the Prize" by a woman on Johns Island, South Carolina, thereby becoming one of the prominent anthems of the movement.[17] But even in its traditional form, the song conveyed a sense of determination and perseverance that spoke directly to foot-sore blacks in Montgomery. Other singers would become far better known as the civil rights movement gathered steam, but the Montgomery Gospel Trio has been credited by Bernice Reagon with having "stimulated a growing awareness of the existence of a body of song unique to the struggle."[18]

The Montgomery bus boycott of 1955–56 thrust Martin Luther

King into the national spotlight—his picture appeared on the 18 February 1957 cover of *Time* magazine. Pete Seeger met him at the close of that summer, when they were gathered with others for a twenty-fifth anniversary of the Highlander School. A photograph taken that weekend of King in the company of some Communist Party members would cause him trouble a few years later. More significantly, however, Seeger introduced him to the song "We Shall Overcome," which King immediately embraced. "There's something about that song that haunts you," he commented that evening on the drive to his next destination.[19]

King was just the sort of maverick, history-making figure Asch appreciated. He wrote to King in September to propose that he interview him for a recording. King's secretary responded, informing Asch that King was busy working on a book and would be out of the office for six weeks. He would be sure to bring the letter to King's attention upon his return. Actually, King did not begin to work in earnest on the manuscript that became *Stride Toward Freedom: The Montgomery Story* until Christmas, but in any case the proposed interview never occurred.

The bus boycotts of the mid-fifties were crucial for mobilizing broad segments of the black community and for grounding its efforts in the ritual of the black church. But the full emergence of the movement as it is remembered today awaited the addition of one further ingredient: the students. On 1 February 1960 four freshmen at predominantly black North Carolina A&T staged a "sit down protest" at the whites-only lunch counter of Woolworth's department store in Greensboro. It was not the first such sit-in, but for whatever reason it was the one that attracted national attention and caused a proliferation of similar lunch-counter sit-ins in North Carolina and bordering states, primarily by black college students.[20] The spread of the sit-ins to Nashville later in the month was probably inevitable. A black seminarian by the name of James Lawson who had spent time in India studying Ghandian revolutionary principles had been schooling students from the four black campuses in Nashville in nonviolent direct-action tactics since the autumn.

The first Nashville sit-ins were staged deliberately by 124 students from American Baptist Theological Seminary, Fisk University, and Tennessee A&I State University on 13 February. Three downtown lunch counters were targeted. As sit-ins continued on the eighteenth, twentieth, and twenty-seventh, the number of participants grew to as many as four hundred in a day, affecting more than ten lunch counters. Arrests began late in the month; as one contingent was hauled off to jail, fresh recruits were called. Refusing bail, the students swelled the local jails until their trials began in early March.

The sit-ins in Nashville received the strong support of the city's adult black community, coming particularly from the clergy-dominated Nashville Christian Leadership Council (NCLC). Following the pattern established in Montgomery, there were again mass meetings at which the ministers solicited financial and legal assistance for the students, urged the boycott of downtown businesses, and buoyed the spirits of the community with prayer, sermons, and song. Traditional music was again pressed into service, but with their more secular musical tastes, the students now at the forefront of the movement found it inadequate. The sit-ins themselves were not initially the sight of much movement singing; instead, it was the jails that became the birthplace of several new movement songs, and mass jailings continued to stimulate the creation of new movement songs through subsequent years of sit-ins and freedom rides. Four student leaders from the American Baptist Theological Seminary—Joseph Carter, Bernard Lafayette, James Bevel, and Samuel Collier—formed the Nashville Quartet, which became a central vehicle for developing and disseminating a new strain of civil rights music in Nashville grounded in popular musical forms. One song, based upon a current rhythm and blues hit by Little Willie John entitled "You Better Leave My Kitten Alone," became "You Better Leave Segregation Alone" at the hands of the Quartet. Another, "Moving On," was a parody of a popular Ray Charles recording of a Hank Snow song (this was Nashville, after all), and "Your Dog Loves My Dog" (or "Dog Dog") was an original composition by Bevel and Lafayette.[21]

The possibilities of expanding the genre of civil rights music became even more apparent to several of the Nashville student leaders in early April, when they attended the seventh annual College Workshop at Highlander in Monteagle, Tennessee. The members of the Nashville Quartet were among them, as well as Guy Carawan, a young folk singer from California who had joined the Highlander staff as its musical director, its first since the death of Myles Horton's wife Zilphia in 1956. Carawan's repertoire of political material was eclectic, and in 1960 black college students did not find all of it to their liking. Many of the songs Carawan had drawn from the old IWW material, as well as Woody Guthrie songs he had learned via Pete Seeger, left the students cold. Even some traditional African American songs were largely unappreciated. Most of them were attending traditionally black colleges where faculty and administrators approved of only one form of traditional black cultural expression—the highly Westernized performance of spirituals by such choral groups as the Fisk Jubilee Singers. Having been weaned from more "authentic" forms of African American song, the students were not immediately responsive to it when they heard it from a white northern folk singer. But a few of these songs met with the students' approval. One was the reworked spiritual "Keep Your Eyes on the Prize," which Carawan had learned recently on Johns Island, South Carolina. Another was an old Baptist hymn originally entitled "I'll Be Alright" or "I Will Overcome," which had been refashioned into a freedom song during a food and tobacco workers' strike in Charleston, South Carolina, in 1945. Two members of the striking Food, Tobacco, and Agricultural Workers Union brought the song to Highlander in 1947, where it was taken up by Zilphia Horton and made into the school's theme song. There it was later taught to Pete Seeger and Frank Hamilton, who in turn taught it to Guy Carawan, each of them putting his stamp on it before it entered into the musical canon of the civil rights movement.[22]

In very short order "We Shall Overcome," as it was now called, became the anthem of the Nashville sit-in movement. Though not yet thirty, the man from whom they had learned it was regarded as the senior mentor of the song movement and was consequently invited by Nashville's student leaders to join them in the ongoing battle there. Carawan readily agreed—it was the battle he had been looking for, arguably all his life.

Carawan was himself something of a hybrid. Although his childhood was spent in working-class sections of Los Angeles, his mother was a Charlestonian (South Carolina) blue blood who regarded her husband from the North Carolina hill country as her social inferior. Guy was born in 1927, and his mother arranged for him to attend a public school outside of their district so that he would not have to go to school with the black children from his own neighborhood. His early musical experiences were limited to the clarinet and the songs of the American Legion Marching Band. Later, while earning a degree in mathematics at Occidental College, he picked up the ukelele and expanded his repertoire to include songs such as "Ain't She Sweet" and "Eyes of Blue."

It was also at Occidental that Carawan met the family of Bill Oliver. Oliver was a professor at Occidental and a member of

People's Songs. Guy would later marry his daughter Noel. Through the Olivers Carawan became involved with other Los Angeles People's Songsters, including Vern Partlow and Frank Hamilton, and first learned about the music of Leadbelly, Woody Guthrie, and Pete Seeger. Seeger himself passed through town as Carawan was completing a master's degree in sociology at UCLA, and he accepted an invitation to spend an afternoon with Guy and Frank Hamilton. Guy and Frank were working out some material as a folk duo and played some of their material for Seeger; Seeger showed them a new finger-picking technique for the banjo that had been developed by Earl Scruggs. By the time he left, he had invited the young men to visit him and Toshi in Beacon, New York, should they ever come east.

Carawan was in fact east in a matter of months. With his master's degree completed and his interest in folk music growing steadily, he wished to see New York which seemed to be the heart of the folk-song movement. And he had a second reason: part of the American folk tradition—that part that had taken root in the thin soil and rich coal veins of Appalachia—was *his*, to be reclaimed by an encounter with his father's North Carolina family. He stayed with the Seegers in Beacon for a while and was also frequently in the city, spending weekends at the great Washington Square jam sessions where he met Mary Travers, Erik Darling, and many others whose names would soon be affiliated with the folk revival. Lee Hays welcomed him to his apartment above Earl Robinson's place in Brooklyn. Ethel Raim and the other members of the Jewish Young Folksingers welcomed Guy into their ranks, and for about a year he joined them in the singing of Robinson's "Lonesome Train," choral arrangements of Yiddish folk songs, and a thoroughly eclectic mix of domestic and international folk songs. To make ends meet, he worked in an orphanage for some weeks. But Seeger kept urging him to travel south and visit the holy places of American folk music, as he and many others had done before. Guy convinced Frank Hamilton to join him, and Jack Elliot signed on for the trip as well. Elliot, rather more road-hardened than the others, was also their direct link to Woody Guthrie and the entire tradition of politically progressive folk music. Early in the summer of 1953 the three of them loaded up Guy's old car with musical instruments and assorted belongings.

Their first destination was the home of Guy's aunt and uncle in Mesic, North Carolina. He and his friends were received warmly, as members of the family, and were encouraged to stay as long as they wanted until they mentioned their desire to attend a Negro worship service. Guy wrote in his diary: "I spoke to my aunt and uncle about visiting the Negro church and some of the people in their homes, and they said 'this is the deep South and unless you plan on leaving Mesic and not coming back you better not get mixed up with neggers. The people here won't stand for it.'" It was Guy's first taste of a sobering contradiction. Here were honest, hard-working, God-fearing people rooted in the folk culture that had generated much of the music that Guy had come to adore. But somehow this did not add up to the kind of progressive outlook that he had always associated with folk music. "Authentic" did not mean politically enlightened. To honor their "tradition" he would have to abide by southern racial customs that were highly distasteful to him.

Having learned to tread carefully when it came to racial issues, the three set off in search of their musical heroes. A. P. Carter did not let them down, regaling them with stories of his life as a hillbilly musician and showing off his vast family of singers and players. Some days later, Bascom Lamar Lunsford was another matter. Despite his great admiration for his banjo playing and singing, Guy concluded that Lunsford was "a reactionary aristo-crat." On first meeting, Lunsford had immediately asked the three young men whether they were Communists and had accused them of being part of a vast conspiracy of song collectors who were misappropriating country people's music for leftist causes that were ruining the country. "Telling him we were friends of Pete and Woody and from New York didn't help matters any," Carawan wrote in his diary. "He thinks Lomax is pink, and went on and on about the subversion that's taking place." Lunsford thawed very little the next morning, when they played some music with him. Guy was furious when Lunsford asked for proof of their political affiliation, and he was more furious with himself for letting Lunsford get away with it without an argument. When they saw Lunsford again, at the festival he hosted in Asheville, North Carolina, suspicions on both sides had not dissipated. "He's a shit—and how," wrote Guy.

The disparity between the beauty of unadulterated rural music and the ugliness of many of its practitioners' political views had begun to eat at Guy. He was confused and disturbed, and was particularly bothered that neither of the others shared his distress. Thus it was with particular relief that they finally arrived at High-lander in Tennessee, where Myles Horton put them to work shelling beans and urged them to use the place as a home base for a while. Guy was palpably relieved to be among "politically akin people" and was all the more pleased to discover that Highlander was accepted and at least occasionally appreciated by its neighbors. Guy, Jack, and Frank joined a local fiddler in playing at a square dance and later surprised themselves by taking up with local trumpet and tenor banjo players with whom they cranked out some New Orleans–style jazz. Myles Horton's wife Zilphia was not there at the time, but her dedication to "cultural work" suffused the place and Guy found it particularly contagious.

But the satisfaction Guy experienced from the music and politics of Highlander evaporated almost as soon as they left the place. Even at avant-garde Black Mountain College Guy found himself out of step. One evening the college showed Elia Kazan's anticommunist film *Man on a Tight Rope*, which Frank Hamilton and most of the others passed off as a kind of grim joke. But Guy could not dismiss it so easily. "I felt alone as hell," he wrote, "almost as if there were something wrong with me." Later he got into an argument with a literature professor who held that political folk singers were ruining the genuine art of folk music by attempting to use it as a weapon: "He got my ire up slightly and I sounded off somewhat in front of a number of kids."[23]

At the end of their ten-week southern tour, Guy's enthusiasm for folk music was undiminished, and he remained equally dedicated to the cause of working people of all races. But the effect of his "southern pilgrimage" included a sobering aspect that had not to the same degree troubled others who either had preceded or would succeed him on this road—Pete Seeger, Fred Ramsey, Harold Courlander, John Cohen, Ralph Rinzler. Guy saw the tragic contradiction between traditional white southern music, its spirit of pride and independence, and the racial attitudes of many of its practitioners. The struggles of poor whites and poor blacks often paralleled each other, but this only too rarely had translated into cooperative political engagement. Instead, the commonality of their political interests was obscured by a centuries-old racial caste system and its accompanying etiquette of avoidance, mistrust, deference, and humiliation. The music of southern blacks and whites often expressed their best impulses and highest aspirations—but not always. The meanings imputed to folk songs were often ambiguous, often left to be determined by the context of a given performance. Sometimes the folk music of southern whites was unambivalently mean-spirited and reactionary.

The political climate in New York upon his return could hardly have been worse. On 19 June, just before heading south, he had been in Union Square when news came through of the execution of the Rosenbergs at Sing Sing, perhaps the Old Left's grimmest moment. The blacklisting of the Weavers had caused them to disband that spring, and Seeger turned from more commercial audiences to performances for left-wing gatherings, summer camps, college campuses, and public school assemblies.[24] Carawan was not himself immediately affected by the witch hunting. He was able to perform occasionally in New York, sometimes with the Jewish Young Folksingers with whom he had taken up again upon his return, or, with increasing frequency, as a solo act. While his reputation grew, it was still necessary to work day jobs. And when he could, he continued to travel. On one trip back to Los Angeles he finally met Zilphia Horton, at a leftist social gathering. He saw her again on a second trip to Highlander in 1956, the year she died of an apparently accidental poisoning. She had become in many respects his mentor, and the idea of combining folk music and political activism was deeply appealing. But how to do it? There was the matter of earning a living, and even the most dedicated folk audiences would probably not be receptive to a steady diet of political songs. And then what would be his cause? Who was he to inspire?

Some additional direction was provided in 1957 when Carawan grabbed the opportunity to attend the World Youth Festival in Moscow. Along the way he spent time with Alan Lomax in London, who was still sitting out the anticommunist hysteria in England in the company of his friend and field assistant Shirley Collins, the fine traditional British singer. Altogether his experiences in Europe that year provided him with an international perspective on the struggle for human dignity among working people. He returned to the States later in the year with a broadened musical repertoire, several dozen slide photographs he had taken in the People's Republic of China, and a renewed sense of the importance of cultural work.

Paul Endicott, a Detroit-based folk music promoter who had managed Pete Seeger for a short time after the breakup of the Weavers, had agreed to represent Carawan before he left for the Soviet Union. He soon had Guy on the road, presenting a multimedia lecture/performance that included both music and a show of slides from his recent travels. Carawan's reputation was sufficiently established by 1958 that Endicott was able to arrange to have Guy record an album for Folkways. Asch and Carawan had met each other as early as 1953, during Guy's first visit to New York. There was no particular meeting of minds—the combination of Carawan's extreme humility and Asch's unself-conscious egotism did not make communication easy. Early encounters were cordial but businesslike. Carawan decided that he needed the support of another instrumentalist on the session and arranged for guitarist John Cohen—who had not yet recorded the first New Lost City Ramblers album for Folkways—to join him. That first album, *Songs with Guy Carawan*, recorded by Mel Kaiser at Cue Studios that spring, was sufficiently successful that Asch agreed to sign an exclusive contract with Carawan that called minimally for six albums from Guy between the start of 1959 and the end of 1961. Two more Guy Carawan albums were recorded at Cue in 1959, *Guy Carawan Sings Something Old, New, Borrowed and Blue*, and *This Little Light of Mine*. The material on these albums was terrifically eclectic—Woody Guthrie songs were well represented, as were traditional African American blues and ballads. But they were the last albums Carawan made for Folkways as a solo artist.

Before Carawan could proceed with his career as a folk singer, Highlander intruded yet again. In May 1959 Carawan arrived at Highlander for a stay that he expected would last through the summer. Once again, he felt that this was the place that held the best hope for the kind of cultural work that he had been envisioning. With Zilphia Horton's death, music at Highlander had largely disappeared, and Carawan saw a ready-made niche for himself. In late June he wrote Asch: "I'm sold on this place completely. There is such a great potential here for developing a program around folk music and to make the integration movement in the South into a singing movement. . . . I'm going to spend all of my time between concert tours here at Highlander and in the South." He added that he hoped Folkways might consider releasing some albums of integration songs, and saw the possibility of distributing them through organizations such as Highlander, NAACP and CORE.[25]

Carawan was busy one week out of the month at Highlander, when various labor and civil rights activists came to the facility to receive training in the philosophy and tactics of nonviolent direct action. Highlander was also working on the first citizenship school, under the direction of Septima Clark, which would teach literacy and political activism within targeted rural communities. The first beneficiary of the program was the black community on Johns Island, one of the remote South Carolina Sea Islands, and Guy planned to assist in the effort there later in the year. He implored Asch in his letters to send him a portable tape recorder "like Tony Schwartz uses" so that he could record songs, folk tales, and rituals on Johns.

Since the Civil War, when northern abolitionists traveled to the Sea Islands around Beaufort to assist emancipated slaves in their transition to citizenship, the remote coastal islands had been regarded as an ideal laboratory for the study of African American culture. Particularly in recent decades, the relative isolation of the islands had suggested to social scientists that there was probably no better setting in which to study African retentions in the culture of black Americans. The Gullah and Geechee speech of the Sea Islands had long been regarded as the most African-influenced of black English dialects in North America, and researchers had identified African origins in Sea Island kinship patterns, songs, and basketry. But Carawan was less interested in the scholarly debates over the origins of Sea Island culture than he was in its reported richness.

Carawan continued to write to Asch, describing his activities at Highlander and around the South. With one letter he enclosed a song sheet he had used at a recent NAACP meeting in Charleston. The NAACP had prepared its own song sheet, he explained in his letter to Asch, but it consisted of "very uninspirational stuff—parodies and limericks to songs like Sweet Adeline, Old Mill Stream, etc. There were no songs of negro background." Carawan's own song sheet included folk songs from white folk music traditions that would not have particular currency in the civil rights movement: "If We Could Consider Each Other," "Passing Through," "This Land Is Your Land." Other "white" folk songs—notably Seeger and Hays's "The Hammer Song"—would fare better. But Guy's list also included several songs of African American origin that would become staples of the movement: "Keep Your Hand on the Plow," "We Shall Not Be Moved," "Oh Freedom," and, of course, "We Shall Overcome." "The singing really filled a need there," he wrote. "The group was very enthusiastic. Me too."

True to form, Asch did not respond to Carawan's several long letters. A note finally arrived from Marian Distler in mid-July. She mentions neither a tape recorder nor the problems Guy had encountered in trying to get Folkways to send copies of his album ahead to places where he was performing. Instead, Distler passed along Asch's criticism of Guy for having used a small *n* and *j* in writing of *Negroes* and *Jews* in his letters: "I believe that you must give dignity and understanding to ALL people. The small 'n' is the Southern approach of minimizing peoples."[26] Carawan was thoroughly irritated by Asch and Distler's self-righteous scolding but was prevented from responding by a raid at Highlander at the end of the month. A group of civil rights leaders had been attending a Highlander workshop when the local police showed up intent on finding evidence of alcohol sales—not a trivial offense, as the county was dry. The police burst in on the showing of a movie and held the fifty conference participants in the dark for a couple hours while the compound was searched. The result was the confiscation of a small amount of whiskey found in Myles Horton's residence (he was away during the raid) and the arrest of Septima Clark, Guy Carawan, and a few others.

Carawan wrote a letter to Asch, Seeger, Silber, and the others at Folkways and *Sing Out!* from jail, requesting that they raise $250 for bail and explaining that the raid had been a frame-up intended to put Highlander out of business. In fact, the Highlander facility at Monteagle remained padlocked much of the next two years and was eventually auctioned off by the state of Tennessee in late 1961. Guy also took the opportunity to complain to Asch about his recent criticism and general lack of responsiveness.

When Guy's letter arrived Paul Endicott happened to be in the Folkways offices, so it was a simple matter to arrange for the bail. But for some reason Guy's letter hit a nerve with Asch, who fired off an angry response. On the face of it he had found fault with Carawan for having referred to songs as "Negro" or "white": "Please in your letters to me do *not* refer to songs as Negro or white but as peoples songs or American songs. Do not use the term segregation when you mention music or dance or song." It was a remarkable criticism, coming from a man who had by then released several volumes of *Negro Folk Music of Alabama* as well as anthologies of Negro poetry. It is difficult to imagine that, in a calm moment, Asch would not have been willing to credit African American culture with its particular contribution to the field of American music, dance, or song. Something else had gotten under his skin, most likely Carawan's inadvertent claim to a martyrdom that Asch would have wished to declare as his own. Asch had never learned to accept criticism graciously and almost always responded, as he did this time, by going on the offensive:

> As to your experiences you should thank the Lord for having
> had them because, perhaps now when you sing one of these

songs they will not mean to you Negro songs or white songs
but songs of protest, confidence and experience. The problem
with you is that you seem to indicate that its only you in relation to the songs. For your information people like me and
I'm sure many many others have had the same experiences
at a very early date and these experiences helped to shape
their lives.

He went on for two pages about the hardships he had encountered in his life—the Cossack raids on his grandparents' apartment
in Warsaw, the "basket cases" he saw from the train during the First
World War, the wretched conditions of the fruit pickers in Kingston,
New York, the rape of a German girl by Senegalese troops that he
witnessed in the twenties, the day he spent in a Brooklyn jail for
refusing to pay a speeding ticket. By the end he had even thrown
in Basha Spiro's ostensible banishment to Siberia. "I hope that this
letter is not in vain," he wrote in a postscript. "I often wonder."[27]

Carawan's reply reflected both his bafflement at Asch's outburst
as well as a good deal of hurt. He defended himself by insisting that
he had "never put on a false front of being something other than
what I am" and had never claimed to have a privileged relation to the
material he performed: "I know that what I'm going through here is
a drop in the bucket compared to what many people have gone
through. I'm still relatively wet behind the ears and have a lot of
living to do. I'm aware of it. But I don't appreciate your rubbing it in,
even if you have been through the mill." Asch's insistence on ob-
scuring the ethnic source of a song, and on avoiding any mention of
segregation in folk music, made no sense to Carawan. Although
noting the frequent interethnic influences of a song, it still seemed
to him that there was merit in crediting the tradition from which a
particular version had derived. To do so did not, in his view, contribute to segregation. At the same time, it was naïve to ignore the fact
that most folk music was, in fact, highly segregated: "Segregation
does influence song, dance & music and I don't see why you don't
think I should mention it. But I'm willing to listen if you've time to
elaborate." Carawan concluded with the hope that they might communicate better in the future: "We have a lot of interests and goals in
common and it is important for us to understand one another if we
are going to work together." He thanked Asch for helping post bail
and hoped that he had not irritated him further.[28]

Songwriter Ernie Marrs had come down to Highlander from
Atlanta around the time that Carawan was drafting his reply to

Asch, and Carawan showed him Asch's letter as well as his response. Marrs took it on himself to facilitate a reconciliation between the two by assuring Asch that Carawan was sincere and dedicated, and that his work in the South was well received:

> He's trying his level best to learn all he can from these folks here—and to help in any way that he possibly can. They have sensed this, taken him as one of themselves, as nearly as possible. . . . I guess you know something of what my feeling for Pete is—I'm glad that Guy is also part of the Folkways family. . . . And any pointers that you may be able to give him would not, in my opinion, be in vain. He has a lot to learn—we all do—but I don't think he'll let you down.

Marrs had, perhaps, conceded a bit too much to Asch. Carawan had, after all, seen a good deal more of American folk music in its native habitat than Asch ever would. But Asch surely was a force to be reckoned with in American folk music and it would not do for Carawan to alienate him.

What Carawan and Marrs may not have known was that although Asch's temper was ferocious, it burned out quickly. Releasing it seemed to provide him with a kind of catharsis, after which he rarely bore a grudge. Carawan's letters to him were restrained and formal in the weeks following their tumultuous exchange, but business continued to be conducted in the fashion that Asch had come to regard as "normal."

As planned, Carawan spent the winter of 1959–60 on Johns Island, arriving on Christmas Eve and remaining until the college workshop necessitated his return to Highlander around Easter. His involvement with the literacy and citizenship school was largely limited to functioning as Septima Clark's chauffeur, as she did not have a car and could not drive, and to occasionally teaching folk songs to the students. A good deal more of his time was spent in acquainting himself with the social life of the island's black community, particularly its religious observances, which centered around the praise house called Moving Star Hall. His first night on Johns was spent at the praise house, attending the "Christmas Watch" service that began at midnight and continued until daybreak. He was altogether entranced by the singing, testimony, praying, preaching, moaning, dancing, and clapping that he heard and saw that night—it was a thoroughly collective endeavor in which shifts of mood and tempo seemed to be intuited.

The islanders had had little to do with whites up to then and for the most part regarded them with suspicion and some fear. But Carawan was gradually able to win their trust and acceptance, largely thanks to Esau Jenkins, with whom he was staying. Jenkins had founded the school on Johns Island with Septima Clark in 1957, and as a lifelong island resident his assurances bought Carawan a great deal of good will. For his part Carawan found on Johns a treasure of odd, haunting melodies, lyrics, and games whose African pedigree appeared to shine through the centuries of Europeanization. Already there were signs that the old worship style, characterized by the repetitive singing and sideways shuffling of the "shout," were falling out of favor among the island's younger citizens. It would be Carawan's self-appointed task over the next few years to preserve much of the island's folklore as best he could, through tapes of conversations, of song performances, of folk tales, and of church services. He saw it as a rear-guard action against the acculturating ravages of modern life. Some on the island—particularly the families of Esau Jenkins and Janie Hunter—understood his project and recognized its intrinsic value. Yet others regarded the inheritance of slavery as a reminder of a bitter and shameful history and would rather have allowed it to fade away.[29]

The return to Highlander in April required a substantial shift of gears, but Carawan plunged back into the "cultural work" with a new sense of the importance of grounding this work in the traditions of black Americans. The energy that weekend was nearly overwhelming; the enthusiasm of the many singers was matched by the intellectual acumen of the students, including Nashville sit-in leaders Diane Nash and Marion Barry. Another student from Nashville there was Candie Anderson, a white woman who was attending Fisk as an exchange student from Pomona College in California. She had come from a politically progressive family of Unitarians; her father was a professor of geology at Harvey Mudd.

In the middle of the month many of the students who had met at Highlander found themselves together again in Raleigh, North Carolina, for the first organizational meeting of what became the Student Non-Violent Coordination Committee (SNCC). It had been called by Ella Baker, the embattled executive director of SCLC, who believed that the students should be allowed to make their own decisions and thus would require a significant degree of independence from the adult, clergy-dominated organizations. Perhaps, had he wished to push the matter, Reverend King could have seen to it that the student movement became an arm of SCLC. But he chose not to, and SNCC was born with Marion Barry as its first chairman.[30] Carawan was there as well, and he used the occasion to bring his growing repertoire of freedom songs to an audience of two hundred student leaders. Some of those who had been with him at Highlander earlier in the month joined him in teaching "We Shall Overcome" to the others, and consequently Raleigh became the next critical moment in the dissemination of the movement's anthem.[31]

When Carawan joined the students in Nashville the next week, he found a highly organized movement in full swing. The arrests that had started late in February were swelling the jails; at the first trial on Monday, 29 April, Diane Nash announced that she would serve time rather than pay the fines that would have, in her view, lent legitimacy to the entire ridiculous proceeding. It was a gesture consistent with the Ghandian principles of nonviolent direct action, which she, John Lewis, and others had learned from James Lawson. Nash, Lewis, and fourteen others declared their intention to serve jail sentences, and they were soon joined by sixty others who changed their minds about paying the fines. Here in the jails Nashville's singing movement took form. Several rhythm and blues–based songs took shape, reflecting the prevailing musical interests of the college students. When it was her turn to contribute a song, Candie Anderson reached into her leftist roots and produced an old IWW song, "They Go Wild Over Me," to which she added new words.[32]

The situation in Nashville came to a sudden head on the evening of 19 April. A bomb destroyed the front portion of the home of Z. Alexander Looby, a black attorney who had been defending the student demonstrators and the only black member of the Nashville City Council. Neither Looby nor his wife were seriously injured, despite the fact that the blast was powerful enough to break 147 windows of the Meharry Medical School across the street. The following morning three thousand marchers, many of them white, wove a ten-mile path through the city of Nashville to the city hall, where they were met by mayor Ben West. Pressed by Diane Nash, West agreed that the desegregation of Nashville's lunch counters was desirable. The crowd was jubilant and drowned out West's effort to equivocate. The following evening Reverend King was scheduled to speak at a Fisk University gymnasium, but a bomb threat forced the postponement of the event for hours. Most of the interracial crowd remained outside while the police searched the gym, and when the meeting finally resumed they heard King

deliver a rousing endorsement of Lawson's troops and their tactics. And they heard Guy Carawan perform "We Shall Overcome"
in its reworked version for the first time in Nashville. Early the
following month six lunch counters as well as four movie theaters
agreed to seat their clientele without regard to race.[33]

Carawan spent a total of about two months in Nashville. Toward
the end of his stay, he conceived of the idea of creating a record
album that would capture some of the music of the Nashville sit-ins
by placing the songs in the context of those history-making events
through dramatic recreations. Most of the major figures in Nashville's sit-in movement agreed to participate—Reverend C. T. Vivian,
the vice president of the Nashville Christian Leadership Council,
John Lewis, Diane Nash, Marion Barry, James Bevel, Bernard Lafayette, and Candie Anderson. Several of the movement leaders
were assigned the task of writing scripts for the various scenes: "the
lunch counter incident," "jail sequence," "court room scene," "scene
on Mayor's steps." The group rehearsed a couple of times and then
convened in a Nashville recording studio. Much of what transpired
there was ad libbed, and although the spoken portions were somewhat stilted, they captured some of the immediacy of the events as
experienced by those who had lived through them a short time
earlier. The singing was much more effective. The Nashville Quartet
performed the songs they had developed in the three months of
the sit-ins—"You Better Leave Segregation Alone," "Moving On,"
"Your Dog Loves My Dog"—and Candie Anderson performed her
Wobblies parody. The album opened with a moving rendition of "We
Shall Overcome," listed on the album as "an old spiritual with new
words—the theme song of the Nashville sit-ins." In the summer
Guy took the tape to New York and spent a day with Mel Kaiser at
Cue, who spliced in crowd noise and did his best to fashion an
orderly whole from the various pieces. Asch released the album late
that summer. The Nashville Sit-in Story (5590) was the first commercially
available documentary recording of the civil rights movement. Over
the next couple of years, Carawan bought dozens of copies of the
album from Asch and then sold them at concerts and civil rights
gatherings, where interest in the documentary inevitably ran high.
Despite the tensions between SCLC and SNCC, Carawan managed
to stay loyal to both and was called upon to lead singing when either
organization met. He found that the sit-in record, as well as other
Folkways recordings, such as Langston Hughes's The Glory of Negro
History (7752), were terrific educational tools for use with Septima
Clark's citizenship and literacy schools.[34] There were the usual

problems in seeing that Folkways sent copies to the right place at the appropriate time. Carawan had insisted on retaining the copyright to the record rather than turning it over to Folkways, and Asch grumbled in a letter to him that summer that doing so "necessarily limits the dissemination of the material from all viewpoints."[35] Later, in September, Carawan had an angry telephone conversation with Marian Distler over albums that had never arrived and had hung up on her. Distler, who seemed to bear Asch's grudges longer than he did himself, complained about it in a letter to Pete Seeger—with a copy to Carawan—claiming that Carawan seemed to want to enrich himself from sales of the album: "If Guy thought we issued it so he could make money on it he is sadly mistaken in the purposes of our issue." She felt that Guy's distribution plan for the album relied too heavily on Highlander and ignored other outlets.[36]

Carawan responded in a long and detailed letter to Asch and Distler in early November. He would be in New York in the middle of the month and wanted to straighten out all of the outstanding financial matters. He had several ideas for resolving the problems of distributing the sit-in recording and specifically instructed them to send one hundred copies to Reverend C. T. Vivian in Nashville. Negro college bookstores, Baptist churches, and Negro newspapers could all serve as outlets for the record. Folkways remained an esoteric, northern, liberal outfit largely unknown and undistributed in the South, Carawan declared. The higher price of Folkways albums compared with other labels was an additional handicap, and the steep discount Asch offered his artists when purchasing their own albums was not extended to organizations such as SCLC and SNCC. Guy also by now felt quite dissatisfied with his first three solo albums, and he expressed the hope that he might have an opportunity to record a fourth that would reflect the work in which he was currently engaged. Another item was minor but irritating—Guy had deposited some commercial recordings of Russian and Chinese vocal music that he had acquired while overseas in 1958 with Asch and hoped now to retrieve them, but Asch continued to insist on his intention to release them (which he would, in 1980). Finally, however, it was Distler's accusation of greed that Carawan most wanted to address. He had sold all the copies of the sit-in album at cost, or very close to it, and was still out two hundred dollars in expenses from the making of the record (not to mention his own time and labor):

> So your statement was untrue and pretty thoughtless. I can understand why you were mad at me for hanging up in a

storm. I apologize for my impoliteness. But still I had reason
to be mad. . . . I realize that you'll have a lot to tell me about
what I do that's wrong in working with you. Well, please
do—and where it's justified I'll try to change my ways.[37]

It continued to mystify Carawan that his motives were so misunderstood. Most of the problems he was encountering with Folkways were a function of the hand-to-mouth way in which Asch
and Distler conducted business. But the very personal anger he
encountered first from Asch and then from Distler seemed to
expose the contradiction between their political dedication and
the apparent necessities of a business on the margins of the
recording industry.

Candie Anderson returned to Pomona that autumn to complete
her senior year. She and Guy had formed a romantic attachment
during the months of the Nashville movement, and he followed
her out to California. In the winter Carawan fulfilled a promise to
spend a second winter on Johns Island, but they continued to visit
each other whenever possible throughout the year. Guy had by
then divorced his first wife, and when Candie graduated college,
they were married. Candie immediately fulfilled a critical organizational role in Guy's work, and most of what they produced in the
succeeding years was collaborative.

In the middle of Carawan's second winter on Johns Island, he
arranged a benefit concert at Carnegie Hall in collaboration with
Highlander in order to celebrate the first anniversary of the sit-ins.
The members of the Montgomery Gospel Trio and the Nashville
Quartet would travel to New York for the first time in their lives,
where they would share a bill with bluesmen Memphis Slim and
Willie Dixon as well as Carawan himself and the Reverend Fred
Shuttlesworth from Birmingham. The odd pairing of the overtly
political and the apolitical, the sacred and the thoroughly secular
might have reminded some of Hammond's From Spirituals to
Swing concert in the same hall twenty-two years earlier. It raised
the same kinds of questions about the relationship between entertainment and cultural work, between musical "escape" and musical messages. The concert was scheduled for 10 February, and
Carawan wrote to Asch the week before suggesting that he might
want to record it.[38] Asch rarely recorded at remote locations any
longer, and he made no exceptions for this performance. But the
morning before the two groups were scheduled to leave for the
South, Asch phoned Carawan and asked him to bring them

around to the studio. The sterile confines of Cue Studios did not elicit the most energetic performances from the singers; without an audience the music sounded flat, if technically proficient. Robert Shelton wrote in a *New York Times* article on the freedom songs the following year that "this use of folk music has to be heard in context to be fully understood. Recordings and Northern 'concerts' tend to make freedom songs seem like stale tub-thumping and sloganeering."[39] Still, when *We Shall Overcome: Songs of the "Freedom Riders" and the "Sit-Ins"* (5591) was released on Folkways the following year, it stood almost alone as a testament to a growing body of movement music and the leadership that was disseminating it.

Ironically, despite the album's subtitle, the freedom rides did not begin for almost three months, following the Carnegie Hall concert. James Farmer's CORE had decided to test the legality of segregated facilities on interstate bus routes, for which the federal government's Interstate Commerce Commission (ICC) had jurisdiction. The plan was to assemble an integrated team of freedom riders who would travel by bus from Washington to New Orleans, integrating the seating on the buses, in the public washrooms, and in bus terminal restaurants. The CORE contingent first encountered violence at the Alabama state line; half a dozen white thugs entered the bus, knocked one freedom rider unconscious, and kicked the head of a sixty-year-old white academician until he suffered a cerebral hemorrhage that left him wheelchair-bound for the remainder of his life. Bloody violence flared again at the bus terminal in Birmingham. A second bus carrying freedom riders was stopped by a crowd of more than two hundred in Anniston, Alabama, where the passengers were forced from the bus by a firebomb that reduced it to a charred shell. Refused access to a bus the next day in Birmingham, the remaining CORE freedom riders decided to conclude their journey by airplane to New Orleans.

It was at the insistence of Nashville SNCC leader Diane Nash that the freedom rides continued. The students, primarily veterans of the Nashville sit-ins, jumped into the breach and did their best to continue on from Birmingham. Driven once to the Tennessee state line by Chief of Police Bull Connor and his deputies, they returned again to the Birmingham bus station to confront the worst violence of the freedom rides. Guy and Candie Carawan learned from California that several of their Nashville comrades and friends had sustained serious injury, and they knew it was time to travel east again to rejoin the fight.

Some days later, reinforced once again, the freedom riders continued to Jackson, Mississippi, where upon using the white rest rooms and waiting areas they were summarily arrested for "breach of peace, refusal to obey an officer."[40] All twenty-seven riders were found guilty of the charges and fined two hundred dollars or two months in jail; following the growing consensus of the student leadership, they all opted for the latter. Through the summer freedom riders continued to descend on the Deep South. Despite the efforts of attorney general Robert Kennedy, the violence continued and southern jails and prisons began to fill. Many protesters were transferred from the relatively benign city jail to notorious Parchman Farm, where for decades black inmates were reduced to a condition that was essentially indistinguishable from slavery.[41] And in the jails and prisons, the next wave of freedom songs took shape. Among the most enduring was James Farmer's reworking of a song by Florence Reece that came out of "Bloody Harlan" (Kentucky) in 1932, "Which Side Are You On?"[42] Robert Kennedy's announcement in late May that he had asked the ICC to ban segregation in all interstate transportation facilities took much of the steam out of the freedom riders, and King's SCLC effectively withdrew from the effort. But CORE, whose project it had been from the start, continued to call attention to the hundreds of riders who were doing time that summer—three hundred in Parchman Farm alone.[43] Thus it was fitting that CORE produced the first commercial recording of genuine freedom rider songs. Crediting neither singers nor producers, *Sit-in Songs: Songs of the Freedom Riders* (Dauntless 4601) was far closer musically to the gospel choir sound of southern churches than either of the two Folkways albums that had appeared. Although it was, like the Folkways releases, a studio production, it was helped along substantially by very able gospel-style piano and organ accompaniment.

Immediately in the wake of the freedom rides Albany, Georgia, emerged as the next prominent arena in the civil rights drama. Albany has been identified as a watershed in the development of freedom songs. "Albany was the first singing movement," wrote Josh Dunson. "Every song that entered Albany was changed in the process, for here the whole community sang—a community dominantly influenced by the older church traditions."[44] This description could very well have fit several hundred Deep South communities in the early 1960s, and certainly the Montgomery bus boycott, the Nashville sit-ins, and the freedom rides could all have been described as "singing movements." But Bernice Johnson (later Reagon), then a student at predominantly black Albany State College, has insisted that there was something unique about Albany: "Southwest Georgia represented inland Black American cultural traditions at its best. Especially in religious culture, the Black churches in and around Albany preserved and carried out statements of Black American traditional music of the highest quality."[45] SNCC's first field secretary, Charles Sherrod, and SNCC staffer Cordell Reagon came to Albany in October 1961 to confront the city's vicious reputation as the center of southwestern Georgia's feudal sharecropping empire. Their program was broader and more deliberate than those previously undertaken. The centerpiece of their effort was to be a voter registration drive; here, as throughout the South, blacks had been prevented from voting for decades through poll taxes, literacy tests, white-only Democratic primaries, and the ever-present threat of violence. Additionally there would be attempts to integrate public transportation facilities, parks, libraries, schools, and lunch counters, as well as to address job discrimination in city, county, and federal employment. Though sympathetic, the city's adult black establishment was too fearful of reprisal to lend much of a hand to the SNCC organizers; moreover, members of the local NAACP chapter were frequently resentful of the SNCC interlopers, from whom they expected a degree of deference. Instead Sherrod and Reagon approached the students of Albany State College, who became their army of protesters, canvassers, and *singers*. Once the students had demonstrated their determination, they were joined by their elders in a coalition that became the Albany movement.[46]

SNCC had a formidable foe in Albany chief of police Laurie Pritchett. Pritchett understood that violence, in the end, served the protesters very well, providing them with media coverage and the consequent sympathy of the nation. Pritchett's strategy was to see that violence was minimized, and he did this in part by arresting protesters by the hundreds, filling the jail in Albany and those in all of the surrounding counties. By mid-December 737 had been arrested, and there were additional mass arrests the following summer. Without beatings and bombings on the evening news, there was little pressure on the federal government to intervene, and by and large it did not. Consequently the gains of the Albany movement were slow in coming. The train and bus stations were integrated in a matter of months, but this had been dictated by federal regulations. A boycott of the city bus line had led to its being shut down, but not integrated. Martin Luther King was ultimately critical of the Albany movement for having attended too much to the political process without attending sufficiently to the economic dimensions of the problem: if white business interests had been sufficiently affected, the white politicians would have capitulated.

By August the Albany movement appeared to have lost steam, and the attention of the press and public turned elsewhere; many concluded that the movement had ended in failure. Pritchett's strategy had indeed succeeded in eliminating violent confrontations. SCLC was disappointed because they had failed to touch the hearts and minds of Albany's white leadership despite frequent appeals to their sense of justice. The hard lesson of Albany was that southern whites would give up racist privileges only when forced to do so by legal pressure, not by having their consciences pricked. But in point of fact, integrationist initiatives continued in Albany through 1963 and 1964. The groundwork for changes that would occur in succeeding years had been established, and if tangible results were few, there was nonetheless palpable growth in the black community's self-esteem, in its ability to respond collectively to intolerable circumstances, and in its recognition of the need for change.[47]

Guy and Candie Carawan were in Albany intermittently. There was much less need now for outside musical support for the movement. Pete Seeger's effort to move a church full of movement supporters there had resulted in awkward embarrassment.[48] Cordell Reagon and Charles Sherrod were both strong song leaders, and they had hit a responsive chord with broad segments of the black community. Highlander's contribution to the music was becoming inseparable from those of the Nashville sit-ins and the Mississippi freedom rides, and all of the freedom songs were quickly becoming the common property of the entire movement. The importance of Guy Carawan's particular contribution was quickly being obscured, a development that troubled him not at all. At the same time the Carawans were anxious to see that the history of the freedom songs was not lost, and to that end they were becoming its careful chroniclers. Guy set up his ubiquitous Ampex tape recorder at church meetings in order to capture the sound of congregational singing and ministerial preaching.

When there was a moment to reflect back upon the history-making events of the preceding months, the Carawans asked movement leaders to set down their recollections of the events on tape. Charles Sherrod's account of the Albany movement was particularly thoughtful and rich in detail. With several hours of unedited interviews as well as the church recordings, Guy was again left with the problem of how to distill his material into a manageable documentary. His experience with the Nashville album had not convinced him that his talents lay in this area. This time Alan Lomax came to the rescue. It has been suggested that Lomax "had no patience" with the demonstrations of the civil rights era, but if this was so, it was a choice that pertained only to his own participation.[49] As for the tactics of the students demonstrators, he was all for it. "While I was squirreling round in the past," he wrote Carawan in April 1960, "you were busy with the present, and how I envy you. It must be wonderful to be with those kids who are so courageously changing the South forever."[50] Lomax put to use the skills he had acquired as a radio show producer in the 1940s and using the facilities of Maynard Solomon's Vanguard recording studio created a dramatic and seamless blend of narration, preaching, and choral and individual singing.

Questions arose about the marketing of *Freedom in the Air: A Documentary of Albany, Georgia.* Asch expressed an interest in releasing it on Folkways even before Lomax was involved: "I think . . . [this] is the type of material I have been asking for." But SNCC, for whom Carawan was making the record, did not want it on Folkways. Carawan wrote Asch to apologize for this turn of events, but Asch was rarely bothered when Folkways artists used other outlets and responded by saying that he did not blame them, and that he would buy copies of the record from SNCC in order to help with its distribution.

Bernice Johnson, along with thirty-nine other students from Albany State College, was expelled by the dean for her participation in the Albany demonstrations. It may have been the most auspicious moment in her young life. She lent her powerful voice and personality to the movement without restraint and was soon a major figure in the Albany movement. Having been reared in Albany, she was immersed in the liturgical musical traditions that were being appropriated for the movement. The strength of the Baptist traditions in Albany meant that those movement songs based on secular musical traditions were proscribed in church meetings, and religious musical traditions consequently played all the more central a role. Bernice Johnson Reagon later reported having transformed the traditional hymn "Over My Head" ("I hear music in the air" or "I see trouble in the air") into the movement standard "Freedom in the Air" as if it were divinely inspired, requiring no effort on her behalf at all.[51]

Pete Seeger was particularly taken by Johnson's big voice and presence; he met her in the autumn of 1962 at a SNCC benefit concert in Atlanta for which they were both performing. Johnson had transferred to Spelman College, but between Seeger's encouragement and the contagion of the movement, her academic career was soon on hold again. In Albany she joined an a cappella quintet—consisting of her future husband Cordell Reagon, Chuck Neblett, Rutha Harris, and Bertha Gober—that became the first version of SNCC's Freedom Singers, and she promptly recruited Toshi Seeger to manage and book them through a grueling tour that winter and spring. Toshi capitalized on the many contacts she had made for Pete, primarily on college campuses. The Freedom Singers became an important way for SNCC to raise money and disseminate news of the movement.

The music of the Freedom Singers, which included substantial elements of rhythm and blues as well as modern gospel music, was too eclectic to be called simply "folk music." But in part because of the company the group kept—Bernice especially was a frequent guest of the Seegers in Beacon—they were regarded as folk musicians and attracted folk music audiences. Pete arranged for Bernice to record an album for Asch at Cue Studios; the title reflected Asch's current state of mind by identifying her musical tradition regionally rather than ethnically: *Folk Music: The South* (2457).

The first record album of the civil rights era that was a genuine commercial success belonged to Pete Seeger. Seeger had Harold Leventhal arrange a concert at Carnegie Hall that would be taped and released as a live album on Columbia. Entitled *We Shall Overcome,* it included many of the traditionally based songs that were acquiring anthem status in the movement as well as songs by several contemporary song writers. Bob Dylan's "Who Killed Davey Moore," about the death of a boxer, seemed only peripherally related to the theme of civil rights, and Malvina Reynolds's satire of middle-class conformity, "Little Boxes," was still less relevant. But the album succeeded in bringing movement song to a still broader audience.

By the time the Freedom Singers succeeded in attracting the attention of a major record label, Bernice and Cordell Reagon had left and there was a whole new lineup. Mercury Records released a concert recording of the new group entitled *Freedom Now,* featuring the topical songs of Matt Jones—"Demonstrating G.I.," "Oginga Odinga," and "The Prophesy of a SNCC Field Secretary." It was rather slicker than any of the other civil rights music that had found its way to vinyl, and with the support of a major label it reached a far broader audience.

In April and May 1963 the police of Birmingham, Alabama, were using dogs to repel demonstrators while the fire company was training its hoses on school children. The tactics of Public Commissioner Bull Connor created a riveting drama for television viewers throughout the country. When the Carawans arrived the first weekend in May, the tension in the city had become extreme. Martin Luther King had been released two weeks earlier from the Birmingham jail after a stay of almost nine days. That Saturday afternoon SCLC planned a string of "surprise" demonstrations by young people throughout the city, with the intention of filling the jails with the city's black children. Connor retaliated by blocking the exits to the churches where the demonstrators had gathered and mowed down the few who escaped with the fire department's water guns. Adults unschooled in nonviolent tactics watched the entrapment of the children from across the street in Kelly Ingram Park. SCLC leader James Bevel, fearful that rock-wielding adults would spark a riot, called off demonstrations for the following day. With Martin Luther King back in Atlanta to preach at his own Ebenezer Baptist Church, Sunday would be a day of cooling off in preparation for renewed demonstrations on Monday.

With some kind of explosion apparently inevitable, Birmingham swelled on Sunday with reporters, activists, and celebrities. Among the latter was Joan Baez, whose manager, Manny Greenhill, had enlisted the Carawans' help in having her make contact with the local movement. Her destination in Birmingham was Miles College. She was fascinated by and lured to the civil rights movement but was unnerved by both the helmeted police patrolling the streets and the palpable racial tension. At the Gaston Motel she encountered the Carawans, who offered to accompany her to the morning worship service. There and at the afternoon mass meeting at the New Pilgrim Church she was transported by the choir's blues-inflected gospel music. Full of the inspiration of the movement and the music, Baez—hidden under a blanket on the floor of

a taxi's back seat—proceeded to an uneventful concert for a surprisingly apolitical audience at Miles College.[52]

The Carawans were less lucky. Andrew Young interrupted the
mass meeting that afternoon to announce that Guy and Candie
Carawan—"the ones who taught us many of the songs that we sing
in the movement"—had been arrested on the steps of the church
for the crime of having attempting to enter a black church.[53] With
their infant son at a babysitter's house, the Carawans spent two
anxious days in jail. They were released in time for the next mass
meetings on Monday evening. Despite Bevel's directive, a spontaneous demonstration the previous afternoon had led to a nearly
calamitous confrontation with Connor and the fire hoses. But the
firemen ignored Connor's command to fire the water guns on the
demonstrators, who proceeded instead to a segregated park
where they prayed, and their restraint was interpreted by marchers and reporters alike as a great moral victory for the movement.
Thus the meeting on the following evening found Birmingham's
black community in a jubilant mood. The meeting spilled over into
a second church, a third, and finally a fourth. The preachers
pushed their way into each of the four churches and took turns
exhorting the throngs. Guy Carawan, carting around his ungainly
Ampex, positioned himself beside Martin Luther King, Ralph Aber-
nathy, Wyatt T. Walker, and others as each spoke. Though embarrassed at having to be so pushy, he knew that this was a moment
that demanded documentation. The result was a snapshot of the
civil rights movement on one of its most jubilant and hopeful
occasions.

Bob Dylan was also anxious to see the struggle for himself
firsthand, but Pete Seeger brought him to Greenwood, Mississippi,
in July rather than Birmingham, where a quieter—if no less vicious—drama had been playing itself out during the preceding
months. Dylan played "Blowin' in the Wind" as well as "Only a Pawn
in Their Game," a composition in which he expressed some sympathy for poor white racists who, in Dylan's view, were manipulated by more powerful political forces. Bernice Reagon recalled
that the SNCC workers took some interest in his lyrics, but "didn't
have much of an affinity with his singing."[54] The following month
he would sing "Only a Pawn" for a crowd of several hundred
thousand at the March on Washington. Dylan's sudden departure
from politically inflected music in 1965 made some wonder
whether his brief foray into civil rights music had been a cynical
manipulation of the movement for his own purposes. But that is

too severe a judgment: Dylan remained a man of strong convictions for years afterward, exploring many other political terrains as well.

Greenwood is a small town in the heart of the rural, sharecropping Mississippi River delta. The movement's agenda in more urban areas, where blacks and whites lived at relatively close quarters, remained largely integrationist—the integration of lunch counters and transportation facilities, of police and fire departments, of colleges and eventually schools. But in the more sparsely populated rural South, where blacks and whites rarely encountered each other outside of kitchens, front porches, and, occasionally, the office, civil rights workers concentrated their efforts on voter registration. The year before a voter registration drive had been initiated by SNCC workers Sam Block and Willie Peacock in Greenwood, and local whites had used every available means of intimidation to keep them from succeeding. SNCC workers and their sympathizers were shot at in their cars and in their homes, were arbitrarily arrested, and were attacked by police dogs. It was little wonder—blacks outnumbered whites by three to two in LeFlore County, and anything resembling equitable voter registration threatened to create a second reconstruction.

Guy Carawan came to Greenwood in early April to record the accounts of several players in the Greenwood saga as well as some of the area's strong congregational singing. The SNCC office had been torched on 24 March, and two nights later a local activist was shot as he entered his home. A spontaneous gathering of protesters the following day turned into a march to the courthouse. Greenwood police turned the marchers back with dogs, as they would again the following day—this time for the benefit of several news photographers whose dramatic shots received front-page exposure throughout the country.[55] The press coverage brought several prominent figures to Greenwood that weekend, including Dick Gregory and the NAACP's Medgar Evers, who would be murdered in his driveway in Jackson, Mississippi, a few weeks later (and in his martyrdom become the subject of Dylan's "Only a Pawn in Their Game"). At a mass meeting on Sunday, Carawan recorded Gregory, Evers, and Fannie Lou Hamer, more than a year before she attracted the country's attention at the 1964 Democratic National Convention in Atlantic City with her moving appeal to allow the seating of the Mississippi Freedom Democratic Party delegation. The Carawans would get to know Hamer much better in the succeeding months. She participated in two of Highlander's citizenship schools that spring, now run by Andrew Young and the SCLC, in part because of the precarious condition of Highlander. The first was in Dorchester, Georgia. Guy, Candie, and their baby were in attendance at the second, in Charleston, South Carolina, teaching freedom songs to the participants and learning new ones from the likes of Hamer and others brought up in traditions of fine congregational singing. It was on the trip home from Charleston in June that Hamer and others were arrested in Winona, Mississippi, after requesting service at a white lunch counter. During her several days in jail, Hamer was brutally beaten. Although the justice department brought charges against Hamer's jailers, an all-white jury declined to convict them.[56]

The Story of Greenwood Mississippi, released in 1965, was the last of the Carawan's civil rights recordings to appear while the movement was still in flower. It was thus the last that could be used as an organizing tool; the remainder appeared fifteen years later as historical footnotes. They had produced it for SNCC, and this time Asch was permitted to release it on Folkways (5593). Greenwood activists recounted the story of organizing and resistance there, and their narrative is interspersed with the public oratory of Dick Gregory, Fannie Lou Hamer, and the sad, ghostly presence of Medgar Evers.

By the spring of 1964 there was a growing sense that a canon of civil rights song was developing. An important part of the process of canon formation was the publication the previous year of the Carawan's *We Shall Overcome!* by Oak Publications. Of the fifty songs in the slim book, twenty, according to Carawan, constituted a "basic repertoire." As a means of further disseminating this basic repertoire, the Carawans, in conjunction with Highlander, SNCC, and SCLC, planned a workshop for the month of May in Atlanta that would bring together movement song leaders as well as northern singers who had been writing songs for the movement. The former, it was hoped, would profit from hearing "vital and exciting songs from elsewhere," and the northern songwriters (Phil Ochs, Tom Paxton, Len Chander, Theo Bikel) would be encouraged to continue to make contributions in the area of protest song, revitalized by the southern musical traditions that were already so thoroughly implicated in the movement. The southern song leaders would include members of the Freedom Singers, the Birmingham Movement Choir, Doc Reese, and a group of traditional singers from St. Simons Island, Georgia, led by Bessie Jones.

In the year of the Sing for Freedom workshop, revisionist history of the antebellum South was in its infancy. While Kenneth Stampp's *Peculiar Institution* had been published eight years earlier, it would be another eight years before publication of Blassingame's *Slave Community,* ten before Genovese's *Roll, Jordan, Roll* would appear, and twelve before Herbert Gutman's *Black Family in Slavery and Freedom* finally saw light of day. Each of these books widened the public consciousness of slave history as an era of cultural inventiveness and political resistance and enabled the reappropriation of that history in the interest of a strong and positive African American identity. But until the work of these historians and those who followed them began to eclipse that of southern apologists such as U. B. Phillips in the popular imagination, there remained a persistent feeling that slavery was the most shameful and degrading chapter in African American history. Not until the publication of Melville Herskovits's *Myth of the Negro Past* in 1941 was there *any* broad recognition of African contributions to slave culture. Consequently, from language to song to family life, it was regarded as an impoverished approximation of white European patterns, which ostensibly constituted the only available cultural models for Africans and their descendants, whose own culture, it was argued, had been stripped from them by the trauma of the middle passage.

In 1964 slavery was consequently a chapter of their past about which most African Americans preferred not to be reminded. Thus the Carawans were taking a calculated risk in inviting the Georgia Sea Island Singers to the workshop. They performed songs and children's play parties that were said to have been handed down to them from their slave ancestors, and they included little overt "protest" content. To Josh Dunson, who was covering the workshop for *Broadside,* many participants seemed embarrassed by the old slave songs, and on Saturday morning an emotional debate ensued. Some did not see a connection between the old songs and the freedom songs: "'I can hear the old songs anytime I want back home. What do people back home want with it? Why should I bring it back?'" Bessie Jones of the Sea Island Singers defended the songs by insisting that they were the one available means—however muted—for slaves to express discontent. Others, including Len Chandler and SCLC secretary Andrew Young, saw the rejection of the slave songs as part of the hegemonic process by which the dominant culture separated blacks from sources of racial pride and dignity. "'We all know,'" declared Young, "you can't trust a Negro on a negotiating committee who doesn't like his people's music."[57]

In the end some were convinced, some were not, and some never needed convincing.[58] Regardless, it was a poignant moment. The most prominent voices in civil rights music were faced with the tangled question of how it was that music—particularly song—"worked" in the world. How was meaning imputed to songs such as those of Bessie Jones, and who had the authority to do so? Did meaning reside with the singer or the listeners, or were there forces beyond the control of either that determined how these songs were understood? If there was a struggle over who was permitted to determine meaning, Guy Carawan under-stood—as Seeger and others had previously—that a community or congregation singing songs at moments of intense, common, and undeniable purpose had the authority to establish meaning as they wished. That is, songs with ambiguous referents could take on clear and unambiguous meanings as a consequence of the contexts in which they were sung. Who could deny the suggestive power of "This Little Light of Mine" when sung on a picket line, at an organizational meeting, in a jail cell?

The Carawans had arranged to tape the proceedings of the Sing for Freedom workshop, but the resultant recording—released fifteen years later on Folkways (5488)—became a historical docu-ment rather than an organizing tool. When it was released in 1980, *Sing for Freedom* was a curious relic. Here were whites and blacks, southerners and northerners, youngsters and oldsters appreciat-ing each other's music across social boundaries that seemed not so very difficult to traverse. Something had happened in the inter-vening years to make the idea of common, interracial purpose difficult to imagine. Bernice Reagon had organized a conference in Washington, D.C., called Voices of the Civil Rights Movement and timed it to coincide with the release of a three-record set (and accompanying booklet) of civil rights music subtitled *Black American Freedom Songs, 1955–65.* The Carawans judged it a good moment to release some of the material in their archives, and Asch concurred. They titled the series Lest We Forget; the material from the mass meeting in Birmingham with Martin Luther King and Ralph Aber-nathy constituted one volume in the series (5487), and the Sing for Freedom workshop another.

The Sing for Freedom workshop occurred about halfway through the Carawan's two-year stay on Johns Island (1963–65).

This was a time of great productivity for them; they recorded sixty hours of songs and religious rituals that were condensed into two Folkways albums, *Sea Island Folk Festival: Moving Star Hall Singers and Alan Lomax* (3841), released in 1964, and *John's Island: Been in the Storm So Long* (3842), released the following year. The former resulted from the first of the many folk festivals they staged on Johns Island in the autumn of 1963 and after; Alan Lomax was in attendance, and his commentary is heard on the album. In an article for a Charleston newspaper the following January, Lomax wrote eloquently about the music he had heard and its importance for America:

> There were more good folk singers among the 300 attending the Johns Island festival than among the 45,000 people who attended the Newport, Rhode Island festival a month earlier. . . . My prophesy is that . . . the musical genius of the South, which has helped to give Southern life its flavor in spite of our special problems, will be alive again—that the strong, sweet music of our world will be linking us together and will be one of the symbols by which the South will be known and of which we will be most proud.[59]

The Carawans sent the festival tape to Asch, as well as to Ralph Rinzler, who promptly invited the Moving Star Hall Singers to the Newport festival the following summer.

Transcribed portions of interviews with several island residents, along with the photographs of Robert Yellin, became the Carawans' book *Ain't You Got a Right to the Tree of Life?* For their efforts, the Carawans have recently been uncharitably (and inaccurately) characterized as "white observers who were untrained social scientists—who lived among the people for a short time."[60] Their critics have maintained that researchers on the Sea Islands should be dedicated to serving the Sea Island community *first*, with research "coincidental to service." Yet although the Carawans were criticized for generating an atmosphere of hostility to future researchers, it is difficult to imagine two people more dedicated to serving the political and educational interests of the island residents. Other criticisms—that only black researchers should study black subjects—are equally fatuous. Only in one sense do the Carawan's detractors have a point worthy of consideration; that is, to what extent are researchers responsible for characterizing the "whole" culture as opposed to just those aspects that appear to have historical pedigree?

It is a quandary that folklorists (and, for that matter, biographers) frequently face. How do you select particular "moments" in the life of a people that are to serve as symbols of something larger? What is representative, and *what* is being represented? To whom is one responsible—the community being studied, a community of scholars, a political movement, or an ideological position? Do you portray "the other" precisely as they would wish to be portrayed, or are there other criteria that take precedence? The Carawans made no bones about their intentions; they were focusing upon those aspects of Sea Island culture that appeared to have historical authenticity and deliberately ignoring the intrusions of the mass market in the lives of islanders. In so doing they believed they were providing the islanders with the best means of confronting their contemporary predicament. Their commitment was to a *movement*, which could not help but imply a *people*. The old traditions were the real traditions, and they had a utility in the modern context that they were intent upon revealing to those who may have forgotten them:

> As the Civil rights movement has reached rural people who are accustomed to folk-style church meetings, songs, and folk philosophy, the civil rights workers have had to adapt their means of communication. Fortunately this has resulted in a two-way exchange, and while rural people have begun to look to the future. . . . Negro leaders who had left their folk heritage behind them have begun to be moved by the fresh contact. Old songs now speak in depth of immediate problems and the message of a folk sermon is suddenly relevant. Today a main object of the civil rights workers in the Deep South is to convince rural Negroes that they do indeed have something important to offer this country.[61]

The equation of "folk culture" with "authentic" black culture introduced its own complications; obscured were other authentic black traditions that embraced intellectualism, modernism, and mass culture. Yet it is an equation that continues to be reflected in most African American literature and theater in the 1990s, and if there is a price being paid for deemphasizing other vital threads of African American culture, it is not yet apparent what that is.

In early 1965 Asch made a second effort to correspond with Martin Luther King, although the admiration that had motivated his attempt seven and a half years earlier had withered somewhat with

King's growing prominence. On 16 January the *New York Times* published a letter from King in which he endorsed an open letter to the Soviet Union that had been signed by a large interfaith roster of prominent Americans in a paid advertisement two days earlier. The open letter had condemned the anti-Semitic tone of the recent "economic trials"in the Soviet Union and called for the right of Soviet Jews to practice their religion. King added:

> The struggle of the Negro people for freedom is inextricably
> interwoven with the universal struggle of all peoples to be
> free from discrimination and oppression. The Jewish people
> must be given their full rights as Soviet citizens. . . . In the
> name of humanity, I urge that the Soviet Government end all
> discriminatory measures against its Jewish community. I will
> not remain silent in the face of injustice.

It would have been difficult to have predicted what Asch might have found objectionable in King's letter. It apparently galled him that King might add his voice to a list of "distinguished" Americans. "I do not consider myself among distinguished Americans," Asch responded to the editor of the *Times*. "I believe first of all that all Americans are distinguished. Does the acceptance of the Nobel Prize make you better or more distinguished than others? If so, please remove your robe and collar for you have fallen for the golden idol." Yet Asch writes hopefully that "associates of yours know of me and my background."

It appears that Asch was bothered still more that King had affiliated himself with a group of pro-Zionist American Jews:

> I do not hold brief with Jews who use the temple of religion
> as a propaganda forum in the guise of God and the Bible by
> saying one is not a Jew unless one lives in Israel (Palestine) as
> the Hebrewites in Israel have us believe. I am against the nar-
> row and archaic concept that the Bible meant physical Israel
> and not the spiritual. . . . I did not read of your protest of the
> displaced Arabs by the Israelites, but of course they are Mo-
> hammedans and not Christian (Jews); my father would have
> loved to see the faces of the Orthodox Jews which you de-
> fend had you done so. Now please don't mix the professional
> Hebrews with the Jewish heritage.

The *Times* refrained from publishing Asch's intemperate outburst. Like much of Asch's communication, it was highly elliptical. "I have done my best to be as controversial as possible," he wrote, which was largely true. But there is no reason to think that he was unsympathetic to the plight of Soviet Jews, and nothing in King's letter suggests that the civil rights leader was pro-Zionist.[62] Some years previously Asch had staked out his own anti-Zionist position and connected it to the struggle of African Americans to claim their rightful place in the fabric of American culture:

> I do not believe that Israel is the hope for the Jewish people any more than I believe that Africa is the hope for the American Negro or that Chicago slums are the answer to a better life. The Negro like any one else I feel must resolve that he is part of the whole and his shame is everyone's shame. That his glory is everyone's glory.

Negro music of the sharecropping South represented a vital contribution to our common American culture, he argued, and everyone's conscience should be bothered by the economic plight of those who offered this gift to the country.[63] Asch was consistent in rejecting nationalist claims for "homelands" and in embracing the rich possibility of life in a diaspora. For a man who had spent his formative years in a state of perpetual exile, it was not a surprising position. The place in which he found himself at any given moment was, finally, the place where he belonged.

By 1966 whites had been largely elbowed out of the civil rights movement by the nationalist impulses of young black leaders, a development that bothered Asch less than one might have predicted. Highlander and the Caravans began to turn to social justice issues that affected their more immediate neighbors in New Market, Tennessee—poor, predominantly white farmers and miners. It was around that time that Stokely Carmichael (known today as Kwame Toure) appeared in the office of Harold Leventhal to harangue him about the way in which white folk singers were co-opting the music of the civil rights movement for their own purposes.[64] The movement itself was being stalled by the daunting problems of urban poverty and eclipsed by the Vietnam War. The riots in Watts, Chicago, Newark, and Detroit in the summers of 1965 and 1966 created a different mood, better reflected in Jimmy Collier's "Burn, Baby, Burn" than in the more conciliatory songs that he and Rev. Federick Douglass Kirkpatrick had recorded on their Broadside album *Everybody's Got a Right to Live* (5308). The nationalist themes of the movement's black power phase were reaching a broad audience through popular black recording artists such as Curtis Mayfield ("Keep on Pushing," 1964; "People Get Ready," 1965), Nina Simone ("Mississippi Goddamn," 1965), James Brown ("Say it Loud—I'm Black and I'm Proud," 1968), and Aretha Franklin ("Young, Gifted and Black," 1971). In 1971 and 1972 Asch released documentary recordings featuring the voices of Angela Davis (*Angela Davis Speaks*, 5401), Huey Newton, Bobby Seale, and Eldridge Cleaver (*Listen Whitey*, 5402), and various anonymous prison poets from Attica, Rikers, and the Tombs (*From the Cold Jaws of Prison*, 5403). The folk music establishment was left once again to contemplate the irony that mass audiences were reached by popular musical forms and that, by the late sixties, the collective consciousness of African Americans was being reflected on Top Forty radio rather than folk music.[65] Still, the early sixties had shown what folk music enthusiasts had always maintained: music created and performed collectively by ordinary people had the means of moving a nation.

8. FINDING THE FINAL PIECES

O n his own again in 1970, without the distraction of a second office or collaborators who seemed to understand little about his method or purposes, Asch was able to return to his accustomed mode of making records. His business practices were rapidly becoming obsolete, and his production process was only made possible by businessmen who had a soft spot for Asch and his quixotic enterprise. Who else would have been permitted such minuscule production runs and repressings? But for another fifteen years Asch more or less carried on in the same manner he had since the 1950s.

He came into the offices very early in the morning. Things were quiet at that time of day; it was not an atmosphere in which gossip was easily exchanged anyway, and the silence was ordinarily broken only by the ring of the telephone or Asch's gruff bark: "Is the mail here yet?" His work day began with the opening of the mail, and no one else was to touch it. He sorted the circulars from the bills and from the orders, although it was primarily for the latter he was looking. He sat at a desk in the front office and placed orders in one drawer, checks in another. If an order arrived without payment, he would write the required sum on the order and have a secretary return it to the sender. Sometimes an order came with payment based on an old price list; occasionally Asch would instruct the warehouse to send the order out anyway, but more often he would write to the customer requesting the balance of payment before the records were shipped. Periodically the phone would ring and Asch would patiently explain to a customer how to fill out an order form or calculate the shipping charges. Once all the mail had been opened, Asch could size up the day: an ample number of large checks meant it had started well and Asch was content.

Frequently Asch would go out for breakfast after he had been in the office for a couple hours, and then the other parts of the office would come alive. After Marian Distler's death Marilyn Conklin—whom Irwin Silber had hired as a secretary in March 1959—gradually began to fill the role once occupied by Asch's late partner. Asch very deliberately taught her the fundamentals of the business, the significance of the catalogue, the meaning of the enterprise; and she was a quick and perceptive learner who developed an instinct for working around his temper and anticipating what needed to be done. Conklin was able to monitor the record production and sales with the help of mammoth ledgers. The production logbook listed each new recording as it was prepared for manufacture, and dates were entered each time one part of the production process had been completed. Master tapes were the special responsibility of Gerson Traub, a warehouse employee who retrieved the tapes from a vault, transported them to the plant that manufactured the mother disks, and saw to it that they were returned to the vault. Another manufacturer produced the stampers from the mothers, and it was a daily matter to determine whether the stampers had been delivered to the pressing plants. Asch did business with at least three pressing plants, of which Plastylite in New Jersey was the most important, especially in the earlier years.

From the late fifties most Folkways cover art was produced by Ronald Clyne, a free-lance graphic artist who worked primarily with book jackets. Asch had met him through Sam Goody, for whose LP record guides Clyne had designed covers. Asch would give Clyne a general description of the album's content and leave it up to him to design a jacket that would reflect it. Clyne kept a file of artwork images in the public domain that he collected from the National Archive and the New York Public Library, and he would frequently design a cover around a photograph or print that he deemed appropriate for the album. Unlike Irwin Rosenhouse, who drew wonderful covers for Folkways releases throughout the fifties, Clyne almost never incorporated his own artwork. A rare exception was a 1958 record of compositions by John Cage and Henry Cowell (among others) entitled *Sounds of New Music* (6160), for which Clyne used one of his own paintings. Sometimes Asch provided Clyne with a photograph that he wished to have incorporated into the cover art, but otherwise he rarely interfered or suggested changes. Nor did Clyne ordinarily communicate with the record's producer or artist. In most instances, he was confined to working in two colors—only very occasionally three—but he did not find it an impediment. When Asch periodically reprinted a cover he would use just one color in order to save money with results that Clyne found disappointing. When the artwork was completed, Clyne would deliver it to Asch's office and present him with a bill. The cover designs were then delivered to a printing plant, and it was to the pressing plants that the printers delivered the album notes and the "slicks" that were pasted over the plain black sleeves. There the final product was assembled. When a new release was finally available, Asch would instruct his warehouse to send a specified number—generally between five and fifteen—to each of his steady retail outlets.

In the mid-1970s Asch moved his operation to West Sixty-first Street, in the vicinity of the Lincoln Center. The WEVD building at 117 West Forty-sixth Street had been demolished some years earlier. In the early 1960s Asch had moved his offices down Forty-sixth Street, closer to Broadway; and in the late 1960s until 1976 he used a set of offices on Seventh Avenue, overlooking Times Square. On Sixty-first Street he had ample space and no longer depended upon Sam Goody to warehouse his inventory as he once had. In the 1970s the warehouse was a three-man operation; between them they filled orders, packed boxes, wrote invoices, and conducted an inventory three times a year. Arguably the warehouse's most surprising feature was a wall in the shipping room that had been covered from floor to ceiling with magazine pornography of the most graphic nature. Because it was necessary to walk through the shipping room to see any other part of the warehouse, the pornography was in plain view of any visitor Asch might have taken on tour. Many commented on it later and found it remarkable that Asch seemed to take no notice of it whatsoever. One observer speculated that although Asch never discussed sexual matters himself and did not appear to take any particular interest in them, his libertarianism required of him a tolerance for other people's interests and tastes. Although the warehouse pornography appeared altogether out of character for Asch and so contrary to the control that he otherwise demanded over his environment, he would not judge what it might require for others to feel comfortable in their work environment. If this was how the warehouse employees chose to decorate their work space, Asch would not interfere.[1]

Marilyn was assisted in the office by two secretaries who took orders, prepared bills, responded to inquiries, transmitted orders to the warehouse, and made periodic trips to the bank. Additionally they tabulated record sales for each album in a large ledger with tiny tick marks in groups of five, from which they calculated royalties. One artist recalls examining the sales ledger one day and expressing disappointment over the sales of one of his albums; the secretary looked at him slyly and added a few pencil marks.[2]

For some of the more prominent Folkways artists the secretaries undoubtedly prepared semiannual royalty statements; others received royalty statements only when they prodded Asch to do so. Conklin recalled that Asch instructed her *not* to include mail-order sales in the calculation of royalties, and overseas royalties were calculated at half-rate. He never offered her an explanation for this practice; it was simply how he did business.[3]

Asch continued to receive tapes from artists and collectors throughout the world—far too many for him to audition them all. Periodically he would close himself in his office to audition a tape; if he felt that he did not have the expertise to judge the quality or importance of a particular tape, he would send it to someone whose judgment he trusted. Scholars who simply wanted to ensure that their recordings were made available to the public continued to send tapes to Asch and were generally content to receive a couple hundred dollars advance to defray their production costs.

By the seventies, however, Asch's competition for the recording of professional folk musicians had increased considerably. Elektra and Vanguard had become enormously successful and had branched out well beyond folk music (particularly Elektra), and smaller operations were springing up to occupy the position in the recording industry that had once belonged to the folk label pioneers. Rounder Records released its first album in 1972, and Bruce Kaplan established Flying Fish in Chicago a couple years later. Other small operations such as Arhoolie, Yazoo, and Herwin were already serving highly specialized markets for esoteric country blues and ragtime. Whether they knew it or not (and many did), all of them were students of Moe Asch and had modeled their operations in certain respects on Folkways. At the same time Rounder particularly came to operate on more contemporary—and more rational—business practices. Especially with respect to distribution, many potential recording artists recognized the advantages of the younger companies.

For the most part, performing artists who sent audition tapes to

Asch in the seventies were either naïve or discouraged by having exhausted other avenues. Kevin Roth was probably a little bit of both. Only fifteen when he sent a tape to Asch in 1974, he thought he recognized an opportunity to capitalize on the current interest in the mountain dulcimer and hoped that Asch would too. Asch had not released a recording of a dulcimer player since Jean Ritchie had left the label and Paul Clayton had committed suicide, and the playing of Richard Fariña and Joni Mitchell had indeed created a flurry of interest in the instrument. Perhaps Asch was also intrigued by a young man whose chutzpah rivaled his own. "I've never known anyone like you," he remarked with grudging respect. On the first visit to the Folkways offices, Roth took the train from his suburban Philadelphia home with his father. Asch made it clear that he would not spend money to promote his records, but he would ensure their availability. He released Roth's first album on Folkways, *Sings and Plays Dulcimer* (2367), before the year was out, advancing him $425 to help cover recording costs. Over the next decade Asch advanced him sums up to $800 to produce an additional dozen albums.

Roth was no less frightened than others by Asch's constant gruffness and periodic screaming, but rather than withering under the attacks he kept coming back for more. During the second half of the seventies, Roth spoke to Asch on the phone several times a week about recording projects and album sales. It was unusual for Asch to make suggestions for the content of an album, so when for his second album Roth wanted to use electric instruments for a more commercial recording, Asch was skeptical but did not interfere. The resulting album, *The Other Side of the Mountain* (31045), sold poorly, and Roth went back to the use of acoustic instrumentation. "Kevin is trying to be popular, but he can't, thank God," laughed Asch during an interview with Fred Ramsey for National Public Radio a few years later.[4]

At about the same time as his first meeting with Roth, Asch received a tape of English concertina music from an Oberlin College freshman by the name of Richard Carlin. Carlin had written a history of the concertina that was published while he was still a high school student in Princeton, New Jersey, and he had acquired an NEH Youth Grant in the fall of 1974 that enabled him to travel throughout England to record aging concertina players during the winter term of his first year of college. Carlin had first sent the tape to Rounder and Philo; the former expressed interest in it until, on listening to it, they discovered that rather than traditional jigs and reels it contained marches and other kinds of "classical" music that constituted the repertoire of English players of the vaudeville era. Philo offered to release it on their vanity label, Fretless, but it would have required Carlin to put up the money for its production. Although Carlin had enormous admiration for Folkways, he knew Asch did not take the same care with the production of his albums that his young competitors did and that, in some respects, it was now less prestigious to have a recording on Folkways than on some of the young upstart labels.

Some months later, having heard nothing, Carlin went to the Folkways offices on Sixty-first Street to retrieve his tape. Asch agreed to return the tape and went back to his tape library to retrieve it. But when he returned, he demurred. "No," he said, "this is one I want to put out." Carlin was elated. In the intervening months, Asch had sent a copy of the tape to an expert on concertinas in England for an evaluation and he had been waiting for a reply. When Carlin arrived in his offices, Asch still had heard nothing but decided to go ahead without a second opinion.

When *The English Concertina* (8845) was released a few months later and Carlin received his complementary copies, he was disappointed to discover that the mastering process had not included any alteration of his original tape—cuts were reproduced at different volume levels and the length of time between songs varied considerably. Carlin learned that for subsequent albums he would have to work with the man at Sound Wave who mastered the tapes to ensure that they were released as he wanted them to appear. He also learned that it was advantageous to submit his album notes to Asch in a fairly sloppy fashion, because then Asch, rather than simply having them reproduced precisely as Carlin had presented them, would have them typeset.

Carlin developed an intuitive understanding of Asch that was much like Roth's—he was a vaguely familiar type, a Jewish grandfather who showed interest in the activity of the youth and was supportive but did not have much kindness to spare them. Asch advanced Carlin the sum of two hundred dollars for each of the additional eight albums that he made for Folkways while still in college. Occasionally Carlin would receive a handwritten royalty statement. But he also recalled being in Asch's office before the start of the new semester one year: Asch asked him how much his textbooks would cost him and wrote out a check for the sum.

Asch seemed to Carlin to be extraordinarily inattentive to the quality of the albums he released. Although Asch agreed to put out an album of Carlin's own renditions of Irish tunes [8846] in the company of his college friends Evan Stein and Grey Larsen, Carlin doubted that Asch listened to it until it had been pressed. By Carlin's own later admission, his playing was then immature and probably unworthy of release. Asch asked to listen to Carlin's second album of his own playing before committing to it, but it did not seem to make any difference.

Carlin, Larsen, and Stein discovered a couple of middle-aged Irish musicians in nearby Cleveland and brought them to Oberlin to perform at the campus coffeehouse and to record them in an Oberlin studio. Asch agreed to release an album of *Irish Music from Cleveland* (3517), and a second and third volume followed. The *Sing Out!* reviewer for the first volume, Miles Krassen, was not complimentary and particularly faulted Carlin for having included himself, Larsen, and Stein—"underqualified revivalist musicians"—on several cuts.[5] For the cover of the third volume, Carlin sent Asch a color photograph of the musicians. But Asch could not use a color photograph and, in any case, did not grant Carlin the kind of control over the albums he produced that he had once conceded to John Cohen and others. Rather than inform Carlin, however, he proceeded to have Clyne use a Library of Congress photograph by Walker Evans of two wooden doors intricately carved with Irish motifs. When Carlin saw the album cover he phoned Asch to determine what had happened. Asch was sympathetic and agreed to change the cover to include a photograph of the musicians, but subsequently the musicians contacted Asch directly and threatened to sue. Asch was furious that Carlin had exposed him to such threats and yelled at him unsparingly. Abruptly their relationship ended.

Before the rupture Carlin had contributed some recordings of French Canadian music to the reissue series on Folkways' subsidiary RBF label, which had once been Sam Charters's exclusive territory (RF 110, 111). His collaborator was a Canadian collector of 78s whom he had encountered through a magazine advertisement. Another collector of 78s, Dave Jasen, had also started to make additions to the RBF series in the seventies, derived from his huge collection of ragtime recordings. Jasen had the great advantage of being both an enthusiast and a highly credible player of ragtime piano in his own right, which made him acutely sensitive to the musical evolution of the ragtime genre. Asch had sought out Jasen in 1971 because there was suddenly a surge of interest in ragtime piano music. Joshua Rifkin's *Piano Rags of Scott Joplin* on

Nonesuch Records was released in November 1970 and became a huge and altogether unexpected commercial success. Although ragtime had gone through several previous revivals, this one was distinguished by both its enormity in market terms and the serious attention the music received as a kind of American classical music. That was Rifkin's intention, in part, in releasing it on a classical label. But he could not have foreseen either its astonishing commercial success or its warm reception from such eminent classical critics as Harold Schonberg of the *New York Times*.[6] Asch phoned Nick Perls of Yazoo Records to see whether it might be possible to add some ragtime to the Folkways list, and Perls put him on to Jasen.

Jasen was initially leery of Asch; he had heard stories about his temper and his treatment of artists and producers, and Jasen in any case was already producing albums for Perls. But Asch offered Jasen an additional enticement; along with the production of LPs from the reissue of 78s in his collection, would Jasen have any interest in working with material—issued and unissued—that Asch had on acetate from his recording activity in the forties? Jasen was more than intrigued; Asch's unexplored acetates were almost as famous as his temper, and the opportunity to issue material that had not been heard in thirty years was more than he could resist.

Jasen began to work in two areas simultaneously. On receiving approval (and an advance of four hundred dollars) from Asch, he prepared the tapes and the notes for a series of ragtime reissue collections. The first was *Ragtime Entertainment (Original Recordings)*, released in 1973. Over the next twelve years he produced more than twenty-five albums for the RBF series, eventually including *They All Played Tiger Rag*—the ragtime equivalent of Ken Goldstein's *Unfortunate Rake*—with multiple versions of one of ragtime's most famous compositions, including a rendition by Eubie Blake recorded especially for the album. There was never any effort to pay royalties to composers or licensing fees to the original record labels; to have done so would have made the projects prohibitively expensive. As always, Asch was confident of his right to make material that other labels had neglected available to the public. He had fought skirmishes from time to time over Harry Smith's *Anthology*, Frederic Ramsey's History of Jazz series, and Charters's many RBF releases, but he knew that it was rarely worth the trouble for the major labels to collect from him. This remained so for ragtime as well, until the field became sufficiently lucrative that Columbia started to go after Asch and the other small reissuers.

Jasen eventually stopped using Columbia material. Asch never turned down a project that Jasen proposed to him, although Jasen remained careful to check with Asch first before investing any labor. If Asch had not heard from Jasen for a few months he would phone him to see what he was working on. Later Jasen recorded some contemporary ragtime revivalists for Folkways, and he was particularly delighted when Asch agreed to release an album of Jasen's own playing.

Jasen's first encounter with Asch's recorded archive was discouraging. The acetates, which had never been previously transferred to tape, were poorly stored and covered with dirt. In many instances they had deteriorated badly or had been broken in Asch's many moves. Jasen nonetheless began to piece together the material that was salvageable, and the results were often enchanting. The first reissue consisted of James P. Johnson piano solos (*The Original James P. Johnson*, 2850), followed by Asch's recordings of Joe Sullivan (2851). Jazz historian Len Lyons described the Johnson reissue in his *101 Best Jazz Albums* as "a small legacy of his piano style but a crucial one."[7]

Jasen's work was that of a second-generation revivalist; in the ragtime, boogie-woogie, and dixieland fields he was preparing material from Asch's archives that was self-consciously revivalist when it was recorded in the forties (Doc Evans, Muggsy Spanier). Asch occasionally purchased air-shot recordings of the big band era, including a Chick Webb and Ella Fitzgerald recording, and Jasen would dutifully prepare these for release as well. Sometimes Asch would ask him to prepare material for reissue about which Jasen knew relatively little or, in some instances, cared rather little—such as Asch's Disc-era recordings of chanteuses Stella Brooks and Greta Keller (2830).[8]

Jasen knew enough about Mary Lou Williams to recognize her importance to the history of jazz and was sufficiently modest to allow others to prepare the album notes. Thirty years after Williams had recorded her *Zodiac Suite* in Asch Studios with drummer Jack Parker and bassist Al Lucas, Jasen prepared a master tape from the old acetates and enlisted the help of Dan Morgenstern at the Rutgers Institute of Jazz Studies for the notes. Asch had been urged back in 1959 by jazz critic Al Close to reissue *Zodiac Suite*, but Asch had responded that the record had been issued originally by Stinson and all that he had in his possession were unreleased alternate takes on acetate. "I will be in touch with you again as I would like you to hear them sometime," was the best he could offer Close.[9] But fifteen years later Asch was no longer bothered by the question of ownership.

The reissue of *Zodiac Suite* in 1975 (32844) was all the more remarkable because it occurred at a time when Williams remained musically active. As she herself recognized, her place in jazz history was unique in that she had been an active participant in most of its important movements, with the exception of the earliest New Orleans era. She had abruptly abandoned her jazz career in 1954 and in 1955 converted to Roman Catholicism, to which she devoted herself for the remainder of her life. In 1957 she came out of retirement in order to play at the Newport Jazz Festival, but she did not record again until 1964, when she prepared an album of new recordings for Folkways. *Mary Lou Williams* (2843) was an eclectic mix of unaccompanied piano solos, ensemble work with a rhythm section, and piano with choral accompaniment. The new compositions were largely dedicated to religious themes. "Fungus Amungus" showed Williams venturing into "free jazz."

Three years earlier Williams had contracted with Asch to record "the story of jazz in your own words (and music)" and was given a small advance.[10] But the project languished for many years. In between she did what she could to promote the new Folkways recording, sending it to a disc jockey in France (where it won the Grand Prix du Disque Français) and hiring a publicist to place it in New York department stores. "Well, 'Sweetie,' the reason I'm writing you is that I too, am working hard for the LP," she wrote Asch in late 1964.[11]

In 1966 Williams wrote Asch in part to inform him that she had enrolled him as a Perpetual Member in the Franciscan Mass League, which, she explained, entitled him to receive more than five thousand prayers a year. "Please may I see you soon?" she added. Despite her own meager existence she was working to raise money through record sales and performances for charitable causes and needed his help. Still, the history of jazz project faltered. In 1968 she received an additional advance for the recording, as well as the sum of $150 for a taped interview with her mother that she intended to include.

Of all the jazz musicians Asch had recorded in the forties, Williams was the only one who remained in touch. Their persistent fondness for one another was genuine and unforced. Moe's least troubled relationships continued to be with women, whose friendship was untempered by rivalry. In late 1968 she wrote him from a cloister in Holland, where the presence of the nuns did not dampen her humor: "Went on a diet . . . must be doing alright 'cause my dress fell off my rump a few days ago, ha!" She urged

Asch to read the works of Thomas Merton, explaining that he had a special understanding of the place of artists in the world: "He also says what you and I have. An honest artist is in a different world, away from greed, hatred of the commercial world—this is you also. I like you because you think with, and are like an artist." She wrote him again the following month, and again the next. The European stores were full of bootlegged copies of the records she had made for him (and others) over the years, and there seemed nothing to be done about it.

Finally, in April 1971, Peter O'Brien, a Jesuit priest who had become Williams's manager and tireless supporter, delivered a completed tape to Asch for the history of jazz recording. Yet it would be an additional *seven* years before the album was actually released. Through the seventies, Asch was only very slowly pulling material off his shelves that had been waiting years for release. He released a second portion of his 1959 interview with W. E. B. Du Bois with the title *Socialism and the American Negro* in 1972 (5514). An LP version of Woody Guthrie's *Struggle* album came out in 1976; Asch added six Guthrie cuts from his archives to the original Asch Records three-disc set. "I waited for the bicentennial to give the struggling people a chance to know that one of their own did not let them down and his songs go on and on and on," wrote Asch in his album notes. But timing was not always the primary constraint; it was largely cash flow difficulties that delayed the release of Williams's history of jazz record until 1978. The previous year, Father O'Brien had produced a reissue of Mary Lou Williams's *Asch Recordings, 1944–47*, and John S. Wilson reviewed both for the *New York Times* along with, appropriately, a new recording of Williams's on Norman Granz's Pablo label. Wilson validates Williams's claim to have "played through all the eras of jazz" and notes how rare it is for jazz artists to move beyond the style that brought them prominence: "The uniqueness of the course Miss Williams has followed through jazz, her ability to be constantly contemporary without betraying her own musical personality, is underlined when one considers other notable jazz musicians whose careers, chronologically, have paralleled her own." Wilson concludes that, in combination, the three albums "capture more of her personality than we usually get on record." He also cannot refrain from commenting on an unintended joke that resulted from Asch's occasional sloppiness:

> One nonmusical highlight of the albums appears in a brochure for "The History of Jazz" which, in paying tribute to the

pioneering recordings of Moe Asch of Folkways Records,
notes that the artists he recorded included Leadbelly, Woody
Guthrie and "a great concert pianist, Bella Bartop [sic]."
   Good old Bella! She really made those beer bottles jump![12]

Another old friend returned to record for Folkways after an absence of many years. Pete Seeger was increasingly frustrated with
Columbia, particularly after they refused to release a single of his
rendition of Country Joe and the Fish's antiwar anthem, "Feel Like
I'm Fixin' to Die Rag."[13] In truth, with the exception of the *We Shall
Overcome* album, Seeger's Columbia albums had never sold particularly well, and with John Hammond no longer involved with his
recording projects Seeger concluded that they may as well just
"call it quits." Early in 1974 he began work on a new Folkways album
but had to interrupt the work in order to have surgery for a hernia.
That summer he resumed recording at Fred Hellerman's studio in
Connecticut. "I recorded more for Fred today, but will have to go
back again July 22 to record again," he wrote Asch. "I need direction
from you. Have you ideas for this LP—is it just 'one more Pete
Seeger LP?'" Seeger also had another recording project in mind for
which he hoped to enlist Asch's enthusiasm. He wanted to record
a series of eight-inch flexible children's discs to be entitled "The
Litterbag Songbook." Each copy would include not only the printed
music and words but also a plastic bag: "I wanted to relate a
mundane task like picking up litter to larger ones of life on earth."
It was a Seeger idea that was longer on idealism than marketing
savvy and did not see light of day.[14]
   A new Pete Seeger Folkways album did result, however—"just
one more Pete Seeger LP," but a very fine one at that. Fred Hellerman joined him on the title track, the People's Song classic
"Banks of Marble." At approximately the same time Seeger and
Asch were talking about rereleasing Seeger's *God Bless the Grass* LP,
which Columbia had allowed to go out of print and which Seeger
wished to make available once again. Columbia was willing to
allow Asch to rerelease the album from the original masters, but
they would charge Folkways two dollars for each record sold.
Seeger wondered whether this would make the project prohibitively expensive and suggested that he simply rerecord the entire
album. Asch grumbled about the cost, but eventually a suitable
agreement was reached and the original 1966 Columbia album,
produced by Tom Wilson, appeared in 1982 on Folkways.
   Two final Pete Seeger albums had come out on Folkways by the

end of the decade. The first resulted from an encounter with William Gekel, an "advertising man" from New York's Dutchess County who approached Seeger one day while he was at work on a dugout canoe by the shore of the Hudson River. Seeger's attention had been drawn to the cause of conservation in the late sixties and with the launching of the sloop *Clearwater* in June 1969 he began to dedicate much of his time and energy to cleaning up the river that ran by his Beacon home. Gekel had written lyrics for several songs that traced the history of the Hudson River, and he hoped that Seeger might be willing to put them to music. He was, and the result was the 1976 album *Fifty Sail on Newburgh Bay,* which Seeger recorded with the help of Ed Renahan. Of the fifteen cuts on the album, only the title song would be picked up by other performers, although Seeger would remember "The Burning of Kingston" as the best of the lot.[15]

The last of his albums on Folkways resulted from Seeger's decision to record a concert for an album release "before my voice, memory and sense of rhythm and pitch were too far gone." He was sixty and his voice was still strong, but he was right that it would become wobbly and weak within a few years. Although Asch had released several albums of Seeger's live performances, Seeger did not feel that any of them had captured the singing of an audience as he would have liked. He arranged for sound engineer John Nagy to place twenty microphones in Harvard's Sanders theater—six on the stage and fourteen in the audience. On a cold day in January 1980 he and Toshi drove up to Cambridge from Beacon and prepared for a capacity audience of "parents, grandparents and pre-schoolers. They all sang like angels," reported Seeger in his album notes. Seeger hoped that the result would demonstrate one of his most enduring beliefs, that there was a special power in group singing that enabled people to transcend (but not obliterate) cultural boundaries. Group singing was peace making, just as it was an exploration of common human purposes:

> I find group sounds inspiring, especially "untrained" voices. I often think, as I face an audience, that here are people whose great-grandfathers were trying to chop off each other's heads. Yet here we all are, harmonizing. Likewise, who knows if one hundred years from now the descendants of present-day Americans, Russians, Chinese, Jews, Arabs, Pakistanis, Hindus, Afrikaners, Bantu, indigenous and invaders, may sometimes

sing together. . . . Technology and industrialization, if used
right, could free us and not destroy us. So far, the profit mo-
tive has proved too powerful. But countertrends are everywhere. Perhaps some of the ideas in this record may
encourage those who are working on those countertrends.[16]

Folklorist Henrietta Yurchenco was another who returned to Folkways after a protracted absence. Asch had released her *Indian Music
of Mexico—Tzotzil, Yaqui, Huichol, Sei Cora* (4413), which had resulted
from a 1948 field trip for the Library of Congress, in 1952. Yurchenco
was musically trained and produced radio shows with Woody
Guthrie and Leadbelly on WNYC during the Second World War.
Shortly after Guthrie's death, she was asked to write the first
Guthrie biography, for the youth market.[17] She did not return to
Asch until the late sixties, when he released an album of her *Latin
American Children's Game Songs* (7851). But thereafter she brought a
string of recordings to Asch, most of which had resulted from
various collecting expeditions she had taken with her Hunter
College students. A trip to Johns Island, South Carolina, in 1970
failed to add much to the body of work that the Carawans had
produced some years earlier, and the album notes did not make
any mention of the previous work (3840). But Nat Hentoff cited it
favorably in a *Village Voice* review, adding that "Moe Asch, who is
Folkways, has as usual made sure there are full texts as well as
essays on the music and its social context. Wouldn't you think
Moe would have gotten a Grammy Award by now?"[18]

Asch was miffed that Yurchenco brought the first results of a
mid-sixties expedition to Mexico and Guatemala to the Nonesuch
Explorer series, which resulted in *The Real Mexico,* Yurchenco's most
commercially successful album. But she subsequently brought
additional material from the same expedition to Asch, which he
released as *Music of the Maya-Quiches of Guatemala* (4226). And he was
particularly excited by her 1983 album of songs by Sephardic Jews
of Morocco (4208) and balked only briefly at the cost of reproducing her twenty-five pages of notes.[19]

Verna Gillis was another fine field collector who began to bring
Caribbean and African material to Asch in the mid-seventies. Unlike Stinson, Elektra, Riverside, and Asch's other competitors in the
mid-fifties who periodically took a chance on esoteric recordings,
Rounder, Philo, Flying Fish, and his other competitors twenty years
later readily conceded the field of ethnographic recordings to
Folkways. And increasingly in the final years this was the material

that dominated Asch's lists of new releases. Only very rarely did he expand his list in relatively new directions.

Jon Appleton, a composer of electronic music, represented one foray into a field not previously well represented in the catalogue. True, Asch had released John Cage's *Indeterminacy* in 1959, and Sam Charters had produced a series of recordings for Folkways in the mid-sixties of works by Charles Ives, one of America's most important composers, whose atonal compositions were then only very rarely recorded. But Asch had previously released avant-garde music only haphazardly, when he was presented with an opportunity to do so. Appleton had met Sam Charters in Sweden in 1970, and Charters suggested that he approach Asch about releasing some of his material. A couple albums of his work had appeared previously on Bob Thiele's Flying Dutchman label (including one with jazz trumpeter Don Cherry), but the label had gone bankrupt and Appleton had to resort to legal threats in order to retain the rights to his material. He sent Asch a tape in the fall of 1973: "I am doing so because I understand that you have specialized in one-of-a-kind recordings and I do not think there is a precedent for my work." Asch was "very intrigued." He agreed to release it as an album, but it would have to wait until spring of the following year because of the vinyl shortage. *The World Music Theatre of Jon Appleton* (33437) consisted of a series of pieces constructed from sounds that had been manipulated through the use of tape recorders, mixers and other sound processing equipment, and included "Times Square Times Ten" from one of his previous Flying Dutchman albums.[20]

Appleton was a professor of music at Dartmouth and the director of the college's electronic music studio. Over the next few years he collaborated with a research assistant and a student from Dartmouth's engineering school to develop a digital synthesizer. Some of the earliest fruits of this collaboration appeared on a 1976 Folkways release entitled *The Dartmouth Digital Synthesizer* (33442), which included compositions by Appleton and other members of the electronic music studio. Still later, out of a desire to produce an instrument that could produce music for concerts in real time, Appleton and his collaborators developed an enormously successful digital synthesizer for the commercial market that they called the synclavier. Appleton produced three additional Folkways albums using the synclavier, including a charming set of children's stories—"The Tale of William Mariner" and "The Snow Queen"—set to music and released as *Two Melodramas for Synclavier* (37470).

In 1981 Dartmouth inaugurated a new president, David McLaugh-lin, a former executive with Toro Mowers who was interested in finding ways to facilitate cooperation between the Dartmouth faculty and business enterprises so that the former might bring a degree of practical "realism" to their scholarship. McLaughlin ar-ranged for the establishment of a fund that would support faculty while they interned in relevant businesses, and he undoubtedly imagined that this would primarily benefit faculty in the sciences. But Appleton had recognized an opportunity, and he applied to be allowed to spend a summer working with Asch at Folkways. Their letter of agreement specified that Appleton would work for Folk-ways in the areas of "planning and marketing," and that he would determine how the company might "reach a wider audience in view of the changing technologies facing the record industry." Asch also hoped that Appleton would identify ethnomusicologists who could facilitate the release of his still-growing backlog of field recordings, and that he might help him market the electronic music in the catalogue. Since the release of Appleton's first Folk-ways recording eight years earlier, Asch had issued more than a dozen additional electronic music recordings, occasionally having called upon Appleton to evaluate them.[21]

Starting in June 1982 Appleton spent three days a week in New York, staying at the Empire Hotel. In some respects he was aghast at what he found. Asch's health was failing, and his hearing had become quite poor. In the late seventies, he had been diagnosed with diabetes and was consequently attempting to adhere to a very strict diet. He also seemed frequently disorganized, with visitors arriving at the door for meetings of which Asch had no memory. Asch squandered time on menial tasks and was extraor-dinarily uncomfortable with technological innovations for some-one who had once regarded himself as a pioneer of sound technology. Appleton attempted to have him adopt new marketing strategies, such as accepting credit cards or the use of an 800 phone line; when Asch learned what they would entail financially, he rejected them. It appeared hopeless.

But on one subject Asch was eager for any and all proposals, that is, the development of arrangements for the perpetuation of Folk-ways upon his death. Asch had not even reached retirement age when, in 1969, Fred Ramsey first approached the Rutgers Institute of Jazz Studies to see whether there might be some interest in its taking over the Folkways collection in some manner. There was. The institute's William Weinberg, a professor of industrial relations, met with Ramsey and Dean Ernest Lynton over lunch in late February the next year and developed the outlines of an initial strategy. Asch had a "fairly successful business," it seemed to them, which brought him a "good income" and which had "major assets in the form of masters and copyrights to a large number of recordings." Rutgers was not interested in entering into the record business, so it seemed wise to try to separate questions about the business from the future of the archive. Perhaps, they concluded, Rutgers might purchase the archive as a source of scholarship and thereby ensure its perpetuity; to Asch they would provide space and equipment, and maybe a partial salary in order to free him from some of his business obligations so that he could concentrate on the archives and perhaps even occasionally teach.[22] Ramsey drafted a proposal partly in order to secure NEH funding for the purchase of the archive:

> As Moe Asch approaches the official age for "retirement," he contemplates many unissued materials, many projects that require completion and publication, that are already housed in his private archives. There is hardly time left without help for him to complete many valid, essential projects for general release; and much less time than this for putting the whole house of his material in order. . . . Without the earliest possible assistance, there remains the serious threat that his private collections and archives of unissued materials will be either lost, or scattered.

Ramsey appended a partial list of prominent scholars who had contributed to the Folkways collection over the years.[23]

Asch traveled to Rutgers and met with representatives of the university and the Institute of Jazz Studies over lunch at the faculty club that May. But although the administration of the institute remained enthusiastic, money for the purchase was not forthcoming and the proposal floundered for a couple of years. Weinberg revitalized the proposal in the spring of 1973, and Asch again took the bus to New Brunswick in order to talk with him and Dean Lynton. Another proposal was drafted to the university, this one including the management of the business operation out of Rutgers' facilities. Still the collaboration foundered; Dean Lynton had become an important supporter, but he left the university at the end of the year to take a post at the University of Massachusetts. Weinberg tried again to interest Rutgers in the Folkways collection in 1975 and met with representatives of the Rockefeller Foundation from whom he received hopeful signals about funding. A date in February was established for a formal presentation to Rockefeller, but at the end of March Rutgers had still not moved. There matters would rest for the next eight years.[24]

But Appleton's growing involvement with Folkways opened up another possibility. Felix Powell, the chair of the Department of Music at the University of Maryland, became interested in the early eighties about the possibility of moving the operation to Baltimore and establishing it within the structure of that university. There were discussions about having Appleton step in to direct it. At the same time Asch's son Michael, who had been teaching anthropology at the University of Alberta since 1971, had become involved in efforts to find a home for Folkways. Asch tried to arrange a meeting between Powell and his son in March 1983, when Michael was coming east for a symposium. It seemed to Appleton that Asch would have liked nothing better than to have his son take over the operation, but neither Asch nor Michael ever broached the subject with the other. Each knew that the moment had long since passed when Michael could have entered the business. He was now tenured, and even had he been interested he could not gamble his family's financial stability on the unlikely prospects of Folkways Records. Under other circumstances might he have been interested? His father would never precisely know, and perhaps dared not inquire for fear of discovering that his son might have preferred to do other things with his life. Additionally, however, Asch was torn by warring impulses: he wanted to be certain that Folkways would outlive him, but even well into his seventies he was having a difficult time letting go of it.

By early 1984 Powell had drafted a letter to Asch on behalf of Maryland's vice president for university development, Robert G. Smith. Ostensibly based upon a conversation Powell had had with Asch and his son at a Greenwich Village restaurant the previous year, it outlined the university's intentions to assume responsibility for the Folkways archive as well as the management of the business, and they accepted Asch's stipulation that the entire catalogue continue to be made available to the public. Asch would be retained as a consultant, although his salary would be "tied to the profits of the company." And they held out the possibility of a faculty position for Jon Appleton, which would enable him to take over the running of the business. The following August, with little movement on the Maryland negotiations, Appleton wrote to Asch:

I do not know the state of your negotiations with the University of Maryland Foundation. I was encouraged by our meeting in New York and I hope any differences can be worked out. It would be a dream come true if I could come to work with you at Folkways and eventually see that the direction you have taken is continued. Frankly, I worry a lot about what will happen to the company if you cannot come to some agreement on transferring the operation in the near future.[25]

At the same moment, there were also signs of interest from yet another quarter—the Smithsonian Institution—and the letter from Maryland added a note of caution on that score:

The Smithsonian is a very well known institution, but it is also a very large institution. I would urge you to be careful in this regard. At the University of Maryland, Folkways and all you have built it to mean, would receive a major share of our attention. One can only wonder if this would be true at an institution the size of the Smithsonian.[26]

Michael Asch recalled that there was an important missing ingredient in the discussions with Maryland; the representatives of the university imagined that the archives and the business would essentially be donated to them. Asch, with his financial future (and that of Frances) very much on his mind, had no intention of simply donating it.

At the time of the negotiations with Maryland Asch was in the process of moving once again. He had been working in the vicinity of Lincoln Center for about seven years, and it had become his neighborhood. Just as in the old days on Forty-sixth Street, he had become a regular at nearby restaurants, where he was greeted by name and his dietary requirements were well known. But the area had become upscale, and Asch could no longer afford his spacious offices. Although then seventy-eight years old, Asch optimistically had his accountant negotiate a lease of several years for office space on lower Broadway, in the Village. The new space had one important advantage—he was now within walking distance of his home and would no longer have to ride the subway in the morning. But Appleton recalled that the move from West Sixty-first Street was a blow to Asch; although the Village was his "home," he had spent few waking hours there over the years, and it was not an easy matter at his age to reestablish his work environment in a new place.

Rutgers had entered the picture once again in the summer of 1983. Irving Louis Horowitz, the prominent sociologist, was running Transaction Books in collaboration with the university and saw the possibility of adding Folkways to his publishing operation. He wrote to Asch suggesting that Transaction had marketing and production facilities that could as "easily accommodate the sale and distribution of recordings no less than books," and he persuaded Asch to pay yet another visit to Rutgers that summer. In August Michael Asch drove his father and mother down to New Brunswick for a meeting with Weinberg. Signs were not auspicious. Asch had recently had eye surgery because of a problem related to diabetes; afterward he had vainly neglected to wear an eye patch, and then hit his eye while exiting a taxi cab and as a consequence the surgery was not successful. In a memo to Horowitz, Weinberg wrote, "Mrs. Asch sat quietly but was more inclined to shake her head rather than nod; it was hot; a thunderstorm broke out and Asch's son and I managed to get Moe's attention over a period of several hours."[27]

Still, Michael and his father returned at the end of September in order to talk with Horowitz—the meeting of two legends, as Michael later recalled. Asch toured the Transaction operation and declared that he was not impressed with its efficiency: he did more business annually than did Transaction, with less than half the publisher's staff. Horowitz later wrote him, expressing his pleasure at having met Asch and his son: "It is not often that one has the opportunity of lunching with a legend; and certainly a pioneering spirit who over the course of a half century has provided a solid foundation to the study and enjoyment of folk, ethnic, and popular culture." But Horowitz seemed no more than mildly hopeful that the arrangement would work out; although a proposal was sent to Asch in October by Transaction's publisher, there was still no provision for the purchase of the collection, which Michael Asch had then estimated to be worth $1.5 million. Transaction was prepared to put Asch on salary and would provide for an annuity for him and, if necessary, Frances. But Horowitz had made it clear that Transaction would ultimately want to own the label, its inventory, and archive, and there was no provision for the purchase of the assets.[28]

Asch continued to communicate with anyone who expressed the slightest interest in taking over the company—universities, foundations, publishers, entrepreneurs. In late 1984 it appeared that Asch was on the verge of selling Folkways outright to a company in California—then nothing.[29] Asch seemed almost in a panic to find the right means of perpetuating his creation, but he could not commit to an arrangement with anyone. Remarkably, he was still regularly releasing albums. In some instances it was a matter of pulling long-neglected material off his shelves and releasing it at long last. He found a Northern Illinois University professor who could write notes to accompany the albums of Chinese folk music that Guy Carawan had brought back from the People's Republic in 1958 and released them in 1980 as the *Vocal Music of Contemporary China*, volumes 1 and 2 (4091, 4092). That same year the Carawans approached him about releasing some of the material from their archive of civil rights material, to which he readily agreed. The result was a series of three documentary albums about the movement entitled *Lest We Forget*. Ossie Davis, who had recorded the autobiography of Frederick Douglass for a two-volume set produced by Philip Foner in the mid-sixties, recorded two additional volumes of the speeches of Frederick Douglass for Foner, which Asch released in a series of recordings in 1975 and 1977. Ruby Dee recorded a series of speeches by prominent African American women that were released at the same time (5522, 5526, 5527, 5528, 5537, 5538). In the mid-seventies Don Molnar, a Scholastic employee who had worked with Asch during the years of that collaboration, proposed making a series of albums based on the Watergate testimony that he had taped off the radio, which Asch agreed to release with typical contrarian glee (5551, 5552, 5553, 5554, 5555).

Still other recordings were coming to him through the mail from hopeful young musicians. Although Asch would have denied it, he was permitting a few musicians to use Folkways as a vanity label. With a small advance on royalties that was almost never sufficient, musicians would record an album on their own; sales of the resultant album were dependent upon the energy and entrepreneurship of the musicians, who sold them at concerts or through their own mail-order efforts. Sometimes the results were surprisingly good. Lucinda Williams, whose "Passionate Kisses" would become a country and western hit for Mary Chapin Carpenter in 1993, recorded her first two albums for Folkways before going on to her own substantial commercial success. More typical was Bob Everhart, a country singer and songwriter for whom Asch released five albums between 1978 and 1985, the Bergerfolk, who released four albums on Folkways between 1971 and 1978, or Tom Parrot (a *Broadside* songwriter), of whose *Neon Princess* album Asch either optimistically or accidentally pressed two thousand copies (Rounder Records still had eighteen hundred of them in 1990 and tried in vain to locate the artist in hopes of unloading them [31009]).

By sheer will power (and occasional financial contributions) Gordon Friesen and Sis Cunningham were managing to keep *Broadside* alive into the 1980s. There clearly was not going to be a "next" Bob Dylan or Phil Ochs coming out of the magazine, but they occasionally encountered a singer-songwriter who wrote with sufficient political conviction that they would prevail upon Asch to release an album or two. Asch released Jeff Ampolsk's *God, Guns and Guts* (5350) in 1977 and *Brown Water and Blood* (5261) in 1979. By the late seventies, trenchant rhetoric of this kind was beginning to sound more than a little anachronistic, and there was too little market for political material to contribute much to the solvency of the magazine. Friesen's health was beginning to fail; the one "star" of the early *Broadside* years who remained in touch into the seventies was Phil Ochs, but his health had also been deteriorating and his musical career had essentially ended. But not so his political engagement.

Ochs's political convictions ran far deeper than those of any of the other early *Broadside* songwriters, and long after Dylan had ceased to be a "topical" songwriter Ochs was singing for political rallies throughout the country, including most of the major anti–Vietnam War rallies and the protest against the 1968 Chicago Democratic National Convention. Some have dated his gradual mental collapse to the disillusionment of the Left that followed the debacle in Chicago. The album he recorded for A&M Records that year, *Rehearsal for Retirement,* featured a grave marker on the cover with the inscription "Phil Ochs (American), born: El Paso, Texas 1940, died: Chicago, Illinois, 1968." Others have attributed it to his inability to attain the commercial success of his hero Elvis Presley or his rival and occasional antagonist, Bob Dylan. Ochs was famished for a popular recognition that became increasingly elusive. When in 1970 he donned a gold suit made by Presley's tailor and arranged a series of concerts in which he would perform Presley and Buddy Holly songs, his audience may well have regarded it as a put-on. It wasn't.

Perhaps the contradictions between these impulses was irreconcilable, but the impulses were no less genuine. By 1973 Ochs was frequently drunk in public, his behavior erratic, sometimes menacing. But he arranged a tour of South America that year with his former yippie compatriot Jerry Rubin, where in Chile he hoped to view firsthand the effects of the region's only democratically elected Marxist government. There he came to know Victor Jara, the revolutionary singer-songwriter who would shortly be tortured to death when Allende's fragile democracy was overthrown. Later in the year he traveled to Africa, where, years before Paul Simon's *Graceland* album, Ochs recorded a single in collaboration with a local Kenyan band. One evening some days later he was badly beaten on a beach in Tanzania, with the effect that he lost much of his vocal range.[30]

Through it all the Friesens remained loyal friends. They had encountered a young singer-songwriter named Sammy Walker who was identified as yet another "new Dylan" and arranged for WBAI to play some tapes that he had made in their apartment on a show one evening in 1975. Ochs heard him over the radio and became wildly enthusiastic, so Sis Cunningham arranged to have him meet Walker at her apartment.[31] It was Ochs's idea to produce an album of Walker for *Broadside*, and Sis received Asch's support to book a basement recording studio in the Village that Ochs had chosen. But Ochs arrived drunk and an hour late for the session; Asch was furious about the wasted studio time, maintaining later that Ochs was the only Folkways artist who had ever shown up drunk for a recording session. Although Ochs sang harmony on a couple songs, his presence became a hindrance over the course of the session and they could not finish until he had been ejected. Ochs was generously listed as the producer of *Songs for Patty* (5310), which featured a photograph of Patty Hearst on the cover, an unlikely representative of genuine political engagement but perhaps a fitting symbol of the confusing twists that Ochs and others had taken in an effort to find a successor to the New Left politics of the late sixties. Asch had Walker record an album of Woody Guthrie songs later in the decade (Logan English, Jack Elliott, Will Geer, and Pete Seeger had all by then produced Folkways albums dedicated to Woody Guthrie material), and Walker would go on to record two albums for Warner Brothers. But as usual the sighting of a new Dylan was a mirage.

The same year Ochs offered to perform a concert as a benefit for *Broadside*. The concert earned the struggling magazine five hundred dollars, and Ochs turned a poorly recorded tape of the event over to the Friesens with the suggestion that they "give 'em one more Broadside." They responded that there was not sufficient material to fill an album, and in any case many of his "best and strongest" songs were not represented. Ochs laughed. "Look," he said, "you've got other tapes of mine. I don't think there's a single song I ever wrote that I didn't tape for you. Just splice on what you want. It's all yours. Have Moe Asch put it out."[32]

In the final months of his life, Ochs often arrived at the Friesen's door first thing in the morning, having spent the night in the park. Dirty, his shoes untied and without socks, he would ask whether they might allow him to lie down somewhere and sleep. Late in the day he would wake up, ask for something to eat, and talk with Friesen for hours. Much of what he talked about was the surveillance he felt sure that the FBI was keeping on him. He would take them to the window and point out a figure on the street: "See that man down there. He's FBI, he followed me here."

The Friesens believed him, and they had some reason to. The FBI had compiled a file of more than four hundred pages on Ochs and clearly regarded him as a subversive. Sis and Gordon procured his file through the Freedom of Information Act and published some of it in *Broadside*. There was little doubt at this point that Ochs was manic-depressive, and it was his illness that had caused his deterioration. But the Friesens felt that it was neither his commercial failure nor his political disillusionment that had hastened his end but the constant hounding of the FBI. After all, it had happened before, to Paul Robeson, a man similarly crushed emotionally by the constant harangue of the U.S. intelligence apparatus. On 9 April 1976 Phil Ochs hanged himself in his sister's home in Far Rockaway.

Sis and Gordon did as they were bidden and arranged for Asch to release the tape of one of Ochs's last concerts as a memorial album, volume 10 in the Broadside series (5320). Later in the year they had Asch release a recording of interviews with Ochs that they had compiled over the years, which contained his thoughts on the state of the music business and of American politics (5321).

In 1980 Sis and Gordon culled through their library of tapes to produce a second volume of Phil Ochs songs (5362), and then there was a second volume of interviews. The second volume of songs consisted of material that Ochs had recorded in their apartment between 1962 and 1964; on one he is accompanied by Eric Andersen. This set off a long and angry correspondence with Ochs's brother Michael, who attempted to stop the sale of what he regarded as illegal, bootleg albums. Friesen responded that the albums were intended merely to "do what little we could to keep Phil's name alive":

> Phil did more for us that we ever did for him, although you
> must remember back in 1963 when we managed to get him

onto a workshop at the Newport Folk Festival at the last moment. You drove him there, with you and Mike Asch and Arlo
Guthrie in the front seat of your compact and Phil, sick, lying
on the back seat. Phil received a standing ovation when he
sang "Birmingham Jam." He said many times that this was the
key factor in starting him on his career.

Friesen went on to insist that he had consulted with Ochs's sister
Sonny about the release of the first interview album, and she had
in fact provided a photograph for the cover:

> It was purely a labor of love. We haven't received a red cent as
> yet for the last LP. Meantime, Sis and I are both in ill health
> with heart trouble and living on measly Social Security checks
> and foodstamps. Sis even was mistaken for a bag lady the
> other day. . . . You know Moe Asch's situation as well as we
> do. His is a small firm with no advertising, promotion or distri-
> bution to speak of. There is no way these records will ever
> pay for themselves. Nor did we or Moe ever expect them to.

Michael Ochs persisted, instructing his lawyer to write to both
Asch and the Friesens. Ochs was in "diminished mental capacity
during the last several years of his life and thus did not have the
means of acting reasonably in turning tapes of interview over to
Broadside," maintained the lawyer. The sales of the Broadside series
albums were harming the sales of Ochs's A&M albums. It was a
claim that would be hard to prove, but the second interview
album—perhaps because of some potentially libelous things that
the interviewer had said about Bob Dylan—was eventually taken
out of the catalogue.[33]

Sam Charters came back into Asch's life in the early eighties,
having lived and worked in Sweden for some years. Few people
ran as hot and cold on the subject of Moe Asch as did Charters.
He and his wife Ann Charters had become close to Marian Distler
in the years prior to her suicide, occasionally attending an art
opening with her or some other Village cultural event. Charters
believed that Asch had driven Distler to suicide with his violent,
belittling temper and he remained appalled at the sadistic bullying
to which Asch subjected his immediate employees—particularly
the women. "I've never known a more vicious man in my life,"
recalled Charters without hesitation.[34]

On the other hand Charters felt that Asch treated his "creative"
collaborators—Ramsey, Courlander, Langston Hughes, himself—

with nothing less than the measured respect that was due them. Simultaneously, though he sometimes felt that Asch got his due and then some, Charters would express unbound, almost fawning, admiration for Asch's work. In 1959 he dedicated his *Country Blues* book to Asch in an extraordinarily encomium:

> I don't really know whether your work could be called "creative" in an artistic sense, but the continued effort you have made to document the music of the world's peoples seems to me to include a creative concept that has given us a new awareness of both the music around us and the life that has produced it. Is this "Art?" I think so—in the fullest sense of the word.

In 1981 Charters wrote to Asch proposing that he assemble a kind of recorded "festschrift" for him, which would include a compendium of cuts from his most important recordings as well as a booklet containing statements from the many people whose work Asch had released over the years:

> For some time I've been trying to think of some way to say something about all of your work over these long years and I've decided, every time, that simply writing something wouldn't give the feeling of all that you've done, since you have worked with music and sound. I have been thinking now of doing something with all the things you've been responsible for—as a kind of testimony to what you've created.[35]

In a subsequent telephone conversation, Asch asked to hear more about Charters's proposed project, and he responded with more details that February. It would consist of a box set entitled "A World of Music: A Tribute to Moses Asch," with each of four LPs dedicated to "songs of America's people," "music of the world's people," "jazz," and "new voices and new worlds." He would ask Ronald Clyne to contribute a cover and Dave Gahr to contribute some photographs. Finally, he would interview Asch in order to write a biography to be included in the booklet.

Charters set to work, writing to a great many Folkways artists and producers, asking them to contribute a short written piece honoring Asch for inclusion in the booklet. Some material started to come in, including a poem for Asch written by Nikki Giovanni, who had recorded three albums of poetry for Folkways in the seventies. But Asch remained noncommittal and ultimately could not bring himself to support the project. Charters was left with the embarrassing task of informing the contributors that he would not be using their material. It seemed surprising for a man who had had little difficulty celebrating his own accomplishments in the past. Yet on the brink of the most deliberate celebration to date of his life work, Asch hesitated. Perhaps he feared that his name was not sufficiently recognizable to render the project commercially viable; or maybe he found it unseemly to draw attention to himself so publicly.

In 1985, at the age of eighty, Asch recognized that his health would not enable him to work much longer. Negotiations with the Smithsonian had picked up, and with Ralph Rinzler pushing hard for the purchase of the collection things appeared hopeful. Simultaneously, however, Asch had a detailed conversation with Walter Handelman, his lawyer, about the perpetuation of Folkways as a nonprofit trust. Michael would be the executor of the trust, and it would be established as a means of ensuring the perpetuation of the company for as long as possible. Asch was asked in the course of the conversation whether Folkways was profitable. "Folkways is able to continue," he replied cautiously. "Whether it is profitable—that's a question of semantics."

Asch had been forced over the preceding year to plow $250,000 back into the business, because it was not meeting its financial obligations. Although in the preceding six months it had not been necessary to invest any additional capital in the company, neither was he drawing any salary. Rather, he was drawing a sum of money against the "loan" he had made to the business. But business had hit bottom, and he was not billing sufficiently to pay his debts. What might have surprised even some of his closer collaborators, however, was the fact that he had a quarter of a million dollars at hand to reinvest in the company.[36]

Rinzler began to work furiously, suspecting that Asch's health would give him very little time. In the spring of 1986 he had to convince the regents of the Smithsonian of the wisdom of purchasing Folkways and of making a long-term commitment to its perpetuation. Equally daunting was the task of convincing Asch to relinquish his life work on terms the Smithsonian would find acceptable. Asch's own conditions remained largely unchanged: he wanted to be paid a sufficiently generous sum for the business to ensure his and Frances's financial future and to be able to leave an inheritance to Michael and his children. The entire catalogue would have to remain available, although Asch conceded that it might not be necessary or practical to retain LP stock on all the titles. Rather, some titles might be kept available by making cassette copies on demand, and in any case the compact disc could render the LP obsolete by the end of the century. And the supervision of the business and accompanying collection would be overseen by an advisory committee consisting of Asch, his son Michael, Toshi Seeger, Harold Courlander, Sam Charters, and Ralph Rinzler.

Asch and his lawyer drafted a proposal on 9 June and gave the Smithsonian ten days to accept or reject it. They let the Smithsonian know that there were still other interested parties but assured Rinzler that the Smithsonian had "first preference."[37] Rinzler responded four days later:

> As you know, we are pushing ahead on lining up supporters with a view towards completing these arrangements as rapidly as possible. In the interest of speeding up this process, please call me as soon anytime something we send you . . . may pose a question. . . . I hesitated to bother you
> at home, but perhaps, in the future, I will not hesitate to call you directly to keep things moving more quickly.[38]

In July Rinzler met with the Asches in their Village apartment. The negotiations at the Smithsonian were preceding apace, but he needed a little additional time to secure the regents' approval. They agreed. In early August the financing from the Smithsonian had been secured, and Rinzler wrote to Asch and his wife to deliver the good news. The approval of the regents seemed to Rinzler to be nothing more than a formality: "It remains my firm view that the Regents will approve the transaction without hesitancy; I have absolutely no reason to suspect otherwise." But they would not meet until 3 September, and he begged their patience for another month. Rinzler proposed a signing date of 1 October, with a good-faith deposit on the initial payment should the Smithsonian be responsible for any delay beyond that.[39]

The regents approved the purchase of Folkways in early September, as Rinzler had predicted.[40] But Asch had been suffering a series of strokes and was becoming progressively incapacitated. Finally confined to a wheelchair, he still insisted on coming into the office every day. His wife Frances would wheel him in and attempt to help him sort through his business obligations. Yet Frances, although integrally involved with the Smithsonian negotiations, had little sense of the day-to-day operation and could only add to the chaos that began to swirl around Asch and Folkways in his final days. For the first time in his thirty-year collaboration with Sam Charters, Asch put him on salary and had him work out of the offices on lower Broadway in an effort to put the business and the archives into some semblance of order in preparation for its sale. But the combination of Charters and Frances Asch was hopelessly volatile, and Marilyn Conklin Averett, attempting to play peacemaker, received fire from both sides. Frances accused Charters of using the Folkways premises to conduct his own business; Charters claimed that Frances presided over the sale of objects from Asch's art collection over her husband's feeble but heart-wrenching protests.[41]

It was a sad finish, and then the true end came very suddenly. The signing of the papers with the Smithsonian had to be postponed. Another stroke had put Asch in Lenox Hill Hospital eleven days earlier, and on 19 October he died of a heart attack. At his death he knew that the Smithsonian agreement was imminent, but he was prevented from witnessing its conclusion.

Word went out very quickly to the Folkways faithful. Rinzler was one of the first to hear and immediately sent Frances a note of condolence:

> Moe and his work have had a profound impact on the way people here and abroad think about art, peace, other people and other people's art. He has changed the lives of many and given voice—beyond life—to literally thousands of musicians. Beyond *all of our lives,* his work will continue, but at this moment of grief that is surely no consolation. My own life's work was shaped by his influence—decisively—and I promise you his work will take on new energy in its new incarnation here.[42]

Irwin Silber and Barbara Dane sent Frances a telegram from California: "Moe Asch's life was a never-ending demonstration of how a determined imaginative irascible and ultimately irresistible individual can influence the way in which the world looks at itself. The wonderful thing is that Folkways recordings will continue to carry out Moe's mission for many decades to come."[43]

Obituaries in the *New York Times,* the *Village Voice,* and *Rolling Stone* were equally magnanimous. *Times* music critic Jon Pareles acquired an unusually generous quotation from Alan Lomax: "Moe was an explorer . . . but an eminently practical explorer, and vox humana was his terrain. As an engineer, and a very canny businessman, he used the record business to keep his rather isolationist country-men sensitive to the wide range of the world. He's been extremely important in keeping America humane and urbane."[44]

The service was held in a funeral home on the Lower East Side, in the old Yiddish theater district where his electronics career had first flourished. Ella Jenkins arrived early and went into a deli to get a bite to eat. She approached some others there whose faces were not familiar to her but whom, she suspected, had also come for Asch's funeral.

"Are you going to Moe Asch's funeral?" she asked them.

"Yes, how did you know?" they responded.

"You just look like it." And what did that mean? "I don't know, you just look . . . folky." They introduced themselves, and she recognized the names: Ralph Rinzler, Bess Hawes.

The faithful had come to say goodbye. Hastily organized in the Jewish tradition, it was a modest and rather ordinary funeral. But a year later, when Jewish tradition would have otherwise dictated the unveiling of a headstone, Frances and Michael, with Marilyn Averett, Harold Leventhal, Ralph Rinzler, and Toshi Seeger, planned a joyful send-off and celebration of Asch's life and work. It was to be a grand concert, held at Symphony Space on Upper Broadway, with old friends, old antagonists, old collaborators, and comrades. Music critic Robert Palmer wrote a piece about the upcoming tribute for the *Times* the day before. "Without Moe," Harold Leventhal had told him, "we might never have heard of Woody Guthrie, Pete Seeger and their contemporaries; we might never have had a folk revival." But, Palmer continued, Asch's contribution extended beyond the shaping of Americans' idea of their musical vernacular:

> Folkways was issuing records of music from Africa, Asia and other cultures years before it became chic to mention pygmy music in dinner-party conversations; before Indian ragas in-spired the minimalist harmonies and cyclical rhythms of Terry Riley and Philip Glass; before field recordings of East Euro-pean choral singing and African drumming became required listening for jazz and rock musicians. Moses Asch probably did more than any other individual to create a climate for the appreciation of world music.[45]

Eighty-seven individuals and organizations contributed to the sponsorship of the concert, many of them performers or business colleagues. A couple dozen shared the stage in order to make music, to lead the audience in singing, and—most important—to tell Moe Asch stories. It seemed that everyone had one. They were told with humor, with exasperation, with fond recollection. It was the folk process at work.

NOTES

INTERVIEWS

Jon Appleton, interview with author, Hanover, New Hampshire, 15 August 1991, cassette tapes in possession of the author.

Frances Asch, interview with author, New York City, 9 August 1991, cassette tape in possession of the author.

John Asch, interview with author, New York City, 24 July 1990, cassette tape in possession of the author.

John Asch, interview with Gary Kenton, New York City, 20 March 1983, transcript in possession of Gary Kenton, Greensboro, North Carolina.

Michael Asch, interview with author, New York City, 29 March 1991, handwritten notes in possession of the author; also Princeton, New Jersey, 16 April 1992, cassette tape in possession of the author.

Moses Asch, interview with Jon Appleton, New York City, 7 November 1982, cassette tape in possession of Jon Appleton, Hanover, New Hampshire.

Moses Asch, interview with David Dunaway, New York City, 8 May 1977, cassette tapes in possession of David Dunaway, Albuquerque, New Mexico.

Moses Asch, interview with Ashley Kahn, New York City, January 1983, cassette tape in possession of the author.

Moses Asch, interview with Joe Klein, New York City, December 1977, cassette tapes in Woody Guthrie Archive, New York City.

Moses Asch, interview with lawyer, New York City, n.d., acquisition no. FP-1988-0196, cassette tape in Folkways Archives and Collections, Smithsonian Institution.

Moses Asch, interview with Guy Logsdon, New York City, 8 July 1974, cassette tape in possession of Guy Logsdon, Tulsa, Oklahoma.

Moses Asch, interview with Tony Schwartz, New York City, 11 March 1971, cassette tapes in Folkways Archives and Collections, Smithsonian Institution.

Moses Asch, interview with Israel Young, New York City, 13 June 1970, typescript in *Sing Out!* Archives, Bethlehem, Pennsylvania.

Moses Asch and Frederic Ramsey, interview for National Public Radio with Elisabeth Perez Luna, New York City, 10 February 1983, transcript in possession of Elisabeth Perez Luna, Miami, Florida.

Marilyn Conklin Averett, interview with Anthony Seeger, Jeff Place, Lori Taylor, and Matt Walters, Somerville, Massachusetts, 30 July 1991, cassette tapes in Folkways Archives and Collections, Smithsonian Institution.

Guy Carawan and Candie Carawan, interview with author, New Market, Tennessee, 28 and 29 December 1991, cassette tapes in possession of the author.

Richard Carlin, interview with author, Lawrence, New Jersey, 9 July 1990, cassette tape in possession of the author.

Sam Charters, interview with author, Storrs, Connecticut, 27 June 1996, cassette tape in possession of the author.

John Cohen, interview with author, New York City, 12 June 1991, cassette tapes in possession of the author.

Harold Courlander, interview with author, Bethesda, Maryland, 7 August 1991, cassette tapes in possession of the author.

Sidney Cowell, interview with author, Shady, New York, 3 January 1992, cassette tapes in possession of the author.

Agnes (Sis) Cunningham, interview with author, New York City, 22 March 1991, cassette tapes in possession of the author.

Kenneth Goldstein, interview with author, Philadelphia, 3 September 1991, cassette tapes in possession of the author.

David Jasen, interview with author, Greenvale, New York, 4 September 1990, cassette tapes in possession of the author.

Ella Jenkins, interview with author, Chicago, 22 August 1991, cassette tapes in possession of the author.

Mel Kaiser, interview with author, Teaneck, New Jersey, 29 August 1991, cassette tape in possession of the author.

Harold Leventhal, interview with author, New York City, 14 March 1991, cassette tape in possession of the author.

Frederic Ramsey, interview with author, Stockton, New Jersey, 17 July 1990, cassette tapes in possession of the author.

Frederic Ramsey, interview with Gary Kenton, Stockton, New Jersey, September 1983, cassette tape in possession of Gary Kenton, Greensboro, North Carolina.

Ralph Rinzler, interview with author, Washington, D.C., 13 June 1991, cassette tapes in possession of the author.

Kevin Roth, interview of the author, Princeton, New Jersey, 20 September 1991, cassette tapes in possession of the author.

Ruth Rubin, interview with author, New York City, 9 October 1990, cassette tapes in possession of the author.

Tony Schwartz, interview with author, New York City, 18 July 1991, cassette tape in possession of the author.

Pete Seeger, interview with Gary Kenton, New York City, March 1983, cassette tape in possession of Gary Kenton, Greensboro, North Carolina.

Pete Seeger and Toshi Seeger, interview with author, Washington, D.C., 11 October 1996, handwritten notes in possession of the author.

Irwin Silber, interview with author, New York City, 7 August 1992, cassette tape in possession of the author.

Irwin Silber, interview with Gary Kenton, New York City, June 1983, cassette tape in possession of Gary Kenton, Greensboro, North Carolina.

Harry Smith, interview with Gary Kenton, New York City, March 1983, cassette tape in possession of Gary Kenton, Greensboro, North Carolina.

Adam Spiro, interview with author, Wayne, New Jersey, 2 July 1991, cassette tapes in possession of the author.

Henrietta Yurchenco, interview with author, New York City, 26 June 1992, cassette tapes in possession of the author.

INTRODUCTION

1. In anthropology, the concept of "cultural broker" developed out of an effort to understand the relationship between local, culturally homogenous communities and emerging national structures of economic and political power. Thus in the wake of the 1910 revolution in Mexico, a class of entrepreneurs developed who stood precariously between local community interests and powerful national interests, knowledgeable about the cultural practices of both and invested in neither. They carved a niche for themselves that was dependent on enabling the two levels of Mexican society to negotiate with one another and pursue their interests without altogether resolving the tension between them, for the resolution would put the broker out of a job. The broker concept was first articulated in Eric Wolf's "Aspects of Group Relations in a Complex Society: Mexico," *American Anthropologist* 58, no. 6 (December 1956): 1065–78.

2. Terry Turner, "Representing, Resisting Rethinking: Historical Transformations of Kayapo Culture and Anthropological Consciousness," in *Colonial Situations: Essays on the Contextualization of Ethnographic Knowledge,* ed. George Stocking (Madison: University of Wisconsin Press, 1991), 301.

3. Moses Asch, interview with Jon Appleton.
4. Janet Malcolm, *The Silent Woman: Sylvia Plath and Ted Hughes.* (New York: Knopf, 1994), 8–10.

1. REVOLUTIONARY BEGINNINGS

1. Sholem Asch, "Kola Street," in *A Treasury of Yiddish Stories,* ed. Irving Howe and Eliezer Greenberg (New York: Viking Press, 1954), 261.
2. See particularly the figure of Reb Israel Zychlinski in "Kola Street" and Reb Yechezkiel Gumbiner in "The Little Town." *Tales of My People* (New York: Putnam, 1948.)
3. S. Asch, "Kola Street," 261.
4. *Encyclopedia Judaica,* s.v. "Sholem Asch" (Jerusalem: Macmillan, 1971), 684.
5. Irving Howe, *World of Our Fathers* (New York: Simon and Schuster, 1976), 9.
6. S. Asch, "Little Town," 97.
7. Ibid., 101.
8. Ben Siegel, *The Controversial Sholem Asch* (Bowling Green, Ohio: Bowling Green University Popular Press, 1976), 15.
9. Sholem Asch, "I Adopt an Ancestor," *American Mercury* 56 (January 1943): 47.
10. Sholem Asch, "The Guilty Ones," *Atlantic Monthly* 166 (December 1940): 713–14.
11. Howe, *World of Our Fathers,* 21.
12. Nora Levin, *While Messiah Tarried: Jewish Socialist Movements, 1871–1917* (New York: Schocken Books, 1977), 15.
13. Levin, *While Messiah Tarried,* 17–19.
14. Sholem Asch, *The Mother* (1930; rev. ed., Garden City: Sun Dial Press, 1950), 62.
15. Howe, *World of Our Fathers,* 19.
16. Siegel, *Controversial Sholem Asch,* 18.
17. S. Niger, quoted in Charles A. Madison, *Yiddish Literature: Its Scope and Major Writers* (New York: Frederick Ungar Publishing, 1968), 222.
18. Siegel, *Controversial Sholem Asch,* 236 n. 2.
19. Ibid., 18.
20. Sholem Asch, *Three Cities* (New York: G. P. Putnam's Sons, 1933), 285, 310–11.
21. Jeff Schatz, *The Generation: The Rise and Fall of the Jewish Communists of Poland* (Berkeley and Los Angeles: University of California Press, 1991), 76.
22. Matilda Asch to Nathan Asch, 29 January 1936, Nathan Asch Papers, Winthrop College, Rock Hill, South Carolina (hereafter cited as Nathan Asch Papers).

23. Nathan Asch, "Grandfather," unpublished MS, Nathan Asch Papers.
24. Adam Spiro, interview with author.
25. N. Asch, "Grandfather."
26. Nathan Asch, "My Father," unpublished MS, pp. 4, 8, Nathan Asch Papers. (A greatly reduced version of this manuscript appeared as "My Father and I" in *Commentary*.)
27. Nathan Asch, "My Father and I," *Commentary* 39 (January 1965): 56.
28. S. Asch, *Three Cities*, 565.
29. Abraham Ascher, *The Revolution of 1905: Russia in Disarray* (Stanford, Calif.: Stanford University Press, 1988), 53, 157.
30. Levin, *While Messiah Tarried*, 308.
31. Ascher, *Revolution of 1905*, 157.
32. *New York Times*, 28 January, 8 February 1905, pp. 1 and 2, respectively.
33. S. Asch, *Three Cities*, 536.
34. N. Asch, "Grandfather," 2.
35. *New York Times*, 2, 3 May 1905.
36. Nathan Asch reported in his sketch "Grandfather" (4) that Menachem Mendel traveled to St. Petersburg in order to appeal to the czar's representatives for his son's life. However, he apparently confused his uncle's imprisonment with that of Isaac Weinberg (his eventual brother-in-law), whose mother *did* appeal to the government in St. Petersburg in a successful bid to have her son's life spared. In *Three Cities*, the character of Weinberg's mother is conflated with that of Bruha Spiro, whose fictional counterpart, Rachel-Leah, likewise travels to St. Petersburg to have her son's life spared.
37. Siegel, *Controversial Sholem Asch*, 34.
38. Quoted in Ascher, *Revolution of 1905*, 134.
39. Ibid., 135.
40. Ibid., 193.
41. Levin, *While Messiah Tarried*, 327; Simon Dubnow, *History of the Jews in Russia and Poland*, trans. I. Friedlaender (Philadelphia: Jewish Publication Society of America, 1916–20), 3:127.
42. Ascher, *Revolution of 1905*, 192.
43. *New York Times*, 3, 4, 5 December 1905, pp. 1, 2, 1, respectively.
44. N. Asch, "My Father," 2.
45. Madison, *Yiddish Literature*, 227; Siegel, *Controversial Sholem Asch*, 34.
46. Matilda Asch to Nathan Asch, 29 January 1936, Nathan Asch Papers.
47. *New York Times*, 7, 9, 11, 12, 16 December 1905, pp. 2, 1, 2, 2, and 4, respectively.
48. *New York Times*, 16, 19 December 1905, pp. 4 and 1, respectively.
49. N. Asch, "My Father and I," 56.
50. Siegel, *Controversial Sholem Asch*, 35–39.
51. John Asch, interview with author.
52. Israel Young, "Moses Asch: Twentieth Century Man, Part II," *Sing Out!* 26, no. 2 (July–August 1977): 26.

53. Dubnow, *History of the Jews* 3:157.

54. Sol Liptzin, *A History of Yiddish Literature* (Middle Village, N.Y.: Jonathan David Publishers, 1972), 148.

55. Adam Spiro, interview with author. See also Nathan Asch's description in "My Father and I," in which Sholem comes to retrieve him in Lodz and brings him to Paris by way of Berlin, where they ostensibly encounter the kaiser.

56. N. Asch, "My Father and I," 56.

57. Moses Asch, interview with Israel Young.

58. N. Asch, "My Father and I," 55.

59. N. Asch, "My Father," 10.

60. Matilda Asch to Nathan Asch, 29 January 1936, Nathan Asch Papers.

61. John Asch, interview with Gary Kenton.

62. N. Asch, "My Father," 13.

63. Melech Epstein, *Profiles of Eleven* (Detroit: Wayne State University Press, 1965), 328–36.

64. Siegel, *Controversial Sholem Asch*, 54.

65. Howe, *World of Our Fathers*, 276–77.

66. Ibid., 132–33.

67. John Asch, interview with author.

68. N. Asch, "My Father and I," 57.

69. Howe, *World of Our Fathers*, 155.

70. Ibid., 80–81, 156–57.

71. Sholem Asch, *East River* (New York: Putnam, 1946), 149–50.

72. Howe, *World of Our Fathers*, 309; Liptzin, *History of Yiddish Literature*, 93–96.

73. Moses Asch, interview with Israel Young. Moe Asch to Guy Carawan, 8 August 1959, Folkways Archives and Collections, Center for Folklife Programs and Cultural Studies, Smithsonian Institution, Washington, D.C. (hereafter cited as Folkways Archives and Collections).

74. Howe, *World of Our Fathers*, 483.

75. N. Asch, "My Father," 15.

76. Howe, *World of Our Fathers*, 325–27, 542.

77. N. Asch, "My Father and I," 57.

78. John Asch, interview with Gary Kenton.

79. W. M. Dalton, *The Story of Radio, Part 2: Everyone an Amateur* (London: Adam Hilger, 1975), 39–56; Hugh G. J. Aitken, *The Continuous Wave: Technology and American Radio, 1900–1932* (Princeton, N.J.: Princeton University Press, 1985), 512.

80. Oscar Handlin, *A Continuing Task: The American Jewish Joint Distribution Committee, 1914–1964* (New York: Random House, 1964), 34–37.

81. Moses Asch, interview with Tony Schwartz.

82. Siegel, *Controversial Sholem Asch*, 81.

83. Murray Friedman, ed., *Jewish Life in Philadelphia, 1830–1940* (Philadelphia: Ishi Publications, 1983), 8, 21, 141.

84. N. Asch, "My Father," 19.

2. RADIO DAYS

1. Warren B. Morris, *The Weimar Republic and Nazi Germany* (Chicago: Nelson-Hall, 1982), 82.
2. Warren, *Weimar Republic,* 87.
3. Peter Fritzsche, *Rehearsals for Fascism: Populism and Political Mobilization in Weimar Germany* (New York: Oxford University Press, 1990), 96.
4. Morris, *Weimar Republic,* 127–28.
5. Moe Asch to Guy Carawan, 8 August 1959, Folkways Archives and Collections.
6. Gene Bluestein, "Moses Asch, Documentor," *American Music* 5, no. 3 (Fall 1987): 293.
7. Morris, *Weimar Republic,* 14–15.
8. Ibid., 152. Sholem Asch described the experiences of German Jews in this era in his novel *The War Goes On* (New York: Putnam, 1936).
9. See N. Asch, "My Father."
10. John A. Lomax, *Cowboy Songs and Other Frontier Ballads* (New York: Sturgis and Walton, 1910).
11. John A. Lomax, *Adventures of a Ballad Hunter* (New York: Macmillan, 1947), 20.
12. Lomax, *Adventures of a Ballad Hunter,* 34.
13. Bluestein, "Moses Asch, Documentor," 295.
14. Moses Asch, interview with Tony Schwartz.
15. Moses Asch, interview with Israel Young, MS in *Sing Out!* Archives, Bethlehem, Pennsylvania.
16. Fritzsche, *Rehearsals for Fascism,* 154–57.
17. Moses Asch, interview with Joe Klein.
18. Robert Sobel, *RCA* (New York: Stein and Day, 1986), 21–35.
19. Kenneth Bilby, *The General: David Sarnoff and the Rise of the Communications Industry* (New York: Harper and Row, 1986), 34–35.
20. Sobel, *RCA,* 47–48.
21. Moses Asch, interview with Tony Schwartz.
22. Moses Asch, interview with Israel Young.
23. Moe Asch to Hugh S. Johnson, 23 February 1934, Folkways Archives and Collections.
24. Asch maintained in his interview with Israel Young that it was for the Madison Square Garden speech in the *first* Roosevelt campaign (5 November 1932) that he set up the address system. This is unlikely. There is no evidence that he was substantially involved in the public address business before joining Mearns and Zolnier in 1934.
25. Moses Asch to Hugh S. Johnson, Washington, D.C., 24 February 1934, Folkways Archives and Collections.
26. Moses Asch, interview with Israel Young.
27. Howe, *World of Our Fathers,* 487–88.
28. Phillip Kapp to Moses Asch, 25 August 1936, Folkways Archives and Collections.

29. John Hammond, *John Hammond on Record* (New York: Summit Books, 1977), 75.

30. Anna Goldblatt to Moses Asch, 26 April 1935, Folkways Archives and Collections.

31. Moe Asch to Charney Vladeck, 3 December 1937, Folkways Archives and Collections.

32. Charney Vladeck to Jack Sullivan, copy to Moses Asch, Folkways Archives and Collections.

33. Bluestein, "Moses Asch, Documentor," 297.

34. *American Standards Yearbook, 1930,* 36–37.

35. Moses Asch, interview with Israel Young.

36. John Borwick, *Microphones: Technology and Technique* (London: Focal Press, 1990), 10–11, 89.

37. Charles Edward Smith claimed in his notes to *Asch Recordings/1939–1945, Volume 2* (Asch Records AA 3/4) that Asch and his colleagues at Radio Laboratories "developed the first electric condenser microphone" (3). This is undoubtedly not true, although they may have made some modifications on the existing design. Mearns and Zolnier's letterhead listed "condenser microphones" among their products, so they were clearly working in this area before Asch joined them.

38. Moses Asch, interview with Israel Young.

39. Moses Asch, interview with Israel Young.

40. Chet Flippo, "I Sing the Solid Body Electric: The Rolling Stone Interview with Les Paul," *Rolling Stone,* 13 February 1975, 45–50.

41. Moses Asch, interview with Israel Young; invoice for twenty-five AC/DC guitar amplifiers, Folkways Archives and Collections.

42. "Jimmy Smith is in the Spotlight," publicity brochure, Folkways Archives and Collections.

43. *New York Times,* 2 October 1938, sec. 9, p. 1.

44. Harold Beaver, "Proletarian or not?" *Times Literary Supplement,* 17 May 1991, 7.

45. *New York Times,* 20 June 1930, p. 15.

46. N. Asch, "My Father."

47. Frances Asch, interview with author.

48. Nathan Asch, "My Father."

49. *New York Times,* 17 May 1938, p. 26.

50. Siegel, *Controversial Sholem Asch,* 127.

51. Drafts of letters from Sholem Asch to his children, Folkways Archives and Collections.

52. Reginald Shaffer to Moses Asch, 1 July, 18 August 1938; Moses Asch to Reginald Shaeffer, 25 July 1938, Folkways Archives and Collections.

53. David Lifson, *The Yiddish Theatre in America* (New York: Thomas Yoseloff, 1965), 375–79.

54. *New York Times,* 2 October 1938, sec. 9, p. 1.

55. R. Serge Denisoff, *Great Day Coming: Folk Music and the American Left* (Urbana: University of Illinois Press, 1971), 66–67.

56. *New York Times,* 2 October 1938, sec. 9, p. 1.

57. Lifson, *Yiddish Theatre in America,* 433.

58. Robbie Lieberman, *"My Song Is My Weapon": People's Songs, American Communism, and the Politics of Culture, 1930–1950* (Urbana: University of Illinois Press, 1989), 28.

59. Philip S. Foner, *The Case of Joe Hill* (New York: International Publishers, 1954), 13.

60. Quoted in Lieberman, *"My Song Is My Weapon,"* 30.

61. Mark Naison, *Communists in Harlem During the Depression* (Urbana: University of Illinois Press, 1983), 211.

62. Martin McCall, "Handy Concert for Milk Fund," *New York Daily Worker,* 24 November 1938, 7.

63. "The W. C. Handy Birthday Concert; Daily Worker Editorial Board Issues Statement on Review of Last Thursday," *New York Daily Worker,* 2 December 1938, 9.

64. Hammond, *John Hammond on Record,* 202.

65. Martin McCall, "'From Spirituals to Swing' Major Event in Current Musical Season; New Masses Brings Together Galaxy of Negro Artists, *New York Daily Worker,* 29 December 1938, 7.

66. Mike Gold, "Change the World: What Is the Place of Swing in the Great Tradition of World Music," *New York Daily Worker,* 3 January 1939, 7.

67. Joe Klein, *Woody Guthrie: A Life* (New York: Knopf, 1980), 152.

68. Andrew Ross, *No Respect: Intellectuals and Popular Culture* (New York: Routledge, 1989), 23.

69. Frances Asch, interview with author.

70. Siegel, *Controversial Sholem Asch,* 143.

71. Epstein, *Profiles of Eleven,* 105.

72. Siegel, *Controversial Sholem Asch,* 142–44.

73. *New York Times,* 21 May, 1 June, 11 June, 31 October 1938, pp. 2, 3, 4, and 1, respectively; Epstein, *Profiles of Eleven,* 355. Frances Asch, interview with author.

74. "Proposal on Phonograph Records," memo, Folkways Archives and Collections.

75. Sholem Asch to Albert Einstein, telegram, 26 October 1949, doc. 30-807, Albert Einstein Papers, Princeton University.

76. Joseph R. Brodsky to Herman Yablakoff, 30 December 1941, Folkways Archives and Collections.

77. Asch's recording of the Bagelman Sisters was technically his first recording, but it was never sold commercially on the retail market.

78. Howe, *World of Our Fathers,* 193.

79. John A. Lomax and Alan Lomax, *Negro Folk Songs as Sung by Lead Belly* (New York: Macmillan, 1936), 15–33.

80. Frederic Ramsey, "Leadbelly: A Great Long Time," *Sing Out!* 15, no. 1 (1965): 17; Richard D. Smith, "Huddie Ledbetter: King of the Twelve-string Guitar Players of the World," *Pickin* 6, no. 11 (December 1979): 12.

81. Lomax and Lomax, *Negro Folk Songs,* 60–62.
82. Oscar Brand, *The Ballad Mongers* (New York: Funk and Wagnalls, 1962), 201.
83. Lomax and Lomax, *Negro Folk Songs,* xi.
84. Julius Lester and Pete Seeger, *The 12-String Guitar as Played by Leadbelly* (New York: Oak Publications, 1965), 79.
85. Richard Wright, "Huddie Ledbetter, Famous Negro Folk Artist, Sings the Songs of Scottsboro and His People," *New York Daily Worker,* 12 August 1937, 7.
86. Jay Williams, *Stage Left* (New York: Scribner's, 1974), 155.
87. Smith, "Huddie Ledbetter," 13.
88. Quoted in Bluestein, "Documentor: Moses Asch," 299.
89. Israel Young, "Moses Asch: Twentieth Century Man," *Sing Out!* 26, no. 1 (May–June 1977): 6.
90. Frederic Ramsey Jr. and Albert McCarthy, "Huddie Ledbetter Discography," in *A Tribute to Huddie Ledbetter,* by Ramsey and McCarthy (London: Jazz Music Books, 1946), 10.
91. Asch Recording Studios to Huddie Ledbetter, 14 May 1941, 29 April 1942, 28 September 1942, Folkways Archives and Collections.

3. ASCH RECORDS

1. Nathan Asch, "Olek," unpublished MS, Nathan Asch Papers.
2. "Pioneer Jazz Writer in 30's," *New York Times,* 17 December 1970, p. 50.
3. Frederic Ramsey Jr. and Charles Edward Smith, eds., *Jazzmen* (New York: Harcourt, Brace, 1939), xiii.
4. Marshall Stearns, *The Story of Jazz* (New York: Oxford University Press, 1956), 159–67.
5. Charles Edward Smith, *The Jazz Record Book* (New York: Smith and Durrell, 1942), 3.
6. Cf. Paul Oliver, *Songsters and Saints: Vocal Traditions on Race Records* (Cambridge: Cambridge University Press, 1984), 257 ff.
7. The one exception was an impromptu 1944 session entitled "Until My Baby Comes Home," featuring vocalist Nora Lee King, accompanied by Mary Lou Williams. It appeared on Asch album 550, *Blues,* featuring performances by Josh White, Jack Dupree, Woody Guthrie, and Sonny Terry.
8. John Lucas, "Rating the Gitmen Who 'Git Wit It': Tracing the Evolution of Jazz Guitars, Appraising Musicians Who Play 'Em," *Down Beat,* 1 September 1943, 15.
9. Smith, *Jazz Record Book,* 250–71.
10. James Dugan, "How Jazz Happened," *New Masses,* 10 March 1942, 28.
11. "Records without Shellac," *Newsweek,* 17 August 1942, 73.
12. "Ransacking for Records," *Newsweek,* 27 July 1942, 65.

13. Mike Levin, "Recording Sliced One-Third: Industry Recovers from Shellac Jitters," *Down Beat*, 1 May 1942, 1.

14. "AFM Confab Blows Hot," *Billboard*, 20 June 1942, 3.

15. Bruce Bastin, *Red River Blues: The Blues Tradition in the Southeast* (Urbana: University of Illinois Press, 1986), 261.

16. Mike Levin, "Showdown Looms on Discs: Petrillo Resolved to Halt Recording," *Down Beat*, 1 July 1942, 1; Mike Levin, "All Recording Stops Today: Disc Firms Sit Back, Public's Next Move," *Down Beat*, 1 August 1942, 1.

17. "Record Firms Have Hot Race on Vocal Discs: Columbia and Decca Wax Sinatra, Haymes sans Orchestra," *Down Beat*, 1 July 1943, 1.

18. Lou Cooper, "Our Singing Country," *New Masses*, 17 February 1942, 29.

19. Marian Distler, notes to *Work Songs of the U.S.A. Sung by Lead Belly* (Asch Records).

20. Charles Edward Smith, "King of the Twelve String Guitar," *Jazz* 4 (1942), reprinted in Ramsey and McCarthy, *Tribute to Huddie Ledbetter*, 4–6.

21. Harvey Klehr, *The Heyday of American Communism* (New York: Basic Books, 1984), 376.

22. Hammond, *John Hammond on Record*, 207–10.

23. Dorothy Schainman Siegel, *The Glory Road: The Story of Josh White* (New York: Harcourt, Brace, Jovanovich, 1982), 66–67; Klein, *Woody Guthrie*, 175; Denisoff, *Great Day Coming*, 70.

24. Siegel, *Glory Road*, 45–59.

25. Bastin, *Red River Blues*, 323.

26. Peter M. Rutkoff and William B. Scott, *New School: A History of the New School for Social Research* (New York: Free Press, 1986), 57–58.

27. Denisoff, *Great Day Coming*, 87.

28. Klein, *Woody Guthrie*, 168–69.

29. Denisoff, *Great Day Coming*, 133.

30. Mike Gold, "Change the World," *Daily Worker*, 2 January 1933, 5.

31. Woody Guthrie, *Pastures of Plenty: A Self-Portrait*, ed. David Marsh and Harold Leventhal (New York: Harper Collins, 1990), 31.

32. David Dunaway, *How Can I Keep from Singing: Pete Seeger* (New York: Da Capo Press, 1990), 63.

33. Pete Seeger, personal communication with the author. Dunaway reports that the president of Berkeley "all but fired Seeger." Dunaway, *How Can I Keep from Singing*, 32.

34. Ibid., 41.

35. Quoted in ibid., 65.

36. Moses Asch, interview with Joe Klein.

37. See particularly Victor Turner, *Dramas, Fields, and Metaphors* (Ithaca, N.Y.: Cornell University Press, 1974), chap. 5, "Pilgrimages as Social Processes."

38. The paregoric story is related by both Guthrie's and Seeger's biographer. See Klein, *Woody Guthrie*, 166, and Dunaway, *How Can I Keep from Singing*, 66.

Notes to Pages 121-129

39. Klein reports that "Pete stayed a few days and then begged off" (*Woody Guthrie*, 167). Seeger maintains that this was not so.

40. Dunaway, *How Can I Keep from Singing*, 74.

41. Klein, *Woody Guthrie*, 189–90. Seeger recalls that Guthrie left New York again shortly before he had begun to sing with Hays and Lampell, which would render this early meeting between Guthrie and the future Almanac Singers apocryphal (personal communication with the author).

42. Guthrie, *Pastures of Plenty*, 55.

43. Almanac Singers, "Ballad of October 16," *New Masses*, 20 May 1941, 20, quoted in Denisoff, *Great Day Coming*, 90.

44. Klein, *Woody Guthrie*, 196.

45. Sis Cunningham, *Red Dust & Broadsides* (privately printed, 1990), 14–15, reprinted from the *Cimarron Review* (Stillwater: Oklahoma State University, January 1977).

46. Klein, *Woody Guthrie*, 220–21.

47. Naison, *Communists in Harlem*, 291.

48. Ibid., 300–303.

49. *Billboard*, 1 July, 15 October 1944.

50. "Hill-Billy Defy on Disc Ban," *Down Beat*, 1 September 1943, 2.

51. Moses Asch, interview with Israel Young. See also Moses Asch, interview with David Dunaway.

52. "Petrillo Lifts Ban on Discs," *Down Beat*, 1 October 1943, 1.

53. Wanda Marvin, "Waxing Is Everybody's Business," *Billboard*, 22 April 1944, 12.

54. See Scott E. Brown, *James P. Johnson: A Case of Mistaken Identity* (Metuchen, N.J.: Scarecrow Press and the Institute of Jazz Studies, Rutgers, 1982), 4–5. Also Charles Edward Smith, notes to Johnson's "Boogie Stride" and "Impressions," Asch Records 1001.

55. See David Schiff, "A Pianist with Harlem on his Mind," *New York Times*, 16 February 1992, sec. 2, p. 1.

56. Brown, *James P. Johnson*, 220–36. The Johnson discography compiled by Robert Hilbert (and included in the Brown volume) suggests that this session occurred in July 1942, and this speculation is repeated in the Walter Bruyninckx discography, *Sixty Years of Recorded Jazz, 1917–1977*. Hilbert also speculates that the October 1943 date might have been when the sides were mastered rather than recorded. However, Asch's log shows almost no activity in 1942, during the AFM recording ban, and there is evidence that Asch was moderately scrupulous in adhering to these and other AFM regulations.

57. Connie's Inn, operated by Connie Immerman, was one of the two most prominent Harlem nightclubs of the prohibition era—the other being the Cotton Club.

58. "Righteous Jazz Rears Its Head on Discs Again," *Down Beat*, 15 December 1943; also *Down Beat*, 15 February 1944, 8.

59. Most of this account comes from Asch's own reminiscences in an interview with Tony Schwartz. See also Bob Woody, "Burl Ives: Folksinger, Actor, Gentleman," *Pickin* 5, no. 10 (November 1978): 6ff, and Alan Lomax's notes to *Burl Ives (The Wayfaring Stranger)*, Asch album 345.

60. Asch was under the impression that Ives had come from Ohio rather than Illinois.

61. Woody, "Burl Ives," 8.

62. The sequence of the Ives session is derived from a list of matrix numbers that Asch prepared in November 1945. Folkways Archives and Collections.

63. *Billboard*, 7 October 1944, 19.

64. "Granz Inaugurates LA Sunday Swing Shows," *Down Beat*, 1 March 1944, 6.

65. Leonard Feather, "Jazz Millionaire," *Esquire*, January 1957, 99–100.

66. Mary Lou Williams, interview with John S. Wilson, 26 June 1973, Smithsonian Institution, Jazz Oral History Project. Transcript in the Rutgers Institute of Jazz Studies, Newark, New Jersey (hereafter cited as Rutgers Institute of Jazz Studies), 77.

67. Peter F. O'Brien, S.J., notes to *Mary Lou Williams—The Asch Recordings 1944–47* (2966), 1977.

68. "Mary Lou Williams writes about Mili and Martin," *Melody Maker*, 29 May 1954.

69. "Covers Up," *Newsweek*, 25 December 1944, 70–72.

70. "Mary Lou Williams writes about Mili and Martin," *Melody Maker*, 29 May 1954.

71. See *People's Songs* 2, no. 10 (November 1947): 8.

72. *People's Songs* 2, nos. 6 and 7 (July and August 1947): 7.

73. Moses Asch, interview with Joe Klein.

74. Lomax believes that the radio shows alone would have made it impossible for Asch to have been unaware of Guthrie by 1944. Author's telephone conversation with Lomax, 28 October 1992.

75. Moses Asch, interview with Guy Logsdon.

76. Joe Klein identifies these as "Hard, Ain't it Hard," which Guthrie recorded again for Asch some weeks later under this title and "More Pretty Gals than One." *Woody Guthrie*, 285.

77. Klein, *Woody Guthrie*, 282–83.

78. Cisco Houston in *People's Songs* 2, no. 10 (November 1948): 8.

79. Moses Asch, interview with Guy Logsdon.

80. Alan Lomax, ed., *Folk Song U.S.A.*, collected, adapted, and arranged by John A. Lomax and Alan Lomax (1947; reprint, New York: New American Library, 1975).

81. Lomax and Lomax, *Folk Song U.S.A.*, 355.

82. Guthrie, *Pastures of Plenty*, 149. The original manuscript for "This Land is Your Land," also reproduced in this volume, renders the verse slightly differently: "Was a big high wall there that tried to stop me

/ A sign was painted said: Private Property / But on the back side it didn't say nothing."

83. Woody Guthrie, *American Folksong,* ed. Moses Asch (1947; reprint, New York: Oak Publications, 1961), 6–7.

84. Frances Asch had no recollection of friends or acquaintances of her husband's who might have fought in the Abraham Lincoln Battalion. Interview with author.

85. Pete Seeger, interview with Gary Kenton.

86. Pete Seeger to Moses Asch, postmarked 8 March 1944. Seeger had forgotten Asch's address and consequently sent the letter care of Alan Lomax. Folkways Archives and Collections.

87. Pete Seeger to Moses Asch, 18 April, 25 July 1944, Folkways Archives and Collections.

88. *New York Herald Tribune,* 11 February 1945, sec. 4, p. 5.

89. Walter Bruyninckx, in his *Sixty Years of Recorded Jazz, 1917–1977,* maintains that there were six short takes of the title "If I Had You" and three of "Soft Winds." However, the matrix numbers in Asch's log (1251–1257) do not reflect the large number of alternate takes.

90. See Charles Fox, Peter Gammond, and Alan Morgan, *Jazz on Record: A Critical Guide* (London: Hutchinson, 1960), 296–97, and Stanley Dance with Yannick Bruynoghe et. al., *Jazz Era: The Forties* (London: Collins, 1961), 219.

91. Siegel, *Controversial Sholem Asch,* 152–62.

92. Nathan Asch, "My Father," 41.

93. Arnold Rampersad, *The Life of Langston Hughes* (New York: Oxford University Press, 1988). See, for example, 2:102–3.

94. Rampersad, *Life of Langston Hughes* 2:95.

95. Ibid. 1:34–35.

96. Ibid. 1:56, 66; 2:106–7.

97. Peter Silvester, *A Left Hand Like God: A Study of Boogie-Woogie* (London: Quartet Books, 1988), 90–98; 127–65.

98. Ibid., 169–70.

99. *Down Beat,* 15 March 1945, 8.

100. Joe Klein credits a different album—Asch 347—with being the first Guthrie album on Asch, maintaining that it appeared in March 1945 (Klein, *Woody Guthrie,* 299). In point of fact, the album was announced in Asch advertisements in late 1944, and its release was noted in *Billboard* the following 13 January. But for all intents and purposes, *Folksay* was a Guthrie album, and it appeared the previous autumn.

101. *Down Beat,* 1 January 1945, 8. Guthrie's review of "Folksay" is among the Woody Guthrie papers in the Folkways Archives and Collections.

102. Klehr, *Heyday of American Communism,* 410–11.

103. Woody Guthrie to Moses Asch et al., 24 September 1944, Folkways Archives and Collections.

104. Woody Guthrie to Moses Asch et al., 14 October 1944, Folkways Archives and Collections.
105. "Mary Lou Rolls 'Em for FDR's Vanguard," *Billboard,* 15 October 1944, 2.
106. *Down Beat,* 15 October 1944, 9.
107. *Billboard,* 3 March 1945, 97; *Down Beat,* 15 March 1945, 8; *New York Herald Tribune,* 14 January 1945, sec. 4, p. 5.
108. Ruth Rubin, interview with author.
109. *Billboard,* 12 May 1945, 66.
110. Alan Lomax, telephone conversation with author, 20 October 1992.
111. Scott Knowles DeVeaux, "Jazz in Transition: Coleman Hawkins and Howard McGhee, 1935–1945" (Ph.D. thesis, University of California, Berkeley, 1985), 55.
112. Moses Asch, interview with Israel Young.
113. DeVeaux, "Jazz in Transition," 2.
114. Ibid., 299–313.
115. *Down Beat,* 15 October 1945, 8.
116. Howard McGhee, interview with Ira Gitlin, 16, 23 November, 6 December 1982, quoted in DeVeaux, "Jazz in Transition," 298.
117. Klein, *Woody Guthrie,* 299; *Billboard,* 20 January 1945, 21; *Down Beat,* 15 March 1945, 8–9.
118. Woody Guthrie to Moe Asch and Marian Distler, 12 February 1945, Folkways Archives and Collections.
119. Lomax and Lomax, *Folk Song U.S.A.,* 208–10, 226–27.
120. Asch's album notes to Woody Guthrie's *Struggle* (2485), 1976.
121. Guthrie to Moe Asch, Marian Distler, and Herbert Harris, 17 June 1945, Folkways Archives and Collections.
122. Klehr, *Heyday of American Communism,* 411.
123. Moses Asch to Marian Distler, 17 November 1944, 8, 10 June 1945, 11, 15, 19, 20 July 1945. Folkways Archives and Collections.
124. Guthrie to Asch from Scott Field, Illinois, 8, 10 July, 19 August 1945, Folkways Archives and Collections.
125. Klein, *Woody Guthrie,* 313–14.
126. Charles H. Nichols, ed., *Arna Bontemps–Langston Hughes Letters, 1925–1967* (New York: Dodd, Mead, 1980), 184.
127. Brown, *James P. Johnson,* 449–53.
128. Dan Morgenstern, album notes for reissue of *The Zodiac Suite* (32844).
129. Samuel Charters and Leonard Kunstadt, *Jazz: A History of the New York Scene* (New York: Doubleday, 1962), 303; George T. Simon, *The Big Bands,* 4th ed. (New York: Schirmer, 1981), 508.
130. *New York Herald Tribune,* 24 June 1945, sec. 4, p. 4.
131. "Signature Threat to Big Disc Firms," *Down Beat,* 1 June 1945, 5; "New Recording Firm Cuts Logan, De Vol," *Down Beat,* 15 June 1945, 8; "Granz and Adams Jazz Bash Combo," *Down Beat,* 15 September 1945, 7.
132. Feather, "Jazz Millionaire," 99ff.

4. THE DISC ERA AND BANKRUPTCY

1. See, for example, Donald M. Marquis, *In Search of Buddy Bolden, First Man of Jazz* (Baton Rouge: Louisiana State University Press, 1978).
2. Christopher Hillman, *Bunk Johnson: His Life and Times* (New York: Universe Books, 1988), 9.
3. Hillman, *Bunk Johnson,* 8.
4. This is the date that is reported by Pete Seeger in *People's Songs Bulletin* 1, no. 10 (November 1946): 2. Serge Denisoff (*Great Day Coming*) gives the date as 31 December (107), and this date is repeated in Robbie Lieberman's *"My Song Is My Weapon"* (67).
5. Pete Seeger, "Report to Members," *People's Song Bulletin* 1, no. 10 (November 1946): 2. There have been two lengthy accounts of the history of People's Songs and, consequently, it does not bear retelling here. Serge Denisoff's account in *Great Day Coming* (chap. 5) is a rather cynical dismissal of the organization for its quixotic misreading of the contemporary political climate. A far more sympathetic account, written by the daughter of a prominent People's Songster, is Robbie Lieberman's *"My Song Is My Weapon."*
6. Denisoff, *Great Day Coming,* 109.
7. See, for example, "On Parodies, Permission, Protection and the Law," *People's Songs* 1, no. 5 (June 1946): 10.
8. From a People's Songs recruiting document, quoted in Lieberman, *"My Song Is My Weapon,"* 68.
9. Pete Seeger, personal communication with the author.
10. Moses Asch, interview with Israel Young.
11. Lieberman, *"My Song Is My Weapon,"* 98.
12. Moses Asch, interview with Israel Young.
13. Donald R. Hill, *Calypso Calaloo: Early Carnival Music in Trinidad* (Gainesville: University Press of Florida, 1993), 161–63.
14. Ruth Reinhardt, "Calypso Fan Burned by Network Banning," *Down Beat,* 1 March 1945, 2; "Rum & Coke Title Cleared," *Down Beat,* 15 July 1945, 13.
15. "Writes Another Calypso Item," *Down Beat,* 11 March 1946, 13.
16. *People's Songs Bulletin* 3, no. 3 (April 1948): 9.
17. Hill, *Calypso Calaloo,* 186–92.
18. "A 'Hootennany' Is Given by People's Songs, Inc.," *New York Herald Tribune,* 10 May 1946.
19. "Carnegie Bash Hits $4,000 Pot: Buck, Trummie, Lester Spark Granz Concert," *Down Beat,* 1 July 1946, 8.
20. "Granz Jazz Grabs Good Grosses," *Down Beat,* 17 June 1946, 7.
21. James M. Doran, *Errol Garner: The Most Happy Piano* (Metuchen, N.J.: Scarecrow Press and the Institute of Jazz Studies, 1985), 177.
22. Hillman, *Bunk Johnson,* 94. "Bunk's Master's Sold to Asch," *Down Beat,* 26 March 1947, 2.
23. "Kiddie Albums Flood Market," *Down Beat,* 7 October 1946, 12.

24. Lawhon Milford, "Guthrie Songs for Kids Win 'A' for Disc Records," *People's World,* 21 August 1946.
25. Klein, *Woody Guthrie,* 326.
26. Woody Guthrie to Moses Asch, 2 January 1946, Folkways Archives and Collections.
27. Moses Asch, interview with Joe Klein.
28. In an article in the *New York Post* (4 December 1947) on the advent of the Disc Ethnic series, Asch was reported to have recognized parallels in the most disparate folk musics: "Listen to a real cowboy song . . . and you'll hear a musical beat from old China. Through the music of the West Indies, of the Central East and of Africa runs a common rhythm. Because he believes that the real folk music of the whole world is interrelated in a hundred similarly curious ways, Moe Asch has been making that music his hobby and his vocation for years."
29. *Sing Out!* 17, no. 6 (December–January 1967–68): 12–13.
30. Woody Guthrie to Moses Asch, 4 November 1946, Folkways Archives and Collections.
31. Frederic Ramsey, ed., *A Tribute to Huddie Ledbetter,* (London: Jazz Music Books, 1946).
32. Arnold Shaw, *Honkers and Shouters: The Golden Years of Rhythm and Blues* (New York: Macmillan, 1978), 388–89.
33. Frederic Ramsey, interview with Gary Kenton.
34. *Billboard,* 29 June 1946, 34; *Down Beat,* 15 July 1946, 22.
35. Studs Terkel to "Disc," 17 July 1946, Folkways Archives and Collections. Terkel wrote a similar letter to *People's Songs Bulletin* that was published the following April (vol. 2, no. 3).
36. Nathan Asch to Moses Asch, 26 September 1946, Folkways Archives and Collections.
37. Joseph Corn to Moses Asch, 31 July 1946, Folkways Archives and Collections.
38. Joseph Corn to Jaffe and Jaffe, 30 December 1946. Julius Schein to Joseph Corn, 26 December 1946. All in Folkways Archives and Collections.
39. Joseph Corn to Moe Asch, 13 August 1946. Stipulation of settlement filed with Supreme Court, New York County, between Moses Asch, plaintiff, and Irving Prosky and Herbert Harris, defendants, Folkways Archives and Collections.
40. *Down Beat,* 1 January 1947, 17.
41. James Haskins with Kathleen Benson, *Nat King Cole* (New York: Stein and Day, 1984), 40–41; Leslie Gourse, *Unforgettable: The Life and Mystique of Nat King Cole* (New York: St. Martin's Press, 1991), 66–67.
42. *Down Beat,* 26 February 1947, 17.
43. Asch recalled in an interview with Tony Schwartz that he had paid $10,000 for the rights to the Nat Cole sides, but existing records suggest that it was more like $750.

44. *New York Herald Tribune,* 21 December 1946, p. 1; *Billboard,* 19 June 1948; Michael Asch, interview with author.
45. Shaw, *Honkers and Shouters,* 12–14.
46. Samuel Charters, *The Country Blues* (New York: Rinehart, 1959), 84.
47. Shaw, *Honkers and Shouters,* 12. *Rhythm and blues* was actually a term invented at the close of the decade by Jerry Wexler—then a writer for *Billboard,* later a prominent R&B producer for Atlantic Records—to take the place of the objectionable "race" category. By the time it had entered general usage, it had taken on its own musical and sociological dimensions. See xv–xvi.
48. Fox, Gammond, and Morgan, *Jazz on Record,* 294. Other critics have been far kinder to Sullivan, describing him in one instance as "one of the best American white jazz pianists." Silvester, *Left Hand Like God,* 200.
49. *Down Beat,* 15 January 1947, 19.
50. *Down Beat,* 26 February 1947, 17; *Billboard,* 1 March 1947, 33.
51. See Klein, *Woody Guthrie,* 33; "A 'Hootenanny' Is Given by People's Songs, Inc.," *New York Herald Tribune,* 10 May 1946; "People's Songs Give Pre-concert Party for Josh White," *Down Beat,* 2 December 1946, 9.
52. *Red Channels: The Report of Communist Influence in Radio and Television,* published by *Counterattack,* June 1950.
53. Huddie Ledbetter to Moe Asch, 25, 28 October 1946, Folkways Archives and Collections.
54. Document on Disc Records stationery, dated 17 June 1947 (signature illegible), Folkways Archives and Collections.
55. *Seeds of Man* was published in 1976 (New York: E. P. Dutton).
56. W. B. Seabrook, *The Magic Island* (New York: Harcourt, Brace, 1929).
57. Harold Courlander, "Recording in Eritrea, 1942–43," *Resound: A Quarterly of the Archives of Traditional Music,* 6, no. 2 (April 1987); Harold Courlander, interview with author.
58. "Disc's New Series," *Down Beat,* 12 March 1947, 9.
59. *Billboard,* 20 September 1947, 48.
60. "Indies Losing Out in Wax Race," *Down Beat,* 7 May 1947, 1.
61. The press release from Disc also mentions a second Nat Cole release to which Asch was entitled, although it never appeared.
62. J. J. Corn to Norman Granz, 29 April 1947, Folkways Archives and Collections.
63. "Granz Suit Takes a Different Twist," *Down Beat,* 2 December 1949, 15.
64. Bill Gottleib, "Cover Art Sells Albums," *Down Beat,* 9 April 1947, 12.
65. "Granz Released from All Deals—Except Taxes," *Down Beat,* 18 June 1947, 1; "Granz Explains Everything," *Down Beat,* 16 July 1947, 7.
66. *Down Beat,* 8 October 1947, 15; *Down Beat,* 31 December 1947, 15; *Down Beat,* 25 February 1948, 19.
67. John Lucas, "Traces Heritage of Today's Jazzman," *Down Beat,* 25 February 1946, 12. Lucas published a second column ("1946–48 Era Produces 57 Significant Albums," *Down Beat,* 2 June 1948, 12) in which he

expands his list of "significant" historical recordings by including fifty-seven additional releases of the previous year and a half. Twelve of them are on Disc and include his Doc Evans albums.

68. *Down Beat,* 19 November 1947, 15.
69. *Down Beat,* 10 March 1948, 22.
70. *Billboard,* 22 March 1947, 160. The album notes incorrectly report that the revolt had occurred in North Carolina in the 1860s. A portion of *Denmark Vesey* was performed in oratorio by the Juanita Hall Singers as part of a Federal Theatre Project production in 1937.
71. Christopher Sawyer-Laucanno, *An Invisible Spectator: A Biography of Paul Bowles* (New York: Weidenfeld and Nicolson, 1989), 22.
72. Tony Wilson and Gerry Wexler, "Specialized Disk Sales Advance," *Billboard,* 19 June 1948, 21. See also Cecil Smith, "Little Record Companies," *New Republic,* 24 February 1947, 42.
73. *Billboard,* 10 July 1948, 111.
74. Leon Wagman to Moses Asch, 12 December 1947, Folkways Archives and Collections.
75. G. P. Putnam's Sons to Moses Asch, 29 May 1947, Folkways Archives and Collections.
76. Moses Asch to Allied Record Manufacturing, 26 April 1948, Folkways Archives and Collections.
77. Henry Wallace, "The Singing People," *New Republic,* 28 June 1948, 11.
78. Quoted in Klein, *Woody Guthrie,* 359. According to Klein, Guthrie directed this tirade at Alan Lomax, although Lomax is not associated with the song in People's Songs publications.
79. Walter Wallace, currently professor of sociology at Princeton University, recalls having encountered Asch at Progressive Party meetings in New York that summer. If this is so, it was an extraordinarily rare instance of Asch's involvement with organized politics.
80. "Distribs Sold on LPs, But Big Sales Bally Lies Ahead," *Billboard,* 3 July 1948, 48; George Hoefer, "'Play It 'Till 1953'—Geo. After Which LPs Get It," *Down Beat,* 28 July 1948, 11.
81. "'Round 'Round We Go on RPMs," *Down Beat,* 11 March 1949, 7; "Indies Work on All-Speed Record Field," *Down Beat,* 8 April 1949, 3.
82. "Death of Kapp Ends Colorful Disc Career," *Down Beat,* 6 May 1949, 2. Moses Asch, interview with Israel Young. Asch also described the deaths of Woody Guthrie, Leadbelly, and Cisco Houston as suicides and held that each had abandoned life because of political and personal disappointments in the postwar years.
83. Undated document, Folkways Archives and Collections.
84. "Moe Asch Declared Bankrupt by Referee," *Billboard,* 22 January 1949, 19.
85. "It's a Hell of a Note," *People's Songs Bulletin* 3, no. 12 (January 1949): 2.
86. Woody Guthrie to Moses Asch and Marian Distler, 16 August 1948, Folkways Archives and Collections.
87. "Folkways, New Label, Headed by Moe Asch," *Billboard,* 24 December 1949, 38.

88. "Cub Hits Market: New Kidisk Label," *Billboard*, 4 December 1948, 19.
89. Leonard Feather to Moses Asch, 19 May 1948, Folkways Archives and Collections.
90. Moses Asch to Paul Reiner, 4 February 1949; Marian Distler to Moe Asch, memo, 24 February 1949, Folkways Archives and Collections.
91. Shaw, *Honkers and Shouters*, 343.
92. Moses Asch to Allied Record Mfg. Co. Inc., 26 April 1948, Folkways Archives and Collections.
93. Distler to Asch, memo, 24 February 1949, Folkways Archives and Collections.
94. Moses Asch and Marian Distler to Paul Reiner, 22 June 1949, Folkways Archives and Collections.
95. Shaw, *Honkers and Shouters*, 228.
96. Paul Reiner to Moses Asch, 29 June 1949, Folkways Archives and Collections.
97. Moses Asch to Paul Reiner, 4 August 1949; Reiner to Asch, 9 August 1949, Folkways Archives and Collections.
98. See, for example, Lieberman, *"My Song Is My Weapon,"* 136; Denisoff, *Great Day Coming*, 115–17.
99. Victor Navasky, *Naming Names* (New York: Viking, 1980), 29–30.
100. Brand, *Ballad Mongers*, 136.
101. Dunaway, *How Can I Keep from Singing*, 193. Pete Seeger to the author, personal communication.
102. Lieberman, *"My Song Is My Weapon,"* 143–44.
103. Howard Fast, *Being Red* (Boston: Houghton Mifflin, 1990), 226–38.
104. "48 Hurt in Clashes at Robeson Rally; Buses are Stoned," *New York Times*, 5 September 1949, p. 1.
105. Denisoff, *Great Day Coming*, 124–26; Dunaway, *How Can I Keep from Singing*, 13–23; Lieberman, *"My Song Is My Weapon,"* 140; Pete Seeger, conversation with the author, 2 January 1997.
106. Denisoff, *Great Day Coming*, 119.
107. Dunaway, *How Can I Keep from Singing*, 148.

5. FOLKWAYS IN THE FIFTIES

1. Harold Courlander, interview with author.
2. David Halberstam, *The Fifties* (New York: Villard, 1993), x.
3. "Sholem Asch to Sail to Rejoin Ailing Wife," *New York Times*, 27 November 1953, p. 25.
4. Siegel, *Controversial Sholem Asch*, 198.
5. Dan Wakefield, *New York in the Fifties* (Boston: Houghton Mifflin, 1992), 307–12.
6. Wakefield, *New York in the Fifties*, 7.
7. Ibid., 7.

8. Marian Distler to American Federation of Musicians, 12 April 1949, Folkways Archives and Collections.
9. Frederic Ramsey Jr., *A Guide to Longplay Jazz Records* (New York: Long Player Publications, 1954), 105.
10. Ramsey, *Guide to Longplay Jazz Records,* 58–59.
11. Woody Guthrie to Moses Asch, 2 December 1950, Folkways Archives and Collections.
12. Album notes for *Talking Dust Bowl* (2011); Klein, *Woody Guthrie,* 376.
13. J. L. Hallstrom to Woody Guthrie, 26 July 1948, photocopy in Folkways Archives and Collections.
14. Klein, *Woody Guthrie,* 370–73.
15. Woody Guthrie to Moses Asch, 23 October 1950, Folkways Archives and Collections.
16. Harold Courlander, interview with author.
17. Moses Asch to Woody Guthrie, 29 October 1950, multiple drafts found in the Folkways Archives and Collections.
18. Woody Guthrie to Moses Asch, n.d., Folkways Archives and Collections.
19. Woody Guthrie to Moses Asch, 3 December 1950, Folkways Archives and Collections.
20. Sam Charters, interview with author.
21. Notes on Eastern Airlines stationery, 7 April 1952, Folkways Archives and Collections.
22. Henry Cowell, notes to *Music of the World's People* (4504).
23. Percy Grainger to Henry Cowell, 9 September 1952, Folkways Archives and Collections.
24. Harold Courlander, interview with author.
25. Harold Courlander, "Recording in Alabama in 1950," *Resound: A Quarterly of the Archives of Traditional Music* 4, no. 8 (October 1985): n.p.
26. Ibid.
27. Harold Courlander, album notes for *Negro Folk Music of Alabama,* vols. 1 and 2 (1417 and 1418).
28. Harry Smith, interview with Gary Kenton; Josh Dunson and Ethel Raim, eds., *Anthology of American Folk Music* (New York: Oak, 1973), 18.
29. Howard W. Odum and Guy B. Johnson, *Negro Workaday Songs* (Chapel Hill: University of North Carolina Press, 1926).
30. John Cohen, "A Rare Interview with Harry Smith," pt. 1, *Sing Out!* 19, no. 1 (January–February 1969): 3.
31. Harry Smith, interview with Gary Kenton.
32. Cohen, "Rare Interview," pt. 1, 10.
33. John Cohen, "A Rare Interview with Harry Smith," pt. 2, *Sing Out!* 19, no. 2 (March–April 1969): 27.
34. Ibid., 3; Klein, *Woody Guthrie,* 211.
35. Harry Smith, interview with Gary Kenton.
36. Dunson and Raim, *Anthology of American Folk Music,* 18.

37. Harry Smith, interview with Gary Kenton.
38. Ibid.
39. Ralph Rinzler, interview with author.
40. Robert Cantwell, *When We Were Good: The Folk Revival* (Cambridge: Harvard University Press, 1996), 190, 237–38.
41. Cantwell, *When We Were Good*, 192.
42. Woody Guthrie to Moses Asch and Marian Distler, 27 May 1953, Folkways Archives and Collections.
43. Klein, *Woody Guthrie*, 386–411.
44. Woody Guthrie to Moses Asch and Marian Distler, 26 August 1953, Folkways Archives and Collections.
45. Nichols, *Arna Bontemps–Langston Hughes Letters*, 300.
46. Asch to Mrs. James Weldon Johnson, 24 April 1952; Asch to Arna Bontemps, 29 October 1952, Folkways Archives and Collections.
47. Nichols, *Arna Bontemps–Langston Hughes Letters*, 293.
48. Arna Bontemps to Margaret Walker Alexander, 12 December 1952, Folkways Archives and Collections.
49. Nichols, *Arna Bontemps–Langston Hughes Letters*, 310–11.
50. Quoted in Rampersad, *Life of Langston Hughes* 2:232.
51. Langston Hughes to Marian Distler, n.d., Folkways Archives and Collections.
52. B. A. Botkin and William G. Tyrrell, "Upstate, Downstate," *New York Folklore Quarterly* (Autumn 1953): 231–34.
53. That the inclusion of urban material in folklore studies might still be a matter of debate fifteen years later is suggested by the title of Richard Dorson's paper, "Is There a Folk in the City?" presented at a symposium at Wayne State University in May of 1968. Of course he answered his question in the affirmative. See Americo Paredes and Ellen J. Stekert, eds., *The Urban Experience and Folk Tradition* (Austin: University of Texas Press, 1971).
54. Ben Shahn to Moe Asch, 24 July 1954, copy of letter in the possession of Tony Schwartz.
55. Marshall Stearns to Moses Asch, April 26 (no year given), Folkways Archives and Collections.
56. Stearns, *Story of Jazz*, 255.
57. Moses Asch, "Folk Music," *Music Library Association Notes* 14, no. 1 (December 1956): 29–32.
58. Long Player, Inc., to Moe Asch, 31 December 1953, Folkways Archives and Collections.
59. "Stockton Man to Record Afro-American Music," *Trenton Evening Times*, 2 June 1953.
60. Frederic Ramsey, "A Study of the Afro-American Music of Alabama, Louisiana and Mississippi, 1860–1900," *Ethnomusicology* 6 (September 1956): 28.
61. Frederic Ramsey to Moses Asch, 11 April 1954, Folkways Archives and Collections.

62. Frederic Ramsey to Moses Asch, 29 April and 9 May 1954, Folkways Archives and Collections.

63. Frederick Ramsey to Moses Asch, 25 April 1954, Folkways Archives and Collections.

64. Moses Asch to Frederic Ramsey, 23 April 1954, Folkways Archives and Collections.

65. Frederic Ramsey to Moses Asch, late April or early May, 1954 [date obscured], 9 May 1954, Folkways Archives and Collections.

66. Frederic Ramsey to Moses Asch, 19 June 1954, Folkways Archives and Collections.

67. Frederic Ramsey to Moses Asch, 30 May 1954, Folkways Archives and Collections.

68. Frederic Ramsey to Moses Asch, 6 June 1954, Folkways Archives and Collections.

69. Marquis, *In Search of Buddy Bolden.*

70. Frederic Ramsey, interview with author.

71. Frederic Ramsey to Moses Asch, 29 September 1954, Folkways Archives and Collections.

72. Frederic Ramsey to Moses Asch, 14 September 1954, Folkways Archives and Collections.

73. Abraham L. Lowenthal to Frederic Ramsey, Abraham L. Lowenthal to Bill Grauer, 16 December 1954, Folkways Archives and Collections.

74. Frederic Ramsey to Moses Asch, 4 March 1955, Folkways Archives and Collections.

75. Ralph Rinzler, interview with author.

76. Dunaway, *How Can I Keep from Singing,* 162.

77. Robin Denselow, *When the Music's Over: The Story of Political Pop* (London: Faber and Faber, 1989), 17–25.

78. Mel Kaiser, interview with author.

79. John Cohen, interview with author.

80. Ralph Rinzler, interview with author. The story of Rinzler's first encounter with Ashley and subsequently with Doc Watson has been recounted in Richard D. Smith, "Ralph Rinzler: Preserving American Folk Arts," *Pickin'* 6, no. 10 (November 1979). See also Rinzler's notes to *The Original Folkways Recordings of Doc Watson and Clarence Ashley, 1960 through 1962,* Smithsonian/Folkways 40029/30.

81. Barry Miles, *Ginsberg: A Biography* (New York: Simon and Schuster, 1989), 257–58.

82. "Record Reviews," *Journal of American Folklore* 73, no. 290 (October–December 1960): 357.

83. Roscoe Holcomb to Moses Asch, 27 August 1965, Folkways Archives and Collections.

84. Dick Spottswood, "Mike Seeger," *Bluegrass Unlimited* 19 (May 1985): 61. See also Mark Greenberg, "Mike Seeger," in *Artists of American Folk Music,* ed. Phil Hood (New York: William Morrow, 1986), 106.

85. D. K. Wilgus, "Record Reviews," *Journal of American Folklore* 73, no. 288 (April–June 1969): 186.

86. Alice Gerrard, "Elizabeth Cotten," in Hood, *Artists of American Folk Music,* 41–46. Pete Seeger believes that the Seeger family discovered Elizabeth Cotten's musical talents earlier than this, in the late forties. Personal communication with the author.

87. Loyal Jones, "Buell Kazee," *JEMF Quarterly* 14, no. 49 (Spring 1978): 65.

88. Sam Charters to Moses Asch, 23 August 1958, Folkways Archives and Collections.

89. *New York Times,* 23 August 1959, sec. 2, p. 8.

90. Sam Charters to Moses Asch, 13 January 1960; Sam Charters to Marian Distler, 30 January 1959, Folkways Archives and Collections.

91. Lightening Hopkins to Folkways Records, 26 November 1959, Folkways Archives and Collections.

92. Moses Asch to Sam Hopkins, 4 December 1959, Folkways Archives and Collections.

93. Samuel Charters, *The Legacy of the Blues* (New York: Da Capo Press, 1977), 182–83.

94. Samuel Charters, "An Introduction to RBF Records," printed on the back page of Folkways' album notes of this era. See, for example, the notes for *Leadbelly's Last Sessions* (2941 and 2942).

95. D. K. Wilgus, "Record Reviews," *Journal of American Folklore* 73, no. 289 (July–September 1960): 277.

96. Gene Lees, *Meet Me at Jim & Andy's: Jazz Musicians and Their World* (New York: Oxford University Press, 1988), xi–xiv; Gene Lees, letter to author, 6 April 1991.

97. Michael Asch, interview with author.

98. "Recordings," *Journal of American Folklore* 68, no. 269 (July–September 1955): 278.

99. Jac Holzman, recorded reminiscences, 30 September 1991; in the possession of the author.

100. John Cohen, "John Cohen II," in *"Wasn't That a Time": Firsthand Accounts of the Folk Music Revival,* ed. Ronald Cohen (Metuchen, N.J.: Scarecrow Press, 1995), 177.

101. Kenneth Goldstein, interview with author.

102. Ralph Rush, "An Interview with Dave Van Ronk," *Sing Out!* 27, no. 5 (September–October 1979): 5.

103. Marian Distler to Kenneth Goldstein, 9 January 1960, Folkways Archives and Collections.

104. "Folkways Records" to Kenneth Goldstein, 29 February 1960, Folkways Archives and Collections.

105. Kenneth Goldstein to Marian Distler, 9 March, 11 April 1960, Folkways Archives and Collections.

106. Marian Distler to Kenneth Goldstein, 31 March 1960, Folkways Archives and Collections.

107. Sidney Cowell would later claim that Ruth Crawford was some-

what miffed at Pete for having put out a recording of her songs, since she had had intentions of doing the same. However, it is difficult to imagine that there was enough money at stake for either of them to have bothered with, and Pete's recording would not have prevented Ruth Crawford from releasing her own. Sidney Cowell, interview with author.

108. Moses Asch to Alan Mills, 16 January 1952, Folkways Archives and Collections.

109. Ella Jenkins, interview with author.

110. Ella Jenkins to Moe Asch, 16 April, 31 July 1958, Folkways Archives and Collections.

111. Ella Jenkins to Marian Distler, 24 September 1958, Folkways Archives and Collections.

112. John Cage, album notes for *Indeterminacy* (3704).

113. Lieberman, *"My Song Is My Weapon,"* 140–46; Irwin Silber, "Folk Magazines," in Cohen, *"Wasn't That a Time,"* 100–101. Dunaway, *How Can I Keep from Singing,* 122. Personal communication from Pete Seeger to the author.

114. Irwin Silber, interview with author. See also Irwin Silber, interview with Gary Kenton.

115. Irwin Silber, notes to *American Industrial Ballads* (5252), Pete Seeger.

116. While "Tom Dooley" may not have been the Kingston Trio's proudest musical moment, folklorists and folk music enthusiasts have been far more generous to them over the last ten years in reassessing their role in the folk revival. See William J. Bush, "The Kingston Trio," *Frets* 6, no. 6 (June 1984), and Dave Samuelson, "Overviews," in Cohen, *"Wasn't That a Time,"* 79–85.

117. D. K. Wilgus, "Record Reviews," *Journal of American Folklore* 72, no. 286 (October–December 1959): 368.

118. Lomax and Lomax, *Folk Song U.S.A.,* xi.

119. Pete Seeger to Moses Asch, 6 September 1958, Folkways Archives and Collections.

120. Dunaway, *How Can I Keep from Singing,* 202.

121. Moses Asch to Pete Seeger, 19 September 1958, Folkways Archives and Collections.

122. Howard Richmond to Moses Asch, 30 October 1958, Folkways Archives and Collections.

123. Moses Asch to Howard Richmond, 10 November 1958, Folkways Archives and Collections.

6. I COULD'VE HAD JOAN: THE FOLK REVIVAL

1. Cantwell, *When We Were Good,* 42–43.

2. Moses Asch, interview with Israel Young.

3. Raymond Williams, *Marxism and Literature* (Oxford: Oxford University Press, 1977), 62.

4. "PM Interviews 'Mr. Offbeat,'" *Popular Mechanics*, April 1961, 204–7.

5. "Sibyl with Guitar," *Time*, 23 November 1962, reprinted in David A. DeTurk and A. Poulin Jr., eds., *The American Folk Scene: Dimensions of the Folksong Revival* (New York: Dell, 1967), 223.

6. Cantwell, *When We Were Good*, 318.

7. Ibid., 324.

8. Simon Frith, *Sound Effects: Youth, Leisure, and the Politics of Rock 'n' Roll* (New York: Pantheon, 1981), 36.

9. Cantwell's postmodernist cultural analysis leads him to conclude that, in the fifties, "the new fissure in American society was not primarily one of class or ethnicity. . . . Rather it was a cleavage of memory, a division between the historical cultures formed before, during, and after the war" (*When We Were Good*, 270).

10. "Folk Songs and the Top 40," *Sing Out!* 16, no. 1 (February–March 1966): 12–21.

11. Frith, *Sound Effects*, 6.

12. Cantwell, *When We Were Good*, 313.

13. Moses Asch, interview with Tony Schwartz.

14. Frith, *Sound Effects*, 50.

15. Ibid., 48.

16. Document written on BOAC stationery, 26 May 1962, Folkways Archives and Collections.

17. Robert Shelton, "Folkways in Sound . . . or the Remarkable Enterprises of Mr. Moe Asch," *High Fidelity*, June 1960, 43ff.

18. Sam Charters to Marian Distler and Moe Asch, 6 July 1960, Folkways Archives and Collections.

19. Robert Shelton, *No Direction Home: The Life and Music of Bob Dylan* (New York: Morrow, 1986), 74–76.

20. Bob Spitz, *Dylan: A Biography* (New York: McGraw-Hill, 1989), 173; Shelton, *No Direction Home*, 134, 137.

21. From FBI documents released to Gary Kenton under the Freedom of Information Act on 3 October 1983.

22. Moses Asch to Barry Goldwater, 2, 14 July 1962; Barry Goldwater to Moses Asch, 6 July 1962, Folkways Archives and Collections.

23. Edward de Grazia, "FBI Checks FolkSongs—Then Mum's the Word," *Washington Post*, 6 November 1965, 6.

24. FBI files on Oak Publications, procured by Gary Kenton under the Freedom of Information act.

25. Notes to Pete Seeger, *Gazette*, vols. 1 and 2 (2501 and 2502).

26. Denselow, *When the Music's Over*, 18–27.

27. Sis Cunningham, interview with author; Gordon Friesen, "Songs of Our Times from the Pages of *Broadside* Magazine," in DeTurk and Poulin, *American Folk Scene*, 130–33, reprinted from *Broadside*, 1964.

28. Friesen, "Songs of our Times," 133; Shelton, *No Direction Home*, 139.

29. Shelton, *No Direction Home*, 141.
30. Marc Eliot, *Death of a Rebel: A Biography of Phil Ochs* (New York: Franklin and Watts, 1989), 71.
31. Toshi Seeger to Moses Asch, 5 November 1963, Folkways Archives and Collections.
32. Eliot, *Death of a Rebel*, 53.
33. Hammond, *John Hammond on Record*, 245–46.
34. Shelton, *No Direction Home*, 104.
35. Ibid., 405.
36. Cantwell, *When We Were Good*, 285.
37. Eliot, *Death of a Rebel*, 40–42.
38. Eric von Schmidt and Jim Rooney, *Baby Let Me Follow You Down: The Illustrated Story of the Cambridge Folk Years*, 2d ed. (Amherst: University of Massachusetts Press, 1994), 37.
39. Irwin Silber, notes for *The Folk Music of The Newport Folk Festival: 1959–1960* (2431 and 2432).
40. John Cohen, interview with author.
41. Moses Asch, "Folk Music—A Personal Statement," *Sing Out!* 11, no. 1 (February–March 1961): 26–27.
42. Gordon Friesen to Michael Ochs, 16 September 1981, Folkways Archives and Collections.
43. Harold Courlander to Moses Asch, 9 September 1963, Folkways Archives and Collections.
44. Sidney Cowell, interview with author.
45. Guy Carawan to Moses Asch, 25 February 1964, Folkways Archives and Collections.
46. Sam Charters, interview with author.
47. Draft of royalty arrangement for the estate of Langston Hughes, n.d., Folkways Archives and Collections.
48. Langston Hughes to Moses Asch, 16 June 1962, Folkways Archives and Collections.
49. Langston Hughes to Moses Asch, 23 April 1964, Folkways Archives and Collections.
50. Rampersad, *Life of Langston Hughes* 2:365, 372–73. Notes to *Jerico–Jim Crow* (9671).
51. Langston Hughes to Moses Asch, 9 February 1965, Folkways Archives and Collections.
52. Harry Smith, draft of notes for *Kiowa Peyote Meeting* (4601), Folkways Archives and Collections.
53. Cohen, "Rare Interview," pt. 2, 26.
54. See Dunson and Raim, *Anthology of American Folk Music*, 18–19.
55. David Evans, "Record Reviews: North American Indian Music," *Journal of American Folklore* 90, no. 357 (July–September 1977): 369.
56. Allen Ginsberg, album notes for *First Blues* (37560).
57. Robert Shelton, notes to *The Folk Box*, Elektra Records.
58. Harold Courlander to Moses Asch, 11 November 1964; Moses Asch

to Harold Courlander, 18 November 1964, Folkways Archives and Collections.

59. Cantwell, *When We Were Good,* 302; Eliot, *Death of a Rebel,* 80–81; Shelton, *No Direction Home,* 293–96.

60. Moses Asch to Toshi Seeger, 24 December 1964, Folkways Archives and Collections.

61. Moses Asch to Pete Seeger, 23 January 1965, Folkways Archives and Collections.

62. Moses Asch, interview with Tony Schwartz.

63. Dunaway, *How Can I Keep from Singing,* 247.

64. Denselow, *When the Music's Over,* 61.

65. Sis Cunningham, interview with author.

66. Notes to Jimmy Collier and Frederick Douglass Kirkpatrick, *Everybody's Got a Right to Live* (5308).

67. Gordon Friesen, "John Wesley Harding *Is* Bob Dylan," *Broadside* 93 (July–August 1968): 6.

68. Notes to *Bob Dylan vs. A. J. Weberman* (5322).

69. Denselow, *When the Music's Over,* 81.

70. Charles Edward Smith to Moses Asch, 21 May 1957, Folkways Archives and Collections.

71. Moses Asch, interview with Israel Young.

72. Evans, "Record Reviews: North American Indian Music," 365.

73. Moses Asch to Jack Weinstein, 14 January 1965, Folkways Archives and Collections.

74. *Broadside* 64 (15 October 1965).

75. Gordon Friesen to Moses Asch, 18 October 1965; Moses Asch to Gordon Friesen, 19 October 1965, Folkways Archives and Collections.

76. "Expand Verve/Folkways Base . . . " *Cash Box,* 18 December 1965.

77. Morris Goldberger, telephone conversation with author, 1 July 1992.

78. Moses Asch to John Studebaker, 8 May 1966; John Studebaker to Moses Asch, 19 May 1966, Folkways Archives and Collections.

79. Moses Asch to John Cohen, 18 February 1967, Folkways Archives and Collections.

80. John Cohen to Moses Asch, n.d., Folkways Archives and Collections.

81. John Cohen to Moses Asch, 15 February 1967, Folkways Archives and Collections.

82. Moses Asch to John Cohen and the New Lost City Ramblers, 18 February 1967, Folkways Archives and Collections.

83. Todd Gitlin, *The Sixties: Years of Hope, Days of Rage* (New York: Bantam, 1987), 213.

84. Moses Asch, album notes for *Nativity* (35001).

85. "One other thing is this," Asch said to W. E. B. Du Bois during the 1959 interview. "This business of Africa in relation to the American Negro—that I never could understand." Asch interview with W. E. B. Du Bois, Folkways Archives and Collections.

86. Michael Asch, interview with author, 16 April 1992.
87. *Sing Out!* 15, no. 5 (September–October 1965): 77.
88. Irwin Silber, interview with author.
89. Pete Seeger to Irwin Silber, 13 November 1967, quoted in Dunaway, *How Can I Keep from Singing,* 265.
90. Harold Courlander to Moses Asch, 16 May 1967, Folkways Archives and Collections.
91. Miles Lourie to Metro-Goldwyn-Mayer, Inc., 19 December 1967, 16 January 1968, Folkways Archives and Collections.
92. Moses Asch, interview with Joe Klein.
93. Harold Leventhal, interview with author.
94. Toshi Seeger to Moe Asch, note on Paris hotel stationery, n.d., Folkways Archives and Collections.

7. RECORDING THE CIVIL RIGHTS MOVEMENT

1. W. E. B. Du Bois, *The Souls of Black Folk* (1903; reprint, New York: New American Library, 1969), 267, 274.
2. Sterling Brown, *Negro Poetry and Drama* (Washington, D.C.: Associates in Negro Folk Education, 1937); John Lovell Jr., "The Social Implications of the Negro Spiritual," *Journal of Negro Education* 8, no. 4 (October 1939): 634–43.
3. John Lovell Jr., *Black Song: The Forge and the Flame* (New York: Macmillan, 1972), 196.
4. John Greenway, *American Folksongs of Protest* (Philadelphia: University of Pennsylvania Press, 1953), 78.
5. Lawrence W. Levine, *Black Culture and Black Consciousness* (Oxford: Oxford University Press, 1977), 51.
6. Albert J. Raboteau, *Slave Religion: The 'Invisible Institution' in the Antebellum South* (Oxford: Oxford University Press, 1978), 250.
7. Levine, *Black Culture,* 51; Raboteau, *Slave Religion,* 246.
8. Dena J. Epstein, *Sinful Tunes and Spirituals: Black Folk Music to the Civil War* (Urbana: University of Illinois Press, 1977), 187.
9. Sterling Stuckey, "Through the Prism of Folklore," *Massachusetts Review* 9 (1968): 478.
10. John A. Lomax, "Self-Pity in Negro Folk-Songs," *Nation* 105, no. 2719 (9 August 1917): 141ff.
11. August Meier, *Negro Thought in America 1880–1915* (Ann Arbor: University of Michigan Press, 1963), 135; John Hope Franklin, *From Slavery to Freedom,* 3d ed. (New York: Vintage, 1967), 446–49; Judith Stein, *The World of Marcus Garvey: Race and Class in Modern Society* (Baton Rouge: Louisiana State University Press, 1986), 227.
12. Robin D. G. Kelly, *The Hammer and the Hoe: Alabama Communists During the Depression* (Chapel Hill: University of North Carolina Press, 1990), 164–69.

13. Kelly, *Hammer and the Hoe,* 105–6, 135.
14. Mike Honey and Pat Krueger, "John Handcox: Union Song Writer," *Sing Out!* 35, no. 3 (Fall 1990): 14–19.
15. Aldon D. Morris, *The Origins of the Civil Rights Movement* (New York: Free Press, 1984), 18–24.
16. Bernice Johnson Reagon, "Songs of the Civil Rights Movement, 1955–1965: A Study in Cultural History" (Ph.D. diss., Howard University, 1975).
17. Guy Carawan and Candie Carawan, *Sing for Freedom: The Story of the Civil Rights Movement Through Its Song* (Bethlehem, Pa.: Sing Out!, 1990), 111.
18. Reagon, "Songs of the Civil Rights Movement," 98.
19. David J. Garrow, *Bearing the Cross: Martin Luther King, Jr., and the Southern Christian Leadership Conference* (New York: William Morrow, 1986), 98.
20. Taylor Branch, *Parting the Waters: American in the King Years, 1954–63* (New York: Simon and Schuster, 1988), 271ff.
21. See Folkways 5590, *The Nashville Sit-in Story,* and Carawan and Carawan, *Sing for Freedom,* 30–42.
22. Guy Carawan and Candie Carawan, interview with author. This interview was the single most important source for this chapter.
23. Guy Carawan, unpublished diary of his travels in the South in 1953. In the possession of Guy Carawan, New Market, Tennessee.
24. Dunaway, *How Can I Keep from Singing,* 156–57.
25. Guy Carawan to Moses Asch, 28 June 1959, Folkways Archives and Collections.
26. Marian Distler to Guy Carawan, 11 July 1959.
27. Moses Asch to Guy Carawan, 8 August 1959, Folkways Archives and Collections.
28. Guy Carawan to Moses Asch, 12 August 1959, Folkways Archives and Collections.
29. Charles Joyner, Preface to Guy Carawan and Candie Carawan, *Ain't You Got a Right to the Tree of Life* (1966; rev. and exp. ed., Athens: University of Georgia Press, 1989), x.
30. Garrow, *Bearing the Cross,* 131–34; Morris, *Origins of the Civil Rights Movement,* 215–21.
31. Pete Seeger and Bob Reiser, *Everybody Says Freedom* (New York: Norton, 1989), 8.
32. Carawan and Carawan, *Sing for Freedom,* 20–21.
33. Howard Zinn, *SNCC: The New Abolitionists* (Boston: Beacon, 1964) 22–23; Branch, *Parting the Waters,* 295.
34. Guy Carawan to Moses Asch, 9 January 1960, Folkways Archives and Collections.
35. Moses Asch to Guy Carawan, 19 August 1960, Folkways Archives and Collections.
36. Marian Distler to Pete Seeger, 7 September 1960, Folkways Archives and Collections.

37. Guy Carawan to Moses Asch and Marian Distler, 3 November 1960, Folkways Archives and Collections.

38. Guy Carawan to Moses Asch, 3 February 1960, Folkways Archives and Collections.

39. Robert Shelton, "Songs as a Weapon in Rights Battle; Vital New Ballads Buoy Negro Spirits Across the South," *New York Times,* 20 August 1962, p. 1.

40. Zinn, *SNCC,* 51.

41. David M. Oshinsky, *"Worse than Slavery": Parchman Farm and the Ordeal of Jim Crow Justice* (New York: Free Press, 1996).

42. Carawan and Carawan, *Sing for Freedom,* 45; Lieberman, *"My Song Is My Weapon,"* 94.

43. Seeger and Reiser, *Everybody Says Freedom,* 64.

44. Josh Dunson, *Freedom in the Air* (New York: International Publishers, 1965), 61.

45. Reagon, "Songs of the Civil Rights Movement," 133.

46. Garrow, *Bearing the Cross,* 173–79.

47. Ibid., 217–19, 226; Zinn, *SNCC,* 136.

48. Dunaway, *How Can I Keep from Singing,* 221–22.

49. Ibid., 223.

50. Alan Lomax to Guy Carawan, reprinted in notes for record album *Freedom in the Air: A Documentary on Albany, Georgia, 1961–62,* SNCC-101.

51. Reagon, "Songs of the Civil Rights Movement," 134.

52. Joan Baez, *And a Voice to Sing With: A Memoir* (New York: Summit, 1987), 103–6.

53. Branch, *Parting the Waters,* 765–66.

54. Denselow, *When the Music's Over,* 38–39.

55. Branch, *Parting the Waters,* 718–20.

56. Kay Mills, *This Little Light of Mine: The Life of Fannie Lou Hamer* (New York: Dutton, 1993), 51–77; Zinn, *SNCC,* 4–95.

57. Josh Dunson, "Slave Songs at the 'Sing for Freedom,'" *Broadside 46* (30 May 1964), reprinted in album notes for *Sing for Freedom: Lest We Forget,* vol. 3 (5488). See also Dunson, *Freedom in the Air,* 103–4.

58. Bernice Reagon, personal communication with author, 14 January 1991. Reagon insists that she always understood the value of Bessie Jones's music and counted Miss Bessie as her teacher and mentor.

59. *Charleston (S.C.) News and Courier,* 19 January 1964.

60. Juanita Jackson, Sabra Slaughter, and J. Herman Blake, "The Sea Islands as a Research Area," in *Sea Island Roots,* ed. Mary A. Twining and Keith E. Baird (Trenton, N.J.: Africa World Press, 1991).

61. Carawan and Carawan, *Ain't You Got a Right,* 10.

62. Draft of letter from Moses Asch to Editor of *New York Times,* 25 January 1965, Folkways Archives and Collections.

63. Moses Asch to Doris Saunders, n.d., Folkways Archives and Collections. This letter (which may never have been mailed) concerned a

CBS television program based upon Ramsey's "Music of the South" series, which aired in early 1961.
64. Denselow, *When the Music's Over,* 44.
65. See Reebee Garofalo, "Popular Music and the Civil Rights Movement," in *Rockin' the Boat: Mass Music and Mass Movements,* ed. Reebee Garofalo (Boston: South End Press, 1992), 231.

8. FINDING THE FINAL PIECES

1. Jon Appleton, interview with author. The description of Asch's work practices and routine derives primarily from this interview and an interview with Marilyn Conklin Averett conducted by Tony Seeger, Jeff Place, Lori Taylor, and Matt Walters.
2. Kevin Roth, interview with author.
3. Marilyn Conklin Averett, interview with Tony Seeger, Jeff Place, Lori Taylor, and Matt Walters.
4. Moses Asch and Frederic Ramsey, interview with Elisabeth Perez Luna.
5. *Sing Out!* 26, no. 4 (1978): 46.
6. Terry Waldon, *This Is Ragtime* (1976; reprint, New York: Da Capo, 1991), 184.
7. Len Lyons, *The 101 Best Jazz Albums: A History of Jazz on Records* (New York: William Morrow, 1980), 53.
8. David Jasen, interview with author.
9. Al Close to Moses Asch, 14 February 1959; Moses Asch to Al Close, 26 February 1959, Folkways Archives and Collections.
10. Moses Asch to Mary Lou Williams, 14 September 1961, Folkways Archives and Collections.
11. Mary Lou Williams to Moses Asch, 7 October 1964, Folkways Archives and Collections.
12. John S. Wilson, "The Ageless Jazz of Mary Lou Williams," *New York Times,* 18 February 1979, p. 10.
13. Dunaway, *How Can I Keep from Singing,* 302.
14. Pete Seeger to Moses Asch, 11 March and 10 July 1974, Folkways Archives and Collections.
15. Pete Seeger and Toshi Seeger, interview with author.
16. Pete Seeger, album notes for *Pete Seeger Singalong* (36055).
17. Henrietta Yurchenco, *A Mighty Hard Road: The Woody Guthrie Story* (New York: McGraw-Hill, 1970).
18. Nat Hentoff, "Roots: Jewish and black," *Village Voice,* 2 May 1974, 74.
19. Henrietta Yurchenco, interview with author.
20. Jon Appleton to Moses Asch, 17 October 1973; Moses Asch to Jon Appleton, 15 November 1973, Folkways Archives and Collections.
21. Moses Asch to Jon Appleton, 29 December 1981, Folkways Archives and Collections.

22. Memo from Dean Ernest Lynton to Dr. William Weinberg, 2 March 1970, Rutgers Institute of Jazz Studies.

23. Frederic Ramsey, "Notes on Rutgers University and the Asch-Folkways Archive Collection," 15 April 1970; "A Partial List of Persons Who Have Contributed to Growth and Development of the Moses Asch–Folkways Archive," 20 April 1970, Rutgers Institute of Jazz Studies.

24. William Weinberg to Moses Asch, 29 March 1972; William Weinberg, memo on meeting with Moses Asch, 28 March 1973; David Cayer, memo to Drs. Ardath Burks and Richard Wilson, 29 November 1973; William Weinberg to Moses Asch, 10 December 1973; William Weinberg to Provost Kenneth Wheeler, 31 March 1975, Rutgers Institute of Jazz Studies.

25. Jon Appleton to Moses Asch, 21 August 1984, copy in the possession of Jon Appleton.

26. Robert G. Smith, draft letter to Moses Asch, with covering memo from Powell to Smith, dated 31 January 1984. It is not apparent whether this letter was ever sent to Asch. Copy in the possession of Jon Appleton.

27. Irving Louis Horowitz to Moses Asch, 25 July 1983; William Weinberg to Dave Cayer, Henk Edelman, and Irving Horowitz, memo, 17 August 1983; William Weinberg, interdepartmental memo on "Meeting with Asch Family," 19 August 1983, Rutgers Institute of Jazz Studies.

28. Irving Louis Horowitz to Moses Asch, 30 September 1983; Scott Bramson to Moses Asch, 24 October 1983, Rutgers Institute of Jazz Studies.

29. John W. Dorsey to Moses Asch, 7 December 1984, copy in the possession of Jon Appleton.

30. Denselow, *When the Music's Over,* 83, 117–21; Eliot, *Death of a Rebel,* 204–6, 221–22, 292.

31. Ochs's biographer reports that Ochs introduced Walker to Sis Cunningham; Cunningham insists that it was the other way around, and that Eliot fabricated a telephone conversation between herself and Ochs that never occurred. Sis Cunningham, interview with author; Eliot, *Death of a Rebel,* 248.

32. Gordon Friesen, album notes for *Phil Ochs Sings for Broadside* (5320).

33. Gordon Friesen to Michael Ochs, 16 September 1981; Ochs's lawyer to Moses Asch and Agnes Friesen, 23, 26 August 1981; Moses Asch to Michael Ochs, 15 September 1981, Folkways Archives and Collections.

34. Sam Charters, interview with author.

35. Sam Charters to Moses Asch, 15 December 1981, Folkways Archives and Collections.

36. Moses Asch, interview with his lawyer.

37. Moses Asch to Ralph Rinzler, 9 June 1986, Folkways Archives and Collections.

38. Ralph Rinzler to Moses Asch, 13 June 1986, Folkways Archives and Collections.
39. Ralph Rinzler to Moses and Frances Asch, 6 August 1986, Folkways Archives and Collections.
40. Ralph Rinzler to Frances and Moses Asch, 3 September 1986, Folkways Archives and Collections.
41. Frances Asch, interview with author; Sam Charters, interview with author.
42. Ralph Rinzler to Frances Asch, 26 October 1986, Folkways Archives and Collections.
43. Irwin Silber and Barbara Dane to Frances Asch, 21 October 1986, Folkways Archives and Collections.
44. Quoted in Jon Pareles, "Moses Asch, Who Founded Folkways Records, Dies at 81," *New York Times,* 21 October 1986, p. D31.
45. Robert Palmer, "A Tribute to a Pioneer of Folk," *New York Times,* 9 October 1987, p. C28.

INDEX